Oracle8 Minimum, Maximum, and Default Val

Objects

Item	Minimum	Maximum
Columns per table	1	1,000
Columns per b*tree index	1	32
Columns per bitmap index	1	30
Index column(s) length	1	40% of block size
Tables per database	Data dictionary	Unlimited tables
Tables per cluster	1	32
Rows per table	0	Unlimited
Partitions per table	0	64KB – 1
Columns per partition key	1	16
Partitioning key length	1+overhead	4KB – overhead
Rollback segments per database	1	No limit
Stored PL/SQL code lines	3	2,000–3,000

Database Files

Note: Some operating systems may not allow the maximum values listed.

Item	Minimum	Maximum
Data file size	2 blocks	2^{22} or 4MB
Data files per tablespace	1	1,022
Data files per database	1	65,533
Control files per database	1	Unlimited
Redo log files per database	2	OS dependent
Redo log files per group	1	Unlimited
BFILE size	OS dependent	4GB

Physical Storage

Note: Some operating systems may not allow the maximum values listed.

Item	Minimum	Maximum	Default
Database block size	2,048 bytes	32KB	
Database blocks per data file	2	2^{22}	
Tablespaces per database	1	64KB	
Tablespace default initial extent	2 blocks	OS dependent	5 blocks
Tablespace default next extent	1 block	OS dependent	5 blocks
Tablespace default PCTINCREASE	0	$2^{32} – 2$	50

continues…

Item	Minimum	Maximum	Default
Tablespace default MINEXTENTS	1	OS dependent	1
Tablespace default MAXEXTENTS	1	Unlimited	1
Rollback optimal size	bytes in MINEXTENTS	2,047MB	NULL
PCTFREE	0	99	10
PCTUSED	1	99	40
INITRANS	1	255	1 for table, 2 for index or cluster
MAXTRANS	1	255	255

Datatype Lengths

Item	Maximum
CHAR	2,000 bytes
CHAR VARYING	4,000 bytes
CLOB	4GB
Literal	4,000 characters
LOB	4GB
LONG	$2^{31} - 1$
NCHAR	2,000 bytes
NCHAR VARYING	4,000 bytes
NUMBER	22 bytes; value range is $-999\ldots(38\ 9s) \times 10125$ to $999\ldots(38\ 9s) \times 10125$
RAW	2,000 bytes
VARCHAR[2]	4,000 bytes

Miscellaneous

Note: Some operating systems may not allow the maximum values listed.

Item	Minimum	Maximum	Default
Constraints per table	0	Unlimited	None
Nested queries	0	255	0
SQL statement length	N/A	64KB	N/A
Trigger cascade limit	N/A	32	N/A
Users and roles (combined)	N/A	65,525	N/A
Instances per database	0	OS dependent	1
SGA size	Approx. 10KB	2–4GB (32-bit OS), >4GB (64-bit OS)	OS dependent
Job queue processes	0	36	0 per instance
I/O slave processes	2	15	2
Sessions per instance	0	32KB	0

Using

Oracle8

David Austin

Vijay Lunawat

Meghraj Thakkar

Tomas Gasper

Ari Kaplan

Raman Batra

Joseph Duer

que

A Division of Macmillan Computer Publishing, USA
201 W. 103rd Street
Indianapolis, Indiana 46290

Contents at a Glance

Using Oracle8

International Standard Book Number: 0-7897-1653-4

Library of Congress Catalog Card Number: 98-84811

Printed in the United States of America

First Printing: July 1998

00   99   98   4   3   2   1

Trademarks

Credits

Executive Editor
Bryan Gambrel

Acquisitions Editor
Angela C. Kozlowski

Development Editor
Susan Shaw Dunn

Managing Editor
Patrick Kanouse

Project Editor
Andrew Cupp

Copy Editors
Tonya Maddox
Patricia Kinyon
Sean Medlock

Indexer
Bruce Clingaman

Technical Editors
Sundar Rajan
Sakhr Youness

Production
Carol L. Bowers
Mona Brown
Ayanna Lacey
Gene Redding

Cover Designers
Dan Armstrong
Ruth Harvey

Book Designers
Nathan Clement
Ruth Harvey

Contents

III Managing Data and Index Segments

IV Managing Users and Database Security

V Backing Up Your Oracle Database

About the Authors

David Austin has been in the data processing profession for almost 25 years. He had worked with many database architectures, including hierarchical, network, and relational, before becoming an Oracle DBA about 10 years ago. For the past five years, David has worked for Oracle Corporation, where he's now employed as a senior principal curriculum developer. His previous positions at Oracle include senior principal consultant and senior principal instructor. David has completed multiple Masters programs with Oracle Education and is a Certified Oracle Database Administrator. David is a contributing author for Que's *Special Edition Using Oracle8* and wrote Chapters 3, 5–8, 10–11, 16–17, and the glossary for this book. He obtained both of his degrees—a B.A. with a double major in mathematics and English and a minor in computer science and an M.S. in applied mathematics—from the University of Colorado.

Vijay Lunawat is a technical specialist with Oracle Corporation; he resides in Orlando, Florida. He has a bachelor's degree in electronics engineering. He has worked with Oracle databases for more than 10 years as a developer, database administrator, consultant, and support. A specialist in Oracle Parallel Server, he's now working with the Center of Expertise in Oracle Support Services. He develops and frequently teaches Oracle Internals classes at Oracle. He was a contributing author for Que's *Special Edition Using Oracle8* and wrote Chapters 1, 13, 18, 27, and Appendix A for this book.

Meghraj Thakkar works as a senior technical analyst at Oracle Corporation. He has been working with various Oracle products for the past six years. He has a master's in computer science and a bachelor's in electronics engineering. He has several industry vendor certifications, including Microsoft Certified Systems Engineer (MCSE), Novell Certified ECNE, and Lotus Certified Notes Consultant. He has taught several courses at the University of California, Irvine; developed and presented a two-day course, "Supporting Oracle on Windows NT," to internal Oracle employees; and presented two papers at the ECO'98 held in New York City in March 1998. He also coauthored several books for Macmillan Computer Publishing— *Special Edition Using Oracle8*, *Oracle8 Server Unleashed*, and *Oracle8 for DBAs*—and contributed Chapters 2, 4, 14, and 21–23 for this book.

Tomas Gasper, the author of Chapters 9, 12, and 20, is an Oracle DBA for Energizer Battery Company in St. Louis, Missouri. He has worked in a variety of system support roles, including DBA, UNIX, and Windows NT administrator and systems programmer. As a refugee from the defense industry, Tomas enjoys learning about exotic and unique computer systems. His hobbies include experimenting with Linux systems, Web-based applications, and, of course, exploring the Internet. Tomas can be reached at tgasper@highlandil.com or TomasM.Gasper@energizer.com.

Ari Kaplan, the author of Chapter 25, is an independent computer consultant specializing in Oracle product design, development, and management. Ari, coauthor of Que's *Special Edition Using Oracle8* and Waite Group Press's *Oracle8 How-To*, both for Macmillan Computer Publishing, has played pivotal roles in implementing some of the nation's largest and most visible Oracle applications for various industries. Ari worked for Oracle before becoming a consultant in 1994, and since 1990 he has worked as a consultant for several Major League Baseball clubs (currently for the Montreal Expos), where he has developed and managed their scouting department's software systems. Ari graduated from the California Institute of Technology in Pasadena and was granted the school's prestigious "Alumni of the Decade" distinction for his contributions in the computer industry. He has appeared on NBC's *Today Show* and CNN, and is a frequent guest speaker on Oracle in the United States and abroad. Ari lives in Chicago and can be reached at akaplan@interaccess.com or through his Web site of Oracle tips at http://homepage.interaccess.com/~akaplan.

Raman Batra, the author of Chapters 24 and 26, is a database administrator for the Cessna Aircraft Company in Wichita, Kansas, where he has been working since 1994. In the past, Raman has developed client/server and intranet applications using Developer/2000 Forms, Pro*C, and Oracle Web Application Server. As a DBA, he is administering Designer/2000 applications and application suites for engineering, supply chain, and parts distribution systems on Oracle7 and 8. He is also designing an advanced replication architecture on Oracle8 for failover and disaster recovery. Raman is a member of the Oracle Technology Network, ACM, IOUG-A, and the Wichita Area Oracle Users Group. Raman can be reached at rrbatra@feist.com.

Joseph Duer, the author of Chapters 15 and 19, is a technical analyst and Oracle database administrator at a technology-driven corporation based in southern Connecticut. He specializes in Web development using Oracle Database Server and Oracle Application Server. He has developed object-oriented systems that utilize C++, Java, and JavaScript, as well as Oracle Application Server's Java, PL/SQL, and VRML cartridges. He can be reached via email at joeduer@ix.netcom.com and via his Web page at http://www.netcom.com/~joeduer.

Dedication

To Doris and Derrick, for being such loving and supportive parents for so many years.—David Austin

To my parents, who always inspire me to accept new challenges.
—Vijay Lunawat

Tell Us What You Think!

As the reader of this book, *you* are our most important critic and commentator. We value your opinion and want to know what we're doing right, what we could do better, what areas you'd like to see us publish in, and any other words of wisdom you're willing to pass our way.

As the Executive Editor for the Client/Server Database Team at Macmillan Computer Publishing, I welcome your comments. You can fax, email, or write me directly to let me know what you did or didn't like about this book—as well as what we can do to make our books stronger.

Please note that I cannot help you with technical problems related to the topic of this book, and that due to the high volume of mail I receive, I might not be able to reply to every message.

When you write, please be sure to include this book's title and author as well as your name and phone or fax number. I will carefully review your comments and share them with the author and editors who worked on the book.

Fax: 317-817-7070

E-mail: cs_db@mcp.com

Mail: Executive Editor
           Client/Server Database Team
           Macmillan Computer Publishing
           201 West 103rd Street
           Indianapolis, IN 46290 USA

Acknowledgments

From David Austin:

Thanks to the many professionals who have helped and encouraged me in my career and my work on this book, particularly my various managers, instructors, and colleagues at Oracle, including Deborah West, Chris Pirie, Nick Evans, Vijay Venkatachalam, Larry Mix, Beth Winslow, Sue Jang, Scott Gossett, and Scott Heisey. I would also like to say thank you to some of my earliest mentors in this business—Bob Klein, Donald Miklich, and Roland Sweet, wherever they might be.

Thanks also to the various editors at Que who helped shepherd this work from its inception to the book you now have in your hands, with a special mention for Angela Kozlowski and Susan Dunn. I also want to thank my coauthors, without whose efforts this work could never have been finished.

Finally, a thank you to my family for putting up with the long hours I spent ignoring them while working on this project. My wife, Lillian, is now bracing for the revisions, while my kitten is just happy that she once again gets some petting when she sits in my lap.

From Vijay Lunawat:

Most thanks go to my two children, Siddharth and Sanchi, and my wife, Sushma, for their patience and for putting up with my long and weekend working hours while I was writing for this book.

From Meghraj Thakkar:

I would like to give a special thanks to my wife, Komal, for her patience and understanding.

From Raman Batra:

To my lovely wife, Sarika, for her understanding and admirable patience in keeping my daughter, Nikita, away from me, when I was writing. Nikita had a real hard time understanding why Daddy was working with such "boring" text stuff with no music, when she could be watching her Winnie the Pooh CD on Daddy's PC.

From Joe Duer:

I would like to thank once again the Tuesday night crew at Shelton EMS: Jason, Betty, John, and Denise. Your help covering all the shifts I missed because I was writing is greatly appreciated.

I would like to thank everyone at Que—in particular, Angela Kozlowski and Susan Dunn—for their help and guidance during the development of this book.

Welcome to *Using Oracle8*! This book identifies the many functions an Oracle DBA needs to perform on an Oracle8 database and explains how to do them as efficiently and effectively as possible. You learn about the key functions of database administration, including installing the product, designing and creating a database and its tablespaces, designing and creating the tables and other objects that make up an Oracle database, designing and executing a good backup strategy with a recovery methodology, and monitoring and tuning performance. You also learn about creating and maintaining users and performing an upgrade to Oracle8, as well as other tasks that you may need in your position as DBA. You also learn when and how to use the various tools Oracle8 provides to assist you in database management, performance monitoring and tuning, data loading, backup and recovery, and data export and import.

The book is designed to let you read about a topic at length when you have the time and the inclination, or to use as a quick reference guide when you need an answer to a pressing technical question or an example to follow when performing a specific task.

Using Oracle8 contains cross-references to related topics so that you can look at all aspects of a topic, even if they're covered in different chapters. These cross-references also enable you to read the book in any order you choose. If you run across a subject you don't fully understand, you can easily switch your attention to the area(s) identified and carry on your reading there.

Where applicable, the book also references the Oracle documentation materials, so you can find even more detail if you need it.

Don't forget to keep this book handy at work, just in case you need to check something in a hurry that you haven't read about yet or is a new topic to you. Be sure also to use the tear-out card inside the book's cover. It contains some of the most common, but difficult to remember, information you'll need.

Who Should Use This Book

You'll get the most out of this book if you have some background in the SQL language and some knowledge or experience with relational databases. Because Oracle's SQL language is based on the ANSI standard, it's not discussed in detail in this book, but numerous examples use SQL statements. The theory of relational databases is also outside the scope of this book, as are the internal structures within Oracle, except where they're needed to help you understand how or why to perform a specific task.

This book is intended primarily for DBAs who have some knowledge of relational databases. Much of this book will be familiar if you've worked with earlier releases of Oracle—but you'll find the new Oracle8 features discussed. If you've worked with other relational databases, you may need to refer to the glossary if you find brand new terms or terms that have different meanings in Oracle. If you haven't worked with any relational databases, you should expect to follow the frequent cross-references to sections of the book; this will fill in background information as you read about a topic.

Why This Book?

Have you ever purchased a *Using* book from Que? The *Using* books have proven invaluable to readers as both learning guides and as references for many years. The *Using* series is an industry leader and has practically become an industry standard. We encourage and receive feedback from readers all the time, and consider and implement their suggestions whenever possible.

This book isn't a compiled authority on all the features of Oracle8; instead, it's a streamlined, conversational approach for using Oracle8 productively and efficiently. This book has many features:

- *Improved index.* What do you call tasks and features? As we wrote this book, we anticipated every possible name or description of a feature or database activity.

- *Real-life answers.* Throughout the book you find our real-life examples and experiences. We recommend how to organize your database on the logical as well as the physical level. We suggest what values to use when assigning physical storage attributes to your tables, indexes, and other database objects, and how to determine if you have made a good set of choices. After all, we've been there, done that! We understand that how to perform a task is only one question you may have, and perhaps the bigger questions are "Why?" and "What for?"

- *Relevant information written just for you.* We have carefully scrutinized which features and tasks to include in this book and have included those that apply to your everyday use of Oracle. Why invest in material that teaches you how to perform tasks you may never need to perform?

- *Reference or tutorial.* You can learn to quickly perform a task using step-by-step instructions, or you can investigate the why and wherefore of a task with our discussions preceding each task.

- *Wise investment.* We don't waste your valuable bookshelf space with redundant or irrelevant material, nor do we assume you "know it all" or need to know it all. Here is what you need, when you need it, how you need it, with an appropriate price tag.

- *Easy-to-find procedures.* Every numbered step-by-step procedure in the book has a short title explaining exactly what it does. This saves you time by making it easier to find the exact steps you need to accomplish a task.

How This Book Is Organized

Using Oracle8 has task-oriented, easy-to-navigate tutorials and reference information presented in a logical progression from simple to complex tasks. It covers features of the program you use in your daily work. Examples are real life. You can work through the book lesson by lesson, or you can find specific information when you need to perform a job quickly.

Using Oracle8 is divided into nine parts:

- *Part I, Building Your Oracle Database*. Part I introduces you to relational databases in general and to the basic tools used to build and manage an Oracle8 database, whether you're creating a database from scratch or converting from an earlier release.

- *Part II, Customizing Your Oracle Database*. Part II shows you how to build the appropriate storage units for your database objects. It's here you also find out how to manage the shared structures required for Oracle to function in the multiuser environment, including redo log files, rollback segments, and temporary segments.

- *Part III, Managing Data and Index Segments*. Part III provides the details needed to build Oracle database tables and indexes, including information on sizing them and assigning appropriate physical characteristics and alternate structures. You find out about the logical and physical design of data and index information, including optional segment structures such as index-organized tables.

- *Part IV, Managing Users and Database Security*. Part IV explains how to create user ids and manage user access to the database and its objects. You are also introduced to methods for monitoring and controlling resource usage. The chapters in this section include detailed information on the new password-management features introduced in Oracle8.

- *Part V, Backing Up Your Oracle Database*. Part V covers the various options available for protecting your database contents against loss due to hardware failure. You learn how to restore data that's lost when failures occur. The chapters in this section also cover the Recovery Manager tools, introduced as part of Oracle8.

- *Part VI, Tuning Your Database Applications.* In Part VI you learn about the various tools and techniques that DBAs and application developers should consider when building and tuning applications. These include performance-analysis tools and various resource-saving design considerations such as indexes, clustering techniques, optimizer selection, and constraint management.

- *Part VII, Tuning Your Database.* Part VII addresses the issues related to gathering and analyzing performance information about your database. The chapters in this section include information on tools available for these tasks, as well as how to interpret various statistics available to you and how to respond to performance degradation caused by various factors.

- *Part VIII, Using Additional Oracle Tools and Options.* In Part VIII you learn about the various tools provided by Oracle as part of the base product that can help you manage your database and the data within it, plus network access between your applications and the database. This section also summarizes the features available with the products that you can optionally license for added functionality if needed, such as Oracle Parallel Server and the Object option.

- *Additional information available at our Web site (www.mcp.com/info).* Appendix A, "Essential PL/SQL: Understanding Stored Procedures, Triggers, and Packages," includes a comprehensive guide to the PL/SQL language and the database constructs you can build with it. Appendix B, "What's New to Oracle8," lists the Oracle8's new features for those of you who are familiar with earlier Oracle releases and just need to identify what changes you may want to study and implement in your own database. Appendix C, "Installing Oracle8," covers the basic steps you need to follow in order to install a new version of the database, whether you're upgrading from Oracle7 or installing Oracle8 directly.

Now look at the detailed table of contents, decide what you want to read now or in the near future, and begin getting comfortable with Oracle8.

Conventions Used in This Book

The following items are some of the features that will make this book easier for you to use:

- *Cross-references.* We've looked for all the tasks and topics related to a topic at hand and referenced them for you. If you need to look for coverage that leads up to what you're working on, or if you want to build on the new skill you just mastered, you have the references to easily find the right coverage in the book:

SEE ALSO
➤ *Information on tablespace usage for different segment types, see page xxx*

- *Glossary terms.* For all terms that appear in the glossary, you'll find the first appearance of that term *italicized* in the text.
- *SideNotes.* Information related to the task at hand or "inside" information from the authors is offset in SideNotes, so they won't interfere with the flow of the text, yet make it easy to find valuable information. Each SideNote has a short title to help you quickly identify the information you'll find there.

Oracle's syntax for commands, scripts, and SQL statements also incorporate special elements. Look at the following syntax example:

```
ALTER DATABASE [database_name]
    ADD LOGFILE [GROUP [group_number]]
    filename [SIZE size_integer [K¦M]] [REUSE]
```

- Terms that are *italicized* are considered placeholders. When you use the command, you replace the italicized word with an appropriate value. For example, *database_name* in the preceding code would be replaced with an actual database name.

- Square brackets ([ ]) in command syntax indicate optional clauses. The brackets around [*database_name*] in the preceding code indicate that you aren't required to provide a database name. Don't include the brackets when you use the command.

- The ¦ character indicates that you choose one item or the other, not both. (For example, you can choose either K for kilobytes or M for megabytes for the preceding command.) Again, don't use this character in the actual command.

- Ellipses (. . .) in listings indicate either a clause that can repeat or skipped code that's not pertinent to the discussion. Don't use the ellipses in the actual code.

- Line numbers are included in some code listings to make discussion about the code easier to reference. Don't include the numbers with any command-line commands, as part of any Oracle scripts, or within SQL statements.

Introducing Relational Databases and Oracle8

Functions performed by a database management system

Physical architecture of an Oracle database

Identify the major components of an Oracle instance

Overview of database tools: Oracle Enterprise Manager, SQL*Plus, PL/SQL, Net8, Developer 2000, and precompilers

Understand the Oracle8 data dictionary and dynamic performance views

What's a Database Management System?

A *database* can be defined as a collection of information organized in such a way that it can be retrieved and used. A *database management system (DBMS)* can further be defined as the tool that enables us to manage and interact with the database.

Most DBMSs perform the following functions:

- Store data
- Create and maintain data structures
- Allow concurrent access to many users
- Enforce security and privacy
- Allow extraction and manipulation of stored data
- Enable data entry and data loading
- Provide an efficient indexing mechanism for fast extraction of selected data
- Provide consistency among different records
- Protect stored data from loss by backup and recovery process

Several different types of DBMSs have been developed to support these requirements. These systems can broadly be classified in the following classes:

- *A hierarchical DBMS stores data in a tree-like structure*. It assumes a parent-child relationship between the data. The top of the tree, known as the root, can have any number of dependents. Dependents, in turn, can have any number of subdependents, and so on. Hierarchical database systems are now obsolete.

- *A network DBMS stores data in the form of records and links*. This system allows more flexible many-to-many relationship than do hierarchical DBMSs. Network DBMSs are very fast and storage-efficient. Network database management systems allowed complex data structures but were very inflexible and required tedious design. An airline reservation system is one example of this type of DBMS system.

- *Relational DBMSs (RDBMSs) probably have the simplest structure a database can have.* In an RDBMS, data is organized in tables. Tables, in turn, consist of records, and records of fields. Each field corresponds to one data item. Two or more tables can be linked (joined) if they have one or more fields in common. RDBMSs are easy to use and have flourished in the last decade. They're commonly used on low-end computer systems. In the last few years, however, their use has expanded to more powerful computer systems. Oracle, Informix, and Sybase are some popular RDBMSs available in the market.

- *Object-oriented DBMSs were designed to handle data such as numbers and words.* During recent years, however, object-oriented DBMSs are emerging. These systems can handle objects such as videos, images, pictures, and so on.

Oracle8 stores objects in relational tables

Oracle8 is an object relational database management system, which allows objects to be stored in tables, in a manner similar to numbers and words being stored in an RDBMS system.

Oracle Database Files

An Oracle database physically resides in various files. Figure 1.1 shows the physical structure of an Oracle database.

The Initialization Parameter File

The parameter file, commonly known as INIT.ORA, contains initialization parameters that control the behavior and characteristics of the database and the *instance* that accesses the database. You can edit this text file in your favorite editor.

Changing the parameter file

The initialization parameter file is read by the instance only during startup. Any changes made in the initialization file take effect only after you shut down and restart the instance.

Oracle supplies a sample INIT.ORA file in the $ORACLE_HOME/dbs directory. $ORACLE_HOME is the top-level directory under which Oracle software is installed; it doesn't need to be the user Oracle's home directory. The default name of an instance's parameter file is init*SID*.ora, in which *SID* (System IDentifier) is a character string that uniquely identifies the instance on the system.

You can override the defaults by using the PFILE parameter of the Server Manager's startup command. The IFILE parameter in this file allows you to nest multiple initialization files for the same instance.

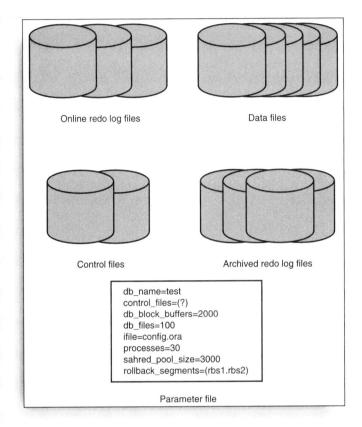

FIGURE 1.1

An Oracle database system

The Control File

Oracle updates the control file

Oracle automatically records any structural changes in the database—for example, addition/deletion of a data file—in the control file(s). An Oracle instance updates the control file(s) with various status information during its operation.

The control file contains information about the database's physical structure and status. It has information about several things: the total number of data files; log files; redo log groups; redo log members; current redo log to which the database is writing; name and location of each data file and online redo log files; archived log history; and so on. Starting from Oracle8, the control file also contains information about the backup of the database.

The control_file initialization parameter specifies the name and location of a database's control file. It's strongly recommended that you specify multiple files in the control_file initialization parameter to mirror the control file to multiple locations. The V$CONTROL_FILE data dictionary view contains information about the database's control file.

The V$CONTROLFILE_RECORD_SECTION dynamic performance view contains detailed structure information about the control file. This view gives the information about all records contained in the control file.

The Data File

An Oracle database stores user information in physical data files. A data file can contain tables, indexes, clusters, sequences, data dictionary, rollback segments, temporary segments, and so on. At the logical level, Oracle manages space in terms of *tablespace* (a group of one or more data files). When an Oracle database is created, it has only one tablespace: SYSTEM. Other tablespaces and the associated data files are added later, as needed.

You can specify the name, location, and size of a data file while creating the tablespace to which the data file belongs. Oracle uses control files to store the name and location of the data files. Use the data dictionary views V$DATAFILE and DBA_DATA_FILES to retrieve the information about a database's data files.

Redo Log Files

Oracle records all changes against the database in the redo log file and uses the contents of the redo log file to regenerate the transaction changes in case of failure. An Oracle database has two or more redo log files. Oracle allows you to mirror the redo log files, thus a redo log group contains one or more files (members). Oracle writes to all the members of a redo log group simultaneously. An Oracle instance writes to redo log groups in cyclical order—that is, it writes to one redo log group and then to the next when the earlier one is filled up. When the last available redo log group is filled, it switches over to the first one.

SEE ALSO
➤ *For detailed information about redo log files, see p. 162*

You can specify the name, location, and size of the redo log files during database creation. The V$LOGFILE data dictionary view contains redo log files' information. You can also add, delete, and relocate redo log files by using the ALTER DATABASE command.

Archived Redo Log Files

The archived log file contains a copy of the redo log file. Archived redo log files are useful in recovering the database and all committed transactions in case of failures (such as disk failure). When an Oracle database is operating in archive log mode, it needs to archive the recently filled redo log file before it can reuse it.

You can enable automatic archiving by setting the initialization parameter LOG_ARCHIVE_START to TRUE or by issuing the archive log start command after the instance startup. When automatic archiving is enabled, the ARCH (archiver) process copies the filled redo log files to the directory specified by LOG_ARCHIVE_DEST. The LOG_ARCHIVE_FORMAT parameter defines the default names of archived log files.

Understanding Database Instances

An Oracle database stores data in physical data files and allows controlled user-access to these files through a set of operating system processes. These processes are started during the instance startup. Because they work silently, without direct user interaction, they're known as background processes. To enable efficient data manipulation and communication among the various processes, Oracle uses shared memory, known as *Shared Global Area (SGA)*. These background processes and the shared memory segment together are referred as an Oracle *instance*. In a parallel server environment, a database can be accessed by multiple instances running on different machines.

An Oracle instance consists of the following background processes:

- *The process monitor process (PMON).* This background process cleans up after a user process terminates abnormally. It rolls back the uncommitted transaction left behind and releases the resources locked by the process that no longer exists.

- *The database writer process (DBWR).* To ensure efficient and concurrent data manipulation, Oracle doesn't allow a user process to directly modify a data block on the disk. The blocks that need to be modified or in which the data is inserted are first fetched in a common pool of buffers, known as *buffer cache*. These blocks are then written to the disk in batches by the DBWR background process. Thus, DBWR is the only process with write access to the Oracle data files.

- *The log writer process (LGWR).* Whenever an Oracle process modifies an Oracle data block, it also writes these changes to the redo log buffers. It's the responsibility of the LGWR process to write the redo log buffers to the online redo log file. This process reads the contents of the redo log buffers in batches and writes them to the online redo log file in sequential fashion. Note that LGWR is the only process writing to the online redo log files. Oracle's transaction commit algorithm ensures that the contents of redo log buffers are flushed to the online redo log file whenever a transaction is committed.

- *The system monitor process (SMON).* This background process does operations such as freeing up the sort space and coalescing the adjacent free extents in one big extent. SMON is also responsible for performing transaction recovery during the instance recovery (during instance startup after a crash or shutdown abort). In a parallel server environment, it also detects and performs instance recovery for another failed instance.

- *The archiver process (ARCH).* This process is started when the database is in archive log mode and automatic archiving is enabled. It copies the recently filled online redo log file to an assigned backup destination.

Oracle background processes that are always started

The LMON, PMON, DBWR, and LGWR processes are always present for an instance. Other processes are started by setting up a related initialization parameter.

- *The checkpoint process (CKPT)*. During a checkpoint, the DBWR process writes all the modified blocks to disk. DBWR also tells LGWR to update the header information of all data files with the checkpoint information. Because a database containing a larger amount of data files might be a time-consuming task for LGWR, the CKPT process starts during instance startup to help LGWR update the file headers during the checkpoint. This process is started only when the CHECKPOINT_PROCESS parameter is set to TRUE or when the number of data files in the database is more than a certain number.

- *The recoverer process (RECO)*. This process is responsible for recovering the in-doubt transaction in a distributed database environment. This process is started only when the initialization parameter DISTRIBUTED_TRANSACTION is set to greater than 0.

- *The parallel query slave processes (pxxx)*. Under favorable conditions, Oracle can reduce the execution time for certain SQL operations by dividing the operation among several dedicated processes. The processes used for parallel execution of SQL statements are known as parallel query slaves.

- *The snapshot process (SNPn)*. The snapshot or the job queue processes are started when the parameter JOB_QUEUE_PROCESSES is set more than 0. These processes execute jobs in the job queue, refresh any snapshot that's configured for automatic refresh, and so on.

- *The dispatcher process (Dxxx)*. Oracle supports multithreaded servers on some operating systems. When enabled, these processes receive the user request and put it in the request queues for execution. They also collect the results of the execution from the dispatcher queues and pass them back to users.

- *The shared server process (Sxxx).* In a multithreaded server environment, the dedicated server process executes the SQL operations from the request queues and puts back the results in the corresponding dispatcher queue.

If you're running Oracle's parallel server option, you also see the following background processes on each instance:

- *The lock process (Lckn).* This Oracle parallel server process coordinates all the lock requests from the local and remote instances. It communicates with user processes and the lock daemon process.

- *The lock monitor process (LMON).* This Oracle parallel server process is responsible for reconfiguring the Integrated Distributed Lock Manager (IDLM) during instance startup and shutdown in an OPS environment. It also performs lock cleanup after abnormal death of a user process.

- *The lock daemon process (LMD0).* This Oracle parallel server process is part of the IDLM. It handles all lock requests from remote instances for the locks held by a local instance.

Figure 1.2 shows the components of an Oracle instance: the SGA and background processes.

Starting and Stopping Instances

An Oracle database isn't accessible to users until it's opened by an Oracle instance. In an Oracle parallel server environment, an Oracle database is accessed by more than one instance. Each instance has its own set of background processes and the SGA. An instance startup operation involves starting all the background processes and allocating the shared memory area (see Figure 1.3).

How Oracle starts instances

1. Oracle starts all the background processes and allocates the SGA. Oracle reads the initialization parameter file during this step.

Who can start up and shut down an Oracle instance?

An instance startup operation can be done only by users with the requisite OS privileges or who have been assigned an **OSOPER** or **OSDBA** role.

FIGURE 1.2

An Oracle instance consists of the SGA and background processes.

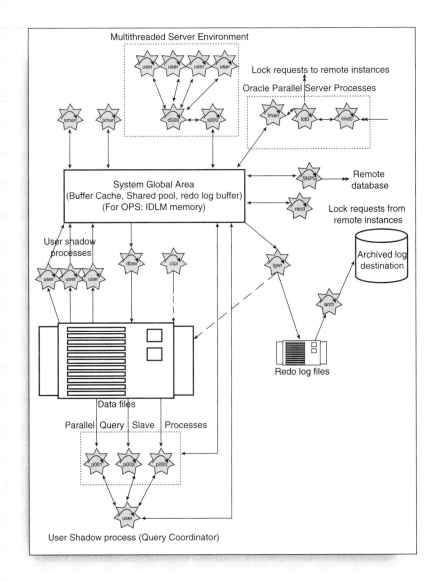

2. Oracle reads the control file and associates the control with the instances. It detects the conditions of the database from the last shutdown/crash.

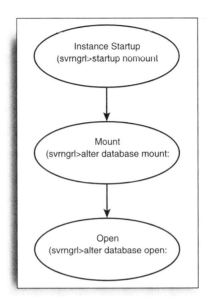

FIGURE 1.3

Oracle instance startup consists of three steps.

3. Oracle reads the file headers of all the data files and redo log files. It ensures consistency among all data files. If the instance is being started after a crash or shutdown abort, Oracle also applies all the redo log since the last successful checkpoint. Oracle database is accessible to users after completing this step.

If the instance is started after a crash or shutdown abort, Oracle needs to perform rollback operations for the uncommitted transaction. This operation is performed by SMON in the background while the database is open and available for use.

An Oracle instance shutdown closes the database, dismounts it, and then removes the SGA and the background processes. Shutdown offers three modes: normal, immediate, and abort. Shutdown normal and shutdown immediate are used most often, whereas shutdown abort should be used with caution. During shutdown normal, Oracle waits for all users to disconnect, writes all modified data to the data files, and then updates files headers, online redo log files, and control files. Shutdown immediate disconnects all users and then proceeds similarly to shutdown immediate. Shutdown abort just removes all the background processes and the SGA; all cleanup work is done during the next startup.

Table 1.1 lists Server Manager commands to start and stop an Oracle instance.

TABLE 1.1   **Server Manager startup and shutdown commands**

Command:	Description:
startup and startup open	Uses the default parameter file to start the instance, mount the database, and open it
startup pfile=*file*	Starts the instance by using the specified parameter file
startup nomount	Allocates the SGA and starts the background processes; doesn't mount and open the database
startup mount	Allocates the SGA, starts the background process, and mounts the database; doesn't open the database
alter database mount	Mounts the database after the instance is started with startup nomount command
alter database open	Opens the database after it's mounted by the startup mount command
shutdown	Closes the instance after all users disconnect (normal shutdown)
shutdown immediate	Doesn't allow any new transactions to start; rolls back uncommitted transactions and closes the instance
shutdown abort	Immediately removes the SGA and the background processes

SEE ALSO
➤ *To learn how to start and stop database instances with Oracle Enterprise Manager, see page 109*

Oracle8's Tools

Oracle provides various tools for application development and for performing administrative functions:

- Oracle Enterprise Manager (OEM)
- SQL*Plus
- PL/SQL
- Net8
- Developer 2000
- Precompilers

Oracle Enterprise Manager (OEM)

Oracle Enterprise Manager is a graphical system management tool that allows you to perform multiple tasks in a complicated database environment. OEM comes with several components. Some components, such as Oracle Expert and Performance Manager, are priced separately. Chapter 4, "Managing with Oracle Enterprise Manager (OEM)," explains how to use these components. OEM's major components are as follows (see Figure 1.4):

- *Backup Manager* lets you perform backup and recovery operations associated with the database. It lets you interface with Oracle8's advanced backup and recovery utility, the Recovery Manager.

- *Data Manager*, a data transfer and loading tool, lets you invoke export, import, and load utilities. Use the Export utility to extract data in Oracle's operating system-independent format. The exported data can be loaded in another Oracle database or later in the same database. You also can use Export as the database's logical backup. The Loader utility is used to insert data in the Oracle database from text files.

- *Instance Manager* lets you manage instances, user sessions, and in-doubt transactions. It lets you start and shut down Oracle instances. You can manage multiple instances in an Oracle parallel server environment. It also lets you manage the initialization parameter file used during instance startup.

- *Lock Manager* lets you view the locks held in an instance. It's a helpful tool for analyzing hung sessions and other, similar situations.

- *Oracle Expert* lets you tune instance and database performance. It generates a listing of recommendations that can be implemented automatically to improve the performance.

- *Performance Manager* lets you monitor an Oracle instance performance. It provides you with graphical representation of various performance statistics.

- *Schema Manager* lets you perform Data Definition Language (DDL) operations, which let you create, alter, drop, and view database objects such as tables, indexes, clusters, triggers, and sequences.

- *Security Manager* lets you perform user-management tasks such as adding, altering, and dropping users, roles, and profiles.

- *Software Manager* allows you to administer in an distributed environment and to automate database administration tasks.

- *SQL Worksheet* behaves mostly similar to a SQL*Plus session. You can use it to enter and execute SQL commands.

- *Storage Manager* lets you perform database space-management tasks such as creating, altering, and dropping tablespaces. It also lets you create online/offline and drop rollback segments.

- *Tablespace Manager* lets you view the space usage within a tablespace at object level. You can also get information about used and free space within the database.

- *TopSession Monitor* lets you monitor active user sessions and view user resource utilization. This information can be used to address slow performance.

- *Oracle Trace* lets you drill down the execution of SQL statements to improve performance of the system.

FIGURE 1.4
Oracle Enterprise Manager consists of
several modules.

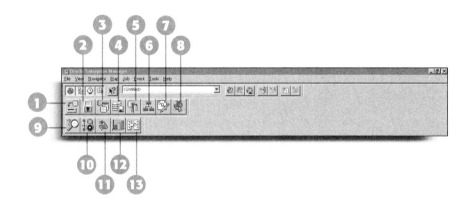

①	Backup Manager	⑧	Software Manager
②	Security Manager	⑨	Oracle Expert
③	Data Manager	⑩	Lock Manager
④	Storage Manager	⑪	TopSession Monitor
⑤	Instance Manager	⑫	Performance Manager
⑥	Schema Manager	⑬	Tablespace Manager
⑦	SQL Worksheet		

SQL*Plus

SQL*Plus can't start or stop an instance

A database administrator can't start and shut down an Oracle instance by using SQL*Plus.

The only interface available between end users and an RDBMS is Structured Query Language (SQL). All other applications and tools that users utilize to interact with the RDBMS act as translators/interpreters. These tools generate SQL commands based on a user's request and pass the generated SQL commands on to the RDBMS.

SQL*Plus, Oracle's version of SQL, is one of the most commonly used Oracle tools. SQL*Plus enables users to instruct the Oracle instance to perform the following SQL functions:

- Data definition or DDL operations, such as creating, altering, and dropping database objects
- Data query to select or retrieve the stored data
- Data manipulation or the DML operations to insert, update, and delete data
- Access and transfer data between the databases
- Allow user to enter data interactively
- DBA functions or the database administrative tasks such as managing users (creating, altering, and dropping users), managing space (creating, altering, and dropping tablespaces), and backup and recovery

In addition to these basic SQL functions, SQL*Plus also provides several editing and formatting functions that enable users to print query results in report format.

Setting Up the SQL*Plus Environment

SQL*Plus has many advanced functions that you can use to present data in a visually pleasing format. You can set various environment variables in order to control the way SQL*Plus outputs a query. Table 1.2 lists some of the most common commands to set up the environment, which you can enter at the SQLPLUS> prompt.

TABLE 1.2 **SQL*Plus environment commands**

Command:	Description:
`set pagesize`	Sets the number of lines per page
`set linesize`	Sets the number of characters in a line
`set newpage`	Sets the number of blank lines between pages
`set pause`	Causes SQL*Plus to pause before each page
`set array`	Sets the number of rows retrieved at a time
`set feedback`	Displays the number of records processed by a query
`set heading`	Prints a heading at the beginning of the report
`set serveroutput`	Allows output from `DBMS_OUTPUT.PUT_LINE` stored procedure to be displayed
`set time`	Displays timing statistics
`set term`	Allows you to suppress output generated by a command executed from a file

Set up the environment automatically

You also can use the LOGIN.SQL and GLOGIN.SQL files to set up the environment for the current session while invoking SQL*Plus.

PL/SQL

PL/SQL stands for Procedural Language/Structured Query Language. It allows a user to utilize structured programming constructs similar to third-generation languages such as C, Fortran, and COBOL. PL/SQL enhances SQL by adding the following capabilities:

- Define and use variables
- Control the program flow (`IF`, `IF...THEN...ELSE`, and `FOR LOOP` constructs)
- Use of cursors and arrays
- File I/O
- Functions and procedures
- PL/SQL tables to move larger amount of data

With PL/SQL, you can use SQL commands to manipulate data in an Oracle database and also use structured programming constructs to process the data.

PL/SQL is embedded in Oracle8 tools

Although you can use PL/SQL as a programming language, it's also available as part of Oracle tools such as Oracle Forms and Oracle Reports. The PL/SQL engine embedded in these tools acts as the preprocessor.

Net8

Net8, formerly known as SQL*Net, is Oracle's networking interface. It allows communication between various Oracle products residing on different machines. It enables communication among client, server, and Oracle databases in a distributed environment. At the client end, the client application code passes messages on to the Net8 residing locally, and the local Net8 transfers messages to the remote Net8 via the underlying transport protocol. These messages are received by Net8 at the server, which sends them to the database server for execution. The server executes the request and responds to the client following the same path. Figure 1.5 shows the communication between client and server using Net8.

FIGURE 1.5

The client and the server communicate with each other through Net8.

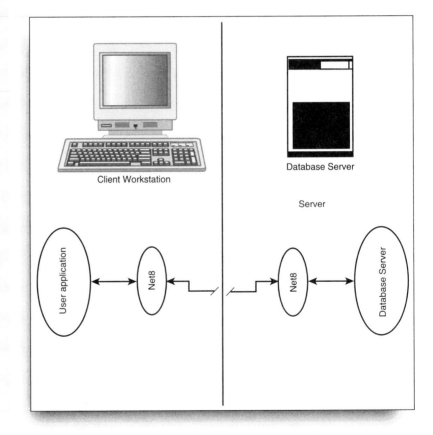

Net8 has many enhancements over its predecessor SQL*Net, such as connection pooling, multiplexing, listener load balancing, and caching the network addresses at the client end. Net8 is backward-compatible and can coexist with SQL*Net version 2.

Precompilers

A third-generation language compiler doesn't recognize the SQL needed to interface with the RDBMS. Therefore, if you need power and flexibility of a language such as C, C++, Fortran, or COBOL and also want it to interface with the Oracle8 RDBMS, you need a tool that can convert the SQL statements to the calls that a language compiler can understand. As Figure 1.6 shows, a precompiler program reads structured source code and generates a source file that a language compiler can process. Oracle provides several precompilers, such as Pro*C, Pro*Cobol, Pro*Fortran, and Pro*Pascal.

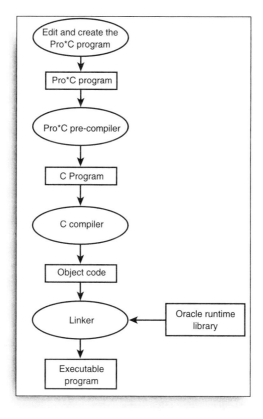

FIGURE 1.6

You develop programs by using a precompiler.

You might want to use precompilers to get better performance while developing long-running batch programs and time-critical programs. You can do the following by using precompilers:

- Use dynamic SQL.
- Better control cursor and program flow.
- Develop program libraries and use them in multiple applications.
- Concurrently access the data from multiple databases.
- Write multithreaded applications by forking processes.

Developer/2000

Developer/2000 provides the complete set of tools to develop applications that access an Oracle database. It consists of tools for creating forms, reports, charts, queries, and procedures. It also enables you to deploy existing and new applications on the Web. Developer/2000 consists of the following component tools:

- *Project Builder.* You can track and control application documents, source code files, charts, forms, reports, queries, and so on.
- *Forms Builder.* Forms are one of the easiest and most popular means for end users to interact with the database. End users totally unfamiliar with the database and the SQL language can easily learn a forms-based application to access the Oracle database. Forms Builder is the tool application developers can use to develop forms.
- *Report Builder.* Although forms give users online/immediate interaction with the database, the Report Builder allows users to queue the data extraction request in a queue at a remote report server. The report server, in turn, interacts with the database to generate the reports. You can also embed the reports in other online tools such as Web browsers, graphics, and forms.
- *Graphics Builder.* Graphical and visual representation of the data is much more effective than raw data. You can use Graphics Builder to produce interactive graphical displays.

Graphics Builder also allows you to include graphs in forms and reports.

- *Query Builder.* Query Builder allows you to interact with database tables in tabular form onscreen. The tables involved in the query are available onscreen, and users can construct the desired query by pointing and clicking. Formatted query results are also displayed.

- *Schema Builder.* Schema Builder is a graphical DDL (data definition language) tool. You can use it to create, alter, and drop database objects such as tables, indexes, clusters, and sequences.

- *Procedure Builder.* The Procedure Builder helps you build procedures interactively. You can use its graphical interface to create, edit, debug, and compile PL/SQL programs. The PL/SQL programs unit, which can be generated with the Procedure Builder, includes packages, triggers, functions, and program libraries.

- *Translation Builder.* The Translation Builder allows you to extract translatable strings from Oracle or non-Oracle resources and perform the desired transaction. For example, you can translate Microsoft Windows (.RC) and HTML files to Oracle resource files.

Traditionally, Developer/2000 supported the client/server architecture, where the client tools and the application reside on one machine (usually the end-user PC) and the database server resides on another machine. With the proliferation of the Web, however, Oracle has introduced a three-tier architecture in which an additional server that runs the application code has been introduced.

Client/server, or the three-tier, architecture for installing Developer/2000 is highly recommended because the workload is distributed among the client, database server, and application servers in this structure. In addition, the application, Developer/2000, and the database software are independent of each other, thus making maintenance easier. SQL*Net or Net8 needs to be installed on the client and the database server to enable the connectivity between the two.

The Oracle8 Data Dictionary

Data dictionary tables are created
when the database is created

Oracle automatically updates these
tables whenever it needs to. Users
should never update any table in
the data dictionary. Several Oracle
and non-Oracle tools also create
some objects in the data dictionary
that are used for storing operational,
reference, and configuration information.

Oracle stores information about all the objects defined by the
users, structural information about the database, and so on in its
internal tables. These Oracle internal tables and associated
objects are collectively referred as the *data dictionary*. The data
dictionary is owned by the user SYS and always resides in the
SYSTEM tablespace.

Information stored in the data dictionary is available to users
through data dictionary *views*. A database administrator or a user
can use the data dictionary to view the following information:

- Definitions of the database objects such as tables, partitions,
  indexes, clusters, views, snapshots, triggers, packages, proce-
  dures, functions, sequences, and synonyms
- Users defined in the database
- Storage allocation for the objects in the database and quota
  assigned to each user
- Integrity constraints
- Database links
- Privileges and roles
- Replicated objects, snapshots, and their refresh charac-
  teristics
- Auditing information such as access patterns for various
  objects
- Jobs in the job queue
- Locks and latches held in the database
- Alerts and table queues (advance queues)
- Rollback segments
- SQL*Loader direct load
- NLS settings

Oracle's data dictionary views can broadly be defined in the following classes:

- *Views with the DBA prefix.* These views contain information
  about the entire database. For example, the view DBA_TABLES

gives information about all tables in the database. By default, these views are accessible only to users with the DBA role.

- *Views with the USER prefix.* USER views contain information about the objects owned by the user. For example, USER_TABLES gives information about the tables owned by the user.

- *Views with the ALL prefix.* These views contain information about all objects accessible to the user. Objects accessible to a user include the objects created by the user plus the objects on which he has received grants from other users. For example, the ALL_TABLES view contains information about all tables accessible to a user.

Table 1.3 lists important Oracle8 data dictionary views. Similar views with DBA and ALL prefixes are available.

TABLE 1.3   **Important data dictionary views**

View Name:	Description:
USER_ALL_TABLES	Contains descriptions of all tables available to the user
USER_CLUSTERS	Contains information about clusters created by the user
USER_CONSTRAINTS	Contains information about the constraint defined by the user
USER_DB_LINKS	Contains information about the database link created by the user
USER_ERRORS	Gives all current errors on all stored objects for the user
USER_EXTENTS	Lists all the extents used by the objects owned by the user
USER_FREE_SPACE	Lists all free extents in the tablespaces on which the user has privilege
USER_INDEXES	Gives information about indexes created by the user
USER_IND_COLUMNS	Gives the name of all the columns on which the user has created indexes

continues…

TABLE 1.3 **Continued**

View Name:	Description:
USER_JOBS	Gives all jobs in the job queue owned by the user
USER_RESOURCE_LIMITS	Gives resource limits applicable for the user
USER_SEGMENTS	Gives information about all segments owned by the user
USER_SEQUENCES	Lists information about all sequences owned by the user
USER_SNAPSHOTS	Gives information about all snapshots the user can view
USER_SYNONYMS	Gives the name of all private synonyms for the user
USER_TAB_COLUMNS	Gives the name of all columns in all tables the user owns
USER_TAB_PARTITIONS	Gives information about all table partitions owned by the user
USER_TABLES	Gives information about all tables the user owns
USER_TRIGGERS	Gives information for all triggers created by the user

Statistics and the Data Dictionary

Several data dictionary views contain columns with statistics information for the object. For example, the USER_TABLES view contains columns NUM_ROWS (number of rows in the table), BLOCKS (number of data blocks used in the table), AVG_ROW_LEN (average row length of a row in the table), and so on. These columns are populated only when you analyze the object by using the ANALYZE command. You should analyze the objects at regular intervals to keep the statistics up-to-date.

Dynamic Performance Tables

An Oracle instance maintains comprehensive information about its current configuration and activity. These statistics are accessible to the database administrator through dynamic performance views. Most of these views are based on in-memory table-like structures known as virtual tables (because they aren't real tables). The majority of these views have names starting with V$. These virtual tables don't require disk storage space and aren't stored in any tablespace. By default, the dynamic performance views are accessible to the SYS user or to the users having a SYSDBA role. Contents of these views are updated continuously while the instance is active.

Table 1.4 describes important dynamic performance views. These views are for Oracle8; some may not exist in Oracle7.

TABLE 1.4 Dynamic performance views

View Name:	Description:
V$ACCESS	Displays information about locked database objects and the sessions accessing them
V$CONTROLFILE	Lists names of the database control files
V$DATABASE	Contains miscellaneous database information such as database name creation date, archive/no archive log mode, and so on
V$DATAFILE	Contains information about the data files that are part of the database (This information is from the control file.)
V$DATAFILE_HEADER	Similar to V$DATAFILE, except that information is based on the contents of each data file header
V$DB_LINK	Lists information about all active database links
V$FILESTAT	Displays read/write statistics for each database data file
V$FIXED_TABLE	Contains names of all fixed tables in the database
V$FIXED_VIEW_ DEFINITION	Lists definitions of all the dynamic performance views; you can see how Oracle creates dynamic performance views based on its internal x$ tables; these x$ tables are known as fixed tables
V$LICENSE	Lists license-related information
V$LOCK	Shows the locks held and requested; information in this view useful while tuning the database performance or hanging issues
V$LOCKED_OBJECT	Lists all the objects locked in the database and the sessions that are locking the objects

continues…

Use TIMED_STATISTICS to gather timing information

Many dynamic performance views contain columns, such as WAIT_TIME and TOTAL_WAITS, that contain timing information. Such columns are populated by Oracle only when the TIMED_STATISTICS parameter is set to TRUE.

Global dynamic performance views

In a parallel server environment, every V$ view has a corresponding GV$ view. These views, known as global dynamic performance views, contain information about all active instances of an Oracle parallel server environment. The INST_ID column displays the instance number to which the information displayed in the GV$ view belongs.

Use fixed tables with caution!

Oracle doesn't encourage the use of fixed tables listed in V$FIXED_TABLE because their structure isn't published and can be changed.

TABLE 1.4   **Continued**

View Name:	Description:
V$LOG	Lists information about the online redo logs
V$LOG_HISTORY	Contains information about the archived redo log file
V$MYSTAT	Lists statistics about the current session
V$PARAMETER	Lists current values of the initialization parameters; the ISDEFAULT column indicates whether the parameter value is the default
V$PROCESS	Lists all Oracle processes; a value of 1 in the BACKGROUND column indicates that the process is an Oracle background process; a NULL value in this column indicates a normal user process
V$RECOVER_FILE	Used to query the information about the files needing media recovery; this view can be queried after the instance mounts the database
V$ROLLNAME	Lists names of all the online rollback segments
V$ROLLSTAT	Lists statistics for all online rollback segments
V$SESSION	Contains information about all the current sessions; this view, one of the most informative, has about 35 columns
V$SESSION_EVENT	Contains information about waits each session has incurred on events; use this view if you're experiencing slow performance
V$SESSION_WAIT	Lists the events and resources Oracle is waiting on; information in this view can be used to detect performance bottlenecks
V$SESSTAT	Contains performance statistics for each active session
V$SESS_IO	Lists I/O statistics about each active session
V$STATNAME	Gives names of Oracle statistics displayed in V$SESSTAT and V$SYSSTAT
V$SYSSTAT	Contains performance statistics for the whole instance
V$SYSTEM_EVENT	Contains information for various Oracle events
V$TABLESPACE	Lists names of all tablespaces in the database
V$TRANSACTION	Lists statistics related to transactions in the instance
V$WAITSTAT	Contains block contention statistics

Creating a Database

Prerequisites for Creating a Database

Before you can create an Oracle database, you need to configure the kernel for shared memory. In UNIX, shmmax needs to be set properly to allow for the total SGA set in the initialization file. In Windows NT, make sure that virtual memory isn't more than twice the physical memory on the system.

You also need to make certain decisions regarding how the database will be used and configured. These decisions should include the following:

- *Database sizing.* Proper sizing of the database files can help you choose your initialization parameters. It will result in an optimally tuned database to start with.

- *Changing passwords for* SYS *and* SYSTEM. These passwords will be used to log onto the database and perform administrative tasks. This can be done after database creation. The passwords of the SYS and the SYSTEM users should be changed as soon as possible. Use the ALTER USER command to change these passwords. It's recommended that you create a new account with SYSDBA privileges and use that account to create and own the database.

- *MTS configuration.* The multithreaded server (MTS) pools connections and doesn't allocate a single thread per connection. As a result, it avoids stack overflow and memory allocation errors that would occur from a dedicated connection per thread. A multithreaded server configuration allows many user threads to share very few server threads. The user threads connect to a dispatcher process, which routes client requests to the next available server thread, thereby supporting more users. (You can configure MTS after database creation.)

- *Setting the environment variables.* Setting the ORACLE_SID, ORACLE_HOME, and path variables to the correct values will allow you to start the correct instance.

Protect the password for SYS

Because **SYS** is the owner of the data dictionary, you should protect that password. Allowing the password for **SYS** to get into the wrong hands can lead to tremendous damage to the database to the point that all data can be lost. The default password for **SYS** is CHANGE_ON_INSTALL, whereas the default password for **SYSTEM** is MANAGER.

Prepare the operating system environment for database creation

The operating system memory parameters should also be set properly. Check your operating system–specific documentation for the parameters to set.

Prepare for and create a database (general steps)

1. Create the init*SID*.ora parameter file.

2. Create the config*SID*.ora file.

3. Create the database script crdb*SID*.ora.

4. Create the database.

5. Add rollback segments.

6. Create database objects for tools.

Choosing Initialization Parameters for Your Database

The instance for the Oracle database is started by using a parameter file (init*SID*.ora) that should be customized for the database. You can use the operating system to create this file by making a copy of the one provided by Oracle on the distribution media, or by using the init.ora file from the seed database (if installed) as a template. Rename this file as init*SID*.ora (for example, for the SID ABCD, the name of the initialization file would be initABCD.ora), and then edit it to customize it for your database.

The parameter file is read-only at instance startup. If it's modified, you need to shut down and restart the instance for the new values to take effect. You can edit the parameter file with any operating system editor. Most parameters have a default value, but some parameters need to be modified with uniqueness and performance in mind. Table 2.1 lists parameters that should be specified.

The DBA's operating system privileges

Your database administrator login should have administrator privileges on the operating system to be able to create a database.

Change these parameters from their default values

Most people make the mistake of leaving the initialization parameters to their default value. These default values aren't ideal for most systems. You need to carefully choose the initialization parameters with your database environment in mind.

TABLE 2.1   **Initialization parameters that you should modify**

Parameter:	Description:
DB_NAME	Database identifier (maximum of eight characters). To change the name of an existing database, use the CREATE CONTROLFILE statement to recreate your control file(s) and specify a new database name.
DB_DOMAIN	The network domain where the database is created.
CONTROL_FILES	Names of the control files. If you don't change this parameter, the control files of other databases can be overwritten by the new instance, making the other instances unusable.
DB_BLOCK_SIZE	Size in bytes of Oracle database blocks.
SHARED_POOL_SIZE	Size in bytes of the shared pool.
BACKGROUND_DUMP_DEST	Location where background trace files will be placed.
USER_DUMP_DEST	Location where user trace files will be placed.
DB_BLOCK_BUFFERS	Number of buffers in the buffer cache.
COMPATIBLE	Version of the server that this instance is compatible with.
IFILE	Name of another parameter file included for startup.
MAX_DUMP_FILE_SIZE	Maximum size in OS blocks of the trace files.
PROCESSES	Maximum number of OS processes that can simultaneously connect to this instance.
ROLLBACK_SEGMENTS	Rollback segments allocated to this instance. Refer to the Oracle8 tuning manual for information and guidelines on determining the number and size of rollback segments based on the anticipated number of concurrent transactions.
LOG_BUFFER	Number of bytes allocated to the redo log buffer in the SGA.
LOG_ARCHIVE_START	Enable or disable automatic archiving if the database is in ARCHIVELOG mode.
LOG_ARCHIVE_FORMAT	Default filename format used for archived logs.

Database names should be unique

Attempting to mount two databases with the same name will give you the error ORA-01102: cannot mount database in EXCLUSIVE mode during the second mount.

Parameter:	Description:
LOG_ARCHIVE_DEST	Location of archived redo log files.
LICENSE_MAX_USERS	Maximum number of users created in the database.
LICENSE_MAX_SESSIONS	Maximum number of concurrent sessions for the instance.
LICENSE_SESSIONS_WARNING	Warning limit on the concurrent sessions.

The following is a sample init.ora file:

```
db_name = SJR
db_files = 1020
control_files = (E:\ORANT\database\ctl1SJR.ora,
   E:\ORANT\database\ctl2SJR.ora)
db_file_multiblock_read_count = 16
db_block_buffers = 550
shared_pool_size = 9000000
log_checkpoint_interval = 8000
processes = 100
dml_locks = 200
log_buffer = 32768
sequence_cache_entries = 30
sequence_cache_hash_buckets = 23
#audit_trail = true
#timed_statistics = true
background_dump_dest = E:\ORANT\rdbms80\trace
user_dump_dest = E:\ORANT\rdbms80\trace
db_block_size = 2048
compatible = 8.0.3.0.0
sort_area_size = 65536
log_checkpoint_timeout = 0
remote_login_passwordfile = shared
max_dump_file_size = 10240
```

Create an initialization file

1. Copy the template file. In UNIX, copy $ORACLE_HOME/rdbms/install/rdbms/initx.orc to $ORACLE_HOME/dbs/init*SID*.ora. In Windows NT, copy $ORACLE_HOME\database\initorcl.ora to $ORACLE_HOME\database\init*SID*.ora.

Setting the parameters

The ideal values for these parameters are application dependent and are discussed in more detail in Chapter 21, "Identifying and Reducing Contention," and Chapter 22, "Tuning for Different Types of Applications." Setting these values is based on trial and error. For DSS systems, it's recommended that you choose a large value for these parameters; for OLTP systems, choose a small value for these parameters.

2. Edit the init*SID*.ora by changing the following parameters:

Parameter	UNIX Setting	Windows NT Setting
%pfile_dir%	?/dbs	?/database
%config_ora_file%	config*SID*.ora (created next)	config*SID*.ora (created next)
%rollback_segs%	r01, r02, ...	r01, r02, ...
%init_ora_comments%	#	#

Create config*SID*.ora

1. In UNIX, copy ?/rdbms/install/rdbms/cnfg.orc to ?/dbs/config*SID*.ora. In Windows NT, copy configorcl.ora to config*SID*.ora.

2. Edit the config*SID*.ora file with any ASCII text editor and set the following parameters: control_files, background_dump_dest, user_dump_dest, and db_name.

Create the database script

1. Copy $ORACLE_HOME/rdbms/install/rdbms/crdb.orc to $ORACLE_HOME/dbs/crdb*SID*.sql.

2. Modify the crdb*SID*.sql file to set the following to the appropriate values: db_name, maxinstances, maxlogfiles, db_char_set, system_file, system_size, log1_file, log1_size, log2_file, log2_size, log3_file, and log3_size.

When it's run, the crdb*SID*.sql does the following:

- Runs the catalog.sql script, which will create the data dictionary
- Creates an additional rollback segment, r0, in SYSTEM
- Creates the tablespaces rbs, temporary, tools, and users
- Creates additional rollback segments r01, r02, r03, and r04 in rbs
- Drops the rollback segment r0 in SYSTEM
- Changes temporary tablespaces for SYS and SYSTEM
- Runs catdbsyn.sql as SYSTEM to create private synonyms for DBA-only dictionary views

Getting Ready to Create a Database

Creating a database is the first step in organizing and managing a database system. You can use the following guidelines for database creation on all operating systems. Check your operating system-specific documentation for platform-specific instructions.

Before creating a database, take a complete backup of all your existing databases to protect against accidental modifications/deletions of existing files during database creation. The backup should contain parameter files, data files, redo log files, and control files.

Also decide on a backup strategy and the size that will be required for online and archived redo logs. Backup strategies are discussed in Chapter 13, "Selecting and Implementing a Backup Strategy."

Mirror your control and redo log files

The control files and redo log files help you recover your database. To keep from losing a control file, keep at least two copies of it active on different physical devices. Also, multiplex the redo log files and place the log group members on different disks.

Organizing the Database Contents

You organize the database contents by using tablespaces. On some platforms, the Oracle installer creates a seed database, which has a number of predefined tablespaces. The tablespace structure should be carefully chosen by considering the characteristics of the data to minimize disk contention and fragmentation, and to improve overall performance.

In addition to the SYSTEM tablespace provided with the installation, Table 2.2 describes several other suggested tablespaces. You can create these tablespaces by using the CREATE TABLESPACE command, as shown later in the section "Using the *CREATE DATABASE* Command."

Use multiple tablespaces

Production data and indexes should be stored in *separate* tablespaces.

TABLE 2.2   **Suggested tablespaces to be created with the database**

Tablespace:	Description:
TEMP	Used for sorting and contains temporary segments
RBS	Stores additional rollback segments
TOOLS	Tables needed by the Oracle Server tools
APPS_DATA	Stores production data
APPS_IDX	Store indexes associated with production data in APPS_DATA tablespace

Designing a Database Structure to Reduce Contention and Fragmentation

Separating groups of objects, such as tables with different fragmentation propensity, can minimize contention and fragmentation. You can use Table 2.3 as a guideline for separating objects.

TABLE 2.3   **Fragmentation propensity**

Segment Type:	Fragmentation:
Data dictionary	Zero
Rollback segments	Medium
Temporary segments	High
Application data	Low

You can reduce disk contention by being familiar with the way in which data is accessed and by separating the data segments into groups based on their usage, such as separating

- Segments with different backup needs
- Segments with different security needs
- Segments belonging to different projects
- Large segments from smaller segments
- Rollback segments from other segments
- Temporary segments from other segments
- Data segments from index segments

Database sizing issues should be considered to estimate the size of the tables and indexes.

Decide on the Database Character Set

After the database is created, you can't change the character set without recreating the database. If users will access the database by using a different character set, the database character set should be the same as or a superset of all the character sets that would be used. Oracle8 uses encoding schemes that can be commonly characterized as single-byte 7-bit, single-byte 8-bit, varying-width multi-byte, and fixed-width multi-byte. Refer to the Oracle8 Server reference guide for limitations on using these schemes.

SEE ALSO

➤ *For more information on Oracle's National Language Support (NLS) feature and character sets, see page 692*

Start the Instance

Make sure that the following parameters are set properly in the environment. If the following parameters aren't set properly, your instance won't start or the wrong instance might start:

- ORACLE_SID. This parameter is used by Oracle to determine the instance to which the user will connect. If ORACLE_SID isn't set properly and the CREATE DATABASE statement is run, you can wipe out your existing database and all its data.

- ORACLE_HOME. This parameter shows the full pathname of the Oracle system home directory.

- PATH. It should include $ORACLE_HOME.

- ORA_NLS. This is the path to the language object files. If ORA_NLS isn't set and the database is started with languages and character sets other than the database defaults, they won't be recognized.

After the following environment variables are verified, you can connect to Server Manager as internal and STARTUP NOMOUNT.

Set the environment variables in UNIX

1. Set the ORACLE_SID variable as follows for the sh shell (*xxx* is your SID):
   ```
   ORACLE_SID XXX; export ORACLE_SID
   ```

2. Set the variable as follows for the csh shell:
   ```
   setenv ORACLE_SID XXX
   ```

3. Verify that ORACLE_SID has been set:
   ```
   Echo $ORACLE_SID
   ```

4. Start up the instance in nomount state:

```
$svrmgrl
SVRMGR> Connect internal
SVRMGR> Startup nomount
```

Set the environment variables in Windows NT

1. Use regedt32 to set the variables in the Registry's \HKEY_LOCAL_MACHINE\SOFTWARE\ORACLE hive. Or, from a DOS prompt, type

```
C: > set ORACLE_SID=XXX
```

where *xxx* is your SID name (maximum of four characters).

2. Use the Services tool in the Windows Control Panel to ensure that the ORACLESERVICE*SID* service is started.

Using Instance Manager on Windows NT

On Windows NT, you can use the **ORADIM** utility (Instance Manager) to create a new instance and service for your database.

Choosing the Method for Creating the Database

You have several options to create the database:

- You can use the Oracle installer to create a database—this is probably the easiest method of database creation because it allows the creation of a *seed* database, which you can use as a template to create new databases. Check your installation guide for platform-specific instructions for creating the seed database which has a fixed platform-specific schema. This method is discussed in the following section.

- You can modify the create database scripts provided with Oracle as desired to create a database with your own schema. The name and location of these scripts varies with the operating system. On Windows 95/NT, the BUILDALL.SQL and BUILD_DB.SQL scripts can be used as a starting point for database creation. On UNIX systems, the crdb*SID*.sql is a similar script for database creation. By using this method, you can copy these mentioned scripts, make necessary changes to create the database, and then run the scripts to create the database. You can specify parameters such as MAXDATAFILES and specify multiple SYSTEM tablespace database files by using this method.

- Manually create the database by executing the CREATE DATABASE command. Refer to the Oracle SQL reference manual for the complete syntax. This method allows for more flexibility by allowing you to specify MAXDATAFILES on parameters or multiple SYSTEM tablespace data files. But, there's also more possibility of syntax errors.

After the database is created, you can run catalog.sql and catproc.sql while connected as the SYS of "internal" account to create the data dictionary views.

After the database is created, the SYSTEM tablespace and SYSTEM rollback segment will exist. A second rollback segment must be created and activated in the SYSTEM tablespace before any other tablespace can be created in the database. To create a rollback segment, from the Server Manager prompt type

```
Svrmgr>Create rollback segment newsegment
Tablespace system
Storage (...);
```

Refer to the SQL Language manual for the complete syntax of the CREATE ROLLBACK SEGMENT command.

Using the Oracle Installer (*ORAINST*) to Create a Database

This menu-driven method is probably the easiest because it runs the necessary scripts for any selected product. You can use this method to create a seed database. The installation guide for your platform should have specific instructions for this purpose.

Oracle's installer isn't very flexible

Using the Oracle installer for database creation isn't as flexible as the preceding methods in terms of specifying param-eters such as MAXDATAFILES. If this method is used, you'll have to create the other standard non-system tablespaces.

Using the *CREATE DATABASE* Command

You also can create a database by using the SQL command
CREATE DATABASE:

```
CREATE DATABASE database
    [CONTROLFILE [REUSE]]
    [LOGFILE filespec[, ...]]
    MAXLOGFILES integer
    MAXLOGMEMBERS integer
    MAXLOGHISTORY integer
    DATAFILE filespec[, ...]
    MAXDATAFILES integer
    MAXINSTANCES integer
        ARCHIVELOG¦NOARCHIVELOG
    EXCLUSIVE
    CHARACTERSET charset
```

Table 2.4 lists the settings available with the CREATE DATABASE command.

TABLE 2.4   *CREATE DATABASE* settings

Option:	Description:
database	The name of the database to be created.
CONTROLFILE REUSE	Specifies that existing control files specified by the CONTROL_FILES parameter can be reused. If REUSE is omitted and control files exist, you'll get an error.
LOGFILE	Specifies one or more files to be used as redo log files. Each filespec specifies a redo log file group containing one or more redo log file members or copies. If you omit this parameter, Oracle will create two redo log file groups by default.
MAXLOGFILES	Specifies the maximum number of redo log file groups that can ever be created for this database.
MAXLOGMEMBERS	Specifies the maximum number of members or copies for a redo log file group.
MAXLOGHISTORY	This parameter is useful only if you're using the PARALLEL SERVER option and in parallel and ARCHIVELOG mode. It specifies the maximum number of archived redo log files for automatic media recovery.

Option:	Description:
DATAFILE	Specifies one or more files to be used as data files.
MAXDATAFILES	Specifies the maximum number of data files that can ever be created for this database.
MAXINSTANCES	Specifies the maximum number of instances that can simultaneously have this parameter mounted and open.
ARCHIVELOG or NOARCHIVELOG	Establishes the mode for the redo log files groups. NOARCHIVELOG is the default mode.
EXCLUSIVE	Mounts the database in the exclusive mode after it's created. In this mode, only one instance can access the database.
CHARACTERSET	Specifies the character set the database uses to store the data. This parameter can't be changed after the database is created. The supported character sets and default value of this parameter are operating system dependent.

Oracle performs the following operations when executing the CREATE DATABASE command:

- Creates the data files as specified (if previously existing data files are specified, their data is erased)
- Creates and initializes the specified control files
- Creates and initializes the redo logs as specified
- Creates the SYSTEM tablespace and the SYSTEM rollback segment
- Creates the data dictionary
- Creates the SYS and SYSTEM users
- Specifies the character set for the database
- Mounts and opens the database

The data dictionary may not be created automatically

You need to run the SQL scripts to create the data dictionary (catalog.sql and catproc.sql) if these scripts aren't run from your database creation script.

The following example shows how to create a simple database:

```
create database test
    controlfile reuse
    logfile GROUP 1
('C:\ORANT\DATABASE\log1atest.ora',
'D:\log1btest.ora') size 500K reuse,
GROUP 2
```

```
( 'C:\ORANT\DATABASE\log2atest.ora',
'D:\log2btest.ora' ) size 500K reuse
    datafile 'C:\ORANT\DATABASE\sys1test.ora'
    ➥size 10M reuse autoextend on
     next 10M maxsize 200M
    character set WE8ISO8859P1;
```

This command creates a database called TEST with one data file (sys1test.ora) that's 10MB in size and multiplexed redo log files with a size of 500KB each. The character set will be WE8ISO8859P1.

Creating a Database from the Seed Database

The following steps can be used to create a database called MARS, using the starter (seed) database ORCL. If you don't have the starter database, you can use the sample initialization file INITORCL.80 in the c:\orant\database directory.

Create a database in Windows NT with BUILD_ALL.sql

1. Create a directory called MARS.

2. Copy C:\ORANT\DATABASE\INITORCL.ORA to C:\MARS.

3. Modify the DB_NAME, CONTROL_FILES, GLOBAL_NAMES, and DB_FILES parameters in the INITMARS.ORA file.

4. Use the ORADIM80 command to create the service. For example, from a DOS prompt, type
   ```
   C: > oradim80 -NEW -SID TEST -INTPWD password
       -STARTMODE AUTO
       -PFILE c:\orant\database\inittest.ora
   ```

   This command creates a new service called TEST, which is started automatically when Windows NT starts. INTPWD is the password for the "internal" account; the PFILE parameter provides the full pathname of init*SID*.ora.

5. Set ORACLE_SID to MARS:
   ```
   C: > Set ORACLE_SID=MARS
   ```

6. Copy the BUILD_DB.SQL script to c:\mars.

When to create Oracle services

An Oracle *service* should be created and started only if you want to create a database and don't have any other database on your system, or copy an existing database to a new database and retain the old database.

7. Edit the BUILD_MARS.SQL script as follows:

- Set PFILE to the full pathname for INITMARS.ORA.

- Change CREATE DATABASE ORACLE to CREATE DATABASE MARS.

- Change the data files and log filenames to the appropriate names.

- Modify the location of the Oracle home directory to point to C:\MARS.

8. Use Control Panel's Services tools to verify that the service ORACLESERVICEMARS is started. If it's not started, start it.

9. Start Server Manager and connect to the database as "internal":

```
C: > svrmgr30
C: > connect internal/password
```

10. Start the database in the NOMOUNT state:

```
SVRMGR> STARTUP NOMOUNT PFILE=c:\mars\initmars.ora
```

11. Turn on spooling to trap error messages and run BUILD_MARS.SQL:

```
SVRMGR> SPOOL build.log
SVRMGR> @BUILD_MARS.SQL
```

If there are errors while running BUILD_MARS.SQL, fix the errors and rerun the script for successful completion.

12. Generate the data dictionary by running CATALOG.SQL:

```
SVRMGR> @%RDBMS80%\ADMIN\CATALOG.SQL
```

13. Run CATPROC.SQL to generate the objects used by PL/SQL:

```
SVRMGR> @%RDBMS80%\ADMIN\CATPROC.SQL
```

14. If you want additional features, run the appropriate scripts, such as CATREP8M.SQL for Advanced Replication.

15. Turn off spooling and check the log for errors.

All the MAX parameters are set when the database is created. To determine what parameters your database has been created with, execute the following:

```
SVRMGR> Alter database backup controlfile to trace
```

This command will create an SQL script that contains several database commands:

```
CREATE CONTROLFILE REUSE DATABASE "SJR" NORESETLOGS
NOARCHIVELOG
    MAXLOGFILES 32
    MAXLOGMEMBERS 2
    MAXDATAFILES 254
    MAXINSTANCES 1
    MAXLOGHISTORY 899
LOGFILE
  GROUP 1 'E:\ORANT\DATABASE\LOGSJR1.ORA'   SIZE 200K,
  GROUP 2 'E:\ORANT\DATABASE\LOGSJR2.ORA'   SIZE 200K
DATAFILE
  'E:\ORANT\DATABASE\SYS1SJR.ORA',
  'E:\ORANT\DATABASE\RBS1SJR.ORA',
  'E:\ORANT\DATABASE\USR1SJR.ORA',
  'E:\ORANT\DATABASE\TMP1SJR.ORA',
  'E:\ORANT\DATABASE\INDX1SJR.ORA'
;
```

CATALOG.SQL and CATEXP.SQL views don't depend on each other

You don't need to run CATALOG.SQL before running CATEXP.SQL, even though CATEXP.SQL is called from within CATALOG.SQL. This is because no view in CATEXP.SQL depends on views defined in CATALOG.SQL.

To generate SQL statements for all the objects in the database, Export must query the data dictionary to find the relevant information about each object. Export uses the view definitions in CATEXP.SQL to get the information it needs. Run this script while connected as SYS or "internal." The views created by CATEXP.SQL are also used by the Import utility. Chapter 25, "Using SQL*Loader and Export/Import," discusses more about Oracle's Export and Import utilities.

Create an identical copy of database but with no data

1. Do a full database export with ROWS=N:

   ```
   C: > exp system/manager full=y rows=n file=fullexp.dmp
   ```

   This will create a full database export (full=y) without any rows (rows=n).

2. Run a full database import with ROWS=N:

```
C: > imp system/manager full=y rows=n file=fullexp.dmp
```

Use Instance Manager to create a new database in Windows NT

1. From the Start menu choose Oracle for Windows NT and then NT Instance Manager. This will start the Instance Manager and show you the status and startup mode of all the SIDs (see Figure 2.1).

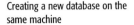

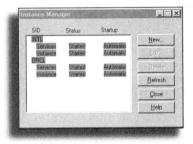

FIGURE 2.1

The Instance Manager dialog box shows the available instances.

Creating a new database on the same machine

If the new database is to be created on the same machine as the old database, you need to pre-create the new tablespaces because the old data files are already in use.

2. Click the New button and supply the SID, internal password, and startup specifications for the new instance (see Figure 2.2).

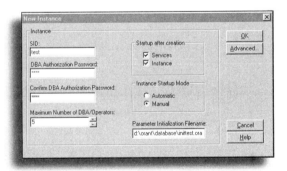

FIGURE 2.2

Provide the specifications for the new instance.

3. Click the Advanced button and choose appropriate database name, logfile, and data file parameters and a character set for the new database (see Figure 2.3).

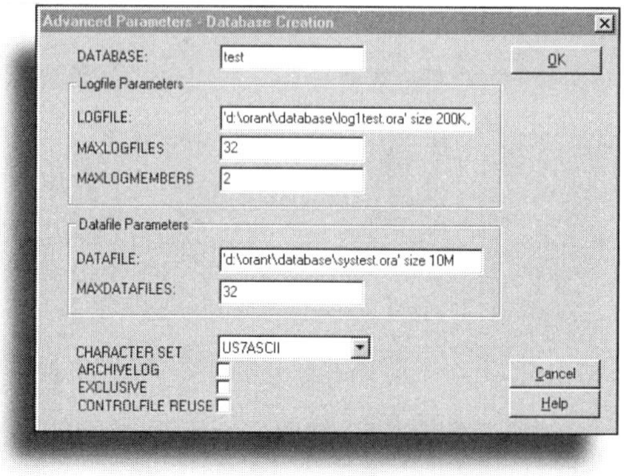

FIGURE 2.3

Provide the specifications for
the new database.

The Oracle Database Assistant can be used to create a database
at any time.

Use Oracle Database Assistant to create a new database in Windows NT

1. From the Start menu choose Programs, Oracle for Windows
NT, Oracle Database Assistant.

2. Select Create a Database and click Next.

3. Choose the Typical or Custom option and click Next. The
Custom option lets you to customize the parameters of the
database that you're trying to create.

4. Choose Finish.

In Windows NT, you can set the default SID by setting the
Registry entry ORACLE_SID.

Updating *ORACLE_SID* in the Windows NT Registry

1. From the DOS command prompt, type REGEDT32.

2. Choose the key \HKEY_LOCAL_MACHINE\
SOFTWARE\ORACLE\HOMEID.

3. From the Edit menu choose Add Value.

4. In the Value Name text box, type ORACLE_SID.

5. For the Data Type, choose REG_EXPAND_SZ.

6. Click OK.

7. Type your SID name in the String Editor text box and
click OK.

8. Exit the Registry.

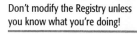

Don't modify the Registry unless
you know what you're doing!

Be extremely careful when working
with the Registry. Improperly set
keys may prevent Windows NT
from booting up.

Checking the Status of Your Database

After the database is created, regularly check the status of the database by examining its data dictionary and the alert log.

Examining Basic Views

The *data dictionary* is one of the most important parts of the Oracle database. The data dictionary is a set of tables and views that you can use to look up valuable information about the database. You can use the data dictionary to obtain various types of information, including:

- General database structure
- Information about schema objects
- Integrity constraints
- Database users
- Privileges and roles
- Space allocated to database objects

The catalog.sql and catproc.sql scripts can be used during or after database creation to create the commonly used data dictionary views and for PL/SQL support, respectively.

The data dictionary contains a set of base tables and associated set of views that can be placed in the following categories:

View Category	Description
USER_*xxx*	Views accessible by any user that provide information on objects owned by them
ALL_*xxx*	Views accessible by any user that provide information on all objects accessible by them
DBA_*xxx*	Views accessible by any user that provide information on any database object

Which data dictionary objects do I have?

All the data dictionary tables and views are owned by SYS. You can query the DICTIONARY table to obtain the list of all dictionary views.

The following examples show how to query the dictionary tables to obtain information about the database:

- To identify all the rollback segments in the current database and their status, use
  ```
  Select * from dba_rollback_segs;
  ```

- To identify all the data files in the current database and their status, use
  ```
  Select * from dba_data_files;
  ```

- To identify all the tablespaces in the current database and their status, use
  ```
  Select * from dba_tablespaces;
  ```

- To identify all the users belonging to this database, use
  ```
  Select * from dba_users;
  ```

- To find out if the database is in the ARCHIVELOG mode, use
  ```
  Select * from v$database;
  ```

- To identify all the parameter values in use for the database, use
  ```
  Select * from v$parameter;
  ```

Checking the Oracle Alert Log

Locating trace files

The trace file would be located in the directory specified by BACKGROUND_DUMP_DEST, USER_DUMP_DEST, or CORE_DUMP_DEST, depending on the exact error and its cause.

When diagnosing a database problem, the first place to look for information and errors is the alert log (the name is operating system dependent). If this file isn't present, Oracle will automatically create it during database startup. This file can point you to the location of trace files, which can give a lot of insight into the problems encountered. It also contains additional information to indicate the status of the database and what's now happening in the database.

SEE ALSO

➤ *For more information on the contents and usage of the alert log, see page 617*

When the database is started, the following information is recorded in the alert log:

- All the init.ora parameters
- Informational messages indicating that the background processes have been started

- The thread used by the instance
- The log sequence that the LGWR is now writing to

In general, the alert log records all important incidents of the database, including:

- Database startups
- Database shutdowns
- Rollback segment creations
- Tablespace creations
- ALTER statements issued
- Log switches
- Error messages

Each entry has a timestamp associated with it, and each non-error message has an entry marking its beginning and another entry marking its successful completion. You should frequently check this file for error messages for which the alert log will point to a trace file for more information.

The following is a sample alert log:

```
Dump file E:\ORANT\rdbms80\trace\sjrALRT.LOG
Thu Jan 29 09:33:46 1998
ORACLE V8.0.3.0.0 - Production vsnsta=0
vsnsql=c vsnxtr=3
Windows NT V4.0, OS V5.101, CPU type 586
Starting up ORACLE RDBMS Version: 8.0.3.0.0.
```

1 File header showing information about your system

```
System parameters with non-default values:
processes               = 100
  shared_pool_size      = 9000000
  control_files         = E:\ORANT\database\ctl1SJR.ora,
                          E:\ORANT\database\ctl2SJR.ora
  db_block_buffers      = 550
  db_block_size         = 2048
  compatible            = 8.0.3.0.0
  log_buffer            = 32768
  log_checkpoint_interval = 8000
  log_checkpoint_timeout  = 0
  db_files              = 1020
  db_file_multiblock_read_count= 16
```

2 Initialization parameters

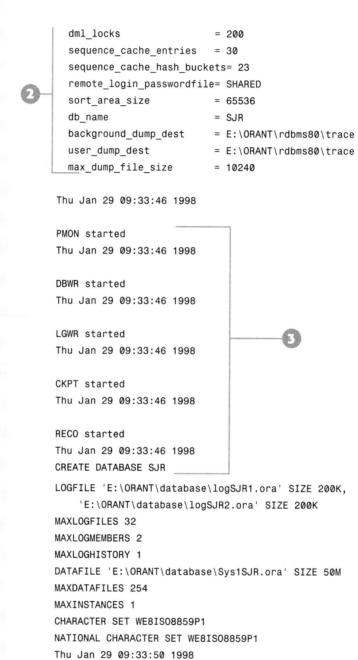

```
dml_locks                 = 200
sequence_cache_entries    = 30
sequence_cache_hash_buckets= 23
remote_login_passwordfile= SHARED
sort_area_size            = 65536
db_name                   = SJR
background_dump_dest       = E:\ORANT\rdbms80\trace
user_dump_dest            = E:\ORANT\rdbms80\trace
max_dump_file_size         = 10240


Thu Jan 29 09:33:46 1998

PMON started
Thu Jan 29 09:33:46 1998

DBWR started
Thu Jan 29 09:33:46 1998

LGWR started
Thu Jan 29 09:33:46 1998

CKPT started
Thu Jan 29 09:33:46 1998

RECO started
Thu Jan 29 09:33:46 1998
CREATE DATABASE SJR

LOGFILE 'E:\ORANT\database\logSJR1.ora' SIZE 200K,
     'E:\ORANT\database\logSJR2.ora' SIZE 200K
MAXLOGFILES 32
MAXLOGMEMBERS 2
MAXLOGHISTORY 1
DATAFILE 'E:\ORANT\database\Sys1SJR.ora' SIZE 50M
MAXDATAFILES 254
MAXINSTANCES 1
CHARACTER SET WE8ISO8859P1
NATIONAL CHARACTER SET WE8ISO8859P1
Thu Jan 29 09:33:50 1998
Successful mount of redo thread 1.
Thread 1 opened at log sequence 1
```

3 Database in nomount state and CREATE DATABASE command.

```
Current log# 1 seq# 1 mem# 0: E:\ORANT\DATABASE\LOGSJR1.ORA
Successful open of redo thread 1.
Thu Jan 29 09:33:50 1998
SMON: enabling cache recovery
Thu Jan 29 09:33:50 1998
create tablespace SYSTEM datafile
   'E:\ORANT\database\Sys1SJR.ora' SIZE 50M
  default storage (initial 10K next 10K) online


Thu Jan 29 09:34:10 1998
Completed: create tablespace SYSTEM datafile 'E:\ORANT\datab
Thu Jan 29 09:34:10 1998
create rollback segment SYSTEM tablespace SYSTEM
  storage (initial 50K next 50K)


Completed: create rollback segment SYSTEM tablespace SYSTEM


Thu Jan 29 09:34:14 1998
Thread 1 advanced to log sequence 2
 Current log# 2 seq# 2 mem# 0: E:\ORANT\DATABASE\LOGSJR2.ORA
Thread 1 cannot allocate new log, sequence 3
Checkpoint not complete
 Current log# 2 seq# 2 mem# 0: E:\ORANT\DATABASE\LOGSJR2.ORA
Thread 1 advanced to log sequence 3
 Current log# 1 seq# 3 mem# 0: E:\ORANT\DATABASE\LOGSJR1.ORA
Thread 1 advanced to log sequence 4
 Current log# 2 seq# 4 mem# 0: E:\ORANT\DATABASE\LOGSJR2.ORA
```

Migrating an Oracle7 Database to Oracle8

Choose a migration method

Design a test plan

Marshall required resources

Perform the migration

Complete post-migration tasks

Why Migrate?

The structural changes in Oracle8

A migration is necessary because the new functionality in Oracle8 requires changes to the basic items in the data dictionary. Until the new dictionary is built, the Oracle8 kernel can't operate successfully. In addition, the structure of the data file header blocks has changed to support some of the new features. These changes must be in place for the code to work correctly. Unlike simple upgrades such as those you might have performed to move from version 7.2 to version 7.3, these structural changes require more than simply installing the new code and relinking the applications.

You may want to *migrate* an Oracle7 database to Oracle8 for a number of reasons. You may want to take advantage of one or more of Oracle8's new features, outlined in Appendix B, "What's New to Oracle8." You may simply want to benefit from the faster processing that the revised code tree should allow. Whatever the reason, you have a number of options regarding the method you can use to complete the migration process. One of them is a migration tool provided by Oracle. Although this chapter concentrates on the migration tool, it also discusses the alternatives. In the following section you learn about all the options. After reading it, you should be able to determine which method is best to use to migrate your database.

For more details and a further discussion of the migration options you should read the *Oracle8 Server Migration* manual, part number A54650-01.

Selecting a Migration Method

The end result of a migration from Oracle7 is a database that contains essentially the same user objects as the original database, but in data files with updated headers and supported by a data dictionary that allows the new Oracle8 features. In some cases, this may not be your ultimate goal. For example, you might want to migrate only a portion of your database for testing purposes, where you want to test only a subset of your applications before migrating the entire database, or because you don't need objects created for now-obsolete portions of the application. On the other hand, you might want to use the downtime required for the migration to make some structural changes to the database. This might include moving segments between different tablespaces or may simply involve coalescing free space in one or more fragmented tablespaces.

We will examine three basic approaches to migration in this chapter: Oracle's Migration utility, export/import, and table copying. You can read the details concerning each strategy in the following sections and decide which best suits you. To get started, look at Table 3.1 to see the basic features of each approach.

Choose your best migration method

Your choice of migration method will depend on how much you want to accomplish as part of the migration and on how much space you have to complete the task. It might also depend on the length of time you can afford to make the database inaccessible, because some methods take much longer than others.

TABLE 3.1   Overview of migration options

Option:	Migrate Only:	Need for Additional Space:	Time Requirements:
Migration utility	Yes	System tablespace	Least
Export/Import	No	Export dump file	Great
Table copying	No	Two databases	Greatest

As you can see, the fastest approach, the one needing the least overhead, is the Migration utility. However, you can't include other database-restructuring or related changes if you use this method. The Migration utility will migrate your entire database as it is. With the two other options, you can make changes to the structure, layout, and tablespace assignments, but you'll need more time and disk resources to complete these tasks. They're also more complicated to complete because you need to perform a number of additional steps.

The details of the steps needed to complete each type of migration (and the reasons for choosing each) are listed in the appropriate sections following. Table 3.2 summarizes these options.

TABLE 3.2   Summary of migration method characteristics

Migration Utility:	Export/Import:	Copy Commands:
Automatic: Requires little DBA intervention	Requires a new database build	Requires lots of attention
Requires minimal extra disk space	Can use large amounts of disk space	Requires both databases to be online
Time is factor of number of objects, not database size	Very slow for large databases	Very slow for large databases

continues…

TABLE 3.2   **Continued**

Migration Utility:	Export/Import:	Copy Commands:
Can only migrate forward	Can migrate forward and backward	Can migrate forward and backward
Can't use for release to release	Can use for release to release	Can use for release to release
All or nothing	Partial migration possible	Partial migration possible
No structural changes can be made	Concurrent defragmentation and reorganization	Concurrent defragmentation and reorganization

Selecting Oracle's Migration Utility

You need to consider several key factors when planning to use the Migration utility:

- Available space in the system tablespace
- Need to migrate only a subset of the database
- Resources to test a full database migration
- Ancillary requirements, such as space defragmentation

Oracle's Migration utility is designed to perform the required structural changes to your existing database. It will actually build a new Oracle8 data dictionary in the same system tablespace as your current Oracle7 dictionary, and it will restructure your rollback segments and the header blocks of the database's data files on disk (see Figure 3.1). Users' objects, such as tables and indexes, stay just as they are, although the ways in which they're accessed—through the data dictionary and then to the files where they really reside—are changed. Again, the new internal structure is designed to make the database more efficient and to support a new set of features.

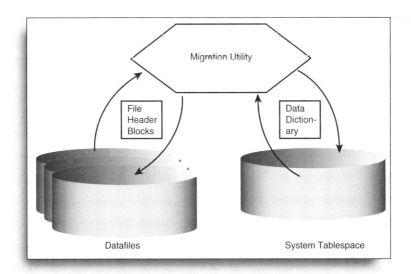

FIGURE 3.1

The Migration utility changes database structures, including the data dictionary, rollback segments, and data file header blocks, in place.

The migration process requires that your current Oracle7 and your new Oracle8 data dictionary reside in the database for a short period of time. This means that the system tablespace, the dictionary's home, must be large enough to hold both versions simultaneously. Therefore, the first item you need to consider before deciding whether to use the utility is the space you have available for the system tablespace. Your Oracle8 data dictionary will be about 50 percent larger than your Oracle7 dictionary. Of course, you may already have some of this space available, but most DBAs will find they need to add more.

Your next decision point for using, or not using, the Migration utility is whether you want to migrate the database as is, or if you also want to make some changes. The Migration utility is an all-or-nothing tool. You can't migrate portions of the database because the database is migrated *in situ*. Similarly, because the data isn't being moved, you can't move segments between tablespaces and you can't coalesce free space in your tablespaces as part of the migration process.

Some DBAs don't like to make too many changes at one time, so even if they want to complete some restructuring tasks, they'll make these changes independently of the migration, completing them before or after the migration itself. Others have limited

Space requirements for the Migration utility

For a period of time, you'll need to have space for two versions of the data dictionary in the system tablespace and for two releases of Oracle in their respective Oracle Home directory structures. The data dictionary will require about 2 1/2 times the space now consumed in your system tablespace. The Oracle8 installation will take 500MB—more if you select many options. If you don't have the required disk space, either consider another migration strategy or wait until you can add the required capacity.

Consider test options for a migrated database

If you want to convert your database to perform functional and similar tests, you can't use the Migration utility for continued work under Oracle7. If you make a copy of it first, you can convert the copy and simultaneously run the production Oracle7 database and the test Oracle8 version. However, making a copy is time-consuming, usually accomplished with the Export/Import tools or with some form of data unloader and SQL*Loader. You can create a partial test database by using the tables for just one or two representative application tasks. You'd still need to complete integrated tests (if you needed them) after a full database conversion.

Piecewise migration with Export/Import

Using this technique to migrate your database one piece at a time requires you to keep both database versions available, which means maintaining the Oracle7 and Oracle8 executables online. Further complications from this approach occur if the data in the different versions is in any way related. You might need to have users switch between databases to perform different functions or temporarily build a distributed database environment. It may also require that parts of both databases be inactive when it's time to move additional segments from Oracle7 to Oracle8. If you're moving only part of your database because you don't need the rest of it, these issues become irrelevant.

time windows in which to complete maintenance work and so try to make all required changes at a single time. You need to consider what else, if anything, you want to achieve as part of the migration processing. You also need to consider how much time you can take away from your user community while working on these steps.

If you only need to perform a migration, Oracle's utility is a good choice. First, it's relatively fast due to the changes being made on the current database structures. They don't have to be copied, moved, or otherwise duplicated—all relatively slow processes. In addition, the only factors that really affect the migration speed are the size of the System tablespace and the number of data files. The System tablespace is typically a small portion of the overall database, and the number of data files is limited to 1,022 in Oracle7. Thus, even the largest databases typically take no more than a day to migrate.

Later in this chapter's "Executing the Migration Process with Oracle's Migration Utility" section you'll find a detailed description of how to complete a migration with the Migration utility. First look at the other migration options and the test plan you need to construct, regardless of the migration approach you'll take.

Using Export/Import

If you decide to use the Export/Import tools to migrate your database, you need to plan for the following resources to be available:

- Space to store the export file
- Time to create the export
- A copy of the Oracle8 executables
- An empty Oracle8 database for the file being exported
- Time to perform the import

The amount of space and time needed for the initial export depends on the amount of data being exported. If you decide to move only part of your database to Oracle8, you need less time than if you are transferring the entire database. The time also depends on the speed of the devices to which you export. A fast disk drive allows a faster export than a slower tape drive. A very large database may also require a file too large for the operating system or for Oracle to handle. In this case you may need to use some form of operating system tool, such as a *pipe*, to move the data onto the appropriate media. Figure 3.2 shows the typical export/import steps. By using a pipe, you can send the output from your Export directly to the Import utility's input.

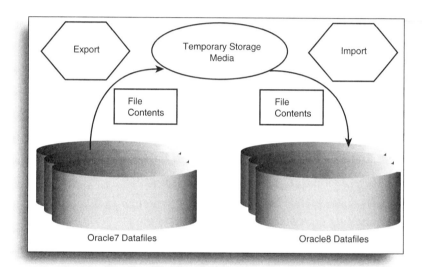

FIGURE 3.2

Migrating your database with export/import requires two distinct steps; the export dump file is the intermediary.

Migrate your database via export/import

1. Perform a full database export from Oracle7, after which you can remove the Oracle7 database and the Oracle7 home directory structure.

2. Install Oracle8 and then alter the environment variables and your parameter file to point to the Oracle8 structures. (See Appendix C, "Installing Oracle8," for installation instructions.)

3. Create an Oracle8 database.

4. Add the required tablespaces to this database.

5. Perform a full import.

Protect your current database

Before beginning your migration, it's recommended that you ensure you have a backup of the home directory and of the database. Minimally, it's recommended that you keep the scripts you used to build the database in the first place; that way you have at least one easy way to reconstruct the database in case you run into problems with the Oracle8 version.

Advantages of unloader/loader technique

The big advantage to the unloader/loader approach is that you can use Oracle's SQL*Loader utility to reinsert the data when the definitions are applied to the database. This utility, running in its direct path mode or–even better if you have the hardware to support it–in parallel direct mode, can complete the job of loading records much more quickly than the Import program.

SEE ALSO

➤ *To learn how to create an Oracle8 database, see page **45***

➤ *To add the required tablespaces to the database, see page **140***

A variant of this method is to use an unload/loader approach to move the data. You can do this by building your own unloader utility or by finding one in the public domain. An unloader utility needs to extract the rows of data from your tables, as well as the definitions of the tables and all the other database objects; that includes indexes, userids, stored procedures, synonyms, and so on. You can also consider a hybrid approach, using the export to create only the object definitions and the unloader simply to create the row entries.

SEE ALSO

➤ *To learn more about the Export and Import utilities, see page **669***

➤ *To learn more about SQL*Loader, see page **679***

Using Table Copying

As with export/import, you can use table copying to move just part of your database, to stage the migration, or simply to avoid migrating unneeded elements. The same caveats for incomplete database migration apply in this context as for the export/import approach.

To perform table copying, you need to have both databases (Oracle7 and Oracle8) available simultaneously, which includes not just the database storage but the two Oracle Home structures and the environments to run them both simultaneously. This makes the approach the most space-intensive of all three methods (see Figure 3.3).

The other drawback to this approach is that it really does only copy table definitions and their contents. To build the same database in the Oracle8 environment that you started with— including all the users, stored procedures, synonyms, views, and so on—you still need to find a method to copy these from Oracle7. It's therefore likely that you'll need to perform a partial export/import or even a data unload/reload, as discussed in the preceding section.

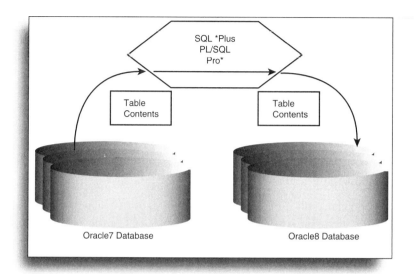

General steps for migrating from Oracle7 to Oracle8

1. Install Oracle8.

2. Create an Oracle8 database.

3. Add the required tablespaces and users.

4. Select the Oracle7 or Oracle8 database as your primary database.

5. Configure SQL*Net or Net8 with a listener to connect to your secondary database.

6. Create or modify a TNSNAMES.ORA file to identify your secondary database.

7. Use SQL*Plus to issue the required COPY commands for your primary database.

8. Add the views, synonyms, stored procedures, and other objects dependent on the tables into your secondary database.

9. Drop your Oracle7 environment.

You find a detailed discussion of these steps later in the section "Executing the Migration with Export/Import or Table Copying."

Warning: Avoid points of no return

As always, before moving or destroying your production system, you should make a backup first.

Copying across database links

Rather than use the SQL*Plus COPY command, you can complete step 7 by creating *database links* in your primary database to access the secondary database and by using SQL CREATE TABLE...AS SELECT commands to copy table definitions and data between your database.

Testing the Migration

Software development and maintenance efforts should always include a good test plan as part of the acceptance strategy. Your migration from Oracle7 to Oracle8 is no different. Indeed, because you already have a working production database, you need to devise a test strategy to ensure that the end results of the migration contain the same, or better, production capabilities. This means testing not only the capabilities, but the performance and results as well.

You can apply a number of types of tests to help assure you and the users that everything is working properly at the end of the migration. In the next sections you see what types of tests you can use and when to use each type. From these selections, you can build a test program and identify the resources needed to complete the tests. Oracle Corporation strongly recommends running all these tests before concluding the migration.

Identifying Types of Tests

You can perform six basic types of tests to validate the migration:

- Migration test
- Minimal test
- Functional test
- Integration test
- Performance test
- Volume/load stress test

Migration Test

This test validates your migration strategy, whether it's to use the Migration utility or one approach to transfer the data from Oracle7 to Oracle8. It's intended to help you determine whether you've allotted sufficient resources for the migration, including disk space, time, and personnel.

Running a migration test

1. Create either a test copy of your whole database, or a subset if you don't have the resources to test the complete database migration. You don't have to complete this step if you're using export/import or table copying.

2. Execute the migration with the utility you plan to use when migrating your production database.

3. Upgrade the tools used by your application.

Minimal Test

This type of testing involves migrating all or part of an application and simply attempting to run it. No changes are made to the application, and performance and value testing should be attempted. This test simply confirms that the application can be started against the migrated database; it's not intended to reveal all problems that could occur.

You should perform this test after a successful migration test and before moving on to the more rigorous tests. It will require *relinking* the tools used by the applications, so you'll need to maintain a separate copy of the application if the users need to continue using the production Oracle7 database.

Running a minimal test

1. Complete the migration test.

2. Have users, developers, or a test suite run selected programs from the applications.

Functional Test

The functional test follows the minimal test and ensures that the application runs just as it did before the migration. This involves having users, or simulated users, executing the different application components and verifying that the outcome is the same as in the pre-migrated database. The results of any queries, reports, or DML should be the same as they were on the pre-migrated database.

Resolving problems with migration tests

If this test fails, you may need to rethink the chosen migration strategy and possibly choose another method. For example, if the time taken is greater than your users are willing to allow, you may need to plan a staged migration, or if you were hoping to use export/import, you may need to consider the Migration utility instead.

Resolving problems with minimal tests

A failure of a minimal test typically indicates problems with the migration itself, such as missing tables, synonyms, views, or stored procedures. It's most likely to fail if you've tried a partial database migration or if you're using one of the data-transfer strategies rather than the Migration utility.

If you're using Oracle8 to enhance the application, you may also want to add the new functionality to each application during this test phase to ensure that the application continues to provide reliable results with the new features in place.

Conducting a functional test

1. Complete the migration and minimal tests.

2. If you intend to add new functionality to your applications, have the developers make these changes.

3. Have users, developers, or a test suite execute the applications, testing all functions and features.

Tracking the cause of errors detected during functional testing may involve close cooperation between the DBA and the application developers. It's important, therefore, to ensure that the development organization is apprised of this testing phase and can commit the necessary resources. If you're running third-party application software, you may need to get help from your vendor should this test fail.

Integration Test

Integrated testing involves executing the application just as you did in the pre-migrated database. This includes establishing client/server connections, using any GUI interfaces, and executing testing online and batch functions. This test ensures that all the application's components continue to work together as before.

Running an integration test

1. Complete the migration, minimal, and functional tests.

2. Install and configure any communication software, such as Net8, for client/server or multi-tier architectures.

3. Install and configure any drivers, such as ODBC drivers, that the applications use.

4. Have the users, developers, or a test suite run the applications across the network, using the same front-end tools and middleware that are now planned for database access.

Testing third-party applications

Some vendors may not be aware of all the changes made in Oracle8. If you're using third-party applications, you shouldn't commit to a completed migration until the functional tests have been rigorously completed.

Resolving problems with integration tests

Should you run into problems with these tests, you'll have to isolate whether the cause is in a single component, such as SQL*Net or Net8, or whether it's part of the overall migration. Generally, if you've completed the functional testing successfully, the likelihood is that the problem is with one component, or the interface between a pair of components.

Performance Test

Although the kernel code tree has been optimized in Oracle8, you might discover that some parts of your applications aren't running as well as before the migration. This could be due to a number of factors, such as tuning efforts that were made to avoid a problem in the earlier release. You need to run the performance tests to ensure that overall processing throughput is at least the same as, if not better than, the Oracle7 performance.

Conducting a performance test

1. Complete the previous tests to ensure that you're running the equivalent of a full production system.

2. Have users run their interactive and batch programs as they would in a production environment.

3. Monitor and record the database performance by using queries against the various dynamic performance tables or by using such tools as the UTLBSTAT.SQL and UTLESTAT.SQL scripts.

4. Solicit feedback from users as to their perceptions of performance and response times compared to the current production system.

If you've been monitoring your Oracle7 database with the various analytic and diagnostic tools, you can easily make comparisons by using the same tools on the migrated database.

SEE ALSO

> *For an overview of the dynamic performance tables, see page* **32**

> *A detailed description of the UTLBSTAT.SQL and ULTESTAT.SQL utilities begins on page* **619**

Volume/Load Stress Test

Ideally, you should be able to test your migrated database against a realistic workload. This includes the amount of data being processed (volume) and the concurrent demands on database (load). To perform such testing, you may need to set up automated procedures rather than expect your user community to test your database under realistic conditions while continuing work on the unmigrated production version. This test will

Resolving problems with performance tests

If you find performance problems, you should attempt to resolve them by using the database tuning techniques described in Chapter 20, "Tuning Your Memory Structures and File Access," through Chapter 23, "Diagnosing and Correcting Problems."

ensure that the database is ready for the workload intended for it and should also display any other problems that the other tests didn't uncover.

Performing volume/load stress tests

Building a load test

If you have software that can capture the keystrokes entered during an interactive session, you can use this to collect the session work completed by the users in earlier tests. You can use these to build scripts that emulate those sessions. Run multiple concurrent copies of these scripts to simulate different levels of system load.

Addressing problems with a volume/load stress test

Problems encountered while testing for volume and load should be addressed by applying the tuning strategies discussed in Chapters 20 through 23 of this book.

1. Assemble either a workforce or automated scripts to represent a normal, everyday workload.

2. Exercise the system by having the users or scripts execute the applications concurrently.

3. Monitor and record the system performance as in the performance testing.

Due to changes in the structure and use of internal structures—the data dictionary, rollback segments, and ROWIDs—you may find that the behavior of the database changes differently from the way it did in Oracle7. Although most resources won't reach a performance threshold as quickly as they might in Oracle7, you can't depend on this. It's therefore not advisable to assume that if you achieve performance equal to or better than Oracle7 with a small number of concurrent sessions manipulating a few tables, this performance level will be maintained under full volume and load.

Setting Up a Test Program

Keeping in mind the various tests you need to perform, your test program should address the when, where, what, who, and how questions associated with each test. The test program should also address the methods you'll use to compare the actual results with what should be expected if the test is successful. This may include creating test suites that can be run on the current production database and on the Oracle8 test database; on the other hand, it could include simply recording the sizes of such objects as temporary segments and rollback segments in the test database so that you'll be prepared to size the associated tablespaces appropriately when the migration is performed for real.

When to perform the tests depends on the resources you need and their availability. For example, DBAs are used to working on major database changes during periods of low activity, such as late at night, weekends, and holidays. If your test needs the participation of developers or end users, however, you may have to plan the test during normal working hours.

Where to perform your tests depends on your computer environment. Ideally, you want to test as much of the database as you can—all of it if possible. This may require using a separate machine if one is available. A test or development machine is probably the best place to run the various tests. Remember, however, that you may have to schedule this machine if it's regularly used by the developers; some tests may require shutting down the Oracle7 database(s) running there.

What to test depends on the test you're performing. By referring to the previous section's descriptions of the different tests, make sure that you have the resources to complete the test and record the findings in a meaningful way. For example, you won't learn anything about whether the Oracle8 performance is equal to, better than, or even worse than the Oracle7 performance if you don't have a method to record the performance characteristics you want to measure in each environment.

Who to involve in the testing also depends on the type of test. The earlier test descriptions should help you identify the type of personnel needed for each one. You may want to form a migration team with members from your system support, developer, and end-user communities if you're going to migrate a large database. This team can help you schedule the tests in such a way that they don't cause major conflicts with other groups. For example, you would want to avoid running a test that needs input from the users during times of heavy workloads, such as month-end processing. The team can also help you find the best resources within their respective groups to aid with the tests and can act as your communication channel back to the various groups regarding the migration progress.

How to complete the tests depends on your environment as well as the test type. You need to decide if you'll run tests on the whole database or on partial applications. This, of course, depends on the resources you have available. Similarly, you need to ensure that you have the resources, including people and

Ensure the integrity of your test environment

There's no point performing a test for validity after migration if the original version is flawed. Similarly, if you plan to test just part of your database, you need to ensure that you'll get a valid subset of the data. For example, if you're going to test a function that adds new records to a table and a sequence generator is used for the primary key values, you'll have to ensure that the sequence generator is available in the pre-migration set of objects.

tools, to fix any problems encountered during the testing so that you can keep the migration project on track. The individuals needed to fix a problem may not be the same as those involved in the test itself.

The how question needs to include how you'll obtain your test data. If you want to test against the entire database, you'll need a method to create an exact copy of it, possibly on a separate machine. This could involve an export/import or some form of Unload/Reload utility. If using the latter, you need a verification test suite to ensure that the copy was successful.

After your test plan is in place, you can begin the process of fully testing a migration. Ideally, you'll run every test on a complete test version of the migrated database before tackling the migration of the production system.

Testing and Retesting

As you complete each test in your test plan, you should be able to determine whether it's successful. If the test is successful, you can move to the next one; if it isn't, you need to fix the problem and retry the test. This part of the testing isn't always as straightforward as it sounds.

Suppose you encounter an error that involves a missing view that should contain the join of two tables. The error could reflect that one of the two underlying tables is missing, or that the view definition is no longer available or valid. If you've performed a full migration, you need to determine whether the Migration utility "lost" the view or table or whether the view (or table) was missing before the migration was performed. If you don't have a copy of the pre-migrated database (or at least a way to reconstruct it), you can't determine the cause of the error. You'll have to go back and redo all the steps you took to get to this testing point, which may include copying the current production database over to your testing environment. Of course, because it has been in active use since you made your initial copy, the current copy you make won't be the same as the one you used for the test that failed. For example, the view may now have been deliberately dropped. You'll have to repeat all the tests to validate this new version of the database.

If you're testing a subset of the database, the missing view or table may not have been created because it wasn't included in the objects selected for migration. In this case, you need to decide whether you can just add it now and continue with your testing. Otherwise, as in the preceding case, you'll need to start over with the migration of the test set from an Oracle7 source and repeat all the testing.

If you run into a problem that you can't easily resolve, you have two options:

- You can continue with further tests to see if a more obvious reason for the problem manifests itself. If you still can't determine the cause of the problem at the conclusion of your tests, you should repeat the entire migration process up to the point where the problem was observed. This time, make detailed notes or keep log files of all your activities so that you can file a detailed report with the Oracle Support organization, should the problem recur.
- Simply restart the process as just discussed, without continuing further testing; keep detailed records in case you need to file a request for help with Oracle Support.

Performing the Migration

After you complete an acceptable test plan, you should use it to migrate and test a non-production version of your database. When you're certain that you're ready, you can perform your production system's migration.

Executing the Migration Process with Oracle's Migration Utility

The database is addressed as a whole in the following, detailed descriptions of the tasks you'll have to perform to complete your

Skip sections that don't relate to your chosen migration approach

If you're planning to use the Migration utility, continue with the following section. If you intend to use export/ import for your migration, skip to "Executing the Migration with Export/Import or Table Copying" in this chapter.

database migration. If you need to migrate only a portion of your production database, you must create a temporary Oracle7 database to hold just that portion. Apply the migration processing to this temporary database only.

General steps for preparing to migrate with the Migration utility

1. Load the Migration utility by using the Oracle8 installer.

2. Ensure that you have sufficient free space in the system tablespace.

3. Recover or remove any offline objects.

4. Remove any user with an ID of MIGRATE.

5. Override any in-doubt transactions.

After you complete the first task (loading the Migration utility), you may want to put your database into restricted mode to prevent users from making unwanted changes as you prepare it for the migration. To do this, perform a shutdown and then reopen it with the RESTRICTED option. This will disconnect all current users and allow only those with the restricted session privilege to reconnect. If you're one of many DBAs with such a privilege, you should coordinate with your colleagues to ensure that only one of you is working on the migration process.

SEE ALSO

➤ *For details on the various options for starting a database, including the* RESTRICTED *option, see page* **17**

Loading the Migration Utility

The Migration utility for converting from Oracle7 to Oracle8 is provided as part of the Oracle8 installation media. You can load just the Migration utility by running the standard installation program for your specific hardware platform (the orainst program in UNIX and the SETUP.EXE program in Windows NT, for example).

Suggested responses to the installer's questions

1. Choose Install, Upgrade, or De-install on the Select the Installer Activity screen.

2. Choose Migrate from Oracle7 to Oracle8 on the Select Installer Option screen.

3. Choose Install Migration Utility on the Select an Oracle7 to Oracle8 Migration Option screen.

The installer will place a number of files into the Oracle7 home directory structure, including the following:

- The Oracle8 Migration utility, placed in the bin sub-directory

- The Oracle8 version of the message file, placed in the MESG subdirectory of the RDBMS subdirectory

- The Oracle8 version of the MIGRATE.BSQ file, placed in the DBS subdirectory

- Any required NLS files, placed in a subdirectory named data, which is in the path from the Oracle home directory that contains the subdirectory tree MIGRATE, NLS, and ADMIN.

Confirm success of your installation

Following the installation, you should check the log file to confirm that the files were successfully installed.

Checking for Sufficient Space in the System Tablespace

The Migration utility needs space for the Oracle7 and Oracle8 data dictionaries in the system tablespace. You can determine whether you have sufficient space available by using a special option in the Migrate utility. Simply run the utility with the CHECK_ONLY option set to TRUE:

- On UNIX, the command is
  ```
  mig check_only=true
  ```

- On Windows NT, the command is
  ```
  mig80 check_only=true
  ```

Depending on your operating system, the name of the utility and the format of the results will vary. You'll typically need free space equivalent to about 1 1/2 times the space consumed by your current data dictionary.

Unusable tablespaces

If you can't bring a tablespace back online because it needs recovery that can't be completed, you need to drop it; it will be unusable under Oracle8 anyway.

Don't have a user called
MIGRATE

The migration process will create a user called **MIGRATE**. Because this user is eventually dropped with the Oracle7 data dictionary objects, you should ensure that you don't already have a database user with this name. If you do, create a new *schema* to contain the **MIGRATE** user's objects, or use a user-level export and plan to reimport the user following the migration. In either case, remember to drop the **MIGRATE** user after you save the objects from the schema. See Chapter 9, "Creating and Managing User Accounts," for information about user and schema management.

Confirming That No Tablespaces or Data Files Need Recovery

All offline tablespaces should be brought back online unless you're certain that they were taken offline by using the TEMPORARY or IMMEDIATE option. After you bring them back online, you can use one of these options to take them back offline.

All data files must also be online. You can check the DBA_DATA_FILES view for the status. If any are offline and you can't bring them back online because they need recovery, the Migration utility will fail with errors.

SEE ALSO

➤ *For a brief discussion of views, see page* **30**

Ensuring That You Don't Have Any Pending In-Doubt Transactions

If you've used distributed transactions in your Oracle7 database, you need to check that none are still pending due to problems with the two-phase commit mechanism, such as lost network connections or offline databases. You can find such transactions by examining the DBA_2PC_PENDING table. If you have any such transactions, you need to commit or roll them back manually. You can find the instructions on how to do this in your Distributed Database documentation, including details on how to determine if you should commit or roll back.

Performing a Normal Shutdown of the Oracle7 Database

When you've readied your database for the migration by performing the preceding tasks, you can shut down your database. You need to shut it down cleanly—that is, with the NORMAL or IMMEDIATE option. If you can't do this and have to use the ABORT option, you need to restart the database and then shut it down again with one of the other options. This ensures that there are no pending transactions or incomplete checkpoints, leaving your database in the appropriate state for the migration.

SEE ALSO
➤ *For details on database shutdown options and commands, see page 17*

Backing Up the Database in Case of Problems

After your database is shut down, you should make a full backup just in case the migration process needs to be repeated, as discussed in the earlier section on testing. The backup needs to be made any time you plan to migrate a database that has been opened subsequent to your last pre-migration backup—unless you don't mind losing the changes made during that period.

SEE ALSO
➤ *For an overview of hot backup strategies, see page 341*
➤ *Detailed descriptions of hot backup steps are available on page 361*

Hot backup option before migration
If you don't have the time to complete an offline backup, you can complete an online backup immediately before shutting it down for the migration. Remember that as soon as it's closed, you should back up the online redo logs as well. If you need to restore the Oracle7 version for another migration attempt, you have to recover the backup to a stable point, which requires the contents of the online redo.

Run the Migration Utility

You may need to set certain system values before running the Migration utility program. These will vary between operating systems, and you need to examine your platform-specific documentation for details on what to set and what values they require. For example, the TWO_TASK and ORA_NLS33 variables have to be set appropriately. You also need to use this documentation to find out how to run the migration program and provide the appropriate options. The options for the migration program are documented in Table 3.3.

TABLE 3.3   **Options for the Migration Program**

Name:	Description and Use:
CHECK_ONLY or NO_SPACE_CHECK	These mutually exclusive options are used to determine whether the System tablespace is large enough to complete the migration or to avoid making this check. You should need the CHECK_ONLY option only in the pre-migration steps, as discussed earlier.
DBNAME	This option specifies the name of the database to migrate.
NEW_DBNAME	This option specifies the new name for the database. By default, the new name is DEFAULT, so you're strongly encouraged to set this value.

continues…

TABLE 3.3   **Continued**

Name:	Description and Use:
MULTIPLIER	This option changes the initial size of one specific data dictionary index. A value of 30 makes it three times larger, for example. The default value (15) should be adequate for most users.
NLS_CHAR	By setting this option, you can change the National Language Standard (NLS) NCHAR character set used for your database. Not setting this option leaves your Oracle7 character set in place.
PFILE	This is the name of the parameter file to be used by the instance in which the migration will occur. Not setting this option causes the default file to be used.
SPOOL	This option names the full path and filename where the Migration utility will write its log file. When the Migration utility completes its processing, you should check the spool file to see if any errors occurred.

Time to take a backup

You should make a backup of this version of the database because it can be used as your first Oracle8 backup, as well as an intermediate starting point for another migration attempt.

Don't open the database as an Oracle7 database at this point; further conversion steps need to be completed before the database is usable again. Prematurely opening the database corrupts this intermediate version and you won't be able to complete the migration process successfully.

Moving or Copying the Convert File

The Migration utility created a *convert file* for you in the Oracle7 environment. This file will be found in the DBS, or related directory, under the Oracle7 home directory and will be named CONV*SID*.DBF (where *SID* is the Oracle7 instance name). You'll need to move this file to the corresponding directory in the Oracle8 home directory, renaming it to reflect the Oracle8 instance name if this is different. If you aren't going to uninstall Oracle7 at this time, you can wait and complete the file transfer in a single step. If you're going to uninstall Oracle7, make a copy of this file outside the Oracle directory structure so that you can find it later.

Installing the Oracle8 Version of Oracle

If you don't have space for the Oracle8 installation, you can remove the Oracle7 directory structure before beginning this step. However, it is recommended that you back it up first, in case you need to use your Oracle7 database again. Use the Oracle7 installer to uninstall Oracle7 and the Oracle8 installer to add the Oracle8 files. Your platform-specific documentation explains how to run the installer for both operations.

When installing Oracle8, be sure to select the Install/Upgrade option in order to prevent Oracle from creating a brand-new database that you won't need.

Adjusting Your Environment Variables and Parameter File

You need to ensure that your operating system is aware of and using the new Oracle8 code before continuing with the migration process. The remaining migration tasks require the Oracle8 executables to manipulate your database. This means resetting the pointers to Oracle Home and related structures, whatever they might be for your operating system. Again, you need to refer to your platform-specific documentation if you aren't sure what these are.

You also need to check your Oracle7 parameter file for obsolete or changed parameters. These are listed in the Oracle8 Server Migration Manual, available as part of the Oracle8 distribution media. Table 3.4 lists the non–platform-specific parameters that you need to address.

TABLE 3.4 **Obsolete and changed parameters**

Oracle7 Name:	Obsolete:	Oracle8 Name:
INIT_SQL_FILES	Yes	
LM_DOMAINS	Yes	
LM_NON_FAULT_TOLERANT	Yes	
PARALLEL_DEFAULT_SCANSIZE	Yes	
SEQUENCE_CACHE_HASH_BUCKETS	Yes	
SERIALIZABLE	Yes	
SESSION_CACHED_CURSORS	Yes	
SNAPSHOT_REFRESH_INTERVAL	No	JOB_QUEUE_INTERVAL
SNAPSHOT_REFRESH_PROCESS	No	JOB_QUEUE_PROCESSES

Use your favorite editor to make any necessary changes to your parameter file. You may also want to move it to a new directory so that it stays with your other Oracle8 files. If you use the default conventions for your parameter filename and location, see the Oracle8 documentation for your specific system to identify what these need to be.

Removing or Renaming the Current Control and Convert Files

You'll perform one conversion step a little later that will create new control files for your database. At this time, therefore, you should remove the control files your database was using. Drop them (if they're safely backed up) or rename them so that you can find them again if needed.

If you've already uninstalled Oracle7, you should have copied the convert file to a safe place as discussed earlier in "Moving or Copying the Convert File." You should now move this copy to the appropriate directory in your Oracle8 Home directory structure. If you haven't uninstalled Oracle7, simply copy the file, renaming it if necessary, to the corresponding directory under Oracle8; see the earlier section titled "Moving or Copying the Convert File" for details.

Starting an Instance

Use Server Manager and the INTERNAL user to start an instance. You should then start a spool file to track the remaining conversion tasks performed on the database. You can use the following script to complete these steps by using Server Manager running in line mode:

```
CONNECT INTERNAL
STARTUP NOMOUNT
SPOOL convert
```

Complete the remaining database conversion activities

1. Issue the command ALTER DATABASE CONVERT to build new control files and update the data file header information.

2. Open the database, which will convert the rollback segments to their Oracle8 format.

This is a point of no return!

After **ALTER DATABASE CONVERT** completes, you can no longer use your database with Oracle7 code or programs.

3. Run the CAT8000.SQL script to do the following:

   - Convert the rollback segments to their Oracle8 format.

   - Update data dictionary components.

   - Drop the MIGRATE user with the Oracle7 data dictionary.

4. Shut down the database if the preceding tasks are all successful.

5. Complete the post-migration tasks.

Perform these steps while still connected to your Server Manager session by using the following commands:

```
ALTER DATABASE CONVERT;
ALTER DATABASE OPEN RESETLOGS;
@CAT8000.SQL
HOST
```

```
SHUTDOWN
```

If you find errors in the log file, you may need to repeat the tasks discussed in this section; you may instead, depending on the severity of the problem, have to repeat most or all of the migration process after correcting the cause of the errors.

If you've completed your migration at this point, you can skip the following discussion of alternate migration techniques. Continue with the section "Completing Post-Migration Steps" to learn how to make your Oracle8 database available to your applications and users.

Executing the Migration with Export/Import or Table Copying

In this section you look at two other options for migrating your database that you may want to use instead of the Migration utility. Both require you to move data between an Oracle7 and Oracle8 database. Therefore, unlike the Migration utility process, you have to build an Oracle8 database yourself, or let the installer build one for you. In all probability, you will need to customize any database you build to match the structure of your Oracle7 database.

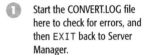

Locating the CAT8000.SQL script and the log file

If you aren't in the directory where the CAT8000.SQL script is located, you need to include the full path name. You'll find this script in the Oracle home directory, under the ADMIN directory, which is under the RDBMS directory. After issuing the host prompt to check for the session's log, you should find the log in your current directory. It will be named CONVERT.LST, but the name may be case sensitive on some operating systems.

Start the CONVERT.LOG file here to check for errors, and then EXIT back to Server Manager.

The main difference between these two approaches is that the export/import option lets you work on each database independently, so you can remove your Oracle7 database before building and populating your Oracle8 database. This can be useful if space is at a premium. The table-copying method requires that the Oracle7 and the Oracle8 databases be online during the migration process. If you have the space, you can also leave both databases in place during an export/import. However, if the Oracle7 database is available to users following the export, the changed data will have to be identified and migrated separately.

In the following sections, it's assumed that you're going to keep your Oracle7 database in place during the whole migration process, but it's pointed out when you could drop it depending on what method you're using. The following steps are based on this assumption.

Step 1: Install Oracle8

Install Oracle8 on your system by using the Oracle installer as described in your platform-specific documentation. You can choose to have the installer build your initial Oracle8 database if you prefer.

Step 2: Prepare Your Oracle8 Database

If you've let the installer build your database, you simply need to add the tablespaces that match your current Oracle7 structure. You should also add the same number of rollback segments and redo logs as you're now using in Oracle7. If you're using the table-copying method, you also need to create the users at this point.

Step 3: Prepare to Migrate

If you're performing the export/import process, you should now create the export file of your full database, or whatever pieces of the database you want to migrate. After this, you can shut down your Oracle7 database and uninstall Oracle7 if you want.

If you're performing table copying, you need to define the network protocol and addresses for SQL*Net or Net8.

Copying tables across database links

If you plan to use **CREATE TABLE...AS SELECT** commands to make table copies, you also need to build database links that allow the Oracle7 and Oracle8 databases to work together. Database links themselves are described in the Oracle8 SQL manual and in the Distributed Database documentation. If you aren't familiar with distributed processing and database links, this is probably not a good method to use for your migration.

SEE ALSO

➤ *If you don't already have these tools configured, you might as well use Net8, which is discussed on page* **635**

Step 4: Move the Data

Now you can move the data into the Oracle8 database. By using export/import, you simply execute the Oracle8 import command and provide the name of the file you exported in step 3. If you're performing table copying, you can use either the COPY command available in SQL*Plus or the SQL CREATE TABLE...AS SELECT command. The former identifies the target (Oracle8) or the source (Oracle7) database, or both, using SQL*Net or Net8 aliases from the TNSNAMES.ORA file. The latter uses a database link name in the new table name or the name of the table being copied, depending on where the command is running. If you're in the Oracle7 database, the link name is appended to the new table name; if you're in Oracle8, the link name goes on the source table name.

Your database should be ready—if you used export/import—after you complete the data transfer. If you performed table copying, you may still need to duplicate the other objects in your Oracle7 database, such as indexes, views, synonyms, and privileges. The simplest way to do this is with an export/import of the full database. In this case, though, you wouldn't export the table rows and would have to allow the import to ignore errors due to existing tables.

Completing Post-Migration Steps

The following sections cover the steps needed to make the database accessible by the applications and the users of those applications. You might not need to follow each step exactly, depending on your system and application mix.

Precompiler Applications

Even if you don't intend to make any changes to your precompiler applications, you need to relink the applications before they will run against the Oracle8 database. You should relink them to the SQLLIB runtime library provided with the Oracle8 precompiler. Of course, if you want to take advantage of some new features of Oracle8, you need to modify your code and observe the standard precompile and compile steps.

OCI Applications

Obsolete OCI calls

Two calls used in OCI programs, **ORLON** and **OLON**, are no longer supported in Oracle8; you should use **OLOG** in their place. Although **OLOG** was originally introduced for multithreaded applications, it's now required for single-threaded code.

You can use your Oracle7 OCI applications with Oracle8 unchanged. If you have constraints in your applications, however, you should relink the applications with the Oracle8 runtime OCI library, OCILIB. You can choose a non-deferred mode to relink, in which case you'll experience Oracle7 performance levels, or you can use deferred mode linking to improve performance. The latter may not report any linking, bind, and define errors until later in the execution of the statements than you're used to seeing. Specifically, they will occur during DESCRIBE, EXECUTE, or FETCH calls rather than immediately after the bind and define operations.

SQL*Plus Scripts

Ensure that your SQL*Plus scripts don't contain a SET COMPATIBILITY V7 command. If they do, change it to SET COMPATIBILITY V8. Also remember to check any LOGIN.SQL scripts for this command.

SQL*Net

The only severe problem you might run into with SQL*Net is if you're still using version 1. Oracle8 will only communicate via SQL*Net version 2 or Net8. The SQL*Net v2.0 *Administrator's Guide* and SQL*Net version 2 *Migration Guide* explain how to upgrade to version 2. As with other Oracle8 products, Net8 gives you a lot of additional features that you may want to consider using.

Enterprise Backup Utility (EBU)

Oracle8 has replaced the Enterprise Backup utility (EBU) with Recovery Manager (RMAN). Therefore, any code and routines you've developed around EBU will need to be replaced. In addition, the backup volumes created under EBU aren't usable by Oracle7. EBU and RMAN both use the same Media Management Language to talk to third-party storage subsystems, so you should still be able to use any tape subsystems and tape management modules that you used with EBU when you convert your backup routines to RMAN.

Standby Databases

A standby database must run on the exact same release as the production database that it mirrors. Therefore, you need to upgrade any standby database after you upgrade your Oracle7 production database.

Migrate your standby database to Oracle8

1. Apply all redo logs created under Oracle7.
2. Ensure that the primary database is successfully opened under Oracle8.
3. Install Oracle8 on the standby database platform.
4. Copy the production database's control file and first data file to the standby site.
5. Make a new control file for the standby database.

Migration: Final Considerations

The following Oracle products will run unchanged against your Oracle8 database:

- Forms
- Developer/2000 applications
- PL/SQL
- Export/Import

Impact of using new Oracle8 features

If you begin using Oracle8's new features, you may have to make further changes to applications by using the products already discussed, and you may have to change code and procedures related to the tools listed here. For example, you have to run a CATEXP7.SQL script if you want to export Oracle8-partitioned tables to an Oracle7 database.

You should consider the possible improvements you might obtain, however, if you begin using some of the appropriate Oracle8 enhancements. This doesn't have to be done immediately, of course, but over a period of weeks or months, as time permits. You should also ensure that the application developers are aware of the possible enhancements to their code.

Managing with Oracle Enterprise Manager (OEM)

Install and configure Oracle Enterprise Manager

Set up the Repository

Manage users and privileges

Manage storage

Tune your database

Introducing OEM Components

Don't install OEM 1.2.2 and OEM 1.5.0 in Oracle 8.0.3 home

OEM v1.2.2 isn't compatible with Oracle Server 7.3.3 and 8.0.x. OEM v1.5.0 shouldn't be installed in an Oracle Server 8.0.3 home directory. OEM's latest version (1.5.5), however, works fine for Oracle 7.3.3 and 8.0.x.

The Oracle Enterprise Manager combines a graphical console, agent processes, and common services to provide an integrated and comprehensive systems management platform for managing Oracle databases on the network. You can perform the following tasks from Enterprise Manager:

- Administer, diagnose, and tune multiple databases.
- Schedule jobs such as executing a SQL*Plus script on multiple nodes.
- Monitor objects and events such as database and node failures throughout the network.
- Integrate third-party tools.

Table 4.1 describes OEM's database application tools that allow you to perform the primary database administration tasks; Figure 4.1 shows these components.

TABLE 4.1   OEM components and their functions

OEM Component	Function
Instance Manager	Manage instances, INIT.ORA file initialization parameters, and sessions
TableSpace Manager	Manage fragmentation and free space in tablespaces
Storage Manager	Manage tablespaces, data files, and rollback segments
Security Manager	Manage users, roles, privileges, and profiles
Schema Manager	Manage schema objects such as tables, indexes, views, clusters, synonyms, and sequences
Server Manager	Perform line-mode database operations from the client
Software Manager	Manage the software distribution process
Backup Manager	Perform database backups and create backup scripts
Data Manager	Perform export/import and data loads

SEE ALSO

➤ *Using the Instance Manager, page 36*

FIGURE 4.1

OEM comprises various components that can be used for specific tasks.

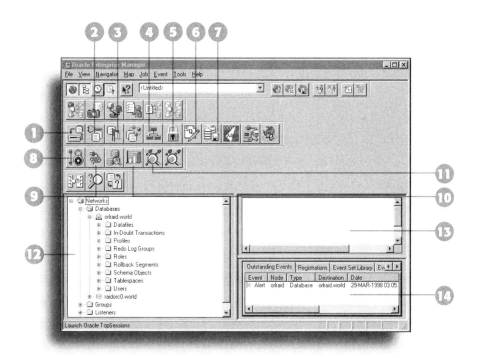

	Backup Manager		Lock Manager
	Data Manager		TopSessions
	Instance Manager		Performance Manager
	Schema Manager		Oracle Trace
	Security Manager		Navigator window
	SQL Worksheet		Job Scheduling window
	Storage Manager		Event Management window

The Enterprise Manager environment consists of the following major components:

- Oracle Enterprise Manager Console
- Services common to all OEM components, such as the Repository, discovery service, communication daemon, and job scheduling and event management systems
- Intelligent agent
- Integrated applications
- Application programming interfaces (APIs)
- Command Line Interface (CLI)
- Online help system

The basic OEM functionality is available to you with Oracle Server; however, you can install several optional management packs: Change Management Pack, Diagnostic Pack, and Tuning Pack.

OEM Console

The console user interface contains a set of windows that provide various views of the system. There's only one console per client machine. Table 4.2 describes the various components of the console.

TABLE 4.2   **Components of the console**

Component	Description
Navigator window	A tree view of all the objects in the system and their relationships
Map window	Allows customization of the system views
Job window	User interface to the Job Scheduling system
Event Management window	User interface to the event management system

Common Services

The following services are common to various OEM components (see Table 4.3 for details on how these components interact):

- *The Repository* is a set of tables in your schema, which can be placed in any Oracle database in the system. Information stored in the Repository includes the status of jobs and events, discovery cache, tasks performed, and messages from the notification queue in the communication daemon.

  To set up the Repository and manipulate it, you need to log on with an account that has DBA privileges. When logging in to Enterprise Manager, you're establishing a database connection into your Repository. At any given time, each user is connected to a single Repository. The connection to the Repository must be active during your working sessions. There can be more than one repository in the system. Repository tables can be installed on any Oracle database accessible to the console. A repository can be moved to another Oracle database. The Repository can be started or shut down from the Instance Manager but not from the console.

- *The communication daemon* is a multithreaded process that manages console communication activities. It's responsible for communicating with agents and nodes for job scheduling and event monitoring, queuing and retrying failed jobs periodically, service discovery, contacting nodes periodically to determine their status, and maintaining a cache of connections to agents on nodes.

- *The Job Scheduling System* enables you to schedule jobs on remote sites by specifying the task to perform, the start time, and the frequency of execution. The Job System isn't usable if Oracle Intelligent Agent isn't installed and configured.

- *The Event Management System* monitors events at remote sites, alerts you when a problem is detected, and optionally fixes it. In Windows NT, the application event log contains many of the errors detected by OEM.

Multiple repositories can exist within the same database

You can use one repository, or you can switch between multiple repositories stored in the same database.

Reactive management is provided by the job and event systems

You can use the Job and Event systems together to provide a reactive management system. This is achieved by allowing certain jobs to get executed when the specified events occur.

- *Security Services* manages administrative privileges for nodes and services in the system. It manages a list of administrators who are notified when an event occurs.

- *Service Discovery* maintains an up-to-date view of the nodes and services being managed. The console's Navigator tree is populated with this information.

TABLE 4.3   Communication between OEM components

Communication Path	Description
Console and communication daemon	The console sends job and event requests to the communication daemon, and the status of these jobs and events are sent back to the console. Authentication requests of users logging in to the console are sent to the daemon. The daemon sends information to update the tree of nodes and services in the Navigator.
Communication daemon and Common Services	Job and event requests are handed to the Job or Event Management systems. The Common Services passes job and event status back to the communication daemon. Service Discovery information is passed from the Common Services to the daemon.
Communication daemon and intelligent agent	Agents communicate with the daemon to report results and status messages for jobs and events from the remote nodes.
Common Services and Repository	The Event Management and Job Management systems write event and job information, respectively, to the Repository.

Figure 4.2 represents the communication path between different components of the Enterprise Manager in terms of the jobs, events, or any other requests logged in to the console.

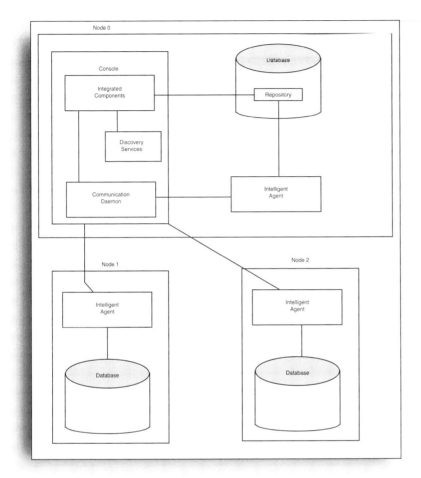

FIGURE 4.2

Interaction between the various OEM components is well-defined.

Intelligent Agents

Intelligent agents are intelligent processes running on remote nodes. Each agent resides on the same node as the service it supports and can support all the services on that node. Intelligent agents perform the following functions:

- Execute jobs or events from the console or third-party applications can be sent to the intelligent agent for execution.

- Cancel jobs or events as directed.

- Run jobs, collecting results and queuing them for the communication daemon.

Use an intelligent agent to manage an older Oracle release

Each intelligent agent is compatible with the database with which it's released and prior database releases. When used to manage an older release of the database, the intelligent agent must be installed in an ORACLE_HOME directory current with the agent release. Older releases of the intelligent agent aren't compatible with newer releases of the database.

- Run autonomously without requiring the console or the daemon to be running.

- Autonomously detect and take reactive measures (as specified by the administrator) to fix problems.

- Autonomously perform specified administrative tasks.

- Check and report events to the communication daemon.

- Handle SNMP requests if supported on the agent's platform.

An agent is required for all or some functionality of these components: Service Discovery; Job Control System; Event Management System; Backup Manager; Software Manager; Data Manager's Export, Import, and Load applications; Oracle Events; and Trace.

Application Programming Interface (API)

The APIs available with Enterprise Manager enable third-party applications—for example, applications that can analyze the data collected through Oracle Expert—to integrate the console with the Common Services. Third-party applications written in C++ that use OLE technology work very well with these APIs. Applications can be integrated at the console, service, or agent level; however, this integration depends on the third-party applications.

Installing and Configuring OEM

Not available for UNIX

OEM is available only for Windows NT and Windows 95. However, the intelligent agent can run on UNIX or Windows NT.

Several issues are involved in the installation and configuration of Enterprise Manager that you should address for the components to work together. Some issues include setting up the client, the server, and the Repository. Configuration involves setting preferred credentials and setting up security, among other things.

Minimum Requirements

You need the following minimum hardware resources to install and use the OEM components:

- Intel 486 PC or higher
- VGA video (SVGA strongly recommended)
- 32MB RAM
- CD-ROM drive
- Windows 95/NT-compatible network adapter
- 25MB of hard disk space for Oracle Enterprise Manager, Net8, and required Oracle support files
- 4MB of hard disk space for Oracle Enterprise Manager online documentation
- 15MB of hard disk space for OEM's Performance Pack
- Disk space for installing a local Oracle database or intelligent agent for Windows NT

The following minimum software resources are needed:

- Microsoft Windows NT version 3.51 or higher, or Windows 95
- TCP/IP services

Installing documentation is optional

The OEM documentation can take a lot of space. If you don't have enough disk space, you can run it from the CD-ROM when needed.

Compatibility Issues

Table 4.4 lists the components of Oracle Enterprise Manager version 1.5.0 and their compatibility with specific releases of Oracle Server.

TABLE 4.4 **Compatibility matrix for OEM 1.5.0**

Feature	Oracle Server 7.2	Oracle Server 7.3	Oracle Server 8.0.3	Oracle Server 8.0.4
Repository				
Local	no	yes	See 1	yes
Remote	yes	yes	yes	yes
Service Discovery	yes	yes	yes	yes
Job Control System	yes	yes	yes	yes
Event Management System	yes	yes	yes	yes

continues…

TABLE 4.4   **Continued**

Feature	Oracle Server 7.2	Oracle Server 7.3	Oracle Server 8.0.3	Oracle Server 8.0.4
Database Applications				
Backup Manager	yes	yes	yes	yes
Instance Manager	yes	yes	yes	yes
Schema Manager	yes	yes	yes	yes
Security Manager	yes	yes	yes	yes
Storage Manager	yes	yes	yes	yes
SQL Worksheet	yes	yes	yes	yes
Software Manager	no	See 2	yes	yes
Utility Applications				
Data Manager/Export	no	yes	yes	yes
Data Manager/Import	no	yes	yes	yes
Data Manager/Load	no	yes	yes	yes
Performance Pack				
Expert	yes	yes	yes	yes
Lock Manager	yes	yes	yes	yes
Oracle Events	no	yes	yes	yes
Performance Manager	yes	yes	yes	yes
Tablespace Manager	no	yes	yes	yes
Top Sessions	yes	yes	yes	yes
Trace	no	yes	yes	yes

[1] *OEM 1.5 must be installed in a different home if there is a local 8.0.3 database.*
[2] *Software Manager can support Oracle Server 7.3.3 agents (Windows NT only) with upgraded OSM job files.*

Performing the OEM Installation

Install and configure Enterprise Manager (general steps)

1. Configure Net8 locally and on the server.

2. Set up the client.

3. Set up the server.

4. Set up the Repository.

5. Install the OEM software on the client.

6. Install the intelligent agent on the server. The agent and the database that it services must be installed on the same node.

Configuring Net8

You can use the following tools to generate the different files required for Net8 and Enterprise Manager:

- Network Manager 3.1 for Windows to generate Net8 files and TNSNAMES.ORA
- Oracle Topology Generator to generate TOPOLOGY.ORA
- ASCII editor

You use Network Manager and Topology Generator to generate the TNSNAMES.ORA file, which will contain the information for the sample database. However, you need to edit this file with the Net8 easy configuration utility or a text editor so it will have information of other databases that you will use from OEM.

Installing and Configuring the Intelligent Agent

You can choose to install the intelligent agent as part of the Oracle Server installation, or you can install it later by running the Oracle installer.

The following is required for the agent to function correctly:

- Sun SPARCstation
- Solaris version 2.4
- 32MB RAM
- Oracle Server version 7.3 or higher
- SQL*Net version 2 or higher (Net8)

Before the agent is started, you must do the following to create a user account with appropriate privileges for the intelligent agent:

- Run the CATSNMP.SQL script (found in the $ORACLE_HOME/rdbms/admin directory) from Server

Net8 must be installed before installing OEM

If Net8 isn't installed on the machine, select it from the OEM installer. You also can choose to install Performance Pack at this point. You need to configure Net8 so that it can use the database you want to access with OEM.

Manager to create a user for the intelligent agent and give that user DBA privileges.

SEE ALSO

➤ *Creating a user, page 261*

➤ *Granting privileges to roles, page 277*

- The SNMP.ORA file must be edited with any text editor. This file contains the address of the agent and other listener information, which is read by the agent. It resides in the $ORACLE_HOME/network/admin directory on the database server.

Install Oracle Enterprise Manager

1. Log in to Windows NT as the administrator or a user with permissions equivalent to an administrator.

2. Change to the \NT_x86\INSTALL directory on the CD-ROM drive.

3. Double-click ORAINST.EXE or SETUP.EXE to launch the Oracle installer.

4. Select Oracle Enterprise Manager to install the base product.

   The Installer will search for the TOPOLOGY.ORA and TNSNAMES.ORA files in the ORACLE_HOME\network\admin directory. If TOPOLOGY.ORA isn't found, an error message appears. If TNSNAMES.ORA is found but not TOPOLOGY.ORA, you'll be prompted to create the TOPOLOGY.ORA file by using the Oracle Network Topology Generator. If the TNSNAMES.ORA file isn't found, you can use the Oracle Network Manager to create the file.

5. Exit the installer after installation is complete.

6. Log off from Windows NT and then log in again.

7. If a local Oracle NT database is being accessed, you need to use Control Panel's Services tool to verify that the Oracle Service is started, and then start up the local NT database.

User and Repository Setup

Before Oracle Enterprise Manager is used, you must create a set of base tables that contain environment information for the managed databases—this is the Repository. You create the necessary tables in the Repository by using the SMPCRE.SQL and XPOCR.SQL scripts found in the $ORACLE_HOME/ rdbms/admin directory.

An Oracle user must be created with appropriate permissions to access the Repository before the scripts are run. For each user that needs to access the console, a separate Repository must be created and setup scripts must be run.

Console and repository compatibility

The Repository must be compatible with the version of the Oracle Enterprise Manager. If the Repository version is older or newer than the console version, you must install a more recent compatible version of Enterprise Manager.

Set up the user and Repository

1. Create a new user with Server Manager:
   ```
   SVRMGR> create user sysman identified by sysman
   ```

2. Grant this user the same privileges as SYSTEM:
   ```
   SVRMGR>grant dba to sysman
   ```

3. Connect as the new user:
   ```
   SVRMGR> connect sysman/sysman@testdb
   ```

4. Execute SMPCRE.SQL and XPOCR.SQL to build the tables and views required by the console and Expert:
   ```
   SVRMRG>@smpcre.sql
   SVRMGR>@xpocr.sql
   ```

The user sysman can now log in to the Oracle Enterprise Manager.

Starting the Intelligent Agent and the Listener

For Enterprise Manager to connect and work successfully, the intelligent agent and the listener must be started on the server. For the client to communicate with the server, the communication daemon must be running.

Starting the daemon

The communication daemon is started and shut down automatically when Enterprise Manager is started.

The following shows how to run the agent and the listener:

Task	Command
Start the agent	`c: > net start oracleagent`
Shut down the agent	`c: > net stop oracleagent`
View agent's status	`c: > net start`
Start the listener on UNIX	`$ lsnrctl start testdblsnr`
Shut down the listener on UNIX	`$ lsnrctl stop testdblsnr`

Start/stop the listener in Windows NT

Use the Control Panel's Services tool to start and stop the listener in Windows NT.

Testing the Configuration

Test the configuration

1. Shut down the listener and the agent.

   ```
   $ lsnrctl stop testlsnr
   $ lsnrctl dbsnmp_stop
   ```

Logging in to OEM doesn't require the agent to be running

Log in is possible without the agent running, because the agent is required only for jobs and events submitted or returned by the remote database or the console.

2. Start up and log in to Enterprise Manager. You should get the message `ORA-12224: TNS: no listener` occurs, and `login is not possible`. Enterprise Manager requires that the listener run on the server at all times.

3. Start up the listener:

   ```
   $ lsnrctl start testlsnr
   ```

4. Double-click the Oracle Enterprise Manager icon from Program Manager and log into the database as `sysman` connected as `sysdba` (see Figure 4.3).

Setting Up Preferred Credentials

You set up preferred credentials to avoid retying the service name, service type, and username for each database, listener, or node that the user intends to access. The Preferred Credentials page of the User Preferences dialog box shows the list of databases, listeners, and nodes in the network (see Figure 4.4).

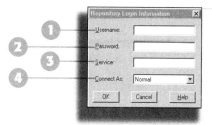

FIGURE 4.3

I og in to OEM by providing the information requested.

1 The username to use for connecting to the database (for example, sysman)

2 The password for the username

3 The Net8 service name for the database to which you're connecting

4 Connect as Normal, SYSOPER, or SYSDBA

Set the preferred credentials

1. From the console's File menu, choose Preferences.

2. Select any service from the list of entries in the dialog box and populate the Username, Password, Confirm, and Role text boxes.

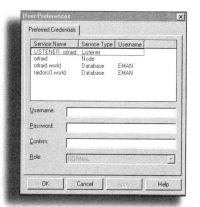

FIGURE 4.4

You can set preferred credentials from the console.

Setting Up Security

The following operations on a remote instance require that security be set up for Enterprise Manager users:

- STARTUP
- SHUTDOWN
- ALTER DATABASE
- OPEN and MOUNT
- ALTER DATABASE BACKUP
- ARCHIVE LOG
- RECOVER
- All system privileges with ADMIN OPTION
- CREATE DATABASE
- Time-based recovery

Set up remote security

1. Create a password file by connecting to the oracle user account, changing to the ORACLE_HOME/dbs directory, and then using the orapwd utility in UNIX:

   ```
   $ orapwd file=orapwtestdb password=testpass entries=10
   ```

   In this example, the SID is assumed to be testdb.

2. Grant appropriate roles:

   ```
   SVRMGR> grant sysdba to sysman
   SVRMGR> grant sysoper to sysman
   ```

3. Edit the INIT.ORA file to add the following entry:

   ```
   REMOTE_LOGIN_PASSWORDFILE=EXCLUSIVE
   ```

4. Shut down the instance.

At this point, the database instance can be shut down from Enterprise Manager, but local security needs to be set up on Windows NT clients to start up the database from OEM.

Set up local security

1. Download the INIT.ORA and CONFIG.ORA files from the server and copy them into the *OEM_directory*\\dbs directory on the Windows NT client.

2. On the client, edit the INIT.ORA file by using any text editor like Notepad, and change the "ifile" entry to the directory in which the CONFIG.ORA file is located, with the "ifile" set to the CONFIG.ORA file.

3. Restart the Enterprise Manager.

Examples of Client Files Required by Enterprise Manager

OEM uses several files on the client side—SQLNET.ORA, LISTENER.ORA, and TOPOLOGY.ORA—in the $ORACLE_HOME/network/admin directory. SQLNET.ORA contains optional parameters that can be used for tracing Net8 connections, whereas LISTENER.ORA is used to provide the address on which the listener listens.

SQLNET.ORA

```
================================================================
AUTOMATIC_IPC=OFF
trace_level_server=off
TRACE_LEVEL_CLIENT=16
trace_file_client=client.trc
trace_directory_client=c:\orant\network\trace
SQLNET.EXPIRE_TIME=0
NAMES.DEFAULT_DOMAIN=world
NAME.DEFAULT_ZONE=world
SQLNET.CRYPTO_SEED="-2089208790-14606653312"
================================================================
```

① ORACLE_HOME is set to c:\orant

② Because the default domain and zone are set to `world`, the service names in TNSNAMES.ORA should have `world` tagged to them

TNSNAMES.ORA

```
============================================================
#Agent Addresses
test_agent.world=(description=
            (address=
                (community=tcp.world)
                (protocol=tcp)
                (host=fastmachine)
                (port=1526)
            )
        )
#Database Addresses
test.world=(description=
            (address_list=
                (address=
                    (community=tcp.world)
                    (protocol=tcp)
                    (host=fastmachine)
                    (port=1701)
                )
            )
            (connect_data=
                (sid=test)
                (global_name=test.world)
            )
        )
============================================================
```

① The domain world must match the SQLNET.ORA file

② Should match the port in the SNMP.ORA file

③ Should match the port in the LISTENER.ORA file

④ The database and SID name is test

The port numbers in TNSNAMES.ORA must be unused by any other service and must be valid port numbers as per TCP/IP standards.

TOPOLOGY.ORA

```
================================================================
# Services of node: test.world
test_agent.world = (oracle_agent, fastmachine)
testlsnr.world = (oracle_listener, fastmachine)
test.world = (oracle_database, fastmachine, testlsnr.world)
#
================================================================
```

1 Should match agent name in TNSNAMES.ORA

2 Should match listener name in LISTENER.ORA

3 Database name should match the one in TNSNAMES.ORA

Examples of Server Files Required by Enterprise Manager

The agent uses several files on the server side—SQLNET.ORA, TNSNAMES.ORA, and LISTENER.ORA—that reside in the $ORACLE_HOME/network/agent directory. SQLNET.ORA contains optional parameters that can be used for tracing Net8 connections, whereas LISTENER.ORA is used to provide the address on which the listener listens.

SQLNET.ORA

```
================================================================
AUTOMATIC_IPC=OFF
trace_level_server=off
TRACE_LEVEL_CLIENT=off
SQLNET.EXPIRE_TIME=0
NAMES.DEFAULT_DOMAIN=world
NAME.DEFAULT_ZONE=world
SQLNET.CRYPTO_SEED="-2089208790-14606653312"

================================================================
```

TNSNAMES.ORA

```
================================================================
#Database Addresses
test.world=(description=
        (address_list=
            (address=
                (community=tcp.world)
                (protocol=tcp)
                (host=fastmachine)
                (port=1701)
```

```
                          )
                        )
                        (connect_data=
                               (sid=test)
                               (global_name=test.world)
                        )
                      )
========================================================
```

LISTENER.ORA

```
========================================================
testlsnr=
    (address_list=
        (address=
            (protocol=ipc)
            (key=test.world)
        )
        (address=
            (protocol=ipc)
            (key=test)
        )
        (address=
            (community=tcp.world)
            (protocol=tcp)
            (host=fastmachine)
            (port=1701)
        )
    )
startup_wait_time_testlsnr=0
connect_timeout_testlsnr=10
trace_level_testlsnr=off
sid_list_testlsnr=
    (sid_list=
        (sid_desc=
            (sid_name=test)
            (oracle_home=/export/home/oracle)
        )
    )
========================================================
```

1 Listener name, domain, host name, and SID are the same in all the other files

2 Must match the port in TNSNAMES.ORA on the client and server machines

SNMP.ORA

```
================================================================
snmp.visibleservices=(test,testlsnr)
snmp.index.test=1
snmp.index.testlsnr=2
snmp.sid.test=test
dbsnmp.address=(description=
            (address=
                (community=tcp.world)
                (protocol=tcp)
                (host=fastmachine)
                (port=1526)
            )
        )
================================================================
```

1. Listener name, SID, and host name are the same in the other files

2. Must match exactly with agent address in TNSNAMES.ORA on client machine

Basic Management Tasks with OEM

As an Oracle DBA, you'll be performing several tasks on a daily basis on OEM, such as starting up shutting down the database and managing users.

Starting and Stopping Your Database

After you set up remote and local security, you can start or shut down an Oracle database from the Enterprise Manager console. To start up or shut down a database, you must have the SYSOPER or SYSDBA role.

Start up the database

1. Start up and log in to the Enterprise Manager.

2. Double-click the database object to be started.

   If you haven't set up preferred credentials for this host, you'll get an error message. Type the correct username and password each time, or set up preferred credentials.

3. In the database property sheet that appears, choose the Startup option.

4. Click the appropriate startup option and specify the location of the INIT.ORA file.

5. Click the startup button.

Shut down the database

1. Start up and log in to Enterprise Manager.

2. Double-click the database object to be stopped.

   If preferred credentials haven't been set up for this host, an error message occurs. Type the correct username and password each time, or set up preferred credentials.

3. In the database property sheet that appears, choose the Shutdown option.

4. Click the appropriate shutdown option and then click the shutdown button.

Managing Users and Privileges

You can easily manage users and privileges by using OEM's Security Manager component (see Figure 4.5). You can manage user information for several databases from one centralized location.

After Security Manager successfully connects to the database, you see a tree structure with three context-sensitive objects. The database name is displayed next to the database container, and the Users, Roles, and Profiles containers branch from the current database container.

You can use Security Manager's User menu to create, edit, or remove existing users on a database.

Manipulate roles and profiles from the menus

Roles and profiles can also be similarly created, edited, and removed by using the Roles and Profiles menus.

Create a user

1. From the User menu choose Create.

2. In the Create User property sheet, enter the new user's username in the Name text box (see Figure 4.6).

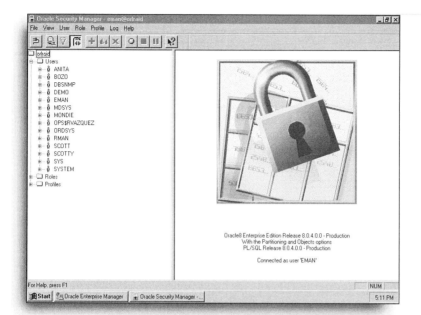

FIGURE 4.5

Security Manager enables you to manage users, profiles, and roles.

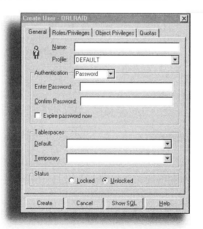

FIGURE 4.6

You can create users from the property sheet.

3. In the Authentication section, enter a password and then re-enter to confirm it.

4. Choose the appropriate default and temporary tablespaces for the user from the Tablespaces section.

5. Click Create.

6. Verify the user creation by checking the Users object in Security Manager's tree structure. This verification can also be done by logging in as the new user with the password.

Quick-edit a user

1. Right-click the username to be modified.

2. Select Quick Edit from the pop-up menu.

3. Make the desired changes to the quotas, privileges, and roles.

4. Click OK.

Remove a user

1. Select the username to be removed.

2. From the User menu, choose Remove.

3. In the confirmation dialog box, click Yes.

The user can also be removed by right-clicking the highlighted username and choosing Remove from the pop-up menu.

The User menu can be used to give privileges to users.

Assign privileges to users

1. From the User menu choose Add Privileges to Users.

2. In the Add Privileges to Users dialog box (see Figure 4.7), select the user to which privileges are to be granted. Ctrl+click additional users in the list to select more than one user.

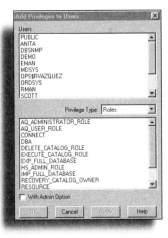

FIGURE 4.7

Privileges can be assigned to users in the Add Privileges to Users dialog box.

3. Select the Privilege Type (Roles, System, or Object).

4. Select the privileges to be granted. Ctrl+click additional privileges in the list to select more than one privilege.

5. Click Apply.

The Security Manager's Profile menu can be used to assign existing profiles to existing users.

Assign profiles to users

1. From the Profile menu choose Assign Profile to Users.

2. In the Assign Profile dialog box (see Figure 4.8), select the user or users to whom profiles are to be assigned.

FIGURE 4.8

Users can be assigned profiles in the Assign Profile dialog box.

3. Select the profile to assign.

4. Click Apply.

5. Additional profiles can be assigned by repeating steps 3 and 4. Click OK when all profiles are assigned.

Using OEM's Navigator Menu to Manipulate Users and Privileges

Create a user with the Navigator menu

1. In OEM's navigator tree, click the + to the left of the Databases folder.

2. Click the + to the left of the database name.

3. Click the + to the left of the Users folder.

4. From the Navigator menu, select Create User.

5. Enter the User information and click OK.

Copy a user between databases

1. In OEM's navigator tree, click the + to the left of the Databases folder.

2. Click the + to the left of the database name.

3. Click the + to the left of the Users folder.

4. Select the username to be copied.

5. Drag and drop the username from one database to the other database folder.

Manage database user properties such as quotas, roles, and privileges

1. In the navigator tree, click the + to the left of the Database folder.

2. Click the + to the left of the database name.

3. Click the + to the left of the Users folder.

4. From the Navigator menu, select Alter User.

5. On any of the four tabbed pages (General, Quotas, Privileges, or Default Roles), select the desired types.

7. Click OK.

Managing Database Storage

You can use Storage Manager (see Figure 4.9) to perform administrative tasks associated with managing database storage, such as managing tablespaces and rollback segments and adding and renaming data files.

You can use Oracle's Tablespace Manager to monitor and manage database storage. It can be used to display graphically how storage has been allocated for the database segments, to defragment segments, and to coalesce free adjacent blocks.

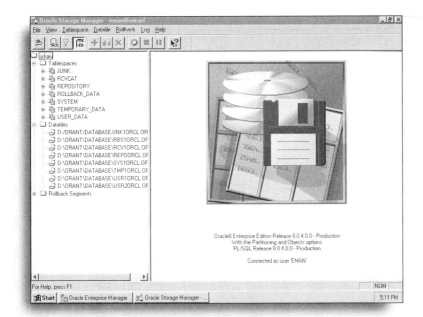

FIGURE 4.9

You can use Storage Manager to manipulate tablespaces, data files, and rollback segments.

Monitoring Tablespaces

Tablespace Manager's main window includes a tree list on the left and a drill-down on the right for a detailed view. You use the Tablespace Manager as follows:

- Click the Tablespaces container to display the space usage for each tablespace in the instance.

- Double-click the Tablespaces container for additional information about the tablespaces.

- Click an individual tablespace container to display the Segments page for that tablespace. Clicking an individual segment graphically displays the space utilization for that segment.

- Click a data file container to find the space usage for a data file.

- Click an individual data file to display the Segments page for that data file (see Figure 4.10).

FIGURE 4.10

Use Tablespace Manager to manage data files.

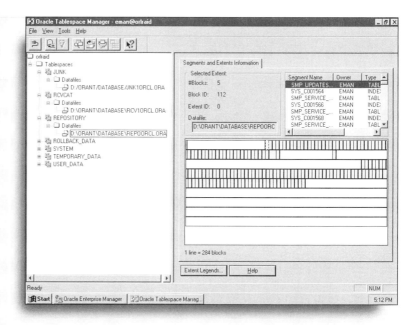

Performing Advanced Management Tasks with the Performance Pack

As a DBA, you should frequently monitor your system resources to identify contention. OEM provides various predefined charts that can help you in monitoring the usage of different resources that can contribute to contention. (For additional information on how to identify and reduce various types on contention, see Chapter 21, "Identifying and Reducing Contention.") Three resources need to be carefully monitored:

My tuning philosophy

Performance tuning shouldn't be treated as a reactive strategy; instead, it should be a preventive action based on trends detected through analysis by using tools such as the Performance Pack.

- *CPU.* Every process that executes on the server needs some time slice of the CPU time to complete its task. Some processes need a lot of CPU time, whereas others don't. You should be able to identify your CPU-intensive processes.

- *Disk access.* Every time a process needs data, it will first look at the buffer cache to see if the data is already brought in. If the data isn't found, the process will access the disk. Disk access is very time-consuming and should be minimized.

- *Memory.* Insufficient memory can lead to performance degradation. When the system falls short on memory, it will start paging and eventually start swapping physical processes.

The Performance Pack is a value-added component of the Oracle Enterprise Manager. It provides various tools to monitor and tune the performance of your database. It's important to understand that taking a point-in-time snapshot of the system doesn't do performance tuning, but it's a way to take into consideration the system performance over a period of time.

You can perform three different types of tuning by using the Performance Pack components (see Table 4.5).

TABLE 4.5 Types of tuning available through the Performance Pack

Tuning Type	Description
Routine Tuning	Used to identify and solve potential problems before they occur
Focused Tuning	Used to resolve known performance problems
What-If Tuning	Used to determine what would happen if a particular configuration change is made

The Performance Pack provides several tools (see Table 4.6) to capture, store, and analyze information so you can improve overall performance.

TABLE 4.6 Performance Pack components and their functions

Component	Function
Performance Manager	Displays tuning statistics on contention, database instance, I/O, load, and memory within predefined or customized charts
Oracle Expert	Collects and analyzes performance-tuning data on predefined rules, generates tuning recommendations, and provides scripts that help with the implementation of tuning recommendations
Oracle Trace	Collects performance data based on events and generates data for the Oracle Expert

continues…

TABLE 4.6   **Continued**

Component	Function
Oracle TopSessions Monitor	Displays the top 10 sessions based on any specified sort criteria
Tablespace Viewer	Displays the free space left on each data file
Oracle Lock Manager	Displays the blocked and waiting sessions
Oracle Advanced Events	Monitors the specified conditions in the databases, nodes, and networks

To start the performance-monitoring applications from the OEM console, use the Performance Pack launch palette or the Performance Pack option on the Tools menu.

Using Oracle Performance Manager

Performance Manager is a tool for monitoring database performance in real-time. It provides a number of predefined charts for displaying various statistics in different formats, including tables, line charts, bar charts, cube charts, and pie charts (see Figure 4.11).

FIGURE 4.11

Read consistency hit ratio is one type of information that can be charted.

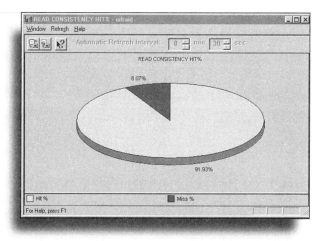

Performance Manager's Display menu includes items for seven different categories of predefined charts. Table 4.7 describes these categories and the set of charts that focus on displaying information of that category.

TABLE 4.7 **Charts used to identify contention**

Category	Charts Included in This Category
Contention	Circuit, Dispatcher, Free List Hit %, Latch, Lock, Queue, Redo Allocation Hit %, Rollback NoWait Hit %, and Shared Server
Database_Instance	Process, Session, System Statistics, Table Access, Tablespace, Tablespace Free Space, #Users Active, #Users Waiting for Locks, and #Users Running
I/O	File I/O Rate, File I/O Rate Details, Network I/O Rate, and System I/O Rate
Load	Buffer Gets Rate, Network Bytes Rate, Redo Statistics Rate, Sort Rows Rate, Table Scan Rows Rate, and Throughput Rate
Memory	Buffer Cache Hit %, Data Dictionary Cache Hit %, Library Cache Hit %, Library Cache Details, SQL Area, Memory Allocated, Memory Sort Hit %, Parse Ratio, and Read Consistency Hit %
Overview	#Users Active, #Users Logged On, #Users Running, #Users Waiting, Buffer Cache Hit, Data Dictionary Cache Hit, File I/O Rate, Rollback NoWait Hit %, System I/O Rate, and Throughput Rate
User-Defined	Charts created by the user

By default, information in the predefined charts is presented in the following manner:

- Charts showing rates per unit of time are presented as line charts.

- Charts showing ratios are presented as pie charts.

- Charts consisting primarily of text information are presented as tables.

- Charts displaying a large number of instances are presented as tables.

The overview charts are a set of 12 predefined charts that give a good overall picture of the system (see Table 4.8).

TABLE 4.8   **Predefined charts**

Chart	Description
Number of Users Active	Shows the number of users actively using the database instance. Obtains information from the V$SESSION view.
Number of Users Logged On	Shows the number of concurrent users logged on to the database instance, regardless of whether any activity is being performed. Obtains information from V$LICENSE.
Number of Users Running	Shows the number of concurrent users logged on to the database instance and now running a transaction. Obtains information from V$SESSION_WAIT.
Number of Users Waiting	Shows the number of users now waiting. Obtains information from V$SESSION_WAIT.
Buffer Cache Hit %	Shows the buffer cache hit percentage. Obtains information from V$SYSSTAT.
Data Dictionary Cache Hit	Shows the Data Dictionary cache hit. Obtains information from V$ROWCACHE.
File I/O Rate	Shows the number of physical reads and writes per second for each file of the database instance. Obtains information from V$DBFILE.
Rollback NoWait Hit %	Shows the hits and misses for online rollback segments. Obtains information from V$ROLLSTAT.
System I/O Rate	Shows I/O statistics including buffer gets, block changes, and physical reads per second for the database instance. Obtains information from V$SYSSTAT.
Throughput Rate	Shows the number of user calls and transactions per second for the instance. Obtains information from V$SYSSTAT.

Get an overall picture of activity on a database with the Overview chart

1. In the navigator window, select the ORCL database and then click the Oracle Performance Manager icon.

2. From the Monitor menu, click Display and then choose Overview.

Monitor disk access, resource contention, and memory utilization

1. Launch the Oracle Performance Manager in the context of the ORCL database, as explained in step 1 of the previous section.

2. From the Charts menu choose Define Window.

3. In the Window Name text box, provide a unique name.

4. Scroll through the list of available charts, select the chart you want, and click the << button.

5. Repeat step 4 for all the charts you need, and then click OK.

If the predefined charts don't suit your needs, you can create your own charts and save them for future use.

Creating your own charts

1. From the Charts menu, choose Define Charts.

2. Click the New Chart button.

3. Enter a name for the new chart.

4. In the SQL Statement text box, enter a statement that will gather the statistics to display in the chart.

5. Click the Execute button.

6. Verify the results in the results field.

7. On the Display Options page, enter the required information for each variable you want to display and click the Add button.

8. Click the Apply button.

9. Click OK.

10. From the File menu choose Save Charts, and save the chart in the Repository.

Recording Data for Playback

You can choose to record data in a chart for analysis at a later time. The collection size varies based on the polling interval, database activity at the time, and the collection interval.

Collect historical data

1. Display the charts from which you want to collect data.

2. From the Record menu choose Start Recording.

3. Provide a unique name in the Data Collection Name dialog box and click OK.

4. When finished with the data collection, choose Stop Recording from the Record menu.

5. Provide the database connect string in the Format/Playback Login dialog box.

Playback recorded data

1. From the Record menu choose Playback.

2. In the Format/Playback Login dialog box, provide the connect string on the database where the formatted data is saved.

3. Select the data collection to play back and click OK.

Using Oracle Expert

Don't run multiple sessions of Oracle Expert against the same repository

You can run multiple sessions of Oracle Expert against the same repository, but it's not recommended because it can lead to data conflicts between sessions.

Oracle Expert is a tool in the Performance Pack that you can use to tune a database. All tuning inputs and recommendations are stored in a tuning repository that allows the review and modification of the data and the rules at a later time. It has a knowledge base of tuning rules, designed through a tight relationship between the Oracle Server, Oracle Trace, and Oracle Expert development teams. It provides an explanation for all the recommendations it makes.

You should use Oracle Expert to complement your tuning experience, not as a tool to replace your function as a database performance tuner. You should instead focus on what to do with the findings and suggestions provided by Oracle Expert and enhance the rules used by Oracle Expert in analyzing the performance data.

You can use Oracle Expert to tune the following:

- *Instance.* It consists of tuning the SGA parameters (which affect the total size of the instance's system global area), I/O parameters (which affect the throughput or distribution of I/O for the instance), parallel query parameters, and sort parameters.

- *Application.* It consists of tuning SQL and access methods, which involves determining the indexes needed and creating, modifying, and deleting them as needed.

- *Structure.* It consists of sizing (recommendations for choosing storage parameters) and placement (recommendations on placing data files and partitioning segments).

For Oracle Expert to perform data collection, the target database being tuned should have the following tables: `dba_tab_columns`, `dba_constraints`, `dba_users`, `dba_data_files`, `dba_objects`, `dba_indexes`, `dba_segments`, `dba_ind_columns`, `dba_tables`, `dba_rollback_segs`, `dba_sequences`, `dba_views`, `dba_tablespaces`, `dba_synonyms`, `dba_ts_quotas`, and `dba_clusters`. Oracle Expert doesn't collect information regarding index-only tables, partitioned tables, partitioned indexes, object types, object tables, and object views.

Use Oracle Expert to gather tuning information (general steps)

1. Set the scope of the tuning session to tell Oracle Expert what aspects of the database to consider for tuning purposes. Oracle Expert collects the following categories of data: database, instance, schema, environment, and workload.

2. The collected data is organized in a hierarchical format. You can view and edit the rules and attributes used by Oracle Expert.

3. Oracle Expert generates tuning recommendations based on the collected and edited data. You can decide to use the recommendations, or ignore them and let Oracle Expert generate a new recommendation.

4. When you're satisfied with the recommendations, you can let Oracle Expert generate parameter files and scripts to implement the chosen recommendations.

Increase the information analyzed by Oracle Expert

Before performing instance SGA tuning, run XPVIEW.SQL (in $ORACLE_HOME\rdbms\ admin) against the database being tuned to get better recommendations from Oracle Expert. Doing so causes Oracle Expert to collect additional information about the database's shared SQL segment.

Don't tune the SYS or system schema

Don't use Oracle Expert to tune the **SYS** or system schema. You should let Oracle tune these items automatically.

Have enough privileges to perform some functions

If the database management functions are grayed out from the menu bar, it may be because you aren't authorized to perform those functions. Reconnect as **SYSOPER** or **SYSDBA**.

Start an Expert Tuning session

1. From the File menu choose New.

2. Define the scope of the tuning session.

3. On the Collect page, specify the amount and type of data to collect.

4. Click the Collect button to acquire the required data.

5. On the View/Edit page are the rules used by Expert. You can modify the rules based on your experience.

6. On the Analyze page, click the Perform Analysis button to begin the data analysis.

7. Select Review Recommendations to review the recommendations provided by Expert.

8. If you agree with the recommendations, you can implement them by generating the requisite scripts and parameter files from the Implement page. If you don't agree with the recommendations, you'll have to change one or more rule and re-analyze (without recollecting) the data.

The collection classes to use are determined by the selected tuning categories for a tuning session.

Reuse collected data

When tuning multiple categories, the common classes need to be collected only once because Oracle Expert will be able to reuse the data for analysis.

Permissions to use Oracle Expert

The user running Oracle Expert must have **SELECT ANY TABLE** privilege for the database in which the repository is stored.

Start Oracle Expert

1. In the OEM map or navigator window, select a database and then click the Oracle Expert icon in the Performance Pack palette. Or double-click the Expert icon in OEM's Program Manager.

2. Connect to a tuning repository.

3. From the File menu choose New to create a new tuning session.

4. Enter the appropriate data in the dialog box pages.

5. Click OK.

Using Oracle TopSessions

You can use the Oracle TopSessions utility to view the top Oracle sessions based on specified criteria, such as CPU usage and disk activity. Before running TopSessions for Oracle8, run $ORACLE_HOME/sysman/smptsi80.SQL to create all the supporting tables.

Identify Oracle sessions that use the most CPU

1. In OEM's navigator window, select the ORCL database and then click the Oracle TopSessions icon.

2. On the Sort page of the Options property sheet (see Figure 4.12), change the Statistics Filter to User and the Sort Statistic to CPU Used by This Session.

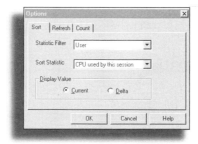

FIGURE 4.12

You can use the Sort page of the Oracle TopSessions Options dialog box to specify the criteria to use for monitoring sessions.

3. On the Refresh page of the Options property sheet (see Figure 4.13), select Automatic for the refresh type, set the Refresh Interval to 10, and reset the Minutes and Hours to 0.

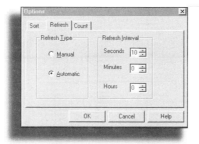

FIGURE 4.13

The Refresh page of the Options dialog box can be used to change the refresh type and refresh interval.

4. On the Count page of the Options property sheet (see Figure 4.14), select the Display Top N Sessions button and change the count to 10.

5. Click OK to show the results (see Figure 4.15).

FIGURE 4.14

The Count page of the Options dialog box can be used to specify the number of sessions to track.

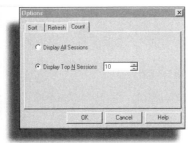

FIGURE 4.15

Oracle TopSessions shows the results as specified by the resource usage criteria.

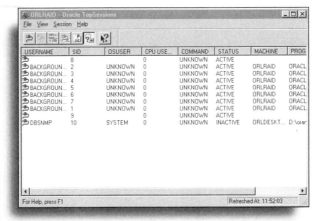

Managing Your Database Space

Identify different segment types

Design tablespaces for different segment types

Manage tablespaces

Make effective use of physical file structures

Control unused and free space

Space Management Fundamentals

The DBA's role in space management

Space management is an ongoing task for most of you. Unless you have a completely static database, tables and indexes will regularly grow, or shrink, in size. You need to ensure that sufficient space is available for this to occur without interruption to the ongoing processing. You also need to help ensure that the space is being used efficiently.

The basic storage unit in an Oracle database is the *Oracle block* (or *database block*). This is the smallest unit of storage that will be moved from disk to memory and back again. Oracle block sizes range from 2KB to 32KB. You obviously couldn't store a complete table on a single block, so blocks are grouped into *segments* to store amalgams of data. There are various types of segments:

- *Data segments* contain rows from a single table or from a set of clustered tables.

SEE ALSO

➤ *See how to use clusters on page **511***

- *Index segments* contain ordered index entries.
- *LOB segments* contain long objects.
- *LOB index segments* contain the special indexes for LOB segments.
- *Rollback segments* store "before" images of changes to data and index blocks, allowing the changes to be rolled back if needed.
- *Temporary segments* hold the intermediate results of sorts and related processing that are too large to be completed in the available memory.
- A single *cache segment* (also known as the *bootstrap segment*) holds boot information used by the database at startup.

You may have very large segments in your database, and it may be impossible to put the whole thing into a set of contiguous Oracle blocks. Oracle therefore builds its segments out of *extents*, which are sets of logically contiguous blocks. "Logically contiguous" means that the operating system and its storage subsystems will place the blocks in files or in *raw partitions* so that Oracle can find them by asking for the block offset address from the start of the file. For example, block 10 would begin at the (10XOracle block size) byte in the data file. It doesn't matter to Oracle if the operating system has striped the file so that this byte is on a completely different disk than the one immediately preceding it. The database always accesses blocks by their relative position in the file.

A large segment may have several, or even several hundred, extents. In some cases it will be too big to fit into a single file. This is where the last Oracle storage construct plays a part. Rather than force users to deal with individual files, Oracle divides the database into logical units of space called *tablespace*s. A tablespace consists of at least one underlying operating system file (or database *data file*). Large tablespaces can be composed of two or more data files, up to 1,022 files.

Every segment or partition of a partitioned segment must be entirely contained in a single tablespace. Every extent must fit entirely inside a single data file. However, many extents can comprise a partition or a non-partitioned segment, and the different extents don't all have to be in the same data file. Only one type of database object, a BFILE (binary file), is stored directly in an operating system file that's not part of a tablespace.

There are six reasons to separate your database into different tablespaces:

- To separate segments owned by SYS from other users' segments

- To manage the space available to different users and applications

- To separate segments that use extents of different sizes

- To separate segments with different extent allocation and deallocation rates

- To distribute segments across multiple physical storage devices

- To allow different backup and related management cycles and activity

The first reason to use multiple tablespaces is to keep the segments owned by user SYS away from any other segments. The only segments SYS should own—and the only ones that Oracle will create and manage for you—are those belonging to the data dictionary.

A second reason to use different tablespaces is to control how much space different *schema*s can take up with their segments.

Recommendation for using multiple tablespaces

Although Oracle doesn't prevent you from creating all your segments in a single tablespace, Oracle strongly recommends against it. You can control your space more easily by using different tablespaces than you can if everything were placed in a single tablespace. Multiple files let you build your tablespace in a manner that helps you improve space usage as well as database performance.

The data dictionary

The data dictionary is the road map to all the other database segments, as well as to the data files, the table-space definitions, the Oracle user-names, passwords and related information, and many other types of database objects. The dictionary needs to be modified as objects are added, dropped, or modified, and it must be available at all times. By keeping it in its own tablespace, you're less likely to run out of room (which would bring the database to a complete halt if it prevented **SYS** from modifying the dictionary).

Each user can be assigned just so much space in any tablespace and doesn't need to be assigned any space at all in some tablespaces. Some end users may have no space allocated to them at all because their database access consists solely of manipulating segments that belong to the application owner.

The third reason to manage your segments in different tablespaces has to do with space usage by the extents belonging to different segments. As you can imagine, most databases have segments that are large and some that are small. To make effective use of the space, you would assign different-sized extents to these objects. If you mix these extents in a single tablespace, you may have problems if you need to drop or shrink the segments and try to reuse the freed space.

Consider the example of a kitchen cabinet where you keep all your canned goods on one shelf (see Figure 5.1). After a trip to the grocery store, you can almost fill the shelf with cans of different sizes. Suppose that during the week you take out half a dozen or so of the smaller cans. After another trip to the grocery store, you couldn't simply put large cans in the spaces where the small ones came from, even if there were fewer large cans. You might have enough space if you rearrange the cans, but none of the spots is initially big enough for a single, large can.

FIGURE 5.1

You may have space management problems if you try storing different-sized objects together.

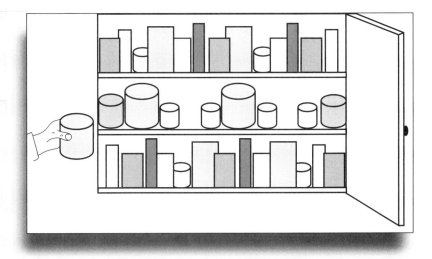

Now suppose that you take out only large cans and then put medium-sized cans in their place. You still have some space around the medium-sized cans, but not enough to store even a small can. Again, you could find room for a small can, but only by shifting things around, as shown in Figure 5.2.

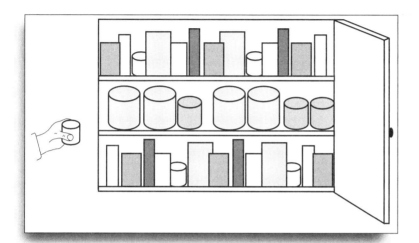

FIGURE 5.2
You'll run into space problems when replacing objects of different sizes.

When large and small extents try to share limited tablespace storage space, they can "behave" like the cans. Space can be freed when extents are removed, but it's not necessarily of a useful size. Unlike you reorganizing the kitchen cupboard, however, the database can't easily shift the remaining extents around to make the space more useful. When space in a tablespace consists of an irregular checkerboard of used and free block groups, it's said to be fragmented. Much of the free space may never be reusable unless the extents are somehow reorganized. You can prevent such *fragmentation* by allowing only extents of the same size in the tablespace. That way, any freed extent is going to be exactly the right size for the next extent required in the tablespace.

A variant of the fragmentation problem provides a fourth value for multiple tablespaces. Some segments are very unlikely to be dropped or truncated. For example, a mail-order business' CURRENT_ORDERS table unlikely will do anything but grow—or at least stay about the same size—as new orders are added and

Avoiding different free space extent sizes requires different tablespaces

To allow different-sized extents in your database without mixing them in the same storage space, you need different tablespaces.

Tables with different propensity to fragment free space

The CURRENT_ORDERS table will never contribute to a fragmentation problem because its extents never go away. The data warehouse partitions, however, are dropped on a regular basis, so they'll have a high propensity to cause fragmentation.

filled orders removed. On the other hand, you may have a *data warehouse* in which you keep the last five years' order records. If you build this table as a series of 60 month-long partitions, you'll be able to drop the oldest one each month as you add the latest month's records.

Thus, the fourth reason to keep segments in different tablespaces is to separate segments with a low, or zero, propensity to fragment space and those with a high likelihood of causing fragmentation. This way, the long-term objects, if they do need to grow, won't have to hunt around for free space of the right size.

The fifth reason to use different tablespaces is to help distribute the data file reads and writes across multiple disk drives. You can use lots of different data files in a tablespace and place them on different disk drives, but you may not be able to control which extents are placed in which file after doing that. If you're lucky, the amount of disk access will be even across all the drives. If you aren't so lucky, you might have a situation where the two busiest extents in your database are in the same file.

For example, if the mail-order house is going into its busy holiday season sale period, it will probably need to use the empty blocks at the end of the CURRENT_ORDER table for the additional orders. If the extent holding these blocks is in the same data file as the index blocks where the newest order numbers are being saved, you'll have excessive disk contention; each new order will use a block from the table extent and a block from the index extent.

If you keep segments that will likely cause concurrent disk access (such as tables and the indexes on those tables) in different tablespaces, you can guarantee that the files making up the different tablespaces are stored on separate disk drives.

Tablespace damage can be pervasive

If any part of a tablespace is damaged, the entire tablespace becomes unusable until the damage is fixed. If every segment belonging to an application were stored in a single tablespace and that tablespace was damaged, nobody could use that application.

A database-management issue is the final reason to use different tablespaces. During its life, a database will need to be backed up and possibly repaired if a disk crashes or otherwise corrupts data.

However, if you split segments that belong to different functional areas of the application (such as order entry and accounts receivable) and use different tablespaces for these, a data file problem may not be so intrusive. A failure with a data file in the accounts-receivable tablespace could be undergoing repair without any impact being felt by the order takers using the order-entry tablespace.

Similarly, a tablespace containing tables that rarely change—such as lookup tables for state codes, part number and part name references, and so on—may not need regular backing up, whereas CURRENT_ORDERS may need very frequent backups to reduce the tablespace recovery time if there were a failure.

SEE ALSO

➤ *To learn more about objects, LOBs, and BFILEs, see page* **731**

Suggested Tablespaces

I recommend that every DBA create certain tablespaces for a production database. The reasons for these different tablespaces stem from the previous discussion. Let's begin with the SYSTEM tablespace, the only mandatory tablespace in every Oracle database.

SYSTEM Tablespace

Every Oracle database must have one tablespace—SYSTEM. This is where the user SYS stores the data dictionary information needed to manage the database. You should create additional tablespaces based on the expected use of your database. If you don't do this and use only the SYSTEM tablespace, you'll violate most of the reasons for using different tablespaces recommended in the previous section. Several other things will happen as well:

- You won't keep the segments owned by SYS out of harm's way by other users.

- You'll have to allow everyone who needs to create objects to take space from SYS in the SYSTEM tablespace.

- You'll cause fragmentation because all extents of all sizes will share the same space.

- You'll have a mix of segments with high and low propensity to fragment space in the same space.

- You can't easily avoid having high-usage extents stored on the same disk drive.

Backing up tablespaces on different schedules

To minimize the time it takes to back up less-often used segments, back up different tablespaces on different schedules. In fact, you can define a truly read-only tablespace to the database and then back it up only once when you've finished loading the required data into it. Of course, if you mix the static tables and the busy tables in the same tablespace, you have to back them all up equally often.

Maintain the integrity of the *SYSTEM* tablespace

You should never need to create any object directly in the SYSTEM tablespace, regardless of which userid you use to connect to the database. This tablespace should be reserved for the recursive SQL executed behind the scenes as part of database creation or the execution of standard SQL statements.

■ You have a single point of failure for the whole database. If the data file in the SYSTEM tablespace is lost or damaged, the entire database will shut down.

I hope this list of possible problems has convinced you to use additional tablespaces, such as those described in the next few pages.

Rollback Segment Tablespaces

The tablespace for rollback segments will contain all the database's rollback segments with one exception—the SYSTEM rollback segment. It is maintained automatically in the SYSTEM tablespace.

Keep your rollback segments separate from other database objects for a number of reasons:

■ They can shrink automatically and therefore create fragmented free space.

SEE ALSO

➤ *For details of the* ALTER ROLLBACK SEGMENT *command, see page* **185**

■ They don't need quotas, so their space can't be managed by schema quotas.

■ They're needed concurrently with data blocks during transaction processing, so they can lead to disk contention.

Rollback segments can be defined to shrink themselves automatically if they grow larger than needed. Thus, they have a very high propensity for fragmenting the free space. Fortunately, a rollback segment is required to use the same size extents as it grows and shrinks, so it can reclaim any empty space it leaves behind when shrinking.

Another reason for using a tablespace for rollback segments is that you create them for use by anyone. Users don't need to have a space quota on the tablespace where the rollback segments reside. This allows the rollback segments to exist without having to contend for space with the segments that belong to an application (suddenly having their free space taken up by a table created with excessive storage requirements, for example).

Rollback segment shrinkage

Although you can define rollback segments to shrink by themselves if they grow too large, you can also use a special **ALTER ROLLBACK SEGMENT** command option to shrink them manually.

Maintaining multiple rollback segment tablespaces

If all the rollback segments in a single tablespace are sized identically, they can even claim the space released by the other segments. You shouldn't have many problems with space overuse or waste in a rollback segment tablespace with this arrangement, as long as they don't try to grow too much all at the same time. Should you need rollback segments of different sizes, therefore, you should consider building a new rollback segment tablespace and keeping the larger ones in one tablespace and the smaller ones in the other.

The final reason for keeping rollback segments in their own tablespace(s) is that you can help avoid contention for the disk. When a table is being modified, not only does Oracle modify the contents of the table block(s), but a set of rollback entries is also stored in a rollback segment. If the table and the rollback segment belonged to the same tablespace, the blocks being changed in each of them could be in the same data file on the same disk.

Temporary Tablespaces

Temporary tablespaces are for the temporary segments built by Oracle during sorting and related operations, when the amount of memory available to the server is insufficient to complete the task. The important characteristic of temporary segments is that Oracle creates and manages them without any input from the users. Consequently, unlike the other segments (except the bootstrap segment), there's no CREATE syntax to identify which tablespace the segment is created in, nor what size or number of extents to use. Neither is there any DROP command, or any other command, that lets you release the space from temporary segments.

By default, temporary segments are dropped as soon as their work is complete. Obviously, the dropping of these segments on a transaction boundary makes them very prone to fragmenting free space. You can help mitigate the fragmentation problems by ensuring that the extents used by the temporary segments are all exactly the same size.

The ephemeral nature of temporary segments by itself makes them candidates for their own tablespace. However, there's one further consideration—you can create a tablespace or alter an existing tablespace to contain only temporary segments. By doing this, you change the default behavior of temporary segments. Rather than drop the segment when it's no longer needed, the server simply records in a special data dictionary table that the extents in the segment are now free. Any other server needing to use temporary space can query this table and locate available temporary extents. In this way, the database will save the space allocated to temporary segments indefinitely and assign it for use as needed by various servers.

Default behavior of temporary segments

Temporary segments obtain their storage characteristics solely from the tablespace definition. Hence, unless you have a tablespace for other types of segments that need identical storage characteristics to your temporary segments, you'll need a dedicated, temporary segment tablespace. Even if you have a tablespace that appears to be able to share storage characteristics for regular segments and for temporary segments, you may want to create a separate one for your temporary segments. The reason for this is that temporary segments are so named because of their default behavior. Because they're being used just to store intermediate values of an ongoing sort, they aren't really needed by the server process when the sort is complete. Hence, they can easily fragment the space in a tablespace as they are created and dropped.

Reduce database overhead with TEMPORARY-type tablespaces

The characteristic of preserving temporary segments in **TEMPORARY**-type tablespaces saves a lot of recursive SQL associated with creating and managing the space for temporary processing. In the long run, reducing recursive SQL speeds the processing of the entire database. It's essential that you have a tablespace dedicated to temporary segments if you want to take advantage of this behavior. You aren't allowed to place anything other than temporary segments in a tablespace defined as a temporary type.

As with the other tablespaces being discussed, you aren't limited to just one temporary tablespace (other than SYSTEM). You can add as many as you need to avoid contention for the space in a single temporary tablespace. Temporary space is assigned to users as part of the user definition. If you need to, you can subdivide your user community to access different temporary tablespaces.

A final benefit of keeping your temporary tablespaces separate from other tablespaces is that because the use of temporary space is the result of processing being performed behind the scenes for the user, you don't need to assign space in temporary tablespaces to your users. You can keep your temporary tablespace(s) clear of other user-created segments by disallowing any storage on them. As with the SYSTEM tablespace, this will avoid problems that could occur should the required space be taken up by segments that don't belong in this reserved space.

User Data Tablespaces

For most of you, the largest amount of storage in your database will be taken by rows in your applications' tables. You should realize that these data segments don't belong in the SYSTEM tablespace, nor should they be stored with your rollback segments or your temporary segments. I recommend that you build one or more tablespaces to store your database tables.

You would need more than one user data tablespace for a number of reasons, all related to the discussion in the section "Identifying Tablespace Uses":

- *Segment and extent sizes.* It's improbable that all application tables will need to be the same size, or even have same-sized extents. To avoid fragmentation, you should place tables into tablespaces only with other tables that use the same extent size.

- *To allow you to manage them differently.* If your database supports more than one application, you may want to protect them from one another by using separate tablespaces for them. In this way only one set of your users would be affected by a disk problem in a tablespace. Users of the applications supported in the unaffected tablespaces can continue their work while the repair work is done to the damaged tablespace.

■ *To keep volatile tables away from static (or almost static) tables.* This way you can organize your backup strategy around the needs of each tablespace—backing up the tablespaces with busy tables more frequently than those with tables less busy. For those tables that never change, or change very infrequently, you can make the tablespaces that hold them READ_ONLY. Such a tablespace needs to be backed only once following its conversion to this status.

■ *To place your very busy tables in tablespaces different from each other.* This way you can avoid the disk-drive contention that could occur if they share the same disks.

By the time you finish planning your user data tablespaces, you may have divided them for a combination of the reasons discussed here. It wouldn't be unreasonable to have two or three tablespaces holding tables with same-sized extents (each with a different backup frequency requirement), and another two or three with the same extent sizes containing tables that have the same backup requirements but have a high contention potential.

Index Tablespaces

Indexes on tables are often used by many concurrent users who are also accessing the tables as part of the same transaction. If you place the indexes in the same tablespace as the tables they support, you're likely to cause disk contention; this would occur as queries retrieved index blocks to find where the required rows are stored and then retrieved the required data blocks. To avoid such contention, you should create a separate set of tablespaces for your indexes.

As with tables, you may find that you need to size your index extents differently, and that you may have indexes supporting tables from different applications. Just as with your user data tablespaces, therefore, you should plan on building multiple index tablespaces to support different extent sizes and backup requirements and to maintain application independence in case of disk failure.

Managing tablespace extent size

You may want to standardize your tables to three or four extent sizes. This will reduce the number of different tablespaces you'll need to manage while allowing you to realize the benefits of having all the extents in a tablespace be the same size. In particular, you won't have to concern yourself with the frequency at which extents are added and dropped. Such activity won't lead to poor space allocation because every dropped extent leaves free space exactly the same size a new extent would require.

If you use the Oracle8 partitioning option, you may need to revise your index and user-data tablespace design. In some cases it's beneficial to build locally partitioned indexes in the same tablespaces as the parent partition. This helps maintain the availability of the partitions during various tablespace maintenance activities.

SEE ALSO

➤ *For additional details on rollback segment management, see page* ***185***

Understanding File Types: File Systems Versus Raw Devices

Raw devices and Oracle Parallel Server

If you're going to use the Oracle Parallel Server option on UNIX or Windows NT, you must create all your database files—including the redo log files, control files, and data files—on raw devices. The various instances can't share the files if you don't do this.

Some operating systems allow you to create raw partitions and use these for your Oracle database files instead of standard file-system files. In certain cases, raw devices can offer you improved performance. In addition, if you're using a UNIX system that doesn't support a write-through cache, you'll have to use raw devices to ensure that every write performed during a *checkpoint* or a *log buffer flush* is actually written to the physical disk.

There are some drawbacks to raw devices:

- On UNIX, sequential data reads from a raw device can't take advantage of read-ahead techniques. This means that a full table scan may be slower if other users are accessing different Oracle blocks on the same disk as the table being scanned.

- Raw partitions aren't as flexible as file-system files. You're generally restricted to a certain number and, hence, fixed partition sizes on each disk. Also, you may not have permission as a DBA to create new raw partitions. This means that you have to work with a system administrator when you need to add a file.

  Although this may be easy enough when you're planning for a new database or a known expansion, it may not be convenient when you need to add or replace a data file in an emergency. Your system administrator may have to prebuild spare raw partitions for you to use in such emergencies. This approach, in turn, requires you to standardize on partition (and, therefore, on data file) sizes. As with extent sizes, you may want to simplify this approach by standardizing just three or four partition sizes across the whole database.

Understanding the Benefits of Striping Data

In some situations, no matter how well you've segregated your data into separate tablespaces, particularly busy tables or indexes will cause "hot spots" on one or more disks. To resolve this, you may need to build your data files by using an operating system *striping* mechanism. Such mechanisms include logical volume manager (LVM) software or redundant arrays of inexpensive disks (RAID). By striping the data file across many disks, you reduce the likelihood that any particular table or index will have all its busiest blocks on one single disk.

If you decide to stripe your data files, you need to determine an appropriate stripe size. Optimal stripe sizes depend on a number of factors, the three key factors being the implementation of the striping software, the Oracle block size, and the type of database processing against the data.

Operating system or disk-striping mechanisms differ widely between vendors. Some offer large, guaranteed cache areas used for reads, writes, or both. A cache can overcome some performance slowdowns that can occur when you need to sequentially read blocks that are scattered across many different disks. Others, such as RAID, provide striping as a side benefit of various levels of disk failure resilience, but can slow certain activities to provide you protection against disk failure. Certain levels of RAID are better left unused for particular file types, such as those with large amounts of data written to them sequentially. For example, redo logs, while not part of a tablespace, may suffer a performance penalty if stored on RAID Level 5. If you have any tables that collect data in a similar sequential fashion, however, you should also try to avoid placing their data files on RAID Level 5 devices.

Oracle block size is an important factor when striping data files that contain tables or indexes that will typically be accessed via random reads or random writes. You'll usually see this type of

Stripe sizes for query-intensive data

If your database is query-intensive—that is, the users are usually executing queries and very infrequently performing INSERTs, UPDATEs, or DELETEs—you need a stripe size that will support sequential processing of data. This will help queries that need to access indexes via range scans (many records with the same value or a set of values between an upper and lower bound) or tables via full table scans. You should set the stripe size for such databases to be a minimum of two times the value of the parameter DB_FILE_MULTIBLOCK _READ_COUNT and, if larger, to an integer multiple of this parameter's value. This will help ensure that all the blocks requested in a single read, when performing a full table scan, will be on the same disk, requiring only one disk read/write head to be moved to the required starting position.

activity when the database is used primarily for transaction processing. In these cases, you should plan to make your stripe size at least twice the size of an Oracle block but, all things being equal, not too much larger. Whatever stripe size you choose, however, make sure it's an integer multiple of your Oracle block size.

Adding New Tablespaces

You automatically create your SYSTEM tablespace when you build your database. As discussed earlier in this chapter, you should add further tablespaces to meet your database's specific requirements. The following sections go over the process of creating tablespaces with various characteristics.

Creating a Tablespace

The very first tablespace you create is the SYSTEM tablespace, always part of an initial database creation. Additional tablespace creation isn't that much different from the SYSTEM tablespace creation. As with the CREATE DATABASE command, the CREATE TABLESPACE command uses a DATAFILE clause to identify the data file(s) and size(s) you want to associate with the tablespace. The syntax for the CREATE TABLESPACE command is as follows:

① Identifies file(s) to be used and their characteristics

② Sets minimum size of used and free extents in tablespace

③ Determines whether certain SQL commands will avoid creating standard redo log entries

④ Controls extent behavior for segments created without defined storage options

⑤ Determines status of tablespace after creation

⑥ Defines tablespace to hold regular segments

⑦ Defines tablespace to hold only temporary segments

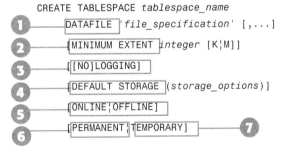

```
CREATE TABLESPACE tablespace_name
①  ──  DATAFILE 'file_specification' [,...]
②  ──  [MINIMUM EXTENT integer [K¦M]]
③  ──  [[NO]LOGGING]
④  ──  [DEFAULT STORAGE (storage_options)]
⑤  ──  [ONLINE¦OFFLINE]
⑥  ──  [PERMANENT¦TEMPORARY]  ──  ⑦
```

We'll examine the DEFAULT STORAGE clause in the following section. In the meantime, look at the DATAFILE clause in more detail. This clause can be applied to any tablespace's data files (including the SYSTEM tablespace), although most DBAs are content to use it simply to name and size the data file(s) for this tablespace. The DATAFILE clause's full syntax is as follows:

```
DATAFILE filename
    [SIZE integer [K¦M]]
    [REUSE]
    [AUTOEXTEND OFF¦ON [NEXT integer [K¦M]]
    [MAXSIZE [UNLIMITED¦integer [K¦M]]]]
```

Recall from the earlier section, "Understanding File Types: File Systems Versus Raw Devices," that you can use native file system files or raw partitions for your tablespace's files. The data file's name will therefore be a file-system filename, a raw partition name, or possibly a link name pointing to one or the other types of file. In the case of a file-system file, the file will be created for you unless you use the REUSE clause. In this case, Oracle will create the file if it doesn't already exist, but will overwrite an existing file as long as the SIZE clause, if included, matches the size of the existing file. If you don't specify REUSE and the file already exists, you get an error message, and the tablespace won't be created.

If you name a raw partition (directly or via a link), the partition must already exist; otherwise, Oracle will attempt to create a standard file with the name of the partition. Because Oracle expects raw partitions to exist before being named in the CREATE TABLESPACE command, the REUSE clause really has no effect. The SIZE clause with raw partitions must be a few blocks smaller than the actual partition size; this allows space for operating system header information. Two operating system blocks are usually sufficient.

The AUTOEXTEND option determines whether a data file can grow automatically should a new extent be required by a segment and there's an insufficient number of contiguous free blocks. You don't have to use this clause (when you create the tablespace) to be able to grow your tablespace, as discussed later in the "Adding and Resizing Data Files" section. If you decide you want your files to be able to grow automatically, you should be aware of the impact of the following behaviors:

- If there are multiple files with the AUTOEXTEND option in a single tablespace, the file chosen to grow when more space is needed will depend on a couple of characteristics. Oracle

The REUSE option can be destructive

Be careful with **REUSE**; any current entries in the file will be overwritten and lost when it's implemented. A raw partition can always be reused, destroying its existing content—even if you don't include the **REUSE** keyword.

Simplify your raw partition sizing

You may want to keep your arithmetic simple when sizing raw partitions for Oracle files by allowing 1MB for the overhead in each partition. Thus, you would create a 101MB partition to hold a 100MB file.

will try to extend the file that can be extended least to obtain the required space. If this results in a tie between two or more files, the one furthest from its maximum size will be extended. If this also results in a tie, the files will be extended in a round-robin fashion as more space is needed.

- If the NEXT option isn't chosen, the files are extended one Oracle block at a time.

- If you don't set an upper limit with the MAXSIZE option or use MAXSIZE UNLIMITED, the file can grow indefinitely until it reaches the limits of the physical storage device.

- You can allow files in raw partitions to grow, but the data will overwrite the adjacent partition(s) if the partition size isn't large enough to contain the extended file; this destroys the contents and integrity of some other file.

SEE ALSO

➤ *For more information on creating a database, see page 41*

➤ *To learn about temporary segments and how they're used in* TEMPORARY-*type tablespaces, see page 190*

Setting Default Storage Values

Your default storage values can be overridden!

After a user has the privileges necessary to build segments, you can't prevent them from overriding the tablespace default storage values. You need to take on the responsibility of building all segments yourself if you don't want to risk this. To reduce the burden of work for yourself you can have the users build script files containing the required **CREATE** commands, which you can simply execute on their behalf. Of course, you should check that

As noted in the earlier sections "Identifying Tablespace Uses" and "Suggested Tablespaces," a tablespace should ideally contain only segments with equal-sized extents. One way to help you maintain such a scheme is to assign to each tablespace the desired storage options as defaults. The CREATE TABLESPACE command's DEFAULT STORAGE clause is the means to achieve this.

Whenever a database segment such as a table, a rollback segment, or an index is created, a set of storage-related information is activated or stored with the segment definition. This storage information defines the size of the first extent belonging to the segment, the size of the second extent, the size of the subsequent extents, and the initial and the maximum number of extents that will be assigned to the segment. In the case of rollback segments, there's also a value associated with the optimal size of the rollback segment, which, if used, will cause extents to be dropped automatically if the overall size exceeds the desired maximum.

SEE ALSO

➤ *To learn more about managing rollback segments and the* OPTIMAL *storage option, see page **180***

Although each user who creates a segment can assign these storage values individually, they also can be inherited from the tablespace's definition. Temporary segments are a little different in that users don't get to create these; they're built as needed by the system on behalf of a user and, as such, always inherit the tablespace storage values. If you've built your tablespaces such that each one is designed to hold only one extent size, you can define the tablespace to provide this size by default. You can then advise those users who create segments (if it's someone other than yourself) that they shouldn't include the STORAGE clause in their CREATE statements. This not only simplifies their work, but keeps your tablespace extents defined as you planned.

You define the inheritable storage values for a tablespace with the DEFAULT STORAGE clause. Here is the syntax for that clause:

```
DEFAULT STORAGE (
        [INITIAL integer [K¦M]]
        [NEXT integer [K¦M]]
        [PCTINCREASE integer]
        [MINEXTENTS integer]
        [MAXEXTENTS integer]
```

① Sets size of initial extent in bytes, with optional K or M to specify kilobytes or megabytes

② Sets size of second extent in bytes, with optional K or M

③ Defines increase, measured as a percentage, by which each extent beyond the second will grow

④ Sets number of extents each segment will be assigned when created

⑤ Sets greatest number of extents that segment will be assigned

You need to set INITIAL equal to NEXT and PCTINCREASE equal to 0 in order for the tablespace to create every extent, by default, with the same size. Remember that even though you set these defaults, every CREATE statement that builds a segment in the tablespace can override them. This is true even if you allow users to include a STORAGE clause simply to change the number of preliminary or maximum extents (MINEXTENTS and MAXEXTENTS). As soon as they can use a CREATE command, you can't restrict what's included in the related STORAGE clause.

The following listing shows a command being used to create a tablespace with three data files, one of which is auto-extendible, and with a default storage clause to build all extents with 10MB of storage:

```
CREATE TABLESPACE extra_room
     DATAFILE      '/d1/oracle/exrm01.dbf' SIZE 1000M,
                   '/d2/oracle/exrm02.dbf' SIZE 1000M,
                   '/d3/oracle/exrm03.dbf' SIZE 1000M
                   AUTOEXTEND ON NEXT 10M MAXSIZE 2000M
     DEFAULT STORAGE (
          INITIAL 10M
          NEXT 10M
          PCTINCREASE 0)
  /
```

Tablespace Management

After you create your tablespaces, you may find that they aren't quite what you needed. To rectify this situation, you can drop and recreate the tablespace. In some cases you can modify it. The latter tends to be the easier solution if segments are already created in the tablespace, because dropping such a tablespace generally requires you to find a way to save and reload these segments.

Changing the Characteristics of a Tablespace

You can see a tablespace's current characteristics by viewing the data dictionary table DBA_TABLESPACES. Many of these characteristics can be changed with the ALTER TABLESPACE command. The syntax for the command is as follows:

ALTER TABLESPACE *tablespace_name option*;

Table 5.1 summarizes the options available with the ALTER TABLESPACE command. (You can only use one option at a time with the command.) Because some of the options are a little more complex than you might infer from Table 5.1, the following sections explain why you might want to use them.

TABLE 5.1 *ALTER TABLESPACE* options

Option:	Purpose:
OFFLINE	Makes a tablespace unavailable for use and prevents access to its contents
ONLINE	Returns a tablespace from OFFLINE to ONLINE accessible status
BEGIN BACKUP	Readies the files in the tablespace for hot backup
END BACKUP	Returns the tablespace's files to normal status following a hot backup
LOGGING or NOLOGGING	Sets the default logging behavior of new objects created in the tablespace
RENAME DATAFILE	Identifies the new name of a data file to a tablespace when the file itself has been changed in the operating system
COALESCE	Coalesces contiguous areas of free space into a single free extent
MINIMUM EXTENT	Sets the minimum size of any extent, used or free, in the tablespace
READ ONLY	Prevents further writes into the tablespace
READ WRITE	Allows writes into the tablespace after it's read-only
TEMPORARY	Converts a tablespace to one that holds only temporary segments
PERMANENT	Converts a temporary tablespace to a permanent one
DEFAULT	Changes the default extent characteristics assigned to any new STORAGE segments built in the tablespace
ADD DATAFILE	Creates one or more additional data files for the tablespace

Removing Access to a Tablespace

You may need to prevent access to a tablespace for a number of reasons. For example, you may want to back it up without users being able to change its contents, or you may need to perform maintenance or recovery on one of its data files. You can take a tablespace offline to prevent further read and write access.

Bringing a tablespace back online

The **ALTER TABLESPACE ONLINE** command will bring an offline tablespace back online, provided that it was successfully checkpointed when it went offline and that all its files are currently online. If one or more of these conditions isn't true, the data file(s) will need recovery before the tablespace can be brought back online. Tablespace and data file recovery are discussed in Chapter 14, "Performing Database Recovery."

The ALTER TABLESPACE OFFLINE command that you use to accomplish this has three options: NORMAL, TEMPORARY, and IMMEDIATE. When you take a tablespace offline with the NORMAL option, Oracle immediately prevents further retrieval from that tablespace. However, it will complete a *checkpoint* on its data files before shutting it down completely; any changed blocks belonging to the tablespace still in the database buffer cache will be copied back to disk. This results in an internally consistent tablespace, so it can be brought back online at any time without any further processing.

The TEMPORARY and IMMEDIATE options of the OFFLINE command don't necessarily complete checkpoints. This can result in a tablespace inconsistent with the rest of the database that therefore may need media recovery when it's brought back online. To guarantee that the redo information required for this recovery is available when needed, the database must be running in ARCHIVELOG mode. The difference between TEMPORARY and IMMEDIATE is that the former will attempt to complete checkpoints on all the files, ignoring any not available for writes, whereas IMMEDIATE won't even attempt to process any checkpoints.

Hot Backups of a Tablespace

A hot tablespace backup is one made while access to the tablespace's data files continues. Even though making a copy of all data files associated with a tablespace may take a number of minutes, Oracle will allow users to read blocks from those files and modify those blocks, as well as allow DBWR to write the changes back to disk. This can result in apparent anomalies in the backup set. A table with blocks in two different data files could have some blocks in each file modified by a single transaction. The backup copy of one file could contain blocks as they were before the change, whereas the backup of the second file could contain changed images of other blocks.

Oracle can resolve such anomalies by applying redo records to the backup files if they're used to replace damaged online files. To do this, the file needs to record the earliest time at which a block may have been changed but not copied into the backup file. This information is automatically available in a file header block, but normally this information will change over time. To prevent such a change from occurring, so as to lock in the time at which the physical backup begins, Oracle needs to freeze the header block for the duration of the backup.

As the DBA, you need to issue ALTER TABLESPACE...BEGIN BACKUP before starting the physical backup of files in the tablespace. This will accomplish the freeze of the header blocks in the data files belonging to the tablespace as discussed earlier. You need to unfreeze these blocks when the backup is completed. You can achieve this with the ALTER TABLESPACE...END BACKUP command. Although you can place a number of tablespaces in backup mode simultaneously, you should understand one other characteristic of a tablespace's backup mode. While in backup mode, Oracle has to create additional redo information to guarantee data consistency within blocks.

The redo logs needed to bring the data back to a consistent state must be available in order for the backed-up files to be useful in a recovery effort. To ensure this, you have to be running your database in ARCHIVELOG mode, which guarantees that all redos written to the online redo logs are copied elsewhere before the entries are overwritten by later transactions. You'll receive an error message if you try to place a tablespace into backup mode and you aren't archiving your redo.

Controlling Logging Behavior

A number of SQL commands can execute in Oracle without generating redo logs. These commands work with an existing set of data and therefore can be re-executed if they fail against the same data source. For this reason, you wouldn't have to rely on the existence of redo entries if there were an instance failure part of the way through the execution of the command. In addition, the SQL*Loader utility can run without logging because—again—the data source will still be available if the instance should fail before the load completes. These commands can be executed without the need for redo log generation:

- INSERT, where data is being selected from another source
- CREATE TABLE...AS SELECT

Block consistency during hot backups

During a hot backup of a data file, it's possible for the operating system to copy different parts of an Oracle block to the backup medium in two separate read/write operations. If **DBWR** happened to write a new image of a block to the data file between the two operations, the backup would contain a fuzzy block image—part of the block would represent integral data at one point in time, while the remainder of the block would contain data from a different time. To ensure that a complete valid block image can be restored when recovering from this backup, Oracle places a complete block image into the redo log before any changes can be made to a block from a tablespace in backup mode. When recovering from the log, this valid block image is first copied over the possibly inconsistent block from the backed-up data file, and then the changes recorded in the redo are applied as usual.

- CREATE INDEX

- ALTER INDEX...REBUILD

- ALTER INDEX...REBUILD PARTITION

- ALTER INDEX...SPLIT PARTITION

- ALTER TABLE...SPLIT PARTITION

- ALTER TABLE...MOVE PARTITION

You can set the whole tablespace to a non-logging mode if your tablespace is going to contain many segments that you'll typically want to manipulate with these commands (and not generate redo entries). You must do this before you build the segments, however, because a segment will acquire only the tablespace's logging mode at the time it's created.

You set the default logging mode for the tablespace with the ALTER TABLESPACE command, using the LOGGING or NOLOGGING option. When set, each new segment you create can accept this default behavior, or you can override it with the appropriate logging clause in the CREATE command.

Moving Data Files

There are generally two reasons to move a data file:

- You're restoring a backed-up copy of the file following a disk failure and need to place the file on a different device or in a different directory structure than the original.

- You've determined from monitoring database read/write performance that you have contention on certain disks. To solve this, you may need to move one or more data files to different disks.

After you move a data file, you need to let the database know that the file has moved. You do this with a RENAME option of either the ALTER DATABASE or the ALTER TABLESPACE command. Generally, you use the former when the database is in a NOMOUNT mode, and you are in the process of recovering from media failure; you use the latter when you've completed a planned file move. In the latter case, you need to take the tablespace offline before physically moving the file and issuing the ALTER TABLESPACE...RENAME 'new_filename' TO 'old_filename' command.

You can rename more than one data file in a single statement as long as they all belong to the same tablespace. Use a comma-separated list of filenames on each side of the TO keyword, ensuring that there's a one-to-one match between the names. For example, the following command will move three files from the /d1 device to three different devices:

```
ALTER TABLESPACE prod_tables
    RENAME '/d1/prod02.dbf',
           '/d1/prod03.dbf',
           '/d1/prod04.dbf'
    TO     '/d2/prod02.dbf',
           '/d3/prod03.dbf',
           '/d4/prod04.dbf'
```

Oracle won't perform operating system file commands

It's important to remember that renaming a file is a two-step process. Oracle doesn't physically move or rename the file at the operating system level; you are responsible for making this change yourself before issuing the ALTER TABLESPACE ...RENAME command.

Coalescing Free Space Manually

When there are multiple adjacent extents of free space in a tablespace, it can take longer for a new extent that spans these free extents to be created. If you monitor DBA_FREE_SPACE and notice that such free extents exist, you can manually coalesce them into one large free extent. You can issue the ALTER TABLESPACE...COALESCE command to combine the contiguous free extents in the tablespace on demand.

Automatic free-space coalescing

If you don't coalesce contiguous free space extents yourself, it will automatically be done for you by the background process SMON. The ALTER TABLESPACE... COALESCE option is provided because SMON may not work soon enough to be useful.

Avoiding Free Space Fragmentation

One way to avoid having free space extents of various sizes is to prevent anyone from creating segments in the tablespace without your supervision. You can then ensure that they use extents of the same size for every segment. If this isn't an option, you can help minimize the problem by setting a "model" size for extents in the tablespace. This model size represents the smallest extent allowed and also controls the size of larger extents by ensuring that they are all integer multiples of the model size. If you decide to set such a model value for your tablespace, use the ALTER TABLESPACE...MINIMUM EXTENT command, providing an integer for the size, in bytes, of the smallest allowable extent.

When MINIMUM EXTENT is set, every new extent added to the tablespace will be exactly the requested size, rounded up to the next Oracle block, or an integer multiple of that number of blocks. This sizing will override the tablespace's default storage clause, if necessary, as well as the storage options of the segment itself. Even manual extent allocations using such commands as ALTER TABLE...ALLOCATE EXTENT (SIZE...) will be controlled by the value MINIMUM EXTENT.

Managing Query-Only Tables

To avoid having to make backups of data files that contain non-changing data, you can define a tablespace and, consequently, its data files as read-only. Similar to putting a tablespace into back-up mode, this freezes the related data files' header blocks. However, because there can be no changes to them, Oracle knows that these data files are current copies, no matter how long ago they were modified as read-only. Consequently, you can take a backup of such files and restore them, following media failure, at any time in the future without them needing any recovery information from the redo log files.

If you later need to make changes to one or more tables in a read-only tablespace, you have to make the tablespace accessible for writes again. You use the commands ALTER TABLESPACE...READ ONLY and ALTER TABLESPACE...READ WRITE to make these changes.

Storage for Temporary Segments

Temporary segments—used to complete sorts too large for the memory allocated to them—are ephemeral objects. They're created when needed and dropped when their work is done. In some databases—particularly query-intensive ones—the over-head of creating and dropping temporary segments can cause a significant performance problem. You can alter this default behavior by defining the tablespace where the temporary seg-ments are stored to contain only this type of segment. Now, rather than drop a temporary segment when its work is finished, Oracle will preserve it for use by another sort in the future.

If you didn't create the tablespace with this characteristic, you can issue the ALTER TABLESPACE...TEMPORARY to convert it to con-tain non-disappearing temporary segments. If the tablespace should happen to contain another type of segment, such as a table or index, you can't make this change. You can convert the

---

Backup guidelines for read-only tablespaces

You should back up the files in the tablespace as soon as possible every time you make a tablespace read-only; an earlier backup will still need to have redo applied to ensure that all changes before the change in status have been applied. Following a change to read/write again, you can still restore from the backup taken while it was read-only, provided that you have the redo generated following its change back to a read/write status.

tablespace if you need to add non-temporary segments or change the storage characteristics of the temporary segments in TEMPORARY tablespace. In this case you use the keyword PERMANENT in the ALTER TABLESPACE command. Any existing temporary segments will be dropped as they are when following their default behavior, and you'll be able to add any other type of required segment to the tablespace. You'll have to drop any of these segments ahead of time to reconvert the tablespace to TEMPORARY.

Modifying Default Storage Values

The command ALTER TABLESPACE DEFAULT STORAGE allows you to change the default values assigned to the storage characteristics of segments created in the tablespace without their own, overriding, STORAGE clauses. You need to take care when issuing this command for a couple of reasons:

- This command affects only segments created after this change is made; it doesn't affect any existing segments. Specifically, if you have a table created with a default MAXEXTENTS value of 20, that table can contain only 20 extents—even if you change the tablespace default MAXEXTENTS to 40, 50, or even UNLIMITED. To change the storage characteristics of any existing segments, you have to alter each one individually; whenever a segment is created, the storage parameters for that object are stored in the data dictionary as part of that object's definition. Changing a tablespace's DEFAULT STORAGE changes only the tablespace definition, not the definitions of the objects within it.

- If you've defined your tablespaces to contain extents of the same size, changing any of the INITIAL, NEXT, or PCTINCREASE default values causes any new object to build extents of sizes different from those of any existing segments. Therefore, unless you're prepared to deal with the possible fragmentation caused by different-sized extents, you shouldn't modify these particular values in anything other than an empty tablespace.

Closing your database releases all temporary segments

Temporary segment space isn't held over database shutdowns and restarts. Even the temporary segments stored in TEMPORARY-type tablespaces will have disappeared when you reopen a closed database.

Adding and Resizing Data Files

You'll occasionally have to add space to an existing tablespace. This may be a planned or an unplanned occurrence:

- Planned expansion is usually the result of an anticipated database growth over time in a system where the full complement of disk drives to support the growth wasn't available at database-creation time. It can also be the result of adding to an application more functionality that requires more rows or columns to be added to a table.

- Unplanned expansion occurs when a segment, such as a table or an index, grows much larger than was anticipated in the database-design phase. This may be due to poor analysis or to a sudden change in the environment, such as an unanticipated doubling of orders for a specific product.

For planned expansion, particularly those involving the addition of new disks, adding more data files is the best method for adding space to a tablespace. This allows you to add exactly the amount of space you need and to place it onto different disks from the existing files, thus avoiding possible disk contention. File-system files and raw partitions can be added by using the `ALTER TABLESPACE...ADD DATAFILE` command. As with the `CREATE TABLESPACE` command, you can add one or many files with the same statement. The file name(s) and size(s) specifications are just the same as in the `CREATE TABLESPACE` command discussed earlier in this chapter.

You can also use additional data files, as just discussed, for an unplanned expansion. In such cases, you may not be able to place the files on new, unused disk drives; you may have to find whatever space is available in the disk farm for the time being. Also, if you need to use raw partitions, you'll have to be able to create them yourself or have the system administrator build them for you—unless you already have spares available.

An alternative for an unplanned expansion is to let the data files grow themselves. This has to be done when you first add them to the tablespace, using the `AUTOEXTEND` clause with the `CREATE` or `ALTER TABLESPACE` commands' file specification. If you didn't set this option when you added the files to the tablespace, you can still increase the file's size by extending it manually. This command is ALTER DATABASE DATAFILE...RESIZE. (Notice that this is ALTER DATABASE, not ALTER TABLESPACE.) The RESIZE clause takes a single argument, indicating the number of bytes that you want the file to contain following successful execution of the command. This can either be a simple integer or an integer followed by K or M for kilobytes or megabytes, respectively.

The ALTER DATABASE DATAFILE...RESIZE command will manipulate only the space requested. It won't cause the file to expand, or shrink, automatically in the future.

Dropping Tablespaces

Although not a common requirement, you may need to drop a tablespace. There are a few reasons you might need to do this:

- You no longer need the segments it contains for any further processing.

- There's enough corruption or damage to the contents of the tablespace that you want to rebuild it from scratch.

- You've moved its contents to another tablespace.

In order to drop a tablespace, it must not contain any rollback segments being used by an active transaction. If it contains any segments at all, you must use the INCLUDING CONTENTS option to force Oracle to drop these segments along with the tablespace.

This is the DROP TABLESPACE command's full syntax:

```
DROP TABLESPACE tablespace_name
     [INCLUDING CONTENTS]
     [CASCADE CONTRAINTS]
```

You'll need the CASCADE CONSTRAINTS option if the tablespace contains tables being dropped with the INCLUDING CONTENTS option and these tables are the parents, via referential integrity constraints, of tables in another tablespace.

Shrinking oversized data files

You can use ALTER DATABASE DATAFILE ...RESIZE to shrink, as well as to increase, the size of a data file. You can't reduce a file, however, unless there's empty space at the end of the file sufficient to remove the number of bytes needed to reach your desired size. The RESIZE option can't remove empty space from the middle of a file, and it won't remove blocks now assigned to a database object.

Dropping online tablespaces isn't recommended

Although you can drop a tablespace while it's still online, I advise you to take it offline first. This will avoid interference with ongoing transactions that are using the contents of the tablespace and save you from dropping a segment that's really still being used.

SEE ALSO

➤ *For a complete discussion of database* ARCHIVELOG *modes, see page* ***334***

➤ *To learn more about temporary segments, see page* ***192***

➤ *To learn about referential integrity constraints and the concepts of parent/child tables, see page* ***494***

Extent Allocation

After you build your tablespaces, you or your users will use them to store various types of segments. Some of these will almost certainly be added by you and some will be automatically created by the Oracle kernel. The others may be created by you or by the users, but their maintenance and space management may still be under your control in either case.

Part of the work involved in managing segment space allocation should be completed during the physical design of your database because it's related to the number and arrangement of your tablespaces. This topic is discussed earlier, in the section "Space Management Fundamentals"; the discussion that follows here assumes that you've already decided what type of segment is being placed where and concentrates on how new extents are added to these segments after they're created, or how unneeded space can be retrieved from segments to which it has already been allocated.

Comparing Dynamic and Manual Extent Allocation

Every type of Oracle segment (except the bootstrap segment, which is fixed in size at database-creation time) can grow automatically by default. The following sections examine how each segment type can have its growth controlled and how best to manage any required growth.

Temporary Segments

We begin this discussion with temporary segments because in many ways these are the easiest to manage—you have so little control over them. Temporary segments are created as needed by Oracle while it's processing SQL statements on behalf of a user's process. Temporary space is generally required by a process if performing a sort operation, although some types of joins and related activities also use temporary segments. This temporary disk space is used only when the SQL statement has insufficient memory in which to complete its processing.

All extent allocation to temporary segments is dynamic. In other words, it occurs automatically, without any specific commands from users. This is true whether a new temporary segment is being created or new extents are being added because the original size was insufficient to complete the task. Due to this completely automatic behavior, users in no way can give explicit instructions about the sizing or the number of extents in a temporary segment. Oracle always uses the storage information defined in the DEFAULT STORAGE clause of the tablespace for its temporary segments. In Chapter 6, "Managing Redo Logs, Rollback Segments, and Temporary Segments," you can find guidelines on how to determine good storage values for temporary segments.

By default, as soon as the operation that required the disk space is finished, the temporary segment is dropped and the blocks used by its extents are returned to tablespaces as free blocks. It's this behavior that gave temporary segments their name; they only acquire space for a short time and then return it.

Another option you should consider for your temporary tablespaces is creating or converting them to the TEMPORARY type. This will prevent Oracle from dropping temporary segments in the tablespace following the completion of the related SQL statements. Instead, the extents used in the segment are tracked in the data dictionary and made available to any server process that needs temporary space. New extents are added to the segments only if all the current extents are now in use by one or more users.

By not forcing users to create and recreate temporary segments each time they're needed, their work can be completed much faster. In fact, you can save your users a lot of time when you first create a TEMPORARY-type tablespace by prebuilding all the extents the tablespace can hold. You can do this by performing a massive sort (if you have a table or set of tables large enough to join), or by running large sorts in a number of concurrent sessions. Make sure that the userid you use for these sorts is allotted to the temporary tablespace you're planning to populate.

Closing your database releases all temporary segments

Temporary segment space isn't held over database shutdowns and restarts. Even the temporary segments stored in TEMPORARY-type tablespaces will have disappeared when you reopen a closed database.

Another benefit to using TEMPORARY-type tablespaces for your temporary segments is that Oracle enforces the use of same-size extents. All extents in such tablespaces are built based on the value of the NEXT parameter in the DEFAULT STORAGE clause.

Rollback Segments

As the DBA, you should create and manage rollback segments. You initially create a rollback segment with two or more extents and with extent sizes taken from the tablespace default values or from CREATE TABLESPACE's STORAGE clause. The behavior of the extents allocated to rollback segments is of interest here.

SEE ALSO

➤ *You can find detailed information about creating rollback segments on page 183*

Rollback segments store information that would be needed if a transaction were to roll back. Every part of a single transaction must be stored in the same rollback segment, and many transactions can share the same segment. In most cases, transactions generate the same amount of rollback information, so when a rollback segment reaches a certain size, its space is sufficient to support all the needed concurrent transactions. As these transactions complete, the space they were using is recycled and made available to new transactions. However, if the database gets very busy or suddenly needs to support one or more very long-running transactions, a rollback segment may need to grow by adding one or more extents. As with temporary segments, this allocation is dynamic; users have no control over it.

OPTIMAL is a special parameter

Whereas all the other storage parameters for a rollback segment can be inherited from the tablespace definition, **OPTIMAL** must be set with the **STORAGE** clause of the **CREATE ROLLBACK SEGMENT** or the **ALTER ROLLBACK SEGMENT** command.

Rollback segments have one unique characteristic of space management not possessed by any other type of segment: They can shrink in size by dropping unnecessary extents. Suppose a rollback segment grew by adding extents in response to an unusual combination of concurrent long-running transactions. If before this it could handle its work load without additional space, it should be able to do so again without the need for additional space. If it's sharing a tablespace with other rollback segments, this space might be better used by one of the others, maybe also for a sudden increase in work. You can cause a rollback segment to return to this preferred size whenever it exceeds it by setting an OPTIMAL parameter value.

Data and Index Segments

Segments designated to store table or index data can be created by you or by userids responsible for the applications that will use them. These segments can inherit all their tablespace's storage characteristics, just some of them, or none of them. When created, their storage characteristics can be changed for the most part; only the INITIAL and MINEXTENTS values are fixed for the life of the segment.

If a data or index segment runs out of space in its current extents, one of two things can occur: A new extent will be added by Oracle dynamically, or the SQL statement that required the extra space will fail. There are a number of reasons dynamic allocation could fail:

- There may be insufficient space in the tablespace, and none of the data files can autoextend.

- There may be space in the tablespace, but there isn't a sufficiently large extent of free space to hold the required extent.

- The segment may already contain the MAXEXTENTS number of extents.

Adding space to allow a new extent to be created automatically when the failed SQL statement is re-executed was discussed earlier in "Adding and Resizing Data Files." This would address the two first causes of dynamic space allocation failure. Another option for handling the second problem is to change the value of the segment's NEXT storage option, causing it to create an extent that fits into a remaining free extent. A third option would be to allocate the extent manually. You use the ALTER TABLE ALLOCATE EXTENT clause to do this. The complete syntax is as follows:

```
ALTER TABLE table_name
     ALLOCATE EXTENT (
          [SIZE integer [K¦M]]
          [DATAFILE 'filename']
          [INSTANCE integer] )
```

① Sets extent size, regardless of table's storage values

② Identifies into which data file extent will be placed

③ Identifies which freelist group will manage blocks in extent (used for databases that use Oracle Parallel Server option)

This command has one additional benefit over changing the NEXT value. If you want, you can execute it a number of times, each time choosing a different size for the extent and a different data

A final note on manual extent allocation

If you don't provide a size when manually allocating an extent, the extent will be sized as though it were created dynamically. If you use the SIZE clause, however, it won't override the dynamic sizing that would have occurred. If a table were going to build its next dynamic extent with 1,000 blocks and you manually add an extent of just 50 blocks, the next dynamically allocated extent would still acquire 1,000 blocks.

file into which it goes. This will allow you to prebuild extents that precisely fit the available free space until you have sufficient space allocated; this allows work on the segment to continue while a more permanent solution, such as additional disk space, is found.

You can take advantage of manual extent allocation with the ALLOCATE EXTENT option for reasons other than overcoming space limitations. For example, you may want to build a segment in a tablespace with many data files so that you guarantee that blocks from each data file will be used by the segment. To do this, you can create the table or index with a single extent and then use the DBA_EXTENTS data dictionary view to find out which data file contains this extent. Then, by successive use of the ALTER TABLE...ALLOCATE EXTENT command, you can place an additional extent into each data file belonging to the tablespace.

Releasing Unused Space

Occasionally you'll build a segment far larger than you need it to be—perhaps because the initial estimates made during the analysis and design phase were wrong, or because the nature of the application changed. If you need to regain the unused space, you have a variety of options.

First, when dealing with the case of rollback segments, you can use the ALTER ROLLBACK SEGMENT command to change the value of OPTIMAL. As long as you don't try to shrink it to a size less than its original size (that is, size of extent 1 + size of extent 2 + ... + size of extent MINEXTENTS), the rollback segment will, as it's used in future transactions, return to this size. As long as it doesn't consistently run out of space, it will attempt to maintain this size even if it temporarily grows beyond it. For a one-time fix, you do have the option of issuing the following command:

```
ALTER ROLLBACK SEGMENT...SHRINK [TO integer [K¦M]]
```

SHRINK can cause free extents of unequal size

This command will remove partial extents. Therefore, even if you've carefully built your tablespaces and segments to have equal-sized extents, the end result of this command can be an extent of a size smaller than planned and a piece of free space larger than the expected extent size.

For table, cluster, and index segments, you can remove unused space with the ALTER command's DEALLOCATE UNUSED clause. This command removes any unused extents and blocks as long as the original extents, set with the MINEXTENTS value in the CREATE command, aren't involved. You can even remove some empty space with the optional KEEP clause. This will save some allocated space to allow for some future growth without further extent allocation.

A second option to remove excessive space from a table—one that will preserve extent sizes—is to move the data into a temporary table, drop all the extents (other than the original ones) from the table, and then move the rows back into it. The following code shows a session that performs exactly these actions on the UNFILLED_ORDERS table. The key commands are the CREATE TABLE...AS SELECT and TRUNCATE commands.

```
CREATE TABLE temp AS SELECT * FROM unfilled_orders
/
TRUNCATE TABLE unfilled_orders
/
INSERT INTO unfilled_orders SELECT * FROM temp
/
DROP TABLE temp
/
```

To drop unused space from an index, you can simply use the ALTER INDEX command's REBUILD option. The only restriction you need to be concerned with when using this command is that the original and the replacement index copies will temporarily have to exist at the same time. This means that you'll need space for the new version of the index to be built in the target tablespace, which may not be the same as the current one.

Defragmenting Free Space

If you have a database that for whatever reason doesn't follow the guidelines discussed in this chapter about maintaining equal-sized extents in a tablespace, you may find yourself with a badly fragmented tablespace. This tablespace contains a lot of free space, but each piece, or extent, of free space is only a few blocks big, too small to be usefully added to any of the segments in the tablespace.

For tablespaces of type TEMPORARY, this will only occur should the default storage settings have been changed before the tablespace is completely filled. To fix it, you can alter the tablespace to be a

PERMANENT tablespace again. This will cause all the temporary segments to be freed over time and new ones built in their place. When all the odd-sized extents have been removed, you can convert the tablespace back to type TEMPORARY and allow the new segments to grow back to the necessary sizes by using fixed-sized extents.

For rollback segment tablespaces, your best option is to temporarily provide additional rollback segments to give you a chance to drop and recreate the current rollback segments, choosing appropriate storage values in your CREATE command. If you already have rollback segments available in another tablespace, you may be able to make the changes without adding temporary ones. If you plan to do this, try to drop and recreate the problem rollback segments during a period of low use. That way users aren't held up because an insufficient number of rollback segments are available to support them.

The most difficult fragmentation problems to fix are those associated with tables and indexes. If you can afford to drop all the indexes in the tablespace temporarily and then rebuild them, this is the easiest way to solve the problem. However, if the tablespace contains tables or other types of segments besides the indexes, you need to deal with the larger problem. Similarly, if the indexes can't all be dropped, you don't have a simple method to solve the issue.

Fragmented tablespaces containing tables, or tables and other types of objects, are very difficult to handle. Some third-party tools are available. Without them, you're going to use a tool to store the contents of the tablespace in some type of temporary storage, drop the tablespace contents, and then restore the original contents by using new segments with appropriate sizes. Oracle offers the Export and Import utilities to help you do this. You can also build your own tools to unload data, table definitions, and the like, and then use a combination of SQL, SQL script files, and SQL*Loader to reload the tablespace.

Need to defragment a tablespace?

If you have to defragment a tablespace, I strongly recommend that you reconsider your tablespace usage before reloading anything. You may want to change all the segment storage clauses so that they all have equal-sized extents, or you may want to add more tablespaces to meet the design suggestions offered earlier in this chapter. As your database grows in size, the inconvenience to you and to your users will increase should you need to perform future defragmentation processing.

Managing Redo Logs, Rollback Segments, and Temporary Segments

Create redo logs for efficient recovery

Manage redo logs for changing needs

Prepare rollback segments for transaction processing

Size rollback segments for transactions and for queries

Control overflow sort space with temporary segments

Database Management Structures

Oracle8 can be forgiving, but don't count on it

Although you can run your database without paying attention to your redo logs and temporary segments, you'll almost certainly pay a performance penalty by ignoring them. In most cases, these penalties will be severe and may cause your database to fail to meet your users' requirements. Rollback segments are a little more intrusive, at least if you pay any attention to Chapter 5's recommendations to use multiple *tablespaces* in your database, because you'll find that the default database structures won't support DBA or user-created segments in new tablespaces.

To most database users, tables are the important elements, with indexes being a second component they might consider as useful. In an Oracle environment, however, some structures are essential to the efficiency and integrity of the database. You need to know how to build and manage these components for your database to run smoothly and to allow your users to be able to work with their tables in an orderly manner.

The three structures you look at in this chapter are *redo log files*, *rollback segments*, and *temporary segments*. If you've already read Chapter 5, "Managing Your Database Space," you'll already be aware of some characteristics of these last two. You have been exposed to the concept of redo log files if you've read Chapter 2, "Creating a Database." Although the purpose of these structures will be touched on in this chapter, the emphasis in the following sections is to help you design, build, and manage them to the benefit of your database.

Managing Redo Log Files

One of the slowest operations performed in a *relational database* is the process of transferring data between disk storage (where it's maintained for long-term safety) and memory (where it needs to reside to be accessed and modified by database users). Although providing you with a number of parameters to tune memory and help avoid unnecessary disk reads, Oracle has its own mechanism—known as *deferred writes*—to reduce the overhead of unnecessary disk writes. Basically, it means that Oracle blocks that have been modified by user processes while sitting in memory will be written back to disk when they can be written most efficiently. This approach takes into account how recently the last change was made, how many blocks can be written with a single write operation, and how much of the space occupied by these blocks is needed for further disk reads.

One key issue to understand about deferred writes is that blocks aren't moved back to disk just because the changes on them have been committed by a user, and that blocks containing uncommitted changes are just as likely to be written to disk as blocks with committed changes. In other words, the act of issuing a COMMIT doesn't override the deferred write considerations. This, in turn, leads to a situation where neither the contents of memory nor the contents of the data files represent a coherent picture of the database transactions. With such a design, it's essential that Oracle provide a mechanism to restore the database to a consistent state should the contents of memory be lost. Of course, disk loss also needs to be protected against, but you can use a number of techniques, discussed in the chapters in Part V, "Backing Up Your Oracle Database," to help ensure that such a loss can be recovered. There's no method to "back up" the contents of memory in case it should suffer a failure.

Understand that Oracle can lose its memory area for many reasons, not just the loss or corruption of memory due to a chip failure, but also due to an unexpected operating system failure, loss of a key Oracle process that prevents further processing (and, hence, further access to memory), or a sudden shutdown of the Oracle instance without normal shutdown activity (a SHUTDOWN ABORT). Anytime Oracle stops operating without being able to complete a requested shutdown command, it's said to have suffered "instance failure." In any such case, there's no opportunity to copy block images from memory down to disk nor to reload blocks that contain uncommitted changes. Instance failure will require that, when the instance is restarted, an *instance recovery* be performed to reapply all changes associated with committed transactions and to remove all uncommitted changes.

The redo log files contain the information needed to complete an instance recovery. They will allow the recovery operation to re-execute every command that produced part, or all, of a committed database change, whether the affected database blocks were copied back to disk before the memory failure or not. Similarly, they contain enough information to roll back any block changes that were written to disk but not committed before the memory loss.

Without delving into the details of what really goes into a redo log and how the recovery process works—information that's

---

The importance of a COMMIT

When users issue the **COMMIT** command and receive an acknowledgment that the command is processed, the changes to the transaction are considered "permanent." This doesn't mean that they can't be changed in the future, but that the assigned values should be available to all other users of the database until they're changed again. This requires that the DBMS guarantees that committed data won't be lost by any fault of the database itself (database vendors can't control the quality of the media on which their databases are stored). Oracle has to employ a method—redo logs—to ensure that the contents of unwritten blocks containing committed data can be restored should unexpected memory loss occur.

Implied SHUTDOWN ABORT

The server manager command **STARTUP FORCE** is used to cycle an instance—that is, it stops the current instance and starts a new one. However, it performs an implicit **SHUTDOWN ABORT** command to stop the running instance. Consequently, this command will cause an apparent instance failure, requiring an instance recovery as part of the requested startup process. You shouldn't use this command to restart an instance quickly, but only when you would normally need to use a **SHUTDOWN ABORT**.

explained fully in the *Oracle8 Server Administrator's Guide* and the *Oracle8 Server Concepts* manuals provided as part of the Oracle documentation—the following sections explain what you need to consider when building your database and preparing it for your users and applications.

Sizing Your Redo Logs

If you make a mistake in the arithmetic in your check register, you can go back to the last time you balanced your account with a bank statement and redo the steps to get a valid current balance. But if you don't know when you last had a valid balance, you can't. Similarly, for Oracle to apply redo information following an instance failure, it must be able to find a starting point at which the status of all data and transactions was known before the failure. This starting point is known as a *checkpoint*.

Very simply, whenever a checkpoint occurs, Oracle forces every changed block now in memory to be written to disk to ensure that the redo records associated with those changes are stored in the redo log. When these steps are complete, a special checkpoint marker record is placed into the redo log. If the instance fails before the next checkpoint completes, the recovery operation knows that the log file and the data files were synchronized at the previous checkpoint. Any changes made to a data block since that checkpoint was completed are recorded in the redo log entries written after its checkpoint marker. Therefore, recovery can begin at the most recent checkpoint marker record.

With this checkpoint mechanism in place, entries older than the most recent checkpoint aren't needed. To conserve disk space, Oracle will reuse the redo logs. When all the logs are filled up, the LGWR process simply starts to write over the first redo log file again. Figure 6.1 shows how this circular use of the redo logs occurs. For this to be successful, Oracle has to ensure that a checkpoint has been taken before reusing a redo, and this is achieved as part of the processing that occurs at a log switch. At this time, LGWR will automatically begin writing new redo information into the next available log file and will also initiate a checkpoint. Therefore, your redo log size has a direct bearing on the frequency of these default checkpoints.

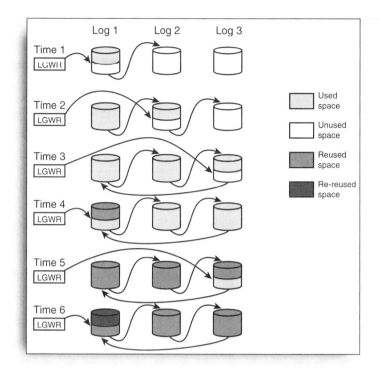

FIGURE 6.1

LGWR reuses the redo log files in a circular fashion, overwriting old records as it goes.

You need to concern yourself with this because the amount of data written to a log file between checkpoints affects the length of the instance recovery process (the act of reapplying changes following an instance failure). If a log file holds a day's worth of transactions, it could easily take a day to reapply them after an instance failure. Assuming that it may take a few minutes to a few hours to research and fix whatever problem caused the instance failure, the total recovery time in such a case could be more than a day. Most businesses can't afford to have a key database unavailable for that long, unless it's a planned period of downtime during which other plans have been made to carry on with essential processing. Instance failure is, by definition, an unplanned event.

Of course, if your database is being used primarily for queries (which, by their nature, don't change the contents of the blocks being read), your redo log could be quite small and still not fill up in a 24-hour period. Only when new data is added, or old

Time to apply redo during instance recovery

If you're running Oracle8 on a multi-CPU platform, it's likely that your users are creating transactions and the related redo log records in parallel. When your database needs instance recovery, only one process—the background process SMON—will be reading the redo logs and reapplying the changes made by your users. This serial processing can take substantially longer, in elapsed time, than the transactions took when being processed by multiple users concurrently.

data is changed or removed, will redo entries be written to the log, and this is very infrequent in read-intensive databases.

Another factor to consider is that you can set parameters to cause additional checkpoints to be performed automatically as a redo log fills up. The LOG_CHECKPOINT_INTERVAL parameter sets the number of blocks that will be written to a redo log file before a checkpoint is forced to occur, whether or not the file is full. If a redo log file is 1,000 blocks in size, setting LOG_CHECKPOINT_INTERVAL to 250 will cause a checkpoint when it's one-quarter, one-half, and three-quarters full. Although such a setting will reduce your instance recovery time for this redo log, it may be inappropriate should you decide to reduce your redo log size, for example, to expedite archiving (as discussed a little later in this section), and then forget to reset this parameter.

There are a number of considerations when setting checkpoint frequency, as the following two examples demonstrate:

- A customer proposed using an Oracle database to track the airborne spread of environmental pollutants during emergencies. During crises, it would be imperative to ensure that the most current information was readily available to emergency response teams. The information was to be loaded from a number of tracking stations in real-time. In case of an instance failure, the customer wanted to restore operations as quickly as possible to continue to collect the most current data and to make it available to users in the field. To minimize downtime during instance recovery, it was recommended that checkpoints be taken every few seconds. Although not necessary for most users, a number of customers that need up-to-the-second real-time data have also instituted checkpoints many times a minute.

- On the other extreme, some commercial customers who experience heavy volumes of transactions for a few hours a day, such as bank counter service operations, have elected to avoid checkpoints during these hours by building large redo logs that can handle a full day's business without switching—and hence without causing any checkpoints. They force a checkpoint every day immediately before the work period to ensure that they have a complete log file available for that day's load.

Ideally, you don't want checkpoints to occur more than once every 15 to 20 minutes, and much less frequently if the database is mainly processing queries. The problem with starting checkpoints too frequently is that a number of very active blocks will still be in use between checkpoints. However, they will have to be written out at each checkpoint. Redundant writes waste the disk I/O bandwidth. You may want to experiment with log file sizes after you finish reading about other considerations, such as archive logging (discussed in a little bit), to come close to the ideal size.

Before leaving checkpoints, you should be aware of one other factor: To perform instance recovery, a checkpoint marker must be available to indicate the start point. If you have two log files and, for whatever reason the checkpoint following a log switch doesn't complete until the second log fills up, the only checkpoint marker is in the first log file. If Oracle began to write redo records into this first log file again, there's no guarantee that this remaining checkpoint wouldn't be overwritten, leaving no starting point for an instance recovery.

Consequently, Oracle will stop writing further redo entries until the checkpoint process completes and the new marker record can be written. If no redo log entries can be written, Oracle can't preserve the integrity of database changes because block images in memory can't be guaranteed to be recoverable. So, rather than let unrecoverable changes occur, Oracle stops any further transaction processing. To the users, the database will appear completely frozen. Of course, after the checkpoint completes, work will continue as normal. You may have to size your redo logs large enough to avoid this problem because a database that freezes out user activity isn't going to meet performance standards.

A second mechanism that may affect your redo log file size decision is whether you're going to archive your log files. Although

Parallel server processes might speed up instance recovery

You can set the RECOVERY _PARALLELISM parameter in your initialization file to an integer value higher than 1 to allow SMON to enlist that number of parallel server processes for recovery. You must also start this number of processes by using the PARALLEL_MIN _SERVERS parameter. These processes will apply the redo in parallel during instance recovery. You may not see significant improvement in recovery time, however, because the parallel server processes must still apply the redo in sequential order, so they're likely to be contending for disk read access to the redo logs as well as contending for space in the database buffer cache.

this is another topic that belongs in the backup and recovery discussions in Chapter 12, "Understanding Oracle8 Backup Options," we'll take a quick look at it here.

Normally, when a redo log is filled and another one is being written to, the contents of the first log are of no use following the completion of the checkpoint started at the log switch. When the other log file fills up, Oracle can safely begin writing over the contents in the first one. Similarly, because a new checkpoint will be under way, the data in the second log file will soon become unnecessary for instance recovery, so Oracle can switch back to it when the current log fills.

Now consider data file backups. They can't be made continuously, so the restoration of a backed-up data file will almost certainly cause old block images to be placed back into the database. Transactions completed since the backup was made won't be represented. However, if you could keep every redo entry made since the data file backup was made, restoring the blocks in that data file would require nothing different than restoring them following an instance failure.

Users and log file switches when archiving

Be sure to understand the pros and cons of archiving before deciding whether to use it, and then be prepared to monitor your system for problems with postponed log switches until archived copies are made. Not only does processing for current users come to a halt during such times, but also new users attempting to connect to the database will be prevented from doing so. This can make the problem very visible to your user community. Even if your users don't let you know, the alter log for your database will show you when you have log-switching problems due to tardy archiving.

Oracle offers the capability to "archive" your online redo log files so that they can be preserved for this very purpose. As each redo log fills up, Oracle still switches to the next one and starts a checkpoint, but also marks the completed redo log file for archiving. Either you or a special background process, ARCH, will copy the redo log to a special location where it can be saved for as long as needed.

When you place your database into the mode that requires completed log files to be saved to an archive location, Oracle becomes very adamant that this work be performed. In fact, it won't let the redo activity switch back into a log file until that file has been safely archived. So, if your files are very big and take too long to archive (particularly if they're being copied to a slow disk drive) or so small that they fill up faster than they can be copied, you can run into problems. If the logs can't be switched because the archiving isn't done, no more log records can be written. Only when the archive is complete can work continue again.

During the time that Oracle is waiting for the archive to finish, your users are experiencing the same situation when checkpoint completion was delayed. To them, the database is stuck and they can't get any work done. You may therefore have to adjust your log file size to ensure that the archiving process will complete sooner than the next switch.

Determining the Number of Redo Log Groups

Besides changing the size of your redo log files to avoid problems with checkpoints and archives not completing in time, you can add the amount of redo that's written before a log file is needed again by adding more log files.

If it takes half an hour to fill each log file, and you have two such files, it will take an hour before you'll fill both logs and need to reuse the space in one of them (refer to Figure 6.1). If this isn't always enough time to complete your checkpoints and archives, you have a serious performance problem and should turn to Chapter 20 to find out about redo log tuning. However, until you can resolve the problem, you could increase the length of time before a log file is reused by adding one more file.

Generally, databases with smaller log files and high DML activity will tend to have peak periods during which their log files fill faster than checkpoints or archives complete. By adding more log files, you increase the time taken to fill up the entire set of logs. This allows time for the checkpoint and archive work to catch up from the overloads during the peak periods.

You need to find a good balance between the size of your log files, which affects default checkpoint intervals (and hence instance recovery times), and the number of your log files, which with the size determines how long each checkpoint and archive has to complete. In general, you're better off having too much online (as opposed to archived, or offline) redo log rather than too little. Too little will likely cause at least an occasional pause while a checkpoint or an archive completes; too much will simply waste disk space.

A suggested option for sizing online redo logs

One approach to redo I've seen work successfully is to keep as much online redo log as can be filled between database backups. This way, should you have to restore a data file from a backup, the redo needed to recover it up to the point of failure will be in the online redo log. The recovery operations can access the online redo logs more directly than they can archived logs, so the recovery time will be reduced.

Oracle requires you to have a minimum of two redo log files. You can have up to 255, unless your operating system sets a lower maximum number. When you create a database, you can reduce the maximum number of redo log files you will be allowed to create by setting the optional parameter value, MAXLOGFILES, of the CREATE DATABASE command. You can even set an initialization parameter, LOG_FILES, to limit the number of log files that an instance can access.

Determining the Number of Redo Log Members

Each log file is given a *log group* number, either by you as you add them or automatically by Oracle. We refer to log files with a group number because a group can contain more than one file. Each member of a group will be maintained by Oracle to ensure that it contains the same redo entries. This is done to avoid making a redo log a single point of failure.

When your log groups contain only one member, you risk having the database become unusable if you lose a redo file. Recall from the earlier section, "Sizing Your Redo Logs," that at least one checkpoint completion marker must be available somewhere in your redo logs. If only one such marker happened to be in a set of logs and the file containing the marker was on a disk that crashed, you would no longer have a way of performing instance recovery. This jeopardizes your database and so Oracle, on detecting a missing log file, will stop processing any more transactions and perform a shutdown.

If each log file is paired with a copy of itself and that copy is on a different disk, a single disk failure won't reduce the database to an unusable state. Even if the only checkpoint record was in the file on a crashed disk, its copy would still contain a valid version of it. Oracle will know to avoid the bad disk for future writes and for any further archiving activity. The term Oracle uses for copied sets of redo logs is *multiplexing*.

You're strongly encouraged, therefore, to multiplex every log group with at least two members. Depending on the criticality of your systems, you may want even more. Rarely do you need to go beyond three members per group; in fact, with more than

Oracle mirrors versus operating-system mirrors for redo logs

There has been much discussion within Oracle and with Oracle's business partners about the pros and cons of using Oracle's multiplexing versus using a mirrored disk controlled by the operating system. The biggest benefit to Oracle mirrors is that they work on any operating system and on any disks; the biggest disadvantage is that Oracle insists that each available copy is written to before it considers a flush of the redo buffer complete. This synchronous write process can be slower than operating-system mirrors. However, as disk subsystems become faster and add intelligent buffering capability, the latter difference becomes less of an issue. My best advice at this time is to use Oracle mirroring if you have no other option, and to experiment with Oracle and operating system-mirroring if you can.

that, you're likely to experience performance problems due to the time it takes to write out of the copies of each redo block. If you can mirror your log files at the operating-system level, you can also use mirroring to guard against a single disk loss. If you rely on operating-system mirroring alone, you still run the risk of having Oracle shut itself down if you lose a disk. System mirrors aren't visible to Oracle, so it may think it has lost its only copy of a log file if the primary disk crashes. System mirroring is a good way to create three- or four-way mirroring, however. Create each Oracle log group with two members, and then mirror either one or both members.

Adding Redo to Your Database

When you created your database, you created at least two redo log groups, the minimum number required to start an Oracle database. You may have created more than that, and you could have created each group with one or more members. This section looks at the commands used to add more log groups or more log members to an existing group. You'll see that the syntax is very similar to the log definition portion of the CREATE DATABASE command.

One option you can use when creating a redo log group allows you to identify a thread number. The thread number is useful only in a parallel server (multi-instance) database, so we won't examine its usage here. For further details on this option, see the *Oracle8 SQL Reference Manual* and the *Oracle8 Parallel Server Administration* manual.

The general syntax for creating a log group with a single member is as follows:

```
ALTER DATABASE [database_name]
    ADD LOGFILE [GROUP [group_number]]
    filename [SIZE size_integer [K¦M]] [REUSE]
```

This code is for a multimember group:

```
ALTER DATABASE [database_name]
    ADD LOGFILE [GROUP [group_number]]
    (filename, filename [,...])
    [SIZE size_integer [K¦M]] [REUSE]
```

Syntax conventions used in this book

Throughout this book, square brackets in command syntax indicate optional clauses and an ellipsis ([. . .]) indicates a clause that can repeat. Another convention used is the ¦ character, which indicates that you choose between one item or the other, not both (for example, choose either K or M). When you actually use commands, don't include the brackets, ellipses, or ¦ character.

The database name is optional if it's included in the parameter file (as the DB_NAME parameter) for the instance. Otherwise, you need to identify the name with which the database was created and which is stored in the control file. If you omit the group clause (the keyword GROUP and the group number), Oracle will assign the next available group number for you. Every group must have a unique number to identify it.

The filename can be a file system filename (which should be fully qualified with a path name), a raw partition name, or a link. In the multimember case, you should put the filenames inside a pair of parentheses and separate the names with commas.

You must include a SIZE or a REUSE clause. You can include both for file system files, as long as any existing file is the same size as the specification. For file system files, you must provide a size if the file doesn't already exist, and you must include the REUSE keyword if the file does exist; the command will fail if either condition is violated. For raw partitions, the REUSE keyword is meaningless because the new contents will always be written over the contents of the partition; therefore, it makes no difference whether you include it. You must include the file size, however, to avoid using the whole partition—two blocks of space must be reserved in each partition for operating-system information—or possibly writing beyond the partition boundaries. The K and M represent kilobytes and megabytes, respectively. Without either, the *size_integer* represents bytes.

Listing 6.1 shows a script file with three commands, each creating a new redo log group.

The SIZE and REUSE options in database redo log groups

If you're creating a log group with multiple members, include the SIZE or REUSE keyword only once for all members of the group. They must all be the same size because they'll all contain the same data. This means—unless you're using raw devices—that if one file exists, they must all exist so that the REUSE option is valid for each named file. If some exist and some don't, you'll have to create the group with only those that exist (or only those that don't) and add the others as additional members. I show you how to do this a little later. No matter how you create them, all the files in a redo log group will have to be same size.

Numbering of code lines

Line numberings were included in Listing 6.1 and other code listings to make discussion about this code easier to reference. The numbers should not be included with any command-line commands, as part of any Oracle scripts, or within SQL statements.

LISTING 6.1   **Create new redo log groups**

```
01: ALTER DATABASE ADD LOGFILE
02: D:\ORANT\DATABASE\log10.ora SIZE 100K
03: /
04: ALTER DATABASE ADD LOGFILE GROUP 6
05: (E:\DATABASE\log6a.ora, F:\DATABASE\log6b.ora) SIZE 10M
06: /
07: ALTER DATABASE ADD LOGFILE GROUP 5
08: (E:\DATABASE\log5a.log, F:\DATABASE\log5b.log) REUSE
09: /
```

On line 1 of Listing 6.1, the first redo log group will be created with a single member in the group, and the group's number will be assigned by Oracle. Group 6 will have two members, and the group is assigned its group number in the command on line 4. In these first two commands, Oracle will create all new files. Redo log group 5, as created by the command on line 7, will contain two members, both of which will replace existing files.

Adding one or more new members to an existing group can be done by identifying the group number (the simplest syntax) or by identifying the group with a list containing the full path names of all the current members. The syntax for the former when adding just one more member is

```
ALTER DATABASE database_name
    ADD LOGFILE MEMBER
    filename [REUSE]
    TO GROUP group_number
```

The database name is optional, as when adding a new group. The group number must refer to an existing group. The filename must be a fully qualified file system name, a raw partition, or a link. The REUSE keyword is needed only if you're using a file system file that already exists, in which case it must be the same size as other files in the group. A SIZE clause isn't needed because every member of the group must be the same size as the existing member(s).

The syntax for using the existing filename(s) to add a single member is as follows:

```
ALTER DATABASE database_name
    ADD LOGFILE MEMBER
    filename [REUSE]
    TO [filename] ¦ [(filename, filename, (,...)]
```

Everything is as described earlier except that for a group with a single member, the filename alone is used in place of the GROUP clause, whereas a comma-separated list of the existing member's filenames (enclosed in parentheses) is required if the group already has more than one member. In either case, the filenames must be fully specified.

Different numbers of members per log group

Oracle doesn't require that you use the same number of log file members in each group. In fact, because you can add a new member or members to only one group at a time with the **ALTER DATABASE** command, you couldn't start mirroring your log files by adding a new member to each group unless they could exist with different numbers of members, at least temporarily. However, even though you could run your database with two members in one redo log, three in another, just one in a third, and so on, I don't recommend this practice. After you decide how many mirrored copies make sense for your requirements, you should use that number in all groups. This way, you won't experience periods of different performance or have to worry, should you lose a disk drive, whether you've lost a single-copy redo log or just one of a mirrored set.

To add multiple members to a group within the same command, you simply change the filename clause to read as follows in either version of the statement:

```
(filename, filename, (,...)) [REUSE]
```

The use of REUSE is, as before, required if the files already exist.

Dropping Redo Logs and Handling Problem Logs

The most likely reason you would want to drop a redo log file is because you want to replace it with one of a different size. Once in a while you may drop a log file because you've determined you have more online redo than you need. This is rarely beneficial, however, unless it's the only log file on the disk, because you generally shouldn't share disks where you're writing online redo logs with other file types. You may also need to drop a redo log member when you're experiencing performance problems due to too many multiplexed copies, or because you want to replace one or more members with operating-system mirrored copies.

To drop an entire log group, the following must be true:

- At least two other log groups will be available after the group is dropped.
- The group isn't currently in need of archiving.
- The group isn't the current redo group (the one to which log entries are now being written).

If these conditions are met, you can drop the entire log group with an ALTER DATABASE command that identifies the group. As with the ADD LOGFILE MEMBER option of this command (discussed in the preceding section), you identify the group with its group number, its member's filename, or with a list of the filenames of its current members:

```
ALTER DATABASE database_name
    DROP LOGFILE
    GROUP group_number ¦ filename ¦
    (filename, filename (,...))
```

The database name is needed only if the parameter file used to start the instance doesn't include the DB_NAME parameter and the ellipsis ([...]) shows a repeatable field.

You can drop one or more members from an existing log group with the DROP LOGFILE MEMBER variant of this command. You can't drop all members with this command, however; you must use the preceding command to drop the group as a whole. The syntax for dropping a group member is

```
ALTER DATABASE database_name
     DROP LOGFILE MEMBER
     filename
```

where the database name has the same requirements as previously discussed, and the filename must be fully qualified, as with all files discussed in these sections.

Once in a while, a redo log group may become damaged to the point where the database can't continue to function and you need to replace the redo group with a clean file or set of members. If the damaged log group isn't yet archived or the log group is one of only two log groups in the database, however, you aren't allowed to drop it. Creating a third log might not help because Oracle will continue to attempt to use the damaged log before moving on to the new one. In such cases, you need to simulate dropping and recreating the log with the CLEAR LOGFILE option of the ALTER DATABASE command. After you do this, you may need to perform a brand new backup of your database because there may be a break in the continuity of your archived logs, and you may have removed the only checkpoint record in the online redo.

If you do have to perform an emergency replacement of an online redo log, use the following command:

```
ALTER DATABASE database_name
     CLEAR [UNARCHIVED] LOGFILE group_identifier
     [UNRECOVERABLE DATAFILE]
```

where database_name and group_identifier follow the same characteristics as described earlier for the DROP LOGFILE option. The UNARCHIVED clause is needed if the group was awaiting archiving before being cleared, and the UNRECOVERABLE DATAFILE option is required if the log would have been needed to recover an offline data file.

To find out about the current status of your redo logs, you can query various dynamic performance views. The V$LOGFILE view will show the names of the members of each redo log group and their status. In this view, NULL is a normal status, INVALID indicates that the file is unavailable, DELETED shows that the file has been dropped, and STALE is used when a file is a new member of a group or doesn't contain a complete set of records for some reason. The V$LOG and V$THREAD provide more detailed status information and include records of the archive and system change numbers related to the redo files. Also, the view V$LOG_HISTORY is used mainly by parallel server databases for recovery operations.

SEE ALSO

➤ *How to set up redo log archiving for your database, page **335***

➤ *Learn about tuning your redo logs for checkpoint and archive processing, page **560***

➤ *More about the alert log and the types of messages it can provide, such as log file switches delayed by checkpoints or archiving, page **617***

Managing Rollback Segments

Rollback segments perform two basic functions, both somewhat related:

- *Allowing changes to be rolled back* (as the name suggests). This activity restores block images to the state they were in before a change was made. The change could be a row INSERT, UPDATE, or DELETE, but could also be simply a change in the header portion of the block to reflect a change in the status of a transaction.

- *Providing read-consistent images of blocks.* These are copies of blocks restored to look just as they did when a query or series of queries began. Known as "undo blocks," they allow a query to read blocks being changed by other users, preventing it from seeing uncommitted changes (dirty reads) or changes that occur while the query is executing (inconsistent reads).

To perform its function, a rollback segment stores a before image of a column, row, or other block element before the change is applied to the block. By using the address of this changed data, also stored with the before image, a rollback or read-consistency operation can overlay the changed information with this record of what it looked like before the change.

During a rollback operation, the before image data is applied directly to the data block image where the transaction had made its changes. Rollbacks can occur for a number of reasons, including, but not limited to the following:

- The user or application issuing a ROLLBACK command

- A single statement failing after making some changes

- A transaction failing because the user is unexpectedly disconnected from the database

- An instance being recovered following an instance crash; the transactions incomplete at the time of the failure are rolled back as part of the instance recovery mechanism

In some cases, particularly the latter, the blocks that need rollback information applied may be stored only on disk rather than in memory.

When a read-consistent block image is needed, Oracle first copies the block into a different memory location inside the database buffer cache. The original block image can continue to be manipulated by any active transactions that need to modify it. Oracle then applies the rollback information to the copy of the block, called the "undo block." In some cases, a long-running query may encounter a block that has been changed by multiple transactions subsequent to the start of the query. In such a case, the undo block will be further modified by applying the before images from each transaction until the undo block resembles how the original block looked when the query began. The query will then read the undo block as opposed to the "real" block.

Rather than allowing rollback segments to grow indefinitely, Oracle reuses the blocks that contain before images of completed transactions. Over time, the entire rollback segment is recycled many, many times as new transactions find space for their

Dirty reads

A "dirty read" is a query that returns value from a row that's part of an as-yet uncommitted transaction. If the transaction is subsequently rolled back, the query has returned a value that's never really been stored in the database. An inconsistent read occurs when a query reads some blocks before a transaction changes them and other blocks after the same transaction changes those.

rollback entries. This reuse of space is controlled rather than haphazard, however. For the read-consistent feature to work, the before images needed by a query need to be available for the whole duration of the query. If a new transaction simply reused any available rollback block, it could be the one needed by an executing query. To help avoid this, the space is used in a circular fashion. The oldest before images are overwritten first. To simplify the code to support this activity, a couple of rules are applied to rollback segments:

- Only one extent is considered to be the active extent. When a new transaction needs to store a before image, it's assigned to a block within the active extent. As soon as the active extent fills up, the next extent is made the active extent. Transactions that run out of space in their assigned block will be given a second block in the active extent or, if none are available, will be assigned a block in the next extent, making it the active extent.

- When an extent fills up, if the next extent still contains at least one block with before images from a still-active transaction, that extent isn't used. Instead, Oracle builds a brand new extent and makes it the active extent. In this way, all the blocks in the extent with the active transaction are left available for queries that might need their contents to build undo blocks.

This behavior is shown in Figure 6.2.

By cycling through the extents or building new ones when necessary, a block in, say, extent 1 won't be overwritten until all the blocks in all the other extents have been reused. This allows before images to remain available for the longest time possible, given the current size of the rollback segment. Preserving the before images for queries is important because, if a query needs a before image that's not available, the query can't continue. Without the before image, the query can't reconstruct the block in question to look as it did at the query start time and it terminates with an error message: ORA-1555 - Snapshot too old.

The ORA-1555 error message

One cause of the **ORA-1555** problem needs to be solved by the application developer rather than by a change in the rollback segment sizing. The error occurs if a program is making changes to many rows in a table by using an explicit cursor data—either in PL/SQL or a 3GL language with Oracle precompiled code—to read through the data and additional cursors to make changes to the required rows. If these individual row changes are committed, the query cursor needs to build read-consistent images of the affected blocks. While this may not involve much rollback information itself, it does require the query to find the transaction entry information in the header blocks of the rollback segments involved. It's the sheer number of transactions, not their size, that causes **ORA-1555** errors in this type of program.

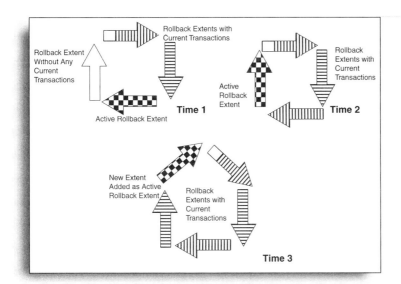

FIGURE 6.2

Oracle uses rollback segment extents in a circular fashion unless they're all busy, in which case it builds a new one.

The message `ORA-1555 - Snapshot too old` is usually a warning that at least one of your rollback segments is too small to hold enough records to provide read consistency. If it occurs very infrequently, however, it may simply indicate that a report, or other query-intensive program, ran into a busy period of transaction processing that it usually avoids. If rerunning the problem program succeeds, you may not need to change your rollback segment sizes for this infrequent occurrence.

The following sections discuss characteristics of transaction rollback and read consistency that you need to consider when determining the size and number of your database's rollback segments.

Determining the Number of Rollback Segments

A rollback segment uses the first block in its first extent to build a list of information about the transactions assigned to it. This list can contain only a fixed number of entries because the block size is itself fixed. Therefore, if your database needs to support lots of concurrent transactions, you should consider adding more rollback segments. Although Oracle will try to balance the workload between the rollback segments as new transactions begin, if every rollback segment is now supporting its maximum number

The SYSTEM rollback segment

When a database is created, the default rollback segment is created in the **SYSTEM** tablespace, and it takes the default storage parameters of the tablespace. You cannot drop this rollback segment. It is used by Oracle for *recursive SQL*.

of transactions, new transactions will be forced to wait until others complete.

For performance reasons, you really shouldn't allow each rollback segment to support its maximum number of transactions. If you do, you'll overwork the header blocks of the rollback segments. Not only do new transactions have to place their entries on these blocks, but the status of ongoing transactions has to be recorded, including information about the extents they're actively using. Finally, when a transaction completes, the status of the transaction—including a system change number for committed transactions—has to be recorded in the transaction's slot in the header block.

There's no absolute rule as to the average number of transactions you should strive for per rollback segment. In most cases, the best number is between 4 and 10. For longer-running transactions that consume more rollback space, you should use a lower number in this range. Similarly, for shorter transactions, a higher number is a better target.

You can get an idea about what your transaction mix looks like by examining the following dynamic performance tables. When you know the total number of concurrent transactions, divide this number by the appropriate value between 4 and 10, based on transaction size, to find a good number of rollback segments to try. You can always adjust this number later.

SEE ALSO

➤ *Determining if you have too many or too few rollback segments by examining contention statistics, page* **566**

➤ *Additional information on rollback segment performance, page* **590**

Sizing Your Rollback Segments

After you determine how many rollback segments you need, you need to figure out how large they should be. For most databases, there is a perfect rollback segment size for the normal workload. At this size, rollback segments will contain sufficient space to hold the rollback data needed for all the concurrently active transactions at any point in time. However, they achieve this without being oversized, which would waste space. Once in a while you may have a special job or program that needs an extra-large rollback segment. If so, you can build one such rollback segment and leave it available at all times, or else leave it offline until needed.

You generally don't have to worry about making your rollback segments too small because, like other segments, they can grow automatically as more space is needed. This growth does depend on whether the segment has reached the maximum number of extents you've defined for it and on the amount of room remaining in the tablespace where it's stored. See the following section, "Adding Rollback Segments," for details on how to set the extent maximums and tablespace allocation.

I don't recommend letting Oracle take care of rollback segment growth for you for a couple of reasons:

- Any such dynamic growth will slow down the process that incurs the overhead of finding the required free space and allocating it to the segment.

- Studies performed at Oracle have shown that rollback segments perform best when they have between 10 and 20 extents. If you rely on Oracle to add extents as needed, you may have segments well outside these ideal limits.

Another problem with automatic growth is that, once in a while, something will occur that will make it grow far larger than is typically necessary. One example I have encountered was a program that, following a minor change, got itself into a processing loop that caused it repeatedly to update the same few records without committing the changes. As a result, the rollback segment handling the transaction kept growing until its tablespace ran completely out of space. At that point, the transaction failed. When that happened, the space in the rollback segment taken up by the runaway transaction entries was freed up for use by subsequent transactions—but the rollback segment was now almost the size of the tablespace. When a different transaction, assigned to another rollback segment, needed more space for its entries, it failed because its rollback segment had insufficient room to grow.

Assigning transactions to specific rollback segments

To ensure that a transaction uses a specific rollback segment, you can take other rollback segments offline, or you can explicitly assign the rollback segment with a SET TRANSACTION USE ROLLBACK SEGMENT *rollback_segment_ name* command. If you have concurrent transactions or the segment is needed by an application that runs outside your control, explicit assignment is better. The SET TRANSACTION command must be executed before every transaction if the same rollback segment is needed for each one.

Rollback segment extents are dropped in a specific order

The extents are dropped in the same order that they would have been reused. This activity results in the oldest rollback entries being dropped, preserving the most recent ones for use by ongoing queries.

Problems to look for when decreasing rollback segment size

When reducing the size of a rollback segment, you need to monitor your users' queries to ensure that the number of Snapshot too old messages doesn't increase. Remember that queries may need rollback information long after a transaction is finished. You can't just size your rollback segments to make them as small as the transaction load requires if this will interfere with standard query processing. Even a report program that runs once a month may require you to maintain larger rollback segments than your records of rollback segment growth and shrinkage would indicate are needed. If the program fails only once or twice a year, the cost of rerunning it may not be as expensive as the cost of the extra disk space needed to support larger rollback segments. But if it fails almost every month, you may need to increase your rollback segment sizes.

By using the OPTIMAL entry in the STORAGE clause of the CREATE or ALTER ROLLBACK SEGMENT command, you can hone in on the best size for your rollback segments. The OPTIMAL value will cause the rollback to perform a special check when it fills up its current active extent. If the sum of the sizes of the current extents is greater than OPTIMAL, rather than just look to see if the next extent is available to be the active extent, the server checks on the one after that, too. If this one is also available, the server will drop the next extent rather than make it current. Now, if the total rollback segment is at its optimal size, the current extent becomes the one following the dropped extent. But if the total size is still greater than OPTIMAL, the extent following this one is checked for availability and the same process is repeated. Eventually, the rollback segment will be reduced to optimal size by the deletion of extents, and the next remaining extent will become the current extent.

You can query the dynamic performance table V$ROLLSTAT to determine how many times a rollback segment has grown through the addition of new extents (the EXTENDS column value), and how many times it has shrunk (the SHRINKS column value). If these numbers are low, or zero, the rollback segment is either sized correctly or it may still be larger than needed. You can adjust the value of OPTIMAL downward and check the statistics again later. If they're still low, or zero, your extent may still be oversized. However, if they have started increasing, it means the rollback segment needs to be larger. If the grow-and-shrink counts are high when you first look at the table, the rollback segment has always been too small.

Due to the automatic nature of the extent additions and deletions, you don't have to recreate a rollback segment that's the wrong size—you can control it with the OPTIMAL value once you find its stable size. As mentioned earlier, however, a rollback segment performs optimally when it has between 10 and 20 extents. This number provides the best balance between the need for transactions to find available space and the availability of required rollback entries for queries needing read-consistent data. Of course, based on the discussion of space management in Chapter 5, we're talking about rollback segments where all the extents are the same size. If your rollback segment's ideal size corresponds to this preferred number of extents, you can leave it as now defined. If the number of extents is below 10 or much above 20, however, you should consider dropping it and re-creating it with around 15 equal-sized extents, such that its total space remains the same.

Adding Rollback Segments

If you've just created a new database, there's only one rollback segment, SYSTEM, and it won't support transactions on segments outside the SYSTEM tablespace. From the discussions in Chapter 5, you should be building all your application tables and indexes in alternative tablespaces, and so you'll need additional rollback segments to support transactions against them.

If you have a running database, based on statistical results from your monitoring and tuning activity, you may determine that you need to add one more rollback segment to the existing set.

In either case, you follow exactly the same steps.

Add rollback segments

1. Create the rollback segment.

2. Bring the rollback segment online.

3. Alter the parameter file to bring it online automatically whenever the instance starts.

Creating a Rollback Segment

Listing 6.2 shows the syntax of the command to create a rollback segment.

LISTING 6.2   **Create a rollback segment**

```
01: CREATE [PUBLIC] ROLLBACK SEGMENT segment_name
02:      [TABLESPACE tablespace_name]
03:          [STORAGE (   [INITIAL integer [K¦M]]
04:              [NEXT integer [K¦M]]
05:              [MINEXTENTS integer]
06:              [MAXEXTENTS integer]
07:              [OPTIMAL  NULL¦integer[K¦M]] ) ]
```

On line 1, PUBLIC causes the rollback segment to be public rather than private. (This distinction is discussed in the next section, "PUBLIC versus PRIVATE Rollback Segments.") *segment_name* is a valid Oracle name.

On line 3, INITIAL is the size of the first extent, in bytes (default) or in K kilobytes or M megabytes.

NEXT on line 4 is the size of the second and subsequent extents, in bytes (default) or in K kilobytes or M megabytes.

Line 5 shows MINEXTENTS, which is the number of extents (minimum two) included in the rollback segment at creation time and the number of extents that must always belong to the segment.

MAXEXTENTS on line 6 is the largest number of extents the segment can acquire. Although MAXEXTENTS can be set to the value UNLIMITED, this isn't recommended for rollback segments. If you've sized your rollback segments correctly, they shouldn't need to grow much larger than this; unlimited growth would result from erroneous processing. Such processing could fill up the available space, restricting the growth of other rollback segments performing valid work, and would take as long to roll back, when it finally ran out of space, as it did to build all the rollback entries in the first place. Until the rollback of this transaction is completed—which could conceivably take many, many hours, if not days—the space consumed by the rollback entries can't be freed.

On line 7 is OPTIMAL, which determines how the rollback segment can shrink. A value of NULL prevents the rollback segment from shrinking automatically; a size (in bytes, kilobytes, or megabytes) causes the rollback segment to shrink automatically by dropping inactive segments.

OPTIMAL must be set to a value no smaller than the sum of bytes in the first MINEXTENTS. This can be computed from the formula

```
OPTIMAL >= INITIAL + (NEXT * (MINEXTENTS - 1))
```

PUBLIC Versus PRIVATE Rollback Segments

The main reason Oracle supports public rollback segments is to help DBAs who manage multiple Oracle instances running against a database with Oracle Parallel Server. The management of rollback segments on some hardware platforms running

No PCTINCREASE option for rollback segments

Every extent, other than the first, must be the same size. With a non-**NULL** value for **OPTIMAL**, any extent with no active transactions assigned to it can be dropped if, by so doing, the total segment size will still be greater than the **OPTIMAL** size. The initial extent is never dropped, however, because it maintains the transaction table in its header block. Also, only the extents that have been inactive the longest are dropped. If there are four inactive extents but an active one between the third and fourth of these, only the first three will be dropped. This is to avoid removing records that might be needed for read-consistent queries.

Parallel Server is almost impossible without them being public, mainly because you don't have to name the rollback segment in a parameter file to make it come online when an instance starts up. Instead, each instance takes one or more segments from the pool of public rollback segments as its own.

Although you can use public rollback segments in a non-parallel database, you're encouraged to use private rollback segments. By naming the rollback segments you want to make active in an instance in your parameter file, you have full control over which ones are active. While you can name public rollback segments in the parameter file, two other parameters—TRANSACTIONS and TRANSACTIONS_PER_ROLLBACK_SEGMENT—can also bring additional ones online, if available. By using private rollback segments, you're guaranteed that only those named in the parameter will be brought online automatically at instance startup.

You can take private and public rollback segments offline and return them to online status while the instance is running, as discussed in the following section.

Altering Rollback Segments

Before working with a rollback segment, you may need to determine its current status. This can be a little confusing due to the number of different data dictionary tables you might need to examine to get the full picture. Table 6.1 shows the various types of rollback segment status and characteristics, along with the data dictionary table and column that contain this information.

How Oracle activates public rollback segments for an instance

Oracle evaluates the quotient of TRANSACTIONS and TRANSACTIONS_PER_ROLLBACK_SEGMENT when it starts up. If these parameters were set to 210 and 25, respectively, the result of this calculation would be 8.4. Oracle rounds up this value to the next integer and attempts to acquire this many rollback segments for the instance. First, it counts the number assigned by the ROLLBACK_SEGMENTS parameter and then calculates how many more are needed. To continue the example, suppose that five rollback segments were named in ROLLBACK_SEGMENTS; 9 minus 5—or 4 more—would be needed. If at least four public rollback segments aren't yet assigned to an instance, the current instance will take four of these and bring them online for itself. If there are fewer than four, it will bring as many online as are available. If no public rollback segments are available, the instance will continue to run with just the five named in the parameter file.

TABLE 6.1 **Identifying the status of a rollback segment**

Status	Data Dictionary Table	Table Column
ONLINE	DBA_ROLLBACK_SEGS	STATUS
	V$ROLLSTAT	STATUS
OFFLINE	DBA_ROLLBACK_SEGS	STATUS
	V$ROLLSTAT	STATUS
PENDING OFFLINE	V$ROLLSTAT	STATUS
DEFERRED	DBA_SEGMENTS	SEGMENT_TYPE
PRIVATE	DBA_ROLLBACK_SEGS	OWNER (= SYS)
PUBLIC	DBA_ROLLBACK_SEGS	OWNER (= PUBLIC)

In an online state, the rollback segment is available for use and may have active transactions running against it. In an offline state, the rollback segment is idle and has no active transactions. A pending offline state is a transition state between being online and being offline. When you alter an online rollback segment to be offline, it won't accept any more transactions, but will continue to process any current transactions until they complete. Until these are all committed or rolled back, the rollback segment remains in the offline pending state.

A deferred rollback segment holds rollback information for transactions that can't complete because the tablespace to which they need to write has gone offline. These transactions will have failed due to the loss of the tablespace, but they can't be rolled back because the blocks in the offline tablespace can't be read or written. To be able to complete the necessary rollbacks when the tablespace comes back online, the associated rollback entries are stored in the SYSTEM tablespace in deferred rollback segments.

Although not truly a status, Table 6.1 also includes an entry for the PRIVATE and PUBLIC rollback segment descriptions so that you know how to identify which is which. As you can see, this is shown indirectly in the OWNER column of the DBA_ROLLBACK_SEGS table, where an entry of SYS indicates that it's a private rollback segment and an entry of PUBLIC shows it to be a public rollback segment.

The ALTER ROLLBACK SEGMENT command lets you change the status of a rollback segment manually. The full syntax for this command is

```
ALTER ROLLBACK SEGMENT segment_name
    [ONLINE¦OFFLINE]
    [SHRINK [TO integer [K¦M]]]
    [STORAGE (storage_clause)]
```

The keywords ONLINE and OFFLINE simply take the rollback segment between the basic states. As discussed earlier, a rollback segment may not go completely offline immediately; it may have to wait until pending transactions complete. If you're taking a rollback segment offline in preparation for dropping it, you may need to wait until it's completely offline, as shown in V$ROLLSTAT. You're not allowed to take the SYSTEM rollback segment offline for any reason.

The SHRINK keyword causes the rollback segment to shrink to its optimal size, or to the size provided when you execute the ALTER ROLLBACK SEGMENT command. As with automatic shrinkage, you can't reduce the size to less than the space taken by MINEXTENTS.

The storage clause of the ALTER ROLLBACK SEGMENT command is identical to its counterpart in the CREATE ROLLBACK SEGMENT statement, with the following provisos:

- You can't change the value of INITIAL or MINEXTENTS.
- You can't set MAXEXTENTS to a value lower than the current number of extents.
- You can't set MAXEXTENTS to UNLIMITED if any existing extent has fewer than four blocks (and you're advised not to use this value anyway, for the reasons discussed earlier).

Dropping and Shrinking Rollback Segments

At times, you may want to change the physical structure of a rollback segment, such as alter its basic extent size or move it to another tablespace. You may even want to remove a rollback segment because you no longer think you need it. If you have a rollback segment that has grown much larger than the optimal size and want it reduced to the optimal size as soon as possible, you can shrink it yourself.

To remove a rollback segment, you must first take it offline, as discussed in the previous section. Recall that even if the command to take it offline works, you may not be able to remove it. Until all the transactions now assigned to the segment complete, the status won't be permanently altered to offline, so you won't be able to drop it. Of course, after you change its status, no further transactions will be assigned to the rollback segment.

As soon as a rollback segment is completely offline—meaning that the status in DBA_ROLLBACK_SEGS and V$ROLLSTAT is OFFLINE—you can remove it. To do this, issue the command

```
DROP ROLLBACK SEGMENT segment_name
```

If you need to reduce a rollback segment to its optimal size, you can just wait until this occurs automatically. However, if the segment is taking up space that might be needed by other segments, you can manually cause the segment to shrink by executing the command

```
ALTER ROLLBACK SEGMENT segment_name SHRINK [TO integer[K¦M]]
```

As soon as you do this, the rollback segment will shrink. If it doesn't shrink to the desired size as specified in the command, or to OPTIMAL if you didn't specify a size, you may need to re-issue the command later. Some extents may still contain active transactions and so can't be dropped. There's also a chance that your command and the SMON background process were both trying to shrink the rollback segment concurrently. To do this, they must both store some rollback information in the segment themselves, and so may be interfering with the extents that each of them are trying to drop.

Working with Temporary Segments

A *temporary segment* is a database object that stores information for a server process that can't fit all the data it needs into memory during a sort, a *hash join*, or other related activities. If it resides in a regular tablespace—that is, one of type PERMANENT—the segment will be available to the server for as long as it's needed. At the end of this time, the segment will be dropped and the blocks it was occupying will be returned to the tablespace for use by another segment.

Any number of server processes can be using temporary segments at one time, each managing its own segment and space allocation. If a temporary segment exists in a tablespace defined as a TEMPORARY type, it's not dropped when the initial server process is done with it. Instead, a list of its extents is maintained in the data dictionary, and any other process needing temporary space is allocated one or more of its extents. As with other segments, if there's insufficient space to meet the demand at any given time, more extents are added automatically. The new extents are added to the list of available extents when the processes using them are done.

In PERMANENT or TEMPORARY tablespaces, temporary segments obtain their storage information from the default storage defined for the tablespace. The user has no opportunity to set extent sizes, maximum extent counts, and so on. Chapter 5 covers the details of setting up tablespaces with default storage sizes.

Sizing Your Temporary Tablespaces

Temporary tablespaces are difficult to plan for when you first build a database. You don't know just how many SQL statements that might need to use the space are likely to be executing concurrently. You probably won't know how much temporary space any one of them will need. A rule of thumb you might consider is to make the tablespace about half as big as the size of your largest table. This will work against the smaller tables to fit into the tablespace concurrently. However, this may not be sufficient space for work on the largest table to complete, particularly if other work is using the space simultaneously.

As your database is used, you can examine performance statistics to see just how many times your applications need temporary segments. Look at the values in the V$SYSSTAT view for the row where the NAME column value is sorts (disk). The number in the VALUE column is the number of sorts since the instance startup that required space in a temporary segment. If you see that the frequency is high enough for multiple such sorts to be occurring simultaneously, you may want to add to your tablespace size.

The number of rows sorted shown in V$SYSSTAT may help you determine whether a few relatively large sorts are requiring the temporary segment space, or if a lot of smaller sorts are just spilling over from the sort memory area. Because the row count is accumulated across memory and disk sorts, however, it can be difficult to tell how many rows are associated with each type. Also, a sort involving lots of rows may not be as memory intensive as a sort of far fewer, but much longer, rows. To take advantage of this statistic, you may have to monitor V$SYSSTAT on a sort-by-sort basis, with some knowledge of the nature of each sort being recorded in this dynamic performance view.

Of course, you may hear from your users if they run out of temporary space, because their applications will fail with an error if they can't acquire sufficient temporary space to complete. You should be careful, however, not to confuse some errors with lack of space in the temporary tablespace:

Disk sorts versus memory sorts

If you query the **V$SYSSTAT** view with the statement `SELECT * FROM v$sysstat WHERE name LIKE '%sorts%';`, you see three rows of data: one for sorts done entirely in memory, one for sorts requiring use of disks (temporary segments), and one showing the total number of rows involved in both types of sorts. If the number of disk sorts is relatively high in comparison to the memory sorts, you may need to tune the memory area provided for sorting, as discussed in Chapter 18.

- A temporary segment may reach its MAXEXTENTS limit and not be able to extend any further, even though the tablespace still has room.

- Certain DML statements use temporary segments inside a standard tablespace to build the extents for a new or changed segment. If the DML statement can't find the required space, it fails with an error such as ORA-01652 unable to extend temp segment by *number* in tablespace *name*. Be sure to check that the named tablespace is really your temporary tablespace before you rush off and try to increase its size; it could be one of your user data tablespaces that's out of room.

Setting Storage Options for Your Temporary Tablespaces

As discussed earlier, temporary segments always build their extents based on the default storage values associated with their tablespace definitions. It's therefore critical that you build your temporary tablespaces with appropriate values in the default storage clause.

To understand what storage values are appropriate for temporary segments, you should think about what's being placed into these segments. It's the data that's being swapped out of the space in memory reserved for the type of activity that might need temporary space—either sorts or hash joins. Generally, the space for sorts is the smaller of these two, and the hash join space should be an integer multiple of the sort space size. Therefore, it makes the most sense to build extents that can hold at least the full amount of data likely to be flushed from memory during a sort.

If the extent is exactly the same size as the sort space, each set of data flushed to disk will need just one extent. If the extent is larger than the sort space but not a multiple of it, every other write or so from disk will probably need to write into two extents, which isn't as efficient as writing to a single extent. The problem is reversed after the sort when the data has to read back from disk. Some reads will need to skip from one extent to another. If the extent is an integer multiple of the sort size, each set of data flushed from memory will fit into some part of a single extent. However, the last set of data flushed may not fill the extent being used, and the additional space will be wasted until the subsequent processing completes and the entire extent is released.

It's almost not worth making each extent in a temporary segment the same as the SORT_AREA_SIZE initialization parameter. If the sort requires more space than this parameter allocates, it will need to write at least two sets of data into its temporary segment—the first set that initially fills up the sort space, and the balance of the sorted data. If no balance were left over to sort, the temporary segment wouldn't have been needed. If the extent size had been double the sort space (2 * SORT_AREA_SIZE), only one extent would have been needed.

You may also want to set MAXEXTENTS based on the type of tablespace you're using. If it's of type PERMANENT, you should ensure that each concurrent disk sort can grow its temporary segment to a size that will let the other segments reach the same size. For example, in a 200MB tablespace where you expect five concurrent disk sorts, each temporary segment should be allowed to grow to 40MB. If your extent size is 2MB, MAXEXTENTS would need to be 20.

If you're using a TEMPORARY type tablespace, there will probably only be one temporary segment. You can ensure this by building it yourself right after you create your temporary tablespace by using the method described in Chapter 5. You may not want to do this if you're using Oracle Parallel Server, but we'll ignore that case here. If you build the temporary segment yourself, you'll know exactly how many extents can be contained by the tablespace, so just set the tablespace default to that number. Of course, if your tablespace is built with files that can autoextend, you should make the MAXEXTENTS value larger.

SEE ALSO
➤ *Building tablespaces specifically for temporary segments, page* **140**

Use large extent sizes for temporary segments

For sorts that almost fit into memory, such as one that uses less than twice the current sort area size, you may well find yourself tuning memory to hold the sort data completely, leaving only the very large sorts in need of temporary space. Such large sorts may need to write a number of *sort run*s to disk, maybe in the tens or twenties. It makes sense, therefore, to make each extent sufficiently large to hold these multiple runs, thus avoiding the overhead of having to find the required extent space more than once. Your temporary extent sizes may well be 10 to 100 times as large as your SORT_AREA_SIZE, depending on your situation and database use.

Managing Your Temporary Segments

Due to their nature, you don't have much control—hence, little management responsibility—for your temporary segments. A couple of issues might affect you: you may run out of space in your temporary tablespace and you may decide to change the value of your SORT_AREA_SIZE parameter.

As with any other tablespace, if you run out of space in your temporary tablespace, you can add a new data file or extend an existing data file, assuming that you have the necessary disk space. After you do this, you may want to look at the MAXEXTENTS value for the tablespace to see whether it can be set higher to take advantage of the additional space.

Should you change the value of the sort space size by altering the parameter SORT_AREA_SIZE, your temporary extents may no longer align with the I/O to and from the sort space. If you're using a PERMANENT type of tablespace, just changing the default storage values for INITIAL and NEXT to the new value will be sufficient to ensure that the next temporary segments will be appropriately sized. If you have a TEMPORARY type tablespace, however, you'll need to drop the segment from it to free up the space to build one with new extent sizes.

> **Converting a tablespace to TEMPORARY requires that all other segments be removed from it**
>
> Anytime a tablespace is of type **PERMANENT**, other types of segments in addition to temporary segments can be created in it. To switch it to a **TEMPORARY** type, all such segments must be removed. This is true whether the tablespace was originally created to hold different types of segments or if it was made **PERMANENT** for only a short time while the storage values were being changed.

To drop the segment(s) from a TEMPORARY tablespace, you need to alter it to be a PERMANENT tablespace. This will cause its contents to be treated as any other temporary segment so they will be dropped automatically. Before a replacement segment is built, you should ensure that the default storage settings are changed to reflect the new extent size you require, as you would do for temporary segments in a PERMANENT tablespace. Therefore, before altering the tablespace back to TEMPORARY status, make sure that you alter the tablespace default storage settings. As when creating a new temporary tablespace of type TEMPORARY, you may want to prebuild the temporary segment to its maximum size as soon as the status is converted. The command to alter the tablespace type is

```
ALTER TABLESPACE tablespace_name PERMANENT¦TEMPORARY
```

SEE ALSO

➤ *More information about setting up temporary tablespaces and their storage options, page* ***140***

➤ *Initialization parameters associated with sorts, page* ***523***

CHAPTER 7

Adding Segments for Tables

Define column datatypes and lengths

Build a basic table

Control your table's space allocation and utilization

Create a table from existing definitions and data

Define views to control user access to tables

Table Structure

Tables are the most common structures in almost all relational databases. They consist of *rows* (also known as *tuples* or *instances* in the worlds of relational theory and modeling, respectively) and *columns* (*attributes*). When queried by Oracle's SQL*Plus tool, they're displayed in a table format, with the column names becoming the headings. Such a display gives the illusion that the data is stored in the database just the way it appears onscreen:

- The columns are lined up under column headings.
- The data in each column is the same width from row to row.
- Numeric data is aligned to the right of the field, other data to the left.
- A fixed number of records fits on each page.
- Each field is separated from its neighbors by a fixed number of bytes.

A query against a table in SQL*Plus could result in the following output:

```
CUST_NUMBER COMPANY_NAME            PHONE_NUMBER LAST_ORDER
----------- ----------------------- ------------ ----------
        100 All Occasion Gifts      321-099-8642 12-MAR-96
        103 Best of the Best        321-808-9753 05-MAY-98
        110 Magnificent Mark's      322-771-3524 11-DEC-97
        111 Halloween All Year      321-998-3623 25-FEB-98
...
```

Although this formatting by SQL*Plus is very convenient and emphasizes the notion that relational databases store data in the form of two-dimensional tables, it doesn't really represent the true internal structure of the database tables. Inside Oracle's data files, the rows are stored very efficiently on Oracle database blocks, leaving very little free space (unless it's believed to be needed) and with little regard for how the data will look if displayed onscreen or in a report.

Helping SQL*Plus format queries

SQL*Plus may not always produce query output just the way you want to see it. For example, a column that's only one character wide will have a one-character column heading by default. Most users won't find the first character of the column name sufficient for identifying the column's contents. Similarly, some columns may be defined to hold many more characters than you need to see when casually querying the table. These longer columns can cause each row to wrap over multiple output lines, making it difficult to read the results. SQL*Plus provides formatting commands to help you produce output that has meaningful column names and column widths. You can even use its advanced features to create subtotals, grand totals, page titles and footers, and other standard reporting features. These are all covered in the *Oracle8 SQL*Plus User's Guide*.

The blocks themselves are stored in a data segment consisting of one or more extents. A very simple table will have a single extent, the first block containing its header information and the other blocks storing the rows themselves. A larger table may contain many extents, and a very large table may have additional header blocks to support the more complex structure. The data dictionary maintains the table definition, along with the storage information and other related object definitions, such as *views*, *index*es, *privilege*s, and *constraint*s, some of which can be created with the table itself. (Views are covered at the end of this chapter, indexes in Chapter 8, "Adding Segments for Different Types of Indexes," privileges in Chapter 10, "Controlling User Access with Privileges," and constraints in Chapter 17, "Using Constraints to Improve Your Application Performance.")

The simplest version of the CREATE TABLE command names the table and identifies a single column by name and type of data it will hold. Its syntax is as follows:

```
CREATE TABLE table_name (column_name datatype);
```

You should, of course, choose a name for the table that's meaningful to you and your user community. Similarly, the column name should provide some useful information about the purpose of the data it will hold.

> **Another trick to create meaningful column names**
>
> It's becoming more and more common to prefix the field names with letters that indicate which datatype is stored in the field—for example, `dtmStartDate` indicates a datatype for the field.

Choosing a Column Datatype and Length

Before building a table, you should know what type of information each column will need to hold. By knowing this, you can select an appropriate *datatype* and, possibly, a length. In some cases, you have a choice of datatypes that could be used for a particular column.

Character Data

You can store freeform character data in a number of formats. Table 7.1 shows the related datatypes and characteristics.

TABLE 7.1   **Definitions of Oracle datatypes**

Datatype:	Max Length:	Preferred Uses:	Notes:
BFILE	4GB	Binary data stored outside the database, allowing fast byte stream reads and writes	1
BLOB	4GB	Variable-length binary objects	1
CHAR	2,000	Short fields or fields that need fixed-length character comparisons	2
CLOB	4GB	Variable-length, single-byte character fields exceeding 2GB	1
DATE	7	Dates and times	3
LONG	2GB	Variable-length character fields that exceed 4,000 bytes	1,4
LONG RAW	2GB	Variable-length, uninterpreted binary data	1,4
NCHAR	2,000	Multibyte characters in short fields or fields that need fixed-length character comparisons	2,5
NCLOB	4GB	Variable-length, multibyte character fields exceeding 2GB; support only one character width per field	1
NUMBER	38	Number, having precision of 1 to 38 digits and scale of –84 to 127	
NVARCHAR2	4,000	Variable-length fields that store single or multibyte characters that don't need fixed-length comparisons	5
RAW	2,000	Variable-length, uninterpreted binary data	4,6
ROWID	10	Extended row IDs	
VARCHAR	4,000	Variable-length fields that don't need fixed-length comparisons	6,7
VARCHAR2	4,000	Variable-length fields that don't need fixed-length comparisons	6,8

[1] *There's no default length and no mechanism to define a maximum length.*
[2] *Trailing blanks are stored in the database, possibly wasting space for variable-length data. Default length is 1 character; to provide a maximum field length, add the required length in parentheses following the datatype keyword.*
[3] *Dates are always stored with seven components: century, year, month, day, hour, minute, and second. They can range from January 1, 4712 BC to December 31, 4712 AD.*
[4] *Supported for Oracle7 compliance and may not continue to be supported; large objects (LOBs) are preferred.*
[5] *The maximum length is the maximum number of bytes. For multibyte characters, the total number of characters will be less, depending on the number of bytes per character.*
[6] *There's no default length. You must always supply your own maximum length value in parentheses following the datatype keyword.*
[7] *Will stay compliant with ANSII standard definition for variable-length character fields.*
[8] *Will stay compliant with the definition from Oracle7.*

Internally, with the exception of the CHAR and DATE datatypes, Oracle stores only the characters provided by the application in the character fields. If you specify a maximum length (when allowed) or use a predefined type at its maximum length, you don't waste any storage space when your records have fewer characters than the field can hold. The CHAR datatype, however, always adds trailing blanks (if needed) when the supplied data is less than the defined field length. The DATE datatype always uses 7 bytes, one for each date/time component, applying a default specific to each missing component.

CHAR Versus VARCHAR2

Besides the storage differences—before being written to the database, CHAR fields are always blank-padded to the full defined length, whereas VARCHAR and VARCHAR2 fields are never padded automatically—the two types of fields sort differently and compare differently. CHAR fields are sorted and compared using their full (padded) length while the variable character fields are sorted and compared on just the characters included in the string.

A simple test is shown in the following few statements:

```
CREATE TABLE test_padding (fixed_col CHAR(5), var_col
VARCHAR2(5));
INSERT INTO test_padding VALUES ('A','A');
INSERT INTO test_padding VALUES ('ABCDE','ABCDE');
SELECT * FROM test_padding WHERE fixed_col = var_col;
FIXED_COL VAR_COL

--------- -------

ABCDE     ABCDE
```

Space management with CHAR and VARCHAR2

Some people prefer to use **CHAR** rather than **VARCHAR2** datatypes to reduce the likelihood that rows will grow in length when updates increase the number of characters in a field. Such growth can cause the row to become too long to fit into the block. However, Oracle provides a **PCTFREE** parameter to allow for row growth. I prefer to use **PCTFREE** to manage space rather than force all character fields to be padded blank characters, which I consider to be wasted space. See the "Creating Tables for Updates" in this chapter for details on the **PCTFREE** parameter.

Only the row where all five characters have been filled in by the VALUES clause is displayed. The row with the single letters doesn't show the two columns having equal values because the FIXED_COL column is comparing all five characters, including trailing blanks, to the single character from the VAR_COL column.

Numeric Data

Numbers are stored by using the NUMBER datatype. By default, a number field can contain up to 38 digits of precision along with, optionally, a decimal point and a sign. Positive and negative numbers have a magnitude of $1.0X10^{-130}$ to $9.9...9X10^{125}$. A number can also have a value of 0, of course. To restrict the magnitude of a number (the number of digits to the left of the decimal point) and its precision (the number of digits to the right of the decimal point), enclose the required value(s) inside parentheses following the NUMBER keyword.

If you include only the magnitude, you actually define an integer. Any numbers with decimal values are rounded to the nearest integer before being stored. For example, NUMBER(3) allows numbers in the range of –999 to +999, and an inserted value of 10.65 is stored as 11. If you provide a precision and scale, you can store a number with as many digits as provided by the precision, but only *precision-scale* digits before the decimal point. Table 7.2 shows some examples of numbers that you can and can't store in a column defined as NUMBER(5,2).

Using a negative precision value

If you use a negative value in the precision field of a number column's length definition, the numbers will be rounded up to that power of 10 before being stored. For example, a column defined as NUMBER(10,-2) will take your input and round up to the nearest 100 (10 to the power of 2), so a value of 123,456 would be stored as 123,500.

How Oracle stores numbers

Oracle stores all numbers, regardless of the definition, by using a mantissa and exponent component. The digits of the mantissa are compressed two digits per byte, so the actual space required to a store a number depends on the number of significant digits provided, regardless of the column definition.

TABLE 7.2   **Valid and invalid numbers for a column defined as *NUMBER(5,2)***

Valid Numbers:	Stored As:
0	0
1	1
12.3	12.3
–12	–12
–123.45	–123.45
123.456	123.46 (rounded to 2 decimal digits)
–12.345	–12.35 (rounded to 2 decimal digits)

Valid Numbers:	Stored As:
123.4567890123456789	123.46 (rounded to 2 decimal digits)
12345	Invalid; exceeds precision (5–2 digits before decimal)
–1234.1	Invalid; exceeds precision (5–2 digits before decimal)

Date Data

Use the DATE format to store date fields or time information. Oracle has a single 7-byte internal format for all dates, and a 1-byte interval for each century, year, month, day, hour, minute, and second. Depending on the format your applications use to store dates, some fields may be left to default. For the time fields, the defaults result in a time of midnight. For century, either the current year (taken from the operating system date setting) is used, or a choice of 1900 or 2000, depending on the year value. The RR format mask causes the latter behavior, with a year in the range 50 to 99 resulting in a value of 19 for the century, and a year in the range 00 to 49 resulting in a value of 20 for the century.

Entering just the time component causes the date portion to be derived from the current operating system date, which uses the RR format mask process as described for the century as well as the current year and month, and defaults the day to the first day of the month.

Oracle can perform extensive date field operations, including date comparisons and date arithmetic. If you need to manipulate dates, check the *Oracle8 Server SQL* manual for detailed descriptions of the available date operators and functions.

One common problem occurs when you use the SYSDATE function to supply the current date when inserting a new record into the database. This would seem to be straightforward, allowing a query such as to select all orders placed on October 10, 1997, assuming that the date is provided in the correct format.

```
SELECT * FROM orders WHERE order_date = '10-OCT-97'
```

Handling the year 2000 problem

Oracle has always stored both the century and the year for any date value in the database. To help distinguish dates in the 20th and 21st centuries when you provide only the last two digits of the year for the TO_DATE function, Oracle provides the RR date format mask. In a statement that stores a date by using the function TO_DATE('12/12/03','DD/MM/RR'), the stored date will have the current century if the current year's last two digits are less than 50, and will have the next century if the current year's last two digits are 50 or greater. Full details of the RR format are given in the *Oracle8 Server SQL Reference* manual.

Default date formats

Oracle uses a format mask when dealing with dates so that each of the seven components of the combined date/time fields can be uniquely identified. The database runs with a default date mask dependent on the setting of the initialization parameters NLS_TERRITORY and NLS_DATE_FORMAT. Generally, these hide the time component so that it defaults to midnight, unless the application or individual statement decides to override the mask and provide its own values for one or more of the time fields. When you're using date arithmetic and date functions, the time component may not be obvious to you or your users and can cause apparent problems.

However, because the SYSDATE function by default always inserts the current time as well as the current date (whereas the query provides only the date, meaning that midnight on October 10 is being selected), there will be no matching records in the ORDERS table. The solution would be to store the data as if the time were midnight by applying the TRUNC function to the SYSDATE on insert.

Binary Data

Binary data is stored without any interpretation of embedded characters. For compatibility with Oracle7, the RAW and LONG RAW datatypes are still usable. However, the LONG RAW datatype is being *deprecated*, meaning that it's gradually becoming unsupported. Oracle8 offers the BLOB and BFILE datatypes to store binary data; these can be used in place of the RAW and LONG RAW datatypes.

SEE ALSO

➤ *For details on large objects (LOBs), see page 691*

The only internal difference between RAW and LONG RAW is the maximum number of bytes they can store. RAW has a maximum length of 2,000 bytes, and you must define the maximum length you need as part of the column definition, even if you need all 2,000 bytes. The LONG RAW datatype can hold a maximum of 2GB. You can't limit this size as you can with RAW column, but, as with variable-character fields, Oracle stores only the characters you supply in RAW and LONG RAW fields, regardless of the maximum possible length.

By using some of the datatypes discussed above, you could create a multicolumn table, SAMPLE1, as follows:

```
CREATE TABLE sample1 (
    sample_id           NUMBER(10),
    sample_name         VARCHAR2(35),
    owner_id            NUMBER(4),
    collection_date     DATE,
    donor_gender        CHAR(1),
    sample_image        BLOB);
```

Tables defined with a variable-length datatype in one or more columns—that is, any datatype other than CHAR or DATE—may

The new syntax isn't very complicated

Compared with the **CREATE TABLE** command included at the beginning of this chapter, the only other new syntax introduced in the listing, in addition to the datatypes, is the comma that separates each column definition.

need some special consideration when they're created if these columns are likely to be updated during the lifetime of any given row. This is because Oracle packs the data into table blocks as tightly as possible. This tends to result in very little, if any, space being left on the block if a row grows in length due to an update that adds more bytes to an existing field. Before creating a table in which you anticipate updates being made to variable-length columns, read the later section "Setting Space Utilization Parameters" to see how to avoid some of the problems this can cause.

Sizing and Locating Tables

Appendix A of the *Oracle8 Server Administrator's Guide* provides a detailed description of calculations you can use to compute how big a particular table will be, based on the column definitions, the average record size, and the expected number of rows. Before the most recent releases of Oracle, a table could contain only a limited number of extents, so it was important to know how big the table would be before creating it in order to provide sufficient extents space. With Oracle8, you can have unlimited extents in a table. Consequently, the only reason to be concerned with table size is to determine if you have sufficient disk space to store it.

Although I won't try to dissuade you from using Oracle's provided sizing calculations, I want to suggest an alternative approach to predicting table size. One key to either approach is to know the average row size. This generally requires that you find or generate some valid sample data. If you have such data, I recommend that you simply load it into your table, measure how much space is used, and then extrapolate the final size based on the ratio of the number of rows in your sample data to the total number of rows you expect the table to contain.

Use sample data to predict table size

1. Put your sample data into a flat file.

2. Create a SQL*Loader control file and run SQL*Loader to load the data. (See Chapter 25, "Using SQL*Loader and Export/Import," for details on SQL*Loader.)

3. Execute the following command to collect current storage information:

```
ANALYZE TABLE table_name COMPUTE STATISTICS
```

4. Execute the following query to find the number blocks now storing data:

```
SELECT blocks FROM user_tables
WHERE table_name = 'table_name'
```

5. Compute the total number of blocks required to store the full table by using this formula:

BLOCKS X (total number of rows) / (number of rows in sample)

You can use the following SQL*Plus script to perform these steps after you load your sample rows:

```
SET VERIFY OFF
ANALYZE TABLE &table_name COMPUTE STATISTICS
/
SELECT blocks * &total_row_count / num_rows
  AS "Total blocks needed"
  FROM user_tables
  WHERE table_name = UPPER('&&table_name')
/
```

After you determine your table's maximum size, you can identify an appropriate tablespace in which to store it. Your choice should be based on the factors discussed in Chapter 5, "Managing Your Database Space," concerning tablespace usage. These include a recommendation to use a limited number of different extent sizes, such as small, medium, large, and huge, for all objects in a given tablespace. You should be able to determine from its maximum size which category of extent sizes would best suit it, assuming that you follow our recommendations. For a very large table, the largest extent size is usually preferable, although if the table is going to grow very slowly, you may want to use smaller extents so that you can conserve disk space in the interim.

Other factors in deciding on a tablespace include the frequency of backup, the likelihood of dropping or truncating the table in the future, and which other segments exist in the candidate tablespaces. The latter might influence your decision when you consider what else the application might need to have access to, besides the new table, if a data file in the tablespace should become unusable.

When you've determined which tablespace to use, you should add the tablespace name to the CREATE TABLE statement. By using the SAMPLE1 table-creation script shown in the preceding command, let's put the table into the SAMPLE_DATA tablespace:

```
CREATE TABLE sample1 (
    sample_id          NUMBER(10),
    sample_name        VARCHAR2(35),
    owner_id           NUMBER(4),
    collection_date    DATE,
    donor_gender       CHAR(1),
    sample_image       BLOB)
TABLESPACE sample_data                    ❶
/
```

Permissions when creating a table

To create a table successfully, you must have the necessary privileges and permissions, including the **CREATE TABLE** privilege and the right to use space in the named tablespace. See Chapter 9, "Creating and Managing User Accounts," and Chapter 10 for more information on these topics.

❶ Moves sample1 table into sample.data tablespace

Of course, if the person creating the table has the SAMPLE_DATA tablespace as his or her default tablespace, the TABLESPACE clause isn't needed. If you include it, you guarantee that the table will be created in the desired tablespace no matter who runs the script.

Setting Storage Parameters

You need to concern yourself with a table's *storage parameters* only if you haven't designed your database's tablespaces according to the guidelines in Chapter 5. These guidelines, along with the correct tablespace selection discussed in the previous section, should allow the table to use the default storage information defined for the tablespace. However, we'll look at each storage option in turn for those of you who may need to consider overriding your defaults. You include these options with the required values in a STORAGE clause as part of the CREATE TABLE or ALTER TABLE commands.

Overriding the defaults

If you have a database that's not designed as rigorously as discussed earlier, you may need to override one or all of the storage parameters. You can find the current default settings for the storage options in a tablespace by querying the **DBA_TABLESPACES** data dictionary view.

INITIAL

This parameter sets the size, in bytes, of the first extent built for the table. Some possible criteria for choosing a size include the following:

- For fast table scans, the extent should hold the entire table.
- For fast parallel table scans, the extent should hold 1/xth of the table, and the rest of the table should be placed in other (x–1) equal-sized extents on different disks.
- To load the table using SQL*Loader in parallel, direct path, the extent should be as small as possible because it won't be used.
- Fit as much of the table as possible into the largest piece of free space available. This is particularly useful when the tablespace has lots of free space but only small amounts of it are contiguous.

NEXT

This parameter sets the size, in bytes, of the second extent. Some possible criteria for choosing a size include the following:

- For fast table scans, the extent should hold all the rows not stored in the first extent.
- For fast parallel table scans, the next extent should be the same size as the initial and all subsequent extents, and each extent should be stored on a different disk.
- To load the table with SQL*Loader in parallel, direct path, the extent should be large enough to hold all the rows from one parallel loader session.
- Fit as much of the table as possible that doesn't fit into the initial extent into the largest piece of remaining free space. This is particularly useful when the tablespace has lots of free space but only small amounts of it are contiguous.

PCTINCREASE

This parameter defines a multiplier to compute the size of the next extent to be created. It's applied to the third, and every subsequent, extent. If you set it to zero (0), each extent will be the same size as defined by NEXT; if you set it to 100, each subsequent extent will double in size. A value of zero is generally to be preferred. You may want to use a non-zero value if you don't know how much your table will grow, so that each extent will be larger than the previous one. This should eventually result in a sufficiently large extent to hold the remainder of the table.

The drawbacks to this include the following:

- An attempt to create an extent larger than can be held by any data file in the tablespace.

- Irregular extent sizes, leading to irregular free extents if the table is dropped or truncated.

- A final extent much larger than required for the number of rows it needs to hold.

- Less predictable space consumption, particularly if there are many tables so defined.

MINEXTENTS

This parameter sets the number of extents built by the CREATE TABLE command. The sizes of the extents are determined by the values for INITIAL, NEXT, and PCTINCREASE. There are some possible reasons for creating only one extent initially:

- You expect the table to fit into a single extent.

- Additional extents will be built by SQL*Loader in parallel, direct mode.

- You'll add extents manually to fit them into differently sized free extents.

- You'll add extents manually to place them on different disks.

There are some possible reasons for creating multiple extents initially:

PCTINCREASE **options**

Oracle allows large values of **PCTINCREASE** to reduce the number of additional extents that might be needed if a table's size was seriously underestimated when it was first created. In earlier releases, this feature was essential because the number of extents that could be added to an existing table was a finite, limited number. With the **UNLIMITED** option now available, the only drawback to having many extents is the overhead associated with adding each new one. In general, I recommend leaving the value at zero whenever the table must share a tablespace with at least one other segment, to preserve uniform extent sizes. In other cases, you should set it to a reasonable value so that it doesn't begin requiring extents significantly larger than the available disk space.

- You have lots of free extents with equal, or nearly equal, sizes, but none large enough to hold the whole table.

- Your tablespace is built with many data files, and you want Oracle to spread the extents evenly among them.

MAXEXTENTS

This parameter sets the maximum number of extents the table will be allowed to use. You don't usually need to worry about this value initially because it can be changed later. Of course, you should be prepared to monitor the use of the space as the number of extents in a table approaches this value, no matter how you've set it. In some situations, however, you may need to set a specific value of MAXEXTENTS, including

Additional storage options that don't affect extent sizes

You can use other keywords in the STORAGE clause of the CREATE TABLE command—FREELISTS, FREELIST GROUPS, and BUFFER POOL. However, these values can't be set at the tablespace level and don't affect the allocation of table extents. The impact of these storage options is discussed in other sections of this book.

- When you have limited disk space.

- When you have fragmented free space in such a way that NEXT and PCTINCREASE can't be set to reasonable values until the next extent is needed.

- In a parallel server environment, when you're manually assigning extents to specific instances (see the Oracle8 Server *Parallel Server Administration* manual for more details on this topic).

SEE ALSO

➤ To see how to use the BUFFER POOL keyword, see page **519**

➤ For more on free lists and free list groups, see page **585**

➤ The buffer pool and table options to use it effectively are covered on page **549**

We end this section by showing the additional lines added to the CREATE TABLE sample1 script to include a STORAGE clause:

```
CREATE TABLE sample1 (
    sample_id          NUMBER(10),
    sample_name        VARCHAR2(35),
    owner_id           NUMBER(4),
    collection_date    DATE,
    donor_gender       CHAR(1),
    sample_image       BLOB)
TABLESPACE sample_data
```

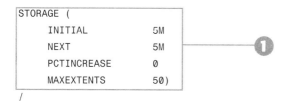

1 The STORAGE clause

Setting Space Utilization Parameters

Each block in an Oracle table can hold as many rows as will fit into the block. When the block is full, Oracle removes it from the list of blocks into which new rows can be inserted. At some point in the future, if enough rows are deleted from the block, it may be added back onto the list of available blocks so that more new rows can be added to it, using the space freed up by the dropped rows.

Some special parameters associated with the table's definition, known as *space utilization parameters*, influence these events. In particular, they control just how full a block becomes before it's moved off the list of available blocks (known as the *free list*), how much space must be made available before it's moved back onto the free list again, and how much space is reserved for multiple *transactions* to access the block concurrently. These settings affect how updates are managed, how much space might be going to waste in a table, and how much transaction concurrency can occur on a block.

Creating Tables for Updates

Unless your table contains all DATE and CHAR columns, any update to a record can cause that record to grow or shrink in overall length. This is because Oracle stores only the bytes that contain information in its variable length fields. A new value, if it has more or less data, changes the amount of storage required. Updating a record with smaller field values doesn't cause any problems, unless this happens repeatedly and the block becomes almost empty, thus wasting space. However, if you add to a field's length, you may run out of space on the block. Even if this doesn't happen the first time you perform such an update, it may occur if you continue to increase the lengths of different columns or rows.

If you run out of space, Oracle will move the row to another block in the table through a process known as *migration*. Although this may sound like a benign solution, it does have performance ramifications. A migrated row leaves behind a forwarding address (pointer) so that it can still be found by an index lookup or by an ongoing query. Subsequent access to that row results in a probe of the row's original home block, which finds the forwarding address, and then a probe of the block where it now resides, known as an "overflow block." Rarely will the original block and overflow block be contiguous blocks in the table, so the disk retrieval for such a row will be slow. Migrated rows, particularly if they are numerous, can affect the overall database performance.

To help you avoid massive row migration, Oracle lets you reserve space on a block into which the data can expand. By default, this space is 10 percent of the data area of the block. When a change to the block leaves less free space than is reserved for row expansion, the block is taken off the free list and no further inserts will occur. For some tables, the 10 percent default may be perfectly adequate. For other tables, 10 percent may be a completely inadequate amount of free space or far more than is needed.

The space is reserved with the PCTFREE parameter, and you should determine a good value for it as best you can before you build any production table. As soon as a table is built you can change this value, but only blocks that aren't being used will adopt the new value and reserve the desired amount of free space.

If you know two pieces of information about the data being stored in the table, you can use the following formula to compute a good value for PCTFREE. The information you need is the average length of the rows when they're first inserted and the average length of the rows when they're at their maximum length. In the following formula, the terms *avg_insert_length* and *max_length* refer to these values, respectively:

$$PCTFREE = 100 * \frac{(max\_length - avg\_insert\_length)}{(max\_length)}$$

In determining the average row lengths, you need to consider only the number of bytes of data per row, not the internal overhead associated with stored rows and fields. If you use just data lengths, the result will be slightly higher and have a built-in margin of error. The size of this error varies depending on the block size, number of rows in the block, and number of columns per row. For a table with 10 columns and a database block size of 4KB, if 10 rows fit into the block, this margin of error will be just over 3 percent.

For rows that don't change over time, or change only fixed-length fields, the expression (*max_length* - *avg_insert_length*) reduces to zero, which in turn causes the entire formula to result in zero. If you're really certain that there will be no updates or just updates that change record lengths, you can set PCTFREE equal to zero without concern for row migration problems.

If you have a table in which the value of (*max_length* - *avg_insert_length*) is negative, you also shouldn't have to worry about migration if you set PCTFREE to zero. However, in such a table, there will be a tendency for the amount of data on each block to become less than is optimal. This will occur when the block gains sufficient empty space, due to record shrinkage, to hold a whole new row. With many blocks in this state, you'll suffer some inefficiency because of this wasted space; more blocks are being taken to store rows than are really needed. To overcome this, you should consider the table in the same category as tables that undergo record deletions over time, and follow the approach to deal with these in the next section.

Creating Tables with High Delete Activity

Over time, tables that have rows deleted or rows that shrink in size can become inefficient. The empty space on the blocks represents additional disk reading and writing that must be done because empty space, rather than data, is being transferred

---

Example of computing the PCTFREE value

If a table has a row with an average length of 153 bytes when it's initially inserted, and it grows by an average of 27 bytes over the course of its time in the table, the average maximum length of a row is 180 bytes. By using these two values in the formula PCTFREE = 100 * (*max_length* - *avg_insert_length*) / (*max_length*), we find that this table should be created with PCTFREE = 100x(180-153) / 180 = 100x27 / 180 = 100x3/20 = 15.

between disk and memory. Oracle provides the space utilization parameter PCTUSED to help you control the amount of empty space allowed to remain on a block.

As mentioned earlier, a block is taken off the free list when it's full so that no further attempts are made to insert more rows into it—that is, when it has less empty space than PCTFREE of the block. PCTUSED sets a threshold value at which the amount of free space becomes sufficient for the block to hold one or more new rows, so it can be placed back on the free list. By default, Oracle sets PCTUSED at 40 percent. In other words, a block that has less than 40 percent of its data area occupied by rows will be put back on the free list.

You can change the value of PCTUSED at table creation time or anytime thereafter. As with PCTFREE, the impact of a change to PCTUSED may be delayed. A block that already contains less than the new PCTUSED amount of data, unless it's already on the free list, won't be placed there until another change is made to it.

What makes a good value for PCTUSED? The first criterion is to set it so that a block goes back on the free list only when there's room to store at least one more new row. In a very volatile table, where rows are frequently added and dropped, it may be worth wasting space on a block until there is room to fit three or four rows. Moving blocks on and off the free list requires some overhead that may not be worth incurring unless more than one row is affected by the change. After you decide how many rows to leave room for before placing a block back on a free list, you can use the following formula to compute a good value for PCTUSED:

```
PCTUSED = 100 - PCTFREE - 100 * row_space / block_space
    where row_space = avg_insert_length * rows_needed
    and block_space = DB_BLOCK_SIZE - 90 - INITRANS * 24
```

- PCTFREE is a space-utilization parameter value discussed in the previous section.

- *avg_insert_length* is the average number of bytes in a row when it's first inserted.

- *rows_needed* is the number of rows you want to be able to fit into the block before returning it to the free list.

Constants used in computing PCTUSED value

The constant 90 is an imprecise measure of the space used by Oracle's header information in a table block, but it has proven to be sufficiently accurate for this calculation. The constant 24 is the number of bytes used to store a transaction entry on a typical hardware platform, and should be adequate for this calculation.

- DB_BLOCK_SIZE is the database block size, set in the parameter file and found by querying the V$PARAMETER table.

- INITRANS is a space-utilization parameter value discussed in the next section.

Following from the example we used to demonstrate the computation for PCTFREE, let's see how this formula would work if we wanted to insert new rows when a block had room for three new rows. In the earlier example, the average length of a row when initially inserted was 153 bytes, and the value for PCTFREE was calculated at 15. Let's use a block size of 4KB and an INITRANS value of 4 to complete the PCTUSED calculation. So we need to compute

```
PCTUSED = 100 - 15 - 100 * (153 * 3) / (4096 - 90 - 4 * 24)
```

- 100 is a constant for computing the percentage.

- 15 is the value for PCTFREE.

- 153 is the number of bytes required to store an average row when inserted.

- 3 is the number of rows we need to have room to store before returning the block to the free list.

- 4096 is the number of bytes on a 4KB block.

- 90 is a constant representing the number of bytes used for block overhead.

- 4 is the value of INITRANS.

- 24 is a constant representing the number of bytes taken by a transaction entry.

This simplifies to the following:

```
PCTUSED = 85 - 100 * 459 / (4006 - 96) = 85 - 100 * 459 /
3910
```

If we round the quotient 459/3910 (= 0.1173913) up to 0.12, the result becomes the following:

```
PCTUSED = 85 - 100 * 0.12 = 85 - 12 = 73
```

The second consideration is how much space you can afford to spare. The lower the PCTUSED value you use, the more empty space will accumulate on a block before it's recycled onto a free list for more data to be added. In very large tables, you may not be able to afford to store blocks with more than a minimal amount of free space. In such cases, even though you may cause additional overhead by moving blocks back onto the free list more often than you might think you need from the preceding formula, you may gain some benefits. Not only will you save disk space, but if the table is queried extensively—particularly when using full table scans—you'll need to read less blocks into memory to retrieve the same number of rows.

Creating Tables for Multiple Concurrent Transactions

For a transaction to add, alter, or drop a row from an Oracle table, it must first obtain a lock on that row. It does this by first registering itself on the block where the row will reside or now resides. The registration is made by updating a special area of the block called the *transaction entry slot*, also known as an *intent to lock (itl) slot*. If a block contains a lot of rows, it's conceivable that more than one transaction will want to work on the same block at the same time. To do this, each must obtain a transaction slot for its own use.

Oracle allows up to 255 transaction slots to be created on a single block, but by default it builds one only when a block is added to a table. When additional slots are needed, the Oracle server process needing the slot has to rearrange the contents of the block to make room for the new slot. If you want to avoid this behavior, you can create a table that will contain more transaction slots on each block as the blocks are added. You can also limit the upper number of slots that can be created, preserving the space for additional row data, albeit at the cost of possibly making users wait for a transaction slot on a very busy block.

You control the allocation of transaction slots with the INITRANS and MAXTRANS space utilization parameters. With INITRANS, you set the number of transaction slots that each block acquires by default. With MAXTRANS, you set an upper limit on the total number of such slots that can be assigned to the block. The difference, MAXTRANS minus INITRANS, is the number of slots that can be added dynamically if needed.

Usually, there's no real need to change the default value for MAXTRANS. Even if you have hundreds of concurrent transactions working against the same table, they're likely to be working on different blocks simply because most blocks don't have room for that many rows. In the rare situation where tens of concurrent transactions all need the same block, they'll probably have to wait for one of the other transactions to release the row-level lock before they can do any work. It's in this case that you might want to set MAXTRANS. Otherwise, each transaction will build itself a transaction slot that it will then occupy idly until it can get to the row it needs. These slots represent wasted space on the block.

You might want to change INITRANS, however, if your can predict that more than one transaction will likely need the same block at the same time. By preallocating the necessary number of transaction slots on each block, you'll help the second and subsequent user get to their resources sooner. Each slot requires about 24 bytes, so don't set the value of INITRANS too high. Otherwise, you'll be taking space that could be occupied by row data.

Adding space utilization parameters to the example SAMPLE1 table requires further modifications to our table-creation command:

```
CREATE TABLE sample1 (
    sample_id          NUMBER(10),
    sample_name        VARCHAR2(35),
    owner_id           NUMBER(4),
    collection_date    DATE,
    donor_gender       CHAR(1),
    sample_image       BLOB)
TABLESPACE sample_data
STORAGE (
    INITIAL            5M
    NEXT               5M
    PCTINCREASE        0
    MAXEXTENTS         50)
    PCTFREE            20
    PCTUSED            25
    INITRANS           4
/
```

1 Space utilization parameters

Building Tables from Existing Tables

One option you may want to exercise is to build a table from the definition of, or the full or partial contents of, another table. Oracle allows you to do this through an AS SELECT clause to the CREATE TABLE command.

The table definition can look just the same as the examples you've seen to this point, except that the datatype isn't included in the column list because the type is inherited from the original table. In fact, if you also want to keep the column names in the new table the same as they are in the original table, you can omit the column list completely. As with the versions of the CREATE TABLE command you've seen listed, you can also include or omit the entire STORAGE clause, or just include it with the required parameters; you can include or exclude any or all space utilization parameters; and you need to include the TABLESPACE clause only if you want the new table to be created somewhere other than your default tablespace.

The AS SELECT clause can include any valid query that will retrieve columns and rows to match the new table's definition. The columns named in the SELECT clause must match the column list, if any, for the new table. If the new table doesn't have a column list, all the columns from the original table are used in the new table. The SELECT clause can optionally include a WHERE clause to identify which rows to store in the new table. If you don't want any rows stored, include a WHERE clause that never returns a valid condition, such as WHERE 1 = 2.

The following shows three different variations of the CREATE TABLE...AS SELECT statement, each one producing a different table definition from the same base table we have been using, SAMPLE1.

```
REM Create SAMPLE2, an exact copy of SAMPLE1, in tablespace
REM SPARE, using default storage and no free space in the
REM blocks.
REM
```

```
CREATE TABLE sample2
TABLESPACE spare
PCTFREE    0
AS SELECT *
    FROM sample1
/
```

① SAMPLE2 is based on entire SAMPLE1 table

```
REM Create SAMPLE3, containing just the ID and IMAGE
REM columns, renamed, from SAMPLE1, placing it in the IMAGE
REM tablespace with unlimited 100MB extents and default
REM space utilization parameters.
REM
```

```
CREATE TABLE sample3 (
id,
image)
TABLESPACE image
STORAGE (
    INITIAL       100M
    NEXT          100M
    PCTINCREASE   0
    MAXEXTENTS    UNLIMITED)
AS SELECT *
    FROM sample1
/
```

② SAMPLE3 is based on two renamed columns from SAMPLE1 table

```
REM Create SAMPLE4 containing all but the IMAGE column from
REM SAMPLE1, and only selecting records from the past year.
REM Use the DEMOGRAPHIC tablespace with default storage,
REM zero free space, a block reuse threshold of 60 percent,
REM and exactly 5 transaction slots per block.
REM
```

```
CREATE TABLE sample4 (
    sample_id,
    sample_name,
    owner_id,
    collection_date,
    donor_gender)
TABLESPACE demographic
PCTFREE        0
PCTUSED        60
INITRANS       5
MAXTRANS       5
AS SELECT *
    FROM sample1
    WHERE collection_date > sysdate - 365
/
```

③ SAMPLE4 is based on all but one column from the SAMPLE1 table and includes only a subset of rows

Monitoring Table Growth

Although you try to determine a table's overall size when it's created to evaluate disk requirements, the actual size may well vary from the predicted size. You should monitor the database tables to ensure that they won't run of out space in the course of normal business. Similarly, you may want to check that the space taken by the table's extents is being used efficiently and that there aren't a lot of empty or near-empty blocks. You may also want to confirm that the PCTFREE value is set appropriately by looking for migrated rows.

Row chaining versus migration

If a row is too big to fit into a single block, the first part of the row is stored in one block and the rest of the row is stored in one or more overflow blocks. Each part of the row is known as a *row piece,* and the first row piece is counted as the row's location for any index entry or when it's examined by the ANA-LYZE command. When a row migrates because it no longer fits into its original block, a pointer is left behind in the original block to identify the row's new location. This pointer is treated as the row's location so that any index entries pointing to the row don't have to be updated. The ANALYZE command treats this pointer as an initial row piece and doesn't distinguish it from a row piece belonging to a chained row. This is why the results of the ANALYZE command don't distinguish between chained and migrated rows.

The ANALYZE command collects statistics and stores them in the data dictionary for you. These statistics include the number of blocks used, the amount of unused space per block, the number of empty blocks, and the number of migrated or chained rows. A *chained* row is one that's simply too large to fit into a single block, and thus will always be spread across multiple blocks. The data dictionary, unfortunately, doesn't distinguish between chained rows and *migrated* rows, the latter being rows that get longer through the use of UPDATE commands and don't have sufficient space on their block for the growth. If the average row length, also shown in the dictionary, is less than the space available on a block (the block size minus the header and transaction slot space), the rows are most likely migrated, not chained.

You can use ANALYZE TABLE *table_name* COMPUTE STATISTICS or ANALYZE TABLE *table_name* ESTIMATE STATISTICS to collect the statistics stored in the DBA_TABLES (and USER_TABLES) data dictionary views. The former command will always give accurate results; the latter will be a good, but not precise, estimate. The COMPUTE option takes longer as the table grows in size, so you may prefer to estimate statistics for your large tables. You can select the percentage of the table or the number of rows you want to include in the estimate with the SAMPLE clause, using SAMPLE *x* PERCENT or SAMPLE *x* ROWS (where *x* is the percentage or the row count, respectively).

When you collect statistics, you may affect how the database performs optimization to determine statement execution plans. If you want to ensure that rule-based optimization is used by default, you should execute the ANALYZE TABLE...DELETE

STATISTICS command after you examine the statistics. If you want to spend more time reviewing the statistics, you can save the results by executing a CREATE TABLE...AS SELECT command against the data dictionary table. In fact, if you do this after you run the ANALYZE command to collect new statistics, using a different table to store the results each time, you will build a history of the table's growth and data distribution. Once you have saved the statistics into a table, you can go ahead and execute the DELETE STATISTICS option to remove them from the base table definition.

Managing Extent Allocation

There are two reasons to monitor how many extents exist in a table:

- You don't want the table to reach its MAXEXTENTS number of extents and thus fail during the execution of a command.

- This may be a table where, for whatever reason, you want to add extents manually, and so you maintain MAXEXTENTS at the current number of extents to avoid dynamic allocation.

To see the number of extents in table, you can query DBA_EXTENTS for the given table (segment) name. If you use the COUNT(*) value in the SELECT clause, the result will show the exact number of extents owned by the table. If you want to see other information, such as the data files in which the extents are stored, you can query other columns in this table.

To allocate an additional extent to a table for which you're using manual allocation, issue an ALTER TABLE...STORAGE (MAXEXTENTS *x*) command, where *x* is one more than the current number of extents. You can then add an extent with the ALTER TABLE... ALLOCATE EXTENT command. The following script manually adds the 12th extent to the SAMPLE10 table, using the third data file in the USR_DATA tablespace:

```
ALTER TABLE sample10 STORAGE (MAXEXTENTS 12)
/
ALTER TABLE sample10
    ALLOCATE EXTENT (
    FILE 'c:\orant\database\samples\usr_data3.ora')
/
```

Reasons to add table extents manually

There are a number of reasons for manually adding extents to a table, although relying on automatic allocation generally makes your work a lot easier. Some of the more common reasons for manual allocation include overcoming a shortage of space in the tablespace that doesn't allow you to choose a good value for the **NEXT** extent to be allocated automatically; placing the extent in a data file of your choice, which allows you to spread the storage around different data files and, presumably, different disk drives; allocating the extent to a specific instance's free list groups if you're using the parallel server option; and ensuring that you fit the largest extent possible into the given space.

For tables to which extents are being added automatically, you simply need to ensure that MAXEXTENTS stays larger than the current number of extents. By monitoring the table over time, you should be able to predict how fast extents are being added and increase the MAXEXTENTS value before the current limit is reached. You use the same command that appears at the start of the preceding script to change the extent limit.

Removing Unused Space

There are two types of unused space in a table:

- Blocks that have been allocated but never used for data.
- Blocks that have become empty or partially empty over time due to row deletions or smaller values updated in variable-length fields.

If you have blocks of the first type—that is, blocks that have never been used—and don't expect this space to be needed, you can remove it with the DEALLOCATE option of the ALTER TABLE command:

ALTER TABLE *table_name* DEALLOCATE UNUSED

If you expect some but not all allocated space to be needed, you can drop a portion of the extra space by using a further option:

ALTER TABLE *table_name* DEALLOCATE UNUSED KEEP *integer* [K¦M]

This removes all but *integer* bytes (or K (kilobytes) or M (megabytes)).

To reclaim the other type of free space—space that has been released by DML activity—you can try increasing the PCTUSED value for the table, as discussed earlier. This will allow blocks to be returned to the free list and used for future new rows sooner than they have been. However, if the table is fairly static and not many more changes will be made, the blocks that are already partially empty can't be touched again and won't be returned to the free list. Even if they were, there might not be enough new rows added to fill all the reusable space. In this case, you may have to rebuild the table.

You can rebuild a table in a number of ways:

- Use the Export/Import utilities explained in Chapter 25.
- Dump the records into an external file and use SQL*Loader (also explained in Chapter 25) to reload them.
- If you have room, you can move the records to a temporary table, truncate the original table, and move the records back again, as shown in the following for the SAMPLE10 table:

```
CREATE TABLE temp AS SELECT * FROM sample10
/
TRUNCATE TABLE sample10
/
INSERT INTO sample10 SELECT * FROM temp
/
DROP TABLE temp
/
```

Using Views to Prebuild Queries

Although you can create tables from the contents of other tables, as discussed in the previous section, in many cases there's no need to consume the space required by the copy just because you need to see a variation of the original table. A *view* is built in the same way that the AS SELECT clause is used to build a table from the contents of another table. With a view, rather than the data be copied to a new location, only the definition of required data is stored in the data dictionary. This amounts to storing the SELECT statement or, to put it another way, storing a query definition.

Views have many uses. The following sections show you how to build a view to meet a specific need you may have. We use a simple EMPLOYEE table as the basis for the examples in these sections. The following shows the CREATE statement for this table:

You can use views without degrading performance

Consider using a view whenever you think it could be useful, for any purpose whatsoever. There is very little overhead involved in storing the definition or in executing a statement against the view.

```
CREATE TABLE employee (
    id              NUMBER(8)
                    CONSTRAINT employee_id_pk PRIMARY KEY,
    last_name       VARCHAR2(35),
    first_name      VARCHAR2(30),
    middle_initial CHAR(1),
    department      NUMBER(5)
                    CONSTRAINT employee_department_fk
                       REFERENCES department_table,
    salary          NUMBER(10,2),
```

```
        title           VARCHAR2(20),
        phone           NUMBER(5) CONSTRAINT employee_phone_fk
                            REFERENCES phone_table,
        hire_date       DATE)
    /
```

For information on the constraints contained in this table definition, see Chapter 17, "Using Constraints to Improve Your
Application Performance."

Changing Column Names with Views

If your table has column names that follow a naming convention—such as a corporate standard or one based on the vocabu-
lary of the primary users—the names may not be meaningful to
other users of the table. For example, the Human Resource
Department may talk about an employee ID number, the Payroll
Department may refer to the same number as a "payroll number," and the Project Scheduling System may use the term "task
assignee." By using views, the same employee table can be used
to provide this number with the preferred name for each group.

The following script, based the EMPLOYEE table created in the preceding script, shows a view being created for the Payroll
Department to give the ID column the name EMPLOYEE_ID, leaving all other columns with their original names:

```
CREATE VIEW  pay_employee (
    payroll_number,
    last_name,
    first_name,
    middle_initial,
    department,
    salary,
    title,
    phone,
    hire_date) AS
SELECT * FROM employee
    /
```

Dropping Columns with Views

Once in a while, you may find that a column originally defined
in a table is no longer needed. The current version of Oracle8

doesn't allow you to drop such a column. Instead, I recommend that you set the column value to NULL in the entire table, which will free up the storage consumed by the column. This doesn't help users who may not know about the column's existence when they try to use the table. An INSERT statement, for instance, would fail if they didn't include a value for the dropped column. If you create a view that excludes the missing column, the view can now be used in place of the table and the dropped column will no longer be a problem.

To make the column's disappearance even more transparent to the users, you can first rename the table and then use the original table name to name the view that excludes the unwanted column:

1. Issue the following command to prevent table access under the old name:
   ```
   RENAME table_name TO new_table_name;
   ```

2. Build the required view with this command:
   ```
   CREATE VIEW table_name (...)
   AS SELECT ... FROM new_table_name;
   ```

   Make sure that you name all but the unwanted column in the list of column names (shown as ... in the preceding statement) and use the new name for the table in the FROM clause.

3. Grant the same permissions on the view that existed on the table.

The following CREATE VIEW statement will result in a view that apparently removes the PHONE column from the EMPLOYEE table:

```
CREATE VIEW emp AS
SELECT id, last_name, first_name, middle_initial,
    department, salary, title, hire_date
FROM
 employee
/
```

> **Updating views may not always be possible**
>
> If you have views that participate in table joins, your users may not be able to update them or perform other DML commands on them. For detailed information on the rules governing updatable views, see the later section "Updating Data Through Views."

Hiding Data with Views

Some tables may contain sensitive data that shouldn't be seen by all users, or rows that aren't useful for some parts of the user community. So, although you may need certain users to see all the contents of a table, others should see only certain columns or rows, or even a subset of rows and columns. You can accomplish this by creating a view that contains only the elements that should be seen by the selected users and then granting them access to the view rather than to the table.

For a view that contains a subset of the columns, you can use the same approach as you would to create a view to hide a dropped column (the example in the preceding section shows the creation of such a view). A view that shows users only a subset of the rows is built by using an appropriate WHERE clause. You can restrict column and row access by building a view with a SELECT clause to identify just the required rows and a WHERE clause to choose the desired rows.

The following command shows the creation of such a view. It's based on the EMPLOYEE table from the earlier section "Using Views to Prebuild Queries," but includes only employees in Department 103. Therefore, it doesn't show the department column, nor does it include salary information:

```
CREATE VIEW dept_103 AS
SELECT id, last_name, first_name, middle_initial,
  title, phone, hire_date
FROM employee
WHERE department = 103
/
```

Hiding Complicated Queries

Your users and applications may need to execute fairly complicated queries that contain multiple table joins, or *subqueries*, and combinations of these. If such a query is needed on a regular basis, you might consider creating a view that embodies the query. The user or application can then simply query the view without being concerned with the complexity of the underlying query. This will reduce the possibility of error as well as save time.

The following code builds a view that could be used for an online phone directory service based on the EMPLOYEE table (for the name and phone number) and the DEPARTMENT table, which it references (for the department name). Although it's not very complicated in terms of the number of columns and tables involved, it does provide a standard format for the output, using SQL functions and operators:

```
CREATE VIEW phone_list (name, department, phone) AS SELECT
    UPPER(last_name) || ', ' ||
    INITCAP(first_name) || ' ' ||
    UPPER(middle_initial) || '.',
    department_name, e.phone
FROM employee e, department d
WHERE department =  d.id
/
```

Although the phone listing might be usefully ordered by the NAME field, a view can't contain an ORDER BY clause. A query against the view PHONE_LIST (created in the previous command) to show an alphabetical listing of all employees' phone information would have to include its own ORDER BY clause. The command would be

```
SELECT * FROM phone_list ORDER BY name;
```

The ordering column is the name from the view definition, not from the columns in the base table on which it's based.

Accessing Remote Databases Transparently with Views

To access a table on a remote database, a statement needs to identify the table name plus a *database link* name for Oracle to find the correct remote database and table. (For information on database links, see the *Oracle8 Server Distributed Systems* manual.) The link name is concatenated to the table name with a commercial "at" (@) symbol. To hide this structure from users and applications, you can create a view that embodies the table and link name. If you needed to reach the EMPLOYEE table in San Francisco from a different database on the network, you could create a database link named SF to point to the San Francisco database and then build a view to hide this link's use. The following shows one version of the command to build the link and then the command to build the view:

```
CREATE DATABASE LINK sf
    CONNECT TO emp_schema IDENTIFIED BY emp_password
    USING 'sfdb'
/
CREATE VIEW employee AS SELECT * FROM employee@sf
/
```

Obviously, you can create a view to meet any one of a number of requirements. In some cases, you may need a view to help with a number of issues. There's no reason that the view to access the remote EMPLOYEE, created in the preceding code, couldn't also restrict access to the salary column while renaming the ID column TASK_ASSIGNEE.

Creating and Handling Invalid Views

In some circumstances, you may need to create a view but find that you don't have the permissions on the base table, or that the table you know should exist isn't available. In such cases, you can create an invalid view that will remain unusable until the underlying table(s) is accessible by you. To do this, use the keyword FORCE following the CREATE keyword in your command to define the view.

A view can also become invalid at a later time due to changes in the underlying table. Whenever a view is invalid, Oracle will return an error message if you try to execute a statement that refers to the view. After the underlying problem is fixed, the view should work normally again.

Dropping and Modifying Views

Dropping a view simply requires issuing the DROP VIEW command to remove the view definition from the data dictionary. No space will be recovered because a view doesn't own any data.

Once in a while, you may need to change the definition of a view. Although this can be done by dropping the view and then re-creating it with the new definition, this might not be a desirable approach. If the view has been granted to users, dropping the view will lose the privileges. Dropping a view that's referenced in triggers or stored procedures causes these objects to be invalidated, requiring a recompile attempt next time they're used, even if you add the new view definition immediately.

To preserve the integrity of the users and objects dependent on a view, you can modify the view's definition without having to drop it first. This is done with the OR REPLACE option of the CREATE command. By issuing the CREATE OR REPLACE VIEW... command, you can use a different SELECT clause from that in the existing view without the view disappearing from the data dictionary at any time.

You can even modify a view such that a valid view becomes invalid or an invalid view becomes valid, or modify an invalid view to become a different invalid view. If the resulting view would be invalid, you must include the FORCE keyword after the CREATE OR REPLACE clause. Otherwise, the view won't be changed from its previous definition.

Updating Data Through Views

Although views are used primarily for queries, they can be used for other types of SQL statements. Rows can be inserted and deleted via a view on a single table when there are no set or DISTINCT operators in the view, nor any GROUP BY, CONNECT BY, or START WITH clauses. For row inserts, no columns excluded from the view can be defined as NOT NULL or be part of the PRIMARY KEY constraint (which implies NOT NULL).

Updates can also be performed via a view on a single table and, in some cases, through a view on joined tables. For a single table, updates are limited by the same restrictions as inserts and deletes. In the case of a view across a join, only one table can be updated in a single statement. Furthermore, there must be a unique index on at least one column in the joined view, and the columns from the table being updated must all be updatable. To see whether a column in a view is updatable, you can query the table DBA_UPDATABLE_COLUMNS (or USER_UPDATABLE_COLUMNS).

Don't expect users to be able to use invalid views

Just as when you create a view with the FORCE option, any modification that requires the FORCE keyword or that otherwise makes a view invalid renders the view unusable. Nobody can use the view name in a SQL statement successfully until the view is revalidated.

Understanding Oracle terminology for updatable join views

Oracle uses the term *key-preserved tables* when discussing the update options on views involving table joins. A table is key-preserved in a join view if every key of the table, whether or not it's included in the view's SELECT clause, would still be a valid key following a change to the columns seen in the view. Only key-preserved tables can be updated through the view.

View Consistency

As we've seen, you can create views to restrict the visible rows in the base table. Also, you've learned that you can update a view on a single table. One concern you might have is how these two characteristics work together. Suppose that I use the view DEPT_103, created earlier in the section "Hiding Data with Views," and update it. If I update the employee's title, there shouldn't be a problem. But what if I update one record to change the department number to 242? Now the row doesn't belong to the view and may not be a row I can officially see.

You can add a refinement to views that restrict access to certain rows within a table. This refinement prevents users from modifying a row that they can see through the view to contain a value that they aren't allowed to see. This is done by including the key phrase WITH READ ONLY or WITH CHECK OPTION to the view definition. WITH READ ONLY doesn't allow any changes to be made to the base table through the view, so you can't perform an insert or a delete, or complete any updates, on the underlying table. WITH CHECK OPTION, on the other hand, does allow any of these operations as long as the resulting rows are still visible under the view definition. If you want, you can give WITH CHECK OPTION a name by using a CONSTRAINT keyword, just as for other types of constraints (see Chapter 17). The following command shows how you can create a view with a named CHECK OPTION:

```
CREATE VIEW dept_103 AS
SELECT id, last_name, first_name, middle_initial,
   title, phone, hire_date
FROM employee
WHERE department = 103
WITH CHECK OPTION CONSTRAINT dept_103_dept_ck
/
```

The name given to the CHECK OPTION here follows a suggested naming standard developed for constraints.

SEE ALSO

➤ *For more information on naming constraints, see page* *477*

Adding Segments for Different Types of Indexes

Create indexes to improve data access

Select index organization scheme

Restructure indexes for performance improvements

Monitor indexes for efficient space utilization

Why indexes are important

Imagine looking for a document in a filing cabinet that contains documents in a random order. You might have to look at each and every document before finding what you're looking for. The effort required to find the document will increase as the size of the filing cabinet and the number of documents within it increases. A database without an *index* is similar to such an unorganized filing cabinet. More than 50 percent of systems reporting a performance problem suffer from lack of an index or from the absence of an optimum index.

Why Index?

Although the primary reason for adding *index*es to tables is to speed data retrieval, you may use indexes for these additional reasons:

- To enforce uniqueness with a *constraint*
- To store data in an *index cluster*
- To reduce locking contention on a *foreign key constraint*
- To provide an alternate source of data

The first and third items are discussed in more detail in Chapter 17, "Using Constraints to Improve Your Application Performance," which is devoted to integrity constraints. Index clusters, mentioned in the second bullet, are covered in Chapter 18, "Using Indexes, Clusters, Caching, and Sorting Effectively." The fourth item needs some additional comments here.

SEE ALSO

➤ *To learn about using indexes with unique constraints, see page **491***

➤ *How to use indexes with foreign key constraints, page **494***

➤ *How to create and manage index clusters, page **513***

Oracle tries to avoid accessing any more blocks than necessary when executing SQL statements. If a query is written in such a way that an index can be used to identify which rows are needed, the server process finds the required index entries. The process usually uses the *rowid*s—pointers to the file, block, and record where the data is stored—to find the required block and move it into memory, if it's not already there. However, if the columns in the query's SELECT clause are all present in the index entry, the server process simply retrieves the values from the index entry and thus avoids the additional block search in the table itself. This technique, the biggest benefit of which is saving time, can also help out if there's a problem with the base table or the file where it's stored. Queries that can be satisfied from index entries will continue to function, even if the base table is unavailable.

Figure 8.1 explains the basic concept of locating data with an index. The user looking for specific information first looks for a keyword in the index. This keyword can be easily located because the index is sorted. The index contains the keyword with the detailed information's address. The desired data is quickly located by using this address information.

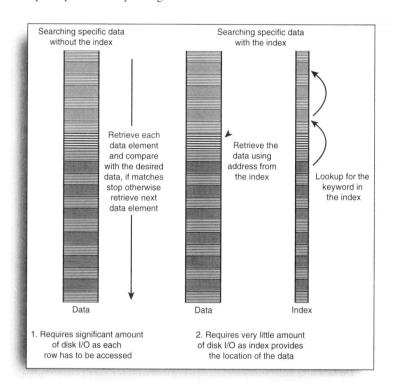

Searching specific data without the index

Searching specific data with the index

Retrieve each data element and compare with the desired data, if matches stop otherwise retrieve next data element

Retrieve the data using address from the index

Lookup for the keyword in the index

Data

Data

Index

1. Requires significant amount of disk I/O as each row has to be accessed

2. Requires very little amount of disk I/O as index provides the location of the data

FIGURE 8.1

Indexes provide a quick access path to the data.

An Oracle index is a structure, maintained as an independent segment, that contains an ordered set of entries from one or more columns in a table. These ordered entries are stored on a set of blocks known as *leaf blocks*. To provide fast access to any specific value in these leaf blocks, a structure of pointers is also maintained in the index. These pointers are stored on *branch blocks*. Each branch block contains pointers for a specific range of indexed values. The pointers themselves may point to a leaf block where the value can be found, or to another branch block that contains a specific subset of the value range.

Oracle uses a *b*tree* index structure, which guarantees that the chain (or number of blocks that must be examined to get from the highest level branch block to the required leaf block) is the same no matter what value is being requested. The number of blocks, or levels, in such a chain defines the height of a b*tree. The larger the height, the greater the number of blocks that have to be examined to reach the leaf block, and consequently, the slower the index. Figure 8.2 shows the logical structure of a b*tree index.

FIGURE 8.2

A b*tree index consists of a set of ordered leaf blocks with a structure of branch blocks to aid navigation to the leaves.

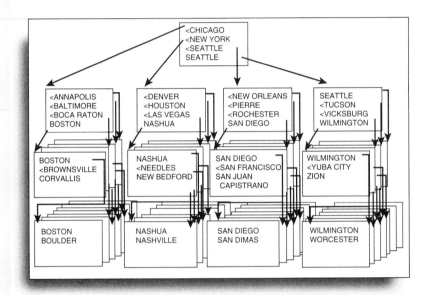

When a leaf block fills up, an empty block is recruited to be a new leaf block; some records from the full block are moved into this new block. This activity is called "splitting a block." The branch block pointing to the original leaf block adds a new entry for the split block. If the branch block doesn't have room for the new entry, it also splits. This, in turn, requires that the branch block pointing to it needs to add a new entry for the split block. The very first branch block, called the "root block," is at the top of the index. If it fills up, it too will split, but in this case the original root block and the split block become the second level in the b*tree. A new root block is created, pointing initially to the two blocks that are now at the next level.

The Mechanics of Index Block Splits

Most indexes will fall into one of two categories—new entries will be randomly inserted between existing values, or new entries will always have a larger value than any existing value. The former is most often found on columns of character data, such as a last name column. The latter would typically be an index on a numeric *primary key* column, where a *sequence generator* or some other tool is used to increment the value of each new entry.

In indexes where values are inserted in an apparent random order, very few entries will be stored on the very last leaf block, but are placed on a leaf block somewhere in the sorted sequence of leaf blocks. When one of these blocks fills up and has to be split, Oracle can't make any assumptions about future entries that might be added in the same value range. Therefore, it splits the block in the middle, leaving the first 50 percent of the entries on the current block and moving the second 50 percent of the entries to the new leaf block. This 50–50 split maximizes the available space for new entries that, statistically, are just as likely to fall in the first part of the range as in the second.

When a new index entry has a higher value than other current entries, it will be added to the last leaf block in the index. When this block fills up and needs to be split, Oracle may not perform a 50–50 block split. If the new entry is the highest value so far, Oracle simply adds a new leaf block and stores just the new record on it. In indexes where all new entries have higher values, this scheme will provide the maximum possible space on the new leaf block. That is where all new entries will be stored. It also saves the overhead of moving 50 percent of the entries from the current leaf block, which would free up space that would never be used anyway.

Splitting the last leaf block

The algorithm for splitting the last index leaf block is optimal when the index is on a column that contains ever-increasing values, such as sequence numbers. Only the last entry is moved to the split block, leaving the preceding entries in place. On rare occasions, the index entry on a column containing unordered data, such as last names, causes the last leaf block to split. If the value is currently the highest in the index in such cases, the split will place just this entry on the new leaf block. This can lead to a further block split if other values need to be inserted in the former last leaf block. Although this is less efficient than splitting the block 50–50 the first time it fills, it occurs too infrequently to be a significant performance factor.

Managing a Standard B*Tree Index

The most common type of index is a standard b*tree index. We will take some time examining the various characteristics of this index type and learn how to build and manage one. If you've read through Chapter 5, "Managing Your Database Space," or Chapter 17, you're already introduced to some index issues. Chapter 5 emphasizes the general usefulness of placing indexes in their own tablespaces, away from the tables on which they're built. Chapter 17 briefly discusses the management of indexes required to support certain types of constraints.

SEE ALSO

➤ *For information on tablespace usage for different segment types, see page* ***133***

➤ *To see when to use b*tree indexes, see page* ***506***

Before proceeding, you need to be introduced to two terms that appear throughout this chapter. A *composite index*, also called a *concatenated index*, is an index that you create on multiple columns within a table.

Sizing an Index

As mentioned in Chapter 5, an index is typically smaller than the table on which it's based. This is because the index generally contains only a subset of the columns from the table and thus requires less storage for each entry than is taken by an entire row. If the index is on many or even all columns, though, it will almost certainly be larger than the table it's indexing. This is because each index entry stores not just the data from the table's columns, but also a rowid, which embodies the physical location of the row in the table. In addition, the index stores one or more branch blocks at every level of the b*tree structure. A table does not need any such blocks; it stores only the data itself.

Another space issue for an index is the use of empty space. When new rows are being added to a table, the rows can be stored on any available block. As blocks fill, rows are placed on empty blocks and continue to be stored there until they too get full. This can't be done with index entries because they're stored in a specific order. Even if a block is almost empty, Oracle can't store an index entry on it if the entry doesn't belong in the range of values now assigned to that block. Following a block split, an index will have two partially full blocks, neither of which can be used for entries outside either block range. A table, on the other hand, doesn't have to move records around when blocks fill up; it simply adds new records to empty blocks, which it can then continue to fill with other new rows, regardless of their values.

As discussed in Chapter 7, "Adding Segments for Tables," Oracle provides detailed descriptions of algorithms that you can

---

Column order in composite indexes can differ from the table

The columns in a composite index may be defined in any order, irrespective of their order in the base table definition. They don't even have to be built on columns adjacent to each other in the underlying table.

use to estimate the total space required by various types of segments. As with computations for table sizes, some of the numbers you have to plug into the formulae are estimates. These include the average lengths of fields stored in indexed columns and estimates of how many rows will have NULLs in the indexed columns, if any. The calculations don't take into account how many block splits might occur while data is being added to the index, so they become less and less reliable for sizing long-term growth. The space required for branch blocks is included for in the calculations, but it's simply based on an expected ratio of branch blocks to leaf blocks. The actual number of branch blocks required depends on the number of distinct values in the index, a factor that isn't included in the space estimate.

You don't really need to know how big an index will be before you create one, unless you're very short of disk space. In this case, you should ensure that you'll have sufficient space for the entire index. Unlike a table, you rarely need to read an entire index from start to finish, so there's no real requirement to keep its blocks on contiguous disk space. Therefore, you don't need to define large extents for an index; you can afford to create it or let it grow via many small extents. Again, you don't need to have very precise sizing predictions if you plan to use small extents— you won't end up wasting too much space even if the last extent isn't very full, something you can't be sure of if you use large extents. If you want to work on the detailed sizing calculations, you can find Oracle's formulae in Appendix A of the *Oracle8 Server Administrator's Guide*.

SEE ALSO
➤ *Get table-sizing details on page* ***201***

Creating an Index

In Chapter 18, "Using Indexes, Clusters, Caching, and Sorting Effectively," you learn what criteria help determine how useful an index would be in optimizing queries or other table access. The other main reasons to use an index were summarized at the start of this chapter. In this section it's assumed you've determined that you need a standard b*tree index on an existing table. You look at the syntax and how to use it to build an effective

Sizing an index with sample data

I recommend that, if you have good sample data, you should consider building a test index with this data and extrapolate the full index size based on the size of the test index. If you don't have good sample data, it's a somewhat pointless exercise to evaluate the index size by using Oracle's calculations— your input will be a guess.

Reuse table-sizing scripts

You may want to look at the sizing section in Chapter 7 and review the scripts that compute sizing requirements for tables based on sample data. These scripts can be modified, if you want to use them, to estimate overall index size.

index. Most indexes you build will use the CREATE INDEX command. In Chapter 17 you can find out about indexes that Oracle builds automatically, if they're needed, to support certain integrity constraints.

SEE ALSO

➤ *For information on constraints that require indexes, see pages 491 and 493*

The syntax for the CREATE INDEX command to build a standard b*tree index on a table is shown in Listing 8.1.

Numbering of code lines

Line numberings were included in Listing 8.1 and other code listings to make discussion about this code easier to reference. The numbers should not be included with any command-line commands, as part of any Oracle scripts, or within SQL statements.

LISTING 8.1   **Creating an index with the *CREATE INDEX* command**

```
01:  CREATE [UNIQUE] INDEX [index_schema.]index_name
02:      ON [table_schema.]table_name (
03:      column_name [ASC][DESC] [,...] )
04:      [parallel_clause]
05:      [NO[LOGGING]]
06:      [TABLESPACE tablespace_name]
07:      [NOSORT]
08:      [storage_clause]
09:      [space_utilization_clause]
```

CREATE INDEX...ON on lines 1 and 2 are the required keywords for the command.

On line 1, UNIQUE creates an index in which every entry must be different from every other entry; by default, an index is non-unique and allows duplicate entries. *index_schema* is the name of the owner of the index; by default, it's the user creating the index. Finally, *index_name* is the name given to the index.

On line 2, *table_schema* is the name of the owner of the table on which the index is being built; by default, it's assumed to be in the schema of the user creating the index. Also on line 2, *table_name* is the name of the table on which the index is being created.

column_name on line 3 is the name of the index's leading column. You can include up to 31 additional columns, as long as the total length of an entry is less than half of the Oracle block size for the database.

Also on line 3, ASC and DESC are keywords provided for compatibility with standards; they have no impact on how the index is created. You can use only one of these two keywords per column, but you can apply either one to different columns in a composite index. Finally, [, . . .] indicates that you can include more than one column in the index, naming them in a comma-separated list.

On line 4, parallel_clause is one of

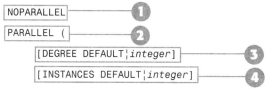

① Causes all access to index to be serialized

② Allows some parallel access

③ Set the number of query slaves to be used in an instance to build index in parallel; only one format can be used per statement

④ Set number of parallel server instances to be used when building index with internode parallel operations; only one format can be used per statement

On line 5 of Listing 8.1, LOGGING and NOLOGGING determine whether creation of the index and subsequent activities will be logged (LOGGING, the default) or not logged (NOLOGGING) into the redo logs. The additional activities subject to this setting are direct loads through SQL*Loader and direct-load INSERT commands.

TABLESPACE *tablespace_name* on line 6 identifies the tablespace where the index will be created. By default, it's built in the default tablespace of the user creating the index.

On line 7 of Listing 8.1, NOSORT is used to prevent a sort when the rows are stored in the table in ascending order by the index key. The CREATE INDEX command will fail if any row is out of order. By default, Oracle assumes that the rows aren't in order and sorts the indexed data.

The *storage_clause* on line 8 is as follows:

```
STORAGE (
    [INITIAL integer [K¦M]]
    [NEXT integer [K¦M]]
    [PCTINCREASE integer]
    [MINEXTENTS integer]
    [MAXEXTENTS [integer¦UNLIMITED]]
    [FREELISTS integer]
    [FREELIST GROUPS integer]
    [BUFFER POOL [KEEP¦RECYCLE¦DEFAULT]]  )
```

When to use CREATE INDEX's NOSORT option

Oracle's tables, like all relational tables, aren't guaranteed to be stored in any specific order. For **NOSORT** to work when you're creating an index, the table must have been loaded by using a single process with no parallel operations, and with a source of data already sorted in the order of the indexed column(s). The rows can be entered manually, one row at a time with **INSERT** statements, or with SQL*Loader in conventional or direct mode. The index needs to be created following such a load, before any additional DML statements are issued against the table; the row order may not be preserved by such commands.

Order of columns in a composite index

If you're building a composite index and aren't sure which columns will be referenced most often, create the index with the columns ordered from the most to the least discriminating. For example, an index on the honorific (Mr., Ms., Dr., and so on), the first initial, and the last name columns: Put the last name first (many different values), the first initial (26 values), and the honorific (a handful of values).

- STORAGE is the required keyword. With no STORAGE clause, or for any optional storage components not included in the STORAGE clause, the value will be inherited from the tablespace's default settings.

- INITIAL *integer* is the size, in bytes, of the first extent.

- K and M change bytes to kilobytes or megabytes, respectively.

- NEXT *integer* is the size of the second extent.

- PCTINCREASE *integer* is the multiplier applied to the size of each subsequent extent following the second extent.

- MINEXTENTS *integer* is the number of extents built when the index is created.

- MAXEXTENTS *integer* and MAXEXTENTS UNLIMITED are the maximum number of extents allowed for the index, where you must provide a number or the keyword UNLIMITED, but not both.

- FREELISTS *integer* is the number of freelists assigned to the index; the default value is 1.

- FREELIST GROUPS *integer* is the number of freelist groups assigned to the index; the default value is 1.

- BUFFER POOL defines the default buffer pool for the index blocks. Only one option is allowed:

KEEP	Assigns blocks to the kept buffer pool
RECYCLE	Assigns blocks to the recycle buffer pool
DEFAULT	Assigns blocks to neither pool; this is the default if you don't include the BUFFER POOL option

The *space_utilization_clause* on line 9 is as follows:

1 Reserves space for new entries on a block (default is 10)

2 Sets number of transaction slots reserved in each block (default is 2)

3 Sets maximum number of transaction slots that can be created in a block (default is 255)

PCTFREE *integer*	——— **1**
INITRANS *integer*	——— **2**
MAXTRANS *integer*	——— **3**

You don't have to name the columns in a composite index in the same order as they're defined in the table—nor do you, as this implies, have to use adjacent columns. Your best option is to include the most queried column first—a query that provides a value for the leading column of a composite index can use the index to find the required rows, even if the indexed columns aren't referenced by the query. You should include the other columns in descending order of frequency of reference for the same reason—Oracle can use as many of the leading columns of an index as are identified in an SQL statement's WHERE clause.

SEE ALSO

➤ *Find out more about parallel operations, page 603*

➤ *For information about SQL*Loader and its options, including direct and parallel direct loads, see page 658*

Unique Indexes

You should rarely need to create an index as UNIQUE. A unique constraint, rather than a unique index, should be used to enforce uniqueness between rows. A unique constraint does use an index, and you can create one for this purpose as discussed in Chapter 17, but it doesn't have to be a unique index.

A composite unique index will ensure only that the set of values in each entry is distinct from all other values. It will allow the same value to be repeated in a column multiple times, as long as at least one other column has a different value from any existing entry. An entry will be stored in the index if at least one column has a non-NULL value. A NULL value in a column will be treated as potentially containing the same value as another NULL value in that same column. Consequently, an entry containing one or more NULLs, but with all the same values in the non-NULL columns, would be considered in violation of the unique condition. A row with these characteristics therefore couldn't be stored.

NULLs aren't considered for uniqueness

A row with a NULL in the indexed column won't be recorded in the index, so a unique index won't prevent multiple rows with a NULL in the indexed column from being stored.

Index Sort Order

All indexes are created with the values in ascending order, regardless of the ASC or DESC options settings on each column. Internally, indexes can be scanned in either direction, due to forward and backward pointers between the leaf blocks.

ASC and DESC index options

The options for ordering indexes in ascending or descending order via the ASC and DESC keywords are included only for compliance with SQL standards. Retrieval from an Oracle index in either direction is equally efficient.

Check availability of parallel server processes

Parallel operations on indexes, as well as any other Oracle objects, will occur only if your instance (or instances) is running with a sufficient number of parallel server processes available. This is determined by the **PARALLEL_ MIN_SERVERS** and **PARALLEL_MAX_SERVERS** parameter settings in your initialization file.

Parallel Operations on Indexes

Unless your index is partitioned, only the creation of the index can be processed in parallel. Subsequent access to the index will be done through a single serial server. Without the parallel clause in the CREATE INDEX command, the creation will also be serial, regardless of the underlying table's definition. The PARALLEL clause's INSTANCES option is of significance only if you're running Oracle Parallel Server.

Parallel creation is usually much faster than serial creation, particularly if you have multiple CPUs on your database server and the table is striped across multiple disk drives. For this reason, you may want to build all your indexes with an appropriate degree of parallelism (and number of instances, if applicable). In particular, you should consider creating any indexes needed to enforce constraints with the CREATE INDEX command so that you can include the PARALLEL clause. You don't have the option of defining a parallel operation when an index is built automatically as a result of creating or enabling the constraint.

SEE ALSO

➤ *Read about partitioned indexes and their parent segments, page* **742**

Logging Index Operations

Index activities affected by the NOLOGGING option

In addition to the creation of the index, the two other activities that aren't logged when the NOLOGGING option is in place are direct loads with SQL*Loader and direct load inserts with the INSERT...SELECT command.

You can speed the processing of your CREATE INDEX commands by not creating redo log entries. After you're done, however, you should try to back up the tablespace where the index is stored—recovery following a media failure can't reconstruct the index correctly without the normally created redo log entries. In addition, you should repeat the backup any time you perform one of the other operations that won't be logged due to the NOLOGGING setting, for exactly the same reason. Of course, in some cases you may not realize that a subsequent operation isn't generating redo entries.

To avoid any problems with future unlogged changes to your index, you might want to turn on logging after its creation. You can still create the index without logs—use the ALTER INDEX command after it's built.

If you don't include the LOGGING or NOLOGGING option in the CREATE INDEX command, the index will be built in, and future activities will use logging mode for non-partitioned indexes. Partitioned indexes will acquire their logging mode from the parent segment.

Index Tablespaces

By default, indexes are created in your default tablespace just like any other segment. Chapter 5 explains why you should consider using different tablespaces for tables and for the indexes on them. Your default tablespace is typically the one where you build your tables, which probably isn't where you want your indexes. It's important to consider where you really want any new index to be created and, if necessary, to include the TABLESPACE clause in your CREATE INDEX command.

Index Space-Utilization Parameters

The space-utilization parameters behave differently for indexes than for tables, which can be confusing:

- PCTFREE sets a percentage of each block aside for use by new index entries. Unlike a table, however, this space is reserved only during the initial index creation. After that, the block will fill up as much as possible—even though each new entry will exceed PCTFREE—because index entries must be stored in a specific order.

  If the initial load filled every block to its capacity, later insertions into the range of values on any block would cause a block split. To reduce the number of such splits, you should reserve space for new entries in indexes where they're likely to occur. Generally, new entries are likely to be needed between other values in alphanumeric data, such as people's names, telephone numbers, or street addresses. Numeric primary keys generally consist of an increasing numeric value, so all new entries will go to the end of the index. Such indexes don't need to reserve free space for new entries into existing blocks.

- Because an index block has to contain entries within a certain value range, deletions from the block don't necessarily make the block available for new entries. The space will be reused only if a new entry has a value that allows it to fit between the dropped entry's adjacent entries. No PCTUSED space-utilization parameter is required to control this behavior.

- INITRANS has to have a minimum value of 2, not 1 (as in a table). The second *transaction slot* is required if the block has to be split. This operation occurs during the user's transaction, which is assigned to one transaction slot and is performed by a second transaction initiated by SYS. SYS is assigned to another slot.

Creating Indexes at the Right Time

Unless you have a table that has all its rows physically stored in the order of an index that you need (in which case you can use the NOSORT option), the indexed columns will have to be sorted as part of the index creation. The only way you can guarantee that rows will be in the required order is if you sort them first and load them in that order, after which you prevent any further DML against the table until the index is built.

Drop indexes that have frequent block splits

Indexes prone to block splitting are good candidates for dropping during periods of heavy DML—either because they're old and have no more free space for new rows on many of their blocks, or because their entries are frequently updated (which results in a DELETE of the old entry and an INSERT of the new, so that ordering is preserved). They can be recreated immediately or, if performance doesn't suffer too much without them, when the underlying table is no longer so busy.

After an index is built, any changes to the underlying table that affect the indexed columns will be automatically included in the index. This adds to the overhead of processing the statements. Unless you need the index to speed the processing or to support concurrent query processing, you should consider dropping it during periods of heavy activity against the table.

Monitoring Space Usage

As mentioned earlier, the space freed in an index when an entry is deleted isn't available to any new entry added. The "hole" left by the deleted entry is in a specific location in the sort order of the index. For a simple analogy, consider a file cabinet. The drawers correspond to an index leaf block and the folders within are akin to index entries, assuming that they're filed in alphabetical order. If you discard a folder labeled BROWN, it leaves room in the file cabinet between the folders labeled BRONX and BRUIN. If you need to file a new folder for GREEN, you won't place it in the drawer from where the BROWN folder was taken, but in the drawer with the other GR... folders—say, between GRAY and GREY. However, a new folder for BROWNING could legitimately occupy the space vacated by the old BROWN folder.

An index works in much the same way. Freed space can be reused only if the entry's value allows it to fit into the value range opened by the deleted entry.

Index leaf entries aren't dropped only when their corresponding row is dropped from the table, but also when the row is updated, if the update affects the indexed column(s). An update is equivalent to taking a folder from the theoretical file cabinet, changing the label (say, from BROWN to WHITE), and then refiling it. The folder is obviously not going to be of any use filed in its original position; it has to be inserted in the correct position among the other folders beginning with W. As far as the index is concerned, the old entry is removed and a new one is created. The space left behind by the removed entry is subject to reuse in the same way as space left by an actual record deletion.

As you can possibly see, an index on a table that undergoes a lot of updates and deletions can end up with lots of free space that may or may not become reusable, depending on the nature of new records being inserted into the table. One type of table and corresponding index will very likely generate lots of free space on the leaf blocks. This is a table with a primary key based on some form of sequence number, either obtained from an Oracle sequence generator or created by the application.

Consider an ORDERS table that has an index on the ORDER_NUMBER column and where each new order is given the next highest unused number. Orders are added to the table when they're received and dropped after having been filled and the invoice paid. Over time the leaf blocks with the older orders start emptying out as they're filled and paid. In most cases they will become completely empty, and then they can be recycled for use with new orders. What if some are from delinquent customers who have never paid the bill, or for standing orders that remain in the system for years? The leaf blocks containing such order numbers will have to be maintained, even if there's just one order on them. The free space on these blocks can't be reused by new orders because they will have numbers much higher than the range reserved for these blocks.

Consider order numbers 1023 and 3345 on two separate index blocks (on blocks 22 and 28, for example). The blocks between these blocks—23 through 27—may have already been emptied and recycled with higher order numbers. However, the pointers between adjacent leaf blocks that allow an index to be scanned in ascending or descending order will "connect" blocks 22 and 28. Any order outside the range of 1023–3345 therefore can't be placed on either block because it would be out of logical order.

It's possible for an index to gradually become burdened by a large number of almost empty blocks. Such an index wastes disk space and results in slow access for values on the sparsely populated blocks. This chapter discusses an index option (reverse-key indexing) that can help you avoid this type of situation.

You should regularly evaluate the space usage—and hence, efficiency—of your indexes. Over time you'll learn which indexes are prone to space problems and which aren't, due to their underlying tables being relatively static or the indexed values being random and, hence, able to reuse space. You can use an ANALYZE command's option to see how well or how poorly an index is using its space, particularly with respect to deleted entries.

The following command will populate the INDEX_STATS view with statistical information about the index:

```
ANALYZE INDEX [schema.]index_name VALIDATE STRUCTURE
```

Of particular interest are the columns LF_ROWS and DEL_LF_ROWS, which show the current number of entry slots in leaf blocks. They also show the total number of entries deleted from leaf blocks, respectively, and LF_ROWS_LEN and DEL_LF_ROWS_LEN, which show the total number of bytes associated with these entries. A rule of thumb is that when the number of, or space used by, deleted entries is greater than 20 percent of total entries, you

---

Using the INDEX_STATS view

INDEX_STATS is a temporary view created by the ANALYZE INDEX...VALIDATE STRUCTURE command. It exists only for the duration of the session that created it and can contain information for only one index at a time. If you execute a second ANALYZE INDEX...VALIDATE STRUCTURE command in your session, the INDEX_STATS view will contain only information about the second index analyzed. Only the session that created it can see the INDEX_STATS view, so another user—or even your userid connected to a different session—won't see the view. When you log out of your session, the view is removed and you'll need to rerun the ANALYZE command to recreate it.

should consider rebuilding the index to reclaim the space. However, you should also check the PCT_USED column. If this is 80 percent or more—an average amount of space you can expect to see used in a typical index—you may not want to incur the work of rebuilding the index. You should continue to monitor it, however, to ensure that the statistics stay in the preferred ranges.

Monitoring the number of keys (leaf entries) versus the number of levels in the b*tree over time is another measure you can apply to an index to see if it's becoming overburdened with deleted entry space. The latter is shown under the HEIGHT column of INDEX_STATS and shouldn't change if the total number of index entries stays the same. If the index height keeps increasing, it indicates that more branch block levels are being added. This behavior is to be expected if more entries are being stored in the leaf blocks. If, on the other hand, the additional branch levels are supporting the same number (or thereabouts) of leaf entries, the structure is becoming top-heavy with branch blocks. This occurs when branch blocks are being maintained for partially emptied leaf blocks.

> **Build a history of index statistics**
>
> If you want to keep a record of an index's statistics over time, you can issue the command CREATE TABLE *table_name* AS SELECT * FROM index_stats, where you use a date or sequence number as well as the index name as part of *table_name*. Remember to do this before you end your session or issue another **ANALYZE** command.

The statistics in INDEX_STATS aren't used by the Oracle *optimizer*s, and the existence of the view in a session won't change the default optimizer behavior. This behavior is different from the statistics collected with the ANALYZE INDEX...COMPUTE STATISTICS or ANALYZE INDEX...ESTIMATE STATISTICS commands. However, if you use these commands, you'll see slightly different values in the DBA_INDEXES than you see in INDEX_STATS. This is because some values in the latter may reflect rows that have been deleted, whereas the values in the former are based only on the current index contents.

SEE ALSO
➤ *To learn more about the use of statistics by Oracle's optimizer, see page **439***

Rebuilding an Index

You may have a number of reasons to rebuild an index. Here are some of the more common reasons:

- To reclaim storage taken by deleted entries
- To move the index to a different tablespace

- To change the physical storage attributes
- To reset space utilization parameters

You can use two methods to make these changes. The first is to drop the index and recreate it by using the CREATE INDEX command discussed earlier in this chapter. The second is to use the REBUILD option of the ALTER INDEX command. Each method has its advantages and disadvantages, which Table 8.1 summarizes.

TABLE 8.1   **Alternatives for recreating an index**

Drop and Rebuild:	Use *REBUILD* Option:
Can rename index	Can't rename index
Can change between UNIQUE and non-UNIQUE	Can't change between UNIQUE and non-UNIQUE
Can change between b*tree and bitmap	Can't change between b*tree and bitmap
Needs space for only one copy of the index	Needs space for duplicate index temporarily
Requires a sort if data exists	Never requires a sort
Index temporarily unavailable for queries	Index remains available for queries
Can't use this method if index is used to support a constraint	Can use this method for an index supporting a constraint

The biggest advantage to dropping and recreating your index is that you don't need space for the original index and the new index to exist at the same time. However, you can't assume that this means the process has no overhead. To build the new version of the index, Oracle will have to perform a sort of the column data in all the existing rows. This will require memory and, for large tables, may even require the use of temporary segments on disk. The sort process will also be time-consuming for a large table, and the index will be unavailable between the time it's dropped and new version is ready. As you may guess, the sort space overhead and time for the work to be done are the biggest disadvantages to this approach.

If you elect to use the drop-and-recreate approach to rebuild an index, you need to issue the DROP INDEX command (discussed in the next section), and then use the appropriate CREATE INDEX command (discussed earlier in this chapter). If the index is now being used to enforce a constraint, you can't use this method—Oracle will prevent you from successfully dropping the index. Of course, you can temporarily disable the constraint as long as you're prepared to deal with any changes to the table that may prevent you from reenabling again.

The biggest advantages and disadvantages to the rebuild option are exactly the opposite of those for the drop-and-create option. When rebuilding an index, Oracle simply reads the leaf block information, which is already in sorted order, to create the new index. When the index is built, it drops the old copy automatically. Because a sort isn't required, the process is relatively fast. Also, it leaves the original index in place for use by queries that may occur concurrently with the rebuild. The disadvantage is that you must have room in your database for the current and new versions of the index simultaneously. This shouldn't be a problem if you're moving the index to a different tablespace, but may be a deterrent if you need to use the same tablespace.

The syntax of the ALTER INDEX...REBUILD command is as follows:

```
ALTER INDEX index_name
    REBUILD
    [parallel_clause]
    [NO[LOGGING]]
    [TABLESPACE tablespace_name]
    [NO[REVERSE]]
    [storage_clause]
    [space_utilization_clause]
```

The parallel_clause takes the same format as that discussed with the CREATE INDEX command. Here it determines whether the rebuilt operation itself can be done in parallel. If it can, each parallel server process will be responsible for retrieving a subset of the current entries and building the new leaf blocks for them. This may cause more extents to be used than a serial rebuild because each slave process will create and use its own extents. Some of these extents may be trimmed back at the end of the operation to remove any unused blocks.

The REVERSE/NOREVERSE option determines whether the replacement index is (REVERSE) or isn't (NOREVERSE) a *reverse-key index*. You read more about reverse-key indexes later in this chapter; for now, simply note that this option allows you to build the replacement either way, regardless of how the current index is structured.

The TABLESPACE option can be used if you want to move the index to a different tablespace. If you don't include this option, the index will be rebuilt in the same tablespace as the original index, not in your default tablespace.

The other clauses in the command all work exactly as they do for the CREATE INDEX command. You can refer to the earlier section, "Creating an Index," where this command and these options are explained in detail.

Dropping an Index

Unless your index was created for you when a constraint was enabled, you should be able to drop it at any time. You may decide to drop an index for any number of reasons, including the need to recreate it (as discussed in the previous section). You may also want to drop an index because it's no longer being used by the statements accessing the table, or because you're going to perform a major data load (or other intensive DML activity) and don't want to incur the overhead of concurrently maintaining the index. Parallel direct data loads, in particular, can't maintain any indexes on a table, so you should always drop them before using this loading technique.

The syntax for dropping an index is very straightforward:

```
DROP INDEX [schema.]index_name
```

You need to include the schema name only if the index doesn't belong to you.

If you need to drop an index that's supporting a constraint, you must first disable or drop the constraint. You can find details on these steps in Chapter 17. If the index had been created automatically as part of the constraint definition and enabling, it will also be dropped automatically.

Back up your work after executing commands without redo entries

If you select the NOLOGGING option, you may want to back up the tablespace in which the new index resides as soon as possible. This option will preclude the creation of redo log entries for the replacement index build just as it does when used with the **CREATE INDEX** command, with the same consequences discussed.

Managing Bitmap Indexes

A *bitmap index* is a special type of index particularly suited to large tables and to columns with a small number of distinct values. Their structure also makes them very efficient when two or more conditions have to be met by a query and the columns involved each have a bitmap index. This structure, however, makes them less efficient than a regular b*tree index when indexed columns are updated, or when rows are added or deleted from the table.

SEE ALSO

➤ *For when to use bitmap indexes, see page* **507**

Bitmap indexes behave like other indexes when created

After a bitmap index is created, it works behind the scenes just like any other index. The users don't have to do anything different to get a bitmap index to be used by a query than they do for a standard index. In addition, bitmap indexes are maintained transparently as records in the underlying table are inserted, updated, or deleted.

Bitmap Index Internals

A bitmap index is actually stored inside a regular b*tree index structure. The entries in the leaf blocks consist of a value, the rowid of the first row represented in the bitmap, the bitmap itself, and some entry-management bytes. These leaf block entries are stored in order by value, just as in a regular b*tree index, and the index can also contain branch blocks to speed access to a required leaf block value.

The value portion of the bitmap entries correspond to the values from the table's indexed column. A small table will have one entry for every distinct value in the column, including an entry for NULLs. The bitmap for each entry will contain a bit for every row in the table. Each bit will be set according to the value in the corresponding row—a 1 if the column's value matches the index value, a 0 if it doesn't. This means that there will be only one index entry with a 1-bit for any given row in the index. Figure 8.3 shows a logical view of a bitmap index on a column with four different values.

Even more bitmap index internals

Before storing them, Oracle applies a compression algorithm to the bitmaps; this reduces the space required to store consecutive bits with the same value. Although this makes the index more compact (and, hence, reduces the number of blocks that have to read into memory when it's being scanned), it slows the process of changing a bit's value. To help reduce the overhead of managing compressed bitmaps, each bitmap actually stores a bit for every potential row in its range rather than just for stored rows. In this way, only the bitmap containing the value for the indexed column(s) of a newly inserted row will need to have its bitmap changed, flipping the bit for the corresponding row from 0 to 1. The other bitmap values stay unchanged.

FIGURE 8.3

A bitmap index consists of index entries (values) and strings of bits (bitmaps) stored in a b*tree structure.

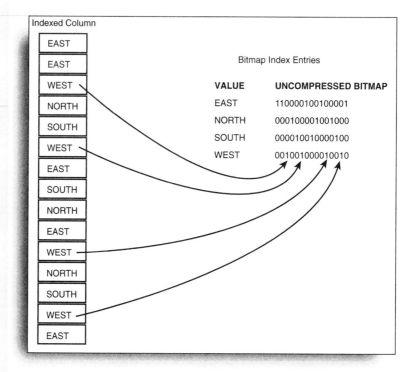

For larger tables, where bitmap indexes are most effective, a single bitmap can't store a bit for every row in the table. This is because each index entry—including the value, the bitmap, and the overhead bytes—must fit into less than half a block, a restriction placed on every Oracle index. To cover a large table, multiple index entries are created for each distinct value. Each entry contains a bitmap that represents a disjoint subset of the rows in the table. These bitmaps work the same way as described earlier—a rowid in each entry points to the first row covered by the entry's bitmap, and each bitmap uses a 1-bit to indicate that the value is in the corresponding row and a 0-bit for all other rows.

Although bitmap indexes are typically built on a single column, they can cover multiple columns. Composite bitmap indexes work exactly as previously described, except that each entry or set of equal-valued entries corresponds to distinct values in the combination of columns.

Using Bitmap Indexes

Bitmap indexes were designed to support the type of tables that are becoming common in data warehouse databases—very large, relatively static, and not normalized. They can support large tables easily because they're relatively compact, even on tables with millions of rows. They're best for static tables because they use compression algorithms that require heavy maintenance when indexed values are added, dropped, or updated. The same values will tend to occur frequently in tables that are not normalized, which wouldn't make their columns good candidates for a standard index.

Bitmap indexes are even efficient when two or more values are requested from a column because the bitmaps from each value can be combined with a Boolean OR. They're very efficient at finding rows based on multiple column queries, such as the following:

```
WHERE region = 'West' AND week = 43 AND salesman = 202 AND
product = 1497 AND color = 'RED'
```

With a bitmap index on each column named in this example, the required rows can be found by performing a Boolean AND on each bitmap. The resulting bitmap will have a 1-bit only in the positions corresponding to rows having all the required values. Boolean ANDs and ORs are some of the most efficient operations a computer can perform.

Building a Bitmap Index

To create a bitmap index, you should use the CREATE INDEX command discussed earlier, except that you have to include the keyword BITMAP where the optional UNIQUE keyword appears. All the other options shown in Listing 8.1 for the CREATE INDEX command can be used for a bitmap index.

You can also rebuild a bitmap index by using the ALTER INDEX...REBUILD command. The only option shown in the previous section that you can't use for a bitmap index is REVERSE. Of course, you can always drop and rebuild a bitmap index by using the standard DROP INDEX command.

Use a large sample size when estimating bitmap index storage requirements

A single bitmap can store only a finite number of bits, representing a fixed number of rows. In a small table, every row can be covered by one bitmap for each distinct value in the indexed column. At some point, the insertion of a new row will require a second bitmap to be built for each value, doubling the number of blocks needed to store the bitmap entries. An insertion will cause the third bitmap to later be built for each value, increasing the number of leaf blocks required by another 50 percent. Until your index is large enough so that the addition of a new set of bitmaps per value doesn't increase its size significantly, you can't extrapolate its final size accurately.

One aspect of bitmap indexes that's difficult to manage is planning how big they will be, using a formula such as the one published by Oracle for regular b*tree indexes. The amount of data compression isn't going to be obvious from an examination of sample data. Your best way to estimate the size of the final index is to extrapolate it from an index built on a sample table.

Managing Reverse-Key Indexes

A reverse-key index is one in which the value portions of the entries in the leaf blocks are saved in reverse bit order. The entries themselves are stored in the order of the resulting bit patterns rather than in the order of the original values. The branch blocks, of course, also reflect the stored values—that is, the reversed bit values rather than the values as found in the tables. The result of this bit reversal is to make somewhat random the locations of entries throughout the index. Values that normally would be stored sequentially are likely to be scattered throughout the index on different blocks.

You use a reverse-key index to help avoid the problem of having an index develop lots of empty spaces because entries were dropped and no new records could reuse the space. This is likely to happen in a normally organized index when new records have increasingly higher values, such as sequence numbers, but not all the older entries are removed from other blocks.

A good example of this type of index is one on an employee ID column. In a growing company, more new employees are added than existing employees leave. The remaining employees have index entries for their ID numbers on the older leaf blocks, which are probably partially empty as a result of some earlier employees leaving. However, the new employees' ID numbers will be too high in value to be stored within the value ranges of these blocks. Over time, the index may become inefficient due to increasing amounts of unusable free space.

As discussed earlier, you would have to drop and rebuild the index to compress the earlier values into full blocks. Rather than have to compress the index regularly, you could build it as a reverse-key index, which should spread high and low values around the used blocks. When entries are removed, new ones stand a reasonable chance of fitting into the ranges opened by the deletions.

SEE ALSO

➤ *To learn when to use reverse-key indexes, see page 508*

Creating a Reverse-Key Index

Use the CREATE INDEX command shown in Listing 8.1 to create a reverse-key index, but include the keyword REVERSE where the optional NOSORT keyword appears. All the other options shown in Listing 8.1 for the CREATE INDEX command can be used for a reverse-key index.

To convert an existing index into a reverse-key index, use the ALTER INDEX...REBUILD command as described earlier. Use the keyword REVERSE as shown in that section. Of course, you can always drop a regular index and rebuild it as a reverse-key index, using the standard DROP INDEX command and the CREATE INDEX command as just described.

Rebuilding Reverse-Key Indexes

To rebuild a reverse-key index, you can drop the original index and create it again. If you decide to use the ALTER INDEX...REBUILD command, you can make any other changes you need, such as changing the tablespace or storage values.

Changing the type of index during a rebuild

A reverse-key index will be rebuilt as a reverse-key index whether or not you use the optional keyword **REVERSE**. However, if you use the **NOREVERSE** keyword, your rebuild index will no longer be a reverse-key index, but will instead be a standard index.

Managing Index-Organized Tables

An *index-organized table* is a hybrid structure consisting of b*tree index and regular table elements. The b*tree components are the use of ordered entries on leaf blocks, and branch blocks that provide fast access to the required leaf blocks. The table-like features include the use of standard SQL commands for table management, such as creation and alteration, and the use of standard DML and SELECT commands to manipulate rows. (See Chapter 7 for information on table creation and management.)

The complete rows—not just the indexed column data—are stored in the b*tree block structure.

Index-organized tables provide the fast data access that's normally achieved only by creating an index on a table but don't require the storage space, or the management, of a separate index. You should consider using an index-organized table for lookup tables, which are almost exclusively used to find a value, or set of values, based on a key. For example, a table containing city names you find by entering the postal zip code are an ideal candidate for an index-organized table.

Indexed-organized tables do have some restrictions. Unlike a regular table, you can't create additional indexes; therefore it's unlikely that you would want to use this structure for tables with columns with different columns that you typically access by specific value. Remember that UPDATE and DELETE commands on specific rows, not just queries, can benefit from indexes on the columns referenced in the WHERE clause.

The ordering of an indexed-organized table is based on its primary key, so the table must have a primary key defined. This, of course, is recommended for all relational tables, but isn't a requirement and makes a second restriction (if you consider it such) on index-organized tables.

Finally, as with a regular index, the space vacated by a dropped row can be reused only if a subsequently inserted row has the same value, or a value that lies between the adjacent column values. This can result in a table with more free space than you would expect to see in a regular table where the PCTUSED setting controls the reuse of released space.

SEE ALSO

➤ *To see when to use index-organized tables, see page 508*

Why Index-Organized Tables Don't Support Additional Indexes

An index uses a rowid to point to a specific row in a table. The rowid identifies where the row is physically stored—the block number within that file and, to ensure that each rowid is unique, the row number on that block. It's this last piece that makes rowids unusable for entries in index-organized tables. The row number for a regular table's row is actually the number of the row's entry in the block's row directory. The row directory is simply an ordered list of byte addresses, entry one containing the byte where row one starts, entry two containing the entry where row two starts, and so on. If the row has to be moved to another location in the block due to an UPDATE that extends its length, for example, Oracle simply moves the row and updates its directory entry to reflect its new starting byte address.

In an index-organized table, the rows have to be stored in sorted order, just as the entries in an index are stored. If a new row is inserted into the table with a primary key value that lies between two existing values, the row must be logically stored between the two rows containing these values. Suppose that the table contains the values "Baltimore" and "Boston," and that they are in row positions 10 and 11 on a particular block—that is, the tenth entry in block directory contains the starting byte address for the row containing "Baltimore" and its eleventh entry points to the "Boston" row.

If we add a row with "Biloxi" as its primary key, it now needs to use the 11th slot in the block row directory for its byte address; the entry for "Boston," and any other rows following it, have to be moved up to the next slot. Were the rows being treated as regular table entries, this action would effectively change the rowid addresses for the "Boston" row and the rows following it on the block. Furthermore, if we had been able to build indexes on this table, Oracle would have to find every index entry that pointed to these rows and update the rowid values, even if the rows themselves didn't move by even one byte from their original locations.

You can help control space usage within an index-organized table by splitting each row into two pieces, the first of which acts more like a regular index entry and the second of which behaves more like a table row. Oracle will build distinct segments to store the index-organized table when you do this. The first segment will hold the portion of each row that constitutes the indexed, or ordered, values; the second segment will hold the

Index-organized tables can't support unique constraints

A unique constraint is enforced by Oracle with an index built on the constrained columns. Due to the limitation that index-organized tables can't have additional indexes, you can't add a unique constraint to such a table.

remainder of each row. This approach reduces the amount of wasted space that can occur when a row is dropped or the primary key value is changed, causing the row to be relocated. Only the row piece in the first of the two segments, the ordered segment, leaves space that has to be reused by an equivalent value. The contents in the second segment are treated like the rows in any other table—space can be reused by any other row piece that fits on the block, and an UPDATE doesn't necessarily cause the row to migrate to a new block.

To build your index-organized table in two such segments, you begin by determining how much of an average row you want to keep in the index portion and how much in the table portion. Generally, you want the primary-key columns in the former and the balance of the row in the latter. You then need to compute the percentage of the block that the index portion consumes for an average row. When that's done, you can build the index-organized table and identify this percentage with storage information for the table's two parts. You can even identify a column that determines where the break between the index portion and the row portion is made; this will ensure that the entire primary key is kept together, even if its length is less than the specified percentage.

Creating an Index-Organized Table

To create an index-organized table, you use the CREATE TABLE command (discussed in detail in Chapter 7) with some additional keywords and certain restrictions. Listing 8.2 shows the syntax for this command.

LISTING 8.2   The *CREATE TABLE* command for an index-organized table

```
01: CREATE TABLE [table_schema.]table_name
02:     ([column_description [,...],
03:     [CONSTRAINT constraint_name]
04:     PRIMARY KEY (column_n¦ame [,...]))
05:     ORGANIZATION INDEX
06:     [TABLESPACE tablespace_name]
07:     [storage_clause]
08:     [space_utilization_clause]
```

```
09:       [[PCTTHRESHOLD integer]
10:       [INCLUDING column_name]
11:       OVERFLOW
12:           [TABLESPACE tablespace_name]
13:           [storage_clause]
14:           [space_utilization_clause]
15:           [PCTUSED integer]]
```

On line 2, `column_description` includes the column name, the column datatype, an optional size, and an optional constraint.

SEE ALSO

➤ *To learn about the column-definition options used when building a table, see page* **195**

➤ *The syntax to add a constraint to a column definition, page* **499**

PRIMARY KEY on line 3 can be a named or an unnamed constraint, defined as a column or a table constraint on a single column or composite key.

SEE ALSO

➤ *For details on primary key constraints, see page* **493**

Line 4's ORGANIZATION INDEX are required keywords.

On line 8 PCTTHRESHOLD `integer` sets the percentage of space in a block that any row can consume; the balance of a row that exceeds this threshold is stored in an overflow area. The default value is 50.

INCLUDING `column_name` on line 9 names the first column that will be placed in the overflow area, if needed; the column must be the last column defined in the primary key or a non-primary key column.

OVERFLOW on line 10 is a required keyword that introduces the definition of the overflow segment on lines 11–through 14:

■ TABLESPACE `tablespace_name`, `storage_clause`, and `space_utilization_clause` all provide the same options as defined earlier in Listing 8.1's CREATE INDEX syntax. These clauses can contain different values for the primary storage segment (the ordered, index portion of the rows) and the overflow storage segment (where the remaining columns of the rows are stored).

Restrictions on constraints in index-organized tables

Because an index-organized table can't have additional indexes, you can't use a unique constraint on any column or column combination. You can include any other type of constraint, however.

Interaction of PCTTHRESHOLD and OVERFLOW clauses

If you include a value for the **PCTTHRESHOLD** option and don't include an **OVERFLOW** clause, any row that exceeds the percentage of block space defined by **PCTTHRESHOLD** will be rejected.

- PCTUSED defines a threshold of space used in a block below, which block is returned to the free list.

Monitoring Index-Organized Tables

The data dictionary stores information about index-organized tables in a number of different tables that you can see through the DBA_/ALL_/USER_TABLES and the DBA_/ALL_/USER_INDEXES views. The *_TABLES views contain the basic definition of the table under the name you provide in the CREATE TABLE command. These views also contain information about the overflow segment, which, if present, contains values for the extent sizes and related storage information. The overflow segment also holds the statistics generated from the ANALYZE TABLE command, whether you name the base table or the overflow table name in the command.

The *_INDEXES views contain most of the segment's description, including its storage and space utilization values, as well as statistics generated with the ANALYZE command. These views also show the name given to the index in which the rows are actually stored. If you don't specify an overflow option, these views will contain the only detailed information about the physical storage of the segment.

Identify the index characteristics' names and, possibly, its overflow segment to find out all the information about an index-organized table in the data dictionary. You can use the following query to find values in the data dictionary columns specific to the objects comprising index-organized tables:

Finding the extents belonging to an index-organized table

If you query the **DBA_EXTENTS** data dictionary view to find the segments belonging to an index-organized table, you won't find them under the segment name you gave to the table. Instead, you find them listed under the Oracle-supplied segment names for the index segment and, if there is one, the overflow table segment. To relate these extents to a specific index-organized table, therefore, you have to use a query, like the one provided, to find the names of its extents.

```
SELECT t.owner AS "Owner",
    t.table_name AS "Table Name",
    i.index_name AS "Index Name",
    i.tablespace_name AS "Index TS",
    o.table_name AS "Overflow Segment",
    o.tablespace_name AS "Overflow TS",
    i.pct_threshold AS "Overflow Pct",
    i.include_column AS "Include Col"
FROM dba_tables t, dba_indexes i, dba_tables o
WHERE i.pct_threshold IS NOT NULL
    AND t.table_name = i.table_name
    AND o.iot_name(+) = t.table_name;
```

You can, of course, restrict this query by naming a specific table or a specific owner (for example, adding the clause AND t.table_name = 'table_name' or AND t.owner = 'owner_name', respectively). Of course, after you use this query to identify the names Oracle has given to the indexes and, when appropriate, to the overflow objects, you can use their names to query the *_TABLES and *_INDEXES views to see other information about them.

To find out how well a specific indexed-organized table is behaving, you can use the ANALYZE INDEX...VALIDATE STRUCTURE on the index built for the table. You should look for the same criteria discussed earlier regarding determining whether a regular index needs reorganizing. However, if you do find problems with an index for an index-organized table, you can't use the ALTER INDEX...REBUILD command to recreate it. If you determine that it does need reorganizing, you may have to drop and recreate the entire index-organized table. However, you can use the ALTER INDEX command on the index itself or the ALTER TABLE command on the base table name in order to make some changes to the index that you could otherwise make to any other primary-key index with the ALTER INDEX command.

You can also monitor the block usage in an index-organized table's overflow segment. To do this, use the ANALYZE TABLE command to compute or estimate statistics on the overflow segment. As mentioned earlier, you can name the base table name or the overflow segment name in the command. If you determine that there are storage problems, you may need to drop and recreate the whole index-organized table. Unfortunately, you aren't allowed to make changes to the overflow segment directly with an ALTER TABLE command in the current release.

Creating and Managing User Accounts

The Key Purposes of a User Account

User accounts in Oracle8 generally provide three distinct and important purposes in the operation of a database:

- They provide security so that you can control who has access to what portions of your database and what operations can be performed.

- Even if someone is allowed access to data, you may want to audit his or her activities as part of an overall security plan or to help diagnose performance problems by identifying who is holding locks, using system resources, or simply logged into the database.

- An Oracle8 account includes a schema wherein all segments (tables, indexes, stored procedures, and so on) owned by the user are stored. The schema name matches the user's userid.

User security is one of the more important functions that you perform. Security in Oracle8 is important not only in keeping prying eyes from your sensitive data, but also in helping keep a developer or normal user from interfering with a production database's operations. Oracle8's security allows you to impose a very granular security profile on every user in the system. This profile allows control over which columns, tables, and rows users can select, update, or insert into, as well as whether users can create segments and where they may be created.

Oracle8 improves user management

User accounts through Oracle7 had been one of Oracle's traditional weaknesses—until Oracle8. Oracle8 truly has an excellent system in place for managing user accounts (and security in general) throughout your enterprise. It's vastly superior to anything Oracle7 DBAs had to work with.

Although security is probably one of the more thankless jobs, it's absolutely essential that you understand what types of security protection are available. Every security permission has some risks and benefits associated with it. It's important that the significance of each permission be understood so you can implement the safest and most flexible security policy possible. It's true that nobody will thank you for expiring his or her password every 90 days, but if someone breaks into the corporate data warehouse, you'll probably be answering some even tougher questions from your organization's upper management.

Creating User Accounts

An Oracle8 user account allows a user to be identified by the database and, optionally, to store segments such as tables and indexes. What users do with their individual user accounts is controlled by permissions that you grant. A user account by itself doesn't allow anyone to even log on to the database. No implicit permissions are given when a user account is initially created.

Oracle, like most RDBMS systems, uses privileges granted to a user account to determine whether a user is allowed to perform a certain function on a particular segment (or in the system at all). A user account without any privileges granted can't do anything at all.

Granting users privilege is covered in depth in Chapter 10, "Controlling User Access with Privileges."

User Authentication

The only means of identifying users to Oracle is their user identification, known as a userid in Oracle8. Anyone could deliberately or accidentally claim to be someone he isn't. Without some means of authenticating who a user is, you could potentially allow someone access to information; that access could be damaging to the company, employees, or worse.

From the earliest of computer days, the password has been a universally accepted means of authenticating who a user is. Central to password authentication is the belief that only a person claiming to be userid GASPERT would know what GASPERT's password is. By making the user produce this secret, you believe that if a user knows the password, he is who he says he is.

The popularity of password authentication is also one of its greatest drawbacks. Most users despise having to keep a different password to each system they use during the day. Users are usually urged to use different passwords on different systems, which leads them to write down passwords or use a single password on all systems anyway. In either case, the password can no longer be considered a secret. You have no way of knowing if someone else had access to the password either in another system or to the piece of paper on which the password was written. Without a doubt, it's at least an irritant to have to log on to multiple systems separately each time you want to use them.

Clearly, it would be most convenient if you could just log on to one system (such as the operating system) and then have all subsystems (such as a database) base their authentication on the first logon. Fortunately, Oracle8 provides this exact capability. Oracle8 allows *external authentication*, which basically links a particular Oracle8 user account to a particular operating system account.

In the modern client/server world, users often aren't actually using a tool such as SQL*Plus on the same machine that the Oracle8 server runs on. External authentication then adds another question to ponder: Can we trust the *remote* operating system to properly authenticate a user? Often, external authentication is practical only if you can trust the database server's OS and the client machine's OS's authentication methods. PCs, again, present a particular problem.

If you want to use operating-system authentication, you need to be aware of two Oracle8 parameters and their customary settings:

```
os_authent_prefix = OPS$
remote_os_authent = true
```

In Oracle8, externally authenticated userids are typically prefixed with OPS$ to distinguish them from users who must log in with the traditional userid/password combination. os_authent_prefix allows you to customize the prefix of externally authenticated userids.

If you plan to allow a remote system to authenticate a user for Oracle8, you must set the remote_os_authent parameter in your INIT.ORA file to TRUE.

Oracle8 introduced a third option for authentication, known as *enterprise authentication*. With the Oracle8 Security Service (OSS), this system creates a global central location for authenticating user logins. If your environment consists of many Oracle8 databases, this may be appealing to you. Although you still must

External authentication's drawback

The only major drawback to external authentication is that you have to trust the operating system to authenticate users properly. Don't take this issue lightly. PC environments in particular are notorious for their lack of credible security. By using external authentication, your database's level of security is no greater than your operating system's. If you can trust your operating system to provide adequate security for your database, external authentication offers an attractive and viable alternative to saddling your users with yet another password.

Remote authentication and Microsoft Windows

Windows 3.x and, arguably, Windows 95 don't offer nearly the level of security that Windows NT or a UNIX workstation offer. If your clients will be using Windows 3.x or Windows 95, you probably should avoid using external authentication.

create a user account in each individual database a user is allowed to access, the authentication and password is stored in a central area. This allows users to have a single logon to all databases. If users change their passwords, the change affects all database systems that use a common OSS.

The installation and configuration of OSS is beyond the scope of this book. The discussions and examples henceforth assume that you aren't using OSS in your environment.

Creating a User Account

Before creating a new user on your database, you must gather some information first. You need to know the following:

- What will the new user's userid be?

- Will the user be externally authenticated? If not, you must choose an initial password for the user.

- If the user will be creating segments, what tablespace will he or she be placed in by default?

- When temporary space is needed for operations such as sorting, which tablespace will be used? In many systems, a tablespace named TEMP will be dedicated for this purpose.

- How much space, or *quota*, will the user be allowed to use on tablespaces in the system?

- If the user will be assigned a security profile, what profile will be used?

To create a user in Oracle8, use the CREATE USER command with the following format:

```
CREATE USER userid IDENTIFIED BY password ¦ EXTERNALLY
        [DEFAULT TABLESPACE tablespace]
        [TEMPORARY TABLESPACE tablespace]
        [QUOTA value ¦ UNLIMITED] ON tablespace] ...
        [PROFILE profile]
        [PASSWORD EXPIRE] [ACCOUNT <LOCK ¦ UNLOCK>]
```

- CREATE USER *userid*   This specifies the userid of the new user you're creating. Using any existing username standards in place at your site is advisable to minimize confusion in

Where to use the CREATE USER command

This discussion of creating user accounts uses SQL*Plus and assumes that you're logged in as a user with the necessary privileges to create another user. This typically means that you're logging in as the **SYSTEM** user or have been granted the DBA role.

Who's looking over your shoulder?

More than one company's security has been breached by someone merely observing a user account being created. After creating a new account, you should always exit SQL*Plus and clear the screen. Remember that SQL*Plus remembers the last command entered. If you create a new user account, clear the screen, and walk off, someone could enter a quick SQL*Plus command and see exactly what password you used to create the new account. Many companies routinely create new accounts with a well-known password, allowing almost anyone access to your system. This is a poor policy from a security standpoint. Always make new user account passwords unique.

Keep the SYSTEM tablespace clean

Never allow users to create segments in the **SYSTEM** tablespace or use it for temporary sort storage. They could bring your database operations to a complete standstill if the **SYSTEM** tablespace fills up!

your user community. If this user will be externally authenticated, be sure to prefix the userid with the value of the os_authent_prefix parameter (typically, OPS$).

- BY *password* ¦ EXTERNALLY   If you aren't using external authentication, you must provide an initial password for the new user. This password should begin with an alphabetical character (a–z) and consist of alphabetical or numeric characters. Be aware that this password will be visible onscreen. You should avoid creating users at a workstation where others could easily see the password(s) you're entering. If you're using external authentication, you must enter EXTERNALLY after the IDENTIFIED clause.

- DEFAULT TABLESPACE *tablespace*   If this new user account will be allowed to create segments, be sure to set a default tablespace for where these segments will go. This won't restrict the user from creating segments in other tablespaces; it just provides a default location for storage if the user doesn't specify otherwise. If you don't specify a default tablespace, the default is to place user segments in the SYSTEM tablespace.

- TEMPORARY TABLESPACE *tablespace*   In the course of sorting functions, Oracle8 will require some scratch space in which it can create temporary segments until a transaction completes. You should dedicate at least one tablespace to this function. Typically, this tablespace will be named TEMP. If you don't specify a location for temporary segments, Oracle8 defaults to the SYSTEM tablespace.

- QUOTA *value* ¦ UNLIMITED ON *tablespace*   Oracle8's quota system allows you to limit the amount of space a user's segments may use on any given tablespace. By duplicating the QUOTA clause as many times as necessary within the CREATE USER command, you can set up quotas on all tablespaces in which the user will be authorized to store segments. You should generally assign an appropriate quota on the user's default tablespace.

  The *value* parameter is an integer followed by K or M (no space) to denote kilobytes or megabytes. If you don't use K or M, Oracle8 will interpret the integer you provide as bytes, which probably isn't what you intended Oracle8 to interpret. For instance, 40M, 40K, 40 will be interpreted as 40MB, 40KB, and 40 bytes, respectively.

■ PROFILE *profile*   Oracle8 allows you to create standard security profiles that can be assigned to users. This greatly simplifies and standardizes the security policies to be enforced. You can specify a security profile by adding PRO-FILE followed by the profile name in the CREATE USER command. Oracle8 provides many new security features that can enhance the security of your Oracle8 database.

SEE ALSO

➤ *For a more in-depth discussion of profiles, see page* ***322***

■ PASSWORD EXPIRE   Oracle8 allows for the initial password to expire immediately. To do this, add PASSWORD EXPIRE to the end of the CREATE USER command. This forces the user to change the password when he or she first logs in to Oracle8.

■ ACCOUNT LOCK ¦ UNLOCK   In some environments, it's desirable to create accounts for new employees but not allow access (by LOCKing them) until they're actually ready to use them (at which time they will be UNLOCKed). By adding ACCOUNT LOCK to the end of your CREATE USER command, the user account will be created but the user can't log in until you explicitly unlock the account.

Basic Example of Creating a User

The following is a basic example of creating a user in Oracle8. Before entering this command, log on to SQL*Plus as a user with DBA privileges (such as the SYSTEM user).

```
SQL> CREATE USER RWILSON IDENTIFIED BY RH0WIL2
        DEFAULT TABLESPACE USERS
        TEMPORARY TABLESPACE TEMP
        QUOTA 100M ON USERS
        QUOTA 0 ON SYSTEM
        PASSWORD EXPIRE
        ACCOUNT LOCK;
```

Statement processed.

1 Used to create user RWILSON

2 Sets password to RH0WIL2

3 Indicates that USERS tablespace will store RWILSON's segments by default

4 Set to store RWILSON's temporary sort segments in the TEMP tablespace

5 Set to allow 100MB in USERS tablespace

6 Set to allow no storage at all on SYSTEM tablespace

7 Forces RWILSON to change password on first logon attempt

8 Prevents user from logging on until you unlock account

After you enter this command, the new user account is created. If the user tried to log in right now, Oracle8 would stop her because she would lack the CREATE SESSION privilege. Chapter 10 discusses the privileges needed by new users to connect and work in the database.

Example of Creating a User with External Authentication and a *PROFILE*

The following example shows how to create a user who will be externally authenticated and has a security profile assigned to him:

① Used to create OPS$BRONC (OPS$ is required because this account is externally authenticated.)

② Indicates that new account will be externally authenticated

③ Set to use security settings in STD_USR_PROFILE profile for new account

```
SQL> CREATE USER OPS$BROHNC IDENTIFIED EXTERNALLY
        DEFAULT TABLESPACE STD_USER1
        TEMPORARY TABLESPACE TEMP2
        QUOTA 20M ON STD_USER1
        QUOTA 0 ON SYSTEM
        PROFILE STD_USR_PROFILE;

Statement processed.
```

Allowing Quotas on Different Tablespaces

Oracle8 allows you to control the amount of space users can consume in tablespaces. By default, there is no quota on the amount of space a user's segments may use in the database. Typically, you'll want to restrict users' storage to prevent someone from consuming all available space. Furthermore, you'll probably have at least one or two special-purpose tablespaces that you'll want to reserve for a specific use. This is particularly true of the SYSTEM tablespace, which should never contain user segments.

The QUOTA parameter, while straightforward, has the potential of greatly affecting the success and efficiency of your database. Too loosely set parameters will usually result in bloated, duplicated segments that have been poorly sized, resulting in wasted disk space, or worse—not enough free space for everyone to continue working. If QUOTA settings are set too tightly, users may waste time with unnecessary workarounds to conserve space.

Coordinating your quota policies

No matter what policy you adopt, it's essential that you coordinate it with your users during the initial policy-making and in regular follow-up discussions. Remember that your job as a DBA is to provide a service to your users. The purpose of quotas is to ensure equal quality system performance for all.

Setting quotas on a user applies only to segments owned by that user. If the user is allowed to create segments in other users' schemas or insert rows into another user's table, only the segment's owner's quota will be applied.

The QUOTA parameter is normally used to provide a fixed limit, such as the following:

```
QUOTA 300M ON USERS
```

There are two special cases, however: no quota limit at all and not allowing any space at all.

To remove quota restriction in a particular tablespace, you must substitute UNLIMITED for the numeric limit:

```
QUOTA UNLIMITED ON USERS
```

This allows a user to use as much space as he or she asks for (as long as there's enough free space to supply the request, of course). If you don't specify a quota limit on a tablespace, Oracle8 will default to an UNLIMITED quota.

To prevent a user from creating segments on a particular tablespace, set the size to 0 as shown in this example:

```
QUOTA 0 ON USERS
```

Because a segment must be larger than 0, it's impossible for a user to create a segment that will satisfy a 0 quota limit.

As explained earlier, you can duplicate Oracle8's QUOTA parameter as many times as necessary within a CREATE USER command. This is useful to easily set quota on many different tablespaces at once. You'll often want to establish quotas on all non-rollback and temporary tablespaces; this is particularly true in production environments.

Suppose that a database has the tablespaces SYSTEM, TEMP, RBS, PROD, DEV, and TOOLS. The PROD tablespace is intended to hold production segments, whereas DEV is used to hold developer's segments. TEMP is used for temporary sort-related segments, and RBS is the tablespace used for rollback segments.

You only want to allow developers to create segments in the DEV tablespace. Remember that they'll need to create segments in the TEMP and RBS tablespaces for normal database activities. A CREATE USER command might look like this:

```
CREATE USER KHEIL IDENTIFIED BY KH1507
DEFAULT TABLESPACE DEV
TEMPORARY TABLESPACE TEMP
QUOTA 0 ON SYSTEM
QUOTA 1024M ON DEV
QUOTA 0 ON PROD
QUOTA 0 ON TOOLS
```

This allows no segments to be created on SYSTEM, PROD, or TOOLS. 1GB is allowed on DEV. An unlimited amount of space would be allowed on TEMP and RBS (because they aren't listed with any quota limits).

Using the *CREATE SCHEMA* Command

CREATE SCHEMA falls short of expectations

Although **CREATE SCHEMA** offers some nice capabilities, Oracle8 doesn't support it very well. Because you can't include a **STORAGE** clause, you most likely can't create optimal tables with this command. Unless you need the capabilities that it offers, you'll probably get along quite well without ever using it.

Sometimes it's useful to group several CREATE TABLE, CREATE VIEW, or GRANT commands into a single operation. You would typically do this to make sure that either everything is created properly or nothing is created. By grouping multiple CREATE TABLE/VIEW and GRANT commands into a single operation, you ensure that even if the first command succeeded, it will be rolled back if the last command fails.

Suppose that you had a script with these operations:

```
CREATE TABLE CUSTOMER
CREATE TABLE SUPPLIER
CREATE VIEW
GRANT
```

If the first CREATE TABLE ran successfully but the second didn't due to disk space, your database would have a CUSTOMER table but no SUPPLIER table. When the disk shortage is corrected, the script can't be used without change because it will abort when it tries to create a CUSTOMER table again. By encapsulating all these commands in a single CREATE SCHEMA transaction, you can correct the problem and restart a script if anything fails; you can do so knowing the database was returned to its original condition.

The syntax of the CREATE SCHEMA command is as follows:

```
CREATE SCHEMA AUTHORIZATION schema
        [CREATE TABLE ...]¦ [CREATE VIEW ...]¦ [GRANT ...]
```

- For CREATE SCHEMA AUTHORIZATION *schema*, provide the name of the schema where the new segments are to be created. This must be the name of the user now logged into the database. You can't use CREATE SCHEMA with someone else's schema name (or userid), even if you're a DBA.

- Use any valid ANSI CREATE TABLE command within a CREATE SCHEMA command. You can repeat as many CREATE TABLE commands as you want within a single CREATE SCHEMA command.

- CREATE VIEW   Just as with the CREATE TABLE command, you may use any number of valid ANSI CREATE VIEW commands.

- GRANT   Any valid GRANT commands can be used with the CREATE SCHEMA command.

Suppose that the SUPPLIER table wasn't created due to an error, but that the CUSTOMER table was created successfully. CREATE SCHEMA wouldn't try to create the view CUSTOMERS_AND_SUPPLIERS or grant permissions. It would drop the CUSTOMER table, thereby returning the database to its original state. This is depicted in the following command:

Watch out for non-ANSI syntax

Many **CREATE TABLE** clauses that you use, such as **STORAGE**, are Oracle extensions to ANSI SQL and aren't supported in the **CREATE SCHEMA** command.

```
SQL> CREATE SCHEMA AUTHORIZATION  TGASPER            ❶
CREATE TABLE CUSTOMER
( NAME            VARCHAR2(30),
  ADDRESS         VARCHAR2(30),
  CITY            VARCHAR2(30),
  STATE           VARCHAR2(2),
  ZIP             VARCHAR2(10) )
TABLESPACE USER_DATA                                 ❷
CREATE TABLE SUPPLIER
( NAME            VARCHAR2(30),
  ADDRESS         VARCHAR2(30),
  CITY            VARCHAR2(30),
  STATE           VARCHAR2(2),
  ZIP             VARCHAR2(10) )
TABLESPACE USER_DATA
CREATE VIEW CUSTOMERS_AND_SUPPLIERS AS               ❸
SELECT C.NAME FROM SUPPLIER S, CUSTOMER C
WHERE S.NAME = C.NAME
GRANT SELECT ON CUSTOMERS_AND_SUPPLIERS TO PUBLIC;   ❹

Statement processed.
```

❶ Used in TGASPER schema (and, of course, run by TGASPER user)

❷ Used to create CUSTOMER and SUPPLIER tables in TGASPER schema (complies with ANSI SQL)

❸ Used to create a view based on CUSTOMER and SUPPLIER tables

❹ Applies appropriate permissions on CUSTOMERS and SUPPLIERS tables

Modifying User Accounts

Like most everything else about your database, user accounts and security properties will inevitably need to be changed. Fortunately, Oracle8 provides the capability to change almost every aspect of a user account after it's created.

Using the *ALTER USER* Command

Oracle8 provides the ALTER USER command to change attributes associated with a user account. You can issue the ALTER USER command with as many clauses as necessary. You need to specify only the attributes you want to change; all other attributes will remain unchanged.

The format of the ALTER USER command is as follows:

```
ALTER USER userid [IDENTIFIED BY password ¦ EXTERNALLY]
   [DEFAULT TABLESPACE tablespace]
   [TEMPORARY TABLESPACE tablespace]
   [QUOTA value ¦ UNLIMITED] ON tablespace] ...
   [PROFILE profile]
   [PASSWORD EXPIRE] [ACCOUNT <LOCK ¦ UNLOCK>]
   [DEFAULT ROLE
   <ROLE [, ROLE]... ¦ ALL [EXCEPT ROLE [, ROLE]...] ¦ NONE >]
```

- ALTER USER *userid*   This will be the userid of the user you want to change. You can't rename a user after he or she is created.

- BY *password* ¦ EXTERNALLY   You can change the password of a user who isn't using external authentication. This password should begin with an alphabetical character (a–z) and consist of alphabetical or numeric characters. Be aware that this password will be visible onscreen. You should avoid changing passwords at a workstation where others could easily see the password(s) you're entering.

- DEFAULT TABLESPACE *tablespace*   You can change the default tablespace for a user at any time. Be aware that this won't move any segments already created. This affects only segments that will be created in the future if the user doesn't explicitly identify a tablespace.

Changing user authentication

Theoretically, you could change a user's authentication from internal (entering a userid/password) to external, or vice versa. However, because the userid will typically be different for users being authenticated internally and externally, this is rarely a practical option. You'll usually need to drop the user and recreate his or her account with the proper authentication.

- TEMPORARY TABLESPACE *tablespace*   The temporary tablespace can be changed for users at any time.

- QUOTA *value* ¦ UNLIMITED ON *tablespace*   User quota values can be changed at any time. Just as in the CREATE USER command, you can repeat the QUOTA clause as many times as necessary. You need to provide a QUOTA clause only for the tablespaces that you want to change the user's quota on.

- PROFILE *profile*   You can change a user's security profile at any time.

- PASSWORD EXPIRE   A user's password can be expired at any time. This should always be done when a user's password is being changed by a DBA, thereby forcing the user to re-enter a password that only he or she knows.

- ACCOUNT LOCK ¦ UNLOCK   Accounts can be LOCKed or UNLOCKed at any time. Many sites require that when accounts are created, they must be LOCKed until the user is actually ready to use them. Use the ALTER USER command with ACCOUNT UNLOCK to unlock the user's account and allow him or her access to the database.

- DEFAULT ROLE   You can use the DEFAULT ROLE clause to make one or more roles enabled by default on a user's account. All roles granted may be enabled by default with the ALL keyword and, optionally, exclude one or more roles from being enabled by default by explicitly listing them. By using the NONE keyword with the DEFAULT ROLE clause, you can specify that no roles are enabled by default.

> **DEFAULT ROLE's limitation**
>
> The **DEFAULT ROLE** clause can't be used to make (as the default) a role that a user hasn't been specifically granted with the relevant **GRANT** command.

Example of Changing a User's Password

Using ALTER USER requires that you first log into SQL*Plus as a DBA user (such as SYSTEM). The following example shows a user's password being changed:

```
SQL>  ALTER USER BJONES IDENTIFIED BY BJ4236
           PASSWORD EXPIRE;

Statement processed.
```

> **①** Indicates that BJONES's user account is being changed
>
> **②** Sets BJONES's password to BJ4236
>
> **③** Forces user to change password the next time she logs in (using new password)

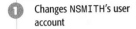

1 Changes NSMITH's user account

2 Changes user's default tablespace to USERS3

3 Denies user any more space on tablespace USERS2 (user's old default tablespace)

4 Allows user 500MB of space on new default tablespace, USERS3

The effect of changing quota

Although Oracle8 allows you to change a user's quota on any tablespace at any time, doing so won't have any effect on space that has already been allocated by a user's segment(s). The only way to change the amount of space already allocated by a user in a tablespace is to copy his or her segment(s) and drop the originals from the database.

Considerations before dropping users

Unfortunately, removing a user from Oracle8 has more implications than removing a user from most operating systems; a segment can't exist without an existing owner. If you must keep the segments in the doomed user's schema, you'll have to keep the schema on the database anyway, or move them to another user's schema. If you choose the former, lock the account with **ALTER USER** to prevent anyone from logging in and posing a security risk. If you want to keep a copy of the segments, you need to use Oracle8's export/import facility.

Changing User's Default Tablespace and Quota Example

The following example shows a user's default tablespace being changed and her tablespace quotas changed accordingly:

```
SQL>  ALTER USER NSMITH ──── 1
────── DEFAULT TABLESPACE USERS3
        QUOTA 0 ON USERS2 ──── 3
4 ───── QUOTA 500M ON USERS3;

Statement processed.
```

Understanding the Results of Changing Quota

Suppose that for the last year, JPOOLE has had a quota limit of 200MB on the USERS tablespace. His segments residing in the USERS tablespace now use around 180MB. If you were to change his quota to 100MB, there would be absolutely no effect on his existing segments—he would continue to use 180MB. He couldn't, however, use any more space.

When a segment needs to allocate an extent (initially or after it exhausts free space in existing extents), Oracle8 checks the respective user's quota against the amount of space he or she is using in the tablespace containing the segment. If allocating another extent for the user won't cause him or her to exceed the quota, Oracle8 will allocate the extent and continue. If not, the transaction will fail and the user will be notified that Oracle8 can't allocate another extent. This is the only time quotas are checked and Oracle8 takes any action based on quotas.

In short, changing a quota affects only future space requests and has no effect on the space a user has already allocated to his segments.

Using the *DROP USER* Command

During the life of a database you'll inevitably need to remove users from the database. In Oracle8, this is accomplished with the DROP USER command.

The format of the DROP USER command is as follows:

```
DROP USER userid [CASCADE]
```

- DROP USER *userid*   Supply the userid of the user to be dropped from the database.

- CASCADE   If you want to remove all the segments owned by the user you're dropping, use the CASCADE option. This tells Oracle8 to first drop all the user's segments before actually dropping the user. Be careful! There's no rolling back this command.

Example of Dropping a User Account

The following example shows a user being dropped, along with his objects from the database.

```
SQL> DROP USER SCOTT CASCADE;
```

1 Drops user SCOTT from database

2 Tells Oracle to drop any tables that SCOTT may have in his schema before actually dropping him from database

```
Statement processed.
```

If you have any doubt whatsoever about needing segments contained in a schema you're about to drop, consider exporting them to a file or tape before dropping the user. That way you can always reload the data if you need it, but your system won't be bogged down with dead wood.

Controlling User Access with Privileges

Guard your database with effective privilege management

Distinguish between system and object privileges

Assign privileges to different categories of users

Build roles to simplify privilege management

Track privilege assignments with your data dictionary

Levels of Access

Oracle protects its database access with passwords that users must know or that the system must validate. Before they can make a connection, users are still prevented from doing any work unless they have been granted the requisite *privileges*.

There are generally two categories of database users: those who need to build and manage database structures and objects (such as files, tablespaces, and tables), and those who need to work with applications that use existing objects. The former users need a variety of *system privileges*, whereas the latter need mainly *object privileges*. As you might guess, system privileges allow you to create, alter, and drop various structures, whereas object privileges allow you to execute commands on specific objects.

Roles allow you to group any number of system and object privileges into a named collection. When you've done this, you can administer roles in much the same way you can manage individual privileges. Typically, you use roles when you have categories of users who need the same sets of privileges to do their work.

System Privileges

Avoid using the default users

Try not to connect to the database with **SYS** or **SYSTEM** any more than necessary. This way you can avoid making mistakes that can have extensive repercussions. Oracle depends on these users having the predefined characteristics with which they were created when your database was built. Instead, you should create a user to act as the primary DBA for your database, give all system privileges to that user, and allow that user to pass those privileges on to others.

When you create a database, you also automatically create two users, SYS and SYSTEM. Both users are equipped with every system privilege and are allowed to add those privileges to any new users you create.

The syntax for managing system privileges is relatively simple. What's much more difficult to deal with, however, is the large number of system privileges that you can assign and understanding just what each one allows (see Table 10.1). You have to decide exactly what subset of these privileges is needed by different users to complete their assigned tasks.

When deciding what privileges to assign to a user, you also need to determine whether that user should be allowed to grant some or all of those privileges to other users, too. Obviously, if you're going to allow them to do this, you must be assured that they can make the same type of decision that you make when giving out the privileges in the first place—that they understand the needs and abilities of the other users to whom they'll be assigning the privileges.

Granting System Privileges

You use the GRANT command to assign system privileges to users. Each GRANT statement can assign one or more system privileges and assign the privilege(s) to one or more users. Furthermore, the command can include an option to allow recipients to grant the named privilege(s) to other users.

The GRANT command can assign the privileges to the "special" user, PUBLIC, as well as to individual users. By so doing, you allow every valid user in the database to take advantage of this privilege. Realize that after you assign privileges to PUBLIC, you can't drop the privilege from individual users while retaining it for all others. Therefore, you can't use PUBLIC grants as a way to simplify the task of assigning a privilege to every user except one or two.

For security reasons, system privileges don't allow users to access the data dictionary. Hence, users with ANY privileges (such as UPDATE ANY TABLE, SELECT ANY TABLE, or CREATE ANY INDEX) can't access dictionary tables and views that have not been granted to PUBLIC.

The following syntax isn't complete because it doesn't include the options for managing assignments associated with roles. (These options are covered later in the section "Granting Roles to Users and to Other Roles.") This abbreviated syntax is complete for assigning individual system privileges to one or more users:

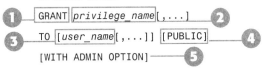

Table 10.1 lists the system privilege names that you can name in the GRANT command, as well as briefly describes what the privilege allows.

Don't take the easy way!

It's not good practice to give every single privilege to anyone who needs to perform some database administrative work, even if this does appear to simplify your work. As the word "privileges" implies, you should treat them as benefits or favors, to be given only to those who have a demonstrated need and appropriate sense of responsibility. You should also ensure that users to whom you assign system privileges know how to perform the tasks that the privileges allow.

① Required keywords

② A valid system privilege name

③ Valid username or userid; must be included if PUBLIC isn't

④ Designates all database users; can be used alone or with a list of one or more named users (required if no username is included)

⑤ Grants the right for recipient(s) to assign the named privilege(s) to, and remove it from, other users

Beware of granting too much to PUBLIC

System privileges should rarely, if ever, be granted to **PUBLIC**. Usually, at least one user shouldn't be allowed to perform the work associated with any privilege. You can't prevent such a user from exercising the privilege, however, if it's granted to **PUBLIC**.

Privilege and usernames can't be repeated in a single GRANT command

Although you can include multiple system privileges in the **GRANT** command, you can't name the same privilege twice. Similarly, you can't repeat a username in the list of users in the **GRANT** command.

TABLE 10.1   **System privileges**

Privilege Name:	Operations Allowed to Grantee:
ALTER ANY CLUSTER	Alter a cluster in any schema
ALTER ANY INDEX	Alter an index in any schema
ALTER ANY PROCEDURE	Alter a stored procedure, function, or package in any schema
ALTER ANY ROLE	Alter any role in the database
ALTER ANY SEQUENCE	Alter a sequence in any schema
ALTER ANY SNAPSHOT	Alter a snapshot in any schema
ALTER ANY TABLE	Alter a table in any schema
ALTER ANY TRIGGER	Enable, disable, or compile any database trigger in any schema
ALTER ANY TYPE	Alter a type in any schema
ALTER DATABASE	Issue ALTER DATABASE commands
ALTER PROFILE	Alter profiles
ALTER RESOURCE COST	Set costs for session resources
ALTER ROLLBACK SEGMENT	Alter rollback segments
ALTER SESSION	Issue ALTER SESSION commands
ALTER SYSTEM	Issue ALTER SYSTEM commands
ALTER TABLESPACE	Alter tablespaces
ALTER USER	Issue ALTER USER commands for any user
ANALYZE ANY	Analyze a table, cluster, or index in any schema
AUDIT ANY	Audit an object in any schema by using AUDIT (schema objects) commands
AUDIT SYSTEM	Issue AUDIT (SQL statements) commands
BACKUP ANY TABLE	Export objects incrementally from the schema of other users
BECOME USER	Become another user (required to perform a full database import)
COMMENT ANY TABLE	Comment on a table, view, or column in any schema
CREATE ANY CLUSTER	Create a cluster in any schema
CREATE ANY DIRECTORY	Create a directory object for BFILEs in any schema

Privilege Name:	Operations Allowed to Grantee:
CREATE ANY INDEX	Create an index in any schema on any table in any schema
CREATE ANY LIBRARY	Create external procedure/function libraries in any schema
CREATE ANY PROCEDURE	Create stored procedures, functions, and packages in any schema
CREATE ANY SEQUENCE	Create a sequence in any schema
CREATE ANY SNAPSHOT	Create a snapshot in any schema
CREATE ANY SYNONYM	Create a private synonym in any schema
CREATE ANY TABLE	Create a table in any schema
CREATE ANY TRIGGER	Create a database trigger in any schema associated with a table in any schema
CREATE ANY TYPE	Create types and type bodies in any schema (valid only with the Object option installed)
CREATE ANY VIEW	Create a view in any schema
CREATE CLUSTER	Create a cluster in own schema
CREATE DATABASE LINK	Create a private database link in own schema
CREATE ANY LIBRARY	Create external procedure/function libraries in own schema
CREATE PROCEDURE	Create stored procedures, functions, and packages in own schema
CREATE PROFILE	Create a profile
CREATE PUBLIC DATABASE LINK	Create a public database link
CREATE PUBLIC SYNONYM	Create a public synonym
CREATE ROLE	Create a role
CREATE ROLLBACK SEGMENT	Create a rollback segment
CREATE SEQUENCE	Create a sequence in own schema
CREATE SESSION	Connect to the database
CREATE SNAPSHOT	Create a snapshot in own schema
CREATE SYNONYM	Create a synonym in own schema
CREATE TABLE	Create a table in own schema
CREATE TABLESPACE	Create a tablespace

continues…

TABLE 10.1   **Continued**

Privilege Name:	Operations Allowed to Grantee:
CREATE TRIGGER	Create a database trigger in own schema
CREATE TYPE	Create types and type bodies in own schema (valid only with the Object option installed)
CREATE VIEW	Create a view in own schema
DELETE ANY TABLE	Delete rows from tables or views in any schema or truncate tables in any schema
DROP ANY CLUSTER	Drop clusters from any schema
DROP ANY DIRECTORY	Drop directory database objects
DROP ANY INDEX	Drop indexes from any schema
DROP ANY LIBRARY	Drop external procedure/function libraries from any schema
DROP ANY PROCEDURE	Drop stored procedures, functions, or packages in any schema
DROP ANY ROLE	Drop roles
DROP ANY SEQUENCE	Drop sequences from any schema
DROP ANY SNAPSHOT	Drop snapshots from any schema
DROP ANY SYNONYM	Drop private synonyms from any schema
DROP ANY TABLE	Drop tables from any schema
DROP ANY TRIGGER	Drop database triggers from any schema
DROP ANY TYPE	Drop object types and object type bodies from any schema (valid only with the Object option installed)
DROP ANY VIEW	Drop views from any schema
DROP LIBRARY	Drop external procedure/function libraries
DROP PROFILE	Drop profiles
DROP PUBLIC DATABASE LINK	Drop public database links
DROP PUBLIC SYNONYM	Drop public synonyms
DROP ROLLBACK SEGMENT	Drop rollback segments
DROP TABLESPACE	Drop tablespaces
DROP USER	Drop users

Privilege Name:	Operations Allowed to Grantee:
EXECUTE ANY PROCEDURE	Execute procedures or functions (standalone or packaged) or reference public package variables in any schema
EXECUTE ANY TYPE	Use and reference object types, and invoke methods of any type in any schema (valid only with the Object option installed); can grant this privilege only to named users or to PUBLIC, not to a role
FORCE ANY TRANSACTION	Force the COMMIT or the rollback of any in-doubt distributed transaction in the local database or induce the failure of a distributed transaction
FORCE TRANSACTION	Force the COMMIT or the rollback of own in-doubt distributed transactions in the local database
GRANT ANY ROLE	Grant any role in the database
INSERT ANY TABLE	Insert rows into tables and views in any schema
LOCK ANY TABLE	Lock tables and views in any schema
MANAGE TABLESPACE	Take tablespaces offline and online, and begin and end tablespace backups
RESTRICTED SESSION	Connect to the database when it's running in restricted mode
SELECT ANY SEQUENCE	Retrieve numbers from sequence generators in any schema
SELECT ANY TABLE	Query tables, views, or snapshots in any schema
SYSDBA	Perform Server Manager STARTUP, SHUTDOWN, and RECOVER commands, perform Server Manager ALTER DATABASE ... OPEN¦MOUNT¦BACKUP¦ [NO]ARCHIVELOG command options, and perform the CREATE DATABASE command; also includes the RESTRICTED SESSION privilege
SYSOPER	Perform Server Manager STARTUP, SHUTDOWN, and RECOVER commands, perform Server Manager ALTER DATABASE ... OPEN¦MOUNT¦BACKUP¦ [NO]ARCHIVELOG command options; also includes the RESTRICTED SESSION privilege
UNLIMITED TABLESPACE	Use an unlimited amount of any tablespace regardless of any specific quotas assigned (can grant this privilege only to named users or to PUBLIC, not to a role)
UPDATE ANY TABLE	Update rows in tables and views in any schema

Uses for assistant DBAs

You can create one or more DBA users who are solely responsible for managing the remainder of your user community, such as adding and dropping users, monitoring and assigning space, and maintaining password integrity. Similarly, you can have an assistant DBA who's in charge of space management, responsible for monitoring the availability of free space, and assigning new files or tablespaces as needed. Grant these DBA users only the system privileges necessary to perform their specific functions–the space-management DBA doesn't need user-related privileges, for example.

To grant a system privilege, you must have been granted that privilege with the ADMIN OPTION yourself, or you must have the GRANT ANY PRIVILEGE system privilege as part of your *privilege domain*. I recommend granting all system privileges to a DBA user with ADMIN OPTION as soon as you've built your database. You can then connect as this DBA user to perform all further system privilege administration duties unless—and until—you create other users and grant them the required privileges. For a small database, you'll probably retain these privileges just for yourself. In a large database environment, however, you may have assistant DBAs who are responsible for subsets of database administration and management.

When you grant a user a privilege, it becomes available immediately. Any user granted the privilege can begin to take advantage of its capabilities. A privilege granted with ADMIN OPTION means that these users can also assign it to or remove it from other users right away. (This includes the ability to revoke the privilege from each other and even from you or the person who granted it to them.) As said earlier, be careful to whom you give system privileges, particularly when you give them with ADMIN OPTION. To restore a system privilege that has been taken from you and to remove it from the destructive user, you need to connect as SYS and re-grant the privilege to yourself.

Revoking System Privileges

Use the REVOKE command to remove a system privilege from a user. If you found the syntax for the GRANT command refreshingly simple, the syntax for the REVOKE command to cancel a user's privilege(s) should be even more delightful. The syntax—again abbreviated to exclude role-related options—is as follows:

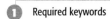

❶ Required keywords

❷ Valid system privilege name

❸ Valid username or userid (must be included if PUBLIC isn't)

❹ Designates all database users; can be used alone or with one or more named users (required if no username is included)

❶ `REVOKE` `privilege_name`[,...] ❷

❸ `FROM` [`user_name`[,...]] [`PUBLIC`] ❹

As with the GRANT command, you can't repeat a privilege name or a username in a statement. You can list as many different names as you need in each command, however, via a comma separator. In addition, as with the GRANT command, you must have the necessary privileges to revoke the named privileges. This again means that it must have been granted to you with ADMIN OPTION or you must have the GRANT ANY PRIVILEGE option. Note that there's no equivalent REVOKE privilege to equate to GRANT ANY PRIVILEGE.

Revoking a privilege from PUBLIC negates the action of the GRANT command that was used to give the named privilege(s) to PUBLIC in the first place. It doesn't affect the privileges granted to individually named users; they will continue to be able to exercise any privileges not specifically revoked from them.

Managing Privileges with *ADMIN OPTION*

We looked briefly at ADMIN OPTION in the preceding two sections. Recall that this option gives the recipients of the system privilege exactly the same rights you have—they not only can perform the tasks associated with the privilege (as listed in Table 10.1), but they can also assign the privilege to other users and revoke it from any user's privilege domain. I've mentioned that one user they can revoke it from is the user who granted it to them in the first place.

Another point to realize about ADMIN OPTION is that when a user with this option grants the privilege to someone else, he or she can concurrently grant ADMIN OPTION for that privilege to the new user. This new user can then revoke it from their donor or from anyone else who has the privilege. The new user, of course, also has the option of granting the privilege to anyone else with or without ADMIN OPTION. It's even possible for a user to grant a system privilege to PUBLIC with ADMIN OPTION, which would allow every user to manage the privilege.

The point of this discussion isn't to recommend a strategy for making privilege management easy by granting system privileges to PUBLIC with ADMIN OPTION, but rather to caution you that this can happen.

It is, of course, perfectly reasonable to expect that a user with a system privilege might need to give that privilege to someone else. The DBA responsible for managing your user information, for example, may need to give the CREATE, ALTER, and DROP USER privileges to a colleague in the Human Resources Department

Don't deprive yourself (of privileges)

Be careful when using the **REVOKE** command because you can revoke a privilege from yourself if you have the necessary privileges.

Manage privileges wisely

I want to emphasize the importance of managing your system privileges and ensuring that they aren't abused. Assign privileges only to the users who need them, and grant to them only the specific privileges you know they will need. Pay special attention to privileges granted with **ADMIN OPTION**.

while they're away on a vacation. If you suspect that there's some misuse of system privileges, however, or you just want to monitor them as part of your security procedures, you can use the data dictionary to help. You can determine who has each system privilege, and which of the users also has the ADMIN OPTION on any given one. DBA_SYS_PRIVS is the view you need to query. A sample query against this view is as follows:

```
SQL> SELECT * FROM dba_sys_privs
  2  WHERE grantee in ('SCOTT','PUBLIC');
```

① Name of the userid (or role, as you see later) to which the privilege has been granted

② Name of the granted system privilege

③ Shows that the privilege can't be administered by the grantee

④ Shows that the privilege can be granted or revoked by the grantee

```
GRANTEE          PRIVILEGE              ADM
--------------   --------------------   ---
SCOTT            CREATE SYNONYM         NO
PUBLIC           CREATE SESSION         NO
SCOTT            CREATE TABLE           NO
SCOTT            CREATE TABLESPACE      YES
```

4 rows selected.

Although you can't necessarily trace who gave whom which privilege, you should be able to identify any users who have privileges you didn't expect them to have. You can begin solving your problems by removing these privileges. You may then want to remove ADMIN OPTION from the other users to prevent the privileges from being re-granted until you can investigate the users involved directly.

To remove ADMIN OPTION from a system privilege, you have to revoke the privilege entirely and then re-grant the privilege without ADMIN OPTION. There isn't a command that lets you remove the administrative capability while retaining the privilege itself.

Object Privileges

Once you have a system privilege, you can use it across the whole database to do whatever the privilege allows. On the other hand, an object privilege is granted on just one object. For example, the right to query the DOCTORS table that you've been given doesn't give you any access to the PATIENTS table. This allows the owners of database tables—and other objects such as stored procedures and packages, sequences, and snapshots—to be very selective about what other users can access them.

Unlike system privileges, the original database users, SYS and SYSTEM, don't own any object privileges by default, except on objects they happen to own. In fact, the owner is the only user with object privileges when an object is created. Most database objects should be accessed only through the object privileges granted by the owner to the users who have a need for them.

If you've read the preceding sections on system privileges, you probably realize by now that some power users have access to all objects without being required to have any object privileges. Such users, however, should comprise a very small segment of your database user community. They need these more powerful privileges to manage the database rather than manipulate data in the applications tables. Even the owner of the tables that contain the application-related data may need only a few, if any, of the system privileges discussed earlier. In some databases I've seen, the application objects are owned by a userid that doesn't even have the privilege to connect to the database, except when an object needs to be built or modified.

The typical user should access the database to perform only specific, well-regulated activities against a set of tables. For instance, a clerk in the medical office may add new patient data, record office visits, and send out statements if payment is due. To do this, he or she may need only to insert or update records in the PATIENTS table and query the ACCOUNTS_PAYABLE table. Medical technicians, on the other hand, may need to read and update the PATIENTS and INVENTORY tables and record charges in the ACCOUNTS_PAYABLE table. Both user types probably won't issue the DML commands against these tables directly, but instead use an application program that further controls their access to the records in these tables.

Protecting application schemas

To protect the objects (tables, indexes, procedures, and so on) that belong to an application, create a schema to hold them. Prevent users from accidentally, or deliberately, connecting to this schema and potentially damaging its contents by withholding the **CREATE SESSION** privilege. Instead, create and manage the objects for the application schema from an account with the necessary **CREATE/ALTER ANY** privileges. You'll temporarily have to give the application schema the ability to connect to the database in order to grant access privileges on the created objects. To minimize the time the account is available for logins, prepare a script to grant all object privileges **WITH GRANT OPTION** to the user who created the objects. All further object privileges can then be granted by this user.

Roles can be used to manage object privileges

As you see later in the "Using Roles to Simplify Privilege Management" section, you can create roles that are granted a subset of privileges, and then grant the role to the users. This minimizes the amount of privilege management on your part.

Typical users require only the subset of object privileges required to complete their work on the objects that are part of the specific application they use. Although there are only nine types of object privileges (compared to about 100 different system privileges), you'll grant many more object privileges—if yours is a typical database—than you will system privileges. Similarly, most work performed in the database will be done under the permissions obtained from object privileges rather than from system privileges.

You allocate and deallocate object privileges by using the GRANT and REVOKE commands, just as for system privileges. However, the two types of privileges have different characteristics and require slightly different syntax to manage them. They're also recorded in different data dictionary tables. You can query the DBA_TAB_PRIVS view to see the privileges granted on database objects:

```
SQL> SELECT * FROM dba_tab_privs WHERE owner = 'SCOTT';
```

① Privilege recipient

② Owner of the object to which the privilege belongs

③ Object to which the privilege belongs

④ User who issued the grant on the privilege

⑤ Name of the object privilege

⑥ YES if the grantee can grant the privilege to another user, NO if the grantee can't make such a grant

⑦ TERRY can grant UPDATE on SCOTT's table because GRANTABLE is YES

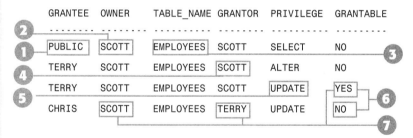

GRANTEE	OWNER	TABLE_NAME	GRANTOR	PRIVILEGE	GRANTABLE
PUBLIC	SCOTT	EMPLOYEES	SCOTT	SELECT	NO
TERRY	SCOTT	EMPLOYEES	SCOTT	ALTER	NO
TERRY	SCOTT	EMPLOYEES	SCOTT	UPDATE	YES
CHRIS	SCOTT	EMPLOYEES	TERRY	UPDATE	NO

Granting Object Privileges

The GRANT command for object privileges has a slightly more complex structure than its system privilege counterpart:

- It must identify not just the privilege, but also the object on which the privilege is being granted.

- For tables and views, some privileges can be limited to a subset of the columns.

- Because the objects belong to a user other than the one issuing the GRANT command, the syntax has to allow for a schema name.

You can see how these factors are incorporated into the object GRANT command by looking at its syntax:

```
GRANT [privilege_name [(column_name[,...])]][,...]]
  [ALL [PRIVILEGES]]
    ON [[schema.]object_name] [DIRECTORY directory_name]
    TO [user_name[,...]] [PUBLIC]
    [WITH GRANT OPTION]
```

- GRANT, ON, and TO are the required keywords to grant object privileges.

- *privilege_name* is an object privilege. It must be included if there's no ALL clause.

- *column_name* is a column name, valid only if the privilege is named and is one of INSERT, REFERENCES, or UPDATE.

- ALL is used to grant all available object privileges. ALL must be included if no privilege is named. The optional keyword PRIVILEGES is used for clarification only and is never required.

- *schema* is the name of the owner of the object on which privileges are being granted. The default is the schema of the user issuing the command.

- *object_name* is the name of the object on which privileges are being granted. It must be included if there's no DIRECTORY clause.

- DIRECTORY *directory_name* identifies a directory object for storing BFILEs. It must be included if no object is named.

- *user_name* is a valid username or userid and must be included if PUBLIC isn't.

- PUBLIC designates all database users and can be used alone or with a list of one or more named users. It's required if no username is included.

- WITH GRANT OPTION grants not just the named privilege(s) but also the right for the recipient(s) to assign it to, and remove it from, other users.

SEE ALSO

> *Learn about* NOT NULL *constraints, page* **490**

Avoid Catch-22 when granting INSERT on selected columns

You should be careful when granting the **INSERT** privilege and restricting the columns to which the privilege allows access. Any column defined with a **NOT NULL** constraint—directly or indirectly through a **PRIMARY KEY** constraint—must be provided a value when a new row is inserted. If the **INSERT** privilege doesn't include all such columns, the recipient of the privilege won't be able use it because it won't allow the inclusion of values into the **NOT NULL** columns.

To complete the syntax options, Table 10.2 shows the names of the available object privileges and indicates on which object types they can be granted. If you use the GRANT command's ALL (PRIVILEGES) option, you can see from this table which privileges are going to be granted, based on the object type.

TABLE 10.2 **Object privileges and related objects**

Object Privilege:	Table:	View:	Sequence:	Procedures Functions Packages:	Snapshot:	Directory:	Library:
ALTER	X		X				
DELETE	X	X					
EXECUTE				X			X
INDEX	X						
INSERT	X	X					
READ						X	
REFERENCES	X						
SELECT	X	X	X		X		
UPDATE	X	X					

The syntax diagram doesn't include the necessary options to grant object options to roles covered later in this chapter. To issue any object grants successfully with this command (with or without the role options), you must be the owner of the named object or have been granted the privilege(s) you're attempting to grant with GRANT OPTION. In the latter case, you need to include the schema name to identify the object's owner.

Although the names of the privileges should indicate what they allow, let's quickly review each one and identify what command or commands it allows the recipient to perform. The capabilities provided by each privilege can vary depending on the type of object to which you're granting the privilege. Table 10.3 summarizes the capabilities each object privilege provides.

TABLE 10.3 **Uses for object privileges**

Privilege Name:	Operations Allowed:
ALTER	Issue the ALTER TABLE and ALTER SEQUENCE commands
DELETE	Delete rows from a table or view
EXECUTE	Execute the procedure, function, package, or external procedure, and access to any program object declared in a package specification
INDEX	Issue the CREATE INDEX command on the table for which the privilege is given
INSERT	Insert rows into a table or view
READ	Read BFILEs from the named directory
REFERENCES	Create foreign-key constraints against the table
SELECT	Select rows from a table, view, or snapshot; extract numbers from a sequence generator
UPDATE	Update rows in a table or view

SEE ALSO

➤ *Read more about foreign-key constraints, page* **494**

To help you understand object privileges, the following examples contain typical user requirements and the commands you would use to provide them:

- Issue the following statement to allow PAT to query all columns in the EMPLOYEES table owned by HR, as well as to updatc and build indexes on them all:

  ```
  GRANT select, update, index ON hr.employees TO pat;
  ```

- Issue the following statement to allow TERRY to execute any procedures or functions in the HR package HIRE_EMPOYEE, or to access any of its publicly defined variables (see Appendix A for details):

  ```
  GRANT execute ON hr.hire_employee TO terry
    WITH GRANT OPTION;
  ```

- Use the following command to allow CHRIS to add new records that contain only the employee's ID number, first and last names, and birth date to the EMPLOYEES table owned by HR:

Remember the ALL shortcut

If you need to assign all the privileges pertinent to a specific object to one or more users, remember that you can use the **ALL** option in the **GRANT** command to grant every privilege appropriate for the object. Table 10.2 lists the privileges associated with each type of object.

```
GRANT insert (id, first_name, last_name, birth_date)
    ON employees TO chris;
```

- Issue the following statement to allow the HR_USER userid to build foreign-key constraints on the ID or SSN columns of HR's EMPLOYEES table, and to grant this right to other users:

```
GRANT references (id, ssn) ON hr.employees TO hr_user
WITH GRANT OPTION;
```

Revoking Object Privileges

You use the REVOKE command to remove an object privilege, just as with a system privilege. Of course, the syntax is slightly different because you need to identify a specific object. You also might have to include options to remove privileges on which other objects depend. The following syntax, as with that for the GRANT command, doesn't include the options for handling privileges assigned to roles:

```
REVOKE [privilege_name [(column_name[,...])][,...]]
  [ALL [PRIVILEGES]]
    ON [[schema.]object_name] [DIRECTORY directory_name]
    FROM [user_name[,...]] [PUBLIC]
    [CASCADE CONSTRAINTS]
    [FORCE]
```

All keywords and options in the REVOKE command are identical to those in the GRANT command, except the following:

- REVOKE, ON, and FROM are the required keywords to revoke object privileges.

- CASCADE CONSTRAINTS indicates that any referential integrity constraints defined by using the privilege being revoked will be dropped. The command will fail if such constraints exist and you don't include this optional phrase.

- FORCE automatically revokes EXECUTE privileges on user-defined object types that have table dependencies. The command will fail if such table dependencies exist and you don't include this keyword.

Revoking specific column grants

The **REVOKE** command doesn't have an option to identify individual columns. If you need to remove a privilege granted for a specific column or change an object privilege from allowing access to the whole table to restrict it to a subset of columns, you must revoke the current privilege and grant it again with the specific column limitations.

Unlike system privileges, which can be granted only to a user or to PUBLIC one time, an object privilege can be granted to the same user by many different grantors. The revocation of a privilege by one grantor doesn't change the status of that privilege as granted by another user to the same grantee. To remove an object privilege from a user's privilege domain or from PUBLIC, every grantor of that privilege must revoke it.

The following examples demonstrate the REVOKE command but also include GRANT commands so that you can see the whole story:

- Assume that TERRY had been granted the privilege to select all columns, to update the SALARY and the JOB_TITLE columns, and to build foreign-key constraints on the DEPT column of the EMPLOYEES table owned by HR with the following command:
  ```
  GRANT SELECT, UPDATE (salary, job_title),
     REFERENCES (dept) ON hr.employees TO terry;
  ```

- The following commands could be used to selectively manage these privileges. Use the following to prevent further queries:
  ```
  REVOKE SELECT ON hr.employees FROM terry;
  ```

- To prevent any further definitions of foreign-key constraints on DEPT, use the following:
  ```
  REVOKE REFERENCES ON hr.employees FROM terry;
  ```

- To allow updates to the DEPT column in addition to the SALARY and JOB_TITLE columns:
  ```
  GRANT UPDATE (dept) ON hr.employees TO terry;
  ```

- To prevent updates on the SALARY column but retain it on the JOB_TITLE and DEPT columns:
  ```
  REVOKE UPDATE ON hr.employees FROM terry;
  GRANT UPDATE (job_title,dept) ON hr.employees TO terry;
  ```

- To remove all privileges on the table:
  ```
  REVOKE ALL PRIVILEGES ON hr.employees FROM terry;
  ```

Mixed PUBLIC and individual privileges

If the same privilege has been granted to PUBLIC and to individual users, revoking the privilege from PUBLIC won't affect users who have been granted the privilege directly. Similarly, revoking the privilege from such a user won't preclude the use of the privilege by that user via the PUBLIC assignment.

Combining REVOKE and GRANT commands

In some situations, you may need to issue a series of REVOKE and GRANT commands to change a privilege mix on an object for a user. This is typically true when you want to remove from a user the capability to grant the privilege but want the user to retain the right to use the privilege.

Automatic Cascading Impacts of Revoked Object Privileges

Dependent objects may be affected by the loss of an object privilege without any further action on the part of the grantor or the grantee. This is in addition to the cascading results of the CASCADE CONSTRAINTS and FORCE options. The situations where this can occur include the following:

- If you revoke a privilege on an object from a user whose schema contains a view requiring the privilege, Oracle invalidates the view.

- If you revoke a privilege that's exercised in a stored procedure, the stored procedure is marked invalid. When this is done, the procedure can't be re-executed or its public variables referenced unless the privilege is regranted. (See Appendix A for details of stored procedures and public variables.) A procedure exercises an object privilege if the object is referenced by one or more SQL statements and the procedure owner isn't the object owner.

- If you revoke a privilege from a user who has granted that privilege to other users, Oracle revokes the privilege from grantees as well as the grantor.

Managing Privileges with *GRANT OPTION*

GRANT OPTION is somewhat like the ADMIN OPTION associated with system privileges. Like that option, it allows the grantee to grant the related privilege to other users. It also allows this grant to be granted with its own GRANT OPTION, thus allowing the new grantee to further grant the privilege, with or without the grant option. However, the two options behave very differently when it comes to the revocation of the privileges.

All object privileges have an ultimate owner—the owner of the object on which the grants have been made. Nobody can remove the object privileges from the object's owner, regardless of what other privileges they may possess. The object owner also has the right to determine who has any privilege on the object, regardless of how that privilege was obtained. For this reason, Oracle

Grantor object privileges can't be revoked by grantee

A user who received an object privilege from a grantor who was assigned the privilege with **GRANT OPTION** can't revoke that privilege from the grantor, even if that user also received **GRANT OPTION**. (This is different from the behavior of system privileges granted with **ADMIN OPTION**.) To execute this **REVOKE** command, the grantee would require, paradoxically, the use of the privilege that the command would have to remove, due to the cascading action. And, were it allowed, the end result of this action would be that that neither the grantor nor the grantee would have the privilege.

tracks the userids of each grantor and each grantee of every object privilege in the data dictionary. This allows the REVOKE command to cascade the removal of the privilege down to everyone who received the privilege from the user named in the REVOKE command. This can include a number of user levels, as shown in Figure 10.1.

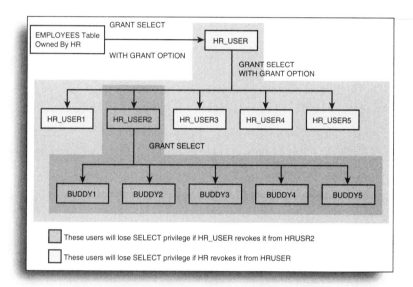

FIGURE 10.1

Object privileges granted to users with the *GRANT OPTION* are removed with an automatic cascading *REVOKE* command.

A user with the GRANT OPTION on an object privilege can revoke it from a user who was granted the privilege through their auspices. For example, the user HR_USER in Figure 10.1 could revoke the SELECT privilege on the EMPLOYEES table from BUDDY1 just as well as user HRUSER2. However, HRUSR1 couldn't successfully revoke the privilege from BUDDY1, even with the GRANT OPTION, because HRUSR1 didn't grant it to that user.

SEE ALSO

➤ *More information on user-defined objects and table dependencies, page 731*

The arithmetic of roles and privileges

Assume that you have some number of privileges (let's say m) and some number of users (let's say n) to whom privileges need to be granted. By granting each user each privilege, you have $m \times n$ relationships between the privileges and the users to manage. If you use a single role, grant the privileges to the role, and then grant the role to the users, you have a total of $m + n$ relationships to manage. The product of m and n will always be larger than their sum, with the difference getting increasingly pronounced as the magnitude increases. Consider just 100 privileges and 50 users. There would be 5,000 individual relationships if you didn't use roles—just 150 with a single role.

Activated roles

By allowing roles to be active or inactive, Oracle provides an extra level of security for the privileges managed by the role. Until the role is active for a user, that user can't take advantage of the privileges associated with the role. If the role is password protected, the user can't activate it without the password. In such cases, the role can be activated by an application program that can supply the password without the user having knowledge of it. This prevents accidental or deliberate use of the privileges while a user is connected to the database through some means other than the application.

Using Roles to Simplify Privilege Management

In a large database with many hundreds, if not thousands, of tables, stored procedures, and related objects, and with many hundreds of users, you can imagine how daunting the task of assigning privileges could be. The task is even more complicated when the database supports more than one application or many different functions within the same application, each requiring different levels of access to various objects. Within a single application or function, there can also be categories of users; some users are only allowed to browse for certain data, while others may have update rights, and yet others can have full DML capability on different subsets of tables.

To help you administer a database with so many different requirements for privileges, Oracle provides a special database object known as a *role*. Most simply, a role is a named collection of privileges. The most important characteristic of a role isn't readily apparent from this definition, however. A role can be granted just like a privilege, and the result of such a grant is that all the privileges assigned to the role will be simultaneously granted to the recipient. If you look at Figure 10.2, you can see how this reduces the number of privilege grants that you need to manage in the very simple case of four privileges being granted to three different users.

Roles have further powerful features:

- A role can contain system and object privileges.
- A role can be granted to another role, allowing you to build meta-roles.
- A role can contain a mix of individual privileges plus roles, or just privileges or just roles.
- A privilege granted to a role becomes immediately usable by any users assigned to the role.
- Revoking a privilege from a role immediately prevents any further use of the privilege by all users associated with the role.

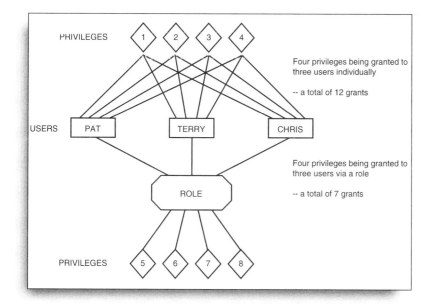

PRIVILEGES

USERS

Four privileges being granted to
three users individually

-- a total of 12 grants

Four privileges being granted to
three users via a role

-- a total of 7 grants

PRIVILEGES

FIGURE 10.2

With roles, you reduce the
number of individual *GRANT*
commands you issue.

- A role can be in an activated or a deactivated state for a user.
- A role can be password-protected to prevent users from activating its privileges for themselves.

Creating Roles

Anyone with the requisite CREATE ROLE privilege can create a new role. As soon as it's created, the role doesn't belong to that user's schema, nor to any other schema. To do anything with a role, however, you must have privileges on it, and only the original creator automatically receives the equivalent of a system privilege's ADMIN OPTION on a role.

If the original creator wants to allow other users to administer the role, he or she can grant it to those users with ADMIN OPTION just as though it were a system privilege. Just as with system privileges, when users have ADMIN OPTION on a role, they can grant the role to others as well as revoke it from other users—including the original creator.

Maintaining the role administration function

At least one user must maintain the ADMIN OPTION on a role at all times. As with system privileges, you can't revoke just the ADMIN OPTION—you must revoke all access to the role. Unlike system privileges, you can't revoke the role from yourself; however, you can remove the role from the database if you have no further use for it, which, of course, eliminates the need for it be administered any further.

The command for creating a role has the following syntax:

```
CREATE ROLE role_name
    [NOT IDENTIFIED]
    [IDENTIFIED [BY password] [EXTERNALLY] [GLOBALLY]]
```

- CREATE ROLE is the command name.

- NOT IDENTIFIED indicates that the role can be enabled without a password. This is the default if the IDENTIFIED clause isn't included, so this clause can be omitted.

- IDENTIFIED indicates that further authorization is required to enable the role. No such authorization will be required if this option is omitted.

- BY password names the password that the user must supply to enable the role. It must be included in the IDENTIFIED clause if the EXTERNALLY and GLOBALLY options aren't.

- EXTERNALLY indicates that the operating system, or a security service running under it, will provide authentication to enable the role. External authentication may or may not require a password. This keyword must be included in the IDENTIFIED clause if the BY and GLOBALLY options aren't.

- GLOBALLY indicates that the user must be authorized by the Oracle Security Service before the role can be enabled. (See *The Oracle Security Server Guide* and the *Oracle8 Server Distributed Systems* manual for further details.) This keyword must be included in the IDENTIFIED clause if the BY and EXTERNALLY options aren't.

You can change the authorization required for a role after it's created by issuing an ALTER ROLE command. This command accepts the NOT IDENTIFIED or IDENTIFIED clause, the latter requiring one of three options listed in the CREATE ROLE syntax. However, before you can alter a role to global authorization, you must revoke the following:

- All other roles granted to the role and identified externally

- The role from all users, except the one altering the role

- The role from all other roles

- The role from PUBLIC

External authentication of roles

Only certain operating systems provide facilities for external authentication of roles. You must check your operating system-specific documentation for information on this topic, including the steps needed to set up specific authorizations. You can also use third-party products for external authentication of roles. Consult the vendor's documentation and *The Oracle Security Server Guide* for more details on such products.

Privileges for altering a role

To alter a role, you must have ADMIN OPTION on the role or the ALTER ANY ROLE system privilege. If you're altering the authentication from global to unrestricted (NOT IDENTIFIED) or to alternate authentication (BY password or EXTERNALLY), you'll be automatically granted ADMIN OPTION on the role if you don't already have it.

Oracle provides this set of predefined roles with included privileges when the database is created:

- CONNECT provides basic privileges for a typical application user.

- RESOURCE provides basic privileges for an application developer.

- DBA provides a full set of system privileges with ADMIN OPTION.

- EXP_FULL_DATABASE and IMP_FULL_DATABASE are for users of the Export and Import utilities.

Oracle doesn't recommend relying on the CONNECT, RESOURCE, or DBA roles, which are included for compatibility with earlier versions of the database and may not be included in later releases.

Granting Privileges to Roles

You grant system and object privileges to roles by using the GRANT commands discussed earlier. The syntax is the same as discussed under each command format, except that you use a role name rather than a username. There's also one restriction on object privileges granted to roles—you can't use WITH GRANT OPTION.

To grant privileges to a role, you must either have the GRANT ANY ROLE system privilege or have ADMIN OPTION on the role, either by being its creator or by being granted the role with this privilege.

As soon as a privilege is granted to a role, it's usable to anyone with the role enabled, and will also be available to anyone enabling the role in the future. There are certain restrictions on the privileges associated with roles. Objects that rely on other object's privileges can't be created when those privileges are available only through a role rather than be directly granted. For example, a view can't be created against a table if the SELECT privilege on that table is available only through a role.

Granting Roles to Users and to Other Roles

A role is granted to a user or to another role by using the same syntax as the system privilege GRANT command. This syntax,

Ghost roles

A number of roles are added to the database when it's created that don't have any associated privileges until work is done that requires them. These roles are undocumented and are included here for completeness: EXECUTE_CATALOG_ ROLE, SELECT_CATA- LOG_ROLE, SNMPAGENT, DELETE_CATALOG_ROLE, AQ_USER_ROLE, RECOV- ERY_CATALOG_OWNER, and AQ_ADMINISTRA- TOR_ROLE.

Grant assignee options

In a single **GRANT** command, you can grant privileges to a user, a list of users, a role, a list of roles, or a list composed of users and roles. The list can even include users who are already assigned to one or more of the roles in the list. **PUBLIC** is also a valid user in this context.

explained in detail earlier in the section "Granting System Privileges," can be followed exactly except that the name of the role is substituted for the name of a system privilege. A single GRANT command can include multiple role names as well as one or more system privilege names. As mentioned earlier, you can't repeat a name in this list.

When a role is granted to another role, the privileges from both roles are combined. The granted role will pass on this superset of privileges to anyone who is granted the role. If this role is itself granted to another role, the privileges from the two original roles will be assigned to the newly granted role; see Figure 10.3 for an illustration of this.

FIGURE 10.3

You can build complex roles from more simple roles.

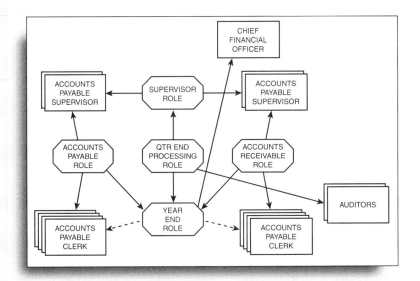

Most application users will have a fixed set of tasks that they need to complete on an ongoing basis. Many of these users will, in fact, perform identical tasks to each other. A single role can be used to provide these users with all the necessary system and object privileges to perform their work. Occasionally, these users may need to perform special projects. A different role can be created to handle the associated privileges and granted to the base role for the duration of the project. One or two users may need both the base role and the special role on a regular basis, in which case you can grant both roles to these users. Other users may perform multiple tasks in a given application.

These users can also be assigned their privileges through a role, but in this case the role will contain the base roles from each independent task. These users' supervisors may have yet another role that contains extra privileges for their supervisory functions, plus the complex role already created for their staff. If you have a situation similar to this, you should plan your roles carefully so that you're allowed the most flexibility in assigning them to the different worker categories.

By this time, you should be able to follow the full syntax of the GRANT command for system privileges and roles. It's shown here without further comment. If you aren't clear on any of the options, refer to the explanation earlier in this chapter.

```
GRANT [privilege_name][,...] [role_name][,...] [,...]
TO [user_name[,...]] [role_name][,...] [,...] [PUBLIC]
[WITH ADMIN OPTION]
```

If the GRANT command includes the WITH ADMIN OPTION clause, any role being granted by the command will be available to the grantees just as if the role had been granted to them directly. In other words, the grantees have the right to grant and revoke the role to and from other users as well as the right to grant and revoke other roles and privileges to and from the role.

There are some limitations on grants associated with roles. In particular, you can't grant the following:

- A global role to a user or to any other role
- A role IDENTIFIED EXTERNALLY to a global user or to a global role
- A global role to PUBLIC
- A role to itself, directly or through a circular set of grants

Setting Default Roles

A role is automatically active for a user to whom it's granted, even if it's a passworded role. To restrict access to the privileges awarded through a role, you have to change the privilege domain of each granted user for whom you don't want the role active by default. You have to use the ALTER USER command's DEFAULT ROLE

Avoid granting roles circularly

A circular grant would occur if Role A were granted to Role B, Role B were granted to Role C, and Role C were granted to Role A. This would result in a grant of Role A to itself. Oracle doesn't support granting a role to itself, however, and will prevent you from doing this accidentally by issuing an error message if you try.

Why identify default roles?

As noted, all granted roles are active by default whenever a user logs into the database. You don't want these roles enabled all the time if you've created roles with password protection to prevent users from using the related privileges unless under the control of an application. The only way to prevent them from being active is to identify all the roles that should be active in the **ALTER USER** command's **DEFAULT ROLE** clause. Any role not named, or any role named in the **ALL** option's **EXCEPT** clause, will remain disabled.

Password versus external or global authentication of roles

You should use password protection for roles that assign privileges you never want the user to be able to take advantage of directly. The privileges granted by the role are used only inside programs that use SQL to activate the role when needed—supplying the password, of course—and deactivate it before exiting. External and global authentication offer a layer of security for roles as long as the operating system account isn't compromised. Adding passwords to the roles gives an added layer of security, but users must know the passwords to activate them at any time. Passworded roles using external or global authorization can't be activated from a program.

option to do this. In a single statement, you can identify exactly which roles granted to the user you want active or inactive whenever the user first connects to the database.

The syntax for only the DEFAULT ROLE option of the ALTER USER command is as follows:

```
ALTER USER user_name
    DEFAULT ROLE
        [role_names]
        [ALL [EXCEPT role_names]]
        [NONE]
```

- ALTER USER *user_name* identifies the user's name.

- DEFAULT ROLE is the required option.

- *role_name*s is the name of a single role, or a comma-separated list of role names, which should be active at connect time.

- ALL indicates that all granted roles are to be active at connect time.

- EXCEPT *role_names* identifies a single role, or a comma-separated list of role names, that shouldn't be active at connect time. This phrase can be used only with the ALL option.

- NONE causes no roles to be active at connect time.

You must include one—and only one—of the *role_name* (or list), ALL, or NONE options in a single command. You can't enable roles with the ALTER USER command if any of the following apply:

- The role hasn't been granted to the user.

- The role was granted to another role (unless it was also granted to the user directly).

- The role is managed by an external service or by the Oracle Security Service Certification Authority.

Here are some examples of the commands you would use to set up the default roles for different users:

- To activate only the ACCT_PAY role for Kim:
  ```
  ALTER USER kim DEFAULT ROLE acct_pay;
  ```

- To activate all but the MONTH_END role for Pat:
  ```
  ALTER USER pat DEFAULT ROLE ALL EXCEPT month_end;
  ```

- To prevent Terry from having any active roles at connect time:

```
ALTER USER terry DEFAULT ROLE NONE;
```

SEE ALSO

➤ *A detailed description of the* ALTER USER *command, page* ***270***

Enabling and Disabling Roles

To activate a role that has been granted to you but isn't available to you now, you have to issue the SET ROLE command and identify the role you need enabled. This will generally be done inside an application, where the role can be enabled without you having to know its password. The SQL command to enable a role is as follows:

```
SET ROLE
    [role_name [IDENTIFIED BY password][,...]]
        [ALL [EXCEPT role_name[,...]]
        [NONE]
```

Notice that this command is very similar to the ALTER USER command's DEFAULT ROLE clause discussed in the previous section. The only differences are the keywords SET ROLE and the optional IDENTIFIED BY password clause. The latter is required to activate a password-protected role. As with the ALTER USER command, you must include one of three optional clauses—role name or list, ALL, or NONE—in the SET ROLE command. Because the SET ROLE command works only for the user who issues it, there's no provision to include a username.

Another similarity between the SET ROLE command and the ALTER USER...DEFAULT ROLE command is that the statement overrides the default behavior. The command activates only the named roles or all the roles not listed in the ALL option's EXCEPT clause. All other roles are disabled by default.

In some cases, the application that needs to change your active roles will be executing a PL/SQL routine rather than a program that can issue the SET ROLE command. To accommodate this eventuality, Oracle provides the procedure SET_ROLE as part of the DBMS_SESSION package. The procedure accepts one string as an input parameter; this string should contain a valid SET ROLE command option, just as shown in the preceding syntax.

Using the ALL EXCEPT clause

You can't use the ALL option if one or more of your roles requires a password to enable it. If even just one of them requires a password, you'll have to list each role—including the password when necessary—in the SET ROLE command. The EXCEPT clause allows you to use the ALL option by excluding the role or roles with passwords.

The SET ROLE command disables roles

SET ROLE disables all roles for the user—including those identified as default roles— except those specifically enabled by the command. Before issuing this command, you should identify any other roles you may need to remain active along with the additional ones you're trying to enable. Include all these roles in the SET ROLE command by naming them or by using the ALL option.

The following listing shows an anonymous PL/SQL block that activates the ACCT_PAY and MONTH_END roles:

```
BEGIN
DBMS_SESSION.SET_ROLE('ACCT_PAY,MONTH_END');
END;
```

The DBMS_SESSION procedure can't be used in a stored procedure or trigger, and the role(s) it activates may not be accessible until after the PL/SQL block completes successful execution.

Revoking Role Privileges

The REVOKE command is used to revoke privileges from roles, roles from roles, and roles from users or from PUBLIC. To revoke an object or a system privilege from a role, use the appropriate version of the REVOKE as discussed earlier, substituting a role name anywhere a username can be used. You shouldn't need the CASCADE CONSTRAINTS or FORCE clause for object privileges because no objects can be created by using object privileges granted via a role.

If you revoke a role to which other roles have been granted, the entire set of privileges associated with every role will be revoked. Of course, if any of those roles and privileges had been granted directly to a user or a role affected by the revoke, they can still exercise the related privileges through the direct grant.

Dropping Roles

You can drop a role at any time as long as you have the role granted to you with ADMIN OPTION or have the DROP ANY ROLE system privilege. The DROP command takes effect immediately, revoking the role from all granted users and other roles and then removing it from the database. The command is as follows:

```
DROP ROLE role_name
```

It has no options. Any roles granted to the dropped role will remain defined but won't be available for use by anyone unless they have been granted those roles directly.

Data Dictionary Tables and Privilege Tracking

The data dictionary uses a number of tables to manage all the possible relationships due to the complexity that can result from the granting of multiple privileges to single users and to roles, and then the granting of roles to users and to other roles. To help you and your users keep track of what has been assigned to whom and to what, and what is or isn't currently active, Oracle provides a number of views on these data dictionary tables. Table 10.4 briefly summarizes the data dictionary views related to privileges and roles.

TABLE 10.4   **Data dictionary views to monitor privileges and roles**

View	Description
ALL_COL_PRIVS	Shows grants on columns for which the user or PUBLIC is the grantee
ALL_COL_PRIVS_MADE	Shows grants on columns for which the user is the owner or the grantor
ALL_COL_PRIVS_RECD	Shows the grants on columns for which the user or PUBLIC is the grantee
ALL_TAB_PRIVS	Shows grants on objects for which the user or PUBLIC is the grantee
ALL_TAB_PRIVS_MADE	Shows grants on objects for which the user is the owner or the grantor
ALL_TAB_PRIVS_RECD	Shows the grants on objects for which the user or PUBLIC is the grantee
COLUMN_PRIVILEGES	Shows grants on columns for which the user is the owner, grantor, or grantee, or PUBLIC is the grantee
DBA_COL_PRIVS	Shows all grants on columns in the database
DBA_PRIV_AUDIT OPTIONS	Shows all system privileges being audited
DBA_ROLES	Shows all roles in the database
DBA_ROLE_PRIVS	Shows the roles granted to users and to other roles
DBA_SYS_PRIVS	Shows system privileges granted to users and to roles

Views for compatibility

The COLUMN_PRIVILEGES and TABLE_PRIVILEGES views are provided only for compatibility with earlier versions. Oracle recommends avoiding the use of these views.

continues…

TABLE 10.4 **Continued**

View	Description
DBA_TAB_PRIVS	Shows all grants on objects in the database
HS_EXTERNAL_OBJECT PRIVILEGES	Shows information about privileges on non-Oracle data stores
HS_EXTERNAL_USER PRIVILEGES	Shows information about granted privileges that aren't tied to any particular object related to non-Oracle data stores
ROLE_ROLE_PRIVS	For roles to which the user has access, shows roles granted to other roles
ROLE_SYS_PRIVS	For roles to which the user has access, shows system privileges granted to roles
ROLE_TAB_PRIVS	For roles to which the user has access, shows object privileges granted to roles
SESSION_PRIVS	Shows privileges now available to the user
SESSION_ROLES	Shows roles now available to the user
SYSTEM_PRIVILEGE MAP	Maps system privilege names to privilege codes numbers
TABLE_PRIVILEGES	Shows grants on objects for which the user is the owner, grantor, or grantee, or PUBLIC is the grantee
TABLE_PRIVILEGE_MAP	Maps object privilege names to privilege codes
USER_COL_PRIVS	Shows grants on columns for which the user is the owner, grantor, or grantee
USER_COL_PRIVS_MADE	Shows the grants on columns of objects owned by the user
USER_COL_PRIVS_RECD	Shows the grants on columns for which the user is the grantee
USER_ROLE_PRIVS	Shows the roles granted to the user
USER_SYS_PRIVS	Shows the system privileges granted to the user
USER_TAB_PRIVS	Shows the grants on objects for which the user is the owner, grantor, or grantee
USER_TAB_PRIVS_MADE	Shows the grants on objects for which the user is the owner
USER_TAB_PRIVS_RECD	Shows the grants on objects for which the user is the grantee

Auditing Database Use and Controlling Resources and Passwords

Control what's audited

Interpret audit results

Control consumption of system resources

Enforce password management

Why Audit?

For an Oracle DBA, *auditing* is the process of recording what's being done in the database. *Audit records* can tell you what system privileges are being used and how often, how many users are logging during various periods, how long the average session lasts, what commands are being used against specific tables, and many other related facts. However, you shouldn't treat auditing as an idle gatherer of data—you simply add unnecessary overhead by doing that. You should use auditing when it's the easiest, fastest, and least intrusive means of collecting information that you need to perform your job.

The types of activities you can perform as a DBA where auditing could help include the following:

- Preparing database usage reports for your management (how many users connect per day/week, how many queries are issued per month, or how many employee records were added or dropped last week)

- Recording failed attempts to break into the database if you suspect hackers

- Identifying the busiest tables that may need additional tuning

- Investigating suspicious changes to critical tables

- Projecting resource consumption by an anticipated increase in user load

Depending on your requirements, you should be able to target exactly what level of auditing you need to invoke. In some cases, you may need to begin by gathering general data before you can identify critical areas that need closer attention.

You may suspect, for example, that the fragmentation in your index tablespace is the result of excessive index creation and deletion over the weekends. You don't know with which tables the indexes are associated because they don't stay in place long enough to find them. You can audit the general activity of index creation in order to identify the specific table or tables involved. You can then audit the indexing activity of the users who have permission to add and drop indexes on these tables. From these detailed audit records, you may be able to identify which user is causing the problem, or at least the specific times the activity is occurring. You can then run a program or log in yourself during these periods to capture data dictionary information about the indexes while they're still in place.

Preparing the Audit Trail

When you decide you need to audit, you must configure your database to handle the task. This requires a special entry in your parameter file. The audit task can be activated—and similarly deactivated—only when the database instance is stopped and restarted.

The parameter you need to modify is AUDIT_TRAIL. By default, it has a value of NONE, which disallows any auditing regardless of any other auditing options that may have been set. You have two additional choices of setting for AUDIT_TRAIL—DB or OS— although the values TRUE (corresponding to DB), and FALSE (corresponding to NONE), are also supported for backward compatibility. With AUDIT_TRAIL set to DB, the audit records are written to a database table named AUD$, which is owned by SYS. If set to OS, the audit records are written to an external operating system file. You can control the location of the audit file by setting an additional parameter, AUDIT_FILE_DEST, to identify the full path name of the directory where you want it to be written.

By default, the AUD$ table is built in the SYSTEM tablespace. This can cause problems if you do extensive auditing because it's possible to fill up this tablespace very quickly. The number of audit records created depends on just how many different actions you audit and what level of detail you require. You should be prepared to monitor your audit table or file on regular basis, even if you collect only minimal data, because other users may turn on additional auditing (by design or by accident), which can generate far more data than you were anticipating.

Protect your audit trail

If you're auditing for any reason—particularly if you're suspicious of hackers—you should make sure that you protect your audit trail from potential tampering. If you're using an external file, make sure that it's in a protected directory. If you're using the internal **AUD$** table, don't give privileges on the table to any user unnecessarily. Just to make sure that you have a record of any attempts to tamper, audit any activity, DDL or DML, against the audit trail by using the commands you learn in the upcoming sections.

Maintaining the Audit Table

**Controlling the capability to per-
form auditing**

There are two levels of auditing: on
statements and on objects. You can
control the auditing of statements
by granting only the **AUDIT
SYSTEM** privilege to users whom
you want to be able to perform this
type of auditing. Object auditing is a
little more difficult to control
because an object's owner can
request that auditing be performed
against the use of that object.
However, you should be able to
prevent any unwanted auditing if
you allow objects to be created only
by a restricted set of users and protect the schemas where those
objects are created by removing
connection privileges to them. If the
objects do need to be audited, you
can grant the **AUDIT ANY** system
privilege to the user(s) responsible
for this task and remove it again
when the required auditing is established.

Although you're never supposed to modify the contents or the
definition of the tables in the data dictionary (meaning any
objects owned by SYS in the SYSTEM tablespace), this restriction is
removed from the AUD$ table. You can change its storage parame-
ters for it to grow larger than set by default, or to make better
use of the free blocks in its tablespace. You also may need to
remove old or other unwanted records to reclaim space. You can
even copy records you do want to analyze to some other location
(including an external file) and then drop them from the AUD$
table. In fact, doing this on a regularly scheduled basis prevents
the table from growing uncontrollably.

You can store records from the AUD$ table a number of ways:

- Issue the SQL statement CREATE TABLE audit_day1 AS SELECT
  * FROM sys.aud$. This will create a table called AUDIT_DAY1
  and copy all the records from AUD$ into it.

- Run the Export utility as user SYS and select the table AUD$ to
  export.

- Use the SQL*Plus SPOOL command and execute a query
  against the sys.aud$ table or against an audit view. (See
  "Reviewing Audit Views" later in this chapter.)

After you save the records you need from AUD$, you can remove
the records you no longer need via different commands, depending on what you're trying to accomplish. Use the following command to remove all records from the table:

```
DELETE FROM sys.aud$;
```

Execute the following command to remove all records and
return the table to its initial extent size:

```
TRUNCATE TABLE sys.aud$;
```

Use the following to remove all records associated with the user
Kim:

```
DELETE FROM sys.aud$ WHERE userid = 'KIM';
```

You can issue the following command to remove all records
except those associated with the EMPLOYEES table:

```
DELETE FROM sys.aud$ WHERE obj$name <> 'EMPLOYEES';
```

SEE ALSO

➤ *Discover the specifics of starting and stopping a database, page **17***

➤ *An introduction to the parameter file, page **11***

Controlling System Auditing

You can audit the use of system privileges or the use of SQL statements used to either administer the database or to manage database objects with a pair of commands. You can also audit the use of DML and DCL statements on specific objects by using a slightly different version of these commands (described in the next section). In both cases, the two commands are AUDIT and NOAUDIT; the former begins an audit and the latter terminates it. Whether you're auditing at the database or object level, the AUDIT command won't generate any audit records unless the instance is running with auditing enabled, as described in the previous section.

The AUDIT command, which begins auditing on system privileges or database administrative commands, has the following syntax:

```
AUDIT
    [system_privilege] [,...]
    [statement_option] [,...]
    [shortcut_name] [,...]
    [BY [user_name [,...]]]
    [BY [SESSION] [ACCESS]]
    [WHENEVER [NOT] SUCCESSFUL]
```

> **Default auditing of the SYS user**
>
> Although you can't audit the user **SYS** yourself, Oracle does track the key work done by **SYS** or using **SYS**'s privileges. This auditing is written to a special file that varies by name and location depending on your operating system. Instance start-up, instance shutdown, and connection as administrator are among the key items audited.

- AUDIT is the keyword to turn on auditing.

- *system_privilege* [,...] is a system privilege or a comma-separated list of system privileges. You can audit any of the privileges listed in Table 10.1. You must include at least one system privilege if you don't list any statement options or shortcut names.

SEE ALSO

➤ *Table 10.1 lists privileges on page **278***

- *statement_option* [,...] is a statement option or a comma-separated list of statement options from Table 11.1. You must include at least one statement option if you don't list any system privileges or shortcut names.

- *shortcut_name* [,...] is a shortcut name or a comma-separated list of shortcut names from Table 11.2. You must include at least one shortcut name if you don't list any system privileges or statement options.

- BY *user_name* [,...] identifies a user, or a list of users, on whom the auditing of the chosen actions will be performed. All users will be audited if you omit this option.

- BY SESSION/ACCESS determines whether all use of an audited action is summarized in a single audit record per user session (BY SESSION), or if a separate audit record will be generated each time the action is performed (BY ACCESS). Audited actions will be summarized at the session level if you omit this option.

- WHENEVER [NOT] SUCCESSFUL determines whether only successful (SUCCESSFUL) or unsuccessful (NOT SUCCESSFUL) attempts to use the audited action are recorded. If you omit the WHENEVER option, all actions—successful and unsuccessful—are audited.

Default auditing for DDL statements

Even if you audit at the session level (by default or with the **BY SESSION** option), you can still generate access-level audit records. This is because all Data Definition Language (DDL) statements, audited as a result of selected system privileges or statement options, will be audited by access.

TABLE 11.1   **Statement options for the AUDIT command**

Statement Option:	Audited SQL Statements and Operations:
ALTER SEQUENCE[1]	ALTER SEQUENCE
ALTER TABLE[1]	ALTER TABLE
CLUSTER	CREATE CLUSTER, AUDIT CLUSTER, DROP CLUSTER, TRUNCATE CLUSTER
COMMENT TABLE[1]	COMMENT ON TABLE for tables, views, or snapshots COMMENT ON COLUMN for table columns, view columns, or snapshot columns
DATABASE LINK	CREATE DATABASE LINK, DROP DATABASE LINK
DELETE TABLE[1]	DELETE FROM tables or views
DIRECTORY	CREATE DIRECTORY, DROP DIRECTORY
EXECUTE PROCEDURE[1]	Execution of any procedure or function, or access to any variable, library, or cursor inside a package
GRANT DIRECTORY[1]	GRANT privilege ON directory REVOKE privilege ON directory

Statement Option:	Audited SQL Statements and Operations:
GRANT PROCEDURE[1]	GRANT privilege ON procedure, function, or package REVOKE privilege ON procedure, function, or package
GRANT SEQUENCE[1]	GRANT privilege ON sequence REVOKE privilege ON sequence
GRANT TABLE[1]	GRANT privilege ON table, view, or snapshot REVOKE privilege ON table, view, or snapshot
GRANT TYPE[1,2]	GRANT privilege ON TYPE REVOKE privilege ON TYPE
INDEX	CREATE INDEX, ALTER INDEX, DROP INDEX
INSERT TABLE[1]	INSERT INTO table or view
LOCK TABLE[1]	LOCK TABLE table or view
NOT EXISTS	Any SQL statement failures because referenced objects don't exist
PROCEDURE	CREATE FUNCTION, CREATE LIBRARY, CREATE PACKAGE, CREATE PACKAGE BODY, CREATE PROCEDURE, DROP FUNCTION, DROP LIBRARY, DROP PACKAGE, DROP PROCEDURE
PROFILE	CREATE PROFILE, ALTER PROFILE, DROP PROFILE
PUBLIC DATABASE LINK	CREATE PUBLIC DATABASE LINK, DROP PUBLIC DATABASE LINK
PUBLIC SYNONYM	CREATE PUBLIC SYNONYM, DROP PUBLIC SYNONYM
ROLE	CREATE ROLE, ALTER ROLE, DROP ROLE, SET ROLE
ROLLBACK STATEMENT	CREATE ROLLBACK SEGMENT, ALTER ROLLBACK SEGMENT, DROP ROLLBACK SEGMENT
SELECT SEQUENCE	Any statement containing a *sequence*.CURRVAL or *sequence*.NEXTVAL phrase, where *sequence* is the name of an Oracle sequence generator
SELECT TABLE[1]	SELECT FROM table, view, or snapshot
SEQUENCE	CREATE SEQUENCE, DROP SEQUENCE
SESSION	All database logins
SYNONYM	CREATE SYNONYM, DROP SYNONYM
SYSTEM AUDIT[3]	AUDIT, NOAUDIT
SYSTEM GRANT[4]	GRANT, REVOKE
TABLE	CREATE TABLE, DROP TABLE, TRUNCATE TABLE

continues…

TABLE 11.1   **continued**

Statement Option:	Audited SQL Statements and Operations:
TABLESPACE	CREATE TABLESPACE, ALTER TABLESPACE, DROP TABLESPACE
TRIGGER	CREATE TRIGGER ALTER TRIGGER with ENABLE and DISABLE options DROP TRIGGER ALTER TABLE with ENABLE ALL TRIGGERS and DISABLE ALL TRIGGERS clauses
TYPE[2]	CREATE TYPE, CREATE TYPE BODY, ALTER TYPE, DROP TYPE, DROP TYPE BODY
UPDATE TABLE[1]	UPDATE table or view
USER	CREATE USER, ALTER USER, DROP USER
VIEW	CREATE VIEW, DROP VIEW

[1] *Not included in the* ALL *shortcut*
[2] *Available only with the* Object *option*
[3] *When used with system privileges or statement options*
[4] *When used with system privileges and roles*

Not all AUDIT options can be named in a single statement

You can mix statement options and shortcuts in the same statement when issuing the **AUDIT** command, but you can't include most system privileges with statement options or shortcuts. Other than this restriction, you can include as many auditing choices as you want in a single statement. You can even include a shortcut and the statement options covered by the shortcut. Similarly, you can either include as many users as you want or allow the statement to default to all users.

To save you from having to enter a series of related system privileges or statement options in an AUDIT statement, Oracle provides a series of shortcuts. Each of these, when referenced in an AUDIT statement, causes auditing to occur on the related items. Table 11.2 lists these shortcuts and the system privileges and statement options included when you use them in an audit command.

TABLE 11.2   **Shortcuts for system privileges and statement options**

Shortcut Name:	System Privilege (P) or Statement Option (O):	Privileges and Options Included:
CONNECT	P	CREATE SESSION
RESOURCE	P	ALTER SESSION
	P	CREATE CLUSTER
	P	CREATE DATABASE LINK
	P	CREATE PROCEDURE
	P	CREATE ROLLBACK SEGMENT
	P	CREATE SEQUENCE
	P	CREATE SYNONYM
	P	CREATE TABLE
	P	CREATE TABLESPACE
	P	CREATE VIEW

Shortcut Name:	System Privilege (P) or Statement Option (O):	Privileges and Options Included:
DBA	P	AUDIT SYSTEM
	P	CREATE PUBLIC DATABASE LINK
	P	CREATE PUBLIC SYNONYM
	P	CREATE ROLE
	P	CREATE USER
	O	SYSTEM GRANT
ALL	O	All statement options listed in Table 11.1, except those noted as not being part of the ALL shortcut
ALL PRIVILEGES	P	All system privileges

Use the NOAUDIT command to cease auditing of the actions you defined with the AUDIT command. The syntax is identical to the AUDIT command except that there's no BY SESSION or BY ACCESS option; the NOAUDIT option turns off whatever option is in effect.

The NOAUDIT command's syntax is as follows:

```
NOAUDIT
    [system_privilege] [,...]
    [statement_option] [,...]
    [shortcut_name] [,...]
    [BY [user_name [,...]]]
    [WHENEVER [NOT] SUCCESSFUL]
```

The various options are described in the syntax description for the AUDIT command.

You can use the NOAUDIT command to stop auditing successful or unsuccessful actions if your AUDIT command had enabled both options (the default) when you executed it. However, you can't alter the auditing behavior from successful to unsuccessful with this command; you have to disable the auditing and re-enable it with your preferred option by issuing a new AUDIT command. If, on the other hand, you were auditing only successful or only unsuccessful actions, the NOAUDIT command can turn off the auditing if you issue it with no WHENEVER option.

Turning off auditing with the NOAUDIT command won't affect any records already created as a result of the previous AUDIT

The NOAUDIT default doesn't necessarily stop all auditing

If your NOAUDIT command doesn't include a list of users, auditing enabled by an AUDIT command also issued without a user list will be terminated. However, any users being audited for the same action(s) for whom you turned on auditing (by naming them in an AUDIT command) won't be affected.

command, but will prevent any further audit records from being created as a result of the audited actions.

Let's end this section by looking at some examples of how the AUDIT and NOAUDIT commands are used:

- The following three commands, in turn, activate the auditing of all connections to the database, the auditing of any successful attempt by Kim to use the ALTER ANY TABLE system privilege, and any attempt by other users to use this privilege:

  ```
  AUDIT create session;
      AUDIT alter any table BY kim WHENEVER SUCCESSFUL
      AUDIT alter any table;
  ```

- To audit just unsuccessful connection attempts, you could now issue this command:

  ```
  NOAUDIT create session WHENEVER SUCCESSFUL;
  ```

- To audit just successful attempts by all other users (as well as Kim) to use the ALTER ANY TABLE privilege, you could issue this command:

  ```
  NOAUDIT  alter any table WHENEVER NOT SUCCESSFUL;
  ```

- To stop the auditing of successful uses of the ALTER ANY TABLE privilege by everyone, you would enter either one of these two statements:

  ```
  NOAUDIT alter any table;
  ```

  ```
  NOAUDIT alter any table WHENEVER SUCCESSFUL;
  ```

  However, Kim's successful use of this privilege would still be audited due to the separate AUDIT command issued earlier. To discontinue this auditing, you also need these two commands:

  ```
  NOAUDIT alter any table BY kim;
  ```

  ```
  NOAUDIT alter any table BY kim WHENEVER SUCCESSFUL;
  ```

Controlling Object Auditing

The command that starts auditing activity against specific database objects has the following syntax:

```
AUDIT
object_option[,...]
    [ALL]
ON
    [[schema.]object_name]
    [DIRECTORY directory_name]
    [DEFAULT]
    [BY [SESSION] [ACCESS]]
    [WHENEVER [NOT] SUCCESSFUL]
```

Object auditing isn't user-specific

You can't select specific users when auditing on objects. All users performing an audited task on an object will cause audit records to be written, either a session record per connection or one record per executed statement.

- AUDIT and ON are the required keywords for the object auditing command.

- object_option[,...] is an option or a comma-separated list of options from Table 11.3. You must include at least one object option if you don't use the keyword ALL.

- ALL includes all valid object auditing options. It must be included if you don't include any individual options.

- schema names the object owner. Your own schema is assumed if it's not included.

- object_name is the name of the object on which auditing is to be started, or a synonym for the object. You must include an object name if you don't include the DIRECTORY or the DEFAULT option.

- DIRECTORY directory_name identifies the name of an object directory to be audited. You must identify a directory if you don't include an object name or the DEFAULT option.

- DEFAULT indicates that you want the auditing options to be applied automatically to all new objects created in the schema. You must include the DEFAULT option if you don't include an object name or the DIRECTORY default.

- BY SESSION/ACCESS determines whether all use of an audited action is summarized into a single audit record per user session (BY SESSION), or if a separate audit record will be generated each time the action is performed (BY ACCESS). If you omit this option, audited actions will be summarized at the session level.

- WHENEVER [NOT] SUCCESSFUL determines whether only successful (SUCCESSFUL) or unsuccessful (NOT SUCCESSFUL) attempts to use the audited action are recorded. If you omit the WHENEVER option, all actions—successful and unsuccessful—are audited.

Different object auditing options are available, depending on the type of object you're auditing. Table 11.3 identifies which options can be selected for each object type. The optional keyword, ALL, will begin auditing every option that can be audited for the object type, as shown in Table 11.3.

TABLE 11.3 **Object auditing options**

Object Option:	Table:	View:	Sequence:	Procedure Function Package:	Snapshot:	Library:	Directory:
ALTER	X		X		X		
AUDIT	X	X	X	X	X		X
COMMENT	X	X			X		
DELETE	X	X			X		
EXECUTE				X		X	
GRANT	X	X	X	X	X	X	X
INDEX	X				X		
INSERT	X	X			X		
LOCK	X	X			X		
READ							X
RENAME	X	X		X	X		
SELECT	X	X	X		X		
UPDATE	X	X			X		

Considerations for the *DEFAULT* audit option

Unlike the other options, **DEFAULT** applies to the whole database, not just to the schema of the user issuing the command. Therefore, following the successful completion of an **AUDIT... DEFAULT** command, any object created by any user will begin to be audited if the object audit list in the command included one or more operations valid for that object type. Using the **ALL** option in an **AUDIT...DEFAULT** command will cause every possible audit action to be applied to every new object created subsequent to the command being executed.

You can enable object auditing on only one object at a time with an AUDIT command. The object can be a schema object or an object directory in which BFILE objects are stored. Instead of either of these, you can also enable auditing by default via the DEFAULT option. Default auditing does nothing to any existing objects, but will apply the selected audit options to any new object for which the option is valid.

Any auditing that commences as a result of default auditing can be stopped with the appropriate NOAUDIT command. However, the command has to be issued against each individual object. The NOAUDIT...DEFAULT command will prevent further objects from being audited by default, but won't terminate any auditing already being performed.

There's a version of the NOAUDIT command for terminating object auditing. Its syntax follows that of the AUDIT command, except that it doesn't include the BY ACCESS/BY SESSION option. Just as with the system privilege and statement option NOAUDIT command, you can stop the auditing of successful or unsuccessful actions on the object actions with the appropriate WHENEVER clause option, or end auditing altogether on the chosen action(s) by completely omitting the WHENEVER clause.

Reviewing Audit Records

The data dictionary contains two types of views related to auditing. The first type identifies which items are being audited; the second type, built on the AUD$ table, shows the audit records from various perspectives. Before you turn auditing on for your database with the AUDIT_TRAIL parameter, or anytime auditing is active, I recommend that you monitor the former type of view (listed in Table 11.4). This will help you identify any auditing that you don't think should occur, thus avoiding unexpected and unnecessary accumulation of audit records.

TABLE 11.4   **Data dictionary views showing current audit options**

View Name:	Description:
ALL_DEF_AUDIT_OPTS	Lists the object-auditing options that will be activated by default on all new objects for which they're valid auditing events. This view contains a single-row, one-entry-per-object option in the form of - / -, where either hyphen (-) can be substituted with an S or an A. The first hyphen, S, or A indicates whether the auditing will be performed on successful use of the command, and the second indicates that auditing will be performed on unsuccessful use. A hyphen means this option won't be audited, an S means that the auditing will be by session, and an A means that it will be by access.

continues...

Special privileges for the AUDIT...DEFAULT option

Due to its far-reaching capabilities, you can't successfully issue the AUDIT...DEFAULT command unless you've been granted the AUDIT SYSTEM privilege. The AUDIT ANY system privilege isn't adequate.

Scripts to manage audit-related data dictionary views

Oracle provides two SQL scripts to manage the data dictionary views associated with auditing: CATAUDIT.SQL and CATNOAUD.SQL. CATAUDIT.SQL creates the views and is run as part of CATALOG.SQL, which should be run following database creation. CATNOAUD.SQL drops the audit-related views should you not require them. This script won't drop the base auditing table, AUD$, owned by SYS. If you drop the views, you can recreate them later by running CATAUDIT.SQL again. Remember to run CATAUDIT.SQL and CATNOAUD.SQL while logged in as **SYS** (either directly or through the **INTERNAL** login).

TABLE 11.4 **Continued**

View Name:	Description:
AUDIT_ACTIONS	Lists the values from the ACTION# column from the AUD$ table and the related audit action type.
DBA_OBJ_AUDIT_OPTS	Lists the object-auditing options on all objects. This view contains a single entry for each database object, whether it's being audited or not. The rows are structured like the one in the ALL_DEF_AUDIT_OPTS view, with a two-part value under each option (each part containing a hyphen, an S, or an A).
DBA_PRIV_AUDIT_OPTS	Describes the system privileges being audited. There's one entry if the privilege is being audited systemwide, and a separate entry for each individual user being audited.
DBA_STMT_AUDIT_OPTS	Describes the statement options being audited. There's one entry if the privilege is being audited systemwide, and a separate entry for each individual user being audited.
USR_OBJ_AUDIT_OPTIONS	Lists the object auditing options on all objects owned by the user. This view contains a single entry for each object owned by the user, whether it's being audited or not. The rows are structured like those in the DBA_OBJ_AUDIT_OPTIONS view.

The second type of audit-related views provides formatted access to the audit trail. These views are generally more useful for examining the audit results than querying the AUD$ table directly. Of course, you can't use these views, or any SQL-based retrieval method, to examine audit records that you store in an external audit trail file. You must develop your own techniques to report on audit records created when you set the AUDIT_TRAIL parameter to the value OS.

Table 11.5 describes the views built over the entries in the audit trail generated as the result of a selected audit action. The table shows the view name and the nature of auditing that creates the audit records displayed through the view.

TABLE 11.5 **Data dictionary views for querying audit records**

View Name:	Audit Action(s) Reported:
DBA_AUDIT_EXISTS	All statements resulting in NOT EXISTS errors
DBA_AUDIT_OBJECT	Any object audit option
DBA_AUDIT_SESSION	All connection attempts
DBA_AUDIT_STATEMENT	All uses of GRANT, REVOKE, AUDIT, NOAUDIT, and ALTER SYSTEM commands
DBA_AUDIT_TRAIL	All audit trail entries
USER_AUDIT_OBJECT	All statements concerning objects
USER_AUDIT_SESSION	All connections and disconnections for the user
USER_AUDIT_STATEMENT	All uses of GRANT, REVOKE, AUDIT, NOAUDIT, and ALTER SYSTEM commands by the user
USER_AUDIT_TRAIL	All audit trail entries relevant to the user

Values for audited actions in the AUD$ RETURNCODE column

For the views that show whether the audited action was successful, the **RETURNCODE** column will contain an Oracle message number: a 0 for success or an exception code from the error message if unsuccessful.

SEE ALSO

➤ *Descriptions of the SQL scripts used following database creation to complete the data dictionary table and view definitions, page* **45**

Profiles and System Resources

To help you control the use of system resources by your database users, Oracle provides you with a special type of database object known as a *profile*. Every database is built with one profile, called DEFAULT, but you can add as many others as you need. Within each profile, you set limits on various system resources that can be consumed. When more of a resource has been used than the limit allows, Oracle will stop further processing and issue an appropriate error message. Every profile can define different limits for some or all controlled resources. You can choose to leave certain resources with no limitations on their use in any of your profiles.

Each database user is assigned to one profile, and the user's database sessions can be constrained by the limits set in that profile. Profile resource limits won't be enforced, however, unless the database is running in a special mode. You can set this mode with a parameter in your initialization file or with an ALTER SYSTEM command. The parameter, RESOURCE_LIMIT, takes the

Scope of the ALTER SYSTEM command

The **ALTER SYSTEM** command won't change the value of the related parameter in your initialization file. If you enable or disable resource checking with this command, therefore, you should also modify your **RESOURCE_LIMIT** parameter to the desired value. This will ensure that the database will continue to behave as you want it to should the instance need to be restarted for any reason.

values TRUE and FALSE; you should set it to TRUE if you want to enforce the resource limits assigned to your profiles. You should issue the following command if RESOURCE_LIMIT is set to FALSE but you want to start enforcing resource limits:

```
ALTER SYSTEM SET RESOURCE_LIMIT = TRUE;
```

You can, of course, issue the command with the FALSE option to turn off resource checking, whether it was begun with an earlier ALTER SYSTEM command or due to the parameter value being set to TRUE. The ALTER SYSTEM SET RESOURCE_LIMIT command doesn't change the behavior of any active user sessions when the command is issued, so users can still encounter limits on their work even if the command turns off resource checking with the FALSE option.

If you don't need to restrict your users with resource limits, ensure that you run your database with the RESOURCE_LIMIT parameter set to FALSE. Even if your users are all assigned to a profile that allows them unlimited resource usage, Oracle must locate the related profile and store the limits in the user's session data every time a new session starts when your system is running with resource checking enabled. This overhead can be avoided, and if you discover the parameter is set to a wrong value you should temporarily change the database behavior until you can change the parameter and restart the instance. The following command will prevent resource checks from being initiated in any new sessions:

```
ALTER SYSTEM SET RESOURCE_LIMIT = FALSE;
```

Combined Resource Limits

You can limit the consumption of different system resources through individual settings in a profile or through a combined usage value. You can even include both limit types within a single profile. You should consider setting up a combined usage limit when your database is running on a system where users are being monitored for their consumption of resources with a standardized unit of measure. Typically, these units—known as "computer resource units," "computer billing units," or "computer service units"—are composed of various amounts of one or more of CPU consumption, memory usage, disk I/O, and connection time.

You can use what Oracle calls *composite limits* for your profiles. These can reflect the same ratio of resource usage as your system's service units. With them, you can terminate a user's session after it consumes more than a predetermined number of such service units.

Before you can take advantage of composite limits, you must define the components to be included and their respective weightings. You use the ALTER RESOURCE COST command to complete these definitions and you can query the data dictionary view RESOURCE_COST to see the current settings. The command allows you to set a weight for each of the following:

- The amount of CPU time used by a session
- The session's connect time
- The number of Oracle blocks read during a session
- The amount of memory dedicated to the session (private SGA)

The ALTER RESOURCE COST command's full syntax is as follows:

```
ALTER RESOURCE COST
    [CPU_PER_SESSION integer]
    [CONNECT_TIME integer]
    [LOGICAL_READS_PER_SESSION integer]
    [PRIVATE_SGA integer]
```

integer is the weight assigned to a unit of the resource's consumption, as shown in Table 11.6. You must include at least one resource in the command and as many of the other resources as you need.

Table 11.6 in the following section shows the optional keyword to use in the ALTER RESOURCE COST command for these options and the unit of measure for each one. If you don't include one of the keywords in the command, it will retain its current value (as shown in the RESOURCE_COSTS view). Each resource has an initial value of 0 when the database is created. A composite limit is reached when the sum of the resources, multiplied by their assigned weights, exceeds the value of the limit.

For example, assume you issued the following command and a session has accumulated 10 seconds of CPU time and accessed 2,000 Oracle blocks while being connected for 30 minutes:

Calculating composite service units

Using this example, CPU has a weight of 50 and a unit of measure of 1/100 second, so 10 seconds contribute 50×10/(1/100) = 50,000 CPU per session. Connect time has a weight of 10 and a unit of measure of minutes, so 30 minutes contribute 10×30 = 300. Logical reads have a weight of 100 each, so 2,000 blocks accessed contribute 100×2,000 = 200,000. Private SGA has a weight of 0 per byte, so all bytes contribute nothing more to the overall total. The sum of these factors gives the resulting total composite service units: 50,000+300+200,000+0= 250,300.

```
ALTER RESOURCE COST
    CPU_PER_SESSION 50
    CONNECT_TIME 10
    LOGICAL_READS_PER_SESSION 100
    PRIVATE_SGA 0;
```

It will have consumed the number of service units (shown here) toward a composite limit:

```
50 * 1000 (1/100's seconds CPU time)
  + 10 * 30 (minutes connect time)
  + 100 * 2000 (Oracle blocks accessed)
```

Creating Profiles

You create a new profile by using the CREATE PROFILE command. This command uses different keywords to set limits for the different resources. Table 11.6 identifies these keywords and lists which resources, plus their units of measure, they control. The table also indicates which of these resources contributes to composite limits, as discussed in the preceding section.

TABLE 11.6   Resource limits controlled by profiles

System Resource:	Keyword for *CREATE PROFILE* and *ALTER RESOURCE COST* Commands:	Unit of Measure:	Part of Composite Limit:
Concurrent sessions	SESSIONS_PER_USER	Number	
Session CPU	CPU_PER_SESSION	1/100 second	X
CPU per call	CPU_PER_CALL	1/100 second	
Session elapsed time	CONNECT_TIME	Minutes	X
Inactive session	IDLE_TIME	Minutes	
Oracle blocks accessed in session	LOGICAL_READS_PER_SESSION	Number	X
Oracle blocks accessed per call	LOGICAL_READS_PER_CALL	Number	
Session memory	PRIVATE_SGA	Bytes	X
Service units	COMPOSITE_LIMIT	Number	

For those resources that can be limited by session and by call, the session value includes all work done since connecting to the database, and the call value includes only the work done during a single database call, such as a *parse*, *execute*, or *fetch*.

SEE ALSO

➤ *Information about the parse, execute, and fetch database calls, page 459*

The syntax for the resource management options of the CREATE PROFILE command is as follows:

```
CREATE PROFILE profile_name LIMIT
    resource_key_word [integer][K¦M] [UNLIMITED] [DEFAULT]
[...]
```

- CREATE PROFILE *profile_name* LIMIT are the keywords to create the profile with the given name.

- *resource_key_word* is a valid keyword from Table 11.6.

- *integer* is the value of the limit assigned to the resource; this must be included if neither the UNLIMITED nor DEFAULT options are included for the resource.

- K and M are optional abbreviations for kilobytes and megabytes, respectively, that can be used only with the PRIVATE_SGA keyword.

- UNLIMITED removes any limitation on the resource from the profile. This must be included if neither a resource limit value nor the DEFAULT option is included for the resource.

- DEFAULT indicates that this resource will be limited by the current value in the DEFAULT profile at the time the profile is invoked. This must be included if neither a resource limit value nor the UNLIMITED option is included for the resource.

- [...] indicates that two or more resources can be controlled in a single statement.

> **Privileges to manage profiles**
>
> Profiles aren't members of any schema, so any user with the necessary privileges can issue commands against profiles created by any other user. The system privileges to create profiles, to alter resource limits in existing profiles, and to drop profiles are CREATE PROFILE, ALTER PROFILE, and DROP PROFILE, respectively.

You don't have to include a limit for every resource in a profile when you create it. Any unnamed resource will be treated as though it were assigned the DEFAULT keyword. In other words, any time the profile is used, the values for unassigned resource limits will be taken from the corresponding values in the DEFAULT profile.

Assigning Profiles

To enforce the limits in a profile you've created, you need to assign that profile to one or more users. You can assign a profile by using the PROFILE option of either CREATE USER or ALTER USER. The RESOURCE_LIMIT must also be activated for the profile limits to take any effect, of course, although the profile can be assigned at any time.

When you change the profile assigned to a user with the ALTER USER command, the new profile will become effective the next time someone connects to the database with that userid. However, any currently active session will continue to function under the limits imposed by the profile assigned to the userid at the time they were initiated.

When profile limits are in effect and a user exceeds a limit, the outcome will depend on the specific resource type:

- When a session exceeds the session limit on CPU time, connect time, blocks accessed, memory used, or on the composite limit, the transaction being processed at the time will be rolled back and the user will be disconnected from the database.

- When a statement exceeds a call limit, the current statement is rolled back but the session and the current transaction remain active.

- When a session remains inactive for longer than the idle time limit, any current transaction will be rolled back and the session terminated the next time a statement is attempted.

- The database connection is refused when a new session exceeds the number of concurrent sessions allowed by the profile.

SEE ALSO
➤ *The complete syntax of the* CREATE USER *command, page* **263**
➤ *The complete syntax of the* ALTER USER *command, page* **270**

Altering Profiles

You use the ALTER PROFILE command to change one, some, or all of the resource limits defined in a profile. Use exactly the same syntax as that for the CREATE PROFILE command, substituting only the word ALTER for the word CREATE. The only restriction on the ALTER PROFILE command is on the DEFAULT profile—you can't use the DEFAULT keyword when changing one of its resource limits. You can, however, change any of the resource limits in DEFAULT profile to any other valid value.

Any resource not named in an ALTER PROFILE command will retain the current limit's value. Include the resource name with the keyword UNLIMITED to remove a limit from a specific resource.

As when you assign a profile to a user, any current session settings aren't changed when you execute the ALTER PROFILE command. Only new sessions started by users assigned to the altered profile will be accorded its new resource limits.

Dropping Profiles

You can drop any profile except the DEFAULT profile by using the DROP PROFILE command:

DROP PROFILE *profile_name* [CASCADE]

The CASCADE option must be included if the profile is still assigned to one or more users. As with other changes to profiles, any sessions started with the profile assigned to them will continue to be limited by the profile limits even after it's dropped. The userids assigned to the dropped profile will be assigned to the DEFAULT profile automatically, and any new sessions started by these userids will be constrained by DEFAULT's limits.

Profiles and Password Management

Oracle8 allows you to control your database users' management of their passwords. The password-management features have many capabilities:

- Pre-expire new passwords
- Expire passwords after a specific period of time
- Allow a grace period between password expiration and the deactivation of the userid
- Prevent the reuse of a password for a specific period of time

Watch for unexpected side effects when changing the DEFAULT **profile**

The user **SYS** needs to retain the ability to use unlimited resources to complete essential database activities. These include the execution of recursive SQL statements and processing performed by the background processes. **SYS** uses the **UNLIMITED** resource limits (set by default in the **DEFAULT** profile) when resource limits are activated. Therefore, you shouldn't reduce any of these limits unless you've already built an alternate profile with unlimited resources and assigned it to **SYS**. You also might want to assign this alternate profile to the **SYSTEM** userid and your primary DBA user accounts.

- Lock and unlock accounts manually
- Force a password to meet certain complexity requirements

The same profiles that you utilize to limit system resource use can be used to provide you with password-management tools. The profiles already contain entries for password-management functions, but these aren't enabled unless you run a special script. This script, UTLPWDMG.SQL, can be found in the same location as the other scripts discussed in Chapter 2, "Creating a Database." To activate the password-management features, execute this script after connecting to Oracle with the SYS userid.

The script has two components: The first changes the password-related entries in the DEFAULT profile and the second builds a password-complexity function in the database. The script also causes the database to begin password-checking activities against all profiles.

Creating Password-Management Profile Entries

You use the CREATE PROFILE and ALTER PROFILE commands to set the values in profiles that determine the password characteristics for the users who are assigned to them. The syntax for these commands, when addressing password options, is as follows:

```
CREATE¦ALTER PROFILE profile_name LIMIT
    password_keyword [expression][UNLIMITED][DEFAULT][NULL]
    [...]
```

- CREATE or ALTER will build a new profile or modify an existing one, respectively.
- PROFILE profile_name LIMIT are the keywords to identify the profile being processed by the command.
- password_keyword is a valid password option keyword from Table 11.7.
- expression contains a value valid for the password option, as indicated in Table 11.7. Expressions that represent the numbers of days can contain whole numbers, fractions, or decimal representations of days and partial days.
- UNLIMITED removes any limitation on the password from the profile.

Password management is independent of resource management

Although the password-management features are controlled by database profiles, they aren't enabled and disabled the same way the resource limits are controlled by profiles. Resource limit checks are activated by starting the database with the initialization parameter RESOURCE_LIMIT set, or by issuing ALTER SYSTEM to change RESOURCE_LIMIT to TRUE. Checking can be deactivated by changing the value to FALSE in the parameter file or with the ALTER SYSTEM command. Password management is activated by running the UTLPWDMG.SQL script and stays active from that point on. The RESOURCE_LIMIT value has no impact on password-checking activities.

Representing portions of days for password options

You can set values for password options that provide time limits measured in whole days, or in portions of a day. For example, two weeks would be represented by the number 14, whereas one hour could be represented as 1/24 or 0.0416667. The CREATE and ALTER PROFILE commands accept any of these formats for days, integers, fractions, and decimals. However, you can't mix whole numbers and fractions in a single expression. One and a half days would have to be entered as 1.5, not as 1fi. The smallest time increment you can use for a password option is one second, represented by 1/86400 or 0.000015741.

- DEFAULT indicates that this password option will conform to the current setting in the DEFAULT profile at the time the profile is invoked.

- NULL indicates that no password complexity checking is to be performed. This option is valid only with the PASSWORD_ VERIFY_FUNCTION password option.

- [...] indicates that two or more password options can be controlled in a single statement.

Only one value—*expression*, UNLIMITED, DEFAULT, or NULL—can be entered for any password option in a given statement. If either password option—PASSWORD_REUSE_TIME or PASSWORD_REUSE_MAX— is set to a numeric value, the other must be set to UNLIMITED.

Mixing resource limits and password options

You can issue a single **CREATE** or **ALTER PROFILE** command that contains resource limit and password option values.

TABLE 11.7 **Password management options**

Function:	Keyword for *CREATE* or *ALTER* *PROFILE* Commands:	Expression Values for *CREATE* or *ALTER* *PROFILE* Commands:
Lock an account after a number of tries to log in	FAILED_LOGIN_ACCOUNTS	An integer
Expire an unchanged password after a number of days	PASSWORD_LIFE_TIME	An integer, decimal, or fractional number of days
Prevent reuse of a password for a number of days	PASSWORD_REUSE_TIME	An integer, decimal, or fractional number of days
Prevent reuse of a password before some number of password changes	PASSWORD_REUSE_MAX	An integer
Keep a password locked for a number of days after consecutive failed login tries	PASSWORD_LOCK_TIME	An integer, decimal, or fractional number of days
Provide a number of days for warnings to be given before locking accounts with expired passwords	PASSWORD_GRACE_TIME	An integer, decimal, or fractional number of days
Name a function that examines the password for desired characteristics	PASSWORD_VERIFY_ FUNCTION	Name of a password complexity function

Considerations for password management

You may want to use different password-management rules for different categories of users, which you can easily accomplish by building different profiles for each group and assigning them to the appropriate userids. You should make sure that any users who remain assigned to the **DEFAULT** profile won't have inappropriate password management options defined by it. Pay particular attention to the special database userids, **SYS** and **SYSTEM**, and to other IDs used by your operations staff or associate DBAs, as well as any userids used for processing batch jobs. If the password options applied to **DEFAULT** by the UTLPWDMG.SQL script aren't appropriate for these users, you should either alter the **DEFAULT** profile or build and assign profiles to control their passwords according to their particular needs.

The password-complexity checking (verify) function is explained in detail in the next section.

When you run the UTLPWDMG.SQL script, you can see the password settings in the DBA_PROFILES data dictionary view. This view lists the profile options and the current values for each defined profile, including DEFAULT. The RESOURCE_TYPE column will have the value PASSWORD for the entries associated with password management, and the value KERNEL for the entries associated with operating system resource limits. The keywords DEFAULT or UNLIMITED will appear in the LIMIT column when a specific value isn't assigned. If the PASSWORD_VERIFY_FUNCTION option was entered as NULL, the value in the DBA_PROFILES view will be UNLIMITED in the LIMIT column.

When assigning profiles to manage passwords, the profile options that are checked are those belonging to the user whose password is being assigned or changed, not those in the profile assigned to the user issuing the command. For example, if the userid SYSTEM has a profile with PASSWORD_REUSE_MAX set to UNLIMITED, a user connected as SYSTEM could issue the following command an infinite number of times without error:

```
ALTER USER system IDENTIFIED BY manager;
```

However, if the user SCOTT were assigned to a profile with PASSWORD_REUSE_MAX set to 1, a user logged into the SYSTEM userid with the profile as described couldn't issue the following command more than once successfully:

```
ALTER USER scott IDENTIFIED BY tiger;
```

The limit on password reuse set by Scott's profile takes effect, not the limit in the profile assigned to SYSTEM.

Checking for Password Complexity

If you want to force your users' passwords to comply with certain rules, such as a minimum number of characters or at least one digit in the password, you must use a PL/SQL function to perform the requisite checks. Oracle provides VERIFY_FUNCTION as the default function for checking password complexity. The function returns a Boolean value of TRUE if the password passes all the checks, or exits with a return code in the range ORA-20002 to ORA-20004 if the password fails a check. The function is created by the UTLPWDMG.SQL script, which also adds its name to the PASSWORD_VERIFY_FUNCTION option in the DEFAULT profile.

If you want to create your own password-complexity function(s), you should use VERIFY_FUNCTION as a model. You can examine the function's code by querying the DBA_SOURCE data dictionary view or, more simply, by reading the UTLPWDMG.SQL script. (For more information about the PL/SQL language and the creation and management of PL/SQL functions, see Appendix A, "Essential PL/SQL: Understanding Stored Procedures, Triggers, and Packages.") You can activate your password functions as soon as they're created by naming them in the PASSWORD_VERIFY_FUNCTION option of the CREATE of ALTER PROFILE command. Users assigned to the profile will have any new passwords checked by your function.

You may not want to continue to use the Oracle-supplied VERIFY_FUNCTION in the DEFAULT profile because it has some characteristics that you may not find appropriate. For example, the function would disallow the password tiger, which is used in a number of the demonstration scripts that create or use the SCOTT userid. It also disallows the password manager, which is the password expected in other scripts that Oracle requires you to run under the SYSTEM userid. You have three options for discontinuing the use of the default function by DEFAULT:

- You can replace the VERIFY_FUNCTION with one of your own and change the DEFAULT profile to identify it:
```
CREATE FUNCTION my_password_function
    (username VARCHAR2, password VARCHAR2,
    old_password VARCHAR2) RETURN boolean IS ... END;

ALTER PROFILE default
    PASSWORD_VERIFY_FUNCTION
    my_password_function;
```

- You can modify the VERIFY_FUNCTION:
```
CREATE OR REPLACE FUNCTION
    VERIFY_FUNCTION (username VARCHAR2,
    password VARCHAR2, old_password VARCHAR2)
    RETURN boolean IS ... END;
```

- You can turn off complexity checking for the profile:

```
ALTER PROFILE default PASSWORD_VERIFY_FUNCTION NULL;
```

To test the code in a password-complexity function, I recommend that you build and use the following SQL*Plus script:

```
DECLARE
    status BOOLEAN;
BEGIN
    status := &function_name
              (user, &new_password, &old_password);
END;
/
```

You can then execute this script from a SQL*Plus session by providing the name of the function to be checked and testing values for new and old passwords when prompted. You can replace the USER function with the &USER substitution variable if you also want to test the function against different userids. Note that testing the function with this script won't cause any password changes to be stored in the database.

Before completing this discussion of the complexity function, we should briefly discuss the Oracle-supplied VERIFY_FUNCTION function because, if you look at this code, two of the checks can cause some confusion:

- Consider the check to guarantee that there's at least one each of the three types of character (letter, digit, and punctuation) somewhere in the password. The code uses string variables to hold the valid characters for each type. The string for checking punctuation contains the standard punctuation marks such as the period (.), comma (,), asterisk (*), and so on. This might lead you to believe that users can now create passwords with such characters embedded in them. You might also assume that any of the three character types can be used anywhere in a password. However, Oracle8 passwords must conform to the standard naming convention for Oracle objects. In other words, they must begin with a letter and contain only letters, digits, underscores (_), dollar signs ($), and pound signs (#). In order to use any other format or any other punctuation character, your users would

---

Testing your own password-complexity functions

If you decide to code your own PL/SQL functions to control password structure and complexity, you should develop a structure to test them. I recommend creating a userid and a profile for developing and testing the code. Also use a script file to hold the PL/SQL **CREATE OR REPLACE FUNCTION** command. Use the same name for each function while it's in development so that you don't continually have to modify the profile's **PASSWORD_ VERIFY_FUNCTION** entry. When you're sure that the function is working as you want it, you can copy the test script to a permanent storage location, alter the test name to a production name, and execute the script under the **SYS** userid. Be particularly careful when building your own password functions to be used with the **DEFAULT** profile or other profiles assigned to key userids such as **SYS**, **SYSTEM**, or your DBA accounts.

have to enclose their passwords in double quotation marks
(") each time they used them.

- The other misleading check compares the old and new passwords. The intent of this check is to ensure that they vary by a certain number of characters. You can execute VERIFY_FUNCTION directly, supplying values for the username and the new and old passwords, to confirm that this check does indeed work as documented in the script.

However, if you look closely at the code, you'll see that this particular check isn't performed if the input value for the old password is a zero-length string. Unfortunately, when the function is executed as part of a password-change command (ALTER USER *user_name* IDENTIFIED BY *password*), Oracle doesn't supply the old password because it doesn't know it. Passwords aren't stored in the database directly, but via a one-way encryption algorithm, which means that the current password can't be extracted from its encrypted version. The value for the old password is therefore always sent to the function as a blank string.

The end result, of course, is that the function can't prevent the reuse of the same or similar password. You can overcome part of this limitation by using the PASSWORD_REUSE_MAX option. This can prevent the same password from being used twice in a row, or even from being reused until some defined number of different, intervening passwords have been used. Currently, there's no way to prevent similar passwords from being used right after each other. In addition, you can't code any of your own routines that depend on the value of the old password and have them work outside the test environment.

Understanding Oracle8 Backup Options

Types of Failure

When you're planning a backup strategy, it's useful to consider the day-to-day hazards that eventually cause any database system to fail. No matter how many UPSs or mirrored disks you have, no matter how regulated your computing environment is, every database system will experience an unexpected failure.

Database failures can generally be divided into two categories:

- *Instance failure* is generally the result of an Oracle internal exception, operating system failure, or other software-related database failure. Instance failure will be the diagnosis when the necessary Oracle processes (PMON, SMON, DB Writer, Log Writer) are no longer running and the database wasn't shut down normally. Although instance failures can directly or indirectly lead to database corruption, they're generally nondamaging in nature. Often, simply restarting the database allows operations to continue normally.

- *Media failure*, by contrast, is usually far more sinister. Media failure will usually manifest itself by the database being unable to read data it has previously written. Leading causes of media failure include disk drive failure, bad disk block, deleted data files, and damaged file system(s).

Media failure, unlike instance failure, almost always results in damage to your database that must be repaired before the database can resume normal operations. Fortunately, Oracle8 provides many methods for recovering from data loss.

Archiving Your Database

Impact of ARCHIVELOG mode on disk requirements

Running a database in ARCHIVELOG mode can seriously affect your database's disk needs, depending on how much activity your database has. Because a copy of every write operation is kept, you may need tens or even hundreds of megabytes of disk space to store all the archived redo logs for one day.

Because databases often contain mission-critical information, an organization may not be able to tolerate the loss of any transactions whatsoever. If a database were backed up every night and suffered a disk failure a few minutes before backups were scheduled to begin, you could lose up to around 23 hours' worth of transactions. Oracle provides an elegant solution to this problem in the form of archive logs.

Oracle keeps a record of most every operation in its redo logs in order to guard against loss of database buffers should the database instance fail. Because these logs, in aggregate, contain everything needed to reconstruct a database from any time in the past, they can be used to recover from media failure. By default, Oracle overwrites the redo log groups in a round-robin fashion. This is sufficient for instance recovery because a log switch forces a checkpoint that, in turn, forces all dirty database buffers to be written to disk.

To guard against media failure, however, it's necessary to keep the redo logs archived since at least the last physical database backup (and in practice, you'll want to keep them much longer). Oracle refers to this as running the database in ARCHIVELOG mode; it will archive every redo log file that's filled up.

Starting Archiving

By default, Oracle doesn't create a database in ARCHIVELOG mode. You have to manually place a database into ARCHIVELOG mode as soon as it's created, but when you do so, Oracle will stay in ARCHIVELOG mode until you return it to NOACHIVELOG mode (at which time your database again becomes more vulnerable to media failure).

To check whether a database is running in ARCHIVELOG mode, check the LOG_MODE column in the V$DATABASE table. This is shown in an example:

```
SQL> select * from v$database;

NAME CREATED    LOG_MODE    CHECKPOINT_CHANGE# ARCHIVE_CHANGE#
---- --------- ----------- ------------------ ---------------
TEST 02/14/98 08:03:01 NOARCHIVELOG 12964              12951

SQL>
```

In this example, the database TEST isn't running in ARCHIVELOG mode, as indicated by NOARCHIVELOG in the LOG_MODE column.

Keep archive logs on disk

Although Oracle allows you to spool your archived redo logs directly to tape on many system architectures, you're strongly advised not to do so. Archiving directly to tape is much slower and requires much more effort and testing than does archiving to disk. Disk space is very cheap these days.

Enable *ARCHIVELOG* mode (general steps)

1. Modify the init.ora file.

2. Shut down the database.

3. Start the database in MOUNT EXCLUSIVE mode.

4. Enable ARCHIVELOG mode.

5. Perform a cold backup.

6. Restart the database normally.

Step 1: Modify the init.ora File

You must decide a couple of things before editing the init.ora file:

- In what directory you will store archive logs
- What format you want the filenames of the archived logs to follow

Determining what directory to store the archive logs in is very important. If you exhaust all the space available, Oracle will stop virtually all activity until space becomes available again.

The following parameters must be set in the database's appropriate init.ora file:

- log_archive_start indicates whether Oracle should automatically archive filled redo logs. You should always set this to true.

- log_archive_dest is the directory to which you want archive log files to be written. This directory should hold exclusively archived redo logs and have plenty of free space.

- log_archive_format defines the format of the archived redo log filenames. Use %s to denote the sequence number of an archived redo log file. A good naming convention is to use the database SID followed by %s (to denote each sequence number), and then an .ARC to denote an archive log.

  Here's an example of these settings on a UNIX system:

  ```
  log_archive_start = true # if you want automatic
  archiving
  log_archive_dest = /opt/oracle803/archive/test
  log_archive_format = TEST%s.arc
  ```

When Oracle freezes

If Oracle suddenly freezes and doesn't respond to the most basic SQL statements, first check to make sure that you haven't used up all the space available to your archive logs. If you move some archive logs to another directory, Oracle will automatically resume database operations. If Oracle must wait for space to become available in the archive log directory, it will log this event in the applicable alert.log file.

Monitoring the archive destination

Ideally, you should have a monitoring system in place to constantly keep watch for an archive destination directory that's quickly filling up. By being warned before your destination directory is actually full, you can take corrective measures before database operations are affected. BMC's Patrol product offers this capability, although many other excellent products in the marketplace serve this need.

A typical Windows NT init.ora setting might look like this:

```
log_archive_start = true
log_archive_dest = %ORACLE_HOME%\database\archive
log_archive_format = "TEST%S.ARC"
```

Step 2: Shut Down the Database

A normal (or immediate) shutdown is required to continue. The following example shows how to shut down the database in a UNIX environment. This example will close any open sessions on the database and roll back any transactions in progress.

```
oreo:~$ svrmgrl
Oracle Server Manager Release 3.0.3.0.0 - Production


(c) Copyright 1997, Oracle Corporation. All Rights Reserved.
Oracle8 Enterprise Edition Release 8.0.3.0.0 - Production


SVRMGR> CONNECT INTERNAL;
Connected.
SVRMGR> SHUTDOWN IMMEDIATE;
Database closed.
Database dismounted.
ORACLE instance shut down.
SVRMGR>
```

Who's using the database?

By querying the V$SESSION view, you can see who's logged in to the database. V$SESSION can help you identify whether the database is in use and who's using it.

Step 3: Start the Database in *MOUNT EXCLUSIVE* Mode

Continuing the example from Step 2, this example shows how to use the STARTUP command with the MOUNT and EXCLUSIVE options:

```
SVRMGR> STARTUP MOUNT EXCLUSIVE;
ORACLE instance started.
Database mounted.
SVRMGR>
```

Step 4: Enable *ARCHIVELOG* Mode

The following ALTER DATABASE ARCHIVELOG command will place the database into ARCHIVELOG mode:

```
SVRMGR> ALTER DATABASE ARCHIVELOG;
Statement processed.
SVRMGR>
```

Step 5: Perform a Cold Backup

By following the procedures outlined in Chapter 13, "Selecting and Implementing a Backup Strategy," you must perform a cold backup of the database before continuing. This is necessary because the archived redo logs are useful only when they can be applied to a database backup made since ARCHIVELOG mode was enabled.

Step 6: Restart the Database Normally

In Server Manager, restart the database normally to allow users back onto the database. The V$DATABASE view will now reflect the switch to ARCHIVELOG mode in the LOG_MODE column.

Stopping Archiving

From time to time, it will be beneficial to stop archiving on your databases. For instance, during a maintenance period, you may be importing or deleting large amounts of data that would generate an excessive number of archive logs.

Stopping archiving will still provide recovery in the event of instance failure, but should a media error occur, it will be necessary to restore from the last cold backup.

Stop archiving (general steps)

1. Shut down the database.
2. Start the database in MOUNT EXCLUSIVE mode.
3. Enable NOARCHIVELOG mode.
4. Open the database.

Step 1: Shut Down the Database

Just as when ARCHIVELOG was enabled, the database must first be shut down. The following example shows how to shut down the database in a Windows NT environment. This example will close any open sessions on the database and roll back any transactions in progress:

```
D:\ORANT\BIN\SVRMGR30
Oracle Server Manager Release 3.0.3.0.0 - Production
```

Cold backups and changing ARCHIVELOG mode

You may want to alternate between ARCHIVELOG and NOARCHIVELOG modes. It's absolutely essential that you perform a cold backup after you re-enable **ARCHIVELOG** mode. Failure to do so may render your archive logs useless.

(c) Copyright 1997, Oracle Corporation. All Rights Reserved.
Oracle8 Enterprise Edition Release 8.0.3.0.0 - Production

```
SVRMGR> CONNECT INTERNAL;
Connected.
SVRMGR> SHUTDOWN IMMEDIATE;
Database closed.
Database dismounted.
ORACLE instance shut down.
SVRMGR>
```

Step 2: Start the Database in *MOUNT EXCLUSIVE* Mode

The database must be in MOUNT EXCLUSIVE mode to change
between NOARCHIVELOG and ARCHIVELOG mode:

```
SVRMGR> STARTUP MOUNT EXCLUSIVE;
ORACLE instance started.
Database mounted.
SVRMGR>
```

Step 3: Enable *NOARCHIVELOG* Mode

The ALTER DATABASE NOARCHIVELOG command places the database
into NOARCHIVELOG mode:

```
SVRMGR> ALTER DATABASE NOARCHIVELOG;
Statement processed.
SVRMGR>
```

Step 4: Open the Database

Use the ALTER DATABASE OPEN command to open the database for
normal activity:

```
SVRMGR> ALTER DATABASE OPEN;
Statement processed.
```

At this time, you may want to query the V$DATABASE view to con-
firm the change in log mode.

The Automatic Archive Process

In the procedure for enabling ARCHIVELOG mode, recall that the
following line was added to the init.ora file to allow automatic
archiving of the filled redo logs:

```
log_archive_start = true
```

**Backing up after
NOARCHIVELOG**

Although a cold backup isn't
required when switching to
NOARCHIVELOG mode, it's
recommended that you do so
anyway. By making a cold backup at this time, you'll have a
known fallback point to restore
to should you experience
media failure or data corruption.

By starting the automatic archiver, the database will copy redo logs to the designated destination directory as each redo log is filled. This asynchronous process won't necessarily begin copying at the instant of a logfile switch, but it usually can keep up with your database's transaction load.

Backup Options

The need to back up databases is certainly obvious enough. However, databases—because of their highly structured and transaction-centric nature—have special backup and recovery needs. By carefully reading and understanding the backup strategies Oracle provides, you can implement a reliable backup strategy that meets your organization's needs.

The most important aspect of any backup plan is to thoroughly test database restores in a test environment. Backups can often appear to have run properly but be incorrect for recovery situations. It's absolutely imperative that all DBAs have first-hand experience with backup and recovery plans.

Understanding Cold Backups

The simplest and most straightforward backup in Oracle is known as a *cold backup*. Essentially, a cold backup involves nothing more than shutting down the Oracle database instance and backing up all the relevant database files, including

- Data files
- Control files
- Redo logs
- Archived redo logs
- init.ora and config.ora (if applicable)

The key to cold backups is that you must have the database instance shut down before beginning. Although the backup process may very well appear to work with the database running, it's very possible that the backup will be corrupted and unusable.

Confirming that the archive process is running

On UNIX systems, you can confirm that the archive process is running by looking for a process named `ora_arch_YourSID`.

Document backup and recovery

Backup systems often run for quite some time without any DBA intervention required. Unfortunately, memories fade and staff turnover can lead to confusion when the time comes to restore a database. It's essential that backup and recovery procedures be tested and documented. Chances are that during a high stress database recovery, not everyone is going to remember the subtle details that can make or break a recovery effort.

Backing up redo logs

Oracle doesn't technically need redo logs backed up. Because the database isn't running, however, they can be safely backed up and will prevent you from having to recreate redo logs should you need to restore the database.

When backing up the database, be sure to also back up all the Oracle program files. All these files are typically found under the ORACLE_HOME directory. This directory tree often contains additional configuration files, such as Net8 files and any applied patches.

Unlike many database systems, Oracle doesn't provide a backup and restore system per se. Oracle instead relies on operating system utilities, such as tar in UNIX. Although this may seem to be a weakness at first, it's actually something of a feature. Many organizations spend a great deal of money on complex and robust backup systems far superior to anything any database maker now bundles with their product. Oracle, in keeping with its history of flexibility, lets you use the best backup tools available for your environment to back up the operating system and the database.

The advantages of cold backups are numerous:

- Quick and easy
- Fairly trouble-free implementation; most sites simply back up the database files as part of a full system backup
- Simple restores
- Very little site-specific customization required for implementation

The disadvantage of cold backups is that the database must be shut down. If you can afford to shut down a database for backups, cold database backups usually offer the best and easiest backup strategy.

SEE ALSO

➤ *More details on performing a cold backup, page* ***355***

Understanding Hot Backups

Oracle uses the term *hot backups* to describe the process of backing up the database while it's open and available to users. Hot backups are an essential component of 24-hour, 7-days-a-week operations, as it allows for backups necessary to data security without interrupting mission-critical operations.

Oracle's Enterprise Manager

Oracle's Enterprise Manager includes a backup and restore utility for Windows NT environments. While this utility is functional, most DBAs find that operating system and third-party backup tools work much better for them.

Effects of taking down a database

Shutting down an Oracle database can have lasting effects beyond the actual backup period. When a database is shut down and restarted, the data dictionary cache is blank and there is no data in the database block buffers. The morning database activity following a backup cycle could be slowed down, as Oracle must reload the data dictionary and the working set of database blocks into the SGA.

Hot backups will back up these components in a manner similar to a cold backup system:

- Archived redo logs
- init.ora and config.ora (if applicable)

However, special consideration must be given to data files and control files.

The advantage of hot backups is that the database can continue normal operations while the database is being backed up. On the other hand, hot backups have several disadvantages:

- Much more complex to implement
- Custom site-specific backup scripts must usually be written
- Extensive testing required to prove viability

Despite the obvious advantage of hot backups, they typically require considerably more time and effort to successfully implement. While running a 24/7 operation may be the trendy thing to do these days, make sure that your business needs require this availability before incurring the time and expense of hot backups.

Although database operations can continue during a hot backup without interruption, it's still important for you to schedule backups during the least amount of database activity (UPDATE, INSERT, and DELETE operations, in particular). Hot backups will cause a database to incur additional overhead in terms of CPU, I/O, and higher production of archived redo logs.

If your organization truly needs to run 24/7, hot backups will provide a proven and robust solution to keep your business running and your database safe and secure.

SEE ALSO

➤ *More details on performing a hot backup, page 361*

Don't back up redo logs

Redo logs aren't backed up during hot backups. In fact, doing so can cause serious database corruption.

Testing hot backups

The need to test hot backup/recovery systems can't be overemphasized. It's absolutely essential that backups be periodically restored to test machines in order to verify that hot backups are being taken properly and to ensure that the skills needed to restore are kept sharp.

Recovery Manager for Windows NT Databases

Oracle8 DBAs supporting Windows NT-based databases have a convenient tool for recovering damaged databases: Recovery Manager (see Figure 12.1). Recovery Manager is a GUI-based tool that simplifies database recovery in these cases:

- Recovering from lost or damaged data file(s)
- Replacing lost or damaged control file(s)
- Performing complete restores from a database backup

Recovery Manager also has an automatic recovery option that may be able to automatically recover a database with little or no DBA intervention. This option isn't a silver bullet for solving all database recovery problems, however. Automatic recovery can't work correctly unless the proper up-front work has been done to ensure that database backups are performing regularly and correctly.

FIGURE 12.1

This is the opening window for Oracle's Recovery Manager on Windows NT 4.0.

Using Database Exports as a Backup Strategy

The backup methods discussed here have been physical in nature. That's to say that the backup methods all copy a database's physical data files verbatim to a backup device. These backups provide a fast backup and are relatively easy to use in a restore process should media failure occur.

Backing up just a database's data through Oracle's Export utility is known as a *logical backup*. In many instances it's useful (and necessary) to use logical backups:

- *Object or row recovery.* If someone inadvertently drops a table or deletes rows from a table, it's exceedingly difficult to restore just a particular table or a few rows from a physical backup.

- *Major release upgrade of Oracle.* When Oracle6 was replaced by Oracle7, Oracle changed the underlying database structures. This necessitated that the data contained in Oracle6 databases be exported and then imported into a new Oracle7 system. Oracle will advise when this operation is necessary.

- *Migrating an Oracle database between significantly different database servers.* The physical data structures between different platforms (MVS, VMS, Windows NT, and UNIX) aren't the same. In order to move data between different Oracle databases on different platforms, it's necessary to export data from the source platform and then import the data into the target system.

- *Moving data between two instances on the same physical machine.* Because a physical backup/restore on the same machine would normally overwrite the source instance, it's necessary to export the data from the source instance and then import it into the target instance.

Exports can be performed with the database up and running. Oracle's built-in read consistency allows it to have a read-consistent view of each table in the database. However, referential integrity can't be guaranteed because Oracle's read consistency will be applied only on a table-by-table basis. If at all possible, exports should be run with the database running in restricted mode.

Regular exports should complement hot or cold backups in any backup strategy. Export is a necessary component primarily to provide recovery from the loss of data due to dropped tables or deleted rows. Hot and cold backups are generally useful only for recovery from media failure. User or application errors are often recoverable only from logical backups.

Export is sometimes needed with similar platforms

Using exports is advised sometimes even when moving data between machines of the same platform. If the data, redo, and control files won't be placed in the same location, it's advisable to export data from the source machine and then import it into a target system configured to receive the data.

Understanding Incremental Backups

Keeping an up-to-date export backup on hand doesn't always require that the complete database be exported. Oracle8 provides an incremental-type export that may reduce the time and space required for an export backup by exporting only tables that have changed since the last full or incremental export.

In many database systems, only a few tables are actually updated on a day-to-day basis. Many more tables are relatively static in nature and don't need to be exported during each export cycle to maintain a complete export backup. Many DBAs avoid making export backups regularly because of the time and space required to do so. You may be able to overcome this obstacle by making several incremental export backups between full export backups.

> **Incremental exports work at the table level**
>
> When performing an incremental export, be aware that the full table is exported–not just the changed row(s)–if anything at all changes in a table.

Understanding Standby Databases

Oracle version 7.7.3 introduced the concept of a *standby database*, which allows you to configure a database that's close to being up-to-date with an online production database instance. In case of a production instance/machine failure, the standby database can be opened, which allows normal database activity to continue.

A standby database is, first, an identical copy of the production database (usually this is done by restoring from a cold backup). From this synchronization point, all archive logs generated by the production database machine will be copied to the standby database machine and applied to the database. The standby database is, essentially, always running in recovery mode because it's actively applying archive logs any time the production database is in operation.

Standby databases don't eliminate the need for normal backups on the production database machine. A dropped table or deleted row will also be dropped or deleted on the standby machine.

> **Pitfalls with standby databases**
>
> Standby databases can work only if the delivery of every archive log from the production machine can be guaranteed. If an archive log is lost, it is necessary to resynchronize the standby database machine with a fresh hot or cold backup. For this reason, you need to implement an automated delivery system of archive logs from the production database to the standby database.

Standby databases have several advantages:

- Fairly easy to implement.
- Will work with all datatypes on Oracle7 databases.
- Most database changes will be copied automatically to the standby database.
- Replication has a negligible impact on the production system.

Standby databases also have several disadvantages:

- Almost never completely up-to-date
- Can't be used for load balancing
- Only the entire database can be duplicated; no provision for duplicating just a subset of the production database

Standby databases are usually best suited for disaster-recovery database machines.

SEE ALSO

➤ *Learn how to create a standby database, page* ***368***

Standby databases can't be used for load balancing

Because the standby database is in recovery mode and not open, it's not available for use by any users. You can't use a standby database to help with load balancing on the production machine.

Understanding Replication Strategies

Oracle8 provides two technologies for replicating all or part of a database between two or more instances:

- Snapshot replication
- Symmetric replication

Snapshot Replication

Limitations in Oracle7

If you're working with some Oracle7 databases, be aware that snapshots can't replicate **LONG** or **LONG RAW** datatypes. If a snapshot's base query includes a **LONG** or **LONG RAW** column, the result will be **NULL** values in the target system. All other columns will transfer normally.

Snapshot replication produces a copy of database tables on a target instance based on a query to the source database. At the time a snapshot is initially taken, the specified query (maybe an entire table) is run and the resulting data is loaded into the target snapshot table. Oracle provides a fairly sophisticated facility for updating snapshots based on time or update activity.

Snapshot replication has the following advantages:

- Very easy to implement
- Excellent for producing a static set of data from OLTP systems to DSS systems
- Can be used for some limited load balancing

On the other hand, snapshot replication has the following disadvantages:

- Snapshots may become out-of-date immediately.
- Excessive refreshing can heavily tax system and Internetworking resources.
- Updates can occur only on the master database.

Typical applications can include the following:

- Transferring OLTP system data to a DSS or data warehousing system for thorough analysis
- Transferring data to a dedicated instance to avoid long running batch jobs from adversely affecting the production system
- Disaster recovery
- Creating a test database environment from production systems

SEE ALSO
➤ *More information on snapshots in relation to setting up a read-only failover database, page 374*

Symmetric Replication

Symmetric replication offers a mission-critical and robust means of keeping two or more instances synchronized. Symmetric replication can ensure that a transaction isn't fully committed until all systems being replicated have committed the transaction locally. Alternatively, it can replicate asynchronously, allowing each database node to run at full speed without holding up local updates because of remote database speed issues.

Symmetric replication is one of the most complicated units of Oracle and any other relational database. Issues such as network

Updating rows in snapshots

It's technically possible to allow updates to a snapshot. However, any changes made won't be sent back to the master database and may be overwritten during the next snapshot refresh.

Limitations in Oracle7

If you're working with some Oracle7 databases, be aware that symmetric replication can't replicate LONG or LONG RAW datatypes.

reliability, resolving conflicting updates, and transaction volumes are major design issues that must be planned for and dealt with.

The advantages to symmetric replication are as follows:

- Updates done on any system can automatically be posted on all other replicated and master systems.
- Replicated systems can be configured to be kept completely up-to-date.
- It's ideal for load-balancing most systems.

Symmetric replication isn't without its disadvantages:

- It's more difficult to set up and administer than other replication options.
- A high update transaction volume on one machine may stress other systems' resources.
- Network outages may bring all update-database activity to a halt.
- Potentially very high network resource requirements.

Typical applications may include the following:

- High availability and disaster-recovery systems
- Using many database instances for load-balancing purposes

Impact on network resources

Symmetric replication will transfer each update transaction from any master database to all other machines that subscribe to database updates. Depending on the volume of updates, this can easily saturate wide area networks. Even high-speed local area networks can become bottlenecks during batch update or load cycles.

Selecting and Implementing a Backup Strategy

Using Recovery Manager for backup and recovery operations

Scripts that perform offline and online backups

Implementing a hot standby database

Using replication for failover

Selecting a Backup Strategy

Oracle offers very rich and comprehensive backup and recovery options to suit every application's demand. The key is to implement a suitable strategy to meet the desired service levels between end users and the database operations group. A backup strategy suitable for a database depends on several factors, based on the nature of the application and the availability requirements. These factors will also decide whether your database is running in ARCHIVE LOG mode or in NOARCHIVE LOG mode. Table 13.1 lists the available database options that depend on the database's ARCHIVELOG mode.

The backup option in NOARCHIVELOG mode

Full cold backup is the only backup option available when the database is in **NOARCHIVELOG** mode.

TABLE 13.1   **Database mode and the available backup options**

Backup Type:	ARCHIVELOG	NOARCHIVELOG
Full cold backup	Yes	Yes
Partial cold backup	Yes	No
Hot backup	Yes	No

Recovery Manager

Recovery Manager is Oracle's new backup and recovery tool. Chapter 15, "Using Recovery Manager for Backup and Recovery," gives the details.

Recovery Manager and OS-level backup rely on making a copy of the users' data on a backup media—most commonly tape and disk. These methods preserve the data in a safe, inactive form. The data stored by these methods isn't used unless there's a loss of the current data for some reason. You can also copy the data stored in an Oracle database by using any of the following methods:

- *Export.* Export enables you to make a logical backup of the data. You can export the full database, specific users, or specific tables. It provides a copy of the data stored in Oracle's proprietary format independent of the OS. Incremental backups are supported but aren't incremental in a strict sense, as any table is fully exported even if only one row has been modified. Export is used generally to transfer data from one database to another.

  Consider using Export for preserving contents of small lookup tables. However, the use of Export as a backup method is very limited in large databases due to its slower performance.

- *Hot standby database.* A hot standby database is normally used as part of the disaster recovery plan in mission-critical environments. A hot standby database needs machine resources equivalent to the primary database. Data can be made available to users at very short notice in a hot standby database, even if no other resource from the primary database is available.

  A hot standby database is used only when the cost of downtime for the database is very high and the downtime cost justifies the cost to devote redundant machine resources required to build the standby database.

- *Replication.* With this technique, you can maintain object-level replicas of user data. The data is asynchronously available to all users at all locations after a predefined replication interval. Use this method when the business requires that the same data be available from multiple databases. It uses a trigger-based technique to propagate changes among the database and is a resource-intensive process. "Using Replication as a Failover," later in this chapter, provides more detail on this subject.

In summary, all these methods offer unique advantages and need to be used depending on your business requirements. However, they can also be used to complement each other.

Consider Using Recovery Manager

Oracle8's Recovery Manager is an integrated backup and recovery tool. Consider the following salient features before deciding your backup strategy:

- Recovery Manager is integrated with Oracle. It performs backup operations with spawned Oracle processes. These processes use Media Management libraries, which interface with backup media. You don't have to specify an OS utility such as `tar`, Backup, `dd`, and so on to copy files.

Media management libraries

The Media Management library contains the vendor-supplied software programs that supply the backup Media Manager. If you don't have any backup media installed on the machine, disks can be used to take backups.

- Recovery Manager greatly simplifies administrative tasks associated with backup and recovery. Several tasks—defining backup configurations, keeping a log of backup and recovery operations, automatically parallelizing the backup and restore with the resources available—can be easily automated with Recovery Manager.

- Recovery Manager detects any Oracle block splits and rereads these blocks to get a consistent view. Therefore, it isn't necessary to keep the tablespace in backup mode while performing a backup. However, you may perform a consistent cold backup of the database by using Recovery Manager. (See "What Is a Block Split?" later in this chapter for more information on block splits.)

- Recovery Manager doesn't back up Oracle blocks that have never been used, thus saving considerable backup time and space.

- Recovery Manager stores backed-up data in an Oracle internal format that can't be read by any other utility. Therefore, files backed up by Recovery Manager can be restored and recovered only with Recovery Manager.

If you aren't using Recovery Manager to perform backup and recovery, you can use OS-level physical backups for making copies of the data to protect against loss. This has so far been the most widely used method for backup operations. There are important considerations to make while implementing a backup strategy:

- You must run the database in ARCHIVE LOG mode in an online transaction system, where each and every transaction is important and it's necessary to recover up to the last committed transaction.

- When the database is running in ARCHIVELOG mode, you can perform a full or partial cold or hot backup.

- A full cold backup is the simplest backup to implement and should be the preferred method, unless availability requirements don't allow enough downtime to perform a full cold backup. A full cold backup can also be integrated with other non-Oracle files at the OS level.

- Recovery Manager is a very flexible and powerful backup and recovery tool. Consider using the Recovery Manager for backup and recovery operations. Refer to Chapter 15 for more details on using the Recovery Manager.

- Recovery Manager enables you to take true incremental backup of the database. You can back up only the modified blocks since the last backup was performed at the same or lower level.

Recovery Manager Scripts

Recovery Manager is an easy-to-use tool available in command-line interface (CLI) and graphical user interface (GUI) mode. (The GUI mode of the Recovery Manager is available through Enterprise Manager on the Windows NT platform.) Oracle also provides comprehensive scripts to start with. The scripts case1.rcv and case4.rcv provide comprehensive information about using the Recovery Manager to perform backup. These scripts are located in the $ORACLE_HOME/rdbms/demo directory on a UNIX system and the \ORANT\rdbms\demo folder on a Windows NT system.

case1.rcv

This script contains code for the following backup, restore, and recovery operations using Recovery Manager:

- Archive the current log
- Specify maximum corruption tolerance
- Mount the database
- Back up archived logs, back up the control file, and back up the control file with the copy command
- Back up system tablespace
- Full, whole database backup
- Incremental level 0, whole database backup
- Incremental level 1, whole database backup
- Incremental level 2, whole database backup
- Back up read-only tablespace

Print the script case1.rcv while reading this part

case1.rcv is a long script that shows how to write Recovery Manager scripts. Keep a printout of it handy while reading this section.

- Script to verify backup set isn't corrupt
- Restore and recovery
- Restore control file
- Restore all data files
- Recover all data files
- Restore and recover data files and control file
- Restore and recover data files
- Restore and recover a single tablespace (database open)

Keep the following in mind when you perform these functions:

- Use the `setlimit`, `filesperset` clause to enforce the following restrictions:

No single backup piece is greater than 2GB.	Puts a maximum of 20 archived logs in any one backup set.
No more than 200 buffers are allowed to be read per file per second, which limits the effect the backup file scan has on online users and batch jobs.	A channel can have a maximum of only 32 files open at any one time. Includes, at the most, six files in one backup set.

- Continue even if any of the data files is inaccessible, leaving unavailable data files.
- Skip data files that belong to read-only tablespaces and are offline.
- Back up the tablespace that has just been made read-only; it should be backed up once before being omitted from future backups by the `skip readonly` clause.

case4.rcv

This script has the code for taking a consistent backup of a database using the Recovery Manager. It performs the backup operations with the following considerations:

- Backs up database by using up to two tape drives.
- The Media Manager has a maximum supported file size limit of 2GB, so any backup piece should be no larger than that size.

Making backups on disk with Recovery Manager

To make backup sets to disk with Recovery Manager, change the channel allocation commands to be type `disk` and modify the `format` clause to include the full path name the backup is to be written to. Otherwise, the backup files will typically be written to the dbs directory in Oracle home.

- Each backup set should include a maximum of five files.
- Includes offline data files and read-only tablespaces in the backup.
- Terminates the backup if any files aren't accessible.
- Opens the database after the backup completes.

Performing an Offline (Cold) Backup

Cold backup or consistent backup of a file is the backup taken when the file is offline (not being accessed by the database instance, for instance). Thus, a file's cold backup is its image copy as it existed when the file was taken offline. You can take a partial or full cold backup off the database. The following factors determine whether a full or a partial cold backup is taken:

- A partial cold backup can't be taken if the database is in NOARCHIVE LOG mode; you can't take the files offline for cold backup.
- Size of the database, speed of the backup media, and the time allowed for the database to be unavailable. If the database is in ARCHIVE LOG mode, you can offline tablespaces to back them up while the rest of the database is available to the users.

Taking an Offline (Cold) Backup of a Tablespace

To make a cold backup of a tablespace (other than system tablespace data files), take the corresponding tablespace offline by issuing the following command from Server Manager:

```
SQL> alter tablespace tablespace name offline ;
```

Use any of the OS utilities tar, dd, and cpio on UNIX and Backup on Windows NT to copy the corresponding data files. When the backup is completed, use the following command to put the tablespace back online:

```
SQL> alter tablespace tablespace_name online ;
```

Enabling ARCHIVELOG mode

By default, the database is created in the NOARCHIVELOG mode. Refer to Chapter 12, "Understanding Oracle8 Backup Options," for steps required to alter the database to ARCHIVELOG mode.

You can't take the SYSTEM tablespace offline

To make an offline tablespace backup, the database needs to be shut down. You can't perform a cold backup of the SYSTEM tablespace while the database is running because Oracle requires that it always be available.

Listing 13.1 lists a sample script that performs an offline backup of a tablespace on a UNIX system. This script does the following:

- Lists the data files belonging to the tablespace (lines 9–23)
- Takes the tablespace offline (lines 28–30)
- Backs up the files with the UNIX tar command (lines 38–49)
- Puts the tablespace back online (lines 51–56)

LISTING 13.1   *TS_BACKUP_OFF.SH*–Performing an offline backup of a tablespace

```
01:  # Script to perform offline backup of a tablespace
02:  # on a UNIX system
03:  #
04:  #   Takes two input arguments
05:  #            1. Name of the tar file
06:  #            2. Name of the tablespace to be backed up.
07:  #
08:  #
09:  # Listing database files belonging to the tablespace
10:  #
11:  #
12:  sqlplus -s sys/<password> > tsfile_name.dat <<!
13:  set heading off;
14:  set pagesize 0
15:  set linesize 2048
16:  set feedback off;
17:  REM
18:  REM   Listing datafiles
19:  REM
20:  select file_name
21:  from DBA_DATA_FILES
22:  where tablespace_name='$2';
23:  exit;
24:  !
25:  #
26:  # Offline the tablespace to be backed up
27:  #
```

Contents of offline tablespaces aren't available to users

When a tablespace is made offline, user objects residing in it aren't available for use until it's put back online. Applications trying to use these objects will signal errors while the tablespace remains offline.

```
28: sqlplus -s sys/change_on_install <<!
29: alter tablespace $2 offline ;
30: exit;
31: !
32: #
33: #
34: # Creating the tar file and
35: # backing up the datafiles
36: #
37: #
38: First_file='Yes'
39: for i in `cat tsfile_name.dat`
40: do
41:         echo "----Backing up the datafile $i"
42:     if [ $First_file = Yes ]
43:     then
44:      tar -cvf  $1 $i
45:      First_file='No'
46:     else
47:      tar -rvf $1 $i
48:     fi
49: done
50: #
51: sqlplus -s sys/change_on_install <<!
52: REM
53: REM Bringing the tablespace back online
54: REM
55: REM
56: alter tablespace $2 online ;
57: !
58: # end of the script tablespace backup script
```

Taking a tablespace offline

You can't take offline a table-space that contains an active rollback segment. First take the rollback segment offline, then the tablespace.

Making a Full Cold Backup

To perform a full offline database backup, the database must be shut down. Listing 13.2 shows a script that performs a cold backup of a database on a UNIX system. This script performs the following sequence of operations:

- Generates a list of all the database's data files, control files, and online redo log files (lines 36–53)

- Shuts down the database (lines 59–62)
- Backs up the default parameter file (line 68)
- Backs up the files with the UNIX tar command (lines 72–76)
- Starts the database after the backup (lines 81–84)

LISTING 13.2   *COLD_BACKUP.SH*–**Performing a full cold backup of a database**

```
01: # Script to perform cold backup of a database
02: # on a UNIX system
03: #
04: # Uses environment variable ORACLE_SID to decide
05: #   which database to backup
06: # The database should be up and running.
07: #
08: # Connects to the database using sys account,
09: # to list name of all the
10: # Control files,
11: # online redo log files and
12: # datafiles.
13: #
14: # It also backs up the default INIT.ORA
15: #   file from $ORACLE_HOME/dbs directory
16: #
17: # The script does not backup archived redo logs.
18: # If you are running in the ARCHIVELOG mode
19: # then please be sure to back them up.
20: #
21: # Modify this script to shutdown all the instances
22: # accessing the database in an Oracle Parallel Server
23: # environment. It creates the tar file with the
24: # following naming convent¦ion
25: #       bkp<ORACLE_SID><mmddhh>.tar (month, data, hour)
26: # Creates tar file in the directory specified
27: # by BACKUP_DIR as defined in the
28: # following line
29: ##
30: BACKUP_DIR=/home/oracle/backup ; export BACKUP_DIR
31: BKPTIME=`date '+%m%d%H'`
32: BKPFILE=$BACKUP_DIR/bkp$ORACLE_SID$BKPTIME.tar
33: #
```

Shut down all instances in an OPS environment

In order to perform a cold backup of a database in an Oracle Parallel Server environment, you must shut down all instances accessing the database before copying the data files at the OS level.

```
34: # Creating database file list in the file file_name.dat
35: #
36: sqlplus -s sys/change_on_install > file_name.dat <<!
37: set heading off;
38: set pagesize 0
39: set linesize 2000
40: set feedback off;
41: REM
42: REM  Listing datafiles
43: REM
44: select name from V\$DATAFILE ;
45: REM
46: REM  Listing control files
47: REM
48: select name from V\$CONTROLFILE;
49: REM
50: REM  Listing online redo log files
51: REM
52: select member from V\$LOGFILE;
53: exit;
54: !
55: #
56: # Shutting down the database
57: # Using Shutdown normal.
58: #
59: svrmgrl <<!
60: connect internal ;
61: shutdown;
62: exit;
63: !
64: #
65: #
66: # Backing up the initialization parameter file
67: #
68: tar cvf $BKPFILE $ORACLE_HOME/dbs/init$ORACLE_SID.ora
69: #Backing up the files using the tar command
70: # to the file BKPFILE as defined above
71: #
72: for i in `cat file_name.dat`
73: do
74: echo "Backing up the datafile $i"
75:     tar -rvf $BKPFILE $i
```

Shutdown immediate disconnects all active users

`Shutdown immediate` disconnects users and rolls back all current uncommitted transactions. The data in uncommitted transactions is lost. If you don't want to forcefully disconnect the users for performing backup, use `shutdown normal`.

continues…

LISTING 13.2   Continued

```
76: done
77: #
78: # Starting the database
79: # after backup
80: #
81: svrmgrl <<!
82: connect internal ;
83: startup;
84: exit;
85: !
86: #
87: exit ;
88: # end of the script cold_backup.sh
```

Pay attention to the following points when performing a cold backup:

Don't use Shutdown abort before a cold backup

If you shut down the database with the **ABORT** option, you should restart the database in **RESTRICT** mode and use **Shutdown normal** before copying the database files.

- Use Shutdown immediate or Shutdown normal. Before copying the files, ensure that the database has been shut down properly by looking at the messages in the alert*sid*.log file.

- The sample script shown in Listing 13.2 backs up online redo log files. Be careful while restoring them, however; if you plan to perform recovery by using the archived redo logs after the restore, don't restore the online redo logs from the backup. If you do so, they will overwrite the current online redo logs on the system and you won't be able to perform a complete recovery.

- Always back up archived redo logs at regular intervals.

- Use an automated method to get a list of the files that are part of the database similar to the one used in the sample script cold_backup.sh in Listing 13.2. This will minimize the administrative work and human errors. If you decide to list the files manually for backup purposes, remember to modify the script after you add and delete data files, control files, and online redo log files to and from the database.

- An automated script that picks up the names of the data files from the database doesn't depend on the underlying database file architecture (such as OFA, Optimal Flexible

Architecture) to discover the name of the files to back up. Thus, it doesn't restrict you to placing the database files in a predefined manner.

- If the database contains READ ONLY tablespaces, it's not necessary to back them up each time during a cold backup. A one-time backup of these tablespaces is necessary, however, after making them READ ONLY.

- You don't need to back up tablespaces that don't contain any permanent objects. Thus, you may not back up tablespaces that contain only rollback segments and are used as temporary tablespace. I recommend, however, that you include them in the cold backup for ease of operation during the recovery. If you have to perform recovery after a full restore and haven't backed up the temporary tablespace and the tablespace containing rollback segments, you might have to perform extra steps before completing the recovery.

- Always look at the log generated during execution of the backup script to ensure that the backup process completed properly. The sample script in Listing 13.2 is provided for a quick start; it doesn't include a comprehensive error-checking mechanism. You might want to enhance it for checking the status of the database pre-script, the status of the backup device, the space available at the backup destination, the errors during backup, and so on.

- The initialization parameter file is an ASCII file and can be created with any editor. It isn't necessary to back this up with every cold backup. I recommend backing it up, however, as it involves resources of little significance and can save valuable time in case you lose it.

Performing an Online (Hot) Backup

A hot or online backup refers to the backup of a database's data files taken while the database is still open. Use online backup when business requirements don't permit the database to be unavailable for an interval long enough to perform the offline data files backup. To perform online backup of a data file, you need to put the corresponding tablespace in backup mode by using the following command:

```
SQL>alter tablespace tablespace_name begin backup;
```

Copy the file at the OS level after issuing this command. When the copy operation is completed, the tablespace should be returned to normal mode with the following command:

```
SQL>alter tablespace tablespace_name end backup;
```

Oracle copies entire block images of the modified data blocks on the first change to the blocks; this is done while the tablespace is in the backup mode. This increases the size of the redo log generated while the tablespace is in the backup mode. Follow these guidelines to minimize its impact on the performance:

- Perform the online backup of a tablespace while its DML activity is minimal.

- Don't keep the tablespace in backup mode longer than what's required to copy the appropriate data files. Start copying the files immediately after issuing the `begin backup` command, and issue the corresponding end backup command as soon as copying is done.

- Ensure that a tablespace isn't left in backup mode for a very long period after a failure in backup process during the middle of the backup.

What Is a Block Split?

An Oracle data block consists of multiple OS disk blocks. The Oracle DBWR process writes modified blocks to the disk through OS write calls, which write to the disk in chunks that are multiples of OS blocks. The same Oracle block may be read and written to the storage media at the same time. This simultaneous read/write operation causes what's known as an "Oracle block split."

Figure 13.1 shows three Oracle blocks. Each Oracle block consists of four OS blocks—a total of 12 OS blocks. Assume that time t1, t2, and t3 are in increasing order, and consider the following situation:

View V$BACKUP

Use the dynamic performance view **V$BACKUP** to determine the backup status of the data files at any time. The **ACTIVE** value in this column indicates that the file is marked as now being backed up.

- The backup process writes the first six OS blocks to the backup file at time t1.
- The DBWR process writes Oracle Block 2 at time t2.
- The backup process writes the next six OS blocks to the backup file at time t3.

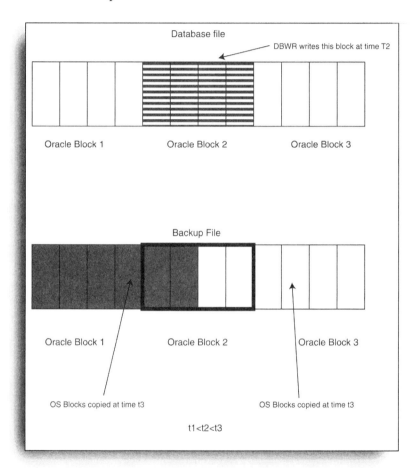

Database file

DBWR writes this block at time T2

Oracle Block 1   Oracle Block 2   Oracle Block 3

Backup File

Oracle Block 1   Oracle Block 2   Oracle Block 3

OS Blocks copied at time t3   OS Blocks copied at time t3

t1<t2<t3

FIGURE 13.1

Oracle blocks splits/fractures as DBWR writes the block while it's being copied at the OS level.

Clearly, the backup file contains the first half of Oracle Block 2 before the update, and the second half after the update. Thus, an inconsistent copy of the Oracle block is present in the backup file. To handle this problem, Oracle writes the complete image of the modified blocks in its redo log while the tablespace is in backup mode. During the recovery process before applying the changes to a block, Oracle copies the block image from its redo log to the disk—making the block consistent—and applies the remaining redo for the block.

Hot Backup Script

You can use the HOT_BACKUP.SH script shown in Listing 13.3 to perform a hot backup of a database on a UNIX system. This script backs up all data files in online mode. It also appends a backup copy of the control file and all archived redo logs present in the archive destination directory. Tailor it to suit your environment. This script calls another script, bkp_ts.sh (shown in Listing 13.4), which issues the necessary begin and end backup commands and copies all the data files belonging to a tablespace.

LISTING 13.3   *HOT_BACKUP.SH*–Performing a hot backup of a database

```
01: # Script to perform hot backup of a database
02: # on a UNIX system.
03: #
04: # Uses environment variable ORACLE_SID to decide
05: #   which database to backup
06: # The database should be up and running.
07: #
08: # Connects to the database using sys account,
09: # to list name of all the
10: # tablespace and the corresponding datafiles.
11: #
12: # It also backs up the default INIT.ORA
13: #   file from $ORACLE_HOME/dbs directory
14: #
15: # The script  performs a log switch at the end and
16: # performs backup of all the archive logs present in
17: # the directory. It creates the tar file with the
18: # following naming convention
19: #       bkp<ORACLE_SID><mmddhh>.tar (month, data, hour)
20: # Creates tar file in the directory specified
21: # by BACKUP_DIR as defined in the
22: # following line
23: #
```

```
24: BACKUP_DIR=/home/oracle/backup ; export BACKUP_DIR
25: BKPTIME=`date '+%m%d%H'`
26: BKPFILE=$BACKUP_DIR/bkp$ORACLE_SID$BKPTIME.tar
27: #
28: # Listing the tablspaces to backup
29: #
30: sqlplus -s sys/<password> > tablespace_name.dat ¦<<!
31: set heading off;
32: set pagesize 0
33: set linesize 2048
34: set feedback off;
35: REM
36: REM  Listing all the tablespaces
37: REM
38: select tablespace_name from DBA_TABLESPACES
            where tablespace_name='SYSTEM';
39: exit;
40: !
41: #
42: #
43: #
44: # Backing up the initialization parameter file
45: #
46: tar cvf $BKPFILE $ORACLE_HOME/dbs/init$ORACLE_SID.ora
46: #Backing up the files using the tar command
47: # to the file BKPFILE as defined above
48: #
49: for ts in `cat tablespace_name.dat`
50: do
51:         echo "Beginning backup of the tablespace $ts"
52:         bkp_ts.sh  $BKPFILE $ts
53: done
54: #
55: # Backing up the control file to a backup file
56: #
57: sqlplus -s sys/change_on_install <<!
58: set pagesize 0
59: set linesize 2048
60: set feedback off;
61: REM
62: REM Backing up control file
63: REM
```

continues...

LISTING 13.3   **Continued**

```
64: alter database backup controlfile to '$PWD/control.bkp';
65: exit;
66: !
67: #
68: #Appending the control file to tar file
69: #
70: tar -rvf $BKPFILE control.bkp
71: rm -f control.bkp
72: #
73: # Performing a log switch to archiving all the
74: # logs
75: sqlplus -s sys/change_on_install <<!
76: set linesize 2048
77: set feedback off;
78: alter system switch logfile;
79: alter system archive log all;
80: exit;
81: !
82: #
83: # Backing up the archive redo logs.
84: # This script assumes that the archive log destination
85: # is set to its default value of $ORACLE_HOME/dbs
86: # This might have to be changed to suit
87: # your environment
88: #
89: FILES=`ls $ORACLE_HOME/dbs/arch*`; export FILES
90: tar -rvf $BKPFILE $FILES
91: rm -f $FILES
92: #
93: # end of the script hot_backup.sh
```

Log switch after a hot backup

Always back up the redo logs generated during a hot backup by forcing a log switch and then copying the generated archived redo logs.

LISTING 13.4   *BKP_TS.SH*–**Performing a hot backup of a tablespace**

```
01: # Script to perform hot backup of a tablespace
02: #
03: #
04: #  Takes two input arguments
05: #              1. Name of the tar file
06: #              2. Name of the tablespace to be backed up.
07: #
```

```
08: #
09: # Listing database files belonging to the tablespace
10: #
11: #
12: sqlplus -s sys/<password> > tsfile_name.dat <<!
13: set heading off;
14: set pagesize 0
15: set linesize 2048
16: set feedback off;
17: REM
18: REM  Listing datafiles
19: REM
20: select file_name
21: from DBA_DATA_FILES
22: where tablespace_name='$2';
23: exit;
24: !
25: #
26: # Putting the tablespace in hot backup mode
27: #
28: sqlplus -s sys/change_on_install <<!
29: alter tablespace $2 begin backup ;
30: exit;
31: !
32: #
33: #
34: # Appending the files to the file
35: # BKPFILE as defined above
36: #
37: for i in `cat tsfile_name.dat`
38: do
39:         echo "----Backing up the datafile $i"
40:     tar rvf $1 $i
41: done
42: #
43: sqlplus -s sys/change_on_install <<!
44: set heading off;
45: set pagesize 0
46: set linesize 2048
47: set feedback off;
48: REM
49: REM Changing the tablespace from hot backup mode
```

continues...

LISTING 13.4 Continued

```
50:  REM to normal mode
51:  REM
52:  alter tablespace $2 end backup ;
53:  !
54:  # end of the script tablespace backup script
```

Creating a Standby Database

The standby database can't be queried

A standby database is constantly in recovery mode and not available for querying the data unless you activate it. Once a standby database is activated, it's no longer available as a standby unless you recreate it as another standby database.

If a database is used for mission-critical applications, you want to avoid downtime at any cost. Modern hardware and software techniques enable you to increase the availability of systems approaching 100 percent. If for any reason the primary production database can't be made available to the end users, however, maintaining a standby may fulfill a business's availability requirements.

A standby database is a copy of the primary database that can be brought online with minimum delay when needed. This feature is part of Oracle's disaster recovery procedures. With this feature, you can maintain a hot standby copy of the production database, preferably at another remote site, which can be activated on short notice. When it's activated, this database will serve as the production database. You might need to start from the beginning to create a standby database for this database.

Create a standby database

  1. Perform an online or offline backup of the production database using the proper procedures. (If your system is mission-critical, however, you would most likely perform an online backup.) It's good practice to perform an online backup while setting up the standby database for the first time; this will give invaluable experience in recreating the standby database whenever the standby database is put into production use.

2. Create a control file for the standby database by using the following command:

```
SQL>alter database create standby
controlfile as control_file_name;
```

The following is a sample command session executing this command. Notice that the filename is included in quotation marks. Because the full path name isn't given for the file, the standby control file is created in the default location—the $ORACLE_HOME/dbs directory.

```
SVRMGR> alter database create standby
     2> controlfile as 'control.std';
Statement processed.
```

3. Archive the production database's current online log files with this command:

```
SQL> alter system archive log current ;
```

This command forces a log switch and then archives the current redo log file group. The database must be open to issue this command. This command may not be required if you've performed an offline backup of the database in Step 1, as data files are checkpointed (synchronized) before an offline backup. If the database is open, issuing this command is important because it ensures consistency among the data files in Step 1 and the control file in Step 2.

4. Transfer all files generated in Steps 1 through 3 to the system where you want to build the standby database.

5. Create the initialization parameter file for the standby database. It's highly desirable and also recommended to have the standby database's parameters similar to the primary database parameters, because the standby database will be used as the primary database after the failover. Keeping most parameters the same will help you avoid any surprises during its operation.

Table 13.2 lists important initialization parameters related to the standby database configuration.

The standby control file

Standby control file contents are different from those in the original control file. You should not use a backup copy of the original control file generated by the backup control file command instead of this file.

The standby should be built on a similar system

The standby database must be built on the same hardware platform as that of the primary database. It's recommended there be similar architecture and software on both machines.

TABLE 13.2   **Parameters related to standby database**

Parameter Name:	Description:
COMPATIBLE	This parameter must be the same on the primary and standby databases.
DB_FILES	This parameter and the MAXDATAFILES clause of the CREATE DATABASE or CREATE CONTROLFILE commands specifies the maximum number of data files for the database. Keep it the same, as the number of data files allowed/needed will be identical at both places.
CONTROL_FILES	This parameter specifies the name of the control files used for the database. Both databases should point to different files. Their names can be the same, as they're located on different machines.
DB_FILE_NAME_CONVERT	This parameter is set only on the standby database. Use this parameter only if the directory paths to the data files are different at both sites.
LOG_FILE_NAME_CONVERT	This parameter is the same as DB_FILE_NAME_CONVERT, except that it applies to the online redo log members.

Maintaining a Standby Database

After transferring all data from the primary database to the host machine for the standby database, you need to keep the standby database closely synchronized with the primary database.

Keep the standby synchronized with the primary database

1. Start the standby database instance in the nomount state with the following command:

```
svrmgrl> startup nomount ;
```

2. Mount the standby database in the standby exclusive mode by using the following command:

```
svrmgrl> alter database mount standby database;
```

3. Prepare the standby database for recovery to apply the archived redo logs received from the primary database:

```
svrmgrl> recover [from location] standby database until
cancel;
```

Automate the archive log transfer to the standby database

Archived redo logs generated at the primary site need to be applied to the hot standby on a regular basis. In a production environment, it's desirable to automate the process of transferring and applying the archived redo log to the standby database. Use the operating system's or Oracle's job-scheduling features to implement this.

4. Oracle will prompt the next log to be applied. Apply all the logs that have been generated so far and then cancel the recovery. If the archived redo logs to be applied are being made available in the directory specified by LOG_ARCHIVE_DEST, the FROM *location* clause doesn't need to be specified. Because it's a recurring process, you might want to automate it by using Oracle job queues or operating system job-scheduling features.

Using the Unrecoverable Option on the Primary Database

Unrecoverable data loads and the no-logging feature associated with tables and indexes that don't generate redo logs aren't propagated to the standby database. If you activate the standby database without paying attention to them, the affected target objects will be marked as corrupted. You can drop the affected tablespace at the standby database after the activation, or recreate it by using a fresh backup of the concerned tablespace at the primary site and transferring it over to the standby database before activation.

Adding and Deleting Data Files

If you add a data file at the primary database, you should make a copy of the added data file and add it to the standby database before applying the redo log that was generated while the file was added. This adds the new file to the standby control file and will allow the standby database's recovery to proceed as normal. A dropped data file at the primary site is also removed from the standby database control file when the corresponding redo log is applied.

Adding, Removing, and Clearing Redo Log Files

Adding and removing online redo logs doesn't have any impact on the configuration of the standby database's redo log configuration.

Performing an incomplete recovery at the primary database and opening it with the resetlogs option will invalidate the standby database, as the resetlogs option initializes all the online redo logs and resets the log sequence number at the primary site.

The standby database's online redo log files

Online redo log files for a standby database are initialized when the standby database is activated. You might consider using the alter database clear logfile command to initialize the online redo logs in advance; this saves time while activating the standby database.

Activating a Standby Database

Standby databases become normal databases after activation

As soon as you activate the standby database, it no longer remains a standby database. It becomes a normal database totally independent of its primary database. If needed, use it to recreate another standby database.

The standby database is mounted and is in recovery mode. Issue the following command to activate it and make it available to the users:

```
svrmgr> alter database activate standby database;
```

Be careful to apply all the archived and unarchived redo logs from the primary database before activating the standby database. Once you activate the standby database, all the transactions from the primary database that are present in the unapplied redo logs are lost.

Using Replication as a Failover

Oracle offers the following solutions for implementing highly available systems:

- Oracle Parallel Server
- Hot standby database (discussed earlier in this chapter)
- Oracle Failsafe option
- Replication

For information on the Oracle Failsafe option, available on Windows NT cluster systems, refer to the *Oracle Fail Safe Concepts and Administration Guide* from Oracle Corporation.

SEE ALSO

➤ *An overview of Oracle Parallel Server options, page* **726**

Oracle's Replication option enables you to maintain the same data in multiple databases. By using replication, you can design applications that are available to end users all the time. If one database fails for any reason—including the unavailability of its host site due to natural catastrophe—the sites having the replicated database can be used by the application. If you're maintaining data at more than two locations, the application can access the data as long as one replicated site is functioning. The nice thing about this scheme is that it can be completely transparent to end users. If the database instance they were working on goes down, the application can connect the users to another replicated site immediately without the users knowing that. Look at this option's important features with respect to a fail-over strategy:

- The Replication option lets you choose the objects to be replicated at the table level. Thus, if only part of the data is critical for the business application, only that data can be replicated.

- There are no restrictions on the hardware and software architecture of the machines hosting the database's participating in a replicated environment. One database could be on a UNIX machine, another could be on a Windows NT box, and so on. You can replicate databases among platforms as long as the Oracle versions residing on them are compatible with each other.

- The systems having replicated databases need not be clustered or part of an MPP (massively parallel platform) system as required while implementing the Oracle Parallel Server or Failsafe option. Common network communication is used for data transfers among the machines having a replicated database.

- Due to the hardware requirements, the machines used for OPS and Failsafe are located in physical proximity; therefore, these two options don't provide protection against site failure. The Oracle Replication option and the hot standby database can have the remote database at different geographical locations and provide protection against site failure.

- The Replication option involves significant overhead in terms of network and other system resources; as a result, it's generally not suitable for a very high volume transaction system.

- Data is propagated to other sites asynchronously. This implies that when a database participating in an replicated environment fails, some transactions committed in it may not be propagated at the other site until the failed database comes back up. Replication shouldn't be used for failover if the application can't tolerate this type of inconsistency.

SEE ALSO

➤ *Information on advanced replication options, page* **696**

Building a Failover Database with Replication

To use replication as a means providing increased availability, you can choose from the following options:

- The read-only snapshots should be used if the backup site is to be used to provide read-only access to the data. In this situation, DML operations can't be performed until the primary site comes back up.

- Provide full access to the data by using multimaster replication. The data is available for read as well as for DML access from all the sites all the time.

Setting Up Read-Only Failover Database with Snapshots

Set up snapshots to provide read-only access to data with the master site

Refer to Oracle8's *Server Replication Manual* for complete details

Detailed instructions on setting up snapshots and replication is beyond the scope of this book. An overview of the tasks to be performed is provided; please refer to the *Oracle8 Server Replication* manual for more details and command syntax.

1. To set up snapshot replication, you need to decide which tables need to be replicated. If the application doesn't require all the tables at the failover site, you can save resources by not configuring snapshots for tables that aren't needed.

2. Create the snapshot schema at the snapshot site and then establish database links to the master site.

3. Create a snapshot log at the master site to allow fast refresh of the snapshots. If you don't create a snapshot log, every refresh will be a complete refresh (which may not be acceptable in most cases).

4. Create a snapshot at the snapshot site. During this process, all the data from the master site is propagated to the snapshot site.

5. Create snapshot groups and assign snapshots to them. This is the process where you define the snapshot update interval.

Setting Up Failover Database with Multimaster Replication

The steps required to set up multimaster replication are very similar to setting up snapshots.

Set up multimaster replication

1. Set up the replication environment at the master definition site. This site includes creating the replication owner and granting necessary privileges to it, defining a database link to be used for replication, and scheduling jobs to replicate changes from one site to another at regular intervals.

2. Decide which tables need to be replicated and who owns them at the master definition site. Create the schema and the tables to be replicated at the master definition site.

3. Repeat the functions from Step 1 on the remote (master) site.

4. Repeat the functions from Step 2 on the remote (master) site.

5. Create a master replication group at the master definition site.

6. Add replication objects to the replication group and generate the replication support for these objects.

7. Start the replication process by enabling changes in the replication group from QUIESCED mode to NORMAL mode.

After the replication is set up, Oracle maintains the data at all participating sites. No additional steps are required to maintain the replicated data, except to resolve error conditions that might result from what's called the CONFLICTS. Refer to the *Oracle8 Server Replication Manual* for more details.

Performing Database Recovery

Determine the extent of system failure

Recover from loss of general data files

Recover from loss of system tablespace

Recover from loss of control files

Recovery Strategies

Analyzing the recovery process involves determining the factors that influence the recovery process. Database size, system complexity, database structure, and application structure are the main factors that influence the mean time to recover (MTTR).

The MTTR can be very critical to the operation of systems that need high availability. You can reduce the MTTR in several ways:

- Reduce the size of components that need to be recovered.
- Use Oracle8's table and index partitioning features. Using partitions will minimize the impact of the failure on the rest of the system.
- Ensure that the backup can be easily and quickly accessed in the event of a failure.
- Test your backups to avoid any surprises.
- Ensure that you are familiar with the recovery procedures that have to be followed based on the type of failure. Keep the common recovery scripts handy.
- Design the database to promote autonomous components. When the components are autonomous, their impact on the rest of the system is minimal and the recovery is faster.

Table 14.1 describes the techniques that can be used for high availability. These strategies should be used to quickly recover in the event of a database failure.

TABLE 14.1   High availability strategies

Technique	Usage	Advantages	Disadvantages
Object-level recovery using Export, Import, and SQL*Loader	Uses Export/Import to protect data	Fast object-level recovery	Difficult to scale; you must be aware of object associations
Failover systems using hardware redundancy	Failover provided by using another node	No data loss due to redundant system	No scalability; costly

Technique	Usage	Advantages	Disadvantages
Oracle standby databases	Primary database's redo log keeps another database updated, which can be used during recovery	Fast recovery; failover; disaster recovery possible	Data loss possible; compli cated setup and maintenance; potential of replicating data-base corruption
Oracle Symmetric Replication	Uses Oracle's replication feature to provide high availability	No data loss; failover; disaster recovery possible; both databases can be used simultaneously	Slow recovery due to use of transactions; use of two-phase commit can lead to additional problems while maintaining the database's consistency
Oracle Parallel Server	Clustering solution that allows failover to another instance; recovery can proceed simultaneously and is done by the surviving instances	No data loss; fast failover; protects against node and cache failures; high scalability; load balancing	Tuning can be difficult; application design plays significant part in strategy's success
Triple mirroring	Uses a third hardware that is a mirror	Fast hot backups; fast recovery	Cost of triple writes and resilvering
EMC SRDF facility	Physical I/O-based replication	No data loss; failover; disaster recovery possible; faster than Oracle Symmetric Replication	Potential of replicating database corruption
Customized store-and-forward replication	Makes use of Oracle8 features such as advanced queuing or trigger-based asynchronous replication	No data loss; fast recovery	Complex; serializing of transactions

General steps to recover a database system

1. Detect the failure. The detection of an outage is usually simple: Either the database isn't responding to the application, or the system has displayed explicit error messages. However, a problem such as a corrupt control file may not be detected while the database is running.

2. Analyze the failure. You should analyze the type and extent of the failure; the recovery procedure will depend on this analysis. This task can take a significant amount of time in large systems.

3. Determine the components of the database that need recovery. This task can also be significant in large systems. You need to determine which components (such as a table) are lost, and then determine whether you need to recover the tablespace or a data file.

4. Determine the dependencies between components to be recovered. Usually the components aren't isolated; loss or recovery of a database object can affect other objects. For example, if a table needs recovery, you'll also have to recreate the indexes. This step isn't done automatically by the recovery of the table.

5. Determine the location of the backup. The closer the backup is to where the recovery is to be performed, the lesser is the MTTR.

6. Perform the restore. This involves restoring the physical file from disk or tape and placing it at a location where the database can access the file for recovery purposes. The time to restore is affected by file location, file size, file format (raw, export, blocks, or extracts), and possibilities of restore parallelism.

7. Replay redo logs (for archived databases) and resync the database components.

Location factors

If the backup is on a disk, is the disk on-site or off-site? Is the disk local or network? Do you have mirrored copies? Are you recovering from a cold or a hot backup? If the backup is on tape, is the tape on-site or off-site? Do you need additional components to access the tape?

Analyzing the Failure and Determining Recovery Options

You need to answer several questions to determine the type and extent of failure. Your answers dictate the steps you take to recover the system:

- What led to the failure: power outage, upgrade, maintenance (OS, hardware, network, database)?
- How did the database go down: shutdown abort, crash, normal shutdown?
- Are there any operating system errors?
- Was the server rebooted?
- Are there any errors in the operating system log?
- Are there any errors in the alert log?
- Were trace files generated?
- How critical is the lost data?
- Are you running Oracle Parallel Server?
- Have you attempted any kind of recovery so far? If so, what steps have already been performed?
- What's your backup strategy?
- If you have cold backups, how was the database shut down when the cold backups were taken?
- Are you running in archive log mode?
- Do you have all archive logs accessible without any break in the sequence numbers?
- Are the online redo logs mirrored?
- Are the control files mirrored?
- Do you have recent full database export?
- What else was running when the system crashed?
- Can you bring the instance up?
- Can you mount the database? Open it?

- What are your system availability requirements?

- What size is the database?

- Are you using raw files?

- What events (if any) are set in your INIT.ORA?

- How many rollback segments do you have?

Database failures can be detected if you get one of various errors. The following list shows some of the common errors encountered and their solutions:

- The message `00205, 00000, "error in identifying controlfile, check alert log for more info"` means the system couldn't find a control file of the specified name and size. Check that all control files are online and that they're the same files that the system created at cold start time.

- The message `00280, 00000, "change %s for thread %s is in sequence #%s"` helps you find the redo log file with the specified change number requested by other messages. Use this information to specify the required archived redo log files for other errors.

- The message `00312, 00000, "online log %s thread %s: '%s'"` reports the filename for details of another message. Other messages will accompany this message; see the associated messages for the appropriate action to take.

- The message `00314, 00000, "log %s of thread %s, expected sequence# %s doesn't match %s"` means that the online log is corrupted or is an old version. You need to find and install correct log versions or reset the log.

- The message `00376, 00000, "file %s cannot be read at this time"` indicates that Oracle is trying to read from an unreadable file—more than likely, an offline file. Check the file's status and bring it online, if necessary.

- The message `00604, 00000, "error occurred at recursive SQL level %s"` indicates that an error occurred while processing a recursive SQL statement (which applies to internal dictionary tables). Usually this error is accompanied by other errors. If the situation described in the next error can be corrected, do so; otherwise, contact Oracle Support.

- The message `01110, 00000, "data file %s: '%s'"` reports a filename for details of another error. See the accompanying errors for analyzing the problem further.

- The message `01116, 00000, "error in opening database file %s"` usually means that the file isn't accessible. The solution is to restore the database file.

- The message `01157, 00000, "cannot identify data file %s - file not found"` means that the background process couldn't find one of the data files. The database will prohibit access to this file but other files will be unaffected; however, the first instance to open the database will need to access all online data files. Another error from the operating system will describe why the file wasn't found. To solve this problem, make the file available to database and then open the database or do an `ALTER SYSTEM CHECK DATAFILES`.

- The message `01194, 00000, "file %s needs more recovery to be consistent"` means that an incomplete recovery session was started, but an insufficient number of logs was applied to make the file consistent. The reported file wasn't closed cleanly when it was last opened by the database. You must recover this file to a time when it wasn't being updated. The most likely cause of this error is forgetting to restore the file from a backup before doing incomplete recovery. Either apply more logs until the file is consistent or restore the file from an older backup and repeat the recovery.

Recovering from the Loss of General Data Files

The procedure to recover from the loss of general data files depends on the type of tablespace from which the data file is lost—rollback tablespace, user tablespace, index tablespace, or read-only tablespace. Several symptoms can indicate this problem. You might get the following errors:

- You're trying to start the database and get error message ORA-1157, ORA-1110 and possibly an operating system error.
- You're trying to shut down the database in normal or immediate mode and get error message ORA-1116, ORA-1110 and possibly an operating system error.

These errors can indicate a loss of a general data file. It's up to you to determine the type of tablespace involved.

Recovering from a Lost Data File in the User Tablespace

If you determine that the tablespace contains user data, the steps you follow to recover the tablespace depend on whether you have a good backup and whether that backup was cold or hot.

Recovering with a Cold Backup

In this case you're in the NOARCHIVELOG mode. The data file recovery will be complete if the redo to be applied is within the range of your online redo logs.

Recover with a cold backup

1. Shut down the database.
2. Restore the lost data file from the backup.
3. Start the database.
4. Execute the following query to determine all your online redo log files and their respective sequence and first change numbers:
   ```
   SELECT X.GROUP#,  MEMBER, SEQUENCE#, FIRST_CHANGE#
   FROM V$LOG X, V$LOGILE Y
   WHERE X.GROUP# = Y.GROUP#;
   ```
5. Determine the CHANGE# of the file to be recovered:
   ```
   SELECT FILE#, CHANGE#
   FROM V$RECOVER_FILE;
   ```

The data file can be recovered if the CHANGE# obtained is greater than the minimum FIRST_CHANGE# of your online redo logs.

6. Recover the data file by using the online redo logs:

```
RECOVER DATAFILE 'fullpath of the datafile'
```

Confirm each log that you're prompted for during the recovery until you receive the message Media Recovery complete.

7. Open the database:

```
ALTER DATABASE OPEN
```

Recovering with a Hot Backup

In this case you're in the ARCHIVELOG mode. The data file recovery will be complete if the redo to be applied is within the range of your online logs.

Recover with a hot backup

1. Shut down the database.

2. Restore the lost data file from the backup.

3. Start the database.

4. Execute the following query to determine all your online redo log files and their respective sequence and first change numbers:

```
SELECT X.GROUP#,  MEMBER, SEQUENCE#, FIRST_CHANGE#
FROM V$LOG X, V$LOGILE Y
WHERE X.GROUP# = Y.GROUP#;
```

The error that reported the failure should indicate the CHANGE# of the file to recover. If this CHANGE# is less than the minimum FIRST_CHANGE# of your online redo logs, the file can't be completely recovered and you have two choices:

- If you can afford losing the database changes since the most recent cold backup, restore the backup and continue with the recovery.

- If you can't afford to lose the database changes, you have to recreate the tablespace as described in the following section, "Recovering with Missing Redo Data."

Use the online redo logs during recovery

If while performing step 5 you're prompted for a non-existing archived log, you need to use the online redo logs to continue with the recovery. Compare the sequence number referenced in the ORA-280 message with the sequence numbers of your online redo logs. Supply the full path name of one of the members of the redo log group whose sequence number matches it.

5. Recover the data file by using the archived and the online redo logs:

   ```
   RECOVER DATAFILE 'fullpath of the datafile'
   ```

   Confirm each log that you're prompted for during the recovery until you receive the message Media Recovery complete.

6. Open the database:

   ```
   ALTER DATABASE OPEN
   ```

Recovering with Missing Redo Data

If redo data is missing, the recovery won't be complete as described in the preceding steps and you'll have to recreate the tablespace. To recreate the tablespace, you can either use a good export script that can easily load the data and recreate the objects in that tablespace or load the data through SQL*Loader.

Recover with missing redo data

1. Shut down the database.

2. Mount the database:

   ```
   Svrmgrl> Startup mount
   ```

3. Offline drop the data file:

   ```
   Svrmgrl> ALTER DATABASE DATAFILE 'fullpath of datafile'
            OFFLINE DROP;
   ```

4. Open the database:

   ```
   Svrmgrl> ALTER DATABASE OPEN;
   ```

5. Drop the user tablespace:

   ```
   Svrmgrl> DROP TABLESPACE tablespace_name
            INCLUDING CONTENTS;
   ```

6. Recreate the tablespace and the tablespace objects.

Recovering from a Lost Data File in a Read-Only Tablespace

Because read-only tablespaces are never modified, the recovery solution is very simple: Restore the data file from its last backup to its original location. No media recovery is required in this case. There are two exceptions to this procedure, however:

- At the time of the last backup, the tablespace was read-only but it has been made read-write since that time.

- At the time of the last backup, the tablespace was read-write but it has been made read-only since that time.

In either scenario, recovery can be performed by following the same steps as described earlier in the section "Recovering from a Lost Data File in a User Tablespace," based on the backup type you have.

Recovering from a Lost Data File in an Index Tablespace

If you determine that the tablespace contains user indexes, you should use the following steps, depending on whether you have a good backup and whether it's a cold or hot backup.

Recovering with a Cold Backup

In this case you're in NOARCHIVELOG mode. The data file recovery will be complete if the redo to be applied is within the range of your online redo logs. To recover from this situation, follow the same steps as described earlier in the "Recovering with a Cold Backup" section of "Recovering from a Lost Data File in a User Tablespace."

Recovering with a Hot Backup

In this case you're in ARCHIVELOG mode. The data file recovery will be complete if the redo to be applied is within the range of your online logs. To recover from this situation, follow the same steps as described earlier in the "Recovering with a Hot Backup" section of "Recovering from a Lost Data File in a User Tablespace."

Recovering with Missing Redo Data

If redo data is missing, the recovery won't be complete. You need to recreate the tablespace. To do so, you can either use a script that can be used to easily create the index or manually create the indexes by issuing CREATE INDEX statements.

Recover with missing redo data

1. Shut down the database.

2. Mount the database:
   ```
   Svrmgrl> Startup mount
   ```

3. Offline drop the data file:
   ```
   Svrmgrl> ALTER DATABASE DATAFILE 'fullpath of datafile'
            OFFLINE DROP;
   ```

4. Open the database:
   ```
   Svrmgrl> ALTER DATABASE OPEN;
   ```

5. Drop the user tablespace:
   ```
   Svrmgrl> DROP TABLESPACE tablespace_name
            INCLUDING CONTENTS;
   ```

6. Recreate the tablespace and all the previously existing indexes in the tablespace.

Recovering from a Lost Data File in a Rollback Tablespace

This recovery scenario is the most critical one, and you should really work with Oracle Support while performing such a recovery. The main issue involved is that you must make sure the active transactions in the rollback segment aren't lost.

In this case, the procedure to follow depends on when the loss was detected.

Database Is Down

You're trying to start the database and get ORA-1157, ORA-1110 and operating system errors, as well as determine that the tablespace contains rollback segments. One thing you have to determine is how the database was shut down.

Database Was Cleanly Shut Down

You're certain that the database was shut down via shutdown normal or shutdown immediate. Check the alert log and look at the last shutdown entry. The following log entry indicates that the shutdown was clean:

```
'alter database dismount
completed: alter database dismount"
```

This may be followed by an attempt you made to start, resulting in the ORA errors and a subsequent SHUTDOWN ABORT by Oracle.

Recover a database that has been shut down cleanly

1. In the INIT*SID*.ORA file, change the ROLLBACK_SEGMENTS parameter by removing all the rollback segments in the tablespace to which the lost data file belongs. If you aren't sure of the rollback segments you need to remove, insert a # at the beginning of the line to comment out the entire ROLL-BACK_SEGMENTS entry.

2. Mount the database in restricted mode:
   ```
   Svrmgrl> STARTUP RESTRICT MOUNT
   ```

3. Offline drop the lost data file:
   ```
   Svrmgrl> ALTER DATABASE DATAFILE 'fullpath of datafile'
   ➡OFFLINE DROP;
   ```

4. Open the database:
   ```
   Svrmgrl> ALTER DATABASE OPEN
   ```

   If at this point you receive a message that the statement has been processed, skip to step 7; otherwise, if you get error codes ORA-604, ORA-376, and ORA-1110, continue to step 5.

5. This step should be performed only if the database didn't open in step 5. Shut down the database and edit the INIT*SID*.ORA file as follows:

   - Comment out the ROLLBACK_SEGMENTS parameter.
   - Add the following line to list all the rollback segments originally listed in the ROLLBACK_SEGMENTS parameter:
     ```
     _Corrupted_rollback_segments
     ➡= (rollback1,rollback2,...,rollbackN)
     ```

   Now start the database in restricted mode:
   ```
   Svrmgrl> startup restrict mount
   ```

6. Drop the rollback tablespace that contained the lost data file:

```
Svrmgrl> drop tablespace tablespace_name including
contents;
```

7. Recreate the rollback tablespace with all its rollback segments and be sure to bring them online.

8. Make the database available for general use:

```
Svrmgrl> alter system disable restricted session;
```

9. If you had to edit the INIT*SID*.ORA file in step 6, shut down the database and edit the file again as follows:

- Uncomment the ROLLBACK_SEGMENTS parameter.

- If you had to perform step 6, remove the following line:

```
_Corrupted_rollback_segments
➥= (rollback1,rollback2,...,rollbackN)
```

10. Start the database.

Database Wasn't Cleanly Shut Down

In this scenario, the database was shut down, aborted, or crashed. You can't offline or drop the lost data file because it's almost certain that the rollback segments with extents in the lost data file contain active transactions; you must restore the lost data file from backup and apply media recovery. If the database is in NOARCHIVELOG mode, a complete recovery is possible only if the redo to be applied is in the range of your online redo log files.

Recover a database that wasn't shut down cleanly

1. Restore the lost data file from a backup.

2. Mount the database.

3. Identify whether the file is offline:

```
Svrmgrl> SELECT FILE#, NAME, STATUS FROM V$DATAFILE;
```

4. If the file is offline, bring it online:

```
Svrmgrl> ALTER DATABASE DATAFILE 'full path of datafile'
         ONLINE;
```

5. Execute the following query to determine all your online redo log files and their respective sequence and first change numbers:

```
SELECT X.GROUP#,  MEMBER, SEQUENCE#, FIRST_CHANGE#
FROM V$LOG X, V$LOGILE Y
WHERE X.GROUP# = Y.GROUP#;
```

6. The file can't be recovered if the CHANGE# is less than the minimum FIRST_CHANGE# of your online redo logs. You now have two options:

- Restore from a full database backup, which may result in data loss.

- Force the database to open in an inconsistent state, and then rebuild the database.

Open the database in an inconsistent state and rebuild it

1. Shut down the database.

2. Take a full database backup.

3. Make the following changes in your INIT*SID*.ORA file:

- Add the following lines:

```
_allow_resetlogs_corruption = true
_corrupted_rollback_segments
      = list of all rollback segments
```

- Comment out the rollback_segments parameter.

4. Do a startup mount.

5. Perform an incomplete recovery of the database:

```
Svrmgrl> RECOVER DATABASE UNTIL CANCEL;
```

6. When prompted for the file, type CANCEL.

7. Reset the logs and open the database:

```
Svrmgrl> ALTER DATABASE OPEN RESETLOGS;
```

8. Rebuild the database by taking a full database export and then importing it to a new database.

However, if the CHANGE# is greater than the minimum FIRST_CHANGE# of your redo logs, recover the data file by using the online redo logs:

```
RECOVER DATAFILE 'fullpath of the datafile'
```

Be careful here!

These steps should be used with extreme caution after taking a full database export–there is a potential for database corruption.

Rebuilding the database

Rebuilding the database is an essential step in this procedure because forcefully opening the database can corrupt the database.

Confirm each log that you're prompted for during the recovery until you receive the message `Media Recovery complete`.

9. Open the database:

```
ALTER DATABASE OPEN
```

Database Is Up and Running

Create new rollback segments

You may have to create additional rollback segments in a different tablespace to continue working with the database while the current problem is being addressed.

Don't shut down the database if you've detected a loss of data file in the rollback tablespace while the database is up and running. It's simpler to resolve the situation with the database up than it is with the database down. You can use two approaches to recover.

Recover a live database in *ARCHIVELOG* mode

1. Offline the lost data file:

```
ALTER DATABASE DATAFILE 'fullpath of datafile' OFFLINE;
```

2. Restore the data file from a backup.

3. Apply media recovery on the data file:

```
RECOVER DATAFILE 'fullpath of datafile';
```

4. Bring the data file back online:

```
ALTER DATABASE DATAFILE 'fullpath of datafile' ONLINE;
```

Recover a live database, no matter what mode (slower method)

1. Offline all the rollback segments in the tablespace to which the data file belongs:

```
ALTER ROLLBACK SEGMENT rollback_segment OFFLINE;
```

Repeat this statement for all rollback segments in the affected tablespace.

2. Execute the following query to make sure that the rollback segments are offline before they're dropped:

```
SELECT SEGMENT_NAME, STATUS
FROM DBA_ROLLBACK_SEGS
WHERE TABLESPACE_NAME = 'tablespace_name';
```

3. Drop all offline rollback segments by running the following command for each segment:

```
DROP ROLLBACK SEGMENT rollback_segment;
```

4. If there are rollback segments that you tried to offline, but step 2 shows that they're still online, it means that they have active transactions in them. Run the following query to determine the active transactions:

```
SELECT SEGMENT_NAME, XACTS ACTIVE_TX, V.STATUS
FROM V$ROLLSTAT V, DBA_ROLLBACK_SEGS
WHERE TABLESPACE_NAME = 'tablespace_name' AND
SEGMENT_ID = USN;
```

If this query returns no rows, all the rollback segments are offline.

If this query returns one or more rows with a status of PENDING OFFLINE, check the ACTIVE_TX column for these rollback segments. Segments with a value of 0 will soon go offline; a non-zero value, however, indicates that you have active transactions that need to be committed or rolled back.

Dealing with Active Transactions

Execute the following query to identify users who have transactions assigned to the rollback segments:

```
SELECT S.SID, S.SERIAL#, S.USERNAME, R.NAME "ROLLBACK"
FROM V$SESSION S, V$TRANSACTION T, V$ROLLNAME R
WHERE R.NAME IN ('pending_rollback1','pending_rollback2',
➥... 'pending_rollbackN') AND
    S.TADDR = T.ADDR AND
    T.XIDUSN = R.USN;
```

After you determine which users have active transactions in the "pending offline" rollback segments, you can either ask them to commit or roll back their transaction or you can kill their session by executing the following:

```
ALTER SYSTEM KILL SESSION 'sid, serial#';
```

The following steps can be performed after you have taken care of the active transactions.

Clean up after active transactions

1. Drop the tablespace including contents.

2. Recreate the rollback tablespace.

3. Recreate the rollback segments and bring them online.

Recovering from Loss of System Tablespace

A good backup strategy can be a lifesaver in a situation where a data file from the system tablespace is lost or damaged. In the absence of a good backup, you may be faced with the undesirable alternative of rebuilding the database with possible data loss.

The symptoms of the scenario in which the system tablespace needs recovery are as follows:

- The database crashed. When trying to start the database, you get ORA-1157, ORA-1110 and possibly an operating system error.
- You're trying to shut down the database in normal or immediate mode and get ORA-1116, ORA-1110 and possibly an operating system error.

You should use the following methods depending on whether you have a good backup and whether that backup is cold or hot.

Recovering with a Cold Backup

In this case you're in NOARCHIVELOG mode. The data file recovery will be complete if the redo to be applied is within the range of your online logs.

Recover with a cold backup

1. Shut down the database.
2. Restore the lost data file from the backup.
3. Start the database.
4. Execute the following query to determine all your online redo log files and their respective sequence and first change numbers:
   ```
   SELECT X.GROUP#,  MEMBER, SEQUENCE#, FIRST_CHANGE#
   FROM V$LOG X, V$LOGILE Y
   WHERE X.GROUP# = Y.GROUP#;
   ```
5. Determine the CHANGE# of the file to be recovered:
   ```
   SELECT FILE#, CHANGE#
   FROM V$RECOVER_FILE;
   ```

If the CHANGE# is greater than the minimum FIRST_CHANGE# of your online redo logs, the data file can be recovered by applying the online redo logs. If the CHANGE# obtained is less than the minimum FIRST_CHANGE# of your online redo logs, the file can't be completely recovered, and you have two choices:

- If you can afford losing the database changes since the most recent cold backup, restore the backup and continue with the recovery.

- If you can't afford to lose the database changes, you have to rebuild the database as described earlier in the section "Recovering with Missing Redo Data."

6. If the CHANGE# is greater than your online redo logs' minimum FIRST_CHANGE#, you can recover the data file by using the online redo logs:

```
RECOVER DATAFILE 'fullpath of the datafile'
```

Confirm each log that you're prompted for during the recovery until you receive the message Media Recovery complete.

7. Open the database:

```
ALTER DATABASE OPEN
```

Recovering with a Hot Backup

In this case you are in ARCHIVELOG mode. The data file recovery will be complete if the redo to be applied is within the range of your online redo logs.

Recover with a hot backup

1. Shut down the database.

2. Restore the lost data file from the backup.

3. Startup mount the database.

4. Execute the following query to determine all your online redo log files and their respective sequence and first change numbers:

```
SELECT X.GROUP#,  MEMBER, SEQUENCE#, FIRST_CHANGE#
FROM V$LOG X, V$LOGILE Y
WHERE X.GROUP# = Y.GROUP#;
```

Use online redo logs for recovery

If you're prompted for a non-existing archived log, you'll need to use the online redo logs to continue with the recovery. Compare the sequence number referenced in the **ORA-280** message with the sequence numbers of your online redo logs. Supply the full path name of one of the members of the redo log group whose sequence number matches.

5. Recover the data file by using the archived and the online redo logs:

```
RECOVER DATAFILE 'fullpath of the datafile'
```

Confirm each log that you're prompted for during the recovery until you receive the message Media Recovery complete.

6. Open the database:

```
ALTER DATABASE OPEN
```

Recovering with Missing Redo Data

The recovery won't be complete if redo data is missing. Your option isn't attractive—you'll have to rebuild the database. For this purpose, you can either use the Export/Import utility to take a full database export, or you can do a user/table-level export. SQL*Loader can also be used for this purpose.

Recovering from the Loss of a Control File

The control file is very important for the database. Usually a problem with the control file isn't detected while the database is up and running. If the control file is lost or damaged in such a way that Oracle can't recognize it, a subsequent database startup will result in ORA-205 (error in identifying control file '%s'), along with an operating system-level error.

The recovery procedure for this situation depends on whether you have lost one of the control files from a mirrored configuration or all copies of the current control file. The following methods should be used to recover the database based on the particular situation.

Recovering with a Mirrored Control File

In this scenario, you can use the other copies of the control file for getting the database up and running.

Recover with a mirrored control file

1. Shut down the instance if it's still running.

2. Find the cause of the loss of control file. Is it due to a hardware problem (disk or controller)?

3. If the hardware isn't a problem, make a good copy of the control file to the location of the lost control file and skip to step 6.

4. If the hardware is the problem, make a good copy of the control file to a reliable location.

5. Edit INIT*SID*.ORA or CONFIG*SID*.ORA to update the `CONTROL_FILES` parameter to reflect the control file's new location.

6. Start the database.

Recovering Without a Mirrored Control File

In this case, the recovery steps are a bit more involved. First you have to analyze the situation and determine the answers to the following questions:

- Do you have a backup trace of the control file that accurately reflects the current database structure?

- If you don't have a backup trace of the control file but the database can mount, proceed with the following steps. In the worst-case scenario, when you've lost all the control files, you have to execute the `CREATE CONTROLFILE` statement.

Recover without a mirrored control file

1. Shut down the instance (if it's not already shut down).

2. Startup mount the database.

3. Get a backup trace of the control file:

```
Svrmgrl> alter database backup controlfile to trace;
```

This command will create a trace file in `USER_DUMP_DEST`. (To find the value of `USER_DUMP_DEST`, use the command `show parameter USER_DUMP_DEST`; at the `Svrmgrl>` prompt.) Listing 14.1 shows an example of such a trace file.

4. Modify the trace file by removing the header information (lines 1–21). Also make any changes desired (such as MAXLOGFILES on line 30 and MAXDATAFILES on line 32) and save the file as create_control.sql.

5. Do a shutdown normal for the database.

6. Take a full backup of the database to protect from any further problems.

7. Execute the following to create a new control file:
Svrmgrl> @create_control.sql

8. Open the database by executing the following at the server manager prompt:
svrmgrl> Alter database open;

9. Shut down the database.

10. Take a full database backup.

LISTING 14.1   **Example control file creation script**

```
01: Dump file E:\ORANT\rdbms80\trace\ORA00167.TRC
02: Tue Mar 31 17:06:56 1998
03: ORACLE V8.0.3.0.0 - Production vsnsta=0
04: vsnsql=c vsnxtr=3
05: Windows NT V4.0, OS V5.101, CPU type 586
06: Oracle8 Enterprise Edition Release 8.0.3.0.0 - Production
07: With the Partitioning and Objects options
08: PL/SQL Release 8.0.3.0.0 - Production
09: Windows NT V4.0, OS V5.101, CPU type 586
10: Instance name: sjr
11:
12: Redo thread mounted by this instance: 1
13:
14: Oracle process number: 8
15:
16: pid: a7
17:
18: Tue Mar 31 17:06:56 1998
19: Tue Mar 31 17:06:56 1998
20:
21: *** SESSION ID:(7.1) 1998.03.31.17.06.56.062
22: # The following commands will create a new control file
```

```
23: # and use it to open the database.
24: # Data used by the recovery manager will be lost.
25: # Additional logs may be required for media recovery of
26: # offline data files. Use this only if the current
27: # version of all online logs are available.
28: STARTUP NOMOUNT
29: CREATE CONTROLFILE REUSE DATABASE "SJR" NORESETLOGS
    ➥NOARCHIVELOG
30:    MAXLOGFILES 32
31:    MAXLOGMEMBERS 2
32:    MAXDATAFILES 254
33:    MAXINSTANCES 1
34:    MAXLOGHISTORY 899
35: LOGFILE
36:  GROUP 1 'E:\ORANT\DATABASE\LOGSJR1.ORA'  SIZE 200K,
37:  GROUP 2 'E:\ORANT\DATABASE\LOGSJR2.ORA'  SIZE 200K
38: DATAFILE
39:  'E:\ORANT\DATABASE\SYS1SJR.ORA',
40:  'E:\ORANT\DATABASE\RBS1SJR.ORA',
41:  'E:\ORANT\DATABASE\USR1SJR.ORA',
42:  'E:\ORANT\DATABASE\TMP1SJR.ORA',
43:  'E:\ORANT\DATABASE\INDX1SJR.ORA'
44:  ;
45:
46: # Recovery is required if any of the datafiles are
47: # restored backups, or if the last shutdown was not
48: # normal or immediate.
49: RECOVER DATABASE
50:
51: # Database can now be opened normally.
52: ALTER DATABASE OPEN;
```

Recover without an accurate trace file

1. Shut down the database.

2. Take a full database backup, including all the data files and redo log files.

3. Use Server Manager and do a STARTUP NOMOUNT of the database.

Full syntax available

For the **CREATE CONTROLFILE** statement's complete syntax, see Oracle's SQL reference manual.

4. Issue a CREATE CONTROLFILE statement such as the following:

```
Create Controlfile reuse database "TEST"
➥noresetlogs noarchivelog
    Maxlogfiles   50
    Maxlogmembers  3
    Maxdatafiles  500
    Maxinstances   8
    Maxloghistory 500
  Logfile
  Group 1 '/u01/oracle/8.0.4/dbs/log1test.dbf' size 1M,
  Group 2 '/u01/oracle/8.0.4/dbs/log2test.dbf' size 1M,
  Group 3 '/u01/oracle/8.0.4/dbs/log3test.dbf' size 1M,
  Datafile
    '/u01/oracle/8.0.4/dbs/systest.dbf' size 40M,
    '/u01/oracle/8.0.4/dbs/data1test.dbf' size 10M,
    '/u01/oracle/8.0.4/dbs/data2test.dbf' size 20M;
```

5. Perform media recovery on the database:

```
Svrmgrl> Recover database;
```

6. Open the database:

```
Svrmgrl> alter database open;
```

7. Do a shutdown normal of the database.

8. Take a cold backup of the database.

Recovering from Loss of Online Redo Logs

Redo logs are important for performing up-to-the-minute database recovery. Several symptoms and errors can indicate that the redo logs are lost or corrupted:

- The database crashed, and you get ORA-1194 upon trying to start the database.

- You're performing media recovery with the following command and get ORA-314, ORA-312, and ORA-376:

```
"RECOVER DATABASE USING BACKUP CONTROLFILE UNTIL CANCEL"
```

These errors indicate that the redo logs are misplaced, removed, corrupt, or from an old backup. The recovery technique that you need to use depends on whether you've mirrored your redo logs.

Recover with mirrored redo logs

1. Identify the files that need recovery:
   ```
   Svrmgrl> select * from V$RECOVERY_FILE;
   ```

2. Shut down the database.

3. Bring all the redo log files to a constant state by copying the archive log with the same sequence number as the redo log that was lost to the original redo log.

4. Start the database.

If you've lost the current redo logs and your archive logs, the only way that you can open the database is by forcing it to open. This involves corrupting the database.

Recover without mirrored redo logs

1. Shut down the database.

2. Take a full database backup.

3. Make the following changes in your INIT*SID*.ORA file:

   - Add the following lines:
     ```
     _allow_resetlogs_corruption = true
     _corrupted_rollback_segments =
     ➡list of all rollback segments
     ```

   - Comment out the `rollback_segments` parameter.

4. Perform a startup mount.

5. Perform an incomplete recovery of the database:
   ```
   Svrmgrl> RECOVER DATABASE UNTIL CANCEL;
   ```

6. When prompted for the file, type `CANCEL`.

7. Reset the logs and open the database:
   ```
   Svrmgrl> ALTER DATABASE OPEN RESETLOGS;
   ```

8. Rebuild the database by taking a full database export and then importing it to a new database.

> **Caution: Database can become corrupt if you force it to open**
>
> These steps use some very dangerous parameters that should be used only on understanding their consequences and with the help of an Oracle Support Services analyst. After the database is opened in this manner, you should rebuild the database at your earliest chance.

> **Rebuild the database after forcing it to open**
>
> Rebuilding the database is an essential step in this procedure because a forced database-open can corrupt the database.

The following parameters can have a very harmful effect on the database and should be used carefully:

- _allow_resetlogs_corruption   When this parameter is set to TRUE, it will allow resetlogs even if there are hot backups that need more redo applied or the data files are out of sync for some other reason. It's effective only if you open the database with the RESETLOGS option:
  ```
  ALTER DATABASE OPEN RESETLOGS;
  ```

- _corrupted_rollback_segments   If a rollback segment isn't accessible because the file it's in is corrupted or offline, you can force the system to come up without the rollback segment by specifying the segment in this parameter. This parameter prevents the rollback of active transactions in the specified corrupted rollback segments.

- _offline_rollback_segments   This parameter prevents the rollback of active transactions in the listed offline rollback segments.

Using Recovery Manager for Backup and Recovery

Learn about Recovery Manager, the newest Oracle utility for ensuring secure restorable backups

Get Recovery Manager up and running

See Recovery Manager in action, performing a full backup and full restore

Defining Recovery Manager

The most important responsibility for any computer system manager is maintaining a good, solid backup procedure. Whether you manage a large data center with many systems or just your own PC, you need to be prepared in case of a system failure.

Recovery Manager is the utility provided with the Oracle Server software that's used to perform database backups and restores. Recovery Manager is supported under Oracle8 and later and replaces the Enterprise Backup Utility (EBU) provided with Oracle7. It offers more than traditional cold backups via the operating system—it even offers online backups with the tablespaces in hot backup mode.

Recovery Manager has two user interfaces; this chapter focuses on the command-line interface, which you access through the rman utility. Most of you will use Recovery Manager and the recovery catalog to back up multiple databases, and will want to automate those operations. You can use the Backup Manager if you prefer a GUI-based interface; it comes with the Oracle Enterprise Manager software shown in Figure 15.1 (for those of you running Microsoft Windows on some of your client PCs). The OEM is covered in Chapter 4, "Managing with Oracle Enterprise Manager (OEM)."

Recovery Manager becomes an indispensable tool when used with a recovery catalog. A *recovery catalog* takes the form of an Oracle schema stored in a database separate from the databases you're backing up; it maintains all information relevant to the structure and backup history of the databases it backs up. What this means is that in case of a system failure, Recovery Manager can handle all tasks relevant to getting the database back up and running.

Recovery Manager can perform backups, store backup and restore scripts that can be executed repeatedly, and offer a wide range of options for backing up your databases.

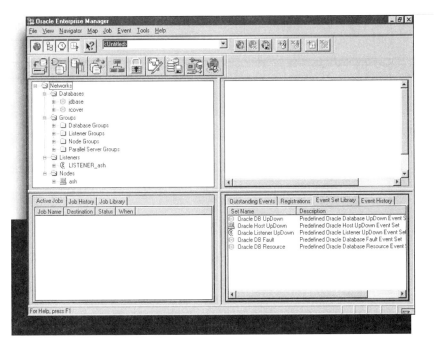

FIGURE 15.1

Oracle Enterprise Manager is your entry point to the GUI version of Recovery Manager.

Recovery Manager will back up and restore Oracle databases that are running Oracle Server version 8.0 and later. You should continue using Oracle Enterprise Backup Utility (EBU) or whatever homegrown backup procedures you have for Oracle7 databases.

Backing Up the Whole Database or Specific Parts

You can back up your database in several different ways via Recovery Manager. By specifying a full backup, Recovery Manager will back up all your data files or all your archive logs, but not both. You can write the backup to disk or tape.

When performing a full backup, Recovery Manager skips over database blocks that have never been used, thus speeding the backup operation. A full backup doesn't reset the individual database blocks' "backup flag." The next incremental backup will back up all database blocks modified since the previous incremental backup. The full backup has no impact on what's backed up during an incremental backup.

Full backup workaround

There's one quick way around the full backup restriction of not being able to back up the archived logs with the data files: Perform a full backup of the archive logs right after the backup of the data files within the same backup script.

You can perform incremental backups on the data file, tablespace, or database level. During an incremental backup, Recovery Manager backs up all database blocks that have been modified since the last incremental backup. Again, database blocks that have never been used are skipped over.

Backup Sets and Image Copies

Recovery Manager supports two different output formats for backup and restore operations:

- A backup set is a single file that contains one or more backed-up database file. The backup is performed serially and may be done to disk or tape.

- An image copy is just what you imagine it is—it's essentially a second copy of whatever database file you're backing up. It's the same as having the database down and using the operating system copy command for your backups. Image file copies can't be used during tape backup operations.

Stored Scripts

Recovery Manager lets you define backup operations in the form of scripts. Those scripts can be stored in disk files or can be loaded into the recovery catalog in much the same way a PL/SQL script is stored in the Oracle server. By using stored scripts, you reduce the possibility of operators performing backups introducing errors. You must have the recovery catalog installed to use stored scripts. You learn about how to create a stored script later in the "Recovery Manager Scripting Commands" section.

Parallel Operations

Recovery Manager can run backups and restores in parallel. If your system has more than one tape drive, Recovery Manager can use both of them at the same time, cutting the elapsed time required for the backup. This will work for disk-to-disk and disk-to-tape backup operations. How the parallelization is done

---

Sizing backup sets

Because multiple database files are written into a single backup set, you run the risk of exceeding your particular operating system platform's maximum file size. For example, if you're using Sun Solaris 2.51, you have a 2GB restriction on file size. Recovery Manager allows you to specify how many files to put in a backup set and how large the backup set file can become. If the backup set reaches its maximum size, the file is closed and a new backup set file is created. By tweaking Recovery Manager backup parameters a little, you shouldn't have any problems with file-system restrictions.

is automatic, and is set on or off in the backup command you use. One sample backup later in this chapter uses parallelization.

Recovery Manager Reports

You use two commands with Recovery Manager to generate reports about the backups you've done and the database objects that need to be backed up: REPORT and LIST. They can give you information on the following:

- Which database files haven't been backed up lately and need backing up
- Which backup sets are obsolete
- Which files are no longer recoverable
- Which database files are in which backup set

You learn how to generate reports from Recovery Manager later in the chapter.

Corruption Detection

The Oracle Server process doing the backup will detect corrupt database blocks during the backup operation and records any corruption in the control file and the alert log. Recovery Manager reads this information after the backup operation completes and stores it in the recovery catalog. Not all types of corruption are detectable at this time, though.

System Performance

With the previous mention of parallelization, you might be thinking, "If I let Recovery Manager operate in this mode, how will I keep it from using all the system's resources?" You can throttle Recovery Manager with the use of the channel control commands. You use the channel control commands to specify limits on disk I/O during backup operations, determine how many threads will be executing concurrently during a parallel operation, and specify the maximum size for the backup pieces you're creating. By using the channel control commands effectively, you can have your backup operations running quickly and efficiently, without affecting the interactive users that may be using the system during your backup.

Setting Up the Recovery Catalog

Recovery Manager flexibility

Recovery Manager gives you a great many options for implementing your database backup strategy. In this chapter you learn about all the software's capabilities, although in some installations you wouldn't use all of Recovery Manager's capabilities.

Using a recovery catalog with Recovery Manager is optional. Recovery Manager becomes much more powerful when a recovery catalog is implemented, which makes database backups and restores much easier.

As mentioned earlier, the recovery catalog takes the form of an Oracle user schema. We will divide the tasks for creating the catalog into two sections. The first section covers the creation of the database schema that will contain the catalog. The second section will handle the steps necessary to create the recovery catalog within the schema.

Creating a Database Schema for the Recovery Catalog

Recovery catalog default tablespace

The recovery catalog database schema should have its own tablespace; it should not have its objects stored in the default user tablespace.

Let's start by making a few quick decisions regarding the catalog and the database schema that we're creating. In this chapter, let's assume that you have many databases to back up, and that your systems must be up 24 hours a day, 7 days a week. Let's also assume that when a system does go down, it needs to be brought back online as quickly as possible.

For the examples in this chapter, the recovery catalog will be created in a separate database whose SID is rcover. The schema that the catalog will reside in will be called recman, and the database that we will be backing up has a SID of jdbase. (Of course, you can and will want to use your own names for these objects.)

Create the Default Tablespace for the Recovery Catalog Schema

Before you can create an Oracle user schema with its own default tablespace, you first need to have the tablespace created. Oracle recommends that the typical recovery catalog require 100MB of storage for one year.

That 100MB value is what we will use to create the tablespace
that will contain our catalog. You create the tablespace from
within SQL*Plus by using the command CREATE TABLESPACE. The
following code shows how the RECOVER tablespace was created on
my test system:

```
SQL*Plus: Release 8.0.4.0.0 - Production on Thu Apr 23
19:44:49 1998


(c) Copyright 1997 Oracle Corporation.  All rights reserved.


Connected to:
Oracle8 Enterprise Edition Release 8.0.4.0.0 - Production
PL/SQL Release 8.0.4.0.0 - Production


SQL> create tablespace recover
  2    datafile '/ora02/oradata/rcover/recover01.dbf'
  3    default storage (initial 1m next 1m pctincrease 0)
  4    size 100m;


Tablespace created.
```

Now, just to double-check that the table is there and created
correctly, use a SELECT command to query the DBA_TABLESPACES
view and look up the new tablespace:

```
SQL> select tablespace_name, status, contents, logging
  2    from dba_tablespaces
  3    where tablespace_name='RECOVER';


TABLESPACE_NAME                  STATUS     CONTENTS   LOGGING
-------------------------------- ---------- ---------- --------

RECOVER                          ONLINE     PERMANENT  LOGGING
```

With the new recover tablespace created and online, you're now
ready to create the schema account that will store the recovery
catalog.

Create the Database Schema

You can also create the new user schema for the recovery catalog
from within SQL*Plus. Let's create the new account with a password for security reasons. Remember to set the default tablespace to be our RECOVER tablespace. Don't forget to grant the
RECOVERY_CATALOG_OWNER role to the schema account, as specified
in the Oracle documentation.

Keep the catalog and target database separate

The database that contains the recovery catalog should never be on the same logical disk drive as the database you're backing up, including RAID and mirrored disk drives. The optimal location for the database containing the recovery catalog is a completely separate system.

Picking an authentication method

A good rule of thumb for deciding whether to use passwords or external authentication for schema accounts is to use passwords for any accounts being accessed from anywhere other than the local system. For databases that will be accessed from the local system itself, you can feel safe in allowing external authentication.

The SQL*Plus CREATE USER command used to create our schema is as follows:

```
SQL> create user recman identified by recman
  2  default tablespace recover
  3  temporary tablespace temp;


User created.


SQL> grant recovery_catalog_owner to recman;


Grant succeeded.
```

Again, you'll want to query the DBA tables to make sure that the account was successfully created. The following code verifies that the default tablespace is correctly set and that the account has a password:

```
SQL>  select username,password,default_tablespace
  2  from dba_users
  3  where username = 'RECMAN';


USERNAME          PASSWORD              DEFAULT_TABLESPACE
- - - - - - - - - - - - - - -    - - - - - - - - - - - - - - - - - - -    - - - - - - - - - - - - - - - - - -

RECMAN            37234A26A0BB0E9F      RECOVER
```

With your database schema created, you can now move on to the next section and create the recovery catalog in the recman schema.

Creating the Recovery Catalog

Use the right schema

You **must** execute catrman from within the **RECMAN** database schema. Don't execute it from the **SYS** schema or your own personal schema; otherwise, you'll see errors when performing Recovery Manager operations.

The creation of the actual catalog is fairly simple after you create the catalog tablespace and schema account. All you need to do is run the catrman script, which is located in the rdbms/admin directory (subdirectory of ORACLE_HOME).

You install the catalog by connecting to the database with the RECMAN schema and executing the script:

```
ash$ sqlplus


SQL*Plus: Release 8.0.4.0.0 - Production on Sat Apr 25
18:37:57 1998
```

```
Enter user-name: recman
Enter password:

Connected to:
Oracle8 Enterprise Edition Release 8.0.4.0.0 - Production
PL/SQL Release 8.0.4.0.0 - Production

SQL> @?/rdbms/admin/catrman
```

The script takes a few minutes. When it's done, you should
select the table names from the DBA_TABLES view to verify that
they are there, in the correct schema:

```
SQL> select table_name from user_tables;

TABLE_NAME
- - - - - - - - - - - - - - - - - - - - - - - - - - -
AL
BCB
BCF
BDF
BP
BRL
BS
CCB
CCF
CDF
CKP


TABLE_NAME
- - - - - - - - - - - - - - - - - - - - - - - - - - -
DB
DBINC
DF
DFATT
OFFR
ORL
RCVER
RLH
RR
```

```
RT
SCR


TABLE_NAME

- - - - - - - - - - - - - - - - - - - - - - - - - - - -

SCRL
TS
TSATT


25 rows selected.
```

Implementing Your Backup Strategy

Recovery Manager provides many different options for backing up and restoring database files. It can perform full and incremental backups, and can use disks and tapes as backup devices. If you have multiple tape drives on your system, Recovery Manager can take advantage of that and run multiple backups concurrently.

Recovery Manager Backup Features

When you read about the creation of the recovery catalog earlier in this chapter, it was mentioned that the catalog is an optional feature and that Recovery Manager can run without it. Let's take a deeper look at this, and the effect that running without a recovery catalog has on the restorability of your database files.

Using the Recovery Catalog with Recovery Manager

As you already know, all information regarding the structure, files, and condition of the database is stored in the database's control file. Recovery Manager reads this information out of the control file and updates the recovery catalog. The maintenance of the information in the recovery catalog isn't dynamic. You update the data in the recovery catalog with the rman command RESYNC CATALOG.

How often you need to perform the resync depends on how active your database is. If your database is in ARCHIVELOG mode and is being updated regularly, you'll want to resync the catalog every few minutes or hours. If your database is static, a greater elapsed time period would probably be sufficient. As an absolute minimum, your resync should be more often than the CONTROL_FILE_RECORD_KEEP_TIME setting in the target database.

When the recovery catalog is fully in sync with the control file, a database restoration after a system failure is very straightforward.

Not Using the Recovery Catalog

Because all the critical data regarding a database's files and structure are stored in the control file, you don't necessarily need to use the recovery catalog when using Recovery Manager. You can simply do your backups and restores the way you always have, and protect the control file to ensure a successful restore.

Without a recovery catalog, however, the following Recovery Manager features will be unavailable to you:

- A point-in-time tablespace recovery.
- Storing any of your backup scripts within Recovery Manager.
- Recovery Manager can't perform restore and recovery operations when your target database's control file is corrupted or deleted.

Also, if you decide not to use a recovery catalog, you have to protect the control file the same way you had to under Oracle7—using multiple copies, frequently performing backups, and keeping a reliable record system of when those backups were done.

Recovery Manager Scripting Commands

Before you can perform any backups with Recovery Manager, you first need to look at how to script the backups. The command-line interface to Recovery Manager is called rman, and all functions relating to database backups and restores are executed through this utility.

Catalog sync frequency

You want to err on the side of syncing the control file and recovery catalog too often. If the recovery catalog isn't current at the time of the system failure, you have to catalog all backups and changes between the last resync and the system failure to bring the database back up.

Do both if it's possible…

Use a catalog with Recovery Manager and continue to maintain your redundant copies of the control file. It's cheap insurance against a prolonged downtime.

You can perform backup and restore operations when you're running rman and are connected to the recovery catalog and the target database. You use rman in very much the same way you use SQL*Plus—you can execute commands from a script file, from a stored script, or by entering it interactively.

Look at Listing 15.1. It's a short script that will add a full backup of a database-to-disk script to the recovery catalog.

LISTING 15.1   *FULLBACK.RCV*–Recovery Manager script to create a full backup stored script

```
01:  replace script fullback {
02:  #
03:  # full backup of database files, excluding archived logs
04:  #
05:      allocate channel d1 type disk;
06:      backup
07:          incremental level 0
08:          tag fullback
09:          filesperset 50
10:          format '/ora03/backup/%d/%d__t%t_s%s_p%p'
11:          (database);
12:  }
```

This simple script performs a full backup of database files, excluding archived logs. You can perform this backup interactively if you replace the statement replace script fullback on line 1 with the command run. The following code shows this script's output. It doesn't execute the backup—it simply stores the script in the recovery catalog as a stored backup script.

```
$   rman target jduer/baseball rcvcat recman/recman@rcover
        cmdfile fullback.rcv

Recovery Manager: Release 8.0.4.0.0 - Production

RMAN-06005: connected to target database: JDBASE
RMAN-06008: connected to recovery catalog database

RMAN> replace script fullback {
2> #
```

```
3> # full backup of database files, excluding archived logs
4> #
5>      allocate channel d1 type disk;
6>      backup
7>              incremental level 0
8>              tag fullback
9>              filesperset 50
10>             format '/ora03/backup/%d/%d__t%t_s%s_p%p'
11>             (database);
12> }
13>
RMAN-03022: compiling command: replace script
RMAN-03023: executing command: replace script
RMAN-08086: replaced script fullback

Recovery Manager complete.
```

Executing a Backup Script

With the sample backup script successfully stored in the recovery catalog, it's time to perform your first backup with Recovery Manager. To execute a stored Recovery Manager script, you first use the rman utility to connect to the recovery catalog and the target database. When connected, you execute the stored script via the rman run command, as follows:

```
ash$  rman rcvcat recman/recman@rcover

Recovery Manager: Release 8.0.4.0.0 - Production

RMAN-06008: connected to recovery catalog database

RMAN> connect target ─────────①
RMAN-06005: connected to target database: JDBASE

RMAN> run { execute script fullback; } ─────②
RMAN-03021: executing script: fullback

RMAN-03022: compiling command: allocate
RMAN-03023: executing command: allocate
RMAN-08030: allocated channel: d1
```

① Connects to the database you're going to back up

② EXECUTE command is encapsulated inside the RUN command; it doesn't work on its own

```
RMAN-08500: channel d1: sid=11 devtype=DISK

RMAN-03022: compiling command: backup
RMAN-03023: executing command: backup
RMAN-08008: channel d1: starting datafile backupset
RMAN-08502: set_count=3 set_stamp=331940454
RMAN-08010: channel d1: including datafile 1 in backupset
RMAN-08011: channel d1: including current controlfile in
backupset
RMAN-08010: channel d1: including datafile 5 in backupset
RMAN-08010: channel d1: including datafile 3 in backupset
RMAN-08010: channel d1: including datafile 2 in backupset
RMAN-08010: channel d1: including datafile 4 in backupset
RMAN-08013: channel d1: piece 1 created
RMAN-08503: piece handle=
/ora03/backup/JDBASE/JDBASE__t331940454_s3_p1 comment=NONE
RMAN-03023: executing command: partial resync
RMAN-08003: starting partial resync of recovery catalog
RMAN-08005: partial resync complete
RMAN-08031: released channel: d1
```

rman Commands

In this part of the chapter, you take a look at the syntax of the main rman commands for backup operations—you look at the channel control commands ALLOCATE CHANNEL and RELEASE CHANNEL. The section follows up with details on the two commands for executing backups: backup and copy.

The *ALLOCATE CHANNEL* Command

The ALLOCATE CHANNEL command establishes a link between Recovery Manager and the target database. The easiest way to visualize an rman channel is to think of it as a thread. You can use multiple channels within your backup script, and Recovery Manager will try to use as many of those channels concurrently as possible.

There are some restrictions, though. A single channel can work on only one image file copy or backup set at a time. If you break your backup into two backup sets, however, and create two channels (one pointing to each tape drive), the parallelization of Recovery Manager kicks in and the software will create both backup sets concurrently.

For disk-to-disk backups, you can create as many channels as you want. For system performance's sake, however, you'll want to spread the backup set destinations over several different disk drives. This way you don't create I/O contention by having the channels compete for system resources. (We will discuss an example of how to use the parallelization of Recovery Manager later in the section "The COPY Command.")

Only one operand is specified with the ALLOCATE CHANNEL command—a name for the channel, such as D1, for the first disk channel. This name comes into play when using the RELEASE CHANNEL command—you use the name to specify which allocated channel to release. Here is a summary of the command parameters the ALLOCATE CHANNEL command accepts:

- connect   You use this parameter to specify a database connect string for Recovery Manager to use when connecting to the target database. Oracle notes that this parameter is intended to give databases that are running the Parallel Server option the capability to execute the database backup across different instances of the database, on different clustered systems. Using this capability greatly increases throughput to the backup output devices and reduces resource contention of the systems performing the backup.

- format   You use this parameter to specify a default filenaming convention for the backup sets created by Recovery Manager on this particular channel. The format specifiers are very similar to those used in the init.ora file for naming archived log files. Using the format parameter in your backup command overrides this default.

Requirements for name parameter

The **name** parameter is only for sequential I/O devices, such as tape drives. You don't use this parameter when opening a channel to disk.

- name   This parameter is used to specify the device name of the system hardware that will be performing the backup or restore. The values for this parameter are port-specific, but in many cases are the physical name of a tape drive.

- parms   This parameter is also port-specific, and is a character string that specifies information about the system device you're allocating. Again, this parameter isn't used when allocating a disk.

- type   This operand specifies your backup device's device type. You can specify this type to be "disk", or a quoted character string specifying some type of platform-specific device (usually "tape"). See your platform-specific Oracle documentation for more information on your particular system.

The following sample code shows how to allocate a disk channel named d1:

```
allocate channel d1 type disk;
```

RELEASE CHANNEL

Freeing system devices

You'll want to use this command if your operating system platform actually allocates resources on the system level during the ALLOCATE CHANNEL command. This way you'll have the system device allocated to you during the time that you need it; you can release this device for others to use during times when other devices are being used.

This command is used to deallocate a channel you created with the ALLOCATE CHANNEL command. This command takes only one operand—the name of the channel to release—which you specified during the ALLOCATE CHANNEL command. The following code line shows a DEALLOCATE command's syntax:

```
deallocate channel d1;
```

SETLIMIT CHANNEL

You use the SETLIMIT CHANNEL command to throttle the use of system resources for a particular channel. This way you can restrict throughput on a per-channel basis. This command takes one parameter, the channel name, and uses any or all of the following three parameters:

- readrate   This parameter lets you control the read I/O rate for the channel. An I/O rate is calculated by multiplying your DB_BLOCK_SIZE and DB_FILE_DIRECT_IO_COUNT. This parameter is specified in I/Os per second. You use this parameter to keep your backups from hammering your disk drives and causing disk contention with other users.

- kbytes   You use this parameter to specify the maximum size of the output files being created during a backup operation. This helps when your backup sets become large and are in danger of exceeding the operating system's largest possible file size. If this threshold is reached when creating backup sets, the current file is closed and a new one is created.

- maxopenfiles   This parameter controls how many files can be opened by the channel at any particular time. This parameter is useful in preventing the backup from exceeding a system- or process-level quota on the number of files that can be open.

The following sample command shows how you would set the channel d1 to open only 48 files at any time, and restrict the read I/O rate to 256:

```
setlimit channel d1 maxopenfiles 48 readrate 256;
```

Controlling file access

If you don't specify the maxopenfiles parameter and don't use the set limit channel command at all, a default of 32 maximum open files is used.

BACKUP

As discussed earlier, there are essentially two types of backups: full and incremental. The default, a full backup, selects all database files with the exception of archived logs. In an incremental backup, only database blocks that have been modified since the last backup are written to the backup set. Database blocks that have never been used aren't written out to the backup set, regardless of whether the backup is full or incremental.

Backup Object List

In your BACKUP command, you use a backup object list to specify which database components you want written into the backup set. There are eight possible values for this backup command operand:

- database   All database data files, including the database control file, are written into the backup set when you specify a value of database.

Understanding backup levels

Incremental backups are multilevel, with incremental level 0 a backup of all database blocks. Incremental level 0 is essentially the same as a full backup, except a full backup doesn't affect subsequent incremental backups. This means that if you want to perform a complete backup followed by a series of incremental backups, you'll want to perform an incremental backup level 0 for your complete (full) backup and use incremental level 1 for your nightly incremental backups.

- `tablespace`   A value of `tablespace` means that you want one or more database tablespaces to be included in the backup set. After the keyword `tablespace`, you follow with a list of tablespace names to specify which will be backed up. The tablespace name is translated into a list of data filenames, whether the tablespace has one data file or many.

- `datafile`   You use the `datafile` keyword to list specific data files that you want backed up. The data files can be specified by their filenames or by their file number as stored in the database control file. Recovery Manager will include the control file if you specify file 1 (the first file in the SYSTEM tablespace).

- `datafilecopy`   The `datafilecopy` specification is a list of data file copies to include in the backup set. Again, the files can be specified by filename or by file number.

- `archivelog`   In the `archivelog` specification, you define a filename pattern that will be used to determine which archived logs to include in the backup set. You can also specify the files to back up by a date/time range.

You can specify three other objects when declaring your backup object list:

`current controlfile`	Use this to back up the current database control file.
`backup controlfile`	Use this to include the backup control file.
`backupset`	Use this to specify that you're backing up a backup set. The backup set must be disk resident and is specified by its primary key.

BACKUP Command Operands

Each operand can be used multiple times within a BACKUP command within your backup script—as long as each one corresponds to a different backup specification:

- `tag`   Use this operand to specify a name for this particular backup. Listing 15.1 uses the tag `fullback` when specifying the incremental backup (level 0). This operand is optional; if it isn't used, it defaults to a null value.

- parms   This operand is used to pass platform-specific information to the operating system during a backup operation. It takes the form of a quoted character string and is passed each time a backup piece is created.

- format   This operand is used by the BACKUP command as well as by the ALLOCATE CHANNEL command. As mentioned earlier, defining the filename format here in the BACKUP command overrides the format you may have defined in the ALLOCATE CHANNEL command. Table 15.1 lists the substitution variables that you can use to help create unique filenames. You can use any or all of these substitution values when creating your output file specs.

Creating output filenames

You use the **format** operand to define the backup objects' output filenames. It's similar to the way you define archived log filenames in your database init.ora file.

TABLE 15.1   Substitution variables for the *format* operand

Variable	Description
%d	The database name is put in the file spec
%p	The number of the backup piece within the backup set
%s	The number of the backup set
%n	The database name (padded)
%t	A timestamp
%u	An eight-character value composed of the backup set number and the time it was created

- include current control file   You use this operand to include the control file in the backup set. During the backup operation, Recovery Manager takes a snapshot of the control file and includes the snapshot in the backup set.

- filesperset   This operand allows you to specify how many data files can be included in a single backup set. You can use this operand to control how large the backup set gets and reduce the likelihood of exceeding the operating system maximum file size. When a backup operation reaches the maximum number of files, the backup set is closed and a new one is opened.

- channel   This optional operand allows you to specify which allocated channel to use when writing the backup set. If you exclude this operand, the channels are assigned dynamically by the software.

- delete input   This operand tells Recovery Manager to delete the input files used during the backup operation after the backup is completed. This operand is valid only when you're backing up data file copies or archived log files; it won't work on your active database data files.

The following code lines show the BACKUP command's syntax:

```
backup
    incremental level 0
    tag fullback
    filesperset 50
    format '/ora03/backup/%d/%d__t%t_s%s_p%p'
    (database);
```

The *COPY* Command

COPY and BACKUP similarities

Because the **COPY** command does essentially the same thing as the **BACKUP** command, the use of the **COPY** command is almost identical to that of the **BACKUP** command. You don't create backup sets with the **COPY** command, however.

You use the COPY command to make an image backup on an individual database file. The actual file can be a database data file, a copy of a data file, a current or backup control file, or an archived log file. You can't use the COPY command to write files to tape; they must be to disk.

The real value of the COPY command is in its capability to multiplex. You can get a large number of files copied in a very short period of time if you list the files to back up individually and create enough channels.

The following sample scripts illustrate the COPY command and the parallelization that it can do. When the COPY command is used as it is in Listing 15.2, Recovery Manager copies the files as five separate operations performed sequentially (lines 7–11). It changes things quite a bit if you use only one COPY command and separate the filenames with commas, as lines 7–11 in Listing 15.3 show.

LISTING 15.2   *COPSAMP1.RCV*—Using the *COPY* command with a single thread

```
01: run {
02:   allocate channel d1 type disk;
03:   allocate channel d2 type disk;
04:   allocate channel d3 type disk;
05:   allocate channel d4 type disk;
06:   allocate channel d5 type disk;
07:   copy datafile 10 to '/ora01/backup/JDBASE/jdbase10.dbf';
08:   copy datafile 11 to '/ora02/backup/JDBASE/jdbase11.dbf';
09:   copy datafile 12 to '/ora03/backup/JDBASE/jdbase12.dbf';
10:   copy datafile 13 to '/ora04/backup/JDBASE/jdbase13.dbf';
11:   copy datafile 14 to '/ora05/backup/JDBASE/jdbase14.dbf';
12: }
```

LISTING 15.3   *COPSAMP2.RCV*—Image *COPY* command with parallelization

```
01: run {
02:   allocate channel d1 type disk;
03:   allocate channel d2 type disk;
04:   allocate channel d3 type disk;
05:   allocate channel d4 type disk;
06:   allocate channel d5 type disk;
07:   copy datafile 10 to '/ora01/backup/JDBASE/jdbase10.dbf',
08:     datafile 11 to '/ora02/backup/JDBASE/jdbase11.dbf',
09:     datafile 12 to '/ora03/backup/JDBASE/jdbase12.dbf',
10:     datafile 13 to '/ora04/backup/JDBASE/jdbase13.dbf',
11:     datafile 14 to '/ora05/backup/JDBASE/jdbase14.dbf';
12: }
```

By specifying the COPY command as a single operation (Listing 15.3), Recovery Manager will use the five disk channels you allocated all at the same time and back up the five files concurrently. There's a great performance gain in this particular case because the output files are all being written to different disks, and will complete far faster than in the example shown in Listing 15.2.

Restores

There's no point in performing backups if there's no way to return the information to the system in case of a system failure.

Recovery Manager provides the RESTORE command to restore the backup sets you created with the BACKUP command, and it's just as easy to use as the BACKUP command. Now it's time to restore the full backup that you performed earlier in the "Recovery Manager Scripting Commands" section.

Restoring the Full Backup

Begin by assuming that some system failure caused corruption or deletion of the database files you backed up earlier. Restoring the files and recovering the database can all be done in a single operation.

First, use Server Manager to start your database instance (not mounted, of course):

```
ash$ svrmgrl

Oracle Server Manager Release 3.0.4.0.0 - Production

(c) Copyright 1997, Oracle Corporation. All Rights Reserved.

Oracle8 Enterprise Edition Release 8.0.4.0.0 - Production
PL/SQL Release 8.0.4.0.0 - Production

SVRMGR> connect internal
Connected.
SVRMGR> startup nomount  ──────────  ①

ORACLE instance started.
Total System Global Area          4749504 bytes
Fixed Size                          47296 bytes
Variable Size                     4218880 bytes
Database Buffers                   409600 bytes
Redo Buffers                        73728 bytes
SVRMGR> exit
Server Manager complete.
```

 Starts the instance nomount; it's mounted by the restore script

With the database started as NOMOUNT, all you have to do is tell Recovery Manager to restore the entire database. Listing 15.4 shows the Recovery Manager script we will use to perform the restore. (I didn't create a stored script because I wanted you to see how to execute an rman script stored on disk.)

LISTING 15.4 *FULLREST.RCV*–Full database restore script using Recovery Manager

```
01: # fullrest.rcv
02: # This recovery manager script will restore the entire
03: # database as backed up
04: # with the fullback script
05: #
06: run {
07:     allocate channel d1 type disk;
08:     restore database;
09:     sql "alter database mount";
10:     recover database;
11:     sql "alter database open";
12:     release channel d1;
13: }
```

That's all it will take to complete the restore and recovery of the database. Notice that you don't even have to specify a location where the backup can be found—this is all handled by Recovery Manager. The following code is a little long but shows all the steps that Recovery Manager took to restore the database and even open it for the users:

```
ash$ rman target jduer/baseball rcvcat recman/recman@rcover
cmdfile fullrest.rcv

Recovery Manager: Release 8.0.4.0.0 - Production

RMAN-06006: connected to target database: jdbase
(not mounted)
RMAN-06008: connected to recovery catalog database

RMAN> # fullrest.rcv
2> # This recovery manager script will restore the entire
database as backed up
3> # with the fullback script
4> #
5> run {
6>      allocate channel d1 type disk;
7>      restore database;
8>      sql "alter database mount";
```

```
9>       recover database;
10>      sql "alter database open";
11>      release channel d1;
12> }
13>
RMAN-03022: compiling command: allocate
RMAN-03023: executing command: allocate
RMAN-08030: allocated channel: d1
RMAN-08500: channel d1: sid=10 devtype=DISK ───────①

RMAN-03022: compiling command: restore
RMAN-03023: executing command: restore
RMAN-08016: channel d1: starting datafile backupset restore──②
RMAN-08502: set_count=3 set_stamp=331940454
RMAN-08019: channel d1: restoring datafile 1
RMAN-08509: destination for restore of datafile 1:
/ora01/oradata/jdbase/system01.dbf
RMAN-08019: channel d1: restoring datafile 2
RMAN-08509: destination for restore of datafile 2:
/ora01/oradata/jdbase/rbs01.dbf
RMAN-08019: channel d1: restoring datafile 3
RMAN-08509: destination for restore of datafile 3:
/ora01/oradata/jdbase/temp01.dbf
RMAN-08019: channel d1: restoring datafile 4
RMAN-08509: destination for restore of datafile 4:
/ora01/oradata/jdbase/tools01.dbf
RMAN-08019: channel d1: restoring datafile 5
RMAN-08509: destination for restore of datafile 5:
/ora01/oradata/jdbase/users01.dbf
RMAN-08023: channel d1: restored backup piece 1
RMAN-08511: piece handle=
/ora03/backup/JDBASE/JDBASE__t331940454_s3_p1 params=NULL
RMAN-08024: channel d1: restore complete

RMAN-03022: compiling command: sql
RMAN-06162: sql statement: alter database mount ───────③
RMAN-03023: executing command: sql

RMAN-03022: compiling command: recover
```

① Disk channel d1 is created and allocated

② RESTORE DATABASE command is executing

③ Newly restored database

```
RMAN-03022: compiling command: recover(1)


RMAN-03022: compiling command: recover(2)


RMAN-03022: compiling command: recover(3)
RMAN-03023: executing command: recover(3)
RMAN-08054: starting media recovery
RMAN-08055: media recovery complete


RMAN-03022: compiling command: recover(4)


RMAN-03022: compiling command: sql
RMAN-06162: sql statement: alter database open
RMAN-03023: executing command: sql


RMAN-03022: compiling command: release
RMAN-03023: executing command: release
RMAN-08031: released channel: d1


Recovery Manager complete.
```

④ Database data files are recovered, completing the restoration

More on Restores

The restore script in Listing 15.4 uses the sql command to mount the database and then to later open it. This very powerful Recovery Manager feature allows for incredible flexibility and programmability of many backup and restore scenarios. For example, if you wanted to recover a tablespace while the database was open, the meat of your restore script would be only three lines:

```
Sql "alter tablespace JDDATA offline";
Recover tablespace JDDATA;
Sql "alter tablespace JDDATA online";
```

The rest of the database would remain available while the restoration was proceeding, and the tablespace in question would be made available again before Recovery Manager exited.

Point-in-time recovery

Oracle documentation dedicates an entire chapter to point-in-time recovery, and there are many prerequisites to performing this operation. Consult the documentation and call Oracle Support for more information; a full discussion is beyond the scope of this book.

Another note on restores is Recovery Manager's capability to perform point-in-time recovery. This is done by using the SET UNTIL TIME command in your restore script. Suppose that today was May 1, 1998, and there was a database problem at 2:01 p.m. that required recovery of one of the database objects. Your restore script would essentially be the same, except for the addition of this command:

```
Set until time '1-MAY-1998 14:00:00'
```

Executing this script would restore the database object to the condition it was in at 2:00 p.m. that day.

Using the *REPORT* and *LIST* Commands

You use the REPORT command to dump information out of the recovery catalog. This command can tell you which database objects need to be backed up, which backup sets are obsolete, and so on.

The LIST command is used to report on the status of backup sets and the like. For example, you use the rman command LIST BACKUPSET OF DATABASE to list information on the full backup script and when it was performed:

```
RMAN> list backupset of database;

RMAN-03022: compiling command: list
RMAN-06230: List of Datafile Backups
Key    File Type          LV Completion_Ckp SCN   Ckp Time
-----  ---- ------------  -- -------------- ----- --------
27     1    Incremental   0  29-APR-98      17900 29-APR-98
27     2    Incremental   0  29-APR-98      17900 29-APR-98
27     3    Incremental   0  29-APR-98      17900 29-APR-98
27     4    Incremental   0  29-APR-98      17900 29-APR-98
27     5    Incremental   0  29-APR-98      17900 29-APR-98
```

The REPORT and LIST commands' full syntax is spelled out on the Oracle documentation CD-ROM.

16

Using Optimizers and the Analytic and Diagnostic Tools

Select the appropriate optimizer

Examine execution plans

Record and interpret processing statistics

Use the AUTOTRACE feature of SQL*Plus

Functions of the Optimizer

Why the Optimizer simplifies
expressions and statements

You can write a SQL statement to
perform a specific task in many
ways, the variety increasing as the
numbers of conditions and different
tables increase. However, you have
a very limited number of choices of
retrieval paths to a table's rows and
to methods for joining multiple
tables. The number of possible
matches that must be checked is
reduced if statements can be converted to a common set of structures.

The Oracle optimizer is responsible for identifying the best
means to execute any SQL statement that needs to be processed.
This includes a number of tasks:

- Simplifying expressions and transforming statements where
  possible
- Choosing a rule-based or cost-based optimization approach
- Choosing an access path to retrieve the data from each table
- Developing a join strategy, which includes defining the
  order in which the tables will be joined and the join operation to be used for each join.

Simplifying and Transforming Statements

The optimizer automatically simplifies certain common constructs in SQL statements if the result will simplify the execution of the statement. Such conversions can range from the very
simple, such as simplifying the expression 2000/10 to the integer
200, to transforming a statement with an OR operation into a
compound query with two *component queries*. The former type of
simplification will always be done; the latter will depend on
whether there are indexes on the columns in the original WHERE
clause and which optimizer approach is being used.

Many different types of transformations can occur, including,
but not limited to, the following:

- Simplifying arithmetic expressions
- Converting the IN operator to a series of OR conditions
- Converting a BETWEEN...AND clause to a pair of comparison
  expressions
- Integrating a view's definition into the statement's condi-
  tions
- Transforming an OR operation into a compound query
- Transforming a *complex statement* into a single statement
  with a join condition

The *Oracle8 Server Concepts Manual* contains detailed explanations of these and all other possible statement simplifications and transformations. You should be aware of them mainly to understand why the optimizer may sometimes choose an execution plan that doesn't appear to be appropriate for the structure of the statement being processed.

Choosing a Rule-Based or Cost-Based Optimization Approach

Oracle chooses an optimization approach for each statement based on several criteria:

- Referenced objects having a defined degree of parallelism
- Hints in the statement
- Session setting of OPTIMIZER_GOAL
- Value of initialization parameter OPTIMIZER_MODE
- Existence of statistics on referenced objects

SEE ALSO

➤ *Find out more about database parameters and the initialization file, page 37*

Figure 16.1 shows how the optimizer uses these criteria to determine whether it uses rule-based or cost-based optimization. The first factor in choosing the optimization approach, when examining a statement to be processed, is to see if it can be executed in parallel. This includes determining if there will be at least one full table scan and if any of the objects referenced by the statement were defined with the PARALLEL option. If both conditions are true, Oracle will use cost-based optimization to create an execution plan containing parallel steps.

For statements that can't be executed, at least partially, in parallel, Oracle looks to see whether the statement contains a hint. If any hint exists (other than the RULE hint), cost-based optimization will be used to process the statement.

Optimization for parallel processing and statements with hints

Oracle must use cost-based optimization to develop execution plans for statements that require *parallel server processes*, because the rule-based optimization approach has never been upgraded to handle parallel execution. Similarly, the only optimization option that can interpret hints is cost-based. Unless the only hint is RULE, Oracle uses cost-based optimization for any statement with one or more hints.

FIGURE 16.1

Oracle examines many factors to determine whether the optimization approach should be rule-based (RBO) or cost-based (CBO).

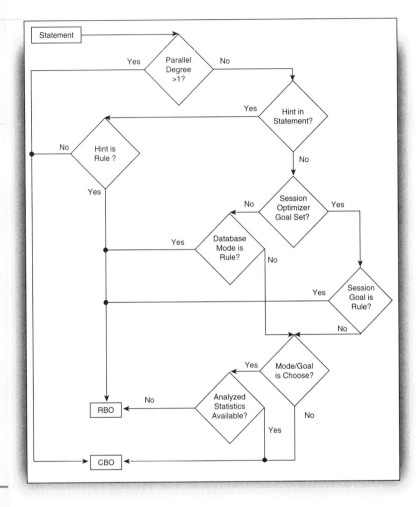

Where you can use the RULE keyword

RULE is the option name (as well as the name of the optimizer approach) used in three different types of syntax to denote the type of optimization required. It's used in hints, in the ALTER SESSION command, and in the database initialization file. It's the same RULE in each case, but in the first situation, it is known as a RULE hint; in the second, it's a RULE goal (because the command sets the OPTIMIZER_GOAL parameter), and in the last case, it's the RULE mode (the parameter name is OPTIMIZER_MODE).

For statements that don't require cost-based optimization because of parallel execution steps or the presence of hints, Oracle checks to see if the session has defined an optimization choice for itself. The command

```
ALTER SESSION SET OPTIMIZER_GOAL = goal
```

allows you to choose from one of the four optimization goals: FIRST_ROWS, ALL_ROWS, RULE, and CHOOSE. The first two options cause Oracle to use cost-based optimization, FIRST_ROWS causing it to find the execution plan that will return the first row as quickly as possible and ALL_ROWS optimizing the overall response time of a statement. The RULE goal always causes rule-based optimization to be used for the session by default. The final option, CHOOSE, as you can see from Figure 16.1, can cause rule-based or cost-optimization to be selected, based on the existence of statistics.

The statistics used to decide which optimization approach will be selected are collected with the ANALYZE command (discussed in the "Collecting Statistics for the Cost-Based Optimizer" section later in this chapter). When Oracle needs to optimize a statement running in a session with its optimizer goal set to CHOOSE, it looks in the data dictionary to see if any one of the segments referenced in the statement have statistics. If statistics are found, the statement will be processed with cost-based optimization, which uses these statistics to help develop its execution plan. If there are no statistics on all the segments to be processed, rule-based optimization is used.

When Oracle has no other indications as to which optimization approach to take, it uses the value assigned to the initialization parameter, OPTIMIZER_MODE. The same four values—FIRST_ROWS, ALL_ROWS, RULE, and CHOOSE—can be assigned to this parameter; they act in the same way as discussed for the ALTER SESSION command. By default, the parameter is set to CHOOSE, which means that the optimization approach chosen for any given statement will depend on the status of the statistics in the data dictionary for the segments processed by the statement. It also means that the optimization approach can change if statistics are added or dropped over time.

Data Access Paths

Table 16.1 lists the access paths available to reach the required rows in a table. The Rank column is included for a later discussion about rule-based optimization.

Choosing FIRST_ROWS versus ALL_ROWS

The **FIRST_ROWS** option is best used for statements executed in interactive applications, because users of such applications are typically waiting for responses from the system as soon as they initiate a process. Even if the overall execution time isn't minimized, a user can probably begin doing useful work with the first row of data returned, so the delay while the remainder of the data is processed isn't detrimental. **ALL_ROWS** should be used when the statement needs to execute as quickly as possible. You should always choose this option when initializing the optimizer for a batch program or for a program that may otherwise have unacceptably poor response time.

Rank column used in rule-based optimization only

The two access paths that show the value "Not ranked" can be used only by the cost-based optimization approach; therefore, they have no rank value for rule-based optimization.

TABLE 16.1   **Optional data access paths to be evaluated by optimizer**

Access Path:	Description:	Rank:
Bitmap Index Scan	Accesses via a bitmap index entry	Not ranked
Fast Full Index Scan	Performs a full scan on the index entries rather than on the table	Not ranked
Single Row by ROWID	Uses the rowid as provided by a current cursor or a WHERE clause with a rowid value	1
Single Row Cluster Join	Returns only a single row from two or more tables in a cluster with a join condition on the cluster key	2
Single Row Hash Cluster	Returns a single row from a hash cluster when the WHERE clause identifies the complete hash key, which is also a unique or primary key	3
Single Row by Key	Returns a single row from a table when the WHERE clause identifies all columns in a unique or primary key	4
Clustered Join	Returns one or more rows from two or more tables in a cluster with a join condition on the cluster key	5
Hash Cluster Key	Returns one or more rows via the cluster-key value	6
Index Cluster Key	Returns one or more rows via the cluster-key value	7
Composite Index	Returns one or more rows when all columns of a composite index are referenced	8
Single-Column Index(es)	Uses one or more single-column indexes	9
Bounded Range Index Search	Uses a single-column index, or the leading column(s) of a composite index, to find values in a bounded range (with a lower and an upper value)	10
Unbounded Range Index Search	Uses a single-column index, or the leading column(s) of a composite index, to find values in an unbounded range (with a lower or an upper value, but not both)	11

Access Path:	Description:	Rank:
Sort-Merge Join	Join of two tables via a join column when the tables aren't clustered together	12
MAX or MIN of Indexed Column	Returns the column maximum or minimum value from an index if the column is indexed by itself or is the leading column of a composite index, if the query has no WHERE clause, and if no other column is named in the SELECT clause	13
ORDER BY on Indexed Column	Uses single column index or leading column of a composite index to find rowids of table rows in order when column is guaranteed not to contain NULLs	14
Full Table Scan	Reads rows directly from a table	15

Using an index to find column minimum or maximum values

An index provides a convenient access path for a maximum or minimum value of a column because the entries are sorted from least (the first entry is the minimum) to greatest (the last entry is the maximum). If the query needs other columns or has other restrictions on which rows are required, this retrieval path is inappropriate because it can't identify any other rows that must be considered. Also, the index can be used only if it's the leading column of a composite index or is the only column in the index.

Table Join Options

A table join occurs when the rows from a table are combined with the rows from another table, or even with the rows from itself. The latter, known as a *self-join*, is used when the value in one column needs to be matched with the same value in another column. Joins typically involve matching a value in a column, or set of columns, in one table with a corresponding value, or set of values, in the other table. When a value in each table must match, the resulting join is known as an *equijoin*. If the join condition is based on an inequality between the columns, the join is called a *non-equijoin*. Other join options are *Cartesian products*, which occur when there's no controlling condition and every row in one table is joined to every row in the other table, and *outer joins*, which include all rows from one table even if there's no matching value on the join column(s).

Consider a table in a manufacturing application. The application records information about individually manufactured parts as well as assemblies—that is, combinations of parts. For example, this book you're reading is an assembly of pages (one type of part) and a set of covers (another type of part). The series, of which this book is a part, is an assembly of the individual books that comprise it. A database table containing assembly information might include, among others, the columns ASSEMBLY_ID and

Left and right joins

Outer joins, when a table having no matching data has its rows included in the result set anyway, are sometimes referred to as left and right joins. Depending on whether the join condition lists the column of the non-matched table on the left or right side of the **WHERE** condition, the join is considered a left or a right join. Although Oracle doesn't allow left and right joins in a single statement, it will allow a view based on a left join to be included in query with a right join, and vice versa.

PART_ID, where PART_ID contains a part identification value and ASSEMBLY_ID is the code number for an assembly that contains one or more parts. If we selected the rows for assembly ID 10-1-AA, we might see the following:

PART_NUMBER	PART_NAME	...
10-1-AA	12-8HY-U-87	...
10-1-AA	9JD7-RT-9	...
10-1-AA	LK-LG-55624	...
...		

If we really wanted to see the part names as well as the part numbers for the parts that comprise assembly 10-1-AA, we would need to code a self-join:

```
SELECT a.part_number, p.part_number, p.part_name
FROM assemblies a, assemblies b
WHERE a.part_number = '10-1-AA'
AND a.part_name = p.part_number;
```

Oracle performs joins in a number of different ways, as summarized in Table 16.2.

TABLE 16.2   Oracle chooses a join method from among a number of options

Join Operation:	Characteristics:
Nested Loops	For each row retrieved from the driving table, looks for rows in the driven table
Sort-Merge	Sorts the rows from both tables in order of the join column values and merges the resulting sorted sets
Cluster Join	For each row retrieved from the driving table, looks for matching rows in the driven table on the same block
Hash Join[1]	Builds a hash table from the rows in the driving table and uses the same hash formula on each row of the driven table to find matches
Star Query[1,2]	Creates a Cartesian product of the *dimension tables* and merges the result set with the *fact table*
Star Transformation[1,2]	Uses bitmap indexes on the dimension tables to build a bitmap index access to the fact table

[1] *Method available only when using cost-based optimization.*
[2] *Any of the other options can be used to join the dimension tables and join that result to the fact table.*

When two tables need to be joined, the optimizer evaluates the methods as well as the order in which the tables should be joined. The table accessed first is the *driving table*; the one accessed next is the *driven table*. For joins involving multiple tables, there's a primary driving table, and the remaining tables are driven by the results obtained from the previous join results. Two situations will always cause the optimizer to select a specific table order when performing table joins:

- If a table is guaranteed to return just one row based on the existence of a unique or primary key, this table will be made the driving table.

- If two tables are joined with an outer join condition, the table with the outer join operator—a plus sign enclosed in parentheses, (+)—will always be made the driven table of the pair.

Using Rule-Based Optimization

Although Oracle8 still supports the rule-based optimizer, Oracle Corporation strongly encourages you to migrate to cost-based optimization. The rule-based optimizer won't be included in later releases of the database, although it isn't clear just when this will be. Support is being maintained to allow customers time to complete the transfer, tuning, and implementation of their applications—in-house and third party—to cost-based optimization.

If you're still using rule-based optimization, you should be planning your strategy to convert to the cost-based approach. You can't take advantage of many new features of the database while using the rule-based optimizer, and you may find that you can improve performance by using the newer optimizer without having to implement these new features, should you not have the resources to investigate them. Beginning, or at least anticipating, the conversion now, before there's a concrete deadline you have to meet, should help you realize a better product overall.

If you haven't set the value of the OPTIMIZER_MODE parameter in your initialization file and haven't executed the ANALYZE command to collect statistics for any of the tables, indexes, or

Features not available to the rule-based optimizer

Some features introduced in recent releases can't be used by the rule-based optimizer. These features include partitioned tables, index-only tables, reverse-key indexes, bitmap indexes, parallel queries, hash joins, star joins, star transformations, *histograms*, and fast full index scans. When the feature is an aspect of an object, such as a reverse-key index, the rule-based optimizer will act as though the object weren't available for use. In cases where there's no choice but to use the feature (such as a index-only table), Oracle will automatically use the cost-based optimizer. Other optional features—such as having a default degree of parallelism on a table—will cause Oracle to use the cost-based optimizer to take advantage of the feature.

clusters used in applications, your applications are probably running against the rule-based optimizer. However, you can't guarantee this because

- Application developers and end users could include hints in the SQL statements.

- Applications and user sessions could set the OPTIMIZER_GOAL.

- Segments could be defined with a default degree of parallelism.

The rule-based optimization approach is so named because it follows a standard set of tests when determining what access path to use to obtain the rows required for each step of a statement's execution. Table 16.1 earlier in this chapter shows the possible access paths to a table and includes a rank number to show which approaches are preferred. During rule-based optimization, the table is tested to see if it can be accessed by each access path in turn, beginning with the rank 1 option, and the first possible path is chosen as the access path.

If the statement requires a table join, the rule-based approach uses an algorithm to determine the two key elements of the join: first, which will be the driving table and which the driven table; and second, which join method will be used. The rules of this algorithm are as follows:

- Choose each table in turn as the driving table and build a possible execution plan for each one.

- In each potential execution plan, add the other tables in order by rank, the lower the rank number, the closer to the driving table.

- Choose a join method for each driven table by looking at its rank number:

  - If its rank is 11 or better, use nested loops

  - If its rank is 12 or lower and

    - There's an equijoin condition in join order (such as an index on the join column(s)), use sort-merge

    - There's no equijoin, or equijoin in join order, use nested loops

---

A good reason to continue using rule-based optimization

Although cost-based optimization is becoming the preferred approach, you shouldn't abandon the rule-based approach, if that is what you have been using, without due consideration. Poor performance can result if your database is using cost-based optimization without any statistical information from which to derive good execution plans. Statistics that are no longer current can also be a detriment to cost-based optimization.

- Select the resulting execution plan with the least nested-loop operations with the driven table being accessed via a full table scan.

- If there's a tie between two or more execution plans, select the plan with the least sort-merge operations.

- If there's still a tie, select the plan with the best (lowest numbered) ranked access path for its driving table.

- If there's still a tie, choose the plan with the most merged indexes for access to the driving table, or else the one that uses more of the leading columns of a concatenated index.

- If this still results in tie, use the plan that uses the last table named in the FROM clause as its driving table.

Using Cost-Based Optimization

As mentioned in the previous section, the cost-based approach will eventually be the only optimization approach available. Meanwhile, it will continue to support new database features that the rule-based approach can't handle. You should plan to convert your applications—if you haven't already—to run under cost-based optimization.

In Figure 16.1, you can see that you can invoke the cost-based optimization in a number of ways. You can do it directly with the FIRST_ROWS or ALL_ROWS setting in the initialization file or in an ALTER SESSION command; you can do it less directly by defining a default degree of parallelism on a segment being accessed in a statement, or by including a hint (other than RULE) in a statement. If you allow Oracle to use its default behavior to select an optimization approach (which means using the CHOOSE option for the OPTIMIZER_MODE parameter), the choice will be based on the existence or non-existence of statistics on the segments referenced in the statement.

The reason for the optimizer approach to depend on statistics is quite reasonable. Cost-based optimization depends on these statistics to compute the relative costs of performing different execution plans in order to choose the most efficient. If the statistics

**Changing the execution plan
under rule-based optimization**

If you don't think the rules will generate the best execution plan for a given statement under rule-based optimization, you can try to improve it. For instance, to stop the optimizer by using an index, you can modify the reference to the column in the WHERE clause by adding a NULL or zero-length string for character columns (such as USERNAME ¦ ¦ ' '), or a zero for numeric columns (such as CUS-TOMER_ID + 0). This won't change the results returned but will prevent use of the index. To force the use of an index that's being ignored, you may have to rewrite the statement to avoid modifying the column reference, such as removing functions such as UPPER.

aren't stored, the likelihood that the optimizer will choose a good plan is reduced significantly, and Oracle would prefer to rely on the rule-based approach.

Of course, if you force the optimizer approach to be cost-based (with a hint, for example), it will work—albeit poorly—in the absence of statistics. It may also perform less than optimally if the statistics it uses are stale and no longer reflect the true nature of the segment they're meant to describe. It's therefore essential that you be prepared to maintain current statistics on the database segments if you want to use cost-based optimization. If you fail to do that, your application developers—and even end users who access the database directly—will have to include hints in many of their statements to ensure that a reasonable execution plan is used.

Statistics are generated and maintained with the ANALYZE command. The syntax for the options related to cost-based statistics is as follows; the other options are covered in other chapters where they are relevant.

```
ANALYZE TABLE¦INDEX¦CLUSTER
    [schema.]table_name¦index_name¦cluster_name
    [PARTITION (partition_name)]
    COMPUTE¦ESTIMATE¦DELETE STATISTICS
    [table_clause][,...]
    [SAMPLE integer [ROWS¦PERCENT]
```

where

- ANALYZE TABLE, INDEX, and CLUSTER identify the type of segment to be analyzed.

- schema. is required if the segment belongs to another user.

- table_name is the name of the table being processed. It's required if the keyword TABLE is included in the command.

- index_name is the name of the index being processed. It's required if the keyword INDEX is included in the command.

- cluster_name is the name of the cluster being processed. It's required if the keyword CLUSTER is included in the command.

- PARTITION (partition_name) identifies the partition name if a single table or index partition is being analyzed. This option isn't valid when analyzing clusters.

What you should analyze

The **COMPUTE** option of the **ANALYZE** command generally consumes more resources than the **ESTIMATE** option and, consequently, can have a greater impact on your application performance. You should compare the results from both options, using different estimated sample sizes, to decide if you really need to incur the extra overhead of computing exact statistics. When analyzing tables with associated indexes, you also can reduce the work performed by the database by estimating the table statistics and then computing exact values on the indexes individually. This will provide the optimizer with the best statistics when accessing the data via the indexes, which is how the data should be retrieved if the indexes are doing their job.

- COMPUTE¦ESTIMATE¦DELETE STATISTICS identifies which operation you want to use. You must include one of the three operations when the keyword STATISTICS is included in the command. COMPUTE provides exact statistics, ESTIMATE uses a sample of the data to generate statistics, and DELETE removes any previously analyzed statistics.

- SAMPLE integer sets the size of the sample used in the estimate. It can be used only with the ESTIMATE option. The sample size will default to 1,064 rows if the ESTIMATE clause is used without the SAMPLE option.

- ROWS¦PERCENT indicates if the sample value should be treated as a row count or a percentage of the table size. It can be used only with the ESTIMATE option.

- *table_clause* is allowed only when the segment being analyzed is a table and you are using the COMPUTE or ESTIMATE option. The format of the *table_clause* is

```
❹  [FOR TABLE] ─────────── ❶
     [FOR ALL] [INDEXED] COLUMNS [[SIZE integer]] ──── ❸
                                                        ❷
❺ ──[FOR COLUMNS [SIZE integer] column [SIZE integer]] [,...]
     [FOR ALL] [LOCAL] INDEXES]                 ❼
                     ❻
```

The TABLE options that create histograms should be used if your table has a very uneven distribution of values in columns used for retrieval. When different values are stored in a column, the optimizer assumes that they will each appear about the same number of times. If some of the values occur only rarely and one or two of the others occur in a large proportion of the records, this assumption may not lead to a good execution plan. The frequently occurring values should be accessed by a full table scan, whereas the infrequently appearing values would be best retrieved via an index.

By building a histogram, you provide the optimizer with the information it needs to distinguish between these two types of values and assist it in building a good execution plan. The number of buckets, or partitions, in the histogram determines how finely the different values are distinguished. The more buckets,

❶ Specifies that the command will create table statistics only; no column or index statistics will be generated

❷ Specifies that the command will create histogram statistics on every column

❸ Specifies maximum number of buckets in the histogram; default value is 75 if option isn't included

❹ Specifies that the command will create histogram statistics only on indexed columns

❺ Specifies that the command will create histogram statistics on the named column(s) or object scalar type(s)

❻ Specifies that the command will create statistics on every indexed column, but not on the table

❼ Specifies that the command will create statistics on every local index partition; must be included if FOR ALL INDEXES and PARTITION options are specified

the greater the chance that the histogram will show the frequency of occurrence of any specific value in the column. If you need to isolate only one or two disproportionately occurring values, however, you need fewer buckets.

You can use the ANALYZE command to recalculate statistics any time you want without having to delete the old ones first. You should plan to perform re-analysis on a regular basis if the segment changes frequently.

When a statement is processed with cost-based optimization, the execution plan will include the table selection access paths and join methods based on the lowest estimated costs. These costs take into account the number of Oracle blocks that have to be manipulated, the number of reads that may need to occur to retrieve these blocks from disk into memory, the amount of additional memory that may be needed to process the data (such as space to complete sorts or hash joins), and the cost of moving data across any networks.

If you've built your database objects with application schemas— that is, where all the objects belonging to an application are owned by the same user—you can simplify the task of collecting statistics for cost-based optimization. Oracle provides a procedure, ANALYZE_SCHEMA, in its DBMS_UTILITY package, which will run the ANALYZE command for you against every segment in a named schema. If you haven't already done so, you need to execute the CATPROC.SQL script, which you can find in the admin subdirectory of your ORACLE_HOME directory, as SYS to build the necessary PL/SQL structures. You can then execute the required procedure by using SQL*Plus's EXECUTE command or by creating your own PL/SQL routine to run the procedure. The SQL*Plus EXECUTE command would look like this:

```
EXECUTE
dbms_utility.analyze_schema('&username','&option',&rows,&pct)
```

SEE ALSO

➤ *Information about the various Oracle-supplied SQL scripts mentioned in this chapter,*
page 9

You would substitute the name of the schema holding the segments you want to analyze at the *username* prompt; the COMPUTE, ESTIMATE, or DELETE keyword at the *option* prompt; and a

Keeping statistics current

You should monitor the statistics on your database segments to make sure that they stay current. I recommend that you begin by executing the **ANALYZE** command and recording the statistics from the related view: **DBA_TABLES**, **DBA_INDEXES**, or **DBA_ CLUSTERS**. Re-execute the **ANALYZE** command a month later and compare the new statistical values; if they're close in value to the previous month's, you shouldn't need to perform another analysis for a few more months. If the statistics are very different, you may need to check again in a week. If they're somewhat different, you should plan to re-analyze the table every month. Over time, you should develop a sense of how frequently each different segment needs to be analyzed. You may need to run a program once a week, once a month, or at some other fixed interval. Your program may analyze just a few segments each time it's run, with additional segments every other time, more every third or fourth time, and so on.

number, the keyword NULL, or an empty string (' ') for the *rows* and *pct* prompts. The last two options are relevant only for the ESTIMATE option, and any values provided are ignored for other options. They indicate the number of rows or the proportion of the table to be included in the sample respectively. If you don't provide a number for either, or set both to zero, the sample uses the default number of rows (1,064). If you provide a number for both, the value for rows is used unless it's zero, in which case the percentage sample size is used.

The statistics collected with the ANALYZE command are used in computing these costs. In cases where the cost-based optimizer is being used for a statement that references one or more—or even all—segments that have no statistics available, it still has to evaluate the potential costs of different execution plans. To do this, it uses basic information from the data dictionary and estimates the missing values. Naturally, the results aren't as accurate as they would be with current statistics collected with the ANALYZE command.

Using Hints to Influence Execution Plans

To overcome poor execution plans—due to missing or out-of-date statistics, or even due to unusual distribution of data in a table or index not anticipated by the optimizer—you can include hints in a statement. Hints are similar to the "tweaks" I suggested you can use to try to modify the behavior of rule-based execution plans, but they're more sophisticated and give you a much wider range of options.

Oracle publishes a complete list of available hints with descriptions of what they do and how to use them in the *Oracle8 Server Tuning* manual, so I won't reproduce that data here. I do include the details required to include a hint in a statement, as this can be confusing:

- Place the hint immediately after the SELECT, UPDATE, or DELETE command statement keyword.

- Open the hint with a comment delimiter and a plus sign concatenated to it. You can use either form of comment delimiter supported by Oracle:

Table names in hints

If you use a table alias in the **FROM** clause of a statement, you must also use that alias in the hint string when referencing the table. Your statement won't fail if you fail to do this, but the hint will be treated as comment text and won't be acted on as you expected.

- A forward slash and asterisk: /*+

- A pair of hyphens: --+

- Include a valid hint or series of hints, with no punctuation (other than the required spaces) between adjacent hints.

- Optionally include comments. Invalid hints and conflicting hints are treated as comment text and ignored. You won't receive an error message for an invalid hint, but the statement will proceed ignoring the intended hint.

- Terminate the hint comment with a string consisting of

  - An asterisk and a forward slash—*/— if the hint comment was opened with a /*+

  - A carriage return if the hint comment was opened with a double hyphen: --+

Here is an example of a hint using some of the features just discussed:

Understand the difference between hint delimiters

A hint enclosed with /*+ ... */ can span multiple lines, whereas a hint introduced with --+ is always terminated at the end of a line.

① Use comment delimiter to begin hint

② Add the plus sign to indicate this string will contain hints

③ Use the hint name in the string

④ Separate additional hints with at least one space

```
① /*+ ORDERED USE_NL(facts) INDEX(facts fact_concat_ix) */
② ③ ④
```

The *EXPLAIN PLAN* Utility

To observe the execution plan that a particular statement would use were it to be executed, you can use Oracle's EXPLAIN PLAN feature. With this utility, you can examine the execution plan of statements you think may run inefficiently and determine if they're using appropriate access paths; you can observe the impact of changing a statement to use, or to avoid using, specific indexes; you can check the execution plans used when including different hints in the same statement; and you can even see if re-analyzing a segment to gather newer statistics or a different sample size results in a different execution plan.

To use the EXPLAIN PLAN feature successfully, you'll need to

- Create a special table to hold the execution plan.

- Know how to use the EXPLAIN PLAN command.

- Learn how to interpret the results.

Creating a Plan Table

The easiest way to create a table to hold the results of an EXPLAIN PLAN command is to run the Oracle script UTLXPLAN.SQL. You can find this script, along with the others mentioned in this chapter, in the admin subdirectory under your ORACLE_ HOME directory. This will build a table, named PLAN_TABLE, in the schema of whichever user is executing the script.

If you want, you can create just one plan table and grant the required privileges on it to any other users who may need to execute the EXPLAIN PLAN command. Minimally, you should grant the INSERT, SELECT, and DELETE privileges if you want the table to be shared.

Although not recommended, you can create your own plan table by hand or change the name of the table to something other than PLAN_TABLE. If you do the latter, you have to include the name in a number of commands that would otherwise use the default name, and you can't use all the features of the AUTOTRACE feature (discussed later). If you build the table by hand, you must ensure that you include the identical column definitions from the ULTXPLAN.SQL script.

> **Create a different PLAN TABLE for different users**
>
> Consider creating this table under every userid that might be used to evaluate statement performance characteristics by executing **UTLXPLAN.SQL** for each one. This will allow users to use the **EXPLAIN** command without having to include the table's schema in the command, or use a synonym to identify a common table. It also will automatically provide a table with the required privileges for use with the **EXPLAIN** command. Finally, it will allow users to manage the contents of the table for themselves, reducing the possibility of confusing different execution plans in a shared table.

Using the *EXPLAIN PLAN* Command

To see the execution plan for a SQL statement, you use the EXPLAIN PLAN command, which has the following syntax:

```
EXPLAIN PLAN
    [SET STATEMENT_ID = 'label']
    [INTO [schema.]table_name[@dblink]
    FOR statement
```

where

- EXPLAIN PLAN and FOR are the required keywords.

Using a plan table identifier

If you're sharing a plan table with other users or want to keep the execution plans for a number of different statements (or versions of the same statement), you need to be able to identify which row belongs to which execution plan. As a regular relational table, the plan table won't necessarily store related rows together but will intermix the rows from different execution plans. Use the statement identifier clause, **SET STATEMENT_ID**, to include a unique string for each statement you explain, which you can then use to identify the rows associated with its execution plan.

Privileges needed for the EXPLAIN PLAN command

Although the statement identified in the **EXPLAIN PLAN** command won't be executed, you must have the necessary privileges to run the statement for its execution plan to be generated. You must also have the privilege to **INSERT** into the plan table. If you don't, you'll receive the same error message as if you tried to execute the statement directly.

- **SET STATEMENT_ID** are optional keywords, required only if you want to flag every row in the plan table with an identifier.
- *label* is an arbitrary string, up to 30 characters long, that you can use to "label" every row in the plan table generated by the current command.
- **INTO** is the option you need to include if the plan table you're using to store your results isn't in your own schema, isn't named **PLAN_TABLE**, or isn't in your local database.
- *schema* is the name of the owner of the plan table you want to use. Your own schema will be targeted if you don't include this option.
- *table_name* is the name of the plan table you want to use. You must include this name if you use the **INTO** option.
- *@dblink* optionally connects you to a *remote database* schema, based on the information in the database link, *dblink*, for you to use a plan table at that location. By default, your *local database* will be used.
- *statement* is any valid **SELECT**, **INSERT**, **UPDATE**, or **DELETE** statement for which you want to examine the execution plan.

The statement you examine in an **EXPLAIN PLAN** command is never executed. It's therefore possible to run the command against an empty table and still see the potential execution plan, although cost-based optimization results may be misleading due to the lack of statistics reflecting real contents. You can also safely rerun the **EXPLAIN PLAN** command multiple times for a statement that would generate extensive overhead if it were actually to run. This is particularly useful when trying to tune a query against massive data warehouse tables (such queries can run for hours, even days) before submitting it for execution.

Interpreting the *EXPLAIN PLAN* Results

Table 16.3 shows the meanings of each operation and options that can appear in the plan table after you execute an **EXPLAIN PLAN** command.

TABLE 16.3   **Operations and options generated by an execution plan**

Operation:	Option:	Description:
AND-EQUAL		An operation that accepts multiple sets of rowids from single-column indexes on the same table and returns the rowids common to all the sets.
BITMAP	CONVERSION	TO ROWIDS converts the bitmap representation to actual rowids in the table. FROM ROWIDS converts rowids into a bitmap. COUNT returns the number of rowids represented by the bitmap.
	INDEX	SINGLE VALUE looks for a single value in the bitmap; RANGE SCAN looks for a range of values; FULL SCAN examines the entire bitmap index.
	MERGE	Merges two or more bitmaps into a single bitmap.
	MINUS	Subtracts the bits of the bitmap for a negated predicate from another bitmap.
	OR	Computes the Boolean OR of two bitmaps.
CONNECT BY		Orders rows for a query containing a CONNECT BY clause.
CONCATENATION		An operation that returns all the rows from two or more sets of rows.
COUNT		An operation to count the number of rows retrieved from a table.
	STOPKEY	A count operation that's terminated by a ROWNUM expression.
FILTER		An operation that removes a subset of the rows from a set.
FIRST ROW		Retrieves the first row only from a query.
FOR UPDATE		An operation that locks the rows retrieved when the query contains a FOR UPDATE clause.

continues...

Operations versus options in the plan table

The operations named in an execution plan are the actual steps performed to process the statement. Options describe why or how the operation is being executed. The results of the operation may or may not be different because of the option. For example, the **INDEX** operation will always return a set of rowids, possibly empty if no rows match the desired criteria, regardless of the option used. On the other hand, a **SORT** operation may only return one row for an **AGGREGATE** or **GROUP BY** option, or may return all the rows in the set as when used for the **ORDER BY** option.

TABLE 16.3   **Continued**

Operation:	Option:	Description:
INDEX	UNIQUE SCAN	An index retrieval guaranteed to find no more than one entry.
	RANGE SCAN	An index retrieval on a non-unique value or a range of unique or non-unique values.
	RANGE SCAN DESCENDING	A range scan performed in descending order.
INLIST INTERATOR	CONCATENATED	Repeats an operation based on the values found in the inlist.
	INTERSECTION	An operation that combines two sets of rows and eliminates any duplicates.
MERGE JOIN		A table join performed by matching values in the tables' join column(s) after they've been sorted.
	OUTER	A merge join operation used to perform an outer join.
	MINUS	An operation that removes rows from a set of records when they appear in a second set.
NESTED LOOPS		A table join that compares each value found in one table with values in the second table and returns rows with matching values in the join column(s).
	OUTER	A nested loops operation used to perform an outer join.
PROJECTION		An undocumented internal operation typically involving views.
REMOTE		Retrieves data from a remote database.
SEQUENCE		An access of values in a sequence generator.
SORT	AGGREGATE	A sort performed to apply a group function.
	UNIQUE	A sort performed to eliminate duplicates.
	GROUP BY	A sort performed to satisfy a GROUP BY clause.
	JOIN	A sort performed in preparation for a merge-join operation.
	ORDER BY	A sort performed to satisfy an ORDER BY clause.

Operation:	Option:	Description:
TABLE ACCESS	FULL	A retrieval that accesses all the rows of a table.
	CLUSTER	A retrieval from a table in an indexed cluster based on a value in the cluster index.
	HASH	A retrieval from a table in a hash cluster based on a hash-key value.
	BY ROWID	A retrieval from a table based on the rowid(s) of one or more rows.
UNION		An operation that combines two sets of rows and returns all the rows from both sets, other than duplicates.
VIEW		Executes a view's query.

Other columns that you may need to review to understand what the execution plan is doing include the following:

- OBJECT_NAME   The name of the table or index being operated on
- OPTIMIZER   The current mode or goal of the optimizer
- OTHER_TAG   Indicates if operations are being performed in parallel with parallel server processes
- COST   The relative cost as evaluated by cost-based optimization
- CARDINALITY   The number of rows that the cost-based optimization estimated will be accessed by the operation
- BYTES   The number of bytes that the cost-based optimization estimated will be accessed by the operation

The other useful columns in the plan table are the ID, PARENT_ID, and POSITION columns. Although you can work out the order of operations in the execution plan by using the values in these columns, you'll find it easier to use them to build a tree-walk output from the plan table, using indentation or other means to show the order in which operations will occur and which operations depend on others. For example, if you explain a query that retrieves a single row through a primary key value, you'll have three entries in your plan table. One will show the primary key index access, one will show the table access using the rowid from the index, and one will show that the whole execution plan was to satisfy a query (SELECT statement). In this case, you could determine in which order the operations would have to occur to produce the desired results.

With a complicated statement that requires tens of operations to complete, however, you may need to see organized rows from the plan table. Oracle has published a number of variations of a query that shows the relationship between each operation through levels of indentation. The query mentioned previously would be formatted to look something like

```
SELECT STATEMENT
    TABLE ACCESS BY ROWID
        INDEX UNIQUE SCAN
```

where the most indented operation is done first, the outermost operation done last, and those in between done according to the amount they're indented. Each level of indentation represents a level of dependency—the outermost operation depending on all the previous levels for it to complete. When two or more operations contribute equally to a parent operation, such as when two sorted sets of table rows are compared in a sort-merge join, they appear under the parent operation at the same level of indentation. Figure 16.2 shows how you can build a tree structure from an execution plan that's formatted in this way. The figure also indicates how you can follow the order of execution from the tree structure if you build it as shown.

To help you get started with the EXPLAIN PLAN utility, Listing 16.1 shows a script you should run from SQL*Plus after you create a plan table. It prompts for the statement you want explained, for a statement ID to keep the results separate, and lets you choose whether to delete the resulting rows from the plan table when you're done.

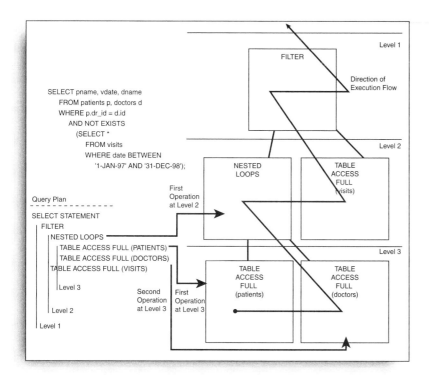

FIGURE 16.2

You can create a tree structure from a formatted plan table query.

LISTING 16.1 **EXPLAIN.SQL—Script to generate and display a formatted execution plan**

```
01:  REM Define column widths to allow columns to fit into
02:  REM 80-character display
03:  COLUMN operation FORMAT A16
04:  COLUMN goal FORMAT A6
05:  COLUMN options FORMAT A10
06:  COLUMN object FORMAT A10
07:  COLUMN parallel_ops FORMAT A12
08:  COLUMN cost FORMAT 9.9EEEE
09:  COLUMN rows FORMAT 9.9EEEE
10:  COLUMN bytes FORMAT 9.9EEEE
11:
12:  REM Turn off distracting feedback from substitution
13:  REM variables
14:  SET VERIFY OFF
15:
16:  REM Get text of statement to be explained, statement id,
```

continues…

Tweak EXPLAIN.SQL

I don't expect you to run the EXPLAIN.SQL script as it stands—I rarely do. But I do have a version of it that I use for checking parallel operations, which I call EXPPAR.SQL, and another version, called EXPROWS.SQL, which allows me to concentrate on the number of rows being handled at each step.

LISTING 16.1 **Continued**

```
17: REM and set delete flag to null for DELETE, to any
18: REM string for no delete
19: PROMPT "Enter statement to be explained --"
20: ACCEPT stmt
21: ACCEPT s_id PROMPT "Enter Statement ID:  "
22: PROMPT "Delete PLAN_TABLE entries when done?"
23: PROMPT "To delete, hit <return>, or else"
24: ACCEPT dlt PROMPT "enter N or n:  "
25:
26: REM     Generate the execution plan
27: EXPLAIN PLAN SET STATEMENT_ID = '&s_id' FOR
28: &stmt
29: /
30:
31: REM     Format the results
32: SELECT SUBSTR(LPAD('  ', 2*(LEVEL-1))||operation,1,16)
33:        AS "OPERATION",
34:        SUBSTR(optimizer,1,6) "GOAL",
35:        SUBSTR(options,1,10) "OPTIONS",
36:        SUBSTR(object_name,1,10) "OBJECT",
37:        DECODE(other_tag, 'serial_from_remote',
38:         'ser from rem', 'serial_to_parallel',
39:         'ser to par', 'parallel_to_parallel',
40:         'par to par', 'parallel_to_serial',
41:         'par to ser', 'parallel_combined_with_parent',
42:         'par w parent', 'parallel_combined_with_child',
43:         'par w child') AS "PARALLEL_OPS",
44:    cost,
45:    cardinality "ROWS",
46:    bytes
47: FROM plan_table
48: START WITH id = 0
49:    AND statement_id = '&s_id'
50: CONNECT BY PRIOR id = parent_id
51:    AND statement_id = '&s_id'
52: /
53:
54: REM Delete the plan table entries matching the statement
55: REM id (if a non-null entry was given at the Delete
56: REM prompt, the WHERE clause will fail to find any rows)
57: REM and clear the substitution variable values
```

```
58: DELETE plan_table WHERE statement_id = '&s_id' ¦¦ '&dlt'
59: /
60: COMMIT
61: /
62:
63: UNDEFINE s_id
64: UNDEFINE stmt
65: UNDEFINE dlt
```

As you'll see, if you run this script, a number of the fields are truncated to fit the data neatly onscreen. You should make any modifications to this script you would find useful, such as removing unwanted columns from the output and displaying more characters from the columns that interest you. Or you can remove the SUBSTR functions (lines 31 through 34) and allow the data to wrap to multiple rows within the defined column widths. You can see from Table 16.3 that you don't need many characters from the entries in the OPERATIONS and OPTIONS columns to be able to tell them apart (although you may need to keep this book open on your desk until you start to remember them all).

When you become familiar with the various execution plans generated by your applications' statements, you can identify useful indexes as opposed to unused ones, spot statements that aren't taking proper advantage of indexes or clustered tables, and locate steps that are causing the most overhead in a statement.

You can also gather useful information from examining the execution plans for statements that you're executing with parallel server processes. You want to ensure that most of the steps in the execution path are processed in parallel and, in particular, that you don't have any serial steps interposed between two sets of parallel steps.

The Trace Facility

If you're having problems with application performance that you can't resolve through the interpretation of the execution plans generated by its statements, you may need to track the actual performance of the SQL commands. The trace facility is designed to help you in this task by recording the basic activities performed by a statement as it executes, along with a record of the resources used to perform those activities. The results of a trace are stored in a file that, although it's a readable text file, isn't in the most convenient format for you to find critical information.

In addition to the trace option itself, Oracle also offers a tool known as TKPROF, which formats the basic trace files into a report format as well as gives you some control over the contents and organization of the output.

If you want to track performance of executing statements, you need to use the trace tool and the TKPROF program.

Creating a Trace File

Setting TIMED_STATISTICS for complete trace data

Some statistics that the trace facility can collect involve the length of time taken by certain activities. These values won't be recorded unless the database is running with TIMED_STATISTICS set to TRUE. You can set TIMED_STATISTICS in your initialization file, with an ALTER SYSTEM file, or in the session where you're planning to run the trace facility. Due to the slight increase in overhead incurred when running with TIMED_STATISTICS enabled, you may want to leave it at its default value of FALSE in your initialization file. However, if your user community will likely use the trace facility and doesn't know about the option to turn on statistics with the ALTER SESSION command, you may need to keep statistics collection turned on for them. Or, if you know when they're likely to be using trace, you can turn it on and off as needed at the database level with the ALTER SYSTEM command.

You can create a trace file in a number of ways. The easiest method to manage is to use SQL*Plus.

Create a trace file

1. Connect to the database in SQL*Plus.

2. Optionally start collecting timing information with the command
   ```
   ALTER SESSION SET TIMED_STATISTICS = TRUE;
   ```

3. Start the trace by issuing the command
   ```
   ALTER SESSION SET SQL_TRACE = TRUE;
   ```

4. Issue the commands you want to analyze. Unlike using EXPLAIN PLAN, the commands will actually execute, so be careful if you use any DML commands that change production tables.

5. Terminate the trace with the command
   ```
   ALTER SESSION SET SQL_TRACE = FALSE;
   ```

6. Disconnect from SQL*Plus and locate the trace file you created.

7. Run TKPROF to format the contents of the trace file.

You might find it more convenient to build a script file containing the statements you want to examine and execute that file while tracing is active in your session. This way, you can test the script ahead of time to ensure that you're going to be working with only the statements you intended. You can also use the script to repeat the exercise to check the impact of any changes you may decide to make as a result of your initial tests.

If you stay connected to the same Oracle session, trace will continue to use the same trace file no matter how many times you turn tracing on and off. Each time you run the same statement in a single Oracle session, trace accumulates its statistics in a single record for that statement, again whether or not you run it in the same trace session. If you want to compare the before-and-after statistics of a single statement, for example, or a query run with and without a certain index in place, you should disconnect from Oracle before tracing the second execution of the statement. This way, each trace file—one for the first and one for the second session—will include only data for the individual executions of the statement you're investigating.

The second way you can initiate the trace facility is to use an Oracle-supplied procedure. This way, you can start the trace on another user's session or start it from within an application program that can execute a PL/SQL block. The procedure, SET_SQL_TRACE_IN_SESSION, is part of the DBMS_SYSTEM package and requires the SID and SERIAL# of the session to be traced supplied as arguments. You can find these values by querying the V$SESSION *dynamic performance view.*

Trace a session for any user

1. Query the V$SESSION table to obtain the SID and SERIAL# for the user's session you need to trace:
```
SELECT sid, serial#
FROM v$session
WHERE username = 'oracle_username'
AND osuser = 'operating_system_userid';
```

2. From within SQL*Plus, execute the procedure to start the trace for the selected session:
```
EXECUTE dbms_system.set_sql_trace_in_session(sid,
serial#,TRUE)
```

Obtaining access to DBMS_SYSTEM

Not all users may be allowed to execute procedures in the **DBMS_SYSTEM** package, which is owned by **SYS**. Other users may need to have the execute privilege on the package granted to them, by **SYS** or by a user with **GRANT OPTION** on the package. Non-**SYS** users will also need to include the schema name, **SYS.**, as a prefix to the package name, or else create a synonym to identify the schema and package.

You simply invoke the procedure by name without the EXECUTE command from within a PL/SQL block.

3. Do nothing while the user continues to work.

4. From within SQL*Plus, execute the procedure to stop the trace for the selected session:

```
EXECUTE
dbms_system.set_sql_trace_in_session(sid,serial#,FALSE)
```

You simply invoke the procedure by name without the EXECUTE command from within a PL/SQL block.

The third, and final, method you can use to start tracing is to set an initialization parameter to cause every session to be traced. The parameter, SQL_TRACE, takes a Boolean value—TRUE turns on database-wide tracing, and FALSE (the default value) causes no default tracing. Just as an individual session can perform its own tracing when the database is running with SQL_TRACE set to FALSE, sessions can disable a statistics collection for themselves even when database-wide tracing is active. In either case, the user issues the ALTER SESSION command as shown earlier.

Formatting a Trace File with *TKPROF*

The TKPROF program uses the data from a traced session to create a formatted report. The program can also create a script file that will store the trace results in a database table or build a script file containing the session's traced SQL statements. Options for the TKPROF program allow you to sort the report in order of the most resource-intensive statements traced, choosing which resource, or resources, you want to influence the ordering. You can request a formatted execution plan, generated with the EXPLAIN PLAN utility, to be included in the report for each SQL statement. You also can include or exclude information about recursive SQL statements, aggregate or separate the statistics for a single statement executed by different users, and limit the number of traced statements that appear in the report. The latter is most useful when used with a sort option, allowing you to restrict the report to the top few resource-intensive SQL statements.

The TKPROF command has two required arguments: the name of the trace file to be processed, and the name of the output file

---

Trace only at the database level under controlled conditions

Setting SQL_TRACE = TRUE in your initialization file forces Oracle to trace every session that connects to the database. You're advised not to try this on a production database due to the volumes of data that will likely be the result. Every DBA I've talked to who has tried this has never had time to review all the trace files produced. Most of them couldn't even decide which of them might contain useful information. You should plan to trace all database sessions only when you're working with a test database and a controlled user community (whether they be users, developers, or even simulation scripts). Even in these situations, make sure that you have the disk space to store the anticipated output.

where the formatted report is to be written. Therefore, to accept all defaults, you can type

```
TKPROF filename1 filename2
```

at your operating system prompt, substituting the trace file for `filename1` and the output file for `filename2`. You don't even need to include an extension for the filenames; TKPROF assumes that .trc will be the extension for the input file and will use .prf as the default extension for the report file.

Table 16.4 describes the options for the TKPROF command. To include an option, type its keyword as shown, followed by an equal sign (=) and the required arguments.

TABLE 16.4   **Optional arguments for *TKPROF***

Argument:	Value(s):	Description:
AGGREGATE	YES (default) NO	Combines statistics for all executions of the command by all users. Separates statistics for the same command by user.
EXPLAIN	*user/password*	Causes an execution plan to be included with each statement in the report, using the named account to run the EXPLAIN PLAN command.
TABLE	*schema.table* (default is user for the schema)	Table used for the EXPLAIN PLAN output if the EXPLAIN argument is set. Will use an existing table, if it exists, deleting any current entries; otherwise, will create the table temporarily, dropping it when the report is completed.
INSERT	*filename*	Creates a script file to build a table and store results in the database. The default file extension is .prf.
SYS	YES (default) NO	Includes recursive SQL in report. Doesn't include recursive SQL in report.

continues…

Recursive SQL in TKPROF reports

Even if you run **TKPROF** with the option **SYS=NO**, certain recursive commands will still appear in the report. These commands are associated with the establishment of the trace environment. You may notice errors listed in the report if you use the **EXPLAIN** option because you may not have permission to access all the tables used by these recursive statements. These errors should be of no concern; they simply indicate that the **EXPLAIN PLAN** command failed when trying to build an execution plan.

TABLE 16.4   **Continued**

Argument:	Value(s):	Description:
SORT	See Table 16.5 (no default)	Determines the order in which SQL statements are listed in the report. Order is in descending order of resource use, where the resource is identified by a keyword from Table 16.5.
PRINT	*integer*	Restricts the report to include only first integer SQL statements, based on the SORT order.
RECORD	*filename*	Creates a script file to execute all non-recursive SQL statements in the trace file. The default file extension is .SQL.

TKPROF execution plans are real time

When you run **TKPROF** with the **EXPLAIN** option, the execution plans will be generated as the report is being created. If the trace file was produced some time before you format it, it's possible that the execution plan used by the command when it executed wasn't the same one you'll see in the report. New statistics—generated with the **ANALYZE** command for cost-based optimization or the creation of deletion of an index, for example—could cause a different execution plan to be used. You're therefore advised to run **TKPROF** as quickly as possible after creating the trace file if you expect to see an execution plan used, in all likelihood, when the statements were actually processed.

An example of a TKPROF command that generates a report containing execution plans built by using the SYS plan table, and also builds a script file to re-execute the statements used in the traced session, might look like the following:

```
TKPROF ora00284.trc jan14hr.rpt TABLE = sys.plan_table
  EXPLAIN = scott/tiger RECORD = jan14hr.sql
```

Table 16.5 shows the keywords, and their meanings, that you can use with TKPROF's SORT option to organize your report with the most resource-intensive SQL statement first, and the remaining statements in descending order of resource usage. You can use just one of the sort options from Table 16.5, or you use more than one, enclosing your list in a pair of parentheses and separating the options with commas, as in the following:

```
TKPROF ora00284.trc jan14hr.rpt SORT = (EXECPU, EXEDSK,
FCHDSK)
```

To generate this report, TKPROF will compute the sum of the values for each statement's CPU usage during its execute phase with the disk reads performed during its execute and fetch phases, and then sort the statements in descending order of the results.

TABLE 16.5 **Sort options for *TKPROF***

Option:	Description:
PRSCNT	Number of times parsed
PRSCPU	CPU time spent parsing
PRSELA	Elapsed time spent parsing
PRSDSK	Number of physical reads during parse
PRSQRY	Number of consistent mode block reads during parse
PRSCU	Number of current mode block reads during parse
PRSMIS	Number of library cache misses during parse
EXECNT	Number of times executed
EXECPU	CPU time spent executing
EXEELA	Elapsed time spent executing
EXEDSK	Number of physical reads during execute
EXEQRY	Number of consistent mode block reads during execute
EXECU	Number of current mode block reads during execute
EXEROW	Number of rows processed during execute
EXEMIS	Number of library cache misses during execute
FCHCNT	Number of fetches
FCHCPU	CPU time spent fetching
FCHELA	Elapsed time spent fetching
FCHDSK	Number of physical reads during fetch
FCHQRY	Number of consistent mode block reads during fetch
FCHCU	Number of current mode block reads during fetch
FCHROW	Number of rows fetched

Interpreting Trace Information

The following is a sample report formatted by TKPROF. The user executed only one statement in the traced session. The report includes this statement and its statistics, but other recursive SQL statements have been edited out.

Watch out for disk space limits when using the trace facilities

You must be careful before performing a trace to check the available disk space on the machine where the trace file will reside. The file could grow tremendously in size because it captures everything you do, even logging off (and back on again). If you then process the file with **TKPROF**, you need the additional disk space to store the formatted output.

```
Sample Trace Report Formatted by TKPROF


*************************************************************
count    = number of times OCI procedure was executed
cpu      = cpu time in seconds executing
elapsed  = elapsed time in seconds executing
disk     = number of physical reads of buffers from disk
query    = number of buffers gotten for consistent read
current  = number of buffers gotten in current mode
            (usually for update)
rows     = number of rows processed by the fetch or
            execute call
*************************************************************
...


*************************************************************


SELECT * FROM patient, doctor
WHERE patient.doctor_id = doctor.doctor_id

call    count    cpu  elapsed  disk  query  current   rows
------- ----  ------ -------- ----- ------ -------- -----
Parse       1   0.00    0.02      0      0        0      0
Execute     1   0.01    0.10      0      0        0      0
Fetch     322   0.01    0.03      5     31        3    322
------- ----  ------ -------- ----- ------ -------- -----
total     324   0.02    0.15      5     31        3    322


Misses in library cache during parse: 1
Optimizer goal: CHOOSE
Parsing user id: 18
Rows     Execution Plan
------- --------------------------------------------------
      0  SELECT STATEMENT   GOAL: CHOOSE
      0   NESTED LOOPS
      0    TABLE ACCESS (FULL) OF 'PATIENT'
      0    TABLE ACCESS (BY INDEX ROWID) OF 'DOCTOR'
      0     INDEX (RANGE SCAN) OF 'SYS_C00551' (NON-UNIQUE)
*************************************************************
...
*************************************************************


OVERALL TOTALS FOR ALL NON-RECURSIVE STATEMENTS
```

```
call      count    cpu  elapsed  disk  query  current    rows
-------   -----   -----  -------- ----- ------ --------  -------

Parse        4    0.00     0.02     0      0        0        0
Execute      5    0.01     0.10     0      0        0        0
Fetch      322    0.01     0.03     5     31        3      330
-------   -----   -----  -------- ----- ------ --------  -------

total      331    0.02     0.15     5     31        3      330
```

Misses in library cache during parse: 1

OVERALL TOTALS FOR ALL RECURSIVE STATEMENTS

```
call      count    cpu  elapsed  disk  query  current    rows
-------   -----   -----  -------- ----- ------ --------  -------

Parse        0    0.00     0.00     0      0        0        0
Execute      0    0.00     0.00     0      0        0        0
Fetch        0    0.00     0.00     0      0        0        0
-------   -----   -----  -------- ----- ------ --------  -------

total        0    0.00     0.00     0      0        0        0
```

Misses in library cache during parse: 0

```
    5   user  SQL statements in session.
    0   internal SQL statements in session.
    5   SQL statements in session.
```
****
Trace file: c:\orant\rdbms80\trace\ora00280.trc
Trace file compatibility: 7.03.02
Sort options: default

```
    1   session in tracefile.
    5   user  SQL statements in trace file.
    0   internal SQL statements in trace file.
    5   SQL statements in trace file.
    5   unique SQL statements in trace file.
   65   lines in trace file.
```

Some key terms from the report that you should recognize are as follows:

- parse is the step in the processing of a SQL statement in which the execution plan is developed, along with checks for valid syntax, object definitions, and user authorization.

- execute is the step in the processing of INSERT, UPDATE, and DELETE statements in which the data is modified, and in a SELECT statement in which the rows are identified.

- fetch is the step in the processing of a query in which rows are retrieved and returned to the application.

- count is the number of times a parse, execute, or fetch step was performed on a statement.

- cpu is the total amount of CPU time used for the parse, execute, or fetch step of a statement. The time is measured in seconds and reported to the nearest 1/100 second. Processing that completes in less than 1/100 second will be reported as zero.

- elapsed is the total amount of elapsed (wall clock) time used for the parse, execute, or fetch step of a statement. The time is measured in seconds and reported to the nearest 1/100 second. Processing that completes in less than 1/100 second will be reported as zero.

- disk is the total number of data blocks read from disk for the parse, execute, or fetch step of a statement.

- query is the total number of buffers retrieved in consistent mode for the parse, execute, or fetch step of a statement. Consistent buffers are usually used for queries and may contain older copies of records for read consistency purposes.

- current is the total number of buffers retrieved in current mode for the parse, execute, or fetch step of a statement. Current buffers are usually used for INSERT, UPDATE, and DELETE activities when the most up-to-date version of the data is required.

- rows is the total number of rows processed by the execute or fetch step of a statement. Any rows processed by a subquery aren't included in this total.

- internal SQL statements is a SQL statement executed by Oracle in addition to the statement being processed by the user to allow the user statement to complete. For example, a CREATE TABLE command will use recursive calls to reserve space for the initial extent(s), to define indexes for unique constraints, and similar actions. The statistics for these statements are totaled under the heading OVERALL TOTALS FOR ALL RECURSIVE STATEMENTS.

- library cache misses means that anytime an object definition is required but not available now in the library cache (part of the shared pool in the System Global Area), it's considered to be a library cache miss.

After you master the trace facility and can generate a formatted report, you should understand what it can tell you about your application code. Obviously, if you're running low on a system resource, such as read/write throughput or CPU cycles, you can use the sort option of TKPROF to help you identify the statements that consume most of these resources. Often, by tuning a few of the worst culprits among all the statements used by an application, you can solve your major resource problems.

You can also make some determinations about a statement's efficiency by looking at the specific statistics listed by TKPROF. Over time, you should easily be able to spot statements that consume more resources than the norm, or statements that appear to use more resources than similar statements require. Some specific indications of a poor-working statement include the following:

- *A large number of blocks being accessed compared to the number of rows being processed.* This generally means that tables are being scanned rather than have a usable index to get to the desired rows. Including the EXPLAIN PLAN output helps you determine if indexes are being underutilized.

- *A large number of parse counts, particularly if for the same user.* This could mean that a cursor is being closed in the application that might be more usefully left open for reuse.

- *A row count in the execute column of a query's statistics, particularly if there's close to or exactly one row per execution.*

Don't jump to conclusions

At certain times, the statistics in a trace report may not indicate the real performance of the statements being monitored. Right after you start up the database, for example, you wouldn't see a lot of additional processing if the statement were executed after the contents of the System Global Area had stabilized. Also, running a statement, or a series of statements, in isolation from the normal work load on the system could bias the results—faster throughput because of less contention on table locks, but with more physical disk reads because the work of loading commonly used data into memory isn't being shared with other users running the same, or similar, statements.

This indicates that an implicit cursor is being used in PL/SQL for single-row queries rather than an explicit cursor. This can cause additional client/server traffic because the implicit cursor has to send a query probe for what should be a non-existent row to set a return code.

- *Fetches equal, or nearly equal, to the number of rows returned.* This is a problem in client/server environments because each fetch requires overhead that could be avoided by fetching the rows in batches.

Certain system-wide tuning problems can also be surmised from the output in a trace file. If the number of disk reads is close to the total number of buffers used (query plus current), for example, it's possible that the database buffer cache isn't large enough. Similarly, if the number of library cache misses is high, your shared pool might be too small.

Using *AUTOTRACE*

Restrictions on AUTOTRACE

AUTOTRACE isn't available when FIPS flagging is enabled, or with TRUSTED Oracle. Also, the formatting of your **AUTOTRACE** report may change if you upgrade your version of Oracle, and it might be influenced by the configuration of the server.

If you are comfortable with SQL*Plus for developing, testing, or tuning your SQL code, you can take advantage of AUTOTRACE. This option causes SQL*Plus to report analytical information after the successful execution of any INSERT, UPDATE, DELETE, or SELECT statement. The information reported is derived from the EXPLAIN PLAN utility and the trace utility, although you can control which elements you want to see. This allows you to see similar information interactively that you otherwise have to collect and format as a separate step. It can, therefore, significantly increase your productivity when you need to monitor the behavior of a particular statement or series of statements.

You control the behavior of AUTOTRACE with the SET AUTOTRACE SQL*Plus command. By itself, the SET AUTOTRACE command won't change the status of the session, but it will return the full syntax of the command, which looks like the following:

```
SET AUTOT[RACE] OFF | ON | TRACE[ONLY]
[EXP[LAIN]] [STAT[ISTICS]]
```

When you choose OFF, AUTOTRACE stops displaying a trace report. If you set it ON, a trace report will be displayed following the standard output produced by each traced statement. The TRACEONLY option will also display a trace report, but it doesn't print the data generated by a query, if any. The EXPLAIN option shows the query execution path by performing an EXPLAIN PLAN command but suppresses the statistical report. STATISTICS, the final option, will display the SQL statement statistics but will suppress the EXPLAIN option output.

If you use ON or TRACEONLY with no explicit options, the output defaults to EXPLAIN STATISTICS. You may find the TRACEONLY option to be useful to suppress the display of rows from large queries. If STATISTICS is specified with TRACEONLY, SQL*Plus still fetches the query data from the server even though the query data isn't displayed. Regardless of the options selected, the AUTOTRACE report is printed after the statement is successfully completed.

To use the EXPLAIN option, explicitly or by default, you must first create the table PLAN_TABLE in your schema. I recommend using the UTLXPLAN.SQL script to accomplish this to ensure that the version of AUTOTRACE and the table definition are compatible. As mentioned earlier, you can find this script in the admin subdirectory under your ORACLE_HOME directory.

To access STATISTICS data, you must have access to several dynamic performance views. The easiest way to handle the necessary privileges—particularly if you'll need to give a number of users access to AUTOTRACE—is to run the PLUSTRCE.SQL script. You can also find this script in the admin subdirectory under your ORACLE_HOME directory. This will create a role called PLUSTRACE and grant the necessary privileges to it. You must run PLUSTRCE.SQL as SYS and grant the PLUSTRACE role to users who will use SET AUTOTRACE.

When SQL*Plus produces a STATISTICS report, a second connection to the database is automatically created. This connection is closed when the STATISTICS option is set to OFF, or you log out of SQL*Plus.

Controlling the *EXPLAIN* Option Output

Each line of the execution plan has a sequential line number. SQL*Plus also displays the line number of the parent operation. Internally, the execution plan consists of seven columns, described in Table 16.6.

Table 16.6   Column definitions used by *AUTOTRACE* for *EXPLAIN* output

Column Name:	Description:	Displayed in Position:
ID_PLUS_EXP	Shows the line number of each execution step.	1
PARENT_ID_PLUS_EXP	Shows the relationship between each step and its parent.	2
PLAN_PLUS_EXP	Shows each step of the execution plan, including the operation and option (from Table 16.3), the object name, and, if using cost-based optimization, the cost and cardinality. Also includes the optimizer choice in the first row. For statements with parallel or remote steps, the bytes value is also included.	3
OBJECT_NODE_ PLUS_EXP	Shows the database links or parallel server processes if they're used.	4
ID_PLUS_EXP	Shows the line number of each parallel or remote execution step.	5
OTHER_TAG_PLUS_EXP	Describes the function of the SQL statement in the OTHER_PLUS EXP column.	6
OTHER_PLUS_EXP	Shows the text of the query for the parallel server process or remote database.	7

Columns in EXPLAIN portion of the AUTOTRACE output

The first four columns—in other words, positions 1 through 3—appear in every execution plan. The last three columns, positions 5 through 7, appear only if the statement involves parallel or remote operations. Although column 4 appears in all execution plans, it's populated only when the same conditions are true that cause columns 5 through 7 to display; in all other cases, it has a value of **NULL**.

You can alter the display of any of these columns with the standard SQL*Plus COLUMN command. For example, to stop the PARENT_ID_PLUS_EXP column from being displayed, enter

```
COLUMN parent_id_plus_exp NOPRINT
```

The default formats can be found in the SQL*Plus site profile (for example, glogin.sql).

When you trace a statement in a parallel or distributed query, in general, the cost, cardinality, and bytes at each node represent cumulative results. For example, the cost of a join node accounts for not only the cost of completing the join operations, but also the entire cost of accessing the relations in that join. If any execution plan steps are marked with an asterisk (*), that denotes a parallel or remote operation. Each of these operations is explained in a separate part of the report, using the last of the three columns described in Table 16.6.

The Statistics Option Output

The statistics are recorded by the server when your statement executes and indicate the system resources required to execute your statement. The client referred to in the statistics is SQL*Plus. Net8 refers to the generic process communication between SQL*Plus and the server, whether or not Net8 is installed. You can't change the default format of the statistics report.

In Table 16.7, you can find the name and description of any of the reported statistics you may not understand.

Table 16.7   Statistics reported by *AUTOTRACE*

Name:	Description:	SQL Trace Equivalent Statistic:
Recursive calls	SQL statements executing on behalf of the user's statement	Internal SQL statements
DB block gets	Database blocks moved into a buffer and used as is	Current
Consistent gets	Database blocks reconstructed in a buffer to a consistent time stamp	Query
Physical reads	Blocks read from disk	Disk
Redo size	Bytes written to redo log buffer	N/A

continues…

Table 16.7   Continued

Name:	Description:	SQL Trace Equivalent Statistic:
Bytes sent via Net8 to client	Bytes sent from the database server to the client (SQL*Plus)	N/A
Bytes received via Net8 from client	Bytes sent from the client (SQL*Plus) to the database server	N/A
Net8 roundtrips to/from client	Messages sent between the database server and the client (SQL*Plus)	N/A
Sort (memory)	Sorts completed entirely in memory	N/A
Sort (disk)	Sorts completed by using temporary segments on disk	N/A
Rows processed	Rows retrieved (query) or processed (DML)	Rows (total)

AUTOTRACE statistics and database tuning

If many statements have high values for the Sort (disk) statistics, it could mean than the sort space allocated in your initialization file is too small. You may need to modify the parameters that control sort space. Similarly, the redo statistic can help you judge an appropriate size for the redo buffer latch parameters in your initialization file. Both topics are discussed in detail in Chapter 20, "Tuning Your Memory Structures and File Access."

SEE ALSO

➤ *Details on tuning the redo log buffer, page 552*

➤ *More about sort space utilization and balancing memory use and disk access for sorting, page 555*

You can use the same criteria to judge the efficacy of a statement from the statistics that equate to those discussed for the trace utility. The additional information from the AUTOTRACE statistics can help you judge whether a statement might be using up excessive bandwidth in a client/server environment (the Net8 statistics), or whether the statement is performing too many large sorts. You may need to examine the execution plan to determine whether any of the sorts could be reduced or even removed.

A Sample Session with *AUTOTRACE*

Listing 16.2 shows a sample SQL*Plus session using AUTOTRACE. The session uses two different queries: one performing a simple table join, the other a join on two tables defined with a non-zero degree of parallelism, causing parallel execution.

LISTING 16.2   Tracing statements for performance statistics and query execution path

```
01:  SQL> REM List statement currently stored in the
02:  SQL> REM SQL*Plus buffer:
03:  SQL> L
04:  SQL> SELECT D.DNAME, E.ENAME, E.SAL, E.JOB
05:    2  FROM EMP E, DEPT D
06:    3  WHERE E.DEPTNO = D.DEPTNO
07:  SQL> REM Turn on AUTOTRACE and execute statement in
08:  SQL> REM buffer:
09:  SQL> SET AUTOTRACE ON
10:  SQL> /
11:
12:  DNAME           ENAME            SAL JOB
13:  -------------- ----------- ---------- ---------
14:  ACCOUNTING      CLARK           2450 MANAGER
15:  ACCOUNTING      KING            5000 PRESIDENT
16:  ACCOUNTING      MILLER          1300 CLERK
17:  RESEARCH        SMITH            800 CLERK
18:  RESEARCH        ADAMS           1100 CLERK
19:  RESEARCH        FORD            3000 ANALYST
20:  RESEARCH        SCOTT           3000 ANALYST
21:  RESEARCH        JONES           2975 MANAGER
22:  SALES           ALLEN           1600 SALESMAN
23:  SALES           BLAKE           2850 MANAGER
24:  SALES           MARTIN          1250 SALESMAN
25:  SALES           JAMES            950 CLERK
26:  SALES           TURNER          1500 SALESMAN
27:  SALES           WARD            1250 SALESMAN
28:
29:  14 rows selected.
30:
31:  Execution Plan
32:  ----------------------------------------------------
33:    0      SELECT STATEMENT Optimizer=CHOOSE
34:    1    0   MERGE JOIN
35:    2    1     SORT (JOIN)
36:    3    2       TABLE ACCESS (FULL) OF 'DEPT'
37:    4    1     SORT (JOIN)
38:    5    4       TABLE ACCESS (FULL) OF 'EMP'
39:
40:  Statistics
```

continues…

LISTING 16.2   Continued

```
41:  ---------------------------------------------------------
42:          148  recursive calls
43:            4  db block gets
44:           24  consistent gets
45:            6  physical reads
46:           43  redo size
47:          591  bytes sent via SQL*Net to client
48:          256  bytes received via SQL*Net from client
49:            3  SQL*Net roundtrips to/from client
50:            2  sort (memory)
51:            0  sort (disk)
52:           14  rows processed
53:
54:  SQL> REM Create two tables with parallel clauses,
55:  SQL> REM and add an index:
56:  SQL> CREATE TABLE testtab1 (testcol1 NUMBER)
57:    2  PARALLEL (DEGREE 6);
58:
59:  Table created.
60:
61:  SQL> CREATE TABLE testtab2 (testcol1 NUMBER)
62:    2  PARALLEL (DEGREE 6);
63:
64:  Table created.
65:
66:  SQL> CREATE UNIQUE INDEX testtab1_col1_ix
67:    2  ON testtab1(testcol1);
68:
69:  Index created.
70:
71:  SQL> REM Prepare to handle long fields in execution plan,
72:  SQL> REM turn off query output and statistics reporting:
73:  SQL> SET LONG 500 LONGCHUNKSIZE 500
74:  SQL> SET AUTOTRACE ON EXPLAIN
75:  SQL>
76:  SQL> REM Define and execute a query against the two
77:  SQL> new tables:
78:  SQL> SELECT /*+ INDEX(B,testtab1_col1_ix) USE_NL  -
79:  > ORDERED */ COUNT (A.testcol1)
80:    2  FROM testtab2 A, testtab1 B
81:    3  WHERE A.testcol1 = B.testcol1;
82:
```

```
83:  Execution Plan
84:  ----------------------------------------------------------
85:   0      SELECT STATEMENT Optimizer=CHOOSE (Cost=1
86:                          Card=263 Bytes=5786)
87:   1    0   SORT (AGGREGATE)
88:   2    1     NESTED LOOPS* (Cost=1 Card=263 Bytes=5785)
89:                                       :Q8200
90:   3    2     TABLE ACCESS* (FULL) OF 'TESTTAB2'  :Q8200
91:   4    2     INDEX* (UNIQUE SCAN) OF 'TESTTAB1_COL1_IX'
92:                   (UNIQUE)                :Q8200
93:   2 PARALLEL_TO_SERIAL   SELECT /*+ ORDERED NO_EXPAND
94:                          USE_NL(A2) INDEX(A2) PIV_SSF */
95:                          COUNT(A1.C0) FROM (SELECT/*+
96:                          ROWID(A3) */ A3."TESTCOL1" FROM
97:                          "TESTTAB2" A3 WHERE ROWID BETW
98:                          BETWEEN :1 AND :2) A1,
99:                          "TESTTAB1" A2 WHERE A1.C0=
100:                         A2."TESTCOL1"
101:  3 PARALLEL_COMBINED_WITH_PARENT
102:  4 PARALLEL_COMBINED_WITH_PARENT
```

Asterisks point to parallel and remote operations

Notice the asterisks next to the **NESTED LOOPS**, **TABLE ACCESS**, and **INDEX** operations (execution steps 2, 3, and 4 respectively in lines 88, 90, and 91). These indicate that the operation is described in more detail later on—in this case, in the lines beginning with the word **PARALLEL**, associated with these same operation numbers (lines 93, 101, and 102).

Notice in Listing 16.2 that the results (line 12) of the initial query (line 4) are displayed along with the execution plan (line 31) and statistics (line 40) from AUTOTRACE due to the choice of the ON option only (line 9). In the second query, on the other hand, the query results and the AUTOTRACE statistics aren't shown because of the TRACEONLY and EXPLAIN options (line 74).

You also can see that the CREATE commands (lines 56, 61, and 66) don't cause any output to be generated by AUTOTRACE, and that the execution plan (line 83) for the second query (line 78) is generated even though there are no rows in either table involved. In this second query, you can also see asterisks, indicating operations performed in parallel, on steps 2, 3, and 4 in the first section of the execution plan. For each of these marked steps, there's a further explanation in the second part of the execution plan output, using the same step numbers to identify them. Here, the nature of the parallel operation is described in more detail, including an entry corresponding to the OTHER_TAG column in the plan table, and a copy of the statement passed to the parallel server processes.

Using Constraints to Improve Your Application Performance

Enforce business rules in your database efficiently

Leverage consistent naming conventions

Activate constraints selectively for different workloads

Manage constraint dependencies

Assign default values to columns

Understanding Constraints

*Constraint*s allow you to define certain characteristics for columns in a table along with the table definition. In effect, they allow you to encode business rules about the data allowed in a table in addition to the table definition. Such business rules could include ensuring that no two customers are assigned the same ID number, or preventing an order from being taken without a customer ID number.

You should plan to use constraints whenever characteristics of a column or group of columns can't be enforced by the chosen datatype. For example, defining a column to hold the minutes portion of a time stamp as NUMBER(2) wouldn't prevent a user from entering a value of 75, even though this wouldn't be a valid number of minutes. You could, however, define a constraint on this MINUTES column to limit the range of values to be between 0 and 59, inclusive. When in effect, the constraint would prevent INSERT and UPDATE statements from creating a record with a value outside the required range in this MINUTES column.

Constraints provide efficiencies for application developers as well as for database operations:

- Simple to code as part of a table definition
- Easy to disable and re-enable as needed
- Always in place, regardless of tools used to access the table
- More or equally efficient execution compared to equivalent SQL statements
- Defined in data dictionary for centralized management
- Constraint names appear in exception messages
- Have to test only when created, not with each application

By using constraints, you reduce the work needed to enforce the related business rules. First, you save application developers a lot of work because they won't need to code an additional check to determine whether the provided value is within the acceptable range. In certain cases—such as ensuring that a value in a column is unique—this check could require coding an SQL statement to query the existing table entries.

This, in turn, provides the second benefit—fewer SQL statements improve your database efficiency because the database will have less work to do.

A third benefit of constraints is that they're part of the definition of the schema to which they belong, and as a result, comprise part of database exports. Naturally, this results in the constraints being passed between database structures when using the Export/Import functions.

In some ways, constraints are to relational tables as methods are to objects—both are integral to each other. As with a good object tool, Oracle8 attempts to process the constraint definitions in memory without generating additional, recursive SQL.

Constraints don't just define the characteristics of a single column, going beyond the type and length of data defined. They can include multiple columns when necessary. Further, you can define the implicit relationships between tables by using constraints. This way, you can maintain integrity between parent and child tables.

Constraint Naming Conventions

When you create a constraint, you can allow Oracle to name it for you or you can choose your own name. I recommend choosing your own names even though it requires more work for you during the design and development phases. Oracle's naming convention doesn't take into account your table's name or the columns to which the constraint refers. This makes it difficult for you to remember the names of the constraints that you create. The default name is even less useful when it's included in exception messages related to the constraint. Neither the user who receives the message nor the person responsible for analyzing the problem can determine the nature of the problem from an Oracle-generated constraint name.

Constraints can help reduce client/server network traffic

In a client/server environment, constraints save a lot of network traffic that would otherwise be needed if the rules were enforced by the application. When an application enforces business rules that require checks against the current database contents, it has to issue additional SQL statements. These must be passed across the network and the results returned across the network. This can take several trips, depending on how the SQL is coded and how much data is returned. If on the other hand you define the rules using database constraints, all the checking occurs on the database server and any required *recursive SQL* is generated and executed at the server, causing no network traffic.

Using Oracle's Naming Scheme

Constraint names can be difficult to change

Before you begin implementing constraints, you should decide if you're going to develop your own naming scheme; if that's the case, you can begin using it right away. Unlike some database objects (such as tables), which you can rename with a simple **RENAME** command, you have to drop and recreate a constraint in order to change its name. As your database grows, even this option can become difficult because some constraints have other constraints dependent on them. Such dependencies can prevent you from dropping key constraints.

Every constraint in an Oracle database must have a name that's unique within its schema. If you don't provide one, Oracle will choose a name for you. These default names have the format SYS_C*n*, where *n* is a five-digit integer with leading zeroes. For example, a constraint could have the name SYS_C00512.

Suppose that you have a constraint on the MINUTES column of a table that allowed only valid minute values (0 through 59), and the system had given this constraint the name SYS_C00512. A user attempting to enter a value of 75 into this column would receive an error message naming the constraint that they violated. Imagine how useful the user would find that error message, stating only that constraint SYS_C000512 had been violated. How would the user, or anyone in a support position, determine the nature of the error from that message?

Along the same lines, suppose that you decided to store the fraction of an hour in the minutes column rather than the actual number of minutes—30 minutes would now be stored as 50, representing 50 percent of an hour. To save a value representing 52 minutes, you would now need to store 86. To allow this value, you would have to disable the constraint restricting the column to a high value of 59. You can find the constraints placed on a table through the view DBA_CONSTRAINTS (or USER_CONSTRAINTS). Looking at the entries in this table, though, it would be difficult for you to determine that constraint SYS_C000512 is the one you need to remove.

Another situation in which you may need to quickly identify a constraint's source is when you're dealing with constraint dependencies. It's very unlikely that you would remember which Oracle-generated name was given to the primary key constraint on a table you created a couple of months ago, but you may need to know when creating another table so that you can verify the constraint's definition. Similarly, if you were to change the status of that primary key constraint, you might be told that your newer constraint was dependent on its current status. Would you know to which constraint the message was referring if it gave you only the name SYS_C00512?

Developing Your Own Naming Schemes

You could adopt a number of possible naming schemes for identifying constraints. Most of them contain three elements in the name: table name, column name, and constraint type. Of course, this may not always be possible if you use long names for either (or both) table and column names. The constraint name is limited to the 30-character maximum set for all Oracle names. If your table name is already 25 characters long, this leaves only five characters for both column name and constraint type. You may therefore need to define a standard set of abbreviations for your table and column names.

The reason to use all three elements should be obvious from the preceding section. If you want to drop or modify a constraint on the values allowed in a MINUTES column in a table, you would like to be able to reference the constraint name directly in the SQL statements needed to effect the change. The most complete naming convention would identify the table name, the column name (MINUTES), and the type of constraint.

As schema objects, your constraints must have names that are unique within their schema. If you used only table name and constraint type as a naming convention, you would limit yourself to just one constraint of each type in any table, or else you would have to differentiate the constraints with some other naming element. Many people gravitate to a numbering scheme when faced with this type of problem, but if you were to use this approach, you're likely to end up with constraint names such as ACTION_UQ_1 and ACTION_UQ_2. This is almost as useless for quick identification as is the infamous constraint named SYS_C00512.

There are only five constraint types; the sections devoted to each type appear later in this chapter. It's quite simple to assign a meaningful two-character string to identify each type. For example, UQ was used in the preceding paragraph. UQ is a widely used abbreviation for the unique constraint. Although this is jumping the gun, Table 17.1 shows the types of constraints, along with a suggested two-character abbreviation for use in your constraint names.

Alternatives for identifying constraint types

You may already have noticed that the five constraint types can be individually identified by the single initial letter of their types. If you use long table and column names, you may need to reduce the constraint-type indicator in constraint names to this single letter. However, you may find yourself using initial letters in other names, such as when naming a column in one table that's related to a column in another table—for example, the column in the **LAB_RESULTS** table that contains the patient's ID number from the **PATIENTS** table. You might name this column **P_ID**. Obviously, such single letters could become confused with a constraint type in some circumstances. The two-character, constraint-type indicators suggested in Table 17.1 are unlikely to be chosen for any other use (hence the **UQ** rather than **UN** for unique), thus avoiding possible ambiguity.

TABLE 17.1 **Constraint types and suggested abbreviations for naming**

Constraint Type:	Suggested Abbreviation:
PRIMARY KEY	PK
UNIQUE	UQ
NOT NULL	NN
FOREIGN KEY	FK
CHECK	CK

Besides deciding to use the three-part constraint names, you also need to determine in which order these parts appear in the name. You should be able to find five distinct abbreviations for the constraint type that won't be confused with either table or column names, so this isn't a major concern. However, it's possible for a table and a column (in the same or a different table) to have identical names. You could mistake constraints based on an ambiguous name unless you have a standard to ensure that these two elements are always included in the constraint name in the same order.

Another point to consider is the use of constraints that cover multiple columns. Consider a constraint name such as PATIENT_TREATMENT_ID_UQ. This could be a unique constraint on the ID column of the PATIENT_TREATMENT table, or on the combined TREATMENT and ID columns of the PATIENT table. You reduce this ambiguity if you separate the table and column names with the constraint-type abbreviation. Thus, the preceding example would become PATIENT_TREATMENT_UQ_ID or PATIENT_UQ_TREATMENT_ID, depending on the name of the base table.

Creating and Managing Constraints

Unlike other database objects that have their own CREATE, ALTER, and DROP commands, constraints are so closely tied to the tables they control that they're manipulated by the commands associated with those tables. As you may remember from Chapter 7, "Adding Segments for Tables," the syntax for creating and altering tables is quite complex in itself. The concepts and the syntax for dealing with constraints is also rather complicated. When you put the two together, the resulting syntax diagram becomes almost impossible to read. Consequently, as you look at each of the options associated with constraints, just the keywords or key phrases required by the syntax to manage that option are introduced. When you're comfortable with these concepts, this chapter ends with a look at the overall constraint syntax and you can see how it fits into the various table management commands.

In the next few sections you examine the options you can apply to constraints that in turn help you and your users make the most effective use of the options. Some options, such as the capability to temporarily turn off constraint checking, apply to all constraint types; other options are specific to one type of constraint. The latter are covered in individual sections devoted to each constraint type. Begin by looking at constraint options that include the options available to all constraints.

An overall syntax diagram for a constraint definition looks like this:

```
[CONSTRAINT constraint_name] constraint_type
[constraint_options]
```

You were briefly introduced to constraint types in Table 17.1, and we will look at each type in detail later in this chapter. The options you look at first, as mentioned, are those valid for all constraint types.

General Constraint Options

In the following sections you look at the various options available to you regarding the enforcement of constraints. These options apply to all types of constraints; they are identified and given values in the segment of the constraint definition labeled *constraint_options* in the constraint syntax diagram.

When a constraint is defined, it stays associated with the table to which it applies. However, it may not always be convenient to have the constraint enforced all the time. You have various options to determine when new records, or even updated records, will be checked for validity against the relevant

---

Table or column name first in constraint name?

Whether you start the constraint name with the table or the column name(s) is your choice. The dictionary views DBA_/ALL_/USER_ CONSTRAINTS don't contain the column names, so if you want to query these tables and report the column names in sorted order, the column name(s) must come first. This approach doesn't help if you have a constraint that covers multiple columns because there will be only a single constraint name; hence, only the first columns in the constraint name will appear in the desired position in the query's sorted output. You can, of course, use the DBA_/ALL_/USER_ CONS_COLUMNS views alone or joined to the *_CONSTRAINTS tables to find the column names and order them in the result set.

CONSTRAINT keyword and constraint name are optional

Leaving these terms out of a constraint definition will cause Oracle to generate a constraint name, in the form of **SYS_C***n*, as discussed earlier. Including these two elements names the constraint with the name you provide.

constraints. In some cases you may want to check as soon as a statement is processed; on the other hand, you may want to wait until a whole work batch is complete before identifying constraint violations.

To determine when and how to force a constraint check when each individual statement or *transaction* executes, you should read the next section, which discusses immediate and *deferred constraint* checking. To look at reasons for turning off constraints for an arbitrary period of time, read the "Disabling and Enabling Constraints" section.

Statement or Transaction Enforcement

When a constraint is in place, every row affected by an SQL statement is examined for constraint violations, and an exception is raised if at least one row remains in violation when the statement completes. This behavior allows *interim violations* to exist for the duration of the statement, but not beyond. An interim violation is one that, although breaking the rules of constraint while processing is under way, is revolved by the time the processing completes. As a simple example, consider a table containing a company's department information. The departments are numbered one by one, but due to a reorganization, the company needs to make the numbers multiples of 10; that allows new subdepartments to be added in the gaps. A partial query of the DEPARTMENTS table's original contents and the UPDATE statement needed to make the required change are shown in this SQL*Plus session:

```
SQL> REM    Examine current values in DEPARTMENT_ID column of
SQL> REM    DEPARTMENTS table
SQL> SELECT department_id
  2    FROM departments
  3    WHERE department_id <= 20
  4    ORDER BY department_id
/
DEPARTMENT_ID

            1
            2
            3
```

```
                                     4
                                     5
                                     6
                                     7
                                     8
                                     9
                                    10
                                    11
                                    12
                                    13
                                    14
                                    15
                                    16
                                    17
                                    18
                                    19
                                    20

20 rows selected.
REM    Multiply each DEPARTMENT_ID by 10 to
REM    change increment from 1 to 10
SQL> UPDATE department
    2   SET department_id = department_id * 10
/
65 rows updated.
REM    Check the work
SQL> SELECT department_id
    2   FROM departments
    3   WHERE department_id <= 20
    4   ORDER BY department_id
/
DEPARTMENT_ID

                                   10
                                   20
SQL>
```

At some point during the execution of this UPDATE statement, the
old DEPARTMENT_ID 1 became 10, the old DEPARTMENT_ID 2 became
20, and so on. If the DEPARTMENTS table had a constraint to prevent duplicate DEPARTMENT_ID values at the time these changes
were made, there would have been constraint violations, because
the original department 1 and the original department 10 both

would have a value of 10 in their DEPARTMENT_ID columns. This would also have been the case for departments 2 and 20, departments 3 and 30, and on up to departments 6 and 60. If Oracle caused the statement to fail due to these anomalies, it would be very difficult for users to make these perfectly valid, albeit infrequent, changes. To avoid this, Oracle marks the duplicates as interim violations and then, when the statement has completed all its changes, it checks them again to see if they remain as violations. By this time, these changes would have included changing the original departments 10, 20, 30... to 100, 200, 300..., hence removing duplicate values for 10, 20, 30.... The statement can therefore complete without any problems.

By default, Oracle checks interim constraint violations at the end of each statement. If one or more are found, the statement fails with an exception and all the changes are rolled back. In some cases, you may want to delay the constraint checking because you need to combine the effects of two or more statements to create consistent records.

Suppose, based on the preceding example, that employees are associated with each DEPARTMENT_ID value in the DEPARTMENTS table. Oracle can enforce a rule (by using a constraint type that's discussed later) that all employees must have a valid department number as part of their records. If we make the preceding change to the DEPARTMENTS table, any employee registered to departments other than 10, 20, 30, 40, 50, or 60 would have an invalid record. To correct this, we would also have to change the employee records. This would take a second statement—thus, the default behavior is of no use because the first statement, the one changing the DEPARTMENTS table, would fail. Changing the employee records first wouldn't help either because we would need to change employees in department 65 (for example) to be in department 650, and such a department number doesn't exist in the unchanged DEPARTMENTS table.

To complete the required changes to both tables—the DEPARTMENTS table and the one with the employee records—we need to defer the constraint checking until the department numbers are changed in both. This is done by using what are known

---

Deferred constraints allow you to code cascading updates

When two tables contain related information—such as a **PATIENTS** table that contains a field for the patient's doctor's ID, stored in the **DOCTORS** table—deleting or updating records can be problematic. For example, to change a doctor's ID value in the **DOCTORS** table would leave the related patient records without a valid doctor. The update to the value in the **DOCTORS** table needs to be cascaded to the appropriate records in the **PATIENTS** table. The ANSI standard doesn't allow such cascading updates when a constraint is used to enforce the relationship between the two tables. By using deferred constraints, however, Oracle will let you make changes to both tables within a single transaction before applying constraint checking. You can use this capability to update the doctor's ID in both tables via two separate statements, thereby coding your own cascading update.

as deferred constraints. If you expect to use deferred constraints for any reason, you must understand what options are available. There are basically two approaches to deferring constraints: one requiring the application user to defer any required constraints at the time the transaction begins, and one allowing the constraint to be deferred automatically in all transactions. Within the constraint definition options, these activities are controlled with the following keywords:

- DEFERRABLE

- NOT DEFERRABLE

- INITIALLY IMMEDIATE

- INITIALLY DEFERRED

The DEFERRABLE keyword determines whether the constraint can be deferred at the time the transaction begins. A constraint can't be deferred by an application when defined as NOT DEFERRRABLE. When defined as DEFERRABLE, the following SQL command will allow any interim violations of the named constraint to remain until the transaction is committed, regardless of when the statement that caused the violations occurred within the transaction:

```
SET CONSTRAINT constraint_name DEFERRED
```

You can make multiple constraints deferrable with the SET CONSTRAINT command by naming them in a comma-separated list. Alternatively, you can issue the following command to defer checking all the constraints encountered in the transaction until it completes:

```
SET CONSTRAINT ALL DEFERRED
```

If you use a list of constraints in the command, they must all be defined as deferrable—otherwise the command will fail. If you use the keyword ALL, only the deferrable constraints, if any, will become deferrable for that transaction. The SET CONSTRAINT command is no longer in force as soon as the transaction completes with a COMMIT or a ROLLBACK.

The INITIALLY keyword sets a deferrable constraint's default behavior. If set to INITIALLY DEFERRED, a constraint is automatically deferred within any transaction that encounters it.

You don't need to issue the SET CONSTRAINT command to defer checking on such a constraint until the end of a transaction; it will be done that way anyway. By default, however, a constraint is INITIALLY IMMEDIATE; this means that all interim violations are checked at the end of each statement and the statement will fail if any are found.

Because the INITIALLY keyword is valid only for constraints already defined as DEFERRABLE, the SET CONSTRAINT command can be used to override DEFERRED or IMMEDIATE. We have already seen that the following statement will defer checking the named constraint until the end of the transaction:

```
SET CONSTRAINT constraint_name DEFERRED
```

Similarly, this command will cause the named constraint to be checked at the end of each statement in which it's invoked during the course of the transaction, even if it's defined as INITIALLY DEFERRED:

```
SET CONSTRAINT constraint_name IMMEDIATE
```

In either case, the scope of the SET CONSTRAINT command is a single transaction; unless you reissue it at the start of your next transaction, the default behavior will apply to all constraints again.

One final note on deferred transactions: During such a transaction, you can issue the following command to see if any interim violations now exist:

```
SET TRANSACTION ALL IMMEDIATE
```

Handling multiple interim violations

If more than one constraint has interim violations when you issue the command **SET TRANSACTION ALL IMMEDIATE**, only one will be reported. Therefore, you can't be sure if you only have one or if you have multiple violations. If you want to address all violations, you have to correct the one that's reported by **SET TRANSACTION ALL IMMEDIATE** and then reissue the command to look for further violations.

If they do, the command will return an error message about the violation, such as ORA-00001: unique constraint (SYS_C00315) violated or ORA-02292: integrity constraint (SYS_C00894) violated - child record found.

Disabling and Enabling Constraints

In the preceding section you saw how to defer constraint checking until the end of a transaction. Sometimes you might find it useful to disable a constraint for an even longer period. Suppose you're building a new medical database in which you have two tables, such as the DOCTORS and the PATIENTS tables, with dependent information. You might want to use a constraint to ensure that every patient is assigned to a doctor. (The section "Validating Data Against Existing Records with Foreign Key Constraints" covers this type of constraint, known as a *foreign key* or *referential integrity constraint* later in this chapter.) If the constraint to enforce this logical relationship between doctors and patients were enforced, you would have to load all doctors' records first and then all patients' records. This would prevent you from running multiple load programs, some storing patient data and some doctor data, to shorten the overall load time.

The data loading problem could become even more complex if the patient table included a field for the financially responsible party and forced a referential integrity check between patients and their financial representatives. If the dependent patient's record were loaded before the responsible party's record, there would be a constraint violation and the load would fail. Even deferred constraint checks couldn't help us if the records for the two related patient records were being stored through two different load programs; each program would be managing just its own transactions.

To help you with such situations, Oracle allows you to temporarily turn off a constraint and then to restart its enforcement later. These actions are known as constraint disabling and enabling, respectively.

Disabling Constraints

In general, there are a number of reasons for turning off constraint checking when performing large data loads, whether into a brand new database or adding to existing data. Rather than make you drop the entire constraint definition, Oracle lets you disable a constraint. The constraint remains defined in the data dictionary while it's disabled, but it's not enforced. You can re-enable a disabled constraint whenever you're ready. At this time, Oracle will check for any violations, and if it finds one or more, will return an exception message and leave the constraint disabled.

When you enable a constraint and expect (or already know) that there will at least violation, you can ask Oracle to save information about which row or rows are causing the exception in a special table. By using data from this table, you can extract the non-conforming rows into a temporary table for later inspection and resolution. With this done, you can then re-enable the constraint on the remaining rows, thus protecting the table from any further violations.

First look at the various ways you can disable a constraint. The methods include the following:

- Creating the constraint in a disabled state
- Disabling an enabled constraint by using the constraint type
- Disabling an enabled constraint by using the constraint name
- Explicitly disabling a dependent constraint

By default, all constraints are created in the enabled state. If you include the keyword DISABLE in the same clause as you define it, however, your constraint will be defined but disabled. To enforce such a constraint, you would have to enable it at a later time.

Certain types of constraints can be disabled by identifying just the constraint type, others by identifying the constraint type and the column or columns on which the constraint is defined. Either type, plus any other type of constraint, can be disabled if you know its name.

Because only one primary key constraint can be defined on a table, the syntax to disable it can be as simple as DISABLE PRIMARY KEY. The syntax that disables a unique constraint is almost as simple. In this case, the key phrase is DISABLE UNIQUE (*column_name*), which identifies the name of the column on which the constraint is defined. In some cases, the unique constraint will span multiple columns. In such cases, the parentheses need to contain not just one column name, but a list of the relevant column names separated by commas.

Primary-key and unique constraints, as well as any other constraint, can be disabled by naming them in the DISABLE

CONSTRAINT `constraint_name` clause. Here, only one constraint can be named in the phrase. You would need to either enter multiple disable phrases or issue multiple SQL commands in order to disable more than one constraint on a table.

In some cases, a constraint may have another constraint that depends on its existence. You can't disable a constraint with such a dependency unless you also disable the dependent constraint. Although you can issue a separate command to disable the dependent constraint first, you can also use the DISABLE clause's CASCADE option to disable any dependent constraints at the same time you disable the parent constraint. DISABLE PRIMARY KEY CASCADE is an example of this type of statement.

One final issue that you should understand about disabling constraints concerns primary-key and unique constraints. Oracle uses an index to enforce these. If the index had to be built when the constraint was enabled, the disabling action will also drop the index. In addition to stopping the integrity checking, the loss of the index may reduce the performance of statements that could normally use the index to reduce the number of rows accessed.

Enabling Constraints

By default, constraints are enabled when they're first defined. As you've just seen, they can be created in a disabled state or disabled at a later time. You need to use one form of the ENABLE constraint clause whenever you need to make a disabled constraint active. In its simplest form, the ENABLE phrase resembles the DISABLE phrase discussed in the preceding section. That is, it can be in one of the following forms:

ENABLE PRIMARY KEY

ENABLE UNIQUE (`column_name`,[`column_name`][,...])

ENABLE CONSTRAINT `constraint_name`

These commands shouldn't have any problems executing if either no changes have been made to the table since the constraint was disabled or if the table is empty. On the other hand, if there are new or changed rows in the table, the constraint may

---

DISABLE...CASCADE has no corresponding ENABLE... CASCADE

If you have to disable a dependent constraint to disable a parent constraint, you need to keep track of which constraints you disable, so that you can re-enable them after you re-enable the parent constraint. This shouldn't pose a problem if you issue explicit SQL commands to disable the dependent constraints—you can perform the disable commands via a script and simply use a modification of the script to re-enable them. You won't have a record of what, if anything, is being disabled if you rely on the **DISABLE** command's **CASCADE** option to disable the related constraints. Although you can query the data dictionary to find which constraints are now disabled, it won't show you which of these were disabled as a result of any particular cascade action. You can't assume that you should re-enable them all after you re-enable the primary constraint— some of them may have been disabled for other reasons.

not be re-enabled due to records that violate the constraint. If this is the case, you have two options:

- Reactivate the constraint with the ENABLE NOVALIDATE phrase rather than just the ENABLE phrase (which actually includes an implied VALIDATE keyword that you could code if you wanted). This will cause all further changes to be subject to the constraint but won't examine the existing data. If you use this approach, you may need to find a way to go back and correct the invalid rows at a later time.

- Identify the rows and deal with them, thus allowing the constraint to be enabled successfully. To do this, you need to add the phrase EXCEPTIONS INTO *table_name* to the ENABLE phrase. The *table_name* can be either just a table name or a schema and table name. Whatever table you use, it must be formatted in a specific way for the command to work.

If you use an exceptions table, any rows that violate a constraint when you try to enable it are identified in this table. Each such row has an entry in the EXCEPTIONS table showing its *rowid*, the name of the constraint that the row violates, and the name and owner of the table to which the row belongs. After you identify the rows that violate a constraint, you need to either update them to fix the problem or delete them, depending on the nature of the problem and the application's requirements. In many cases, you may want to defer the corrections until a later time but still want to enable the constraint to avoid further potential violations. The following script contains a series of commands that attempt to activate a unique constraint in the DOCTORS table and then moves any problem rows out of DOCTORS and into a temporary table, FOR_FIXING, where they can be processed later:

```
ALTER TABLE doctors
ENABLE UNIQUE (suite_number)
EXCEPTIONS INTO exceptions
/
CREATE TABLE for_fixing
    AS SELECT * FROM doctors
    WHERE rowid IN
        (SELECT row_id FROM exceptions)
```

Building a table to hold constraint exception information

The easiest way to build an exceptions table is to run the Oracle-supplied script UTLEXCPT.SQL, which creates an **EXCEPTIONS** table in your own schema. The enable phrase that allows you to use this table while enabling a primary key is **ENABLE PRIMARY KEY EXCEPTIONS INTO** *exceptions*. If you want to use a table with a different name or in a different schema, substitute the appropriate table reference in the **ENABLE** phrase. No matter which table you use, it must defined with exactly the same columns and datatypes as the default table in UTLEXCPT.SQL.

```
/
DELETE doctors WHERE rowid IN
    (SELECT row_id FROM exceptions)
/
TRUNCATE TABLE exceptions
/
ALTER TABLE doctors
ENABLE UNIQUE (suite_number)
/
```

Unless additional invalid changes are made to the DOCTORS table between the time you start this script and the time the final command is executed, the constraint should be enabled when the script completes. When you or your users have updated the FOR_FIXING table created by the script, you can try to put the rows back into the original table with the following command:

```
INSERT INTO doctors SELECT * FROM for_fixing;
```

You may need to address one other option when enabling certain constraints. The unique constraint and the primary key constraint require an index to help enforce them. The index may not exist while a constraint is disabled, in which case it will need to be built when the constraint is enabled. You need to include the USING INDEX phrase as part of the ENABLE clause if you don't want the new index to use your default tablespace, or you want to override one or more of the default storage or space utilization parameters. Should the index already exist, the USING INDEX clause will be ignored. The syntax for the USING INDEX phrase is as follows:

```
USING INDEX
    [PCTFREE integer]
    [INITRANS integer]
    [MAXTRANS integer]
    [STORAGE (
        [INITIAL integer [K¦M] ]
        [NEXT integer [K¦M] ]
        [PCTINCREASE integer]
        [MINEXTENTS integer]
        [MAXEXTENTS integer]
        [FREELISTS integer]
        [FREELIST GROUPS integer] ) ]
```

```
TABLESPACE tablespace_name
NOSORT
[NO[LOGGING]]
```

The terms used in this phrase are a subset of the options for the CREATE INDEX command, which you can find described in detail in Chapter 8, "Adding Segments for Different Types of Indexes."

SEE ALSO

➤ *A complete description of the options when creating an index, page 250*

Forcing Input with the *NOT NULL* Constraint

You use the *NOT NULL constraint* when your table contains a column that's required to hold a value for every single row in the table. If you're familiar with entity-relationship models, an attribute at the mandatory end of a relationship would always have to contain a value. In a business environment, it might be a requirement that every order in the ORDERS table contain a valid method of payment, such as a credit-card number, a bank account number for customers paying by check, or a flag to indicate that cash has been received.

A NOT NULL constraint can't be defined on multiple columns, but you can use a NOT NULL constraint on as many different columns in a single table as you need. To add a NOT NULL constraint, use the clause CONSTRAINT constraint_name NOT NULL. Remember that if you don't mind Oracle naming your constraint for you, you can omit the keyword CONSTRAINT and the constraint's name. You can also include any of the deferrable and validation options discussed earlier if you're assigning the constraint as part of a CREATE TABLE command, or if you're adding a new column to an existing table. However, you can't use these options when you're adding a NOT NULL constraint to an existing column.

NOT NULL constraints in the data dictionary

If you're looking for a **NOT NULL** constraint in the data dictionary tables, such as **DBA_CONSTRAINTS**, you may wonder why you don't see any constraints of type **N**, or some other obvious code letter for these constraints. The reason is that Oracle internally enforces **NOT NULL** requirements with a *check constraint*, such as those you can build yourself (as described a little later). Therefore, the **NOT NULL** constraints are tagged with the code letter **C** (the abbreviation for check type constraints) in the **CONSTRAINT_TYPE** columns of the data dictionary views.

Ensuring Distinct Values with Unique Constraints

You may need one or more columns in a table to contain no duplicate data. A table containing data being collected in real time may need each record to contain a distinct time stamp, for example, so that a user can tell the exact order in which the data was gathered. You may have to ensure that no two employees share the same userid in the company's email system when you add new records to the EMPLOYEES table. A *unique constraint* provides a simple method to enforce such a requirement.

A unique constraint can be defined on a single column or on a collection of columns. In the latter case, it's known as a *composite unique constraint*. If a single column is constrained with a unique key, you can still store multiple records with a NULL value in that column. With a composite unique constraint, two records are considered duplicates if they contain identical values in every column covered by the constraint. The same value can appear in the same column of many records without violating the constraint if at least one column in each record has a different value. NULLs in columns of a composite unique constraint are ignored when comparing two different records, so uniqueness has to be provided by the values in the non-NULL columns. Table 17.2 shows pairs of records from a two-column composite unique constraint and identifies which are considered duplicates.

TABLE 17.2 **Unique and non-unique characteristics of composite constraints**

Column 1:	Column 2:	Uniqueness:
12	13	
14	15	Unique
12	13	
12	14	Unique
12	NULL	
13	NULL	Unique
12	13	
12	13	Duplicates

TABLE 17.2 Continued

12	NULL	
124	NULL	Duplicates
NULL	NULL	
NULL	NULL	Unique

As with other constraint types, you can add unique constraints by using your own name for them, or allow Oracle to name them for you. You also can make them deferrable or not, with the default behavior for deferrable constraints dependent on whether the user begins a transaction as deferrable. Similarly, the constraint can be created in an enabled or a disabled mode. (See the preceding sections for details of these characteristics.) The full syntax of the clause for creating unique constraints is as follows:

```
[CONSTRAINT constraint_name]
    UNIQUE [column_name[, column_name[...]]]
    [deferred_clause]
    [enabled clause]
    [exceptions_clause]
    [index_clause]
```

- CONSTRAINT *constraint_name* applies your name to the constraint. Omitting it will let the name be an Oracle-supplied name.

- UNIQUE is the required keyword for a unique constraint.

- *deferred_clause* contains any required DEFERRABLE and initial phrases and values. (See the detailed syntax in the earlier section "Statement or Transaction Enforcement.")

- *enabled_clause* contains either ENABLED or DISABLED.

- *exceptions_clause* identifies the table where invalid rows can be identified, as discussed in the "Enabling Constraints" section.

- *index_clause* has the following syntax:
```
USING INDEX
    [PCTFREE integer]
    [INITRANS integer]
    [MAXTRANS integer]
```

```
[STORAGE (
    [INITIAL integer [K¦M] ]
    [NEXT integer [K¦M] ]
    [PCTINCREASE integer]
    [MINEXTENTS integer]
    [MAXEXTENTS integer]
    [FREELISTS integer]
    [FREELIST GROUPS integer] ) ]
TABLESPACE tablespace_name
NOSORT
[[NO]LOGGING]
```

The terms in the USING INDEX clause are identical to those involved when building a new index with the CREATE INDEX command; see Chapter 8, where they're described in detail. Without a USING INDEX clause, the required index will be created in the same tablespace as the table if it's a new column and a new constraint; if it's a constraint being enabled it's built in the user's default tablespace. Of course, if there's already an index on the column(s) covered by the unique constraint, you shouldn't include the USING INDEX clause—otherwise the statement will fail.

Indexes created automatically through the addition of a unique constraint are also dropped automatically when the constraint is dropped or disabled. Oracle names these indexes with the same name as the constraint itself, whether it's an Oracle- or a user-supplied constraint name. If the index exists on the table before the constraint is created, it can't be dropped unless the constraint is dropped or disabled. You can't name your constraint with the same name as the index in such cases.

SEE ALSO
➤ *A complete description of the options when creating an index, page 250*

Creating Distinct Rows with Primary Key Constraints

A relational database table can't distinguish between two rows that have exactly the same values in all their columns. It's therefore advisable to create every table with a *primary key constraint*.

Indexes for unique constraints

You should use your own index—rather than rely on the index created as part of the constraint definition—when you need the performance benefits offered by the index. This way, the index will always be available, regardless of the status of the constraint. Depending on your needs and the nature of the data, you can use a unique or non-unique index to enforce a unique constraint. A non-unique index might be useful if you have needs for duplicate values during processing that occurs while the constraint is disabled.

This type of constraint guarantees that every row has some unique value that makes it distinguishable from every other row. Although there can be many columns in some tables that fulfill this requirement, only one primary key constraint is allowed per table.

A primary key constraint has the characteristics of the NOT NULL and the unique constraints. However, if the primary key is a composite constraint (a *composite primary key constraint*)—that is, defined across more than one column—the NOT NULL characteristic is applied to each individual column. Therefore, you can't store a row with a NULL value in a primary key column. This is different from composite unique constraints, which do allow NULLs in one or more columns.

Other than the constraint type keyword, the syntax for a primary key constraint is identical to that for a unique constraint. The syntax is shown here, but you're referred to the preceding section, which discusses unique constraints, for the details of the various clauses:

```
[CONSTRAINT constraint_name]
    PRIMARY KEY [column_name [,column_name[...]]]
    [deferred_clause]
    [enabled clause]
    [exceptions_clause]
    [index_clause]
```

An index is used just as for unique constraints to enforce a primary key's unique qualities. An index enforcing a primary key behaves in exactly the same way as one for a unique constraint, including what happens if it pre-exists or if it's created automatically; see the previous discussion on unique constraints for information about primary key indexes.

Validating Data Against Existing Records with Foreign Key Constraints

Earlier in this chapter, we discussed two tables that contained records with a dependency between them. In case you skipped that section, the tables were for a medical facility and one, DOCTORS, contained information about the physicians who practice there; the second was a PATIENTS table with information that included the ID number of the patient's doctor. To ensure that every patient is assigned to a doctor in the practice, the DOCTOR_ID column in the PATIENTS table needs to be validated against the ID column in the DOCTORS table. This can be achieved with a *foreign key constraint*, also known as a *referential integrity constraint*.

You create foreign key constraints by identifying the column (or columns if it's a *composite foreign key*) in the parent table that contains the data against which new records are to be checked. In the example you would put a foreign key constraint on the PATIENTS table's DOCTOR_ID column. This constraint would identify the DOCTORS table's ID column as the column containing the data against which patient records would have to be checked.

Unlike primary key or unique constraints, an index isn't required to support a foreign key constraint. However, without an index on the foreign key, some SQL statements performed against the parent table may cause locks to be placed on the table with the foreign key. These locks can prevent one or more users from accessing the table concurrently and might slow overall processing as a result. It's therefore recommended that you build an index on any foreign key constraints that you define. This will reduce the number of locks on the table and cause less restrictive locks to be placed on the index instead.

Before you try to add a foreign key constraint to a table, you need to confirm that the parent table has a primary key or a unique constraint defined on the columns you need your foreign key to reference. Oracle relies on this constraint to maintain a valid relationship between the two tables. If the constraint on the parent table is disabled or dropped, the foreign key also has to be disabled or dropped. A CASCADE option for these commands causes the appropriate action on the foreign key to occur. You also need to determine what happens to records in your table if the related record in the parent table is deleted. You have the option of preventing the DELETE from occurring if you have a child record still in place, or you can elect to allow the DELETE to delete any records with the same value in the foreign key column(s).

The syntax for a foreign key constraint is as follows:

```
[CONSTRAINT constraint_name]
    [FOREIGN KEY (column_name[, column_name[...]]) ]
    REFERENCES [schema_name.]table_name
[(column_name[, column_name[...]] ) ]
[ON DELETE CASCADE]
[deferred_clause]
    [enabled clause]
    [exceptions_clause]
```

- The CONSTRAINT clause optionally assigns the given name to the constraint.

- The FOREIGN KEY clause is required only if the constraint is being defined outside the scope of the column definition (a column constraint versus a table constraint, as discussed later in this chapter). When required, it also must name all the columns covered by the constraint.

- The keyword REFERENCES is required and identifies the parent table.

- The schema_name is required if the parent table isn't in the same schema as the table to which the foreign key constraint is being assigned.

- The table_name is the name of the parent table.

- The column_name, or series of column_names, are the columns in the parent table that hold the values being referenced; they're required only if they don't comprise the parent table's primary key.

- ON DELETE CASCADE is an optional clause that allows the deletion of records from the table if the referenced parent record is deleted.

- the deferred_clause, enabled clause, and exceptions_clause perform the identical actions as described in detail for unique constraints.

To explain the action of the ON DELETE CASCADE option, consider the example of the DOCTORS and PATIENTS tables. The PATIENTS table has a foreign key constraint on the DOCTOR_ID column, which references the ID column in DOCTORS. Suppose that a doctor has an ID of 22 in the DOCTORS table and that the PATIENTS table has a number of records for patients of doctor number 22. If this doctor decides to leave the practice, the record for this doctor should be deleted from the DOCTORS table. If this were allowed without any further action the patient records with DOCTOR_ID equal to 22 would violate the foreign key constraint.

By default, Oracle would prevent the deletion of the doctor record because of this resulting constraint violation. However, if the constraint were defined with the ON DELETE CASCADE option, the deletion of the record for doctor 22 from the DOCTORS table would also cause the records with DOCTOR_ID equal to 22 to be deleted from the PATIENTS table. These cascaded deletes occur automatically and without any feedback to the user that any patients are being deleted.

Although you may not need to use them very often, you can also define *self-referencing constraints*. These are foreign key constraints where the constrained column is in the same table as the referenced column, or (to put it another way) where the parent table and the child table are one and the same table. A parts and assemblies table may use such a constraint to ensure that every component listed for an assembly is itself a valid component or assembly as verified by another entry in the table.

Defining Business Rules with Check Constraints

Check constraints allow you to write your own conditions to determine whether the value in a column is valid. The conditions must evaluate to true or false, but they can include comparisons between two different columns in the same row as well as comparisons of column values to constants or functions. There are many uses for check constraints. Some that we've encountered include the following:

- Requiring that the value in a gender column be M or F

Don't allow cascading deletions if they might not always be required

Be careful when allowing cascaded deletes on a foreign key and provide this option only when it's always going to be valid for the child records to be removed automatically. In this example, the business rules are likely to stipulate that patients be assigned to different doctors when a doctor leaves. If the **ON DELETE CASCADE** were in place, an enthusiastic employee could, without even knowing it, delete all the patient records for the departing doctor before such reassignments were completed. If the patients also owned laboratory results and similar records stored in additional tables with foreign key constraints allowing cascading deletes, these would also be lost as a result of the unintended action.

- Ensuring that birth date is at least 18 years less than hire date
- Checking that both or neither of two specific columns contain NULLs
- Avoiding storing a negative quantity-on-hand value

Although they're powerful, check constraints may not be able to define all your needs. For example, they can't compare values in two different rows in the same table, nor check values in a different table. The former restriction also means that you can't include an aggregate function, such as MIN or AVG, in a check constraint because they implicitly obtain data from multiple rows. In addition, check constraints can't include subqueries or functions that return values based on something outside the record being constrained.

These restrictions are all related to the issue that if the constraint were valid at one point in time, a change to some other record could invalidate it. For example, the AVG function is disallowed because any new record in a table could change the average value of a numeric column. Similarly, a subquery that retrieves records from the table could easily return different results after the new row for which the constraint is being checked is stored. Functions such as SYSDATE and USERID and *pseudocolumns* such as ROWNUM will be different depending on when the row is stored, who stores it, or where in the table it's located.

For complex rules, you can add as many check constraints to a column as you need to guarantee valid data. If a business rule becomes too complicated, you might not be able to use a check constraint or any other type of constraint to enforce it. You'll need to add a trigger to the table, or possibly handle the validation in the application code. Although not as efficient as a constraint, these techniques are required for certain types of integrity enforcement.

The check constraint syntax is quite simple compared with other constraints, and consists of the standard naming, deferred, and enabling options as well as the CHECK keyword and the related condition. The condition is placed inside parentheses, resulting in the following structure:

```
[CONSTRAINT constraint_name]
    CHECK (condition)
    [deferred_clause]
    [enabled clause]
    [exceptions_clause]
```

All components of this syntax, except the CHECK clause, were discussed in detail earlier in the section on unique constraints, so this information isn't repeated here. Instead, look at the condition clause by examining some examples. Table 17.3 shows the business rules listed at the beginning of this section and a check condition that could perform the required validation.

TABLE 17.3 **Sample business rules and related check constraints**

Rule:	Check Clause Syntax:
Require that the value in a gender column be M or F	CHECK (gender IN ('M','F')
Ensure that birth date is at least 18 years less than hire date	CHECK (hire_date - birth_date > 18 * 365.25)
Check that both or neither of two specific columns contain NULLs	CHECK ((col1 IS NULL AND col2 IS NULL) OR (col1 IS NOT NULL AND col2 IS NOT NULL))
Avoid storing a negative quantity-on-hand value	CHECK (quantity_on_hand >= 0)

Including Constraints in a New Table Definition

When a new table is created, you can include any required constraints as part of the CREATE TABLE command. For single-column constraints, you can include the constraint definition as part of the column clause or add the definitions following all the column clauses. Constraints defined with their columns are called *column constraints* by Oracle, whereas constraints defined independently of their columns are called *table constraints*. This distinction is made only because the constraints' syntax varies slightly in some cases, depending on whether the constraint is defined at column or table level. Any constraint will work in exactly the same way, regardless of which type of definition was used to create it.

Some constraints can be defined only by using one or the other constraint type. Composite constraints, for example, must be defined as table constraints because they aren't part of any single column definition.

The general syntax for defining a table with constraints is as follows:

```
CREATE TABLE table_name (
    column_name column_datatype [(length)]
        [column_constraint [column_constraint [...]]],
    column_name column_datatype [(length)]
        [column_constraint [column_constraint [...]]],
    ...
    column_name column_datatype [(length)]
        [column_constraint [column_constraint [...]]],
    table_constraint [, table_constraint [...]] )
```

Chapter 7 includes details of the *column_name*, *column_type*, and *length* definitions, as well as other clauses (not shown here) relating to the table's extents, space utilization, and similar characteristics. We want to examine only the constraint clauses here.

You can see from the syntax that a column definition can include one, many, or no constraint clauses. If there are constraint definitions, they all precede the comma that separates one column definition from the next. Table constraints follow the last column definition and are separated from it and from each other by commas. The other major difference in syntax between the two types of constraint definitions is that, because it's implied, a column constraint doesn't need to include the column name as part of its definition. Naturally, a table constraint must include the column name or names to which it applies because there's no syntactical link between the definition and any specific column definition.

Column constraints versus table constraints

Unless the nature of the constraint—a multi-column constraint, for example, which must be defined at the table (not column) level—dictates it, you can use a column and a table constraint interchangeably. The difference in how the constraint is defined is simply a matter of style, not functionality. If you're using scripts to build your tables, you may prefer to define the constraints along with the related columns whenever possible, so that all the pertinent information about each column is in one place in the script. Alternatively, you may want to put all the constraint definitions in one place in the script, using table constraints to achieve this. Again, you can't do this for all constraints because a **NOT NULL** constraint can be defined only at the column level.

There are some specific restrictions regarding constraint definitions when creating a table:

- A NOT NULL constraint must be defined as a column constraint.
- A composite constraint must be defined as a table constraint.
- Only a table-level foreign key constraint requires the FOREIGN KEY clause.
- Constraints enforced through the existence of an index (primary keys and unique constraints) can't violate the limits of an index—namely, they can't include more than 32 columns, and the total key length must be less than half the size of an Oracle block.

As an example of a table using different constraints, look over the following script file, which contains a CREATE TABLE command:

```
CREATE TABLE orders
  id             NUMBER(10)
                 CONSTRAINT orders_pk_id PRIMARY KEY,
  order_date     DATE CONSTRAINT orders_nn_date NOT NULL,
  customer_id    NUMBER(10)
                 CONSTRAINT orders_nn_customer NOT NULL
                 CONSTRAINT orders_fk_customer
                   REFERENCES CUSTOMERS (id),
  status         CHAR(5)
                 CONSTRAINT orders_ck_status CHECK (status
                   IN ('NEW','SHPD','PRTL','CANC','HOLD')),
  total_order    NUMBER(20,2),
  shipped_value  NUMBER(20,2),
  unshipped      NUMBER(20,2),
  payment_type   VARCHAR2(15),
  credit_rating  CHAR(4)
                 CONSTRAINT orders_ck_credit_rating CHECK
                   (credit_rating IN
                   ('EXCL','GOOD','FAIR','POOR',UNKN')),
  sales_rep      NUMBER(10),
  sales_region   NUMBER(10),
  CONSTRAINT orders_ck_ship_total
    CHECK (total_order=shipped_value+unshipped),
```

```
CONSTRAINT orders_ck_payment_rating
  CHECK (payment_type IS NOT NULL
  OR credit_rating IS NOT NULL),
CONSTRAINT orders_fk_sales_rep_region
  FOREIGN KEY (sales_rep, sales_region)
  REFERENCES employees (id, region) )
/
```

Adding a Constraint to an Existing Table

You need to use the ALTER TABLE command to add a constraint to a column in an existing table. You need to use the table constraint definition for all constraint types (except NOT NULL). The command is as follows:

```
ALTER TABLE table_name ADD (
  table_constraint [, table_constraint [...]] )
```

As you can see you can add more than one constraint with a single command; and, as with the CREATE TABLE command, each constraint clause can include any valid option for the constraint type. These options are described in detail in the earlier sections of this chapter.

If you need to make a column NOT NULL, you need to use the ALTER TABLE command with the MODIFY keyword. The syntax for this command is as follows:

```
ALTER TABLE table_name MODIFY (
  column_name column_constraint
  [, column_constraint [...]] )
```

column_constraint is a NOT NULL constraint with any optional clauses you want to use. Again, as with adding new constraints, you can use a single command to add multiple NOT NULL constraints to a table.

If you're adding one or more new columns to an existing table, you also use the ALTER TABLE command but now include the column definition. This definition may also include one or more constraints, or you can include table constraints in the statement following the new column definitions.

Modifying and Dropping Constraints

You might need to modify the constraint definitions you've created for a table. These modifications could include enabling a constraint, disabling or dropping a constraint, or changing a NOT NULL column to allow NULLs. All these changes require the use of the ALTER TABLE command.

The earlier section on enabling and disabling constraints looks at the details of the enable and disable clauses, so they're not repeated here. To perform these actions, you need to embed these clauses in the ALTER TABLE command:

```
ALTER TABLE  table_name enable_clause
ALTER TABLE table_name disable_clause
```

You can include multiple enable or disable clauses in a single ALTER TABLE command, and even use both types of clauses in a single statement. However, you can name only one constraint in each clause.

The following script contains the code necessary to redefine the index used for the primary key constraint defined on the ORDERS table's ID column. It shows the use of both the DISABLE and ENABLE options of the ALTER TABLE command.

```
     ALTER TABLE orders
❶──DISABLE PRIMARY KEY;──────────❷
    °ALTER TABLE orders
       ENABLE PRIMARY KEY ───❸
          USING INDEX
             TABLESPACE large_indx ───❹
       ❻──PCTFREE 0 ───❼
    ❽────────STORAGE (MAXEXTENTS UNLIMITED)
❾──EXCEPTIONS INTO exceptions; ──❿
```

Dropping a constraint is similar to disabling one. You have the same options to identify the constraint: by name or by the keywords PRIMARY KEY and UNIQUE, the latter with the list-included columns. The CASCADE option is also available should you want to force any foreign key constraints that depend on the constraint being dropped concurrently. As with the disable action, you can't drop a constraint if there's a dependent constraint.

❶ To drop the index associated with the primary key constraint, you need to disable (or drop) the constraint

❷ Use the keywords to disable the constraint; because there's only one primary key per table

❸ The index will be rebuilt when you enable the primary key (again using the keywords)

❹ Include this clause to override default index creation

❺ Use this clause to override index creation in your default tablespace

❻ Include other space utilization parameters if needed

❼ You don't need to leave free space if the index is on a column with an ever-increasing value

❽ Use whatever options are appropriate for your index

❾ You may want to include this in case an invalid record was added while the constraint was disabled

❿ You need to name your table if you don't use the default created by ULTEXCPT.SQL

The syntax for dropping a constraint follows. (Refer to the section on disabling constraints if you need clarification on any of the included terms; they perform identical duties in either command.)

```
ALTER TABLE table_name DROP
    [PRIMARY KEY]
    [UNIQUE (column_name[, column_name [...] ] ) ]
    [CONSTRAINT constraint_name]
```

As with the enable and disable clauses, you can include only one constraint in an ALTER TABLE...DROP command.

Again, the NOT NULL constraint doesn't completely conform to the syntactical rules of the other constraint types. Although you can use all the preceding commands to enable, disable, or drop a NOT NULL constraint, you can also use an ALTER TABLE...MODIFY statement to switch a column between allowing and disallowing NULLs. The statement has the following form:

```
ALTER TABLE table_name MODIFY
(column_name [CONSTRAINT not_null_constraint] [NOT] NULL
[,column_name [CONSTRAINT not_null_constraint] [NOT] NULL]
[,...] )
```

As you can see, this command allows you to alter the NULL enforcement for a single column or multiple columns in a single command. You can even include column changes from NULL to NOT NULL and from NOT NULL to NULL within the same statement, although you can't change the same column twice within one command. The command also gives you the option of using the constraint name (if there is one), but works just as well if you don't include it.

One final issue you need to consider when using constraints: Your command will fail if you try to drop a table that's being referenced by at least one foreign key constraint in a different table. The exception message will indicate that the primary key or a unique key in the table is required by the foreign key reference. To drop the table, therefore, you must drop the foreign key constraint. You can do this by manually dropping the foreign key constraint before you attempt to drop the referenced table. You can also elect to include the keyword CASCADE CONSTRAINTS clause

Tablespaces containing tables with dependent constraints

You may have to drop a tablespace that contains tables with foreign key dependencies. You have to use the **INCLUDING CONTENTS** clause in order to drop a tablespace that still contains tables. The **DROP TABLESPACE** command will fail if any of the tables that would be dropped when you issue this statement are parent tables for foreign key constraints belonging to tables in a different tablespace. To override this, you can add the **CASCADE CONSTRAINTS** clause to the **DROP TABLESPACE... INCLUDING CONTENTS** command. As with the use of this option on individual tables, you may want to defer using it until you confirm that you won't affect any applications by indiscriminately dropping all the dependent constraints.

Using Indexes, Clusters, Caching, and Sorting Effectively

Optimize your indexes

How Oracle8 stores data in a cluster and when to use clusters

How buffer pools increase cache performance

Minimize sorting's performance impact

Tuning Indexes

Indexes are transparent to users

Indexes are transparent to the end-user application. Oracle automatically maintains the indexes during a DML operation on the table. Oracle Optimizer chooses the suitable index during a SQL **SELECT** operation.

Indexes are the first in line of means to reduce disk I/O and to provide a short access path to the desired data. Until version 7.2, Oracle used to provide only b*tree indexes. The task for selecting an index was relatively simple then: have one or not? Several indexing options are available with Oracle8, and now it's challenging to select an optimal indexing strategy.

Chapter 8, "Adding Segments for Different Types of Indexes," discusses indexes in more detail; the following sections give you a better idea of how to use indexes effectively with your databases.

When to Use B*Tree Indexes

Balanced tree (*b*tree*) indexes have been part of the Oracle RDBMS since its inception. It's still the most commonly used indexing mechanism. You should create a b*tree index on a table column if it meets any of the following criteria:

Increase data selectivity

Use a concatenated index (that is, an index on multiple table columns) if these columns are involved in any of these situations. You can create a concatenated index to increase the selectivity of the data by using indexed columns. However, ensure that leading columns from a concatenated index are used frequently in an application's SQL statements.

- SQL queries frequently use the column in the `where` clause, and the amount of data returned by the query is very low compared to the table data. Consider a sales order-entry table, `Orders`, which has the following columns:

  ```
  order#
  order_date
  part#
  Quantity
  customer#
  sales_person
  ```

  If you frequently retrieve orders with a query containing `order#` in the `where` clause (as shown in the following SQL command), you must create an index on this table on the `Order#` column.

  ```
  select * from orders where order# = <order number>;
  ```

  Similarly, other columns on the table can be indexed if they're also used in the queries' `where` clause and return very few rows. However, imagine a query like the following:

  ```
  select * from orders where qty = '1'
  ```

If a large proportion of your orders are with this quantity, an index on this column won't be useful because the query will return a large number of rows. Using a full table scan in that situation is more appropriate.

- The column is frequently used to join multiple tables in queries. Again consider the order-entry table mentioned in the preceding example, along with a parts_master table that contains columns describing attributes for parts such as part#, Description, price, and so on. To prepare the invoice for an order, you might have to execute a SQL statement very similar to the following:

```
select ord.order#, ord.customer#, ord.part#,
parts.Description,
ord.Qty, parts.Price
from  orders ord, parts_master parts
where ord.part# = parts.part# ;
```

Indexes on orders and parts_master tables on the part# column are recommended in order for this query to run fast.

- The column is defined as a foreign key to enforce a *referential integrity constraint*. Frequent update operations involve this column on the parent table. The presence of an index on the child table will avoid a table-level shared lock on it, which Oracle acquires while updating the parent key column in the absence of the index.

- Oracle automatically creates unique indexes to enforce primary-key and unique-key integrity constraints.

- You must also create an index on columns in tables that are referred as parent columns in a foreign-key constraints relationship with other tables.

When to Use Bitmap Indexes

Bitmap indexes, first introduced in Oracle 7.3, are very frequently used in data warehouse environments. Creating a bitmap index is recommended in the following situations:

- The column or the set of columns frequently appear in the where clause of SQL statements.

- The column has fewer distinct values as compared to the total number of rows in the table. The ratio of distinct values to the total number of values is known as *cardinality*. Thus, the column has a low cardinality value.

- The column is used frequently to perform joins between multiple tables.

- Updates to the column are infrequent.

When to Use Reverse-Key Indexes

A *reverse-key index* is very similar to a regular b*tree index, except that the byte order for the indexed column is reversed. Consider a table containing the orders where the primary key, order numbers, is generated in increasing sequence order. Because all the entered orders are nearby, all the new values will go to the same index leaf block, thus causing multiple concurrent inserts into the same block. This is especially a problem in an Oracle parallel server environment in which that block will be *pinged* among the instances for insertion of new values. If the byte order for the order number is switched now, the numerically adjacent order number will go to different leaf blocks, and pinging is greatly reduced.

Reverse-key indexes are recommended in the following situations:

- The indexed column is a serially increasing number.

- There are concurrent INSERTs and DELETEs in the table.

- The application is used in an Oracle parallel server environment.

- Queries don't require index range scans—that is, the queries involving the indexed column that use clauses such as between, greater than, lesser than, and like aren't likely to be used.

When to Use Index-Organized Tables

An *index-organized table* (or index-only table) is very similar to a b*tree index. If your table data is very static and will invariably

be retrieved via an indexed key, an index-only table can be a better alternative to combining a regular table and its associated
index—it will save the additional I/O to retrieve the additional
column from the table data after the index lookup. You can't create another index on an index-only table, however.

Use index-organized tables in the following situations:

- The data is frequently retrieved via the primary key.

- A set of columns is most frequently selected during the
  retrieval.

- No other table column will be used in the where clause of
  SQL statements; hence, the index isn't needed on any other
  column.

- Full table scans are very infrequent.

Consider a table containing a Social Security number, name, and
address information. If queries similar to the following are going
to use the table extensively, it is advantageous to create the table
as an index-organized table:

```
Select SSN, Name, Address from cust_info where ssn = <SSN> ;
```

Evaluating Index Usage

The only direct way to confirm the usage of an index is to look
at your application code; do this to determine whether the
indexed column is appearing in the where clause of a SQL statement. You should reconfirm the index usage by looking at the
query's execution plan. However, using an index and avoiding a
full table scan doesn't guarantee the optimal indexing strategy.
You should further examine the possibility of creating a more
selective concatenated index on a table if multiple columns from
the same table are appearing in the SQL statement's where
clause. Decisions could be simple in an OLTP environment
where a transaction deals with a relatively low volume of data
indexing. During batch processing, during report generation, or
in a DSS environment, however, the decision between various
indexing strategies and full table scans performed in parallel
could be tricky and might be greatly influenced by machine
resources, database layout, the nature of the query, and so on.

A full table scan can be faster
than using an index

Under favorable conditions, a
full table scan using the Oracle
parallel query option might be
faster than using an existing
index. This is especially true
while joining multiple tables. At
what point a full table scan
becomes faster than an index
retrieval depends on many factors, including the available
CPU capacity and a table's
physical layout.

Confirm the presence of needed indexes with na execution plan

Look at your time-consuming queries' execution plan to see whether performance can be improved by adding an index or by increasing the selectivity of an existing index (via adding another column to it). In an OLTP system where resource usage by a transaction isn't significant, however, the overall system can reduce the I/O marginally, because every transaction is executed numerous times.

 Index used to retrieve data from ITEM table

The following command sequence shows how to use the auto-trace utility to quickly get the execution plan of a SQL statement and confirm the index usage:

```
SQL> set autotrace on ;
SQL> select * from item where i_id=1000 ;


   ITEM_ID    ITEM_NAME                            ITEM_PRICE
---------- -------------------------- ----------
ITEM_DATA
----------------------------------------------------
      1000    FAbLm1A84sVcZXgkJbZvSVe          7590
HTXSxYlPUMW5HGc5umArHcJofKDlwiOXPN


Execution Plan
----------------------------------------------------------
   0      SELECT STATEMENT Optimizer=CHOOSE
   1    0    TABLE ACCESS (BY INDEX ROWID) OF 'ITEM'
   2    1      INDEX (UNIQUE SCAN) OF 'IITEM' (UNIQUE)
```

To measure the overall effectiveness with which an Oracle instance is using indexes, calculate the Index Use Ratio as follows:

```
Index Use Ratio = 'table fetch by rowid'/
    (table fetch by rowid + table scan rows gotten)
```

table fetch by rowid and *table scan rows gotten* are the statistics from the dynamic performance view V$SYSSTAT.

A value of 90 percent or higher for this ratio is recommended. A lower value might be acceptable in a data-warehousing or decision-support system where the full table scans are frequently used.

Index usage doesn't come without a cost. Before creating an index, consider the following factors along with the advantages you'll gain by the presence of an index:

- The DML operations involving the indexed column will also need to update the index along with the table, thus consuming more resources than used to update the table.

- Indexes require additional disk space.

- Creating an index on a large table could be time-consuming.

Watch for SQL Statements That Don't Use Indexes

Several SQL queries don't use indexes:

- SQL queries that perform calculations or functions on the indexed column. For example, the following SQL statement won't use an index on the name column:
```
Select name, address from persons where
upper(name)='JOHN';
```

- SQL statements that use NOT when testing an indexed column. The following SQL statement won't use the index present on the city column:
```
Select name, street_address, city
from persons
where city not in ('BOSTON','NEWYORK');
```

- SQL statements that use an IS NULL or IS NOT NULL clause.

- SQL statements that perform internal conversion on the indexed column. In a part_master table where part# is defined as a character column, the following query won't use the index on the part# column:
```
select * from part_master where part# = 999999;
```

Instead, use this SQL statement:
```
select * from part_master where part# = '999999';
```

Using Clusters

A *cluster* is a group of tables. If the application SQL statements frequently join two or more tables, you can improve performance by clustering the tables. Oracle stores the clustered tables in the same data blocks. This reduces the amount of I/O required during the retrieval, because the rows needed from multiple tables are available in the same block. Similarly, you can group multiple table rows with the same value for a non-unique column together if you know that these rows will be processed together. This type of cluster—where a key column is used to group multiple rows—is known as an *index cluster*. The key column used to group the rows together is the *cluster key*.

When clusters hurt performance

Using clusters for frequently updated or deleted tables affects performance adversely.

Another type of cluster that Oracle offers is hash clusters—single-table clusters where rows of a table with the same hash value are stored together to enable fast access. These are discussed in detail in a later section.

Consider a telephone billing system where the `calls` table stores information about each customer's usage. If billing rules indicate that all calls made by a customer in a particular month be billed together, you can store these calls in a cluster whose cluster key could be concatenated for the columns `phone_number`, `year`, and `month`.

Figure 18.1 shows the difference between a normal table and a single-table cluster. Figure 18.2 shows the data storage in a three-table cluster.

FIGURE 18.1

Index clusters store the data with the same index key together.

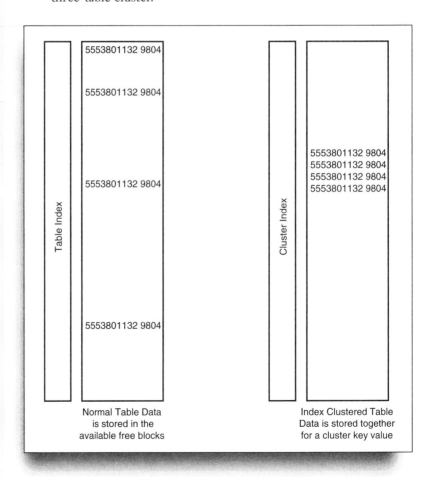

Normal Table Data
is stored in the
available free blocks

Index Clustered Table
Data is stored together
for a cluster key value

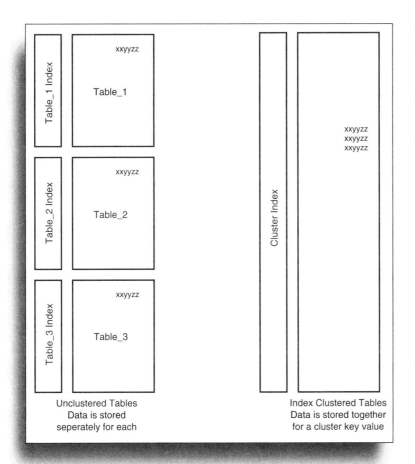

FIGURE 18.2
Index clusters store the data
from multiple tables with the
same cluster key together.

Unclustered Tables
Data is stored
seperately for each

Index Clustered Tables
Data is stored together
for a cluster key value

Creating and Managing Index Clusters

Create an index cluster and its tables (general steps)

1. Create the cluster.
2. Create the cluster index.
3. Create the tables.
4. Insert data and perform DML/query operations.

Creating an Index Cluster

Use the following command to create a single-table cluster for
the previously discussed calls table:

When to use index clusters

If two or more tables are related via referential integrity and frequently used with joins in the SQL operations, create an index cluster for these tables. If multiple rows from a table are frequently fetched together with a non-unique column, create a single-table index cluster with that column as the cluster key to improve performance.

```
SQL> create cluster C_phone_calls ( phone_no number(10),
        year number(4), month number(2))
    pctused 80 pctfree 5
    tablespace users
    storage (initial 10M Next 10M);
```

Creating a Cluster-Key Index

Cluster-key indexes can't be unique

Oracle doesn't allow cluster-key indexes to be unique. You can create indexes on a clustered table's other columns. These indexes are maintained independently of the cluster index.

Oracle Server requires an index on the cluster key before it allows any DML performed against the tables in the index cluster. You can't perform any DML operations until you create the index. To locate a row with a given cluster key, Oracle first looks in the index and reads the corresponding rowid. This rowid is, in turn, used to retrieve the table data for the clustered table(s). The following command creates the cluster-key index I_phone_calls on the c_phone_calls cluster:

```
SQL> create index I_phone_calls on cluster c_phone_calls
    pctfree 10
    tablespace user
    storage (initial 1M next 1M);
```

Creating Tables in an Index Cluster

You can create a table within a cluster after creating the cluster. A cluster-key index can be created before or after the tables within the cluster. However, you can't insert any rows in a cluster's tables until you create the cluster-key index.

The following CREATE TABLE command creates the table phones_calls within the cluster c_phone_calls:

```
SQL> create table phones_calls
        ( phone_no number(10), year number(4),
            month number(2),day number(2),
            duration number(3), .......... )
            cluster C_phone_calls
            (phone_no number(10), year number(4),
            month number(2));
```

Creating and Managing Hash Clusters

Hash clusters are single-table clusters in which rows with the same hash-key values are stored together. Oracle uses a mathematical hash function to choose the location of a row within the cluster.

A cluster key and the data block in which it will be stored are directly related. The space used for a cluster needs to be allocated during cluster creation. Thus, the size and the number of rows should be accurately known.

Consider an item table containing information about 100,000 items and having the following structure:

```
item_id          number(6,0),
item_name        varchar2(24),
item_price       number(5,0),
item_data        varchar2(50)
```

Also assume that the item_id is unique and the average row length is 75 bytes. If a 3,750-byte space is available within each Oracle data block, each data block will accommodate 45 rows (3,750 divided by 75) per block. The total storage space needed for this cluster will be 2,223 data blocks (100,000 divided by 45). Oracle rounds it off to a certain higher number and might allocate a few more blocks. The data stored in the cluster will look similar to Figure 18.3.

When Oracle needs to store or retrieve a row with an item_id, it simply applies the hash function to the given item_id to get its block number. In the example, the hash function is mod(45); to retrieve data for item_id 10576, Oracle looks in data block 236 (10,576 divided by 45), needing to read only one disk block.

Use the following SQL statement to create a hash cluster for this data:

```
create cluster item_cluster (
  item_id          number(6,0)
  )
        hashkeys         100000
        hash is          item_id
        size             75
        tablespace       items
        storage (initial 8M next 1M pctincrease 0);
```

> **When to use hash clusters**
>
> Use hash clusters for lookup tables whose data is static and is retrieved mostly by using their primary key.

1 Total number of cluster keys to be stored

2 Cluster-key column, based on data most frequently retrieved from table

3 Space (in bytes) used to store data for single-cluster key

Carefully choose the size amount

If space used by the rows associated with a cluster key isn't predictable, exercise caution while using clusters. If space usage frequently exceeds allocated space, chaining will take place and will result in wasted disk space and increased I/O.

```
create table item (
item_id               number(6,0),
item_name             varchar2(24),
item_price            number(5,0),
item_data             varchar2(50)
)
cluster item_cluster(item_id);
```

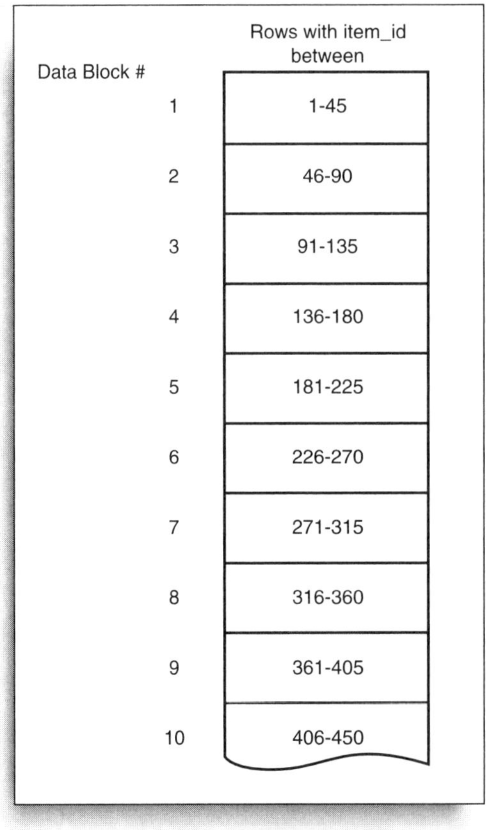

FIGURE 18.3

Hash clusters preallocate the storage location for a row based on the hash-key value.

Data Block #	Rows with item_id between
1	1-45
2	46-90
3	91-135
4	136-180
5	181-225
6	226-270
7	271-315
8	316-360
9	361-405
10	406-450

Restrictions on Clustered Tables

Clustered tables have some restrictions:

- A direct path load can't be used to load tables in a cluster.

- Storage allocation is defined at the cluster level; thus, it can't be defined for each individual table.

- Clusters can't be partitioned.

- The cluster index can't be unique.

- Clustered tables can't contain long, long raw, or LOB object datatypes.

Evaluating Cluster Usage

Oracle Server automatically maintains the clusters once they're created. Oracle will also use the underlying hash or the index cluster key for data retrieval whenever the cluster key is used in a SQL statement's where clause.

The following example uses the autotrace utility to see the SQL query's execution plan. The execution plan shows that the table is accessed via HASH of ITEM, thus using the hash cluster key to retrieve the specified data.

```
SQL> set autotrace on ;
SQL> select item_id,i_name from item where item_id=1000;


   ITEM_ID I_NAME
---------- ------------------------
      1000 FAbLm1A84sVcZXgkJbZvSVe
Execution Plan
----------------------------------------------------------
   0      SELECT STATEMENT Optimizer=CHOOSE
   1    0   TABLE ACCESS (HASH) OF 'ITEM'
```

Caching Data

Caching is the most common approach for improving retrieval rates of large random data. The effectiveness of caching depends on the size of the cache memory available and the access pattern of the data. Oracle uses a significant part of the *Shared Global Area* (*SGA*) as the buffer cache. Its size can be specified by the DB_BLOCK_BUFFERS initialization parameter in terms of total number of Oracle data blocks, and it's generally referred to as the *buffer cache* or *buffer pool*. By default, Oracle uses the Least

Recently Used (LRU) algorithm for maintaining the buffer cache, in which the least recently used blocks are used first.

When an Oracle user process needs a data block it proceeds as follows:

1. It looks in the buffer cache for the desired block.

2. It finds a free buffer in the buffer cache and reserves it.

3. If it doesn't find a free buffer after searching a predetermined number of buffers, it signals the DBWR. The DBWR, in turn, writes the modified data blocks to the disk. The buffers written to the disk are available for reuse.

4. The process reads the block from the disk in the buffer cache.

Figure 18.4 depicts these steps in the form of a flowchart.

FIGURE 18.4

An Oracle process follows this algorithm to access a data block.

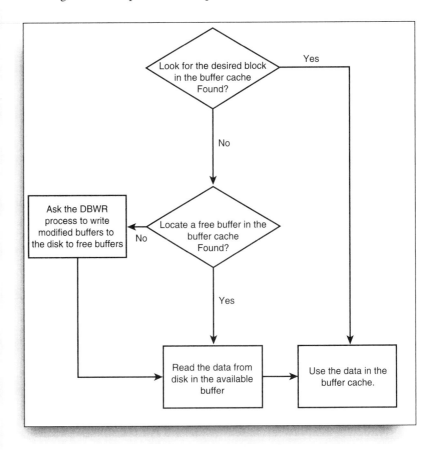

The effectiveness of caching depends on the access pattern for the data. The access pattern may vary vastly from object to object, however. To improve caching effectiveness, Oracle8 offers a multiple-buffer pool and a CACHE attribute for the objects.

Setting Up a Multiple-Buffer Pool

Oracle8 lets you divide the buffer pool into three different pools:

- KEEP As the name suggests, buffers in this pool are kept as long as possible. Frequently accessed objects that contain a small number of blocks should be assigned to this pool.

- RECYCLE Buffers in this pool are recycled after they're used. You should assign to this buffer pool very large, randomly accessed objects whose blocks won't likely be accessed again very soon.

- DEFAULT Data block buffers remaining after assigning the specified buffers to the KEEP and RECYCLE pools are assigned to this pool. Objects that haven't been allocated to any other buffer pool are cached in this pool.

By default, Oracle8 enables only one buffer pool—that is, the default buffer pool and all the buffers allocated to it. To assign buffers to the KEEP and RECYCLE buffers, use the following initialization parameters:

```
DB_BLOCK_BUFFERS        = 10000
DB_BLOCK_LRU_LATCHES    = 10
BUFFER_POOL_KEEP        = (1000,2)
BUFFER_POOL_RECYCLE     = (3000,2)
```

Figure 18.5 shows the buffer pool allocation specified by these parameters.

1. Assigns 10,000 total buffers to the pool

2. Assigns 10 LRU latches

3. Assigns 1,000 buffers and 2 latches to the KEEP pool

4. Assigns 3,000 buffers and 2 latches to the RECYCLE pool

FIGURE 18.5

Oracle8 can divide a buffer pool in three sections.

Keep Buffer Pool 1000 Blocks	Default Buffer Pool 6000 Blocks	Recycle Buffer Pool 3000 Blocks

Assigning Objects to Buffer Pools

By default, all objects use the DEFAULT buffer pool. To cache the objects in other pools, you need to create the object with the desired buffer pool attribute or alter the object's buffer pool attribute by using the ALTER command. ALTER and CREATE for the table, partition, index, cluster, snapshot, and snapshot log support the buffer pool attribute in their storage clause. You can assign different buffer pools to different partitions of a partitioned object.

Use the following command to create and assign the example item table to the KEEP buffer pool:

```
item_id          number(6,0),
item_name        varchar2(24),
item_price       number(5,0),
item_data        varchar2(50)
)
storage (initial 1M next 1M buffer_pool keep);
```

If the table already exists, use the following command to assign it to the KEEP buffer pool:

```
Alter table item storage (buffer_pool keep);
```

Choosing objects to cache

The caching strategy for a particular object depends on its access pattern and the available buffer cache. If the object is a frequently used reference table, assign it to the **KEEP** buffer pool. On the other hand, assign a large, randomly accessed table to the **RECYCLE** buffer pool. The proper caching strategy should factor the available memory, disk I/O, and overall response time for transactions.

Caching Objects with the *CACHE* Attribute

In addition to grouping the objects in the KEEP, RECYCLE, and DEFAULT buffer pools according to their access patterns, you can also specify the CACHE attribute for very frequently accessed tables; this makes it so that buffers for these tables are read at the most recently used end of the LRU during their full table scans.

By default, Oracle always keeps the read blocks at the least recently used end of the LRU list during a full table scan. You can specify the CACHE attribute for the table with the CREATE or ALTER command to keep the read blocks at the most recently used end of the LRU chain. Use this command to alter the item table to use the cache attribute:

```
Alter table item cache;
```

If you don't want to permanently change a table's CACHE attribute but still want to read it at the most recently used end of the LRU list during the current full table scan (due to special processing requirements), use the CACHE hint in the SELECT statement. Similarly, you can use the NOCACHE hint to disable a table's CACHE attribute during the current full table scan.

Evaluating Caching Effectiveness

The effectiveness of a buffer cache is measured in terms of the cache hit ratio or the buffer's hit ratio, defined as the percentage of times a desired data block was found in the buffer cache. You can calculate the buffer hit ratio from the statistics available in the V$SYSSTAT dynamic performance view as follows:

```
Cache hit ratio = 100*(1- 'physical reads'/ 'Logical reads')
```

Logical reads is further derived as the following:

```
Logical Reads = 'db block gets' + 'consistent gets'
```

These statistics from the V$SYSSTAT view give you the combined statistics for the buffer cache as a whole. If you've defined KEEP and RECYCLE buffer pools, it's strongly recommended that you evaluate the hit ratios for them separately. The V$BUFFER_POOL dynamic performance view gives physical reads, block gets, and consistent gets statistics for each buffer pool.

Tuning Sorts

Sorting is the rearranging of a random collection of data sets into an ordered collection—sorting the data in order. You need to sort the data to make it more presentable and usable.

Sorting data consumes memory and CPU resources. The time taken and resources consumed to sort are proportional to the amount of data sorted. If the volume of the data to be sorted is more than the available memory, the sort operations must use disks to store intermediate sort results (further slowing the sort operation). Reducing disk I/O is one primary focus of Oracle8 (or of any computer system for that matter), because disks operations are comparatively slower; they involve movement of mechanical components and should be optimized to the fullest possible extent.

Oracle8 performs the sort operation in memory, allocating memory up to the maximum specified by the initialization parameter SORT_AREA_SIZE. If the volume of the data to be sorted is more than the SORT_AREA_SIZE, it uses temporary disk segments. The amount of disk space it uses depends mainly on the volume of the data to be sorted.

Understanding Sort Behavior

The V$SYSSTAT dynamic performance table contains the statistics sorts (memory) and sorts (disk), indicating the number of in-memory and on-disk sorts the instance has performed since instance startup. It also contains the sorts (rows) statistics, which indicates the total number of rows sorted by the instance. Use the following query to see these statistics:

```
SQL> column name format a20
SQL> select name,value from v$sysstat where name like 'sort%'

NAME                          VALUE
--------------------          ----------
sorts (memory)                11462
sorts (disk)                      3
sorts (rows)                  5187983
```

In this system there were 11,462 sorts in the memory. Three sorts were done by using the disk.

Optimizing Sort Operations

Sorts are one of the most resource-intensive operations in any database. If sorts are taking too much time on your system and

---

When does Oracle perform sort operations?

Oracle8 performs sorts while creating indexes and executing SQL operations that contain order by, group by, distinct, union, join, unique, and aggregate operations such as max, min, and so on. The analyze command also sorts data to calculate statistics.

Calculating the in-memory sort ratio

In an OLTP environment, the sorts (disk) number should be a very low percentage of the total sorts. In Memory Sort Ratio can be calculated as In Memory Sort Ratio = 'sorts (memory)'/('sorts (memory)' + 'sorts (disk)'). A value very near 100 percent is recommended for In Memory Sort Ratio. A lower value of this ratio indicates that the workload is performing too many disk sorts.

are a cause of concern, consider the following options to minimize their impact:

- Eliminate the sorting operation needed during the index
  creation by using the NOSORT clause of the CREATE INDEX command. To use NOSORT, you must presort the data before loading it into the database. Operating-system sort utilities as
  well as third-party sorting tools such as SYNCSORT can be used
  to sort the data before loading it into the database.

- If you're recreating an existing index, use the ALTER
  INDEX...REBUILD command to recreate the index by using the
  existing index rather than the table data:

  ```
  SQL> alter index I_orders rebuild ;
  ```

- Use the ANALYZE command with the ESTIMATE clause rather
  than with the COMPUTE clause:

  ```
  SQL> analyze table orders estimate statistics ;
  ```

- Ensure that the application isn't performing unnecessary
  sorts by using clauses such as distinct and union in the SQL
  commands when not needed. Several third-party tools do so
  very frequently. Trace the suspected queries and look at their
  execution plan to see if they include a sort operation.

Setting Sort-Related Parameters

It's certain that the workload will need some amount of sorting.
You can minimize the disk sorts or enhance performance of disk
sorts by using the following Oracle8 parameters to appropriate
value depending on the application nature:

- SORT_AREA_SIZE indicates the number of maximum memory
  in bytes a user process can allocate for sorting. Sort memory
  is allocated on a per-session basis. Each parallel query slave
  performing sorts has its own sort memory, thus the amount
  of memory used during parallel execution may increase drastically if this parameter is set too high. Ensure that the system has sufficient memory to meet the increased demand
  before increasing this parameter.

- SORT_AREA_RETAINED_SIZE determines the amount of memory retained by the process after completion of a sort. The additional memory used for a sort is released back to the session. (Remember, it's not freed to the operating system.) This parameter has more significance when a session can perform multiple concurrent sorts, especially while using TP monitors or MTS. The default value of 0 for this parameter indicates that it's equal to the parameter SORT_AREA_SIZE.

- Setting SORT_DIRECT_WRITES to TRUE enables the session to allocate additional buffers in memory and to write them directly to disk. This eliminates the use of a buffer cache for sorting operations and increases the performance. When this parameter is set to its default value of AUTO, Oracle8 enables direct sort writes when the SORT_AREA_SIZE is more than 10 times the database block size. Buffer memory used for SORT_DIRECT_WRITES is used from the session memory.

**Should you set
SORT_DIRECT_WRITE to
TRUE or AUTO?**

The values of **SORT_WRITE_
BUFFER_SIZE** and
SORT_WRITE_BUFFER are
considered only when
SORT_DIRECT_WRITE is set to
TRUE. The default values of these
parameters are effective if **SORT_
DIRECT_WRITE** is set to **AUTO**.

- Set SORT_READ_FAC for the disk subsystem in the system to optimize the I/O performance during disk sorts. The formula to calculate SORT_READ_FAC is as follows:

```
SORT_READ_FAC=(avg. seek time + avg. latency time
+ block transfer rate)/(block transfer time)
```

- SORT_WRITE_BUFFER_SIZE determines the size of the I/O buffer used to perform direct sort writes.

- SORT_WRITE_BUFFER determines the total number of buffers used for direct sort writes.

Managing Temporary Segments

Improving sort performance

To improve the performance of sort
operations, assign a **TEMPORARY**-
type tablespace as the user's temporary tablespace, setting the
DIRECT_SORT_WRITE initialization parameter to **TRUE**, or setting the value of initialization
parameter **SORT_AREA_SIZE**
to a larger value.

Oracle8 allocates temporary segments used during sorts from the tablespace defined as the user's temporary tablespace. Because the default value for this tablespace is SYSTEM, you must change it to some other tablespace.

A production system will often need one or several tablespaces dedicated as temporary. To improve performance, you should alter these tablespaces to be of type TEMPORARY. If you use a permanent tablespace as temporary tablespace for sorting, each user has his dedicated sort segments deallocated at the end of the current operation. If you use a TEMPORARY-type tablespace as the temporary tablespace for users, the segments, once allocated by the instance, aren't deallocated and can be reused by other users who have been assigned to the same tablespace. This saves the overhead of allocating and deallocating the extents during the sort operations.

It's recommended that you stripe the temporary tablespace to improve I/O performance during the sort write operations. Striping the temporary tablespace on the number of disks equal to the SORT_DIRECT_BUFFERS will yield the maximum performance benefit.

Set the initial and next extent parameters for the temporary tablespace as multiples of the SORT_AREA_SIZE in order to optimize extent allocation.

View disk sort usage statistics

The dynamic performance view **V$SORT_SEGMENT** provides the usage statistics for the **TEMPORARY** tablespace. The **V$SORT_USAGE** view contains statistics related to the current sort activity in the instance.

Improving Throughput with SQL, PL/SQL, and Precompilers

Maintain a balance between hardware and software to keep your system fast

Learn how to write queries so that multiple users share the same space in the SGA

Remove unnecessary SQL parsing to speed up your system

Understanding SQL Tuning

The true power of SQL

How SQL queries are written have the most impact on the performance of the database. Many times, a small change to a SQL query can make it execute many times more quickly—or slowly.

Because SQL is the most widely used utility for database queries, having a good handle on how to write efficient queries can give your system a great performance boost. You need to determine which database access method will yield the fastest system performance and use the least amount of system resources.

Just because a SQL script accomplishes the task it was assigned to do doesn't in any way mean that it's a good script. A good SQL script is one that uses all the database features available to accomplish the task as fast as possible with as little system resource use as possible. That's where SQL tuning comes into play—how you can increase system throughput by reducing resource usage and contention.

Defining System Performance

Before discussing how to maximize system performance through tuning, you need to answer the question of what exactly good system performance is. The easiest answer is to get the most amount of processing done in the least amount of elapsed time, but that's not always true.

Good system performance is a balance between effective, efficient application code versus available system resources. By using threads and multiple CPUs, a single database application can use all the resources of an entire system. This results in the application executing very quickly, but other users of the system will most probably experience slow or sluggish response time. You create good system performance by writing efficient code and also by considering how system resources are affected.

When thinking about system performance as it relates to software development with Oracle, what you need to keep in mind is how you structure your queries. It's true that database design and maintenance pretty much determines how a database will perform, but you can use a few tricks as a database administrator that will help your scripts and application programs run faster.

Deciding Which SQL Statements to Tune

Before you can begin tuning SQL statements, you need to decide which statements to tune. Your best bet is to start by using the utilities that come with the Oracle Server: TKPROF, Oracle Trace, and the EXPLAIN PLAN utility. You should also query the V$SORT_USAGE and V$SQLAREA views for more information on which SQL statements are using the most system resources.

As a general rule, you should tune statements that do one of two things: take a very long time to execute or execute fairly quickly but are repeated many times (for example, in a loop). Tuning statements such as these will reap the most benefit in terms of system resources because they're using the most resources in your application. When tuning these statements, you want to reduce the resources the statements require, and, if possible, also reduce the number of times the statement is executed.

SQL Statement Tuning

This section focuses on quick suggestions on how to write the most effective SQL code and to perform the same task your code was doing before more quickly and efficiently.

Take a Different Approach

As stated earlier, SQL is a powerful language, and queries that produce the same result can be written in different ways. You can rewrite a query and then run the EXPLAIN PLAN command against the old and the rewritten query to determine the cost of each approach. In a nutshell, the utility analyzes a SQL statement and places the results in a table, which you query. The default name for this table is PLAN_TABLE, and its fields are as follows:

```
SQL> describe plan_table
 Name                             Null?    Type
 -------------------------------- -------- ----
 STATEMENT_ID                              VARCHAR2(30)
 TIMESTAMP                                 DATE
 REMARKS                                   VARCHAR2(80)
 OPERATION                                 VARCHAR2(30)
```

Use joins effectively

How you order your joins in a SQL statement can affect the performance of the statement. When your SQL statement joins two or more tables, you'll want to list the tables that return the most rows first and have the smaller row selections later. You'll also want to use an index if possible to avoid full table scans.

OPTIONS	VARCHAR2(30)
OBJECT_NODE	VARCHAR2(128)
OBJECT_OWNER	VARCHAR2(30)
OBJECT_NAME	VARCHAR2(30)
OBJECT_INSTANCE	NUMBER(38)
OBJECT_TYPE	VARCHAR2(30)
OPTIMIZER	VARCHAR2(255)
SEARCH_COLUMNS	NUMBER
ID	NUMBER(38)
PARENT_ID	NUMBER(38)
POSITION	NUMBER(38)
COST	NUMBER(38)
CARDINALITY	NUMBER(38)
BYTES	NUMBER(38)
OTHER_TAG	VARCHAR2(255)
PARTITION_START	VARCHAR2(255)
PARTITION_STOP	VARCHAR2(255)
PARTITION_ID	NUMBER(38)
OTHER	LONG

SEE ALSO

➤ *How to invoke the* EXPLAIN PLAN *utility, page 445*

Avoid Transformation Where Possible

If you can, avoid using the SQL functions that cast column information to a different data type—for example, numerical text information to a NUMBER. Also, avoid character information where you pull out a specific range of characters. When using the WHERE clause, make sure that the comparison is done on two variables of the same data type.

A good example of what to avoid is the case where you're comparing an integer value with a character numerical value. By default, the optimizer will convert the character data to an integer before comparing, which will cause the SQL statement to fail if a row of character data doesn't translate to an integer. To avoid this, you should cast the integer value as a character value by using the to_char function, as in the following WHERE clause:

1 Declared as a VARCHAR2

2 Declared as a NUMBER

```
WHERE
    OrderNumber = to_char(order_index);
```

Keep SQL Statements Single Purpose

A long time ago there was a book out that contained a collection of programs written in a single line of the BASIC programming language. Because BASIC can do multiple things within a single line, it was possible to encapsulate an entire program in the context of one programming line.

Although these programs worked, they were probably some of the worst examples of software design that have ever existed. Remember that when writing your SQL queries.

Although it's possible to have a single SQL statement perform multiple operations, it's not always the best thing when you're working on improving system performance. Keep your queries to the point and single-tracked; watch out for SQL statements that do different things based on the data being selected. These types of operations bypass the optimizer and in many cases don't run as efficiently as they should.

Make Use of Optimizer Hints

By using optimizer *hints* (such as FULL, ROWID, and HASH), you can steer the optimizer down a particular data access path. Because you know the data and application better than the optimizer does, sometimes you'll override what the optimizer wants to do. By using hints, you can change the way the optimizer accesses data and therefore possibly speed up a query. (You can also slow down a query if it's not done right, so be careful!)

Create Extra Tables for Reference When Necessary

Sometimes you need to use the IN clause to select a group of rows. Suppose you're working at the Internal Revenue Service, and you want to list all the athletes you have in your database. Your query would look something like the following:

```
Select name, gross, occupation from taxpayer
    where
        occupation in ('BOWLER', 'GOLFER', 'BASEBALL PLAYER',
                    'FOOTBALL PLAYER');
```

Be careful when using SELECT with IN

Another possible performance killer is the use of a **SELECT** statement within an **IN** clause. You want to avoid the situation where **SELECT** could return hundreds or even thousands of rows, each one of which is processed with the **IN** clause.

Do you see the problem? You would have a very long list of sports-related occupations to add, and the query would be very long and inefficient. Although there's really no way to tune the query, what you could do is create another table in the database called OCCUPATION_TYPE that would list each occupation name and the type of job that it is. The WHERE clause in your query now becomes

```
WHERE
    Occupation_type = 'ATHLETE';
```

Not only will this run faster, but you won't have to worry about changing your query when a new type of sport gets added.

Combine *INSERT* and *UPDATE* operations

This suggestion is very simple to implement and has a good performance gain. When selecting data and updating it, you can combine those operations into a single SQL statement, so that the data being updated is read from the database only once. This reduces the number of calls to the database server, thereby increasing the performance of the query.

Index Tuning

Consider hash clusters when indexing

Hash clusters group data in the tables by applying a hash algorithm to the cluster key value of each table row. Hash clusters are very useful in the situation where tables are accessed with a **WHERE** clause. Performance can be better than just using an index.

To make the most out of database indexes, you might be adding more indexes or even dropping some. The common thought among software developers is that things will always run faster when using an index. But that's true only most of the time. If there are many indexes on a single set of Oracle data, there comes a point of diminishing returns, and the indexes could actually cause a performance bottleneck. So keep in mind that indexes aren't an answer to poorly written queries—they should be used with efficient code to get the most out of the Oracle Server.

Data Tuning

Believe it or not, how you store the raw data within the database can affect performance. This is particularly true when you're dealing with distributed data and are performing joins over the network. If that's the case, you can minimize processing time by keeping the data local as well by using replication. Also, partitioning the data helps as well by distributing the data across multiple disk drives that can be read in parallel.

Shared SQL

Sometimes you have different users executing the same or similar queries against the database. Each statement is parsed out and uses its own space in the shared pool. If two users submit the exact same query, however, Oracle stores only one copy of the parsed query in the SGA, and that one copy is shared among the processes making that query. This is a performance gain because of the space that this frees up in the SGA—space that can be used for other processing.

Look at the steps that Oracle takes to determine if a query already has an identical copy resident in the shared area:

- First, Oracle takes the query and compares its hash value to that of all the other statements in the shared pool. If it finds a match, Oracle then compares the text of the query to the text of the other queries in the shared pool. The following group of SQL statements all return the same data, but are handled as completely different by Oracle and don't share space in the SGA:

```
SQL> SELECT PLAYER, POSITION FROM TEAM;
SQL> SELECT PLAYER, POSITION  FROM TEAM;
SQL> select player, position from team;
SQL> Select player, position from team;
```

- Oracle then compares the objects referenced in the statement to make sure that they're referencing the same physical objects within the database. Suppose that two users have loaded the demo tables into their personal schemas and are performing the same query on the EMP table. Even though the text is exactly the same, the query is referencing two distinct tables and is treated as two separate queries by the database.

Put common SQL into the shared pool

Take your most common SQL and create stored procedures, which are automatically shared when multiple users execute them. Stored procedures also are parsed only once and stored in memory as parsed. Performance is improved through the elimination of reparsing.

Keep SQL text consistent

When Oracle compares the SQL text, to find a match with an existing statement it must match exactly. The case of each character must be the same, and spaces must match exactly as well. If not, Oracle treats the text as two distinct SQL statements.

- Lastly, the bind variable names in each statement—if they're used—must match exactly. The following shows two SQL statements that do the same thing but aren't shared in the pool:

```
SQL> SELECT * FROM TEAM WHERE NUMBER = :PLAYERNUM;
SQL> SELECT * FROM TEAM WHERE NUMBER = :PLAYERNO;
```

Although the bind variable in the example references the NUMBER field of the TEAM table, it won't be shared in the shared pool because the two queries aren't syntactically the same. Develop a common naming convention for bind variables.

The benefit of shared SQL isn't really that two statements are sharing space in the shared pool; the real benefit comes when you have many application users running the same queries. That's why it's important to keep in mind shared SQL when writing your applications. When you get into the hundreds of users and the same SQL statements aren't shared among the users, you'll end up increasing the size of your shared pool unnecessarily.

The benefit of programming standards

If you get your developers together and decide on some common approaches to writing programs that access the Oracle Server, you can take advantage of being able to share SQL code within the SGA. Although it might be beneficial to change applications so that they use the same queries, you could define a few standards the developers would use and if they're submitting the same query. For example, you can define whether to use upper-case or lowercase and how they're spaced. Oracle will detect the similarity and share them because they will match all the criteria for sharing SQL.

Keeping Shared SQL in the Shared Pool

Now that you've created identical SQL statements and they're being shared, you'll want to take steps to help ensure that they stay in the shared pool. You want to make sure that they're not knocked out of the shared pool because of the LRU (least recently used) algorithm used on the shared pool to keep the pool current. You also want to make sure that a large PL/SQL package being read into the shared pool doesn't overwrite your shared SQL statements. Take a quick look at how to prevent these two things from happening.

How to Handle Large Allocations of Shared Pool

The problem here is when a large PL/SQL script is being loaded for the first time, or that same script was loaded, was knocked out of shared pool because of non-use, and is being reloaded. This has the tendency to cause some of the smaller SQL statements in the shared pool to be knocked out of the shared pool because of the LRU algorithm.

What you can do to prevent this is to use the INIT.ORA parameters to reserve space for large allocations. If this is done, the large allocations will be done in a reserved section of the shared pool and won't overwrite the other statements in the pool. This is done with two initialization parameters: SHARED_POOL_RESERVED_SIZE and SHARED_POOL_RESERVED_SIZE_MIN_ALLOC

First, set SHARED_POOL_RESERVED_SIZE to reserve a chunk of shared pool memory for large allocations. Next, set SHARED_POOL_ RESERVED_SIZE_MIN_ALLOC to the smallest value you want allocated in the reserved space. This means that any request for shared pool larger than the SHARED_POOL_ RESERVED_SIZE_MIN_ALLOC parameter will be allocated in the reserved memory, thus protecting the smaller statements from being pushed out.

Keeping Objects in the Shared Pool

Even if you use the parameters listed in the previous section, this won't prevent commonly used SQL statements from being aged out of the shared pool. There's something you can do about it, however.

You'll want to check out the package DBMS_SHARED_POOL package. You create this package and package body by executing the DBMSPOOL.SQL and PRVTPOOL.PLB scripts, located in the /rdbms/admin directory under ORACLE_HOME. When you use this package, you can load objects into memory early, before memory fragmentation begins, and they can stay there for the duration.

It's the DBMS_SHARED_POOL package that you use to pin a SQL or PL/SQL area. By pinning (locking in memory) large objects, you increase system performance in two ways:

- Response time doesn't slow as the larger objects are read into the shared pool.
- It's less likely that the smaller SQL areas will be aged out to make room for a much larger one.

Sizing the shared pool

Having a large shared pool takes away some of the issues regarding fitting objects into the shared pool. The INIT.ORA parameter **SHARED_POOL_SIZE** sets the size of the pool. You should make it as large as is reasonable, without making it so big that you waste system memory.

To pin objects in the shared pool, decide what you want to pin, start up the database, and then run DBMS_SHARED_POOL.KEEP.

Three procedures come with the DBMS_SHARED_POOL package:

- DBMS_SHARED_POOL.SIZES displays the objects in the shared pool that are larger than the size passed in as a parameter.

- DBMS_SHARED_POOL.KEEP pins a SQL or PL/SQL area in memory.

- DBMS_SHARED_POOL.UNKEEP marks a pinned object as available to be aged out. It's the opposite of the KEEP function, but doesn't actually remove the pinned object from the shared pool.

Speeding Up Access to the Shared SQL Area

Now that you know how to get your SQL into the shared pool and keep it in memory, look at how you can increase the speed of the shared SQL area of the SGA. An INIT.ORA parameter called CURSOR_SPACE_FOR_TIME can speed up execution calls on systems that have a large shared pool and plenty of free memory. It's a parameter set to TRUE or FALSE, and should be used only if your library cache misses on execution calls whose count is 0.

Keep an eye on library cache misses

You don't want to set CURSOR_SPACE_FOR_TIME to TRUE if you're seeing library cache misses. Performance will get worse if you do, and statements may begin failing with out-of-shared-pool errors.

If you have no library cache misses and you set the CURSOR_SPACE_FOR_TIME parameter to TRUE, you'll see a slight performance improvement on execution calls. The way it works is as follows: When the parameter is set to TRUE, a shared SQL area won't be deallocated until all cursors associated with the shared SQL statement have been closed. This saves some time because Oracle doesn't have to check to see if the statement is still in the shared pool when performing an execution call.

SQL and PL/SQL Parsing Reduction

Another tool you can use to increase throughput of your SQL and PL/SQL objects is to tune the private SQL and PL/SQL areas. You can do this by reducing the number of parse calls made to the database. Again, this tuning technique is for systems with available free memory, because reducing parsing by the means suggested in the following sections will require more memory and a larger shared pool.

How to Identify Unnecessary Parse Calls

You need to find out the number of SQL execution calls being parsed compared with the number of statements being executed. Two Oracle tables can help you in this task: V$SQLAREA and V$SESSTAT.

V$SQLAREA

The V$SQLAREA view contains information on the SQL statements in the shared SQL area. One row in this view constitutes one SQL statement. It provides statistics on SQL statements already in memory, parsed and ready for execution. The V$SQLAREA view contains the following field names:

```
SQL> describe V$SQLAREA;
 Name                            Null?    Type
 ------------------------------- -------- ----
 SQL_TEXT                                 VARCHAR2(1000)
 SHARABLE_MEM                             NUMBER
 PERSISTENT_MEM                           NUMBER
 RUNTIME_MEM                              NUMBER
 SORTS                                    NUMBER
 VERSION_COUNT                            NUMBER
 LOADED_VERSIONS                          NUMBER
 OPEN_VERSIONS                            NUMBER
 USERS_OPENING                            NUMBER
 EXECUTIONS                               NUMBER
 USERS_EXECUTING                          NUMBER
 LOADS                                    NUMBER
 FIRST_LOAD_TIME                          VARCHAR2(19)
 INVALIDATIONS                            NUMBER
 PARSE_CALLS                              NUMBER
 DISK_READS                               NUMBER
 BUFFER_GETS                              NUMBER
 ROWS_PROCESSED                           NUMBER
 COMMAND_TYPE                             NUMBER
 OPTIMIZER_MODE                           VARCHAR2(25)
 PARSING_USER_ID                          NUMBER
```

```
PARSING_SCHEMA_ID                    NUMBER
KEPT_VERSIONS                        NUMBER
ADDRESS                              RAW(4)
HASH_VALUE                           NUMBER
MODULE                               VARCHAR2(64)
MODULE_HASH                          NUMBER
ACTION                               VARCHAR2(64)
ACTION_HASH                          NUMBER
SERIALIZABLE_ABORTS                  NUMBER
```

For your purposes, in this section you'll be concerned only with the SQL_TEXT, PARSE_CALLS, and EXECUTIONS fields. The SQL_TEXT field contains the actual text of the SQL statement being executed. The PARSE_CALLS field is the number of times the statement has been parsed, and the EXECUTIONS field is the number of times the statement was executed.

Try the following SQL_TEXT query on one of your databases to get the parsing information:

```
SQL> SELECT SQL_TEXT, PARSE_CALLS, EXECUTIONS
  2> FROM V$SQLTEXT;
```

V$SESSTAT

The V$SESSTAT view stores statistics on the individual user sessions. The individual statistics are stored by number, so you need to query the V$STATNAME view with the statistic name to get the corresponding number. In Oracle8, this table contains more than 200 statistic names. For now, however, you'll be concerned only with the PARSE_COUNT and EXECUTE_COUNT statistics.

First, get the statistic numbers for parse and execute counts. Start by executing the following two queries:

```
SQL> SELECT STATISTIC#, NAME FROM V$STATNAME
       WHERE NAME IN ('parse count (hard)','execute count');
```

You'll see output such as this:

```
SQL> SELECT STATISTIC#, NAME FROM V$STATNAME
  2> WHERE NAME IN ('parse count (hard)','execute count');


STATISTIC# NAME
---------- -------------------------------------------------
```

Interpreting parses versus executions

Look carefully at the ratio of parses to executions of the individual SQL statement. If the number or parses for any statement is close to the number of executions, that means you're continually reparsing that statement.

```
153 parse count (hard)
154 execute count
```

From this output you can tell that the parse count statistic is number 153 and the execute count statistic is number 154.

Now look at the V$SESSTAT view, which has only three fields:

```
SQL> describe v$sesstat;
Name                            Null?    Type
------------------------------- -------- ----
SID                                      NUMBER
STATISTIC#                               NUMBER
VALUE                                    NUMBER
```

Select the parse and execution statistics for all connected Oracle sessions with the following query:

```
SQL> select * from v$sesstat
  2  where statistic# in (153,154)
  3  order by sid, statistic#;
```

This query lists out (by session) the parse count and execution count for each session. You're looking for sessions where the two statistical values are closer rather than further apart. The closer in value the two statistics are, the more potential there is to reduce unnecessary parsing. The output of the query is as follows:

```
SID STATISTIC#      VALUE
---------- ---------- ----------
         1        153          0
         1        154          0
         2        153          0
         2        154          0
         3        153          0
         3        154          0
         4        153          0
         4        154          0
         5        153          0
         5        154          0
         6        153          5

SID STATISTIC#      VALUE
---------- ---------- ----------
```

6	154	46
7	153	1
7	154	14
8	153	52
8	154	395

```
16 rows selected.
```

Oracle Performance Pack

A great tool for interpreting database statistics is Oracle's Performance Pack, which provides a graphical interface to database statistics such as cache rates, disk I/O, and SQL performance.

In the output, look at session ID 8; it had 395 execution calls but only 52 parses. You'll want to find sessions where the parse count is much higher to reduce unnecessary parsing. (This query was run against the test database, which unfortunately doesn't have much of a user load, but this is the query you use to get this information.)

Reducing Unnecessary Parsing

The key to eliminating unnecessary parsing is how you handle the cursors. This is especially true when you're using explicit cursors.

When using explicit cursors, be sure to avoid the situation where you open and close cursors in a loop. Moving the open and close statements outside the loop will keep the statement from being reparsed. Your program also should DECLARE the cursor, reOPEN it each time the value of a host variable changes, and CLOSE the cursor only after the SQL statement is no longer required.

Remember also that when you're using MODE=ANSI with the precompilers, a COMMIT command will close a cursor.

The cursor-management functions HOLD_CURSOR, RELEASE CURSOR, and MAXOPENCURSORS give you additional power in how to control the parsing and reparsing of SQL statements. In a nutshell, these commands help you control how Oracle handles the creation and uses cursors. You use these commands to keep cursors to prevent reparsing and to remove cursors to save memory.

Using Array Processing

Using host arrays in a program is useful when you're updating multiple rows of a table. You get a real performance gain if the rows are contiguous.

You define the arrays the same way you would any other programming array. For example, look at an array of size 100 for the three fields of the table TEAM:

```
int     uniform_no[100];
char    player_name[100][25];
int     position[100];
```

Oracle8 supports only single-dimensional arrays. The player_name array is single dimensional; the 25 is simply the maximum size of each string. The benefit here comes in how you can update the table after the arrays are populated.

Rather than use a FOR loop to update the table in the following example:

```
FOR (counter = 0; counter <=100; counter++)
    EXEC SQL INSERT INTO TEAM
                (uniform_no,player_name,position)
                VALUES(:uniform_no[counter],
                :player_name[counter],
                :position[counter]);
```

you could pass just the array name to the EXEC statement. Oracle not only updates the table with all the elements in the arrays, but also does it as a single operation.

In the preceding example, 100 insert statements are executed. Look at the new code:

```
EXEC SQL INSERT INTO TEAM (uniform_no,player_name,position)
    VALUES(:uniform_no, :player_name, :position);
```

The loop is no longer necessary, and you have a much nicer looking piece of code.

Handling NULL values in a program

You also can use *indicator arrays* to assign NULLs to variables in input host arrays, and to detect NULL or truncated values in output host arrays. Check the Oracle documentation for more information on indicator arrays.

CHAPTER

20

Tuning Your Memory Structures and File Access

How often is Oracle finding data in cache?

Would more memory increase the database's speed?

How large should the shared pool be?

Is disk I/O well spread out across data files?

Are redo logs configured properly?

Would Multithread Server be of value?

Why Oracle Must Be Tuned

One of Oracle8's strongest assets is its rich tuning facility. Oracle8 offers a staggering array of parameters that you can tune to achieve maximum performance for any database system. Because every database has different data structures and different transaction loads, you can maximize the return on your hardware investment only by tuning Oracle. This will minimize the total cost of ownership for your database system and provide users the maximum performance Oracle can deliver.

Although there may be no need initially to dive into the full array of tuning parameters for acceptable performance, the need will become more acute as a database becomes larger and services more transactions. Oracle, out of the box, is tuned to run acceptably well on systems with low memory and CPU resources; most databases of any significant size should be tuned before being considered production quality.

Database Buffer Cache

Beware of swapping

When allocating a larger database buffer cache, pay attention to whether the operating system is swapping real memory pages to disk to alleviate a memory shortage. Swapping is terribly expensive and will, by far, outweigh any benefit you gain from an oversized buffer cache.

Disk I/O operations are hideously expensive when compared to I/O operations performed in memory. In fact, reading information from memory is often thousands of times faster than when reading from disk. Oracle capitalizes on this by caching the most recently used database blocks in a memory segment that resides in the SGA. This memory block is known as the *database buffer cache*, or sometimes as just the *buffer cache*.

When tuning the database buffer cache, bigger is usually better. The more database blocks that Oracle can keep in memory, the faster it will perform. When allocating more memory to the database buffer cache, be aware that as the buffer *hit ratio* approaches 100 percent, it will take increasingly larger amounts of additional memory for the buffer cache's hit ratio to increase noticeably.

Most active database systems have a discernible *working set* of very frequently used database blocks. When tuning a database, the goal is to keep at least the working set of database buffers in memory to maintain acceptable performance. Not surprisingly, as a database grows larger, it will need a larger buffer cache to maintain the same *hit ratio*.

Examining Performance

We're interested in knowing the hit ratio of the buffer cache for a database. To determine this, we must know the number of

- Consistent gets
- Logical block reads
- Physical block reads

The hit ratio is computed as follows:

```
(consistent gets + logical reads - physical reads)
  / (consistent gets + logical reads)
```

The V$SYSSTAT table contains all the needed information since the database was last started. This table is easily accessed through SQL*Plus; the following example uses SQL*Plus to find the database buffer cache hit ratio:

① ```
SQL> SELECT ((SUM(DECODE(NAME, 'consistent gets', VALUE, 0))+
SUM(DECODE(NAME,'db block gets',VALUE, 0)) -
```
**②** ```
SUM(DECODE(NAME,'physical reads',VALUE,0))) /
(SUM(DECODE(NAME, 'consistent gets', VALUE, 0))+
SUM(DECODE(NAME,'db block gets',VALUE, 0))) * 100) "Hit Ratio"
FROM V$SYSSTAT;
Hit Ratio
----------
77.0755025
1 row selected.
SQL>
```

Ideally, a database running OLTP-type transactions should see a hit ratio of 90 percent or more. During long-running batch jobs, the hit ratio may fall into the 70–80 percent range. Anything lower than 70 percent may indicate that a larger database buffer cache is needed.

Many DBAs who are familiar with other database systems on the market will find queries against V$ views to gather performance statistics crude and time-consuming. Fortunately, Oracle has

---

Consistent gets

Consistent gets are logical block reads associated with Oracle's read consistency system. When rollback segment blocks must be read to provide read consistency, they're not included in the normal logical block reads statistic.

---

① Used to read rows from V$SYSSTAT table

② Used to read the value associated with each specified parameter

companion packs for its Enterprise Manager system that will show, graphically, a database's performance health. These tools can also go a long way toward helping you tune your database(s) for optimum performance. Third-party vendors, including BMC and Platinum, offer similar tools that also work quite well for non-Oracle databases; these tools are particularly well suited for DBAs supporting a heterogeneous database environment.

Testing New Buffer Cache Settings

Allocating a larger database buffer cache often also means adding memory to the database server. Before writing a purchase order, it's often useful—if not necessary—to know the benefit more memory will bring to the database.

Oracle8 has a utility that lets you see the effect on the buffer cache hit ratio after a hypothetical change in the size of the buffer cache. By enabling the DB_BLOCK_LRU_EXTENDED_STATISTICS parameter in the INIT.ORA file, Oracle8 will record the hypothetical statistics in the following tables:

Impact of DB_BLOCK_LRU_STATISTICS

Be aware that **DB_BLOCK_LRU_EXTENDED_STATISTICS** has a noticeable impact on Oracle's internal overhead. Don't run **DB_BLOCK_LRU_EXTENDED_STATISTICS** any longer than you must to gather the needed statistics.

- x$kcbrbh records "what-if" statistics to show the number of additional cache hits for each additional block added to the database buffer cache. In this table, the following fields are of interest:

  INDX   Identifies each new phantom block for which you're collecting statistics

  COUNT   Indicates how many additional cache hits would occur if the block number INDX were added to the database buffer cache

- x$kcbcbh records hypothetical statistics to show the effect of reducing the size of the database buffer cache. As this utility is very rarely used, its use isn't covered in this chapter. Oracle's documentation should be consulted for further information.

Enable *DB_BLOCK_LRU_EXTENDED_STATISTICS*

1. Edit the appropriate INIT.ORA file and add the following line:

```
DB_BLOCK_LRU_EXTENDED_STATISTICS = additional buffers
```

2. Shut down the database.

3. Restart the database.

Disable *DB_BLOCK_LRU_EXTENDED_STATISTICS*

1. Edit the appropriate INIT.ORA file and remove the following line:

```
DB_BLOCK_LRU_EXTENDED_STATISTICS = number
```

2. Shut down the database.

3. Restart the database.

Calculating a New Hit Ratio from Additional Buffer Cache

The database is now running an OLTP application that achieves only an 81 percent database buffer cache hit ratio. Let's test the effect on the hit ratio by adding 2,048 blocks to the buffer cache.

First, you set the number of hypothetical new buffers. Use an operating system editor to edit the INIT.ORA file to include the following line:

```
DB_BLOCK_LRU_EXTENDED_STATISTICS = 2048
```

Next, shut down and restart the database. Server Manager is run from the operating system command line. The shutdown and startup session is as follows:

```
SVRMGR> connect internal;

Connected.

SVRMGR> shutdown immediate;

Database closed.
Database dismounted.
ORACLE instance shut down.

SVRMGR> startup

ORACLE instance started.
Database mounted.
Database opened.

SVRMGR>
```

At this time, either normal OLTP database operations should resume or test scripts should be run to simulate normal database load. In either case, make sure that enough realistic activity occurs for the database buffer cache hit ratio to stabilize.

Now calculate the number of additional hypothetical cache hits for all 2,048 phantom database buffers, as shown in this Server Manager session:

```
SVRMGR> SELECT SUM(COUNT) FROM X$KCBRBH;
SUM(COUNT)
- - - - - - - - - -
     43712
1 row selected.
SVRMGR>
```

We now know that 43,712 additional cache hits would occur if the buffer cache were enlarged by 2,048 blocks (rather than force physical reads).

Finally, you need to calculate the hypothetical cache hit ratio. Let's use the same formula used in the last section to compute the cache hit ratio, but this time subtract 43,712 phantom cache hits from the actual physical reads as shown:

```
SVRMGR> SELECT ((SUM(DECODE(NAME, 'consistent gets',
    2> VALUE, 0))+
    3> SUM(DECODE(NAME,'db block gets',VALUE, 0)) -
    4> (SUM(DECODE(NAME,'physical reads',VALUE,0))) -
    5> 43712) / (SUM(DECODE(NAME, 'consistent gets',
    6> VALUE, 0))+SUM(DECODE(NAME,'db block gets',VALUE,
    7> 0))) * 100) "Hit Ratio" FROM V$SYSSTAT;
Hit Ratio
- - - - - - - - - -
92.2935720
1 row selected.
SVRMGR>
```

You can see here that adding 2,048 blocks to the database buffer cache would cause the cache hit ratio to increase from 81–92 percent.

Change the size of the database buffer cache

1. Use any standard operating system text file editor to change the DB_BLOCK_BUFFERS parameter in the INIT.ORA file to reflect the size of the buffer cache in database blocks.

Using X$ tables

X$ tables are owned by the SYS user and usually don't have public synonyms established. These examples use Server Manager because connect internal always connects as the SYS user. You can run these same queries from SQL*Plus, as long as you log in as the SYS user.

What's the next step?

Knowing that there would be a very noticeable rise in the database buffer cache hit ratio, you would want to add 2,048 to the DB_BLOCK_BUFFERS parameter in the INIT.ORA file. Don't forget to turn off DB_BLOCK_LRU_EXTENDED_STATISTICS!

2. Stop the database.

3. Restart the database.

Example of Enlarging the Buffer Cache by 2,048 Blocks

The current INIT.ORA file has the following parameter line:

```
DB_BLOCK_BUFFERS = 8192
```

In the example from the preceding section, it was determined that adding 2,048 blocks would help improve database response time. Now edit the INIT.ORA file to contain these lines:

```
#
# This setting was changed on 2 FEB 98 by TMG x3707. Buffer
# Cache hit ratio rose from 81% to 92% by increasing it
# 2048 blocks
# DB_BLOCK_BUFFERS = 8192
#
DB_BLOCK_BUFFERS = 10240
```

Whenever the `DB_BLOCK_BUFFERS` parameter is changed, the database will have to be shut down and restarted for the changes to take effect.

Comment INIT.ORA file changes

When you're diagnosing sudden changes in the database's performance or reliability, it's often invaluable to know what crucial parameters were changed recently. Any time parameters are changed in INIT.ORA, you should add at least a one-line description of the change, who made it, and when it was done.

Tuning the Shared Pool

Oracle8's shared pool contains the following:

- Execution plans for recent SQL statements, known as the library cache
- Data dictionary cache
- Some miscellaneous session information

LRU in the shared pool

The shared pool, like most of Oracle's caches, is organized in an LRU manner. The information least recently used is purged to make room for new information when the cache is full.

Recall that every SQL statement executed by the database engine must be parsed, evaluated, and executed. This process is relatively time-consuming, because Oracle8 has very sophisticated methods for determining the optimum execution plan. By caching execution plans and the data dictionary, Oracle8 can quickly execute similar SQL statements by retrieving preprocessed execution plans and data dictionary information from the shared pool.

The goal of tuning the shared pool will be to achieve a +95 percent hit ratio on the library cache and a 95–100 percent hit ratio on the data dictionary cache during all operations.

Examining Library Cache Performance

The V$LIBRARYCACHE view contains information on the library cache, including cache hit statistics. The cache hit ratio is determined by issuing the following SQL statement:

```
SELECT SUM(PINS)/(SUM(PINS)+SUM(RELOADS))*100
   "Cache Hit Ratio"
FROM V$LIBRARYCACHE;
```

SQL*Plus will reply with a single row and column that will be the library cache hit ratio.

Example of Calculating the Library Cache Hit Ratio

The following command is issued after you log on to SQL*Plus as a DBA user (the SYSTEM user in this case):

```
SQL> SELECT SUM(PINS)/(SUM(PINS)+SUM(RELOADS))*100
  2   "Cache Hit Ratio"
  3  FROM V$LIBRARYCACHE;

Cache Hit Ratio
---------------
    99.8039216

SQL>
```

Here we can see the library cache hit ratio is almost 100 percent, which is ideal. If the library cache hit ratio were lower than 95 percent, you would probably want to add memory to the shared pool.

Examining Data Dictionary Cache Performance

Data dictionary cache statistics are kept in the V$ROWCACHE view, which categorizes data dictionary cache statistics. However, most DBAs will benefit most from knowing an aggregate hit/miss percentage with the following SQL statement:

```
SELECT (1-(SUM(GETMISSES)/SUM(COUNT)))*100
   "Dictionary Cache Hit Ratio"
FROM V$ROWCACHE;
```

This statement will return the data dictionary cache hit ratio since the database was last started.

Example of Calculating the Data Dictionary Cache Hit Ratio

The following command is issued after you log on to SQL*Plus as a DBA user (the SYSTEM user in this case):

```
SQL> SELECT (1-(SUM(GETMISSES)/SUM(COUNT)))*100
  2   "Dictionary Cache Hit Ratio"
  3   FROM V$ROWCACHE;


Dictionary Cache Hit Ratio
--------------------------
                63.1687243

SQL>
```

Notice that the dictionary cache hit ratio is only 63 percent—far below the ideal ratio of 99 percent and the acceptable threshold of 95 percent. In this case, the shared spool size almost certainly must be increased.

Setting New Shared Pool Parameter Values

Although we examine the shared pool in library cache and data dictionary cache steps, adding memory to either is accomplished by adding memory (in bytes) to the shared pool with the SHARED_POOL_SIZE parameter in the applicable INIT.ORA file. The following line would allocate 3,500,000 bytes (~3.5MB) to an instance's shared pool. This is the default setting found in an INIT.ORA file:

```
shared_pool_size = 3500000
```

Choosing new sizes for the shared pool is something more akin to art than science. Based on the library and data dictionary cache hit ratios, you may need to increase the shared pool perhaps just 25 percent, or to many times the default size.

Considerations with low hit ratios

When a low hit ratio is encountered, always consider how long the database has been up and running. If a database was just started or started a while ago with little or no subsequent application activity, it's very likely that Oracle simply hasn't had the opportunity to cache the information it will need. Oracle caches information only when it's needed; all information contained in the cache was preceded by at least one cache miss.

Library versus data dictionary cache allocation

Oracle8 automatically proportions the shared pool into data dictionary and library cache segments. You can't adjust their respective sizes manually. If either cache hit ratio falls below par, you must increase the size of the shared pool.

When choosing new shared pool sizes, be aware that it will usually take a much larger increase in memory to increase a cache hit ratio from 90 to 95 percent than from 70 to 80 percent.

Change the size of the shared pool

1. Modify the SHARED_POOL_SIZE parameter in the appropriate INIT.ORA file. The following sets the shared pool to 16MB:

```
#
# Original setting increased to 16MB. Library cache hit
# ratio was 61%.
# TMG: 21 Jan 98
# shared_pool_size = 3500000
SHARED_POOL_SIZE = 16777216
```

2. Stop the database.

3. Restart the database.

Redo Log Buffer

The redo log subsystem is probably one of the most heavily accessed components of Oracle; every change to the database system must go through it. Spooling all changes directly to disk would impair transaction throughput, so Oracle8 buffers redo log information in the SGA to better utilize precious I/O resources.

Considerations for SMP systems

In addition to the redo log buffer size, SMP database DBAs must also consider the number of latches needed to prevent latch contention when accessing the redo log buffer area. Consult Oracle's documentation for information on the V$LATCH view.

It's important to size the redo log buffer appropriately to avoid user database processes from having to wait on space in the buffer to continue operations. During high update transaction rates, the log writer process may not be able to keep up with several user processes all submitting redo log information that must be written. The redo log buffer holds redo log information so that user processes can continue; as the log writer process catches up, it will purge information from the redo log buffer.

Examining Performance

When tuning the redo log buffer, focus on these statistics in the V$SYSSTAT view:

- `redo log space requests` is the number of times user processes had to wait for space to become available in the redo log buffer. Ideally, this parameter will be zero; in practice, however, it's acceptable for a few user processes to wait on space in large systems. Size the redo log buffer to keep redo log allocation waits close to zero.

- `redo buffer allocation retries` is the number of times the redo writer had to stop and wait for the log writer to finish writing dirty buffers. Again, this parameter should be zero; however, a low number is acceptable on larger systems.

Use the following SQL command to gather redo log statistics:

```
SELECT NAME,VALUE FROM V$SYSSTAT WHERE NAME IN
('redo buffer allocation retries','redo log space requests');
```

The result of this query will be two rows listing the value of each parameter.

Example of Redo Log Performance Evaluation

The preceding command is issued and the result is shown in the following sample SQL*Plus session for a DBA user (SYSTEM in this case):

```
SQL> SELECT NAME,VALUE FROM V$SYSSTAT WHERE NAME IN
  2  ('redo buffer allocation retries',
  3  'redo log space requests');

NAME                                               VALUE
-------------------------------------------------- ----------
redo buffer allocation retries                       835
redo log space requests                              508

SQL>
```

Because both statistics are quite high in this case, it is advisable to add memory to the redo log buffers.

Set new redo log buffer parameters

Guidelines for LOG_BUFFER
values

Oracle's default will depend on your
platform and database version.
Typically, however, the default is too
small. 64KB to 128KB will usually
work out well for smaller databases.
512KB to 1MB (or even more) may
be needed on larger database systems.

1. Change the LOG_BUFFER parameter in the appropriate
   INIT.ORA file to the new size of the redo log buffer, in
   bytes. Any text file editor may be used for this purpose.

2. Stop the database.

3. Restart the database.

Example of Setting *LOG_BUFFER* in INIT.ORA

The following INIT.ORA file section was changed in an operating system-supplied text editor to increase the size of the
LOG_BUFFER parameter from 16KB to 256KB:

```
#
# 16k Proved to be too small. Increased the size to 256k
# TMG: 03 Mar 98
# LOG_BUFFER = 16384
#
LOG_BUFFER = 262144
```

Process Global Area

Whenever a connection is made to an Oracle database, a unique
section of memory is allocated to store session-level information.
The area of memory allocated for each session is known as the
Process Global Area (PGA).

Tuning the PGA is largely done to allow Oracle to scale well
based on hardware constraints and the needs and use patterns of
the predominate applications. As more and more users begin to
utilize a particular database, it will become more important to
ensure that Oracle is tuned to scale as well as possible with a
given hardware configuration.

Comparing Dedicated Versus Shared Servers

Oracle8 offers two different options for managing each session
connected to the database:

- *Dedicated Server* will create a new server process for each
  connection to the database. This is Oracle's default behavior.

■ *Multithreaded Server* creates a finite number of server processes shared between all the individual connections to the database.

You can achieve the best performance by using the dedicated server process. Because no sharing of the server processes exists, when a database session needs to access the database, a ready server process is guaranteed to service its needs.

In environments where there could be many hundreds or even thousands of simultaneous connections to the database, Multithreaded Server can offer better scalability. Short and infrequent queries are often made to the database server in OLTP environments. In the dedicated server model, each session (which may go for hours between database activity) will have its own server process waiting for SQL commands to execute. Each server uses a quantity of system memory and a slot in the operating system's process table, so there's a real limit to the number of the server processes that may be running at any given time. By using a fixed pool of server processes, you can continue to add concurrent users without consuming any more system memory.

Multithreaded Server's downside exists precisely for the reason it offers increased scalability. Each server process can service only one database connection at a time (despite the deceiving "multi-threaded" adjective); if more connections need servers than there are servers available, the additional connections must wait until a server process becomes available. Obviously, perceived performance can suffer noticeably when a client must wait for a server process to become available.

Managing Sort Space

Sorting will occur if an SQL statement includes ORDER BY or GROUP BY. It can, however, also occur when joining tables and various other Oracle internal operations. Although much can be done to improve sorting performance, the best way to increase performance is to eliminate sorts in the first place when possible.

When Oracle must sort a set of data, it must use a temporary workspace to create the sorted list. Oracle can use two locations:

Use multithreaded only when necessary

Many DBAs mistakenly believe that Oracle's multithreaded server (MTS) will perform better than the dedicated model. This is usually the result of contemporary lingo that almost always associates "multithreaded" with faster. In reality, MTS will slow a database's operation overall. MTS can drastically increase the number of concurrent database sessions—that is the only advantage it offers. Don't use MTS unless scalability requirements dictate its use.

Setting up MTS

Installing and configuring Multithreaded Server can be a rather complex task that's outside the scope of this book. Refer to Oracle's product documentation for installation and configuration instructions.

- Memory
- A segment in the user's defined TEMPORARY TABLESPACE on disk

As you can imagine, sorting in memory is much faster than sorting on disk. The SORT_AREA_SIZE parameter in the INIT.ORA file describes, in bytes, the amount of space available to each server process for performing sorts in memory.

The V$SYSSTAT view keeps statistics on the number of sorts performed in memory and on disk. Use the following SQL statement to retrieve sorting statistics:

```
SELECT NAME,VALUE FROM V$SYSSTAT WHERE
NAME LIKE 'sort%';
```

OLTP applications should perform almost no sorts on disk (user response is paramount). DSS systems may see larger sorts running on disk but, if possible, these too should be run in memory for the best possible performance.

Tune the database for sorting

1. Query the V$SYSSTAT view to determine the number of sorts performed in memory and on disk.

2. If fewer sorts on disk are desired, increase the SORT_AREA_SIZE parameter in the appropriate INIT.ORA file.

3. Stop and restart the database.

4. Allow the database to run at least a full business day for accurate sorting statistics to be gathered.

5. Repeat this procedure until the number of sorts performed on disk is acceptable.

Example of Tuning the Sort Space

The following SQL*Plus session shows the V$SYSSTAT view being checked by the SYSTEM user:

```
SQL> SELECT NAME,VALUE FROM V$SYSSTAT WHERE
  2  NAME LIKE 'sort%';

NAME                                  VALUE
------------------------------- ----------
sorts (memory)                         2922
```

When to read statistics

As with all other statistics, be sure to allow Oracle and the predominate applications to run for a fair amount of time before acting on any statistics gathered. If Oracle and the associated application(s) haven't run long enough (a full business day is typical), the values retrieved may not truly reflect the workings of the database.

```
sorts (disk)                        97
sorts (rows)                        32693
```

```
SQL>
```

Because the primary application is OLTP in nature, the number of sorts performed on disk (97) is a bit high. The following line appears in the relevant INIT.ORA file:

```
sort_area_size = 65536
```

The first test to reduce disk sorts will increase the sort_area_size parameter to 128KB. The new section will be as follows:

```
#
# 97 sorts were being performed on disk. Parameter
# increased to 128k
# TMG: 11 Apr 98
# sort_area_size = 65536
sort_area_size = 131072
```

After the database was stopped and restarted (to activate the new parameter), one full business day elapsed and the V$SYSSTAT view was queried again. These are the results:

```
NAME                            VALUE
------------------------------- ----------
sorts (memory)                  3661
sorts (disk)                    3
sorts (rows)                    34014
```

By increasing the sort_area_size parameter to 128KB, the number of disk sorts has been lowered to an acceptable level.

Managing Data File Contention

Databases often exhibit the characteristic that most data that must be accessed is physically close together. Even though a database may be many gigabytes in size, only a few dozen megabytes or so may be accessed over an hour. If this information is physically close, it's likely that only a handful of database data files are actively being used.

Reducing hot spots by design

When designing a database, try to identify which segments will receive the highest volume of data accesses. Heavily accessed segments ideally should be placed in their own tablespaces with composing data files distributed across different disk drives and controllers.

Data files accessed at much higher rate than most others over a particular time period are known as *hot spots*. From a tuning perspective, hot spots should be minimized if at all possible. Most database servers are designed with data files distributed over many disk drives to maximize the potential for parallel I/O. Hot spots result in just a few disk drives at 100 percent utilization, whereas most others sit idle. When a disk drive (or controller) is fully utilized, any further requests have to wait in a queue to be serviced.

Fortunately, Oracle keeps statistics on each data file's I/O rates to help you identify hot spots. The V$FILESTAT contains the information needed to identify and reduce data file hot spots.

Locating Data File Hot Spots

The V$FILESTAT view will be queried for physical reads and physical writes on each data file. By looking at the number of physical reads and writes in each of a database's data files, you can discern which data files are hot spots. Be aware that the values reported for physical reads and writes are counted from the time the database was last started. To identify hot spots during a particular period of time, it's necessary to compare the contents of the V$FILESTAT view at the beginning and end of the time period of interest.

The following SQL statement shows the physical read and write values for each data file sorted by the total number of physical accesses:

```
select name,phyrds,phywrts,(phyrds+phywrts) Total
from v$filestat s, v$datafile d
where s.file#=d.file#
order by total desc;
```

By looking at data files at the top of the result from this SQL statement, you can identify which physical devices are being accessed the most. If any of the top data files are on the same physical disk drives or controllers, you should consider moving them to different drives or controllers.

V$FILESTAT and V$DATAFILE views

This SQL code uses the V$FILESTAT and V$DATAFILE views. This is necessary because the statistics in the V$FILESTAT view are identified by file number only. By inner joining the V$FILESTAT and V$DATAFILE views, file statistics can be mapped to filenames.

Example of Identifying Hot Spots

The V$FILESTAT view is queried for hot spot information by the SYSTEM user in SQL*Plus. The resulting session is as follows:

```
SQL> select name,phyrds,phywrts,(phyrds+phywrts) Total
  2  from v$filestat s, v$datafile d
  3  where s.file#=d.file#
  4  order by total desc;
NAME                          PHYRDS   PHYWRTS    TOTAL
----------------------------  -------- ---------- ------
/oracle/sapdata4/stabi.data2  322805   6373       329178
/oracle/sapdata2/btabd.data1  108051   666        108717
/oracle/sapdata2/protd.data2  7798     64125      71923
/oracle/sapdata1/stabd.data1  57173    2871       60044
...
/oracle/sapdata5/user1i.data1 11       0          11
/oracle/sapdata2/docud.data1  6        3          9
/oracle/sapdata2/loadd.data1  6        1          7
/oracle/sapdata3/loadi.data1  4        0          4
/oracle/sapdata2/protd.data1  0        0          0
```

① These two data files reside on the same physical device (mounted on /oracle/sapdata2)

Because btabd.data1 and protd.data2 would be considered hot spots and both reside on the same physical device, it's possible they should be moved to different physical devices. As with all statistics, confirm that they are a representative sample before using them to guide any changes to the database.

Using Striping Strategies

Data-access patterns often unavoidably produce data file hot spots no matter how well the database is designed. You can use two key strategies to minimize data file contention caused by these hot spots:

- Rebuilding tablespaces with more data files that are smaller in size and located on different disk drives and controllers
- RAID technology

The simplest and (often) cheapest remedy for contention is to recreate a tablespace identified as housing hot spots with more data files that are smaller in size. The key here is to keep data files smaller than they were in the original; this will force Oracle to spread extents out over more data files (and, therefore, physical devices) and minimize data file contention. This solution is most ideal on servers that have many individual disk drives not being heavily used.

In recent years, RAID technology has been rapidly adopted in many database servers to maximize I/O throughput with little administrative work. Because the hardware automatically stripes physical (not database) storage blocks for each data file across many disk drives, no changes to the database are necessary. RAID technology can help reduce data file contention without causing you much (if any) additional workload.

By implementing one or both of these strategies, the performance degradation caused by data file contention can be reduced to an acceptable level.

RAID technology isn't a magic cure

Inexperienced DBAs sometimes mistakenly believe that RAID technology eliminates the need for them to properly design a database's physical storage layout (such as isolating tables and indexes on different tablespaces and sizing segments). Unfortunately, although RAID can offer perhaps two or even five times the throughput of a single disk, proper database design can offer overall performance increases of several magnitudes. RAID technology will offer the most benefit to properly designed databases.

Maximizing Redo Log Performance

Oracle must keep a log of all its write activity in order to facilitate lossless recovery from instance and media failure. The redo logs contain exceedingly detailed information about most every change Oracle makes to a database's physical file components.

Because so much information is written to the active redo log, it can easily become a bottleneck that can significantly limit the performance of an otherwise well-tuned database. When you're tuning the redo logs for performance, your objective will be to minimize the amount of time the database must spend writing redo information to disk.

Sizing Redo Logs to Allow Checkpoint Completion

Checkpoints, while necessary for system integrity, also can drastically affect system performance depending on their frequency and duration. The system should ideally be tuned such that a checkpoint occurs only during a log switch.

When sizing redo logs, it's absolutely essential that they be sufficiently sized so that checkpoints can finish well before a log switch is necessary. Oracle's V$SYSSTAT view contains the statistical values for background checkpoints started and background checkpoints completed. When the values for these statistics vary by more than 1, at least one checkpoint didn't finish before a log switch was necessary and log sizes must be increased.

Use the following SQL statement to query the V$SYSSTAT view for the background checkpoint statistics:

```
select name,value from v$sysstat
where name like 'background checkpoint%';
```

Two rows will be returned: one with the count of background statistics started and another with the count of background statistics finished.

Example of Checking for Checkpoint Completion

The V$SYSSTAT view is queried for the background checkpoint statistics by the SYSTEM user in SQL*Plus. The example session follows:

```
SQL> select name,value from v$sysstat
  2  where name like 'background checkpoint%';


NAME                                                VALUE
-------------------------------------------------- --------
background checkpoints started                       4521
background checkpoints completed                     4520

SQL>
```

Use the checkpoint process

Most sites should use the optional checkpoint process to take care of updating data file headers during checkpoints. By using the checkpoint process, the log writer process won't be interrupted from writing redo log information during a checkpoint, thereby further reducing performance problems caused by checkpoint activities.

Identifying the problem

The two background checkpoint statistics vary by only 1. This indicates that checkpoints are finishing before a log switch is forced. If the **background checkpoints completed** were 3,788, we would have to increase the size of the redo log files until the two statistics varied by only 1.

Sizing Redo to Allow Archive Completion

When a database is running in ARCHIVELOG mode and a log file switch occurs, the database will immediately begin filling a new redo log group as the ARCH process begins copying one of the completed redo logs to the archive log destination. It's important to make sure that the ARCH process finishes its task well before another redo log group is filled. If the ARCH process can't keep up with redo log generation, Oracle will have to suspend database activity when all redo log groups have filled. Although database activity will resume as soon as ARCH can catch up and release a redo log group, users and batch jobs will most definitely notice the lack of system responsiveness.

You can check the time the ARCH process is using for each filled redo log. Do this by looking at the time of a log switch in the relevant ALERT.LOG file, and then comparing it to the time-stamp of the resulting archived redo log file. If the time required for the ARCH process is close to the time between redo log switches, you should implement one or more of the following options:

- *Increase the size of redo logs.* The ARCH process is more efficient when working with fewer and larger redo logs.
- *Add more redo log groups.* This will give the ARCH process more time to catch up during peak transaction rates without causing the database to suspend activity.
- *Store archived logs on faster physical devices.* By using RAID technology with high-speed disk drives, the ARCH process should be able to keep up with most any realistic redo log generation rate.

Designing Redo to Avoid *LGWR* and *ARCH* Contention

When a log switch occurs in Oracle, the LGWR process will immediately begin writing to the next redo log group in a circular fashion. Meanwhile, the ARCH process will begin reading the last redo log to make a copy in the archive log destination. Because these operations happen concurrently, each should be working with two distinct physical disk drives.

Recall that when redo log group n is filled up, Oracle will always switch to the $n+1$ group (unless n is the last redo log group, in which case Oracle will start with group 1 again). Therefore, when redo log group n is full, a log switch occurs—log group n is read by the ARCH process, while LGWR moves on to writing in group $n+1$.

To ensure that ARCH and LGWR are always working from different physical drives, odd-numbered redo log data files should always reside on completely different disk drives (and, ideally, different controllers) than even-numbered redo log data files.

Remember to isolate redo logs

Because of the high I/O rates on redo log data files, remember to dedicate disk drives exclusively for redo log use. In an ideal system, at least four disk drives (two data files per group on different drives and two groups on completely different devices) will be dedicated for redo log use.

Identifying and Reducing Contention

Identify and reduce contention for rollback segments

Identify and reduce contention for MTS processes

Identify and reduce contention during parallel operations

Use free lists appropriately

Identifying Rollback Segment Contention

Interleaf rollback segments to reduce contention

Interleaf the order of the rollback segments in the initialization file's **ROLLBACK_SEGMENTS** parameter so that the first is in one tablespace, the next one is in the other, and so on. This will reduce the contention for rollback segments.

Rollback segments are concurrently used by one or more transactions; any delays caused by contention on rollback segments affect performance. More transactions per rollback segment cause more contention and use space more efficiently, whereas fewer transactions per rollback segment cause less contention and waste more space.

Rollback segments hold transaction tables in their headers. Concurrent transactions contending for the same rollback segment will show up due to contention for the undo header.

Each time a transaction begins, it's assigned to a rollback segment. This assignment can be done automatically or manually:

- *Automatic.* When the first DDL or DML statement is issued, Oracle automatically assigns the transaction to a rollback segment. Queries are never assigned rollback segments.

- *Manual.* You can use the SET TRANSACTION command with the USE ROLLBACK SEGMENT parameter and manually specify a rollback segment to use for a transaction. The rollback segment is assigned for the duration of the transaction. By using this method, the developers can use the correct size rollback segment for a particular task.

You should create rollback tablespaces to hold rollback segments. In a heavy transaction-based system, you should have at least two rollback tablespaces on separate disks. Rollback segment contention occurs when transactions request rollback segment buffers and those buffers are still busy with previous transaction rollback information.

Rollback segment contention is reflected by contention for buffers that contain rollback segment blocks. V$WAITSTAT contains statistics for different classes of block. The following table shows the different classes of blocks tracked through this view for rollback information:

Block class	Description
System Undo Header	Buffers containing header blocks of the SYSTEM rollback segment
System Undo Block	Buffers containing blocks of the SYSTEM rollback segment other than header blocks
Undo Header	Buffers containing header blocks of the rollback segments other than the SYSTEM rollback segment
Undo Block	Buffers containing blocks (other than header blocks) of the rollback segments (other than the SYSTEM rollback segment)

Use the following queries to determine the number of requests for data and the number of waits for each class of block over a period of time.

The following query gives you the total number of data requests:

```
SELECT SUM (value)   "DATA REQUESTS"
FROM V$SYSSTAT
WHERE name IN ('db block gets', 'consistent gets');
```

This query's output might look like this:

```
DATA REQUESTS
-----------------------
          223759
```

The following query provides the number of waits on rollback segments:

```
SELECT class, count
FROM V$WAITSTAT
WHERE class LIKE '%undo%'
AND COUNT > 0;
```

This query's output might look like this:

```
CLASS               COUNT
--------------------------
system undo header    3145
```

```
system undo block      231
undo header           4875
undo block             774
```

As seen from these results, the number of waits for system undo header is (3145 / 223759)*100 = 1.4%, and the number of waits for undo header is (4875 / 223759)* 100 = 2.1%. Contention is indicated by the number of waits for any class being greater than 1 percent of the total number of requests.

Contention is indicated by frequent occurrence of error ORA-01555, or when transaction table wait events are much greater than 0.

Reducing Contention for Rollback Segments

Increasing the number of rollback segments can reduce contention for rollback segments. After creating the new rollback segments, you must reference them in the init.ora parameter ROLLBACK_SEGMENTS and also make them online. Use the following table as a guideline for determining the number of rollback segments to allocate, depending on the number of concurrent transactions anticipated.

Number of concurrent transactions	Number of rollback segments
Fewer than 16 concurrent transactions	4
Concurrent transactions between 16 and 32	8
More than 32 concurrent transactions	Number of transactions divided by 4

The following query will tell you whether the OPTIMAL setting for the rollback segments is appropriate:

```
SELECT substr(name, 1,20), extents, rssize, aveactive,
                      ave_shrink, extends, shrinks
   FROM v$rollname rn, v$rollstat rs
   WHERE rn.usn = rs.usn;
```

This query's output might look like this:

```
substr(name, 1, 20)
          extents rssize aveactive aveshrink extends shrinks
-----------------------------------------------------------------
SYSTEM          4 207639         0         0        0        0
RB1             2 207489         0         0        0        0
RB2             4 207698         0         0        0        0
```

OPTIMAL is set properly if the average size of rollback segments is close to the size set for OPTIMAL; otherwise, you need to change the value for OPTIMAL. Also, if the value in the shrinks column is very large, that means that the OPTIMAL setting is set improperly.

You can follow several other recommendations with respect to rollback segments to reduce contention:

- Set NEXT to INITIAL.

- Set MINEXTENTS equal to or greater than 20.

- Set OPTIMAL to equal INITIAL multiplied by MINEXTENTS.

- Set the value for INITIAL appropriately after determining the amount of undo generated by transactions, as follows:
  ```
  SELECT MAX(USED_UBLK)
  FROM v$transaction;
  ```

- Set INITIAL equal to or greater than MAX(USED_UBLK).

Identifying and Reducing Contention for Multithreaded Server Processes (MTS)

The components of the MTS configuration consist of the processes on the system, communication software, and the shared global area (SGA). A system using MTS has the following processes (see Figure 21.1):

- A network listener process that connects user processes to dispatchers and dedicated servers. (This functionality is provided by Net8.)

Use rollback segments wisely

Assign large rollback segments to long-running queries and to transactions that modify a large amount of data. Avoid dynamic expansion and reduction of rollback space. Also, don't create more rollback segments than your instance's maximum number of concurrently active transactions.

Use Net8 to connect to shared servers

To use shared servers, a user process must connect through Net8, even if it's on the same machine as the Oracle instance.

■ One or more dispatcher processes. Dispatchers belong to a specific instance and are protocol-specific handlers. (Windows NT currently supports only the TCP/IP protocol.)

■ One or more server processes.

FIGURE 21.1

The components of the MTS configuration consist of the processes on the system, communication software, and the shared global area (SGA).

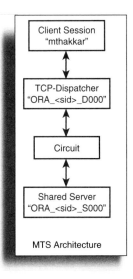

Client Session
"mthakkar"

TCP-Dispatcher
"ORA_<sid>_D000"

Circuit

Shared Server
"ORA_<sid>_S000"

MTS Architecture

When you configure Oracle8 to use Multithreaded Server architecture, you have to deal with the contention for dispatcher and shared server processes. You can configure the number of dispatchers and server processes; there's no direct relationship between the number of dispatchers and shared servers.

SGA enhancements include additional memory structures, such as request and response queues for handling service requests and returning responses to those requests. Session information is migrated from the PGA into the SGA (this section of the SGA is known as the user global area, or UGA), so that the correct response goes to the appropriate client.

PGA in an MTS environment

The program global area (PGA) of a shared-server process doesn't contain user-related data because this information needs to be accessible to all shared servers. The PGA of shared servers contains only stack space and process-specific variables. Session-related information is moved to the SGA, which should have enough space to store all session-specific information.

How MTS server processes are run

1. When the listener is started, it starts listening on the listed addresses. It opens and establishes a communication path through which users connect to Oracle. The only services it's aware of are those defined in listener.ora.

2. When an Oracle instance configured for MTS is started, each dispatcher gets its random listen address and gives the listener this address, at which the dispatcher listens for connection requests. The dispatcher calls the listener by using the address specified in the init.ora parameter MTS_LISTENER_ADDRESS.

3. The listener adds the dispatcher's MTS_SERVICE and address to its list of known services.

4. The network listener process waits for incoming connection requests and determines whether a shared server process can be used.

5. If a dedicated server process is requested, it creates a dedicated server process and connects the user process to it; otherwise, it gives the user process the address of a dispatcher process with the lightest load. (Windows NT now supports only the TCP/IP protocol for MTS connections.)

6. The user process connects to the dispatcher and remains connected to it throughout the life of the user process. After the connection is established, the dispatcher creates a virtual circuit, which it uses to communicate with the shared servers.

7. The user process issues a request, which is placed by the dispatcher in the request queue in the SGA, where it's picked up by the next available shared server process. The request queue is common to all dispatchers.

8. The shared server process does all the necessary processing and returns the results to the response queue of the dispatcher in the SGA. Each dispatcher has its own response queue.

9. The dispatcher process returns the completed request to the user process.

Because dispatchers have few responsibilities, each dispatcher can serve many clients, allowing a significantly high number of clients to be connected to the server.

Identifying Contention for Dispatcher Processes

Contention for dispatcher processes can be identified by the following symptoms:

- *High busy rates for dispatchers.* The V$DISPATCHER view contains important statistics regarding the activity of dispatcher processes. Pay special attention to this view's [BUSY] and [IDLE] fields.

- *A steady increase in waiting time for responses in the dispatchers' response queues.* The V$QUEUE view contains important statistics regarding the response queue activity of dispatcher processes. Pay special attention to this view's [WAIT] and [TOTALQ] fields.

Examining Busy Rates for Dispatcher Processes

You can examine the efficiency of the dispatchers by using the following query over a period of time with the application running:

```
SELECT name, network, owned, status, (busy /(busy + idle))
➡* 100 "% of time busy"
FROM  v$dispatchers
```

NAME	NETWORK	STATUS	% of time busy
D000	TCP	WAIT	.141240092
D001	TCP	CONNECT	.146774237
D002	TCP	WAIT	.04165972
D003	TCP	WAIT	.04052496

Four dispatchers are running on this instance. All have the status WAIT except one (D001), whose status is CONNECTED. This dispatcher is servicing a connect request from a client that will remain connected to this dispatcher for the lifetime of its session. None of these dispatchers have a high percentage of busyness; you could conclude that we could do with fewer dispatchers.

You can use another query to determine the dispatcher that you need in the system:

```
SELECT network                              "PROTOCOL",
       ( SUM(busy) / (SUM(busy) + SUM(idle)) ) * 100
       "% TIME BUSY"
FROM v$dispatcher
GROUP BY network;


PROTOCOL    %  TIME BUSY
==========  ============
decnet          0.5676849
tcp            61.4379021
```

From this result, you can see the following:

- The DECnet dispatcher processes are busy nearly 0.5 percent of the time.

- TCP dispatchers processes are busy nearly 61 percent of the time.

Thus, you can conclude that there's contention for the TCP dispatchers. You can improve the performance by adding dispatchers for the TCP protocol.

Examining Contention for Dispatcher Process Response Queues

You can determine whether you have the correct number of dispatchers by finding the average wait time for the dispatchers of that protocol. You can use the following query for this purpose:

```
SELECT network            "PROTOCOL",
       DECODE( SUM(totalq), 0, 'No Responses',
       SUM(wait)/SUM(totalq) )
   "Average wait time per response (1/100th of seconds)"
FROM v$queue q, v$dispatcher d
WHERE q.type = 'DISPATCHER'
AND    q.paddr = d.paddr
GROUP BY network;
```

This query will return the average time, in hundredths of a second, that a response waits in the response queue. A steady increase in the wait time would indicate that you need to add more dispatchers.

```
Protocol Average wait time per response (1/100th of a second)
-------- -----------------------------------------------------
decnet   0.134180
tcp      235.38760
```

This result shows that the responses in the response queue of the DECnet dispatcher processes wait an average of 0.13 of a second, whereas the wait is much higher for the TCP dispatcher processes.

Reducing Contention for Dispatcher Processes

You have two options for reducing the contention of dispatchers:

- *Add dispatcher processes.* You can dynamically adjust the number of dispatchers to improve performance. Use the ALTER SYSTEM command to change the number of dispatcher processes.

- *Enable connection pooling, a feature implemented with Net8 clients and dispatchers for MTS.* It allows a limited number of physical connections to be shared among a large number of logical sessions. It uses a time-out mechanism to temporarily release an idle transport connection while maintaining its network session. Use of this feature is ideal when many clients run interactive applications such as email, which have high idle time.

Limit the number of dispatchers

The MTS_MAX_DISPATCHERS parameter determines the total number of dispatcher processes across all protocols. The default value of this parameter is 5; the maximum value is operating-system dependent.

Oracle8 provides an optional attribute POOL (or POO), which can be used with the parameter MTS_DISPATCHERS to enable the Net8 connection pooling feature in the init.ora file. The following example allows you to start the database with four TCP dispatchers and enables the Net8 connection pooling feature:

```
MTS_DISPATCHERS = "(PROTOCOL=TCP)(DISPATCHERS=4)(POOL)"
```

Identifying Contention for Shared Server Processes

Contention for shared server processes can be determined by monitoring the wait times for requests in the request queue (V$QUEUE and V$SHARED_SERVERS). A steady increase in the wait time indicates that there's contention and that you need to increase the number of shared server processes.

The query for examining the shared servers is similar to that of monitoring dispatchers but from the dynamic view V$SHARED_SERVERS:

```
SELECT name, status, requests, (busy /(busy + idle)) * 100
➥"% of time busy"
FROM v$shared_servers;
```

```
NAME        STATUS            REQUESTS    % of time busy
--------    ----------------  ----------  --------------
S000        WAIT(COMMON)            1122       .05956579
S001        WAIT(ENQ)                  1      99.1001586
S002        WAIT(COMMON)               0      .000031547
```

Servers S000 and S002 are idle, whereas server S001 is very busy; its client could benefit from a dedicated server. The value of the REQUESTS column is cumulative since instance startup.

You can use the following query to determine the average wait time for the requests in the request queue:

```
SELECT DECODE( totalq, 0, 'No Requests',  wait/totalq )
   "Average wait time per requests (hundredths of seconds) "
FROM v$queue
WHERE type = 'COMMON';
```

```
Average wait time per requests (hundredths of seconds)
-----------------------------------------------------------
                 0.293734950
```

The result shows that there's an average wait time of 0.29 of a second in the request queue.

Reducing Contention for Shared Servers

Oracle8 automatically adjusts the number of shared servers to improve performance. You should try to identify requests that need to be serviced by dedicated servers and not shared servers.

Theoretically, any application can be used with MTS, but in reality some applications will benefit from its usage, whereas others won't. Client/server applications that don't require a lot of processing from the client will benefit from the usage of MTS. An example of such an application is Oracle's own BUG

Limit the number of shared servers

The MTS_MAX_SERVERS parameter determines the maximum number of shared server processes in the system. The default value of this parameter is 20; the maximum value is operating-system dependent.

database. During the day, bugs may be filed, updated, and closed by various people working in any number of departments. These transactions are short and don't tie up the server for an extended period of time, allowing the server to work on many requests simultaneously. However, not all the BUG database's functionality will benefit from MTS, such as running weekend reports and complex SELECT statements, which can tie up the shared servers.

Suppose that an MTS instance has three dispatchers and two shared servers. If one client decides to submit such reports during the day, you are left with just one shared server, because the other will be tied up processing the reports. Now if a second client submits another such report, it will appear to other clients that the instance is locked up, because both shared servers are performing large reports. New requests won't be processed until a server becomes free. It will be better if the clients request a dedicated connection. As you can see, a mixed environment can usually give great benefits.

The following shows the init.ora file with MTS parameters:

```
mts_service= "YOUR_SID"
mts_listener_address="(ADDRESS=(PROTOCOL=tcp)(port=1521)
                       (host=your_machine))"
mts_dispatchers= "tcp, 1"
mts_max_dispatchers=10
mts_max_servers=10
mts_servers=4
```

Identifying and Reducing Contention for Parallel Server Processes

You can use the dictionary view V$PQ_SYSSTAT for determining the appropriate number of parallel server processes for an instance:

```
SELECT STATISTIC, VALUE
FROM v$pq_sysstat
WHERE
    statistic = "Servers Started " or
    statistic = "Servers Shutdown";
```

```
STATISTIC          VALUE
-----------------------
Servers Started      48
Servers Shutdown     45
```

The following statistics can be helpful in identifying the contention for parallel server processes:

- Servers Busy
- Servers Idle
- Servers Started
- Servers Shutdown

Use the following query to determine whether the set numbers of parallel server processes are really busy:

```
SELECT STATISTIC, VALUE
FROM v$pq_sysstat
WHERE statistic = "Servers Busy"

STATISTIC          VALUE
-----------------------
Servers Busy         65
```

If the query's result shows that the number of busy parallel server processes is typically less than PARALLEL_MIN_SERVERS, you should consider decreasing the value of PARALLEL_MIN_SERVERS in init*sid*.ora. If servers are continuously starting and shutting down, however, consider increasing PARALLEL_MIN_SERVERS. This parameter should be set to the number of concurrent parallel operations multiplied by the average number of parallel server processes used by a parallel operation.

Identifying and Reducing Latch Contention

Oracle uses different types of locking mechanisms:

- Latches
- Enqueues

The maximum parallel servers should not exceed your machine capacity

The maximum number of parallel server processes for an instance depends heavily on the capacity of your CPUs and your I/O bandwidth. Set PARALLEL_MAX_SERVERS to the maximum number of concurrent parallel server processes that your machine can manage.

- Distributed locks
- Global locks (used in parallel instance implementations)

You can't control what latches to use and when to use them, but you can adjust certain init.ora parameters to tune Oracle to most efficiently use latches and reduce latch contention. Latches protect internal data structures by maintaining a defined method of accessing them. If a process can't obtain a latch immediately, it waits for the latch, resulting in a slowdown and additional CPU usage. The process, in the meantime, is "spinning."

Latch contention occurs when two or more Oracle processes attempt to obtain the same latch concurrently. You can detect latch contention by using the V$LATCH, V$LATCHHOLDER, and V$LATCHNAME data dictionary views.

The following queries can be used to provide latch information:

- Obtain the name of a latch from the latch address:
  ```
  SELECT name
  FROM v$latchname ln, v$latch l
  WHERE l.addr = '&addr'
  AND l.latch# = ln.latch# ;
  ```

- Obtain systemwide latch statistics:
  ```
  SELECT ln.name, l.addr, l.gets, l.misses, l.sleeps,
  l.immediate_gets, l.immediate_misses, lh.pid
  FROM v$latch l , v$latchholder lh , v$latchname ln
  WHERE l.addr = lh.laddr (+)
  AND l.latch# = ln.latch#
  ORDER BY l.latch# ;
  ```

- Display statistics for any latch X:
  ```
  SELECT ln.name, l.addr, l.gets, l.misses, l.sleeps,
  l.immediate_gets, l.immediate_misses, lh.pid
  FROM v$latch l , v$latchholder lh , v$latchname ln
  WHERE l.addr = lh.laddr (+)
  AND l.latch# = ln.latch#
  AND ln.name like '%X%'
  ORDER BY l.latch# ;
  ```

The following table lists all the latches that are of concern to Oracle DBAs:

Latch Number	Name
0	Latch wait list
1	Process allocation
2	Session allocation
3	Session switching
4	Session idle bit
5	Messages
6	Enqueues
7	Trace latch
8	Cache buffers chain
9	Cache buffers LRU chain
10	Cache buffer handles
11	Multiblock read objects
12	Cache protection latch
13	System commit number
14	Archive control
15	Redo allocation
16	Redo copy
17	Instance latch
18	Lock element parent latch
19	DML lock allocation
20	Transaction allocation
21	Undo global data
22	Sequence cache
23	Sequence cache entry
24	Row cache objects
25	Cost function
26	User lock
27	Global transaction mapping table
28	Global transaction
29	Shared pool
30	Library cache

continues…

...continued

Latch number	name
31	Library cache pin
32	Library cache load lock
33	Virtual circuit buffers
34	Virtual circuit queues
35	Virtual circuits
36	Query server process
37	Query server free lists
38	Error message lists
39	Process queue
40	Process queue reference
41	Parallel query stats

The cache buffers chains latch is needed when user processes try to scan the SGA for database cache buffers. Adjusting the DB_BLOCK_BUFFERS parameter can reduce contention for this latch.

The cache buffers LRU chain latch is needed when user processes try to scan the LRU chain containing all the dirty blocks in the buffer cache. Increasing the DB_BLOCK_BUFFERS and DB_BLOCK_WRITE_BATCH parameters can reduce contention for this latch.

The row cache objects latch is needed when user processes try to access the cached data dictionary values. Tuning the data dictionary cache can reduce contention for this latch. Increasing the size of the shared pool (SHARED_POOL_SIZE) can be used to achieve this result.

Identifying and Reducing Contention for the LRU Latch

Design your applications to reduce LRU contention

Application design can have a significant influence on LRU contention because the design will ultimately determine the queries and DML statements that in turn can affect contention for LRU latches.

The least recently used (LRU) latch controls the replacement of buffers in the buffer cache. Contention for the LRU latch can be identified by querying V$LATCH, V$SESSION_EVENT, and V$SYSTEM_EVENT. V$LATCH shows cumulative values since instance startup.

The initialization parameter DB BLOCK LRU LATCHES specifies the maximum number of LRU latches on your system. Each LRU latch controls a set of buffers. You can use the following guidelines to determine the value for DB_BLOCK_LRU_LATCHES:

- DB_BLOCK_LRU_LATCHES can range from 1 to twice the number of CPUs in the system.
- A latch should have at least 50 buffers in its set.
- Oracle uses only one LRU latch in a single-process mode.

Identifying and Reducing Contention for Space in Redo Log Buffers

Redo information must be written to the redo log before a transaction is completed. Any kind of bottleneck in the redo log can cause the performance of all the processes in the system to be affected. You should therefore check for contention of the redo log buffers and the redo log buffer latches.

The dynamic performance table V$SYSSTAT stores systemwide statistics that can be used to identify contention for various resources. The statistic REDO BUFFER ALLOCATION RETRIES reflects the number of times a user process waits for space in the redo log buffer. The process may have to wait if the LGWR process isn't fast enough to write the redo entries from the redo log buffer to a redo log file. These statistics are available only to the SYS user or users with the SELECT ANY TABLE privilege.

You can use the following query to determine contention for space in the redo log buffer:

```
SELECT name, value
FROM V$SYSSTAT
WHERE name = 'redo buffer allocation retries';
```

The value from this query must be almost 0. If it increases consistently, contention is indicated. You have several options for reducing the contention for space in the redo log buffer:

- Increase the size of the redo log buffer by increasing the LOG_BUFFER parameter. LOG_BUFFER (in bytes) must be a multiple of DB_BLOCK_SIZE.

LRU latches for SMP and non-SMP machines

For SMP machines, Oracle automatically sets the number of LRU latches to be one half the number of CPUs on the system. One LRU latch is sufficient for non-SMP machines.

- Improve the checkpointing process.
- Improve the archiving process.

Identifying and Reducing Contention for Redo Log Buffer Latches

The V$LATCH dynamic performance view contains statistics for the activity of the various latches. A process can request a latch in one of two ways:

- *Willing to wait.* If the requested latch is unavailable, the requesting process will wait for some time and request the latch again. This wait-request cycle continues until the latch becomes available. The following V$LATCH columns reflect willing-to-wait requests:

    GETS   Number of successful willing-to-wait requests for a latch

    MISSES   Number of unsuccessful, initial willing-to-wait requests for a latch

    SLEEPS   Number of times a process waited and requested a latch after an initial request

- *Immediate.* If the requested latch is unavailable, the requesting process doesn't wait but continues processing. The following V$LATCH columns reflect immediate requests:

    IMMEDIATE GETS   Number of successful immediate requests for a latch

    IMMEDIATE MISSES   Number of unsuccessful immediate requests for a latch

The following query can be used to monitor contention of the redo allocation and the redo copy latch:

```
SELECT ln.name, gets, misses, immediate_gets,
immediate_misses
FROM V$LATCH l, V$LATCHNAME ln
WHERE ln.name IN (' redo allocation', 'redo copy')
AND ln.latch# = l.latch#;
```

This query's output might look like this:

```
NAME            GETS   MISSES   IMMEDIATE_GETS  IMMEDIATE_MISSES
.............   .....  .......   ..............  ................
redo alloc...   12580    215                5                 0
redo copy          12      0             1223                 2
```

Contention exists for a latch if either of the following is true:

- Ratio of MISSES to GETS exceeds 1 percent
- Ratio of IMMEDIATE_MISSES to the sum of IMMEDIATE_MISSES and IMMEDIATE_GETS exceeds 1 percent

The example shows a redo allocation latch contention; the ratio of misses to gets is 1.7 percent. The redo allocation latch controls space allocation for redo entries in the redo log buffer. An Oracle process must obtain the redo allocation latch before allocating space in the redo log buffer. There's only one redo allocation latch; therefore, only one process can allocate space in the redo log buffer at a time.

You can reduce contention for this latch by minimizing copying on it, which in turn reduces the time that any single process holds the latch. To do so, decrease the value of the LOG_SMALL_ENTRY_MAX_SIZE parameter, which determines the number and size of redo entries copied on the redo allocation latch.

Whereas the redo allocation latch is held only for a short period of time, the redo copy latch is held for a longer amount of time because the user process first obtains the redo copy latch, and then the redo allocation latch. The process performs allocation and then releases the allocation latch. The copy is then performed under the copy latch, after which the redo copy latch is released.

On multiple CPU machines, the LOG_SIMULTANEOUS_COPIES parameter determines the number of redo copy latches. Multiple redo copy latches allow multiple processes to concurrently copy entries to the redo log buffer. The default value of this parameter is the number of CPUs available to the instance; the maximum value is twice the number of CPUs. To reduce contention, increase the value of LOG_SIMULTANEOUS_COPIES.

Latch contention doesn't occur on single-CPU machines

Only one process can be active at a given time on a single-CPU machine; therefore, latch contention rarely occurs.

Another way in which you can reduce redo copy latch contention is by prebuilding the redo entry before requesting the latch. The LOG_ENTRY_PREBUILD_THRESHOLD parameter can be set to achieve this result. The default value for this parameter is 0. When this parameter is set, any redo entry of a smaller size than this parameter must be prebuilt.

Identifying and Reducing Contention for Library Cache Latches

The library cache latches are required to prevent multiple access to a shared library cache entry. There are three types of library cache latches:

- The library cache latch—the highest latch level—is needed before getting a lock on a handle.
- The pin latch is needed by a process before pinning a heap.
- The load-lock latch is needed to load a library cache entry.

The following query can be used to identify library cache latch contention:

```
SELECT count(*) number_of_waiters
FROM v$session_wait sw, v$latch l
WHERE sw.wait_time = 0
AND sw.event = 'latch free'
AND sw.p2 = l.latch#
AND l.name like 'library%';
```

In this query, a large number of waiters indicates that you have contention.

You can reduce contention for library cache latches in the following ways:

- Minimize shared pool fragmentation.
- Increase the sharing of statements, which in turn decreases the completed reloads.
- Reduce the amount of parsing that's going on in the system. You can use the following query to identify the SQL statements that are receiving a lot of parse calls:

```
SELECT sql_text, parse_calls, executions
FROM v$sqlarea
WHERE parse_calls > 100
AND executions < 2*parse_calls;
```

- Set CURSOR_SPACE_FOR_TIME to TRUE.

- Use fully qualified table names.

Identifying Free-List Contention

Oracle maintains information in memory that allows instanta-
neous access to information on disk. Some of this information
keeps track of the space available in the tablespaces for inserting
new rows. You can indicate at table-creation time how much
information to keep in memory for tracking available blocks for
creating new records. This is the *free list* for the table.

The following code creates a table with 12 free lists:

```
create table test_table (id number,
                  desc varchar2(20))
                  freelist 12;
```

Free-list contention is generally indicated by excessive disk I/O
for block ID requests to create new rows. This contention
occurs when multiple processes are searching the free list at the
same time.

The dynamic view V$WAITSTAT contains statistics for block con-
tention. Free-list contention is reflected by contention for free
data blocks in the buffer cache. You can use the following query
to determine what percentage of the total requests was actually
waiting for free blocks:

```
SELECT class,count
    FROM V$WAITSTAT
    WHERE class = 'free list';
```

This query's output might look like this:

```
CLASS       COUNT
- - - - - - - - - - - - - - - - -
free list      39
```

You can use the following query to determine the number of requests for DB_BLOCK_BUFFERS and consistent reads:

```
SELECT name, value
   FROM v$sysstat
   WHERE name in ('db block gets', 'consistent gets');
```

This query's output might look like this:

```
NAME                VALUE
--------------------
db block gets    14236
consistent gets  10437
```

By using the preceding query, you can determine the number of waits for free lists:

```
free list wait events
  = ( (free list count) /
    (db block gets + consistent gets)) * 100
  = (39/ (14236 + 10437 ) * 100
  = 0.15
```

Identify free-list contention

1. Query V$WAITSTAT for contention on DATA BLOCKS.

2. Query V$SYSTEM_EVENT and determine BUFFER BUSY WAITS.

3. For each buffer-busy wait, use V$SESSION_WAIT to determine the FILE, BLOCK, and ID.

4. The following query shows the segment_name and segment_type for the objects and free lists with buffer busy waits:

```
SELECT segment_name "segment", segment_type "type"
FROM dba_extents
WHERE FILE_ID = file
AND BLOCK BETWEEN block_id and block_id + blocks;
```

5. You can use the segment and type from the preceding query in the following query to determine the free lists having contention:

```
SELECT FREELISTS
FROM DBA_SEGMENTS
WHERE SEGMENT_NAME = segment
AND SEGMENT_TYPE = type;
```

If the number of free-list wait events is greater than 1 percent of the total number of requests, you have contention for free list.

Reducing Contention for Free Lists

Recreating the table with a larger value of the FREELISTS storage parameter can reduce contention for free lists of a table. There are alternative ways for recreating the table that has free-list contention. The first example uses the table TEST.

Using Export/Import to reduce free-list contention

1. Export the table with the grants and indexes.
2. Drop the table.
3. Recreate the table with an increased value for FREELISTS.
4. Import the table with IGNORE=y.

You should have at least enough free lists to accommodate the number of concurrent processes that will be inserting into the table.

Using CTAS (*Create Table as SELECT*) to reduce free-list contention

1. Create a new table with the desired value for FREELISTS and the same structure as the old table.
2. Select data from the old table into the new table.
3. Drop the old table.
4. Rename the new table.

Tuning for Different Types of Applications

Transaction Processing Tuning

Online Transaction Processing (OLTP) systems have several characteristics:

- High throughput
- Insert/update intensive
- Large amount of concurrent users
- Data volume changing rapidly

Typical OLTP applications include airline reservation systems and banking applications. When you design an OLTP system, you must ensure that the large numbers of concurrent users don't affect the system performance. At the same time, you should get high availability, speed, and recoverability. You need to consider several issues when using OLTP systems:

- Rollback segments
- Indexes, clusters, and hashing
- Transaction modes
- Size of the data block
- Transaction processing monitors
- Multithreaded server
- Well-tuned memory structures

Tuning Rollback Segments

In an OLTP environment, an increased number of transactions occur, which may require a lot of rollback segments. When you're using parallel DML statements, the rollback segments become more important. You should have rollback segments that belong to tablespaces with lots of free space. You should also have unlimited rollback segments or a very high value for MAXEXTENTS.

SEE ALSO

➤ *More information on tuning rollback segments, page 568*

Using Discrete Transactions

Discrete transactions can be used concurrently with standard transactions. Discrete transactions are useful for transactions with certain characteristics:

- Transactions are short and non-distributed.
- Transactions modify very few database blocks.
- Transactions don't change individual database blocks more than once per transaction.
- Transactions don't modify data that will be needed by long-running queries for read consistency.
- Transactions don't need to see the new value of data after modifying the data.
- Modified tables don't contain any LONG values.

When you use a discrete transaction, all the changes made to any data will be deferred until the transaction commits. Redo information is generated but undo information isn't generated. The redo information is stored in a separate location in memory and gets written to the redo log when the transaction commits.

Use discrete transactions

1. Set the parameter DISCRETE_TRANSACTIONS_ENABLED to TRUE in the initialization file. (If DISCRETE_TRANSACTIONS_ENABLED is set to FALSE, all the transactions will be run as standard transactions.)

2. Use the procedure BEGIN_DISCRETE_TRANSACTION as the first statement in a transaction.

The example in Listing 22.1 uses a discrete transaction for a movie theater application. The name of the movie, show time, and number of tickets are passed as the arguments to this procedure. The procedure checks the tickets available. If enough tickets are available, it issues the tickets; otherwise, it will indicate the number of tickets available for that movie and show time.

ORA-1555 during discrete transactions

Undo information isn't generated during a discrete transaction. Therefore, you may get "snapshot too old" errors if a discrete transaction starts and commits during a long query, and the discrete transaction modifies blocks used by the long query.

Changes made during discrete transactions

Discrete transactions can't see their own changes. Therefore, they can't perform inserts or updates on both tables involved in a referential integrity constraint.

Scope of a discrete transaction

The procedure BEGIN_ DISCRETE_ TRANSACTION is effective only for the current transaction. As soon as the transaction commits or rolls back, the next transaction will be treated as a standard transaction.

LISTING 22.1 **A movie theater application using a discrete transaction**

```
01:   CREATE PROCEDURE BUY_TICKETS (movie_name IN VARCHAR(25),
02:            num_of_tickets IN NUMBER(10),
03:            movie_datetime  IN DATETIME,
04:            status OUT VARCHAR(5))
05: AS
06: DECLARE
07:   theatre_capacity    NUMBER(3);
08:   tickets_sold        NUMBER(3);
09:   tickets_available   NUMBER(3);
10: BEGIN
11:   dbms_transaction.begin_discrete_transaction;
12:   FOR I IN 1 . .  2 LOOP
13:       BEGIN
14:           SELECT theatre_max, tics_sold
15:           INTO theatre_capacity, tickets_sold
16:           FROM movies
17:           WHERE movie_title = movie_name
18:           AND show_time = movie_datetime
19:           FOR UPDATE;
20:   tickets_available := (theatre_capacity - tickets_sold)
21:   IF tickets_available <= num_of_tickets
22:   THEN
23:       status := "Sorry. Only " & tickets-available &
                   "tickets are available";
24:   ELSE
25:       UPDATE movies
26:       SET tics_sold = tickets_sold + num_of_tickets
27:       WHERE movie_title = movie_name
28:       AND show_time = movie_datetime;
29:
30:       status := "Requested number of tickets available."
31:   END IF;
32:   COMMIT;
33:   EXIT;
34:       EXCEPTION
35:   WHEN dbms_transaction.discrete_transaction_failed THEN
36:       ROLLBACK;
37:   END;
38:       END LOOP;
39:     END;
```

Discrete transaction failure

In this example, if the discrete transaction fails, the DISCRETE_ TRANSACTION_FAILED exception occurs and the transaction is rolled back. The second iteration of the loop will re-execute the transaction but this time as a standard transaction.

Transaction Processing Monitors (TPMs)

When a large number of concurrent users are connecting to the database, the demand for resources can become very heavy. On UNIX, the limiting factor is usually the physical memory. On Windows NT, each process can address a maximum of 4GB address space; 2GB of this 4GB address space is shared between processes. The shadow processes are implemented as threads within a single process; therefore, the limiting factor becomes the 2GB address space limit. There are several solutions to this problem, such as Multi-Threaded Server, concurrent manager, and connection multiplexing.

Another approach is to split the application logic into an application client and application server. The application client becomes responsible for the collection and presentation of the data, whereas the application server becomes responsible for providing business services that it implements through accessing various data stores (resource managers). The application server will normally be written in a 3GL such as C or COBOL, and the interface to the resource manager is using the normal pre-compiler or API mechanisms. This environment is normally managed with a transaction processing monitor (also called a transaction monitor), such as BEA Tuxedo. The TPM will normally provide the following:

Fault tolerance using TPM

The application client isn't aware of the application server servicing it; therefore, fault tolerance can be provided by using the transaction monitor architecture.

- A messaging interface
- Message routing between client and server
- Application server management including registration, startup, shutdown, and load balancing

A typical application server's logic

1. Connect to Oracle:
   ```
   EXEC SQL CONNECT
   ```

2. Wait for the message from the application client (an ATMI call for BEA Tuxedo).

3. Access Oracle:
   ```
   EXEC SQL SELECT
   EXEC SQL UPDATE
   ```

4. Commit:

```
EXEC SQL COMMIT;
```

5. Send a reply to the application client (an ATMI call for BEA Tuxedo).

6. Return to step 2 and repeat the process.

In a high-concurrency environment, many application clients can share the same application server. The TPM is responsible for routing messages. As the load increases, the TPM can also spawn more application servers.

Monitoring transactions in pending state

The `DBA_2PC_PENDING` and the `DBA_2PC_NEIGHBORS` views can be used to monitor if the transaction is in a pending state.

Distributed transaction processing can be obtained in the transaction-processing (TP) architecture by routing messages to different application servers. This can be homogeneous (Oracle-Oracle) or heterogeneous (Oracle-Sybase). The limitation is that the transaction is committed separately on the data stores. Thus, you'll need to use XA to achieve global heterogeneous transactions. In the XA architecture, each resource manager exports an XA API. The TPM becomes the 2PC coordinator and uses the XA API to control the prepare/commit/rollback of transactions within the resource managers. Direct commits and rollbacks from the application servers are replaced with calls to the TPM through the XA interface.

Transaction Recovery in the XA Environment

If the TPM crashes or becomes unavailable while performing a 2PC, a transaction may be left in pending state. In this state, it may be holding locks and preventing other users from proceeding. You can use the commit force or rollback force statements as needed to manually force the transaction to commit or rollback.

Purchasing a TPM

Several vendors provide UNIX TPMs. The following support XA:

- Tuxedo System/T, UNIX System Laboratories
- Top End, NCR Corporation
- Encina, Transarc Corporation

- CICS/6000, IBM Corporation
- CICS 9000, Hewlett-Packard

The following don't currently support XA:

- VIS/TP, VISystems, Inc.
- UniKix, UniKix, Inc.
- Micro Focus Transaction System, Micro Focus

Writing an Oracle TPM Application

The TPM vendor documentation should describe the actual
APIs used to talk to the TPM. However, all of them have a way
to indicate where a transaction begins and ends and a way to
send a request and receive a response from a client to a server. In
the following example, which uses Tuxedo /T verbs, the SQL
COMMIT is replaced with the TPM COMMIT.

The first example is an Oracle managed transaction. For the
client, use

```
Tpcall("debit_credit");
```

Use the following for the server:

```
Debit_credit_service (TPSCVCINFO *input)
{
    extract data from the input;
    EXEC SQL UPDATE debit_data;
    EXEC SQL UPDATE credit_data;
    EXEC SQL COMMIT WORK;
    Tpreturn(output_data);
}
```

The next example is a TPM-managed transaction using XA. Use
the following for the client:

```
Tpbegin();
Tpcall("debit");
Tpcall("credit");
Tpcommit();
```

For server 1, use

```
Debit_service(TPSCVCINFO *input)
{
```

```
    extract data from the input;
    EXEC SQL UPDATE debit_data;
    Tpreturn(output_data);
}
```

For server 2, use the following:

```
credit_service(TPSCVCINFO *input)
{
    extract data from the input;
    EXEC SQL UPDATE credit_data;
    Tpreturn(output_data);
}
```

For the TPM API and programming overview, you can obtain the material from the vendor.

DSS and Data-Warehousing Tuning

DSS systems generally perform queries on huge amounts of data that has been gathered from OLTP systems. You need to consider several issues when using DSS systems:

- Index management
- Data block size
- Star queries
- Parallel execution

Adding Indexes

Using the UNRECOVERABLE option

Using the **UNRECOVERABLE** option during index creation can speed up index creation. Because this won't generate any redo log records during index creation, you should back up after the index is created.

An index is generally used to provide a fast access path to the data. When using indexes in a DSS environment where you would be dealing with a huge amount of data, you need to take several special measures:

- Create indexes after inserting data in the table. Use SQL*Loader or Import to load the data first, and then create the index. This will be faster because the index doesn't have to be maintained for each insertion; instead, it's created at the end when all the data has been inserted.

- Create enough indexes based on the type of queries you'll be running.

In the DSS system, the data changes won't be a lot, so you should be able to create relatively more indexes without worrying about the performance. In general, be careful when creating indexes because unnecessary indexes can degrade performance.

When you're using star queries, the indexes on the fact table can be partitioned or non-partitioned. Local partitioned indexes are the simplest, but their disadvantage is that a search of local non-prefixed index requires searching of all the index partitions.

Managing Sort Space

In a DSS environment, you usually will end up with queries that require some kind of sorting. Several initialization parameters can be manipulated to manage the amount of sort space used by these operations:

- SORT_AREA_SIZE. You can set this parameter from the initialization file. It specifies the amount of memory to allocate per parallel server process for sort operations. If you have sufficient memory on your system, you'll benefit in performance by setting a large value for SORT_AREA_SIZE because the entire operation can be performed in memory. If memory isn't enough, you should set SORT_AREA_SIZE to a lower value and increase the size of the buffer cache so that blocks from temporary sort segments can be cached. The SORT_AREA_SIZE is relevant to parallel query operations and to the query portion of DML or DDL statements.

- SORT_DIRECT_WRITES. You can set this parameter in the initialization file. The recommended value is AUTO. When this parameter is set to AUTO and SORT_AREA_SIZE is greater than 10 times the buffer size, the buffer cache will be bypassed for the writing of sort runs. Avoiding the buffer cache can improve performance by reducing the path length, reducing memory bus utilization, and reducing LRU latch contention on SMP machines. SORT_DIRECT_WRITES has no effect on hashing.

Index creation and sorting

Statements such as CREATE INDEX, direct-load INSERT, and ALTER INDEX... REBUILD perform some sorting during index creation.

Effect of sort area size

As the sort area size decreases, the amount of I/O increases due to the need to perform merges on a large number of runs. A large sort area, on the other hand, can result in a high operating system paging rate.

Release memory after completing sorts

The SORT_AREA_ RETAINED_SIZE parameter allows you to specify the level to which memory should be released as soon as possible after a sort completes. If memory isn't released until the user disconnects, large sorts will create problems in the system.

- SORT_AREA_RETAINED_SIZE. This parameter specifies the maximum amount of User Global Area (UGA) memory retained after a sort run completes. If more memory is required by a sort, a temporary segment is allocated and the sort becomes an external sort. SORT_AREA_RETAINED_SIZE is maintained for each sort operation in a query.

Large sort areas can be used effectively by combining a large SORT_AREA_SIZE with a minimal SORT_AREA_RETAINED_SIZE.

Managing Hash Join Space

If $C_x(Y)$ is used to represent the cost to perform operation x on table Y, the cost to perform a hash join is as follows (provided that you have sufficient memory available):

$$C_{hj}(T1,T2) < C_{read}(T1) + C_{read}(T2) + C_{hash}(T1,T2)$$

When you use *hash join* operations, an in-memory hash table is built from smaller table, and then the larger table is scanned and joined by using a hash table probe. Hash joins are applicable to equijoins, anti-joins, and outer joins. Indexes aren't required to perform a hash join.

Suppose that you have two tables, french and engineers, and want the names of all the French engineers. french is the smaller of the two tables.

```
SELECT /*+ use_hash(french) */ french.name
FROM french, engineers
WHERE french.name = engineers.name
```

To perform the hash join, an area of memory known as the hash memory is allocated (see Figure 22.1).

The first stage of the join involves scanning and partitioning the french table and building an in-memory hash filter and hash table. This is the *build*, and the french table is known as the *build input*. The french table is hash partitioned into smaller chunks so that at least one partition can be accommodated in the hash memory, which reduces the number of comparisons during the join. As the build input is scanned, parts of some partitions may be written to disk (temporary segment).

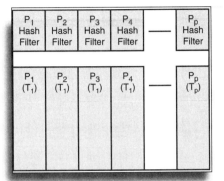

FIGURE 22.1

The in-memory hash table is obtained by using the *french* table.

A hash filter is created for each partition and stays in memory even if the partition doesn't fit. The *hash filter* is used to efficiently discard rows that don't join. After the french table is scanned completely, the size of each partition is known, as many partitions as possible are loaded into memory, and a single hash table is built on the in-memory partitions.

Case 1: The hash memory is large enough for all the partitions of the french table; therefore, the entire join is completed by simply scanning the engineers table and probing the build.

Case 2: The hash memory isn't large enough to fit all the partitions of the french table. In this case, the engineers table is scanned, and each row is partitioned using the same method (see Figure 22.2). Then for each row,

- The "no hope" rows are discarded after verifying them with the hash filter.
- Rows that correspond to in-memory french partitions are joined immediately, and rows that don't are written to an engineers partition on disk (temporary segment).

After the engineers table is scanned, phase 2 begins. In phase 2, the smaller of the french and engineers partitions are scanned into memory and a hash table is built. The larger partition is scanned, and the join is completed by probing the hash table. If a partition won't fit in memory, the join will degenerate to a nested loop type mechanism.

Applying hash functions to data

When applying hash functions to data, $Key1 = Key2 \Rightarrow hash(Key1) = hash(Key2)$ but the reverse isn't true. (*hash* represents a hash function, and *Key1* and *Key2* represent data.)

FIGURE 22.2

Hash joins are performed by using the in-memory hash table and the hash filters.

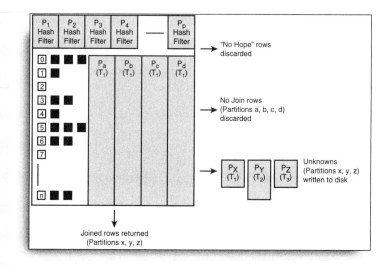

You can set the following parameters in the initialization file or by using the ALTER SESSION command from Server Manager:

- HASH_JOIN_ENABLED (the default is TRUE). Setting this to TRUE allows you to use hash joins.

- HASH_AREA_SIZE (the default is twice the SORT_AREA_SIZE). This parameter specifies the size of the hash memory. It should be approximately half of the square root of S, where S is the size (in MB) of the smaller of the inputs to the join operation. The value shouldn't be less than 1MB. HASH_AREA_SIZE is relevant to parallel query operations and to the query portion of DML or DDL statements.

- HASH_MULTIBLOCK_IO_COUNT (the default is DB_FILE_MULTIBLOCK_IO_COUNT). This parameter specifies the number of sequential blocks a hash join should read and write in a single I/O.

Set the size of hash area appropriately

Each process that performs a parallel join operation uses an amount of memory equal to HASH_AREA_SIZE. Setting HASH_AREA_SIZE too large can cause the system to run out of memory, whereas a setting that's too small can degrade performance.

Designing Tables for Star Queries

Star queries are most suitable for data warehouses, where there's a huge amount of data but relatively few data changes. A star schema is a natural data representation for many data warehousing applications; it consists of one very large table, referred to as a *fact table*, and many smaller tables, called *dimension tables*. (Note that the rule-based optimizer doesn't recognize star schemas.)

Dimension tables aren't related to each other; however, each dimension table is related to the fact table through a primary key/foreign key relationship. Usually, there's a b*tree concatenated index on the columns of the fact table that are related to the dimension tables.

An example of a star schema would be a retail environment (see Figure 22.3).

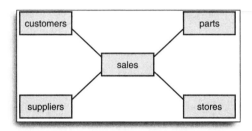

FIGURE 22.3

In a star schema, the relationship between the involved tables represents a star structure.

The following tables can be part of a retail environment:

- `sales` with columns `customer_key, supplier_key, part_key, store_key, date, quantity,` and `total_price`
- `suppliers` with columns `supplier_key, name, address,` and `telephone`
- `customers` with columns `customer_key, name,` and `address`
- `parts` with columns `part_key, name,` and `cost`
- `stores` with columns `store_key, address,` and `telephone`

The `sales` table can be the fact table and contain several millions of records for the different sales transactions. The dimension tables—`suppliers, customers, parts,` and `stores`—are relatively small and provide additional details about a sale.

If you need to find sales information, use a star query. It uses specific details from the dimension tables. For example, if you want to find the total sales of a specific part purchased by a specific group of customers from a specific store and sort the results by suppliers, use the following query:

```
Select supplier.name, sum(total_sales)
from sales, customers, parts, suppliers, stores
where
```

```
sales.customer_key = customer.customer_key and
sales.part_key = parts.part_key and
sales.supplier_key = suppliers.supplier_key and
sales.store_key = stores.store_key and
customers.name in ('IBM','HP','COMPAQ') and
parts.name = '2 GB disk' and
stores.name = 'EGG HEAD SOFTWARE'
group by suppliers.name;
```

Tuning Star Queries

To efficiently use star queries, you must use the cost-based optimizer (set OPTIMIZER_MODE to CHOOSE) and analyze with COMPUTE STATISTICS all the tables involved in the star query. To analyze tables, use the following command from the Server Manager prompt:

```
SVRMGR> ANALYZE TABLE tablename COMPUTE STATISTICS;
```

You can also tune star queries in other ways:

- You can improve the optimizer plan by using hints. The most effective method is to order the tables in the FROM clause in the order of the keys in the index with the large table last. Then use the USE_NL hint or the STAR hint.

- The columns in the concatenated index of the fact table should take advantage of any ordering of the data. If all the queries specify predicates on each dimension table, a single concatenated index is sufficient, but if you use queries that omit the leading columns of the concatenated index, you'll have to create additional indexes.

- Denormalized views can be effective at times when too much normalization of information can cause the optimizer to consider many permutations and result in very slow queries. For example, you have two tables, brands and manufacturers, that can be combined into a product view as follows:

  ```
  CREATE VIEW product AS SELECT /*+ NO_MERGE */ *
  FROM brands,manufacturers WHERE brands.mfkey =
  manufacturers.mfkey;
  ```

  This will improve performance by caching the result of the view and reducing the executions of the small table joins.

STAR hint versus USE_NL hint

The **STAR** hint /*+ STAR */ forces a star query plan to be used if possible. The **USE_NL** hint /*+ USE_NL (*table*) */ causes each specified table to join with another row source with a nested loops join, using the specified table as the inner table.

You also can use a star transformation by setting STAR_
TRANSFORMATION_ENABLED to TRUE in the initialization file and using
the STAR_TRANSFORMATION hint in the query. Tables with the following characteristics can't be used with a star transformation,
however:

- Tables with very few bitmap indexes
- Anti-joined tables
- Tables already used as dimension tables in a subquery
- Remote tables
- Tables that are unmerged views

The star transformation is ideal under any of the following conditions:

- The fact table is sparse.
- There are a lot of dimension tables.
- In some queries, not all dimension tables have constraining
  predicates.

The star transformation doesn't rely on computing a *Cartesian
product* of the dimension tables; instead, it uses bitmap indexes
on individual fact table columns. It works by generating new
subqueries that can be used to drive a bitmap index access path
for the fact table.

SEE ALSO

➤ *More information on using the cost-based optimizer, page 439*

➤ *See how to use hints, page 443*

➤ *More information on bitmap indexes, page 247*

Parallel Operations

Oracle can perform the following operations in parallel:

- Parallel query
- Parallel DML (INSERT, UPDATE, DELETE, APPEND hint, and paral-
  lel index scans)
- Parallel DDL
- Parallel recovery
- Parallel loading
- Parallel propagation (for replication)

You should try to parallelize operations that have high elapsed time or process a large number of rows.

Tuning Parallel Operations in a DSS Environment

You can use several techniques to optimize parallel operations.

One way is to increase the default degree of parallelism for I/O-bound operations and decrease the degree of parallelism for memory-bound operations. Follow these guidelines when adjusting the degree of parallelism:

- Use the ALTER TABLE command or hints to change the degree of parallelism.

- Reducing the degree of parallelism will increase the number of concurrent parallel operations.

- If the operation is I/O-bound, spread the data over more disks than there are CPUs and then increase the parallelism in stages until it becomes CPU-bound.

You also can verify that all the parts of the query plan for SQL statements that process huge amounts of data are executing in parallel. By using EXPLAIN PLAN, verify that the plan steps have an OTHER_TAG of PARALLEL_TO_PARALLEL, PARALLEL_TO_SERIAL, PARALLEL_COMBINED_WITH_PARENT, or PARALLEL_COMBINED_WITH_CHILD. Any other keyword or null indicates serial execution and possible bottleneck. Follow these guidelines to improve parallelism of the SQL statements:

- Because Oracle can parallelize joins more efficiently than subqueries, you should convert your subqueries into joins.

- Use PL/SQL functions in the WHERE clause of the main query rather than correlated subqueries.

- Queries with distinct aggregates should be rewritten as nested queries.

You can create and populate tables in parallel by using the PARALLEL and the NOLOGGING options with the CREATE TABLE statement. For example,

```
CREATE TABLE new_table PARALLEL NOLOGGING
AS SELECT col1,col2, col3 FROM old_table;
```

You also can create indexes by using the PARALLEL and NOLOGGING clauses of the CREATE INDEX statement. Index creation takes place serially unless you specify the PARALLEL clause. An index created with an INITIAL of 5MB and a PARALLEL DEGREE of 8 will use at least 40MB during index creation because the STORAGE clause refers to the storage of each subindex created by the query server processes.

Another technique to optimize parallel operations is to set the initialization parameters correctly:

- OPTIMIZER_PERCENT_PARALLEL. The default value of 0 will cause the least usage of resources and will generally result in a long response time. On the other hand, a value of 100 will cause the optimizer to use a parallel plan, unless a serial plan is faster. The recommended value is 100 divided by the number of concurrent users.

- PARALLEL_MAX_SERVERS. The recommended value is 2×CPUs×Number of Concurrent Users.

- PARALLEL_MIN_SERVERS. It's recommended that you set this to the same value as PARALLEL_MAX_SERVERS.

- SHARED_POOL_SIZE. Oracle reserves memory from the SHARED_POOL for the parallel server processes. You can use the following formula to determine the setting of this parameter:

  (CPUs + 2)×(PARALLEL_MIN_SERVERS)×1.5×(BLOCK_SIZE)

- SORT_AREA_SIZE. Use a large SORT_AREA_SIZE because the parallel queries would generally be doing some sort of sorting. A small SORT_AREA_SIZE could lead to a lot of sort runs.

- PARALLEL_ADAPTIVE_MULTI_USER. The recommended value for this is FALSE. When this parameter is set to TRUE, it automatically reduces the requested degree of parallelism based on the current number of active parallel execution users on the system. The effective degree of parallelism is based on the degree of parallelism set by the table attributes or hints, divided by the total number of parallel execution users.

The number of CPUs can affect the amount of parallelism

If the degree of parallelism isn't specified in the PARALLEL clause of CREATE INDEX, the number of CPUs is used as the degree of parallelism.

Parallelism is influenced by the usage of hints

A non-zero setting of OPTIMIZER_PERCENT_ PARALLEL is overridden if you use a FIRST_ROWS hint or set OPTIMIZER_MODE to FIRST_ROWS.

Set PARALLEL_MIN_ SERVERS appropriately

You can use the V$PQ_ SYSSTAT view to determine if you've set the value of PARALLEL_MIN_SERVER S too low or too high. If the Servers Started statistics are continuously increasing, you need to increase this parameter. On the other hand, if very few parallel server processes are busy at any given time, you should decrease this value.

This parameter works best for a single-node SMP machine but can be used in an OPS environment if all the following conditions are true:

- Users that execute parallel operations connect to the same node
- Each node is an SMP
- Instance groups aren't configured

Diagnosing and Correcting Problems

Identify and recover from database corruption

Use *UTLBSTAT* and *UTLESTAT* to analyze the database

Obtain quality service from Oracle Support

Common Problems in Oracle Systems

People encounter four common types of failures or problems in an Oracle system:

- *Crash (code failure).* This can be seen in the form of ORA-600 errors, exception signals (ORA-7445 in UNIX), or other error messages. When a process crashes, it places diagnostic information in a trace file, and the background process places an entry in the alert log to indicate what this trace file is called. Usually, the trace file contains sufficient information to identify the cause of the problem. If the information isn't sufficient, you may need to get additional trace or dump files as requested by Oracle Support Services. From the trace file, the most useful diagnostic information is obtained from the stack trace and process state dump sections.

- *Hang.* You first have to identify the situation as being a hanging situation. If a process is consuming CPU, it isn't hung; a hang is indicated by a process waiting for something that will never happen. The hung process usually isn't the cause of the problem, so you need to obtain more diagnostic information to find the root cause. The most useful tools to diagnose the hanging situation is to get system state dumps from the trace file and v$session_wait.

- *Looping.* A looping situation is identified by a process endlessly repeating the same task and using all available CPU. Loops are difficult to diagnose because the target is moving continuously. You can diagnose this problem by obtaining stack trace and process state dumps information. You'll need to get multiple dumps to identify the location and scope of the loop.

- *Slow process.* A slow system or process is generally the result of insufficient tuning, an art that requires you to understand the application and the system environment properly. Oracle provides two scripts, UTLBSTAT and UTLESTAT, which you can use to tune the system by identifying the sources of contention.

Data Block Corruption

An Oracle data block is written in an internal binary format and is considered to be corrupt if it no longer conforms to this format. Oracle checks a block for possible corruption before using it in any way. This checking is performed at the cache layer and higher layers of the Oracle code. The cache layer information includes the block type, version, DBA, incarnation, sequence, and block checksum.

If an inconsistency is found, the block is considered to be media corrupt. If a block isn't media corrupt but corruption is identified at the higher layer of the code, the block is considered to be software corrupt.

When a block is found to be corrupt, you normally would see an `ORA-1578` or `ORA-600 [3374]` error. You also can use the following methods to detect and identify corrupt or damaged blocks:

- The most detailed block check available is the following (this command requires the database to be open):

```
Analyze table table_name validate structure cascade;
```

    It checks every table block at the cache and higher levels. It also checks the associated index blocks and checks the one-to-one correspondence between data and index rows.

- You can use the `DB_VERIFY` utility to check the validity of Oracle data files, even if the database is down or all the files aren't available.

Using the *DB_VERIFY* Utility

The `DB_VERIFY` utility lets you to perform integrity verification of database files. It's a command-line utility that performs a physical data structure integrity check on an offline database; you can find it in the rdbms/admin directory. (`DB_VERIFY` checks are limited to cache-managed blocks.) Its syntax is as follows:

```
DB_VERIFY parameters
```

In the syntax, `DB_VERIFY` is an operating system–specific executable: `dbv` on Sun/Sequent systems and `dbverif80` on Windows NT systems. *parameters* is from the following table:

Validate your backups

You also can use `DB_VERIFY` to validate your backups and make sure that you can use them for database recovery.

Parameter	Description	Default
FILE	Name of file to verify	None
START	Starting block address	First block of the file
END	Ending block address	Last block of the file
BLOCKSIZE	Logical block size	2048
LOGFILE	File that logs the DB_VERIFY's output	STANDARD ERROR
FEEDBACK n	Displayed for every n pages verified (0 indicates off)	
HELP	Type Y to display online help	
PARFILE	Name of the parameter file	None

Specify a BLOCKSIZE

If you don't specify **BLOCKSIZE** for non-2KB files, you'll get error DBV-00103.

You can obtain the BLOCK_SIZE by executing the following at the Server Manager prompt:

```
SVRMGR>SHOW PARAMETER BLOCK_SIZE
```

To use the DB_VERIFY utility in Windows NT, enter the following at a system prompt:

```
dbverif80 file=datafile1.ora logfile=dbvlog.out feedback=0
```

DB_VERIFY will verify the file datafile1.ora, starting from the first Oracle block to the last Oracle block, using a block size of 2048 and put the results in the file dbvlog.out. It doesn't send any dots to the screen for verified pages.

Shut down the database before using DB_VERIFY

You must shut down the database before using **DB_VERIFY** against its data files, to prevent the database from getting corrupted.

To use the DB_VERIFY utility on a Sun machine, enter the following at a system prompt:

```
dbv file=datafile2.dbf feedback=10
```

You'll get the following output:

```
DBVERIFY: Release x.x.x.x.x - date
Copyright......

DBVERIFY - Verification starting: FILE = datafile2.ora

DBVERIFY - Verification complete
```

Validating archive logs

You can verify inactive archive log files with **DB_VERIFY**, even if the database isn't offline.

```
Total Pages Examined............................: 9216
Total Pages Processed....(Data).................: 2044
Total Pages Failing.........(Data)..............: 0
Total Pages Processed....(Index)................: 921
Total Pages Failing.........(Index).............: 0
Total Pages Empty...............................: 5442
Total Pages Marked Corrupt......................: 0
Total Pages Influx..............................: 0
```

On other UNIX platforms such as HP and DEC-UX, results should be very similar.

Verifying a Data File Created on a Raw Device

The following shows the contents of a raw device when used with a data file:

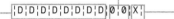

① Data

② Space left in the data file

③ Reserved for non-data file usage

When you use DB_VERIFY to verify a data file on a raw device, you should use the START and END parameters. Otherwise, it will mark the non-database blocks as corrupt:

```
$Dbv testfile.dbf


DBVERIFY: Release x.x.x.x.x - date


Copyright........


DBVERIFY - Verification starting: FILE = testfile.dbf
Page 23548 is marked software corrupt
Page 23600 is marked software corrupt
Page 23601 is marked software corrupt
Page 23602 is marked software corrupt
Page 23603 is marked software corrupt
Page 23604 is marked software corrupt
Page 23605 is marked software corrupt
Page 23606 is marked software corrupt
Page 23607 is marked software corrupt
Page 23608 is marked software corrupt
Page 23609 is marked software corrupt
Page 23610 is marked software corrupt
```

```
Page 23611 is marked software corrupt
Page 23612 is marked software corrupt
Page 23613 is marked software corrupt
Page 23614 is marked software corrupt
Page 23615 is marked software corrupt
Page 23616 is marked software corrupt
Page 23617 is marked software corrupt
Page 23618 is marked software corrupt
Page 23723 is marked software corrupt


DBVERIFY - Verification Complete


Total Pages Examined..............................: 12075
Total Pages Processed....(Data).......................: 0
Total Pages Failing.........(Data)....................: 0
Total Pages Processed....(Index)...................: 462
Total Pages Failing.........(Index)...................: 0
Total Pages Empty................................: 11482
Total Pages Marked Corrupt..........................: 20
Total Pages Influx...................................: 0
```

Ensure that you don't get blocks corrupted when using *DB_VERIFY*

1. At the Server Manager prompt, type the following:

```
SVRMGR> select bytes
        from v$datafile
        where name = 'datafile_name';
```

By using the bytes amount from this query, you can determine the number of database blocks in the data file with the following equation:

```
Number of blocks = datafile bytes/BLOCKSIZE
```

2. Run DB_VERIFY:

```
$Dbv file=datafile end=number of blocks
```

Using the Checksum Facilities

The checksum facilities provided by Oracle can be used to identify corrupt blocks.

Setting DB_BLOCK_CHECKSUM to TRUE causes checksums to be calculated for all data blocks on their next update. A block will always use checksums as soon as it's generated, even if the parameter is removed. The checksums are calculated by the DBWR and the direct loader and stored in the cache header of every data block when writing it to disk.

Setting LOG_BLOCK_CHECKSUM to TRUE causes checksums to be calculated for all redo log blocks.

Setting _DB_BLOCK_CACHE_PROTECT to TRUE in the init.ora file protects the cache layer from becoming corrupted. It will prevent certain corruption from getting to disk, although it may crash the foreground of the database instance. It will help catch stray writes in the cache and will fail with a stack violation when a process tries to write past the buffer size in the SGA.

The checksum utility also provides various events that you can use to check various blocks for corruption. These events "soft corrupt" a block if they find any kind of mismatch during the checking process. To use these events, type the following at the Server Manager prompt:

```
alter session set events '102xx trace name context forever,
level 10';
```

The following events are available:

Event	Purpose
10210	Checks data blocks
10211	Checks index blocks
10212	Checks cluster blocks
10225	Checks information in fet$/uset$ for any corruption; can be used in case your create segment statement is hanging

Recovering from Damaged Data Blocks

There are several causes for a data block getting damaged:

- Bad I/O hardware/firmware
- Operating system I/O or caching problems

Parameters used to check for corrupt blocks can affect performance

Setting DB_BLOCK_CHECKSUM or LOG_BLOCK_CHECKSUM to TRUE can result in CPU time being spent in validating blocks, a process that's normally not performed. The performance hit can be from 5% to 20%, depending on the type of data.

- Disk repair utilities

- Memory problems

- Oracle incorrectly attempting to access an unformatted block

To recover from damaged data blocks, you need to figure out the extent of the damage by looking at the full error message(s), the alert log, and all the trace files generated. If there are multiple errors or you have operating system–level errors, you should first resolve those errors before even attempting to recover the damaged file. After the operating system and hardware errors are fixed, you can use the following steps to recover.

The error is in file# (*F*) and block#

1. Determine the corrupted file by typing the following at the Server Manager prompt:

    ```
    SELECT * FROM v$datafile WHERE file# = F;
    ```

2. Determine the damaged object by executing the following at the Server Manager prompt:

    ```
    SELECT owner, segment_name, segment_type
    FROM dba_extents
    WHERE file_id = F
      AND    B BETWEEN block_id AND block_id  + blocks - 1;
    ```

SEE ALSO

➤ *If the segment returned from this query is a rollback segment, you can recover from the damaged segment by using a certain method, page 388*

3. If the segment is an index, determine the table it belongs to by executing the following:

    ```
    SELECT table_owner, table_name
    FROM dba_indexes
    WHERE index_name = 'segment_name';
    ```

    If the segment is a cluster, determine the table it belongs to by executing the following:

    ```
    SELECT owner, table_name
    FROM dba_tables
    WHERE cluster_name = 'segment_name';
    ```

    If the segment is a table, note the table name and the owner.

SEE ALSO

➤ *If the table is a data dictionary table, recover from the damage by using a described method, page 384*

4. Run the ANALYZE command at least twice to ensure that the problem isn't an intermittent problem.

For an index or a table, at the Server Manager prompt type the following:

```
ANALYZE TABLE owner.tablename VALIDATE STRUCTURE
➥CASCADE;
```

For a cluster, type the following at the Server Manager prompt:

```
ANALYZE CLUSTER owner.clustername VALIDATE STRUCTURE
➥CASCADE;
```

If you encounter potential hardware errors on a particular disk or controller, first relocate the files to a good disk.

Recover from a hardware problem in *ARCHIVELOG* mode

1. Take the affected data file offline.

2. Restore its last backup on a good disk.

3. Rename the data file to the new location.

4. Recover the data file.

5. Put the file back online and start using it.

Recover from a hardware problem in *NOARCHIVELOG* mode

1. Take the affected data file offline.

2. Restore its last backup on a good disk.

3. Rename the data file to the new location.

4. Put the file back online and start using it.

If you have to rename the file, run the ANALYZE command at least twice to verify that the corruption still exists. If ANALYZE still returns an error and you've already fixed the hardware problems, you need to salvage the data.

You can salvage data from damaged data blocks in several ways:

- Media recovery is the easiest method to resolve block corruption problems.

- If the object (table, index, whatever) that contains corruption can be easily recreated, you should drop the object and recreate it.

If you know the file and block number of the corrupted blocks, you can extract the good data by selecting around the corruption. Before attempting to salvage the data this way, check the following:

- Do you have an export that can be used to create the table easily?
- Do you have a backup copy of the database from which you can create an export of the table?

If you have neither, you can extract data around the corrupt block by using the following command at the Server Manager prompt:

```
(a) CREATE TABLE salvage AS
SELECT * FROM corrupt_table WHERE 1 = 2;
(b) INSERT INTO salvage
SELECT /*+ ROWID(corrupt_table) */ * FROM corrupt_table
WHERE rowid <= 'low_rowid_of_corrupt_block';
(c) INSERT INTO salvage
SELECT /*+ ROWID(corrupt_table) */ * FROM corrupt_table
WHERE rowid >= 'high_rowid_of_corrupt_block';
```

You also can set event 10231 in the initialization file and select around the corruption. This event causes Oracle to skip software and media-corrupted blocks when performing full table scans and allows you to extract the good blocks and recreate the database object:

```
Usage: event="10231 trace name context forever, level 10"
```

You can set event 10233 in the initialization file and select around the corruption. This event is similar to event 10231, except it works with index range scans. Note, however, that data in the corrupted blocks will be lost when event 10233 is set.

Finally, you can contact Oracle Support Services, which has access to several tools that you can use to extract data from corrupt database objects. See the later section "Working with Oracle Support" for more information.

Working with the Alert Log and Trace Files

In an Oracle environment, you'll encounter many kinds of logs and trace files, including the alert log, process trace files, core files, application logs, system logs, and network logs.

Oracle Alert Log

The Oracle background and foreground processes log information to a file called the *alert log*. The primary use of the alert log is to understand the progress of the instance, because it captures the following:

- Summary errors
- The important stages the database goes through, such as startup, shutdown, and tablespace creation/drop
- Pointers to trace files when there's a failure

SEE ALSO

➤ *More information on the contents and usage of the alert log, page* **54**

Oracle Trace Files

All the Oracle server processes have a file called a *trace file* to which they record traces, dumps, and error messages. This file isn't written to by any other process.

The trace file is linked to the standard output of the process, allowing the capture of encountered operating system messages. All trace files have a header that contains

- Timestamp
- Oracle version used
- Operating system and version
- Installed options
- Instance name
- Oracle process ID
- Operating system process ID

Locating trace files

You should find the trace file in the directory indicated by **BACKGROUND_DUMP_DEST**, **USER_DUMP_DEST**, or **CORE_DUMP_DEST**, depending on the exact error and its cause.

Application Trace Files

Client-side progress and failure information can be collected in application trace files—for example, spool.lst from SQL*Plus. These files contain useful information, such as the following:

- Application progress and performance
- Alert of application malfunction
- Indications of system, network, or database problems

Extracting the Stack Trace Out of the Core Dump

When a process aborts, it creates a core file in the current directory. This core file contains a dump of process memory. To dump your process state, use the following command:

```
Alter session set events
➡'immediate trace name processstate level 10';
```

You can extract a stack trace from the core file, which can indicate where the process failed. To obtain a stack trace when a certain error XXXX occurs, use the following command:

```
Alter session set events
➡'XXXX trace name errorstack forever, level 10';
```

Get the stack trace from the core file

UNIX versus Windows NT core dump

These steps are UNIX specific. If you use Windows NT, you can find the core dump in an "access violation" file.

1. Log in as ORACLE and change to the $ORACLE_HOME/bin directory.

2. Type the following, where *program* is the program that aborted:
   ```
   file program
   ```

3. Add read permissions to the program. At the operating system prompt, type
   ```
   $Chmod +r program
   ```

4. Log out and then log in as the user who encountered the error.

5. The next step varies, depending on the version of UNIX you're using. One of the following commands should exist on your machine:

Command	Exit Command/Keystroke
dbx	quit
xdb	quit
sdb	q
adb	Ctrl+D
gdb	Ctrl+D

Change to the directory where the core dump is located. In the Bourne or Korn shell, type the following:

```
dbx $ORACLE_HOME/bin/program core 2>&1 ¦ tee /tmp/stack
trace
```

In the C shell, type the following:

```
dbx $ORACLE_HOME/bin/program core ¦ tee /tmp/stacktrace
```

6. The stack trace should be produced in the file stacktrace. Exit the debug tool.

Other Useful Files

Several other useful files can help you diagnose system problems:

- You can use system logs to obtain information about hardware or operating system problems.
- Use network logs to find network messages.

Analyze Your Database with *UTLBSTAT/UTLESTAT*

Oracle provides you with two scripts, utlbstat.sql and utlestat.sql, that you can use to tune a database. The utlbstat component gathers the initial performance statistics and places them in temporary tables; the utlestat component gathers the performance statistics at the end of the observation period and places them in temporary tables. When utlestat is finished, it compares the information in the two sets of temporary tables and places the result of comparison in another set of temporary tables. A report is generated from the results and is placed in an ASCII report.txt file in the current directory.

UTLBSTAT and UTLESTAT don't affect performance

Using **UTLBSTAT** and **UTLESTAT** doesn't result in a performance degradation, except for a few minutes while these scripts run. This is because these scripts simply take a snapshot of the system at the beginning and a snapshot at the end of the period.

Use the *utlbstat* and *utlestat* scripts

1. Determine the time period for analysis. You should choose the time period to represent your normal workload. You shouldn't run utlbstat right after the database is started, for example, because it won't represent the normal working condition of the database. Let the database run for some time so that the system caches can be loaded appropriately and represent a stable running environment.

2. Set initialization parameters. In the init.ora file, set TIMED_STATISTICS to TRUE and then restart the database. Alternatively, if you don't want to restart the database, connect internally and type the following at the Server Manager prompt:

   ```
   ALTER SYSTEM SET TIMED_STATISTICS = TRUE;
   ```

Keep the database running while getting reports

Don't shut down the database between the running of UTLBSTAT and UTLESTAT; otherwise, the results will be useless.

3. Run utlbstat.sql from the Server Manager prompt at the appropriate time:

   ```
   SVRMGR> @%RDBMS80%\admin\utlbstat
   ```

4. Run utlestat.sql from the Server Manager at the end of the time period:

   ```
   SVRMGR>@%RDBMS80%\admin\utlestat
   ```

The resulting report.txt file provides the following information:

- Library cache statistics
- Systemwide statistics
- Wait events
- DBWR statistics
- I/O statistics
- Latch statistics
- Dictionary cache statistics

Let's analyze each section in more detail and determine how to tune the system based on the report's information.

Library Cache

The SQL AREA, TABLE/PROCEDURE, BODY, and TRIGGER rows in the following output show library cache activity for SQL statements and PL/SQL blocks. The other rows indicate library cache activity for object definitions used by Oracle for dependency management.

LIBRARY	GETS	GETHITRATI	PINS	PINHITRATI	RELOADS	INVALIDATI
BODY	972	1	972	1	0	0
CLUSTER	0	1	0	1	0	0
INDEX	0	1	0	1	0	0
OBJECT	0	1	0	1	0	0
PIPE	0	1	0	1	0	0
SQL AREA	3653	1	23462	1	4	0
TABLE/PROCE	153	.98	9169	1	0	0
TRIGGER	0	1	0	1	0	0

8 rows selected.

① How many times object was found in memory (equivalent to # of parses)

② How many times did object was executed

③ Object definition was aged out for lack of space

④ Should be greater than 0.9 for all rows

⑤ Should be (ideally 0) not more than 1 percent of PINS

Your aim is to reduce parsing, enable sharing of statements, reduce aging out, and provide enough space to large objects.

If you have a lot of reloads or the GETHITRATIO is less than 90%, you should increase the SHARED_POOL_SIZE parameter in the initialization file.

System Statistics

The following file also provides several comments (not shown here) that you can read for further information:

Statistic	Total	Per Transa	Per Logon	Per Sec
CPU used by this session	9904	8.94	70.24	27.66
CPU used when call started	9904	8.94	70.24	27.66
CR blocks created	9	.01	.06	.03
DBWR buffers scanned	907	.82	6.43	2.53
DBWR checkpoints	6	.01	.04	.02
DBWR free buffers found	763	.69	5.41	2.13
DBWR lru scans	89	.08	.63	.25

Improving database writer performance

From these system statistics, **DBWR buffers scanned row** and **DBWR checkpoints** should give you a good idea about the amount of load on the **DBWR** process. On operating systems such as UNIX that allow you to have multiple **DBWR** processes, you should increase the parameter **DB_WRITERS** in the initialization file to two per database file. Also, increase **DB_BLOCK_WRITE_BATCH** to reduce the number of times the **DBWR** is signaled to perform a write operation.

DBWR make free requests	76	.07	.54	.21
DBWR summed scan depth	907	.82	6.43	2.53
DBWR timeouts	91	.08	.65	.25
OS System time used	284700	256.95	2019.15	795.25
OS User time used	838900	757.13	5949.65	2343.3
SQL*Net roundtrips to/from	8899	8.03	63.11	24.86
background checkpoints comp	7	.01	.05	.02
background checkpoints star	6	.01	.04	.02
background timeouts	214	.19	1.52	.6
bytes received via SQL*Net	1167468	1053.67	8279.91	3261.08
bytes sent via SQL*Net to c	343632	310.14	2437.11	959.87
calls to get snapshot scn:	5622	5.07	39.87	15.7
calls to kcmgas	1130	1.02	8.01	3.16
calls to kcmgcs	101	.09	.72	.28
calls to kcmgrs	9064	8.18	64.28	25.32
change write time	529	.48	3.75	1.48
cleanouts only - consistent	1	0	.01	0
cluster key scan block gets	334	.3	2.37	.93
cluster key scans	303	.27	2.15	.85
commit cleanout failures: b	1	0	.01	0
commit cleanout number succ	1329	1.2	9.43	3.71
consistent changes	9	.01	.06	.03
consistent gets	5784	5.22	41.02	16.16
cursor authentications	3744	3.38	26.55	10.46
data blocks consistent read	9	.01	.06	.03
db block changes	18659	16.84	132.33	52.12
db block gets	15638	14.11	110.91	43.68
deferred (CURRENT) block cl	1260	1.14	8.94	3.52
enqueue conversions	139	.13	.99	.39
enqueue releases	2472	2.23	17.53	6.91
enqueue requests	2466	2.23	17.49	6.89
execute count	10859	9.8	77.01	30.33
free buffer requested	447	.4	3.17	1.25
immediate (CR) block cleano	1	0	.01	0
logons cumulative	141	.13	1	.39
logons current	1	0	.01	0
messages received	684	.62	4.85	1.91
messages sent	684	.62	4.85	1.91
no work - consistent read g	3291	2.97	23.34	9.19

```
opened cursors cumulative   3655        3.3     25.92   10.21
opened cursors current         3          0       .02     .01
parse count                 5728        5.17    40.62      16
parse time cpu              1602        1.45    11.36    4.47
parse time elapsed          1799        1.62    12.76    5.03
physical reads                29         .03       .21     .08
physical writes             1021         .92      7.24    2.85
recursive calls            25096       22.65    177.99    70.1
recursive cpu usage         5052        4.56     35.83   14.11
redo blocks written         1420        1.28     10.07    3.97
redo buffer allocation retr   11         .01       .08     .03
redo entries                9339        8.43     66.23   26.09
redo log space requests       13         .01       .09     .04
redo log space wait time     856         .77      6.07    2.39
redo size                1796924     1621.77  12744.14 5019.34
redo small copies           1359        1.23      9.64     3.8
redo synch time             5011        4.52     35.54      14
redo synch writes            565         .51      4.01    1.58
redo wastage             1076955      971.98   7637.98 3008.25
redo write time             5529        4.99     39.21   15.44
redo writer latching time      7         .01       .05     .02
redo writes                  994          .9      7.05    2.78
rollback changes - undo rec  278         .25      1.97     .78
rollbacks only - consistent    9         .01       .06     .03
session logical reads      21135       19.07    149.89   59.04
session pga memory       20645272   18632.92 146420.3757668.36
session pga memory max   20645272   18632.92 146420.3757668.36
session uga memory         232400     209.75   1648.23  649.16
session uga memory max    5826432    5258.51  41322.2116274.95
sorts(disk)
sorts (memory)               282         .25         2     .79
sorts (rows)                3414        3.08     24.21    9.54
table fetch by rowid         554          .5      3.93    1.55
table fetch continued row         indicates row chaining
table scan blocks gotten     571         .52      4.05    1.59
table scan rows gotten      3207        2.89     22.74    8.96
table scans (long tables)      1           0       .01       0
table scans (short tables)   833         .75      5.91    2.33
total number commit cleanou 1330         1.2      9.43    3.72
user calls                  7271        6.56     51.57   20.31
user commits                1108           1      7.86    3.09
```

```
user rollbacks   # of rollback calls issued by users. User
      rollbacks/user commits, if high indicates a problem.
write requests             109        .1       .77      .3
```

Use the following formulas to calculate the data cache hit ratio:

```
LOGICAL READS = CONSISTENT GETS + DB BLOCK GETS

HIT RATIO = (LOGICAL READS - PHYSICAL READS) / LOGICAL READS
```

By using these calculations for the preceding output, we get

```
LOGICAL READS =  5784 + 15638 = 21422

CACHE HIT RATIO = (21422 - 29) / 21422 = 99.86%
```

If the cache hit ratio as calculated here is less than 80%, you should increase the DB_BLOCK_BUFFERS parameter in the initialization file.

Use the following equation to check the effectiveness of your application to see if indexes are used properly. The result should be close to zero.

```
Non-Index lookups ratio = table scans (long tables) /
    table scans (long tables) + table scans (short tables)
             =  1/(1+833)
             = close to zero.
```

Wait Events

Event Name	Count	Total Time	Avg Time
SQL*Net message from client	9385	41677	4.44
log file sync	563	5196	9.23
write complete waits	68	1624	23.88
log file switch completion	13	856	65.85
log buffer space	7	301	43
SQL*Net message to client	9385	54	.01
buffer busy waits	10	25	2.5
db file sequential read	36	18	.5
SQL*Net more data from client	139	12	.09
latch free	4	2	.5
control file sequential read	22	0	0
db file scattered read	1	0	0

Your goal is to eliminate all waits for resources:

```
Buffer Busy Waits ratio = Buffer busy waits / Logical reads
                        = 11 / 21422
                        = close to zero
```

For example,

- If the waits are due to data blocks, you should increase the FREELISTS parameter for the heavily inserted table.

- If you see waits for UNDO segments, you should add more rollback segments.

- If the Sorts (memory) are less than 90% of the total sorts, you should increase the SORT_AREA_SIZE parameter in the initialization file.

- If you see a lot of enqueue waits, you should increase the parameter ENQUEUE_RESOURCES in the initialization file.

Minimize the waits for buffers

A ratio of buffer busy waits greater than 4 percent indicates that you need to tune the **DB_BLOCK_BUFFERS** parameter.

Latch Statistics

①

① Anything less than 0.98 indicates a potential problem

LATCH_NAME	GETS	MISSES	HIT_RATIO	SLEEPS	SLEEPS/MISS
cache buffers chai	70230	2	1	0	0
cache buffers lru	1540	0	1	0	0
dml lock allocatio	2545	0	1	0	0
enqueue hash chain	5051	0	1	0	0
enqueues	6574	0	1	0	0
ktm global data	1	0	1	0	0
latch wait list	6	0	1	0	0
library cache	136074	19	1	3	.158
library cache load	2	0	1	0	0
list of block allo	2234	0	1	0	0
messages	4122	2	1	0	0
modify parameter v	140	0	1	0	0
multiblock read ob	6	0	1	0	0
process allocation	139	0	1	0	0
redo allocation	12711	4	1	0	0
row cache objects	15913	0	1	0	0
sequence cache	431	0	1	0	0
session allocation	3361	0	1	0	0
session idle bit	15861	0	1	0	0
session switching	6	0	1	0	0

```
shared pool          10198     0     1     0         0
sort extent pool         1     0     1     0         0
system commit numb   16081     0     1     0         0
transaction alloca    3356     0     1     0         0
undo global data      3440     0     1     0         0
user lock              556     0     1     0         0
26 rows selected.
```

SEE ALSO

➤ *More information on reducing latch contention, page 580*

Rollback Segment Contention

1 If the waits-to-gets ratio is greater than 5%, consider adding rollback segments

2 Used in determining the waits-to-gets ratio

3 Shouldn't be high; set OPTIMAL accordingly

```
UNDO_SEGMENT TRANS_TBL_GETS TRANS_TBL_WAITS UNDO_BYTES_WRITTEN
----------- -------------- --------------- ------------------
          0              2               0                  0
          2            776               0             170900
          3            699               0             153523
          4            727               0             146419
          5            762               0             170326

SEGMENT_SIZE_BYTES XACTS SHRINKS WRAPS
------------------ ----- ------- -----
            202752     0       0     0
            530432     0       0     2
            663552     0       0     1
           1462272     0       0     1
            530432     0       0     2
5 rows selected.
```

Shared Pool Size

The following file also includes columns for COUNT and CUR_USAG (not shown here):

```
NAME           GET_REQS GET_MISS SCAN_REQ SCAN_MIS MOD_REQS
-------------- -------- -------- -------- -------- --------
dc_tablespaces      283        0        0        0        0
dc_free_extent       15        3        3        0        9
dc_segments           3        0        0        0        3
dc_rollback_se       12        0        0        0        0
dc_used_extents       3        3        0        0        3
```

dc tablespace_q	3	0	0	0	3
dc_users	1272	0	0	0	0
dc_user_grants	849	0	0	0	0
dc_objects	166	0	0	0	0
dc_tables	2724	0	0	0	0
dc_columns	596	0	56	0	0
dc_table_grants	1260	0	0	0	0
dc_indexes	2	0	16	0	0
dc_constraint_d	1	0	13	0	0
dc_constraint_d	0	0	1	0	0
dc_usernames	282	0	0	0	0
dc_sequences	7	0	0	0	7
dc_tablespaces	3	0	0	0	3

18 rows selected.

If the GET_MISS to GET_REQS ratio is greater than 15%, consider increasing SHARED_POOL_SIZE.

I/O Statistics

The following file also includes READ_TIME and MEGABYTES columns (not shown). The MEGABYTES column shows the size of the tablespaces. ➊

➊ Try to balance this out over all the tablespaces

TABLE_SPACE	READS	BLKS_READ	WRITES	BLKS_WRT	WRITE_TIME
RBS	1	1	663	663	3546
SYSTEM	38	46	372	372	2186
TEMP	0	0	0	0	0
TOOLS	0	0	0	0	0
USERS	0	0	0	0	0

5 rows selected.

The following file also includes WRITE_TIME, READ_TIME, and MEGABYTES columns (not shown).

TABLE_SPACE	FILE_NAME	READS	BLKS_READ	WRITES	BLKS_WRT
RBS	rbs01.dbf	1	1	663	663
SYSTEM	system01.d	38	46	372	372
TEMP	temp01.dbf	0	0	0	0
TOOLS	tools01.dbf	0	0	0	0
USERS	users01.dbf	0	0	0	0

5 rows selected.

The following actions can be taken to balance out the load:

- Move one or more database files to another disk.
- Frequently accessed tables should be separated from other tables and moved to their own data files on another drive.
- Separate your rollback segments, redo logs, and archive logs.

Working with Oracle Support

You can do several things to obtain quality service from Oracle Support. These things are very simple but important because they tell Oracle Support the exact nature and urgency of your problem, so they can provide you with the best possible resolution:

- *Keep your Customer Support information handy.* Most often, problems occur when you don't want them to happen. Not having contact information readily available can result in loss of valuable time. Keep the contact telephone numbers and your Customer Support Identification (CSI) number around. Also make sure that you understand the type of customer service contract you have with Oracle Support Services.

- *Understand the problem.* This will allow your problem to be addressed by the correct group at Oracle Support Services.

- *Set the correct priority for your problem.* Make sure that the analyst who obtains information from you is made aware how critical your problem is.

- *Provide configuration information.* When contacting Oracle Support Services, you should have as much of the following information as possible:

  - The hardware and operating system release number on which the application(s) is running
  - The release number of all Oracle products involved in the problem
  - A clear problem description

- Any third-party vendor and version in use
- The error messages
- The alert log
- The trace files that you've obtained in relation to the error

- *Provide test cases when requested.* Several times the problem isn't easy to describe, and it helps to provide a test case to Oracle Support. A test case is a collection of trace files, code modules, and steps that can be used to reproduce the problem. You can assume that the analyst at Oracle Support doesn't know much about the application specifics, so you should try to create a very simple test case. If you can, try to use the standard Oracle schema (such as SCOTT) and standard demo tables (such as EMP and DEPT) for your test case. Provide the steps to reproduce the problem and keep the size of the test case minimal.

- *Have your Technical Assistance Request (TAR) number handy.* Oracle Support Services assigns a TAR number (a PMS number in some countries) to every problem you report. If you have multiple issues, a new TAR will be generated for each issue. Every time you contact Oracle Support, you should refer to this TAR number.

Configuring and Using Net8 Features

Understand network location and application transparency

See the structure of Net8's TNSNAMES.ORA, SQLNET.ORA, and LISTENER.ORA configuration files

Configure networking with Net8 Easy Config and Net8 Assistant

Understand dead-connection detection, Oracle Connection Manager, and multiplexing

Use ODBC to connect Windows-based tools to Oracle

Configure and manage the Multithreaded Server option

Introducing Net8

Net8 is an Oracle networking product that facilitates network communication between remote clients and database servers, as well as between two or more database servers. Net8, the successor to SQL*Net 2.*x*, is a software layer that runs on top of standard network protocols such as TCP/IP and SPX/IPX.

Like its predecessor, Net8 enables location, network, and application transparency:

- *Network transparency* enables Net8 and client-side tools to work the same, regardless of network protocols between server and clients. Oracle network protocol adapters that work identically across different network protocols facilitate network transparency. You can change the network structure without making any changes at the application level.

- *Location transparency* is the capability of making remote database objects appear local. This is done with the use of synonyms and links. If an instance is moved from its location, changes are transparent to the application.

- *Application transparency* gives transparency to database objects when they're migrated between systems. An application tested against a test instance and being deployed on a production instance is an example.

Net8 Naming Techniques

You can implement Net8 by using host, local, external naming, and Oracle Names server methodologies. *Oracle Names* is a centralized management system used mostly by larger shops. An Oracle Names Server maintains client configuration information in one location. Oracle Names Server is very similar to Domain Name Service (DNS) on IP-based networks. Each method has its advantages and disadvantages. Host, local, and external naming are most commonly used for smaller installations.

It really doesn't matter what naming convention and technique a shop uses. What really matters is that the technique is unique. Whenever connections are made between clients and servers, there must be no confusion as to what database the connection must be made to. To enable uniqueness, Oracle and Net8 use the convention of *DB_NAME.DB_DOMAIN*.

A domain is a logical collection of machines, hardware, and networked devices in a networked environment. The convention is that, all names must be unique within a domain, but can be repeated across domains. If your shop uses DNS (Domain Naming Service) for defining its network, you can use DNS-type conventions for your Oracle domain. For example, if your server's host name in a DNS architecture is ABCINC.STARSHIP.COM, you could keep the domain name ABCINC.STARSHIP.COM, but it's not necessary to do so. You may want to keep the domain name WORLD for backward compatibility, especially if you have a heterogeneous environment (with several networking operating systems at work). However, if your database server is serving intranets and the Internet, observing DNS naming conventions may be more advantageous to your shop. The *DB_DOMAIN* parameter in INIT*SID*.ORA acts as an extension component to a global database name. WORLD is *DB_DOMAIN*'s default value.

The global name is a unique name that represents the database's name and domain. The representation for the database's global name is *DB_NAME.DB_DOMAIN*. Don't confuse this with the parameter GLOBAL_NAMES in the INIT*SID*.ORA file. GLOBAL_NAMES has to be set to TRUE if you want database links to use the same name as the *DB_NAME*. As seen in Figure 24.1, if you want to refer to table TOASTERS in the MONTHLY schema, the global name that would prefix MONTHLY.TOASTERS would be SALES or SALES.WORLD because there's only one domain. In contrast, Figure 24.2 shows several domains. If you want to refer to table MONTHLY.TOASTERS in the SAMERICA domain, you would use SALES.SAMERICA.ABCINC as the global name (that is, refer to the database SALES in the domain SAMERICA.ABCINC). Similarly, to access the table MONTHLY.TOASTERS in the EUROPE domain, you would use SALES.EUROPE.ABCINC as the global name. This ensures that uniqueness is maintained when you have similar tables and objects in different locations.

FIGURE 24.1

This naming structure uses a single domain name.

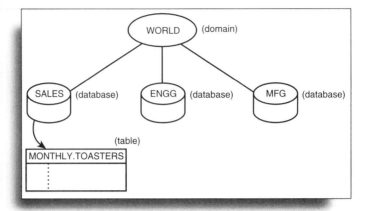

FIGURE 24.2

This naming structure uses multiple domain names.

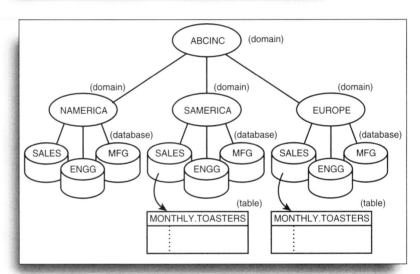

Supported Network Protocols

Net8 works with several industry-standard network protocols. These include but are not restricted to TCP/IP, SPX/IPX, Named Pipes, LU6.2, DECnet, Bequeath, and AppleTalk. The adapters for each protocol are supplied mostly by the vendors of the operating system on which they run.

To configure Oracle networking, you need to know the following:

- Your shop's network protocol
- The Oracle instance name (SID) you want to connect to
- The host name or IP address (if you were using TCP/IP) of the server on which the Oracle instance you want to connect to is running
- Oracle names if Oracle Names Server is being used

Basic Net8 Files

Net8 uses a minimum of three basic files to establish communications between remote clients and server: TNSNAMES.ORA, LISTENER.ORA, and SQLNET.ORA. These files are identical in form, function, and location on all platforms of Oracle. (You may have SNMP.ORA on some platforms and network protocols as well.)

Although you can modify these files by using any text editor, Oracle provides (and recommends) tools to configure these files: Net8 Assistant and Net8 Easy Config. We look at these tools later in the chapter.

TNSNAMES.ORA

This configuration file is used by clients to connect to servers (actually, to a listener service running on the server). Servers also use this file to connect to other servers as clients. A sample TNSNAMES.ORA is created on client software in the ORACLE_HOME/NET80/ADMIN folder. You have to add this file to this folder for server-to-server communications because you will unlikely ever do the standard client installation on the server.

The following is an example of this file. Your systems administrator is a good source of information about the listener's port number on the server.

Testing network connectivity

Because Net8 is a layer on top of an operating system network protocol, it makes sense to ensure that the clients and servers can "see" each other. On IP-based networks, just *ping* the server or the client from the server to verify this. If you can't ping the destination host, Net8 won't work and you'll need to contact your network/systems administrator in such a situation. An Oracle utility named TNSPING80 verifies that the listener is listening on the server. TNSPING80 is verified normally after the operating system ping is verified.

Definition of ORACLE_HOME varies

The definition of ORACLE_ HOME varies on different platforms and depends on the installation. On Windows NT systems, it may be in the form of C:\ORANT. On UNIX servers, an environment variable probably defines ORACLE_HOME. The folder and file structure is virtually identical on all platforms under ORACLE_HOME.

Different platform? Different SID

The naming convention for the system identifier (SID) varies on different platforms. The SID can be up to four alphanumeric characters on Windows NT. The SID can be up to eight alphanumeric characters on most UNIX platforms. Consult your platform-specific documentation for valid SIDs.

```
FinProd.world =
 (DESCRIPTION=
 (ADDRESS_LIST=
  (ADDRESS=
   (PROTOCOL=TCP)
    (Host=STARSHIP)
     (Port=1521)
    )
   )
 (CONNECT_DATA=(SID=finance)
 (source_route=yes)

    )
 )
```

Using Oracle tools to configure networking

Oracle recommends using Net8 Easy Config and Net8 Assistant to configure your network connections on the client side. All changes and new entries made via the Net8 Easy Config and Net8 Assistant tools are reflected in the TNSNAMES.ORA file.

As you can see, the TNSNAMES.ORA file has two main components: the service name and the address/connect descriptor. In the file, FinProd is an alias or service name that represents a connection to the database instance Finance, running on a server/host named STARSHIP and establishing a connection on port 1521; that is the port on which the listener is listening. (The LISTENER.ORA file on host STARSHIP, running an instance called Finance, will have an entry for port 1521.) In general, the connect descriptor contains information specific to the database server, database instance, and network protocol.

LISTENER.ORA

This file is located on the server and acts as a configuration file for the listener service/process. This configuration file runs on the server and "listens" to incoming requests. This file has three major components: address list, Oracle SID, and listener parameters.

When the Oracle product is installed on a database server, the installer gets basic information about the server's network configuration (host name, IP address, or both) and creates a sample LISTENER.ORA in the ORACLE_HOME/NET80/ADMIN folder. If you want more than one listener service on a server, simply add details about the listeners in the listener's

ADDRESS_LIST component. If you have one listener service for several Oracle instances (SIDs) on a server, simply add the instance information in this file's SID_LIST component. You can have multiple listeners for a single database listening on different server ports, or you can have a single listener listening on a port for requests made to different databases on the same server.

LISTENER.ORA defines the listener's address descriptor besides the instance's (SID) name or the global name of the database instances for which the listener is listening. The listener parameter portion is used for tracing and logging the listener process.

The following is a LISTENER.ORA file:

```
################
# Filename......: listener.ora
# Node.........: local.world
# Date.........: 24-MAY-94 13:23:20
################
LISTENER =
  (ADDRESS_LIST =
      (ADDRESS=
         (PROTOCOL= IPC)                    ①
      ②  (KEY= FinProd.world)              ③
      )
      (ADDRESS=
         (PROTOCOL= IPC)
         (KEY= finance)
      )                                     ④
      (ADDRESS=
         (PROTOCOL= TCP)
         (Host= STARSHIP)
         (Port= 1521)
      )
  )
STARTUP_WAIT_TIME_LISTENER = 0             ⑤
CONNECT_TIMEOUT_LISTENER = 10              ⑥
TRACE_LEVEL_LISTENER = 0                   ⑦
```

① Internal network protocol (always needed)

② Service name associated with IPC

③ Domain; follows Internet naming conventions

④ Same as descriptors for TNSNAMES.ORA

⑤ Number of seconds listener sleeps before responding to LSNRCTL80 STATUS command

⑥ Time (in seconds) after which listener request is timed out

⑦ Amount of tracing desired, from 0 to 16 (0 = no tracing, 16 = support-level tracing)

```
SID_LIST_LISTENER =
  (SID_LIST =
    (SID_DESC =
      (GLOBAL_DBNAME = finance_prod)
      (SID_NAME = finance)
    )
  )
PASSWORDS_LISTENER = (oracle)
```

For other configuration parameters that go into the
LISTENER.ORA file, refer to Appendix B of the *Net8
Administrator's Guide* in the Oracle documentation set.

Checking Listener Status

You can verify the status of the listener process by typing
LSNRCTL80 STATUS at the server's command line for UNIX and
Windows NT servers. (The LSNRCTL80 executable was formerly
LSNRCTL with Oracle 7.*x* and SQL*Net 2.*x*.) The command
results in the following output:

```
LSNRCTL80 for 32-bit Windows: Version 8.0.3.0.0 - Production
  on 29-MAR-98 00:43:48


(c) Copyright 1997 Oracle Corporation.  All rights reserved.


Connecting to (ADDRESS=(PROTOCOL=IPC)(KEY=finance.world))
STATUS of the LISTENER
------------------------
Alias                     LISTENER
Version                   TNSLSNR80 for 32-bit Windows: Version
                          8.0.3.0.0 - Production
Start Date                24-MAR-98 21:28:09
Uptime                    2 days 3 hr. 15 min. 38 sec
Trace Level               off
Security                  ON
SNMP                      OFF
Listener Parameter File C:\ORANT\NET80\admin\listener.ora
Listener Log File         C:\ORANT\NET80\log\listener.log
Services Summary...
   FINANCE            has 1 service handler(s)
  The command completed successfully
```

**Starting and stopping the listener
process on different platforms**

LSNRTCL80 is the executable
used to verify and start/stop the listener process. On UNIX servers, you
can start and stop the process with
the **LSNRCTL80 start** and
LSNRCTL80 stop commands,
respectively. To verify that the
process is running, use **ps -ef**
on the server. (You must have the
required privileges.) For Windows
NT servers, use the Services dialog
box, which you access through
Control Panel. You can see whether
the listener is running and set the
listener process's startup to automatic or manual.

SQLNET.ORA

This configuration file, used by clients and servers, contains information about Oracle Names (if used) and information about other client parameters such as diagnostics, naming conventions, and security. This file is installed automatically on the server in the ORACLE_HOME/NET80/ADMIN folder. Net8 client installations also install it in the same folder on the client side. A sample client-side SQLNET.ORA file is as follows:

```
TRACE_LEVEL_CLIENT = OFF
sqlnet.authentication_services = (NTS)
names.directory_path = (TNSNAMES, HOSTNAME)
names.default_domain = world
name.default_zone = world
automatic_ipc = off
```

The settings for TRACE_LEVEL_CLIENT are similar to the TRACE_LEVEL_LISTENER parameter in LISTENER.ORA. The values for both parameters can be either a scale from 0 through 16 or the following predefined names (which correspond to numeric values):

- OFF (value is 0)
- ADMIN (value is 6)
- USER (value is 4)
- SUPPORT (value is 16)

AUTOMATIC_IPC can be turned on or off, depending on whether IPC is wanted.

A new parameter introduced in Net8, SQLNET.EXPIRE_TIME, is used for dead-connection detection. The recommended value for this is 10 (minutes). This parameter must be entered in the server's SQLNET.ORA file. It's a good idea to consult your network administrator before enabling this parameter; a packet—albeit small—would be sent out at the interval specified in the SQLNET.EXPIRE_TIME parameter.

Net8 Features

The following sections cover a few new Net8 features that have improved the product over SQL*Net 2.x.

Distributing the files

In a client/server environment, you may have several hundreds of personal computers that need to be connected to the Oracle database with Net8. You could use Microsoft Systems Management Server (SMS) to distribute the TNSNAMES.ORA and SQLNET.ORA files to each PC. If you want to make a server a client to another server, you can copy or FTP SQLNET.ORA and TNSNAMES.ORA to the database server.

Multiplexing

Oracle8 Enterprise Edition provides the Connection Manager, which facilitates *multiplexing*. Net8 takes in multiple client connections and combines or multiplexes them over a single transport connection through Oracle Connection Manager to the destination database. Multiplexing improves response time and increases the number of client connections. It also better uses resources on the server.

Multiplexing is available only on TCP/IP networks and only if the multithreaded server (MTS) option is used. You examine MTS later in the "Connecting to Multithreaded Servers" section. The Connection Manager uses the CMAN.ORA file to configure multiplexing.

Dead Connection Detection

This new feature identifies and terminates "dead" connections caused by improper client session termination. If dead-connection detection is enabled, a probe packet is sent to the client from the server. The client process is terminated if no response is received within a user-defined interval.

Dead-connection detection makes administration of the database a little bit easier; uncommitted transactions are rolled back and the locks associated with the transaction are released. In addition, resources associated with connection of the "dead" process aren't wasted.

Parallel Server Reconnections

Network configuration files for Oracle Parallel Server (OPS) have to be configured a little differently. In the TNSNAMES.ORA file, the ADDRESS_LIST should include the details of the nodes (host name, port number) and Oracle instance names (SIDs). This enables a client-side application to go through the list and connect to the first available instance for a service name. If an instance in the ADDRESS_LIST is unavailable, the client application simply goes on to the next available instance.

Configuring Net8

The following sections review the predefined configurations of Net8 that are part of the default installation of most Oracle client-side software, such as SQL*Plus 8.0. You also see how to use two tools specifically for client-side network configuration: Net8 Assistant and Net8 Easy Config, both of which are written in the Java programming language.

The Default TNSNAMES.ORA File

The sample TNSNAMES.ORA file created during a standard Oracle client installation has default samples that correspond to different network protocols (such as TCP, IPX, and Bequeath). You can ask your network administrator on what port the listener is listening (the default is normally 1521), as well as other details, such as database instance name (SID). Then you can drop, modify, or add aliases (services) to configure the client with the Net8 Assistant and Net8 Easy Config. This is covered in detail later in this chapter's "Using Net8 Assistant" and "Using Net8 Easy Config."

Oracle8 Server is packaged with a CD-ROM called Oracle8 Client, which creates a standard client configuration, including TNSNAMES.ORA and SQLNET.ORA files on the client. Because your client machine (PC or server) will be connected to the database server with just one networking protocol, you can choose your network protocol during the Oracle8 client installation. If one isn't chosen, the standard client installation creates a TNSNAMES.ORA with the most commonly used network protocols listed. You look at three sections of a default TNSNAMES.ORA file that explain TCP/IP, IPX/SPX, and Extproc:

Use Net8 Easy Config and Net8 Assistant instead of an editor

Although you can modify TNSNAMES.ORA via a text editor such as Notepad, it's highly recommended that you use Net8 Easy Config or Net8 Assistant to modify the client side. Using the tools ensures that only the required changes are made to the existing file. When you use Windows Notepad or a UNIX editor such as `vi`, you might miss a parenthesis or type some extra, unwanted characters.

① TCP section

② Server's host name

③ SPX section

④ Section for calling external procedures

```
TcpExample.world =
  (DESCRIPTION =
    (ADDRESS_LIST =
      (ADDRESS =
        (PROTOCOL = TCP)
        (Host = Production1)
        (Port = 1521)
      )
    )
    (CONNECT_DATA = (SID = SID1)
    )
  )
```

```
SpxExample.world =
  (DESCRIPTION =
    (ADDRESS_LIST =
      (ADDRESS =
        (PROTOCOL = SPX)
        (Service = Server_lsnr)
      )
    )
    (CONNECT_DATA = (SID = ORCL)
    )
  )
```

```
extproc_connection_data.world =
  (DESCRIPTION =
    (ADDRESS =
      (PROTOCOL = IPC)
      (KEY = ORCL)
    )
    (CONNECT_DATA = (SID = extproc)
    )
  )
```

As you can see in the default file, Oracle client-side installation gives you various choices for configuring the TNS alias or service name. The word world represents the domain; the letters prefixing the domain are the service names or aliases. A description of each alias follows each *alias*.world combination. This description varies for different network protocols.

Fortunately, you don't have to remember the syntax for each protocol adapter. It's always useful to know the syntax, though, so that if you have to move the files to a server, you can do so with minimal editing.

Oracle8 and Net8 have "external" stored procedure capability; the last service name (extproc_connection_data.world) describes the address for the external procedure. When stored or internal procedures written in PL/SQL programs call external procedures, the Net8 listener spawns a session-specific process and, using PL/SQL, passes information regarding the external procedure name, shared library name, and arguments (if needed). Examples of external programs are shared libraries written in a language such as C++/C. For more information on external procedures, refer to *Oracle8 Server Administrator's Guide* and *PL/SQL User's Guide and Reference* in the Oracle documentation set.

Using Net8 Assistant

Net8 Assistant, a new tool written in the Java programming language, has a similar look and feel on different platforms. It replaces Oracle Network Manager, which was packaged with Oracle Server through release 7.3.4. As Figure 24.3 shows, Net8 Assistant provides a graphical user interface that helps you administer and configure profiles (groupings of Net8 parameters), service names, and Oracle Names Servers. To launch the Net8 Assistant in Windows NT or Windows 95, choose Start, and then Programs, and then click Oracle for Windows NT/9x; select the Oracle Net8 Assistant icon.

Configuring the Profile

As you can see in Figure 24.3, the Profile branch of the network tree on the left displays a drop-down box and tabbed pages on the right. Each item in the drop-down box presents different configuration pages.

FIGURE 24.3

Create a profile by using Net8
Assistant's general options.

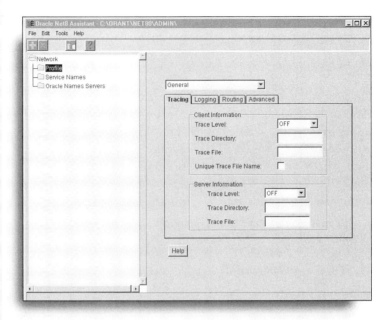

If you select the General option, you can customize Tracing,
Logging, Routing, and Advanced settings:

- The Tracing page gives you more detailed information
  about Net8 than the contents of a log file provides. You
  can activate tracing at the server and client level. You can
  specify the tracing level by choosing from OFF, USER, ADMIN,
  and SUPPORT. You also can specify trace directories and filenames for the client- and server-side files.

- The Logging page lets you specify log directories and filenames on the server and client. Changing the values of the
  LOG_DIRECTORY_CLIENT, LOG_DIRECTORY_SERVER,
  LOG_FILE_CLIENT, and LOG_FILE_SERVER parameters sets the
  corresponding values in the SQLNET.ORA file.

- With the Routing page, you can route connect requests to
  specific processes. You can configure Dedicated Server,
  Interprocess Communication (IPC), Addressing for Client,
  and Source Route Addresses. If Dedicated Server is set to
  ON, the listener on the server spawns dedicated server
  processes for each connection request. The IPC option
  tells the listener to route requests to IPC addresses.

- Use the Advanced page to configure Net8's advanced features. TNS Time Out sets the `SQLNET.EXPIRE_TIME` parameter value (default is 0). With Net8, this also enables dead-connection detection. A small probe packet is sent out at the interval specified to make sure that a client/server connection is alive. Client Registration ID registers a unique client identified during a client request, which is then used for an audit trail. The other two parameters are UNIX Signal Handling (default is NO) and Disable Out-of-Band Break (default is OFF). For more details on these two parameters, refer to *Oracle Net8 Administrator's Guide* in the Oracle8 documentation set.

Selecting Naming from the Profile branch's drop-down list enables you to use various naming methods to configure your client/server connections. The page in Figure 24.4 has three tabbed pages: Methods, Oracle Names, and External.

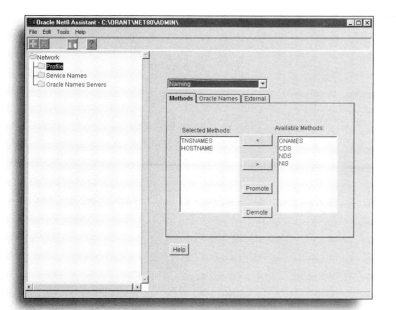

UNIX signal handling

When an event occurs in UNIX, a signal flags a process that executes the relevant process code. Because UNIX doesn't allow events to call more than one signal, it's possible that a signal may not be made properly, and a defunct or dead process may not be cleaned up. The `BEQUEATH_DETACH` parameter in the SQLNET.ORA profile turns UNIX signal handling off or on. The default value, NO, leaves signal handling on.

FIGURE 24.4

Use the Promote and Demote buttons on the Methods page to set the order of the naming convention used.

Disabling out-of-band breaks

The `DISABLE_OOB` parameter in the SQLNET.ORA profile is used to disable out-of-band breaks. This parameter's default value, OFF, keeps the out-of-band breaks on.

The Methods page includes two list boxes: Available Methods and Selected Methods. Oracle and Net8 uses the Naming methods in a top-down hierarchy. You can choose from several networking methodologies:

- *TNSNAMES (Local Naming)*. When a connection request to Net8 is made, the program first looks for the presence of a local TNSNAMES.ORA file with the connection description parameters in the file. If this file isn't present, Net8 tries to use the next naming method in the list.

- *HOSTNAME (Host Naming)*. Host Naming is a simple way of resolving connection descriptors. It's used mainly for clients and servers with the TCP/IP protocol. Host name resolution is done by using Domain Name Services (DNS), network information services, or a host table with the relevant information.

- *ONAMES (Oracle Names)*. This centralized naming system is used generally in larger installations where you have many servers each running several instances of Oracle. This system is relatively easier to administer after it's set up correctly. You can use Net8 Assistant to configure the Oracle Names Server and ensure that all parameters are set up correctly.

- *CDS, NDS, and NIS (External Naming)*. In this method, an adapter of the External Naming Protocol is installed on the client side. You then use Net8 Assistant to add the name of the protocol and the directory path information (`NAMES.DIRECTORY_PATH`) in the client profile. Cell Directory Services (CDS), Novell Directory Services (NDS), and Network Information Services (NIS) are the external naming services supported by Net8.

You use the Oracle Names page when your network configuration is using Oracle Names. This page enables you to set the following values:

- *Database Domain Name* with a default value of WORLD.

- *Maximum Wait Each Attempt* (in the Resolution Persistence section) with a default value of 15 (seconds) on

Windows NT. Default values depend on the operating system. This parameter specifies how long an Oracle Names client waits for a response from an Oracle Names server before trying to re-establish the connection.

- *Attempts Per Name Server* (in the Resolution Persistence section) with a default value of 1. This specifies the number of attempts each Oracle Names client will try in the list of preferred names server before allowing the operation to fail.

- *Maximum Open Connections* (in the Performance section) with valid values between 3 and 64. This parameter specifies the maximum number of open connections an Oracle Names client may have at one time to an Oracle Names Server.

- *Initial Preallocated Requests* (in the Performance section) with valid values between 3 and 256. Oracle Names lets you configure a number of messages in the message pool of the client. These messages can be used for future requests to names servers.

The External page has these parameters available:

- *Cell Directory Service (CDS/DCE) Cell Address.* If you're using Cell Directory Service, add a valid DCE prefix to this field.

- *Netware Directory Service (NDS) Name Context.* Enter a valid NDS name context in this field if you're using Novell's NetWare Directory Service (NDS). Net8 uses the NDS name context to look for a service name.

- *Network Information Services (NIS).* Net8 needs to know the location of the file containing the meta map of NIS to map attributes.

Configuring Service Names

The Service Names branch of the network tree enables you to create aliases or service identifiers for connecting Net8 clients to Oracle8 servers. The dialog box and sequence is exactly the same as detailed in the section "Using Net8 Easy Config."

Configuring Oracle Names Servers

The last option under the network tree, Oracle Names Servers, is used to configure Oracle Names. The administrative functions available for Oracle Names configuration include discovering an Oracle Names Server, Creating a Names Server, Reloading All Names Servers, Navigating Oracle Names Server, and other options.

Using Net8 Easy Config

To launch Net8 Easy Config, choose Start, and then Programs; then select Oracle for Windows NT/9x and Oracle Net8 Easy Config. The first screen is the Oracle Service Name Wizard (see Figure 24.5). You can use this wizard to create a new service, modify an existing service, and test existing services.

FIGURE 24.5

Use the Oracle Service Names Wizard to configure network services.

❶ Type in new service names

❷ Select an existing service

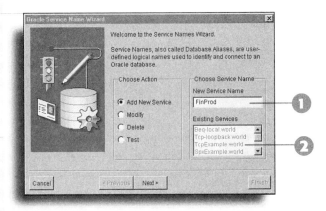

In the following example, you use this wizard to add a service named FinProd. The alias (or service name) FinProd refers to an Oracle instance (SID) called finance running on server STARSHIP.

Add a service with Net8 Easy Config

1. Launch Net8 Easy Config.

2. The Existing Services list box lists all the service descriptors observed earlier in the default configuration file. To add a new service, click Add New Service and type FinProd in the Net Service Name text box. Click Next to move to the next dialog box.

Verifying changes made in TNSNAMES.ORA with a text editor

You can view the TNSNAMES.ORA file in a text editor after changing or adding any information through Net8 Easy Config. You can see a new entry for the finance alias you create in the "Add a service with Net8 Easy Config" steps.

3. Select your network protocol. (Figure 24.6 shows TCP/IP selected.) Click Next.

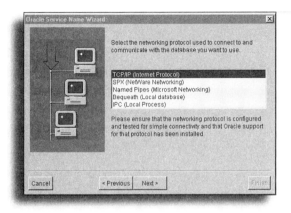

FIGURE 24.6

Select a network protocol for configuring Net8 clients.

4. Enter information about the database server name (Host Name) or IP address (see Figure 24.7). If the listener is set to listen on a port other than 1521, you can make the change here. Click Next.

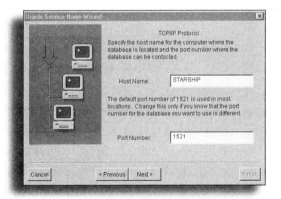

FIGURE 24.7

Select a host name and listener port.

5. Add the database instance name in the next dialog box—in this case, finance (see Figure 24.8).

6. Click Finish to save the service name (see Figure 24.9). However, it's recommended that you first test the service to see if it works (see Figure 24.10). If the test is successful, you can save this information.

FIGURE 24.8

Enter the database SID.

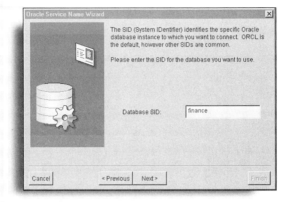

FIGURE 24.9

Test the service to see if a connection can be made.

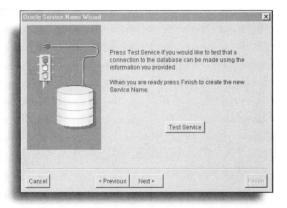

FIGURE 24.10

Verify to see if the created service works.

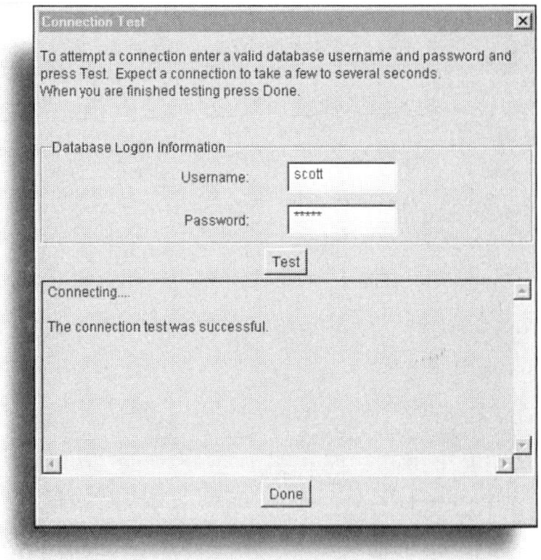

Connecting to Other Products with ODBC

Open Database Connectivity (ODBC) is a programming interface developed by Microsoft for providing Windows client-side products connectivity to ODBC-compliant databases (Oracle, of course, is ODBC-compliant). To enable connectivity to ODBC databases, you must install an ODBC driver, which runs on "top" of Net8 drivers. In other words, you can install the ODBC drivers if you have client-side connectivity working with Net8. Oracle, as well as third-party vendors, make ODBC drivers for Oracle databases. Examples of products connecting to Oracle with ODBC are PowerBuilder (Professional Edition), Microsoft Access, Microsoft Visual Basic, and Seagate Crystal Reports.

For this example, configure an ODBC connection on a PC running Windows NT 4.0. The ODBC configuration utility is found in Control Panel. (When you install a standard Oracle client such as Net8 or SQL*Plus 8.0, you also can access another shortcut for the utility from the Oracle for Windows NT folder.) You also have to install the Oracle ODBC driver on your PC. (You need administrator access if you're using Windows NT.)

The ODBC configuration utility has several tabbed pages (see Figure 24.11).

Some Oracle tools come with ODBC drivers

You may want to verify whether you have an ODBC driver already installed on your PC. The ODBC administrator will list an ODBC driver, if present.

Add an ODBC system data source name

1. From the Windows Start menu, select Settings and then Control Panel. Launch the ODBC tool.

2. On the System DSN page, click the Add button. The Create New Data Source dialog box appears, listing all the ODBC drivers installed locally (see Figure 24.12).

3. Either double-click the Oracle ODBC driver or select it and click Finish.

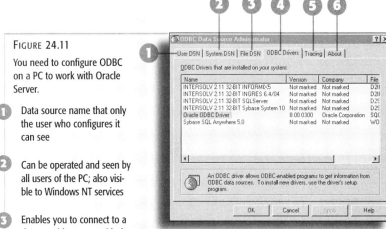

FIGURE 24.11

You need to configure ODBC on a PC to work with Oracle Server.

1 Data source name that only the user who configures it can see

2 Can be operated and seen by all users of the PC; also visible to Windows NT services

3 Enables you to connect to a data provider; users with the same drivers installed can share it

4 Lists all ODBC drivers installed on the PC

5 When tracing is enabled, logs all calls made to the ODBC drivers

6 Lists the core components for the 32-bit ODBC administrator

4. Enter relevant information in the Oracle8 ODBC Driver Setup dialog box (see Figure 24.13). The Data Source Name, Description, and userid can be anything relevant to you. Enter `FinProd` in the Service Name text box. Click OK.

With this, you're done configuring your system DSN. As you can see in Figure 24.14, the DSN `FinanceConnect` is listed as a system data source.

FIGURE 24.12

Create a new data source in the 32-bit ODBC Administrator.

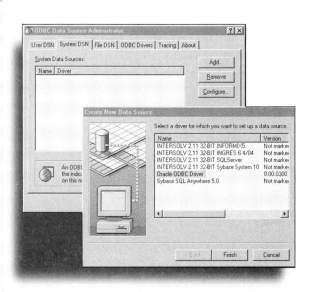

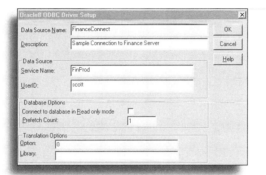

FIGURE 24.13

Enter the data source name, description, and userid.

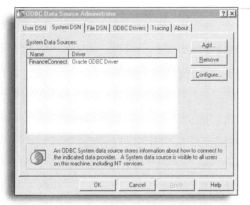

FIGURE 24.14

Within each ODBC front-end product, all you need to do is simply use the name FinanceConnect hereafter as needed.

Connecting to Multithreaded Servers

When a client program such as SQL*Plus connects to an Oracle server with Net8, a process is spawned on the server. This process can be dedicated or shared (multithreaded). By default, the connection is made by using a dedicated server. For most online transaction processing (OLTP) applications, data is retrieved into client applications, operations are performed on the data, and changes are saved. Thus, data processing shifts between the client and the server.

It's not always advantageous in terms of system resources to use dedicated server processes. You should use a dedicated connection, however, for database administration activities and batch loads. If the server operating system can support it, you can use multithreaded or shared server processes (MTS). With the MTS option, a number of small processes share the workload of dedicated server processes. Two processes—shared servers and shared dispatchers—are created in addition to the standard Oracle database server processes.

Setting Net8 Entries and Initialization Parameters

To set up the MTS option, certain initialization parameters must be configured in the database instance's configuration file (INIT*SID*.ORA) on the server. (INIT*SID*.ORA's location varies from installation to installation.) You can use any text editor, such as Windows Notepad or UNIX vi, to configure the parameters:

- MTS_LISTENER_ADDRESS is the address at which the listener listens by using a specific protocol. The syntax is as follows:
  ```
  MTS_LISTENER_ADDRESS = " (addr) "
  ```

  addr is the address from the LISTENER.ORA file. It can take the following form:
  ```
  MTS_LISTENER_ADDRESS =
  " (ADDRESS=
  (PROTOCOL=TCP)
  (HOST=STARSHIP)
  (PORT=1521)
  ) "
  ```

- MTS_SERVICE specifies a service name for the dispatcher. The syntax is as follows:
  ```
  MTS_SERVICE = DB_NAME
  ```

  Oracle Corporation recommends using a unique identifier— the instance's SID if possible. If this value isn't set, it defaults to the DB_NAME value.

- MTS_DISPATCHERS controls the number of dispatcher processes created at startup. You can specify the number of dispatchers for each network protocol supported. The number of MTS dispatchers depends on the capacity of the database server, number of connections per process, and number of connections per network protocol. As a rule of thumb, the more dispatchers, the better the database performance will be. The *Oracle8 Server Administrator's Guide* gives a formula for calculating the initial number of dispatchers:

number of dispatchers = CEIL (maximum number of concurrent sessions/connections per dispatcher) "Connections per dispatcher" depends on the operating system.

- MTS_MAX_DISPATCHERS limits the maximum number of dispatcher processes, including those belonging to all network protocols running on the server. There also may be a setting on the operating system for limiting the number of server processes. The formula for calculating this parameter is as follows:

Max number of dispatchers = (maximum number of concurrent sessions/connections per dispatcher)

- MTS_SERVERS sets the initial number of shared server processes. It's recommended that you use a lower setting because the additional server processes require startup and are automatically deallocated as the load drops.

- MTS_MAX_SERVERS sets a limit on the maximum number of shared server processes.

- SHARED_POOL_SIZE has to be increased by about 1KB per user connecting to an Oracle server with the MTS option.

Connecting to Shared Servers

To connect from client software to a database server running with the MTS option enabled, use regular aliases or services generated with Net8 Easy Config, Oracle Net8 Assistant, or both. The database instance has to be stopped and started after the preceding parameters are introduced in the initialization.

Managing Dispatchers

Oracle8 provides two dynamic views—V$DISPATCHER and V$QUEUE—to monitor load on the dispatcher processes. The number of dispatcher processes can be increased or decreased

Prerequisites for shared servers

The database server's operating system must support the MTS option. Oracle on that platform must also support the multithreaded server option. Oracle on most UNIX and VMS platforms supports the MTS option. The Oracle-to-Windows NT port doesn't support the MTS option.

depending on the load and number of connections. Idle dispatchers are automatically terminated, until the number reaches MTS_DISPATCHERS, which acts as a lower limit for dispatcher processes. You can monitor this process from Server Manager (in motif mode) on UNIX servers.

SEE ALSO

➤ *For a listing of other dynamic views, see page* **32**

Managing Shared Servers

You also can monitor shared servers by using Server Manager in motif mode on UNIX-based systems. Idle shared server processes also are terminated automatically, to a lower limit of MTS_SERVERS.

Using SQL*Loader
and Export/Import

Understand the Purpose and Capabilities of Import/Export and SQL*Loader

The Oracle8 Server comes with three utilities that help you load data into and out of a database: *Export*, *Import*, and *SQL*Loader*. The Import and Export utilities work together; Export sends database definitions and actual data to an export file and Import can read the file to perform many different tasks. You can use Export and Import for many important database tasks, such as restoring a *table*, generating CREATE *scripts*, copying data among Oracle databases, migrating among Oracle versions, and moving tables from one *schema* to another.

SQL*Loader is similar to Import in that it can load data; the main difference is that Import can read only Oracle export files. SQL*Loader can read text files generated by non-Oracle databases. SQL*Loader uses a control file to guide the utility on how to load data.

Export and Import can do the following:

- *Back up and recover objects.* Perhaps the most widely used Export and Import feature is the capability to serve as a useful backup solution. Most Oracle installations use full online or hot backups to back up the entire database in the event of a CPU, network, or disk failure. This works well because all data can be restored to the very millisecond that the database crashed. However, Export and Import provide for extra safety. If just one table in the entire database needs to be recovered during a full backup, the entire database would have to be recovered on another machine, and the one table would be copied back over into the original database. This incredibly time- and resource-consuming task could become a real headache in distributed databases. Export and Import can save you this trouble by exporting the entire database and importing just the tables that need to be recovered. Now that point-in-time recovery is an option for *tablespaces* in Oracle8, Export and Import can also serve as a backup and recovery mechanism for the entire database.

- *Copy objects among schemas.* You can use Export and Import to copy all object types such as tables, *indexes*, grants, *procedures*, and views from one schema to another. You can specify which objects you want to move, and provide the FROM and TO schemas. Oracle does the rest automatically.

- *Copy objects among Oracle databases.* You can export a table in one Oracle database and import that table into another. Many businesses export key tables and send the export files to a remote office location, which can then use Import to load the data into its local database. This is a form of one-way data replication to remote locations.

- *Generate CREATE scripts.* Export and Import contain powerful options that allow you to generate CREATE scripts for tables, *partitions*, indexes, object-type definitions, views, grants, *constraints*, *rollback segments*, tablespaces, and all other objects in the database. This safeguards the structure of your objects, in case one gets corrupted or deleted.

- *Migrate databases from one Oracle version to another.* You can upgrade (or downgrade) the version of Oracle by using the Export and Import utilities. For example, you can export an Oracle7 database, copy the export file to an Oracle8 database server, and then import into the Oracle8 server. This process, called *migration*, makes the data and application function in an Oracle8 environment. Of course, we always recommend complete testing before relying on the results of a migration.

- *Defragment a tablespace.* *Fragmentation* occurs when tables and indexes are created, dropped, enlarged, and reduced in size over time. Fragmentation also occurs when an object's *storage parameters* are sized improperly. To defragment a tablespace, you can export a tablespace, coalesce the free space (or drop and recreate the tablespace), and import the objects again.

What are fixed-length and delimited files?

A *fixed-length file* has a specified number of bytes for each column in the table. For example, if the specification is for 50 bytes and there are only 20 bytes in the *record's* column, 30 blank spaces will be appended. This way Oracle knows which byte range to look at for each column.

A *delimited file* has a special character (usually a tab) separating each column for each record. The character shouldn't be used within the data, so if there's a text *field* that might contain tabs, developers generally choose a different character as the delimiter. Non-Oracle products generally use more delimited files than fixed-length files.

SQL*Loader can do the following:

- *Load data into an Oracle database from a non-Oracle database.* The SQL*Loader utility is used for analyzing and loading text files into Oracle tables. Many non-Oracle products— such as Microsoft Excel, Lotus 1-2-3, Sybase, Access, Microsoft SQL Server, and Informix—can save data in a fixed-length or delimited file.

- *Replace existing data with new data.* SQL*Loader replaces records that exist in a table with records being loaded. This is known as the REPLACE method. Another similar method is TRUNCATE, which is quicker than REPLACE. Again, all records are removed from the table before new data is inserted. The difference is that REPLACE fires any delete triggers, whereas TRUNCATE doesn't.

- *Produce a set of all invalid data.* SQL*Loader can create files that list all records that don't meet the conditions specified, or incorrectly formatted data. These files can be analyzed after the load, and the data can be cleaned up and reloaded, if desired.

- *Perform logic on data while loading.* You can specify WHEN conditions so that only certain types of records get loaded. For example, if you have a file containing Major League Baseball players, you can specify that only catchers get loaded. The rest are discarded.

- *Load data from multiple sources simultaneously.* You can combine multiple physical records into one database record by using the CONTINUEIF... THIS clause in the SQL*Loader control file. It's limited in that the text file must be set up in a special way for this to work. Another method is to load the multiple sources into temporary tables in the database and then join them by using SQL.

- *Load data into multiple tables.* With this powerful SQL*Loader option, you can specify that some columns go into one table, and that other columns go into another table. You can even repeat loading columns into multiple database tables. A benefit is that if the database has a normalized set of tables, each with a joining *primary key*, SQL*Loader can load the appropriate columns into each table while copying the primary key into each table for each record in the text file.

Control and Configure Import and Export

FULL, OWNER, and TABLE are the three types of exports. A FULL export exports all objects, structures, and data within the database for all schemas. OWNER exports only those objects owned by the specified user accounts. TABLE exports only the specified tables and partitions for specific user accounts.

Because dozens of object types can be exported, it's important to distinguish what gets exported with each export category:

- With TABLE, the specified table (or cluster or partition) is exported with its indexes, referential integrity constraints, synonyms, and triggers.

- With OWNER specified, all the specified schema's objects are exported. This includes database links, *sequences*, *packages*/procedures/functions, object-type definitions, clusters/tables/partitions, postable actions, synonyms, views, triggers, snapshots/snapshot logs, job queues, and refresh groups.

- With the FULL option, all objects described in OWNER are exported for every user account, in addition to tablespace definitions, profiles, user definitions (and encrypted passwords), *roles*, resource costs, rollback segment definitions, directory aliases, user history table, and auditing options.

You can use the Export and Import utilities in interactive or non-interactive mode. In interactive mode, Oracle steps you through the process, prompting for basic Import/Export session information. This method, however, limits you to the simple prompts that Oracle provides. You have more flexibility in non-interactive mode because you can supply up to 23 parameters for the Export utility and 24 parameters for the Import utility. The parameters may be supplied at the command line or by specifying a command file that contains all parameters and values. You can automate Export and Import sessions by using a command file, or repeat them over and over again manually.

The syntax of running Export and Import is as follows:

```
EXP80 KEYWORD=value or keyword=(value1,value2,...,valueN)
IMP80 KEYWORD=value or keyword=(value1,value2,...,valueN)
```

Replace KEYWORD with the parameter, and value with what should be the parameter's value. For example, use the following to export the entire database:

```
EXP80 USERID=SYSTEM/MANAGER FULL=Y
```

Use the following to import the EMP and DEPT tables owned by the SCOTT user account:

```
IMP80 USERID=SYSTEM/MANAGER FROMUSER=SCOTT TABLES=(EMP,DEPT)
```

More in-depth Export and Import sessions are discussed later in the section "Walkthroughs of Export and Import Examples."

As mentioned earlier, you can use 23 parameters during an Export session on the command line or in any specified *parameter file*. Table 25.1 lists all parameters that can be used with the Export utility, along with their default values (if any).

Different commands on different operating systems?

exp80 and imp80 are the commands for the Export and Import utilities on a Windows NT environment. exp and imp are the commands for the Export and Import utilities on UNIX and other operating systems. This book's examples include the exp80 and imp80 commands.

TABLE 25.1   **Parameters for the Export utility**

Parameter	Default Value	Description
BUFFER	OS-dependent	The size of BUFFER (in bytes) determines the memory buffer through which rows are exported. This should be larger than the size of the largest record multiplied by the number of rows that you want to fit within the buffer.
COMPRESS	Y	If COMPRESS=Y, the INITIAL storage parameter is set to the total size of all *extents* allocated for the object. The change takes effect only when the object is imported.

Parameter	Default Value	Description
CONSISTENT	N	Setting CONSISTENT=Y exports all tables and references in a consistent state. This slows the export, as rollback space is used. If CONSISTENT=N and a record is modified during the export, the data will become inconsistent.
CONSTRAINTS	N	Specifies whether table constraints are exported.
DIRECT	N	If DIRECT=Y, Oracle bypasses the SQL command-processing layer, improving the speed of the export. Unfortunately, the new object types endemic to Oracle8, such as LOBs, don't get exported.
FEEDBACK	0	Oracle displays a period for each group of records inserted. FEEDBACK defines the size of the group. For example, if FEEDBACK=1000, a period will be displayed for every 1,000 records imported. This parameter is useful for tracking the progress of large imports.
FILE	expdat.dmp	By default, expdat.dmp (stands for EXPort DATa.DuMP) is the filename. For a more meaningful name, change the FILE parameter.
FULL	N	The entire database will be exported if FULL=Y, including tablespace definitions.
GRANTS	Y	Specifies whether all grant definitions are exported for the objects being exported.
HELP	N	No other parameters are needed if you specify HELP=Y. A basic help screen will appear.
INCTYPE		The valid options for this parameter are COMPLETE, CUMULATIVE, and INCREMENTAL. A COMPLETE export lays down a full export for which the other two options rely on for restores of the database. CUMULATIVE exports all tables and other objects that have changed since the last

How can you easily see the Export/Import parameters and syntax?

If you don't have this book handy when necessary and haven't memorized the dozens of parameters, the Export and Import utilities have a handy reference built in. Typing **EXP80 HELP=Y** or **IMP80 HELP=Y** at a command prompt brings up a nice one-page reference manual.

TABLE 25.1   Continued

Parameter	Default Value	Description
		CUMULATIVE or COMPLETE export was taken; if one record in a table is altered, the entire table is exported. INCREMENTAL exports all tables and objects that have changed since the last INCREMENTAL, CUMULATIVE, or COMPLETE export.
INDEXES	Y	Specifies whether user-defined indexes are exported. System indexes created with constraints (primary key, *unique key*) and OID indexes are automatically exported, regardless of this parameter's value.
LOG		Specifies the name of the file to spool the feedback from the export session. Unless otherwise specified, Oracle appends a .LOG extension to the file.
PARFILE		Rather than enter all parameters on the command line, some or all can be kept in a parameter file. This parameter specifies which file to use, if desired. This parameter is especially useful for non-interactive import sessions.
POINT_IN_TIME_ RECOVER	N	Exports information for a point-in-time recovery for the tablespace listed with the TABLESPACES parameter.
RECORD	Y	If you use the INCTYPE parameter with RECORD=Y, the SYS data dictionary tables INCEXP, INCFIL, and INCVID are populated with export data such as owner, type of export, and the time of export.
RECORDLENGTH	OS-dependent	The RECORDLENGTH parameter is used only when you'll import on a machine with a different byte count of the file than on the machine where the export occurs. The default should be used in most import sessions.

Parameter	Default Value	Description
RECOVERY_ TABLESPACES		Used with `POINT_IN_TIME_RECOVER`; specifies which tablespaces can be recovered by using point-in-time recovery. This is important because imports otherwise can't recover transactions past the time of export.
ROWS	Y	Specifies whether table and object data will be exported. If `ROWS=N`, only object definitions are exported.
STATISTICS	ESTIMATE	Specifies whether table and index statistics are to be analyzed with `COMPUTE` or `ESTIMATE` when imported. Only those objects that already have statistics on them will be analyzed during import. Specify `NONE` if no objects should be analyzed.
TABLES		Specifies a comma-separated list of all tables to be exported. This parameter could be used with the `OWNER` parameter to specify which owner to associate the tables with. Tables can also be specified with the *owner.table_name* format. In a non-UNIX environment such as Windows NT, you must enclose the table list within parentheses.
TABLESPACES		List of tablespaces to be exported with the `POINT_IN_TIME_RECOVER` parameter.
USERID		Specifies the username and password for the user conducting the import. The format for the command is *username/password*. You can also use Net8's *@connect_string* format if you want.

You can use 24 parameters during an import session. They may be specified in the command line or any specified parameter file. Table 25.2 lists all the import parameters.

TABLE 25.2   **Parameters for the Import utility**

Parameter	Default Value	Description
ANALYZE	Y	Imported tables have their statistics analyzed if ANALYZE is set to Y. Only those tables that already had statistics on them during the export are computed. The tables will be ESTIMATED by default, unless the export was performed with the STATISTICS=COMPUTE parameter configuration.
BUFFER	OS-dependent	The BUFFER size (in bytes) determines the memory buffer through which rows are imported. This should be larger than the size of the largest record multiplied by the number of rows that you want to fit within the buffer.
CHARSET		An obsolete Oracle6 parameter, indicating whether the export was done in ASCII or EBCDIC. This information is processed automatically in Oracle7 and Oracle8.
COMMIT	N	By default, a COMMIT occurs after each table, nested table, and partition. If you're importing a large table, the rollback segments may grow large. To improve performance while loading large tables, you should set COMMIT=Y.
DESTROY	N	If you set DESTROY=Y and do a full import, Oracle will overwrite any data files that exist. If you use raw devices for your data files, they will be overwritten during a full import, as DESTROY=N won't prevent the overwriting of datafiles! Don't use this option unless you know what you're doing.
FEEDBACK	0	Oracle displays a period for each group of records inserted. FEEDBACK defines the size of the group. For example, if FEEDBACK=1000, a period is displayed for every 1,000 records imported. This parameter is useful for tracking the progress of large imports.

Parameter	Default Value	Description
FILE	expdat.dmp	By default, expdat.dmp (stands for EXPort DATa.DuMP) is the name of the file that Import will import from. If the file is something other than exp-dat.dmp, specify it with this parameter.
FROMUSER		Specifying this parameter imports only those objects owned by the FROMUSER user account.
FULL	N	The entire database will be imported if FULL=Y.
GRANTS	Y	Specifies whether all grants will be created for the exported objects.
HELP	N	No other parameters are needed if you specify HELP=Y. A basic help screen will appear.
IGNORE	N	If IGNORE=Y, object creation errors are ignored, and records are inserted into the table. Duplicate records can result, if no unique constraints exist for the table. Non-object creation errors are still reported, such as operating system problems.
INCTYPE		If you're importing an incremental export, tables are dropped and recreated. You must first restore from the last SYSTEM export (specify INCTYPE=SYS-TEM). Then import every incremental export (specify INCTYPE=RESTORE) until the desired changes are applied to the database.
INDEXES	Y	Specifies whether user-defined indexes are imported. System indexes created with constraints (primary key, unique key) and OID indexes are automatically imported, regardless of this parameter's value.
INDEXFILE		Specifies the name of the file to generate CREATE INDEX statements. Unless otherwise specified, Oracle appends an .SQL extension to the file. (This parameter is explained in more detail later in this chapter.)

continues...

Export/Import and non-Oracle databases

The export file (expdat.dmp by default) is a binary file that only Oracle databases can read. Many databases and PC software can export data into delimited text files, but the Export utility can't. To transfer data from Oracle to a non-Oracle database, you must make a delimited file manually by spooling from within PL/SQL or SQL*Plus and running a custom-made script.

TABLE 25.2   Continued

Parameter	Default Value	Description
LOG		Specifies the name of the file to spool the feedback from the import session. Unless otherwise specified, Oracle appends an .LOG extension to the file.
PARFILE		Rather than enter all parameters on the command line, some or all may be kept in a parameter file. The PARFILE parameter specifies which file to use, if desired. This parameter is especially useful for non-interactive import sessions.
POINT_IN_ TIME_RECOVER	N	Performs a point-in-time recovery for the tablespace exported with the TABLESPACES parameter.
RECORDLENGTH	OS-dependent	Used only when importing on a machine with a different byte count of the file than on the machine where the export occurred. The default should be used in most Import sessions.
SHOW	N	Displays each SQL statement and doesn't apply them to the database. The SQL statements can be viewed and modified when used with the FILE parameter. (The SHOW parameter is explained in more detail later in this chapter.)
SKIP_UNUSABLE_ INDEXES	N	Allows the postponement of index creation until the record data is imported. The indexes affected are only those set to an unusable state, and all other indexes are created if INDEXES=Y (the default value) is set.
TABLES		Specifies a comma-separated list of all tables to be imported. You should use this parameter with the FROMUSER parameter. In a non-UNIX environment, such as Windows NT, enclose the table list within parentheses.

Using the LOG parameter

You can specify a *log file* for the Export and Import sessions with the LOG parameter. The file, which mimics what's output to the screen, reports all successful and unsuccessful messages to be examined at a later point. Some Oracle experts use this file during an automated load process and then checks the file for errors. A database administrator is paged if any appear.

Parameter	Default Value	Description
TOUSER		Specifies the user account into which tables should be imported, if you want it to be different from the original owner of the tables. This parameter needs to be used with the FROMUSER parameter.
USERID		Specifies the username and password for the user conducting the import. The format for the command is *username*/*password*. You may also use Net8's *@connect_string* format if desired.

Walkthroughs of Export and Import Examples

The following sections walk you through a few examples of the Export and Import utilities, to demonstrate some of the most often used features and to point out a few pitfalls that you should avoid. You see how to copy objects among schemas, how Import works when it encounters errors (such as when a table already exists during an Import session), and how to export and import table partitions.

Copy Database Objects from One Schema to Another

The most widespread use of Export/Import is for backup and recovery (as explained earlier). The next is copying data from one schema to another, or from one database to another.

During the import step, you can create the tables into any database you want, as long as the export file is on the database server.

In this first example, assume that there are two tables in the QUE schema: BOOK_DISTRIBUTION and BOOK_SALES. We'll copy these tables from the QUE schema to the SALES schema. You can export all of QUE's objects or specify only the two tables. The latter is done in this walkthrough.

Make sure you have the proper permissions

To copy or move tables among schemas, the user accounts must have proper permissions. **CREATE ANY TABLE** is needed to create the tables in the destination user account. In addition, either the **SELECT** permission on the table(s) or the **EXP_ANY_TABLE** permission must be granted to the user performing the export. All tablespace quotas need to be sufficient for the table to be created.

Copy two tables from one schema to another

1. Export the data with this command:

```
EXP80 USERID=system/manager
TABLES=QUE.BOOK_DISTRIBUTION,QUE.BOOK_SALES
```

You will see the following output:

```
Export: Release 8.0.3.0.0 Production on Fri May 13
10:16:16 1998
Copyright  1997 Oracle Corporation. All rights reserved.
Connected to: Oracle8 Server Release 8.0.3.0.0 -
Production
With the distributed, heterogeneous, replication, objects
And parallel query options
PL/SQL Release 3.0.3.0.0 - Production
Export done in WE8IDO8859P1 character set and
WE8ISO8859P1
 NCHAR character set
About to export QUE's objects ...
. about to export QUE's tables via Conventional Path ...
. . exporting table   BOOK_DISTRIBUTION   3280 rows
exported
. . exporting table   BOOK_SALES        241031 rows
exported
Export terminated successfully without warnings.
```

The data is stored by default in the expdat.dmp export file, or in a different path or export file specified with the FILE parameter. If you specify a log file with the LOG parameter, the output is placed in there as well.

2. Import the exported data. You need to consider three situations when importing: if the tables don't exist in the SALES schema, if the tables do exist in the SALES schema and are empty, and if the tables exist in the SALES schema and already contain data.

- If the BOOK_DISTRIBUTION and BOOK_SALES tables don't exist in the SALES schema, use the following syntax:

```
IMP80 USERID=system/manager FROMUSER=QUE
TOUSER=SALES
TABLES=BOOK_DISTRIBUTION,BOOK_SALES
```

The result will look similar to this:

```
Import: Release 8.0.3.0.0 Production on Fri May 13
10:22:17
1998
Copyright  1997 Oracle Corporation. All rights
reserved.
Connected to: Oracle8 Server Release 8.0.3.0.0 -
Production
With the distributed, heterogeneous, replication,
objects
And parallel query options
PL/SQL Release 3.0.3.0.0 - Production


Export file created by EXPORT:V08.00.03 via
conventional path
. . importing table   "BOOK_DISTRIBUTION"  3280 rows
imported
. . importing table   "BOOK_SALES"       241031 rows
imported
Import terminated successfully without warnings.
```

- Use the IGNORE=Y parameter if the tables already exist in the SALES schema but contain no data:

```
IMP80 USERID=system/manager FROMUSER=QUE
TOUSER=SALES
TABLES=BOOK_DISTRIBUTION,BOOK_SALES IGNORE=Y
```

3. Check the screen output, log files, or database for any possible errors.

How Import Reacts When Encountered with an Error

There's always a chance of errors occurring. As briefly described in the preceding example, you can get errors if a table already exists with data. This is especially true if there are unique or primary key constraints on the data. In addition, errors can occur if a table exists in the database and IGNORE=Y wasn't specified. Read the following example (and don't do this at home or office, as you may end up creating duplicate records in your tables).

What if the table contains data?

If the tables exist in the SALES schema and already contain data, you'll have two options: truncate the tables before beginning the Import session, or risk having duplicate or rejected data. Either way, use the same syntax when you are ready to import the data.

Detect errors in an Export/Import session

1. Export the QUE.BOOK_SALES table into the default expdat.dmp export file:

```
EXP80 USERID=system/manager TABLES=QUE.BOOK_SALES
```

2. At this point, there is the BOOK_SALES table in the QUE schema's database. Assume that there are 241,031 records, and that the table has a primary key called PK_BOOK_SALES. Assume that the following command is entered:

```
EXP80 USERID=system/manager FROMUSER=QUE
TABLES=BOOK_SALES
```

If data from the export file is loaded into the table, it will violate the constraint:

```
Import: Release 8.0.3.0.0 Production on Fri May 13
10:22:17

1998

Copyright  1997 Oracle Corporation. All rights reserved.

Connected to: Oracle8 Server Release 8.0.3.0.0 -
Production

With the distributed, heterogeneous, replication, objects

And parallel query options

PL/SQL Release 3.0.3.0.0 - Production


Export file created by EXPORT:V08.00.03 via conventional
path

. importing QUE's objects into QUE

. . importing table              "BOOK_SALES"

IMP-00019: row rejected due to ORACLE error 1

IMP-00003: ORACLE error 1 encountered

ORA-000001: unique constraint (QUE.PK_BOOK_SALES)
violated

Column 1 4321

Column 2 GREENE

Column 3 ANDREA

Column 4 613

Column 5 16-JUL-70:00:00:00
```

This would also appear in the log file if specified. If other tables were specified, Oracle would continue with the Import session until completed; only those records that defied the primary key wouldn't get loaded.

Exporting and Importing Table Partitions

The table partition is a new Oracle8 object type. The Export and Import utilities have been expanded to handle the export and import of table (and index) partitions. For this example, assume there's a BASEBALL_PLAYER table with five partitions based on the player's last name: A, E, J, O, and V.

To export all partitions, you can simply specify the table's name:

```
EXP80 USERID=system/manager FROMUSER=QUE
TABLES=BASEBALL_PLAYER
```

The result will look like this:

```
Export: Release 8.0.3.0.0 Production on Fri May 13 10:16:16
 1998
Copyright  1997 Oracle Corporation. All rights reserved.
Connected to: Oracle8 Server Release 8.0.3.0.0 - Production
With the distributed, heterogeneous, replication, objects
And parallel query options
PL/SQL Release 3.0.3.0.0 - Production
Export done in WE8IDO8859P1 character set and WE8ISO8859P1
 NCHAR character set
About to export QUE's objects ...
. about to export QUE's tables via Conventional Path ...
. . exporting table              BASEBALL_PLAYER
. . exporting partition          A
342 rows exported
. . exporting partition          E
```

```
172 rows exported
. . exporting partition              J
613 rows exported
. . exporting partition              O
291 rows exported
. . exporting partition              V
716 rows exported
Export terminated successfully without warnings.
```

If you want to export only a specific partition of the
BASEBALL_PLAYER table, use *TABLE_NAME:PARTITION_NAME* as the format of the TABLES parameter specification:

```
EXP80 USERID=system/manager FROMUSER=QUE
TABLES=BASEBALL_PLAYER:J
```

The result will look like this:

```
Export: Release 8.0.3.0.0 Production on Fri May 13 10:16:16
 1998
Copyright  1997 Oracle Corporation. All rights reserved.
Connected to: Oracle8 Server Release 8.0.3.0.0 - Production
With the distributed, heterogeneous, replication, objects
And parallel query options
PL/SQL Release 3.0.3.0.0 - Production
Export done in WE8IDO8859P1 character set and WE8ISO8859P1
 NCHAR character set
About to export QUE's objects ...
. about to export QUE's tables via Conventional Path ...
. . exporting table              BASEBALL_PLAYER
. . exporting partition          J
                613 rows exported
Export terminated successfully without warnings.
```

The syntax for using Import to import partitions is similar to the
Export syntax—specify the partition with
TABLE_NAME:PARTITION_NAME. The following example imports two
partitions from a previous export:

```
IMP80 USERID=system/manager FROMUSER=QUE
TABLES=BASEBALL_PLAYER:A,BASEBALL_PLAYER:J
```

The result will look like this:

```
Import: Release 8.0.3.0.0 Production on Fri May 13 10:22:17
 1998
```

Connected to: Oracle8 Server Release 8.0.3.0.0 - Production
With the distributed, heterogeneous, replication, objects
And parallel query options
PL/SQL Release 3.0.3.0.0 - Production

Export file created by EXPORT:V08.00.03 via conventional path
. . importing partition   "BASEBALL_PLAYER":"A"
       342 rows imported
. . importing partition   "BASEBALL_PLAYER":"J"
       613 rows imported
Import terminated successfully without warnings.

Additional Export and Import Features

The Export and Import utilities have additional useful features. The following sections explain how to generate various CREATE statement scripts with the SHOW option, generate CREATE INDEX statement scripts with the INDEXFILE option, and defragment a tablespace with the Export and Import utilities.

Using the *SHOW* Parameter

The Import utility's SHOW parameter is used to show the SQL statements that Oracle would perform if the import were to occur. It doesn't physically do anything to the database; its purpose is for information only.

Used with the LOG parameter, you can save the SQL statements into a script file, listed in the proper order of dependencies. For instance, a table is created before an index, primary keys are created before *foreign keys*, and so on. A sample portion of the output from specifying SHOW=Y follows:

The purpose of the SHOW option

You can use this parameter to generate all SQL statements used to create the database's data files and all its objects. This includes creating *comments*, tablespaces, users, privilege grants, roles and their assignments, *quota* definitions, *audit* definitions, rollback segments, sequences, tables, constraints, indexes, packages, procedures, partitions, user-defined *datatypes*, and so on.

```
"ALTER SCHEMA = "QUE""
"CREATE UNIQUE INDEX "U_NAME" ON "BASEBALL_PLAYER"
 ("LAST_NAME" , "FIRST_NAME", "MIDDLE_INITIAL" )  PC"
"TFREE 10 INITRANS 2 MAXTRANS 255 STORAGE
 (INITIAL 10240 NEXT 10240 MINEXTEN"
"TS 1 MAXEXTENTS 121 PCTINCREASE 50 FREELISTS 1)
 TABLESPACE "USER_DATA" LOGG"
"ING"
"ALTER TABLE "BASEBALL_PLAYER" ADD CHECK
 (LAST_NAME IS NULL OR FIRST_NAME IS NULL "
") ENABLE"
"ALTER TABLE "BASEBALL_PLAYER" ADD PRIMARY KEY
 ("PLAYER_ID") ENABLE"
"GRANT SELECT ON "BASEBALL_PLAYER" TO PUBLIC"
"ALTER TABLE "BASEBALL_PLAYER" ADD FOREIGN KEY
 ("PLAYER_ID") REFERENCES "STATISTICS" ("P"
"LAYER_ID") ENABLE"
```

Notice that the output's formatting is syntactically incorrect (quotation marks are inappropriately placed and some words are split among two lines). The log file can be modified to change almost any aspect of the database. Each line begins and ends with a quotation mark. Be sure to string these marks from the beginning and ending of each line. In addition, Oracle doesn't wrap words between lines in the output. This results in some statements having words and numbers being cut in two. To remedy this, you must manually join the lines in each statement. The preceding sample portion could be cleaned up to look like the following script:

```
ALTER SCHEMA = QUE;

CREATE UNIQUE INDEX U_NAME
 ON BASEBALL_PLAYER (LAST_NAME, FIRST_NAME, MIDDLE_INITIAL)
 PCTFREE 10 INITRANS 2 MAXTRANS 255
 STORAGE (INITIAL 10240 NEXT 10240 MINEXTENTS 1
 MAXEXTENTS 121
          PCTINCREASE 50 FREELISTS 1)
  TABLESPACE USER_DATA LOGGING;
ALTER TABLE BASEBALL_PLAYER ADD CHECK (LAST_NAME IS NULL OR
   FIRST_NAME IS NULL) ENABLE;
```

```
ALTER TABLE BASEBALL_PLAYER ADD PRIMARY KEY (PLAYER_ID)
 ENABLE;
GRANT SELECT ON BASEBALL_PLAYER TO PUBLIC;
ALTER TABLE BASEBALL_PLAYER ADD FOREIGN KEY (PLAYER_ID)
REFERENCES STATISTICS (PLAYER_ID) ENABLE;
```

Using the *INDEXFILE* Parameter

The INDEXFILE parameter is used to generate CREATE INDEX statements. Unlike the SHOW parameter, which has extra quotation marks and words cut up among different lines, INDEXFILE generates a clean and usable file. The value of the INDEXFILE parameter specifies the name of the file to be created. By default, Oracle appends an .SQL extension unless otherwise specified.

The following is part of the output file X.LOG from an import with INDEXFILE=X.LOG specified. Notice how Oracle wraps all lines appropriately and doesn't add quotation marks before and after each line, as it does with SHOW=Y:

Generic statements don't execute

Generic table-creation statements are shown but are commented out so that they don't execute if the script is run.

```
REM  CREATE TABLE "QUE"."BASEBALL_PLAYER"
 ("PLAYER_ID" NUMBER(6, 0), "LAST_NAME"

REM  VARCHAR2(60), "FIRST_NAME " VARCHAR2(60),
 "MIDDLE_INITIAL " VARCHAR2(5), "START_DATE"
REM  DATE) PCTFREE 10 PCTUSED 40 INITRANS 1
 MAXTRANS 255 LOGGING
REM  STORAGE(INITIAL 10240 NEXT 10240 MINEXTENTS 1
 MAXEXTENTS 121
REM  PCTINCREASE 50 FREELISTS 1 FREELIST GROUPS 1)
 TABLESPACE "USER_DATA" ;
REM  ... 58 rows
CONNECT QUE;
CREATE UNIQUE INDEX "QUE"."U_NAME" ON "BASEBALL_PLAYER"
 ("LAST_NAME ",
"FIRST_NAME", "MIDDLE_INITIAL" ) PCTFREE 10 INITRANS 2
 MAXTRANS 255 STORAGE (INITIAL 10240
NEXT 10240 MINEXTENTS 1 MAXEXTENTS 121 PCTINCREASE 50
 FREELISTS 1)
TABLESPACE "USER_DATA" LOGGING ;
```

Reorganizing a Fragmented Tablespace

Tablespace fragmentation occurs when objects are created, dropped, enlarged, and shrunk. The more often this occurs, the more fragmented the tablespace becomes. This causes free space to be broken into many separated island-like chunks of space. In addition, if an object has multiple extents, they could be spread out over different parts of the tablespace; this causes performance and maintenance problems. With many small blocks of free space instead of fewer large free spaces, you may be unable to create some objects that you otherwise could have. By defragmenting the tablespace, the data is reorganized so that all free space is put into one contiguous area, and each object's extents are grouped next to each other.

The Export and Import utilities can fix fragmentation in two ways:

- They can take a table with multiple extents and resize it into a table with one larger extent. This larger single extent will encompass the total size of all previous table extents.

- They can make all objects within the tablespace adjacent to each other with no island-like characteristics, while at the same time merging all the free space into one larger free space.

The easiest and most dramatic method fixes both fragmentation problems for the entire database. The database is shut down during the process. This forces all sessions against the database to stop (which is why it's the most dramatic method).

Fix both fragmentation problems quickly

1. Export the entire database, specifying FULL=Y and COMPRESS=Y. FULL=Y exports the entire database; COMPRESS=Y changes the INITIAL storage parameter of each table in the database

---

Fixing a storage parameter

Fixing a table's storage parameter is fairly easy compared to the entire tablespace, as only one table is affected. To fix an entire tablespace, you'll have to drop and recreate it, along with all the tables within it.

(if necessary) to fit within one extent each. For example, if a table has five 10M extents, the COMPRESS=Y specification changes the table to one 50M extent when imported.

2. Drop and recreate the entire database.

3. Import the entire database with the FULL=Y parameter.

Defragment just one tablespace (a less dramatic method)

1. Determine which tables exist in the tablespace and export just those tables.

2. Drop all the tables in the tablespace.

3. Issue the ALTER TABLESPACE COALESCE command (or drop and recreate the tablespace). This will coalesce all the free space within the tablespace into one contiguous area.

4. Import the tables. Oracle will create the tables adjacent to each other within the tablespace, and all free space will still be contiguous in one chunk of space.

Control and Configure SQL*Loader

You can call the SQL*Loader utility from the operating system's command line and, if needed, use a parameter file known as the control file. This file contains all the logic and formatting controls that SQL*Loader can use for an automatic loading session.

You can enter the parameters in any order. A sample format of a command-line SQL*Loader session follows. You pass parameters to the SQLLDR command (issued at a command prompt) as follows:

```
SQLLDR USERID=system/manager CONTROL=test_control.ctl

DATA=the_file.txt LOG=the_log.log
```

First, it's important to know what options are available at the command line (see Table 25.3).

TABLE 25.3   **Parameters for the SQL*Loader command line**

Parameter	Default Value	Description
BAD	*control_filename*.bad	Specifies the file in which all bad data is kept. The default filename is the control filename with a .BAD extension.
BINDSIZE	System-dependent	Size of the path *bind array* (in bytes) for conventional loads.
CONTROL		Specifies the name of the control file. If left blank, only command-line parameters are used. If supplied with no extension, Oracle prompts you to enter the extension.
DATA	*control_file*.dat	Specifies the file that contains all data to be loaded. The default filename is the control filename with a .DAT extension.
DIRECT	FALSE	If set to TRUE, direct mode is used. Conventional path will otherwise be used. (Direct mode is discussed at length later in the section "Conventional Path and Direct Path Modes.")
DISCARD		Specifies the file where all discarded data is kept. Discarded records are those that don't meet any conditional settings defined in the control file. Any data inserted before the SQL*Loader utility stops (due to exceeding the discard parameter) will be committed in the database.
DISCARDMAX	ALL	The maximum number of invalid records that may be encountered before the SQL*Loader session is to stop.
ERRORS	50	Specifies how many total errors can be encountered before SQL*Loader stops. Any data inserted before the SQL*Loader utility stops (due to exceeding the ERRORS parameter) will be committed in the database.

What's the BAD file used for?

The **BAD** file is a text file filled with improperly formatted data. For example, if a record in the text file has too few columns or a character where a number was expected, that record won't be loaded into the database and will instead be put into the **BAD** file, if specified with the **BAD** parameter.

What's the DISCARD file used for?

The **DISCARD** file is a text file, like the **BAD** file, but is populated with all records that don't meet an **IF** condition specified in the control file (if any such **IF** clauses exist). For example, if there's a condition that only employees older than 25 get loaded into the database, those who are 25 or younger will be placed into the discard file.

Control and Configure SQL*Loader

Parameter	Default Value	Description
LOAD	ALL	Specifies the maximum number of records to load before stopping.
LOG	*controlfile*.log	Specifies the log file's name, where information on the success or failure of the SQL*Loader session is reported.
PARALLEL	FALSE	If set to TRUE, loads are performed in parallel where possible.
PARFILE		An additional file that contains more parameter specifications.
ROWS	64 in conventional mode	Number of rows to put in the path bind array, for conventional loads. For direct path loads, ROWS specifies the number of rows to read before a data save is performed.
SILENT		You can choose from many options, including ALL, DISCARDS, ERRORS, FEEDBACK, HEADER, and PARTITIONS. The related messages will then be suppressed from the output.
SKIP	0	The number of records to skip before starting the load. This parameter is important for restarting a load process after stopping an earlier session. SKIP can specify how many records were loaded already and where to continue.
USERID		Specifies the username and password for the user conducting the SQL*Loader session. The format for the command is *username/password*. You may also use Net8's *@connect_string* format if desired.

What the different SILENT options mean

The **SILENT** parameter has six possible keywords. **DISCARDS** suppresses messages created for each record written to the discard file. **ERRORS** suppresses Oracle data-error messages that cause entries to be added to the **BAD** file. **FEEDBACK** suppresses all "commit point reached" messages. **HEADER** suppresses header messages from the screen; they still show up in the log file. **PARTITIONS** suppresses the partition statistics messages. **ALL** implements the suppression of all the other five keywords.

SQL*Loader reads in parameters and instructions from a control file and, if requested, generates a bad file, a discard file, and a log file. The control file controls how the external text file will be mapped to the Oracle database. The syntax of several control files are shown later in the "Walkthroughs of SQL*Loader Examples" section. There are so many possibilities that it could take several chapters to describe. In fact, this has already been done; refer to the *Oracle Server Utilities User's Guide* (which comes with your Oracle software) for a full reference. The control file is extremely flexible and consists of many subsections.

The SQL*Loader utility, like the Export and Import utilities, has a log file. The log file has many sections, including the environment, a running account of transactions, and summary statistics at the end.

Walkthroughs of SQL*Loader Examples

The following sections show three of the most common SQL*Loader tasks: loading from a delimited file, loading with conditional checking, and loading into multiple database tables. The examples give you a good idea of the SQL*Loader utility, and give you concrete examples of how control files are set up.

For these examples, assume that two tables are created with the following commands:

```
CREATE TABLE baseball_player (

        player_id               NUMBER(7)      NOT NULL,
        last_name               VARCHAR2(40)   NOT NULL,
        first_name               VARCHAR2(30)   NOT NULL,
        middle_initial          VARCHAR2(5),
        start_date              DATE)
/

CREATE TABLE player_statistics (

        player_id               NUMBER(7)      NOT NULL,
        year                    NUMBER         NOT NULL,
        batting_average         NUMBER,
        home_runs               NUMBER,
        stolen_bases            NUMBER,
/
```

Also assume that there are three text data files. PLAYER.TXT is as follows:

```
0001,Taub,Caleb,S,24-APR-98
0002,Sandor,Penya,,12-MAR-92
0003,Glickman,Gayle,,27-JUN-94
0004,Murphy,Ann,,25-FEB-95
0005,Greene,Donald,G,16-JUL-70
0006,Greene,Jennifer,R,12-SEP-92
0007,Deutsch,Jon,,04-OCT-97
0008,Hurley,John,,02-MAR-98
0009,Klimczak,Rhonda,,09-MAR-70
0010,Kaplan,Todd,R,11-FEB-68
0011,Hudson,Hoyt,,05-AUG-94
0012,Buberel,Jason,,09-NOV-96
0013,Verberkmoes,Ryan,,17-DEC-97
0014,Booey,Baba,,12-NOV-95
```

STATS.TXT is as follows:

```
0001,1996,320,10,4
0001,1997,330,12,7
0002,1997,230,0,3
0003,1995,110,3,0
0003,1996,186,6,3
0003,1997,205,12,7
0004,1997,313,33,9
0005,1997,330,40,35
0006,1995,280,5,12
0006,1996,297,9,20
0006,1997,310,23,20
```

MORE_STATS.TXT is as follows:

```
0001 1996 Taub     Caleb 320
0002 1997 Sandor   Penya 230
0004 1996 Murphy   Ann   186
0007 1997 Deutsch  John  205
```

Comma-delimited files

Notice how a comma separates each field in the PLAYER.TXT and STATS.TXT files. This is a comma-delimited file. Many programs use tab-delimited files, where tabs separate the fields. If the data itself were to contain commas, such as text fields with English sentences in it, SQL*Loader would think those commas were the field separators and get confused. In your case, however, the data is simple enough so that this isn't the case.

Load from a Comma-Delimited File

Use the following example control file to load the PLAYER.TXT data file into the BASEBALL_PLAYER table:

```
LOAD DATA
INFILE 'PLAYER.TXT'
INTO TABLE BASEBALL_PLAYER
FIELDS TERMINATED BY ',' OPTIONALLY ENCLOSED BY '"'
  (player_id,last_name,first_name,middle_initial,start_date)
```

Assume that this control file is named LOAD1.CTL. Notice that it starts with LOAD DATA (all control files start with this). Also note that Oracle automatically converts the date from *DD-MON-YY* to the internal Oracle data format. If dates were stored differently in the data file, you would specify a different default format.

Type the following to invoke SQL*Loader from the command line:

```
SQLLDR system/manager CONTROL=LOAD1.CTL LOG=LOAD1.LOG
 BAD=LOAD1.BAD DISCARD=LOAD1.DSC
```

The output will look similar to this:

```
SQL*Loader: Release 8.0.3.0.0 - Production on
 Fri Apr 09 10:39:32 1998
 Copyright 1997 Oracle Corporation. All rights reserved.
Commit point reached - logical record count 14
```

Load with Conditional Checking

The first example was the simplest form of loading. This example will take it one step further by using conditional checking. Suppose that you want only to load from the STATS.TXT table where the year is 1997. The control file would then have a WHEN clause, like the following LOAD2.CTL file:

```
LOAD DATA
INFILE 'STATS.TXT'
INTO TABLE PLAYER_STATISTICS
WHEN YEAR = "1997"
FIELDS TERMINATED BY ',' OPTIONALLY ENCLOSED BY '"'
  (player_id,year,batting_average,home_runs,stolen_bases)
```

Invoke SQL*Loader with the following statement at the command line:

```
SQLLDR system/manager CONTROL=LOAD2.CTL BAD=LOAD2.BAD
 DISCARD=LOAD2.DSC LOG=LOAD2.LOG
```

This will load only 1997 data, as shown in this output:

```
SQL*Loader: Release 8.0.3.0.0 - Production on
 Fri Apr 09 11:21:16 1998
 Copyright 1997 Oracle Corporation. All rights reserved.

Control File:    load2.ctl
Data File:       STATS.TXT
Bad File:        load2.bad
Discard File:    load2.dsc
(Allow all discards)
Number to load: ALL
Number to skip: 0
Errors allowed: 50
Bind array:      64 rows, maximum of 65536 bytes
Continuation:    none specified
Path used:       Conventional
Table STATISTICS, loaded when YEAR = 1997
Insert option in effect for this table: INSERT

Record 1: Discarded - failed all WHEN clauses.
Record 4: Discarded - failed all WHEN clauses.
Record 5: Discarded - failed all WHEN clauses.
Record 9: Discarded - failed all WHEN clauses.
Record 10: Discarded - failed all WHEN clauses.

Table STATISTICS:
6 Rows successfully loaded.
5 Rows not loaded because all WHEN clauses were failed.

Space allocated for bind array:
                 7168 bytes (64 rows)
Space allocated for memory besides bind array:      0 bytes

Total logical records skipped:         0
Total logical records read:           11
Total logical records rejected:        0
Total logical records discarded:       6

Run began on Fri Apr 09 11:21:16 1998
Run ended on Fri Apr 09 11:21:18 1998

Elapsed time was:     00:00:02.12
Elapsed CPU time was: 00:00:00.35
```

Load Data into Multiple Tables

This example uses the MORE_STATS.TXT data file, which contains the player_id, year, last_name, first_name, and batting_average in a fixed-length format. player_id is stored from position 1 to 4, year from 6 to 9, last_name from 11 to 17, first_name from 19 to 23, and batting_average from 25 to 27. This will be denoted in the LOAD3.CTL control file, as follows:

```
LOAD DATA
INFILE 'MORE_STATS.TXT'
BADFILE 'LOAD3.BAD'
DISCARDFILE 'LOAD3.DSC'
INTO TABLE baseball_player
        (player_id       POSITION(1:4)   INTEGER EXTERNAL,
         last_name       POSITION(11:17) CHAR,
         first_name      POSITION(19:23) CHAR)
INTO TABLE player_statistics
        (player_id       POSITION(1:4)   INTEGER EXTERNAL,
         year            POSITION(6:9)   INTEGER EXTERNAL,
         batting_average POSITION(25:27) CHAR)
```

Each table uses player_id

Note how the **player_id** is used in each table, so that each record in the MORE_STATS.TXT data file is loaded into the **BASEBALL_PLAYER** and **PLAYER_STATISTICS** tables.

The POSITION clause is used because the file is of fixed length. All NOT NULL constraints are met for both tables, so no records will be rejected. This is shown in the resulting log file, as follows:

```
SQL*Loader: Release 8.0.3.0.0 - Production on
 Fri Apr 09 11:38:23 1998
 Copyright 1997 Oracle Corporation. All rights reserved.

Control File:    load3.ctl
Data File:       MORE_STATS.TXT
Bad File:        load3.bad
Discard File:    load3.dsc
(Allow all discards)
Number to load: ALL
Number to skip: 0
Errors allowed: 50
Bind array:     64 rows, maximum of 65536 bytes
Continuation:   none specified
Path used:      Conventional
```

```
Insert option in effect for this table: INSERT

Table BASEBALL_PLAYER, loaded from every logical record.
Column Name       Position    Len   Term   Encl    Datatype
PLAYER_ID         1:4         4                     INTEGER
LAST_NAME         11:17       7                     CHAR
FIRST_NAME        19:23       5                     CHAR

Table PLAYER_STATISTICS, loaded from every logical record.
Column Name       Position    Len   Term   Encl    Datatype
PLAYER_ID         1:4         4                     INTEGER
YEAR              6:9         4                     INTEGER
BATTING_AVERAGE   25:27       3                     CHAR


Table BASEBALL_PLAYER:
        11 Rows successfully loaded.
Table PLAYER_STATISTICS:
        11 Rows successfully loaded.


Space allocated for bind array:          4241 bytes (64 rows)
Space allocated for memory besides bind array:     0 bytes

Total logical records skipped:          0
Total logical records read:            11
Total logical records rejected:         0
Total logical records discarded:        6

Run began on Fri Apr 09 11:38:23 1998
Run ended on Fri Apr 09 11:38:25 1998

Elapsed time was:     00:00:03.18
Elapsed CPU time was: 00:00:00.75
```

Additional SQL*Loader Features

The SQL*Loader utility has many additional features. The most
important include the conventional/direct path modes, the UNRE-
COVERABLE clause, special Oracle8 index usability, and loading
data in parallel.

Conventional Path and Direct Path Modes

SQL*Loader can run in two modes: conventional (the default
mode) and direct path loading. Conventional mode is less

The UNRECOVERABLE Clause

Use the **UNRECOVERABLE** clause to greatly improve performance for direct path loading. That way, SQL*Loader doesn't record changes to the redo logs; it just records a relatively small volume of invalidation redo. This saves overhead, especially for larger data loads.

efficient but is needed if other users are accessing the tables during the load. Direct path mode bypasses some Oracle overhead processing for better performance. More specifically, conventional path loading uses SQL INSERT statements and bind-array buffer processing to load records into the database. This will also fire INSERT triggers if they exist. Direct path load bypasses all this by first formatting the data into Oracle data block format, and then writing directly into the database's data files. Direct path load can also work with the PARALLEL parameter for even better performance. Specify DIRECT=TRUE to use direct path mode.

Oracle8 Index Usability

Oracle8 introduced new index maintenance with SQL*Loader. Specifically, the SKIP_UNUSABLE_INDEXES parameter applies if any tables have indexes in the IU (Index Unusable) state. If this parameter is set to TRUE, these indexes won't be maintained during the SQL*Loader session. The indexes are built one at a time after the load session, which reduces sort processing. In addition, the SKIP_INDEX_MAINTENANCE parameter applies only for direct path mode and, if set to TRUE, stops maintenance on indexes during the load.

Parallel Loading

You can load a table in parallel with SQL*Loader with direct path load. To do this requires some setup, as the text file must be broken into several smaller files. Assume that you're about to load 40 million records into a table with the SQL*Loader utility. You would break the text file (data.txt for this example) into four files: data1.txt, data2.txt, date3.txt, and data4.txt, with about 10 million records each. You can then run four separate SQLLOAD sessions in parallel by issuing the following commands (assuming that the LOAD1.CTL, LOAD2.CTL, LOAD3.CTL, and LOAD4.CTL control files are properly configured):

```
SQLLOAD USERID=system/manager CONTROL=LOAD1.CTL
 PARALLEL=TRUE DIRECT=TRUE

SQLLOAD USERID=system/manager CONTROL=LOAD2.CTL
 PARALLEL=TRUE DIRECT=TRUE

SQLLOAD USERID=system/manager CONTROL=LOAD3.CTL
 PARALLEL=TRUE DIRECT=TRUE

SQLLOAD USERID=system/manager CONTROL=LOAD4.CTL
 PARALLEL=TRUE DIRECT=TRUE
```

The combined result will be about four times faster than if one process were to load the entire 40 million records.

Using Other Oracle8 Features and Functionality

Use National Language Support (NLS) at the server, session, and operating system level

Use advanced replication and Replication Manager

Store and retrieve spatial data with the Spatial Data Cartridge

Review Oracle Web Application Server architecture

Configure PL/SQL and Java cartridges

Use Oracle Advanced Queuing (AQ) to track workflow and applications

National Language Support

National Language Support (NLS) is a feature that enables Oracle database users to interact with the database in their native language. It also enables applications written in different national languages to interact with different NLS configurations.

Oracle's NLS architecture has two main components: language-independent functions used to provide generic language features, and language-dependent data used to work with features for a specific language. Oracle Server uses several encoding schemes to enable NLS capability. In essence, letters typed from a keyboard are displayed onscreen with character encoding. The encoding schemes commonly used by Oracle8 Server are categorized into single-byte 7-bit (7-bit ASCII), single-byte 8-bit (ISO 8859/1), varying-width multi-byte (for Chinese and other Asian languages), and fixed-width multi-byte (a subset of varying-width multi-byte). For more information on encoding schemes and restrictions on character sets, review the *Oracle8 Server Reference* in the Oracle documentation set.

Oracle8 has a new datatype, NCHAR, which facilitates the existence of two character sets in one database instance. Oracle8 also adds support for fixed-length native Unicode 2.0 and Chinese language support.

Setting Database Character Set

Setting the database character set is something you should do before creating a database instance. All database character data is stored in the character set specified during database creation. Although you may be able to change the character set of objects created later, characters in the data dictionary are stored in the character set used during creation and can't be changed later. The database character set is used for the following items:

- Table and field (column) names
- PL/SQL variables
- Data (LONG, CHAR, VARCHAR, and CLOB datatypes)
- Other SQL and PL/SQL scripting commands

The database set must be derived from 7-bit ASCII or EDCDIC character sets. The database character set can be a varying-width multi-byte character set.

Setting National Character Set

The National Character set is used for handling data stored in the NCHAR, NCLOB, and NVARCHAR2 datatypes. You can use a fixed-width or a varying-width multi-byte character set for the National Character Set.

Setting Initialization File Parameters

You can set NLS parameters as default values for the server. The client software can alter the server default values, if desired. The following parameters in the initialization file (INIT*SID*.ORA) set the default NLS values for the server:

- NLS_LANGUAGE sets up the default language of the database. This language sets up default values for several other NLS variables. For example,
  ```
  NLS_LANGUAGE ="US7ASCII"
  ```

  or
  ```
  NLS_LANGUAGE="GERMAN"
  ```

  This important parameter is used in several places internally in the Oracle server, including server messages; language for day-and-month functions and their extensions; abbreviations for time such as AM/PM, AD/BC, and so on; writing direction; and default sorting sequence. The value set for NLS_LANGUAGE in the init*sid*.ora file sets the default for all sessions for that database instance.

- NLS_TERRITORY sets and specifies the conventions to be followed for date and several other numeric formatting characteristics (such as decimal character and group separator, local currency symbol, ISO currency symbol, week start day, ISO week flag, and so on). For example,
  ```
  NLS_TERRITORY="GERMANY"
  ```

> **Some performance improves with the National Character Set**
>
> You might see some performance gain in string operations when you choose a fixed-width character set for the National Character Set versus a varying width character set. Smaller width (varying width) character sets are more efficient in reducing data storage capacity.

- NLS_CALENDAR is a string whose default value is Gregorian. This parameter sets a valid calendar system format that's used by date fields for displaying time and date information. For example,
  NLS_CALENDAR="Gregorian"

  or

  NLS_CALENDAR='Thai Buddha"

- NLS_CURRENCY specifies the local currency symbol. This parameter overrides the value set by the NLS_TERRITORY parameter.

- NLS_DATE_FORMAT sets the date format to be used by the TO_DATE and TO_CHAR built-in functions. NLS_TERRITORY variables provide a default value for NLS_DATE_FORMAT. This string can take any valid date format—for example,
  NLS_DATE_FORMAT = "DD/MM/YYYY"

- NLS_DATE_LANGUAGE sets the values to be used for spelling day and month names (for example, January, Enero, or Janvier) and time abbreviations (such as AM or PM). For example, if NLS_DATE_LANGUAGE="US7ASCII", a query of the form SELECT TO_CHAR(sysdate, 'Day-dd-Month- yyyy') from dual would return Friday-22-May-1998.

- NLS_ISO_CURRENCY provides an explicit definition for ISO currency values, overriding the defaults set by NLS_TERRITORY. For example, this is used to specify Canadian dollars versus US dollars to eliminate ambiguity. For example, if NLS_ISO_CURRENCY="GERMAN", the query SELECT TO_CHAR("Monthly_Total_Sales",'C099G999D999) from SALES (where Monthly_Total_Sales is a column in the table SALES) would give the result DM132,345.345.

- NLS_NUMERIC_CHARACTERS sets up the characters that act as decimal and group separators. These two characters must be single byte and differ from each other. They also can't take the values of the addition sign (+), subtraction sign (−), and equality signs (< or >).

- NLS_SORT specifies the type of sort for character data. The default is set by NLS_LANGUAGE. For example,
  NLS_SORT = Greek

Setting Session Values

Most NLS parameters can be set in an interactive session and as environment variables on UNIX and Windows NT. You can set the following NLS variables as initialization parameters, environment variables, and ALTER SESSION parameters:

NLS_CURRENCY	NLS_ISO_CURRENCY
NLS_DATE_FORMAT	NLS_NUMERIC_CHARACTERS
NLS_DATE_LANGUAGE	NLS_SORT

You can set NLS_LANGUAGE and NLS_TERRITORY as initialization parameters and ALTER SESSION parameters but not as environment variables.

The NLS variables that you can set only as environment variables are

NLS_CREDIT	NLS_LIST_SEPERATOR
NLS_DEBIT	NLS_MONETARY_CHARACTERS
NLS_DISPLAY	NLS_NCHAR
NLS_LANG	

Setting NLS values interactively with the ALTER SESSION command

If you want to set a parameter such as **NLS_DATE_LANGUAGE** to Spanish by using an interactive **ALTER SESSION** command, the syntax would be **ALTER SESSION SET NLS_DATE_LANGUAGE="SPANISH"**. For this particular session, the **ALTER SESSION** command will override the default value of **NLS_DATE_LANGUAGE**.

Using SQL NLS Options

You can use NLS parameters in SQL statements that depend on NLS conventions. Applications using these SQL functions can explicitly call the functions independently of the environment variables or session parameters:

- TO_CHAR (Example: TO_CHAR(Date_of_Birth, 'DD-MM-YYYY', 'nls_date_language = GERMAN'))
- TO_DATE (Example: TO_DATE('01-14-93','DD-MM-YY',nls_date_language = French'))
- TO_NUMBER
- NLS_UPPER
- NLS_LOWER
- NLS_INITCAP
- NLS_SORT

Using environment variables to modify NLS values

If you want to set the value of a variable such as **NLS_CREDIT** by using UNIX environment variables, the syntax would be **setenv NLS_CREDIT="CR"**. This would append the symbol **CR** in financial statements and reports, wherever applicable.

For more details, refer to the *Oracle8 Server Reference* in the Oracle8 documentation set.

Advanced Replication

New replication features in Oracle8

Oracle8 provides several new features that enrich Replication functionality: parallel propagation of deferred transactions, internalized replication triggers, reduced data propagation, LOB (large binary object) support, data subsetting based on subqueries, and primary key snapshots. The number of transactions to be replicated as well as the mechanism have been improved over Oracle7. Oracle8 sends row-level changes over the network to the replicated site, also optimizing bandwidth requirements. Improvements in Replication Manager 1.4 also make it easier to design and manage a replicated environment.

In today's distributed architecture and global economies, organizations have database servers all over the world and need to exchange information in a timely and efficient manner. Oracle Replication is widely used to provide data access to different Oracle databases, as well as provide redundancy in the case of disaster. Replication is also used to distribute processing loads in distributed systems and give mobile workers the capability to work with the master database site.

Oracle provides two forms of replication: basic and advanced. In the most elementary form of replication—basic—replicated sites have read-only access to data being maintained at the master site. Advanced replication gives replicated sites full read/write access to data at the master site.

Advanced Replication Configurations

You can implement Oracle advanced replication by using two basic configurations or a combination of the two:

- *Multimaster replication.* In this configuration, multiple sites act as equals. Depending on the setup, the entire database or groups of objects can be replicated. You can configure multimaster replication so that any change in the replicated group is propagated to all locations.

- *Snapshot replication.* In this configuration, a designated master site and replicated sites can maintain a full copy of the replication group or part of it. Changes in tables can be propagated from the master site to the replicated members, or vice-versa. Changes are made in both directions by using updatable snapshots.

- *Mixed configurations.* This is normally a combination of multimaster and snapshot replication. An example would be an organization having full multimaster replication configured between its regional headquarters and company headquarters, and snapshot replication configured between the headquarters and service centers.

Advanced Replication Components

Replication objects, groups, sites, and catalogs are the basic components of an advanced replication configuration. Let's take a quick look at their definitions:

- *Replication object.* This is a database object (such as a table, package, synonym, or trigger) that exists on multiple database servers in a distributed database system. An example would be an EMPLOYEE table replicated in all regional offices of an international organization. A replication object may or may not be part of a replication group.

- *Replication group.* To ease administration of an advanced replication configuration, replication objects are grouped into replication groups, which can contain replication objects from different database schemas. The only restriction is that each replication object can be included in only one replication group. A replication group at a master site is called a *master group*. A replication group at a snapshot site is called a *snapshot group*.

- *Replication site.* Oracle8 advanced replication classifies replication sites into two categories: master and snapshot sites. A master site contains a full, complete copy of all replication objects and groups. In a distributed advanced replication architecture, there can be only one designated master site, although the configuration may be full multimaster replication. The master site propagates object and data changes to other sites in the configuration. A snapshot site reflects simple read-only and updatable snapshots of tables in a master site.

- *Replication catalog.* In an advanced replication configuration, a separate set of data-dictionary tables are maintained at master and snapshot sites. These tables form the replication catalog. They're used for administrative purposes and help in configuring and maintaining a replicated architecture. Oracle Replication Manager and other tools use the replication catalog to make administration easier.

Advanced Replication User Accounts

An advanced replication configuration requires certain special user accounts: replication administrator, replication propagator, and replication receivers. Each site—snapshot or master—requires a replication administrator. The replication administrator, propagator, and receiver can be the same Oracle account but have to be set up individually.

Managing Job Queues

Oracle8 uses a combination of internal triggers, deferred transactions, and job queues to propagate data and object changes between replicated sites. The internal triggers capture the changes to be propagated and execute them on replicated sites by using remote procedure calls. These remote procedure calls are stored in deferred transaction queues for later propagation. The actual propagation process is managed by using job queues and deferred transactions.

A local job queue is maintained on each database server participating in the replicated configuration containing information about the PL/SQL procedure, the schedule to run the job, and so on. These jobs will probably include but not be restricted to pushing deferred transactions to master sites, purging applied transactions from deferred transaction queues, and refreshing update snapshot groups.

Oracle8 provides data-dictionary views that contain detailed information about deferred transactions. These views are used to administer an advanced replication configuration. Some views are DEFCALL, DEFCALL_DEST, DEFDEFAULTDEST, DEFERRCOUNT, DEFERR, and DEFSCHEDULE.

Transactions that can't be completed are rolled back at the destination site and are logged in the DEFERROR view, which stores the identity number of the transaction that couldn't be applied. The

Use APIs to track advanced replication

Oracle8 also provides a set of application program interfaces (APIs) to track and facilitate advanced replication. Some of these packages are DBMS_DEFER_QUERY, DBMS_DEFER, DBMS_OFFLINE, DBMS_REPCAT, and DBMS_SNAPSHOT. These packages, in combination with the replication data-dictionary views, are used to find out information about a transaction. For a complete listing of these views and packages, refer to *Oracle8 Replication*, which is part of the documentation set published by Oracle Corporation.

DEFCALL view lists each remote procedure call associated with a particular deferred transaction and the number of arguments to the procedure. However, to know the value of the argument, you have to know the type of argument. This is obtained by using the GET_ARG_TYPE function of the DBMS_DEFER_QUERY package:

```
DBMS_DEFER_QUERY.GET_ARG_TYPE (
    call IN NUMBER,
    arg_no IN NUMBER,
    defer_trans_id IN VARCHAR2)
) RETURN NUMBER
```

① Argument number of the remote call

② Identity number of the deferred transaction; get its value from DEFERROR view

For example, in a SQL*Plus session, you would call this package as follows:

```
trans_type := DBMS_DEFER_QUERY.GET_ARG_TYPE(221, 7, '2.4.453')
```

① Numeric variable declared in SQL*Plus session; you can call it anything

② ID number corresponding remote call

This function would return a numeric value that corresponds to a datatype: 1 represents VARCHAR2, 2 represents NUMBER, 11 represents ROWID, 12 represents DATE, 23 represents RAW, and 96 represents CHAR. When you know the value of the returned number and hence the corresponding datatype, you can use another function, GET_VARCHAR2_ARG (if the return value was 1 representing a VARCHAR2), to get the actual value of the datatype.

Preparing for Replication

The process of building a replicated architecture involves several steps that involve planning and making decisions regarding the replicated configuration. At this stage, you define the schemas to be replicated, including tables, packages, and triggers. You also decide the number of sites at which you want your data replicated.

For organizational efficiency and for ease of administration, it's a good idea to group objects into replication groups. With Oracle8, you can turn off replication for replicated groups without affecting the other groups. This helps sometimes when you want to do maintenance on certain schemas and don't want to stop the rest of the database to stop replication.

You also can decide if you want snapshot replication or full multimaster replication or a combination of both. On today's systems, a lot of static tables or metadata tables are meant for lookup only and don't change. You can decide not to replicate such static tables, at least when using Advanced Replication. When configuring snapshot replication, the additional components of the system are snapshot logs and refresh groups. Snapshot logs are created at each master site to support the necessary snapshots. Refresh groups are created at each snapshot site. At each snapshot site, you also create snapshot groups that correspond to master group objects.

Finally, depending on the need for "fresh or refreshed" data at replicated sites, you might want to decide on an interval at which you want the replicated data to go across to the replicated site. As a DBA, you'll have to go through some trial and error to get the exact configuration you want for your shop, depending on your business needs, nature and amount of data, money you can invest in hardware, and so forth.

Using Replication Manager

This tool is available only in Windows

You can install Replication Manager on a PC that acts as client to an Oracle server, and most configuration and management can be done from within Replication Manager. Thus, the platform of the database server doesn't matter, as long you have a PC running Windows. If you still want to configure and track replication from a UNIX server or a workstation, you have to write/modify your own scripts.

Oracle Replication Manager is a GUI tool that helps you build and track a replicated schema. This tool provides graphical shortcuts to several API calls that are normally made from the server, and displays information in a easy-to-understand graphical fashion.

Replication Manager comes with replication wizards that help configure a replication schema. With Replication Manager, you can also connect to a master site and create master replication groups. Replication Manager will also create the Replication Administrator, Propagator, and Receiver accounts. Finally, you can use Replication Manager to create the database links that facilitate communications between sites. You can configure and create multimaster as well as snapshot replication sites with this tool.

To start Replication Manager, from the Start menu choose Programs, Oracle Replication Manager. Click the icon for Oracle Replication Manager. Figure 26.1 shows the startup window of the Replication Manager.

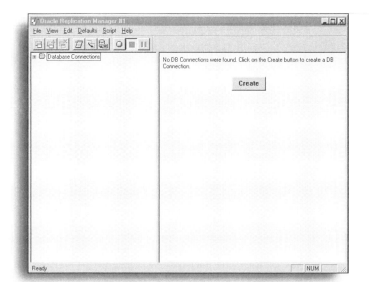

FIGURE 26.1

In Replication Manager's start-up window, the button for creating a database connection is on the right and the database connections are on the left.

Click the Create button on the right. In the Create DB Connection dialog box, you may or may not want to keep the two check boxes checked (see Figure 26.2), depending on how secure your PC and office environment is.

FIGURE 26.2

Selecting the Auto Connect at Startup check box will autoconnect the Replication Manager to the database. Deselecting the Always Prompt for Password check box will store the password locally on the PC, which isn't always recommended.

Set up a master site with the Replication Manager Setup Wizard

1. From Replication Manager's File menu, choose Setup Wizard.

2. The first dialog box lets you choose to set up a master site or a snapshot site (see Figure 26.3). Click the Next button to choose the default, Setup Master Sites.

FIGURE 26.3

You can choose to set up the master site or the snapshot site. For this example, we will look at creating a master site. The steps provided by the wizard are identical for both Multimaster and Snapshot Replication.

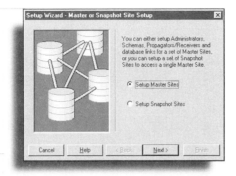

3. In the next dialog box, you can choose from exiting sites or enter a new site name. Click the New button.

4. In the New Master Site dialog box (see Figure 26.4), enter a Site Name. The user is preselected (SYSTEM). Also enter the password for the user SYSTEM, which in this case is the installation default of *manager*. Clicking OK will save your input and return you to the Setup Wizard – Setup Master Sites dialog box with your site name saved.

What's in a site name?

The site name corresponds to a service or Net8 alias with which you can connect to the database. For more information on Net8 aliases, refer to Chapter 24, "Configuring and Using Net8 Features."

FIGURE 26.4

If you want more sites to be made master sites, click Add instead of OK after entering each site name and password. When done, click OK.

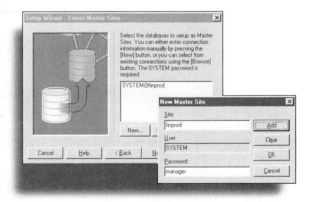

5. After you select all the sites you want, click the Next button to move to the next dialog box, which is for creating default administrators, propagators, and receivers (see Figure 26.5). You can accept the defaults or change them. When done, click Next.

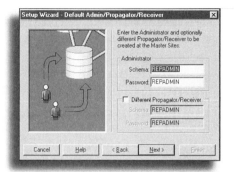

FIGURE 26.5

Enter the Schema name and Password for the administrator account, and optionally different propagator/receiver accounts.

6. In the next dialog box, you can optionally specify schemas to be created at the master sites to contain objects to be replicated (see Figure 26.6). For this example, we don't want any more schemas, so click Next.

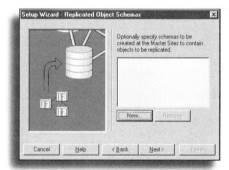

FIGURE 26.6

If you want to create schemas to replicate objects at a master site, click the New button.

7. The next dialog box lets you set values for scheduled links: Next Date, Interval Expression, Parallel Propagation, and Delay Seconds (see Figure 26.7). You can change the defaults if you want to, and then click Next.

8. In the Default Purge Scheduling dialog box (see Figure 26.8), you can set values for Next Date, Interval Expression, and Rollback Segment for default purge schedules. Click Next when done.

FIGURE 26.7

Click the Edit buttons to change the default values for Next Date and Interval Expression.

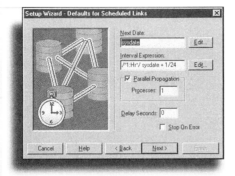

FIGURE 26.8

Clicking the Edit button for Next Date brings up a graphical calendar (similar to the Windows calendar), from which you can select the next date. Clicking the Edit button for the Interval Expression brings up a Set Interval dialog box, in which you can set the interval as seconds, minutes, hours, and days (the smallest allowed value is 1 second).

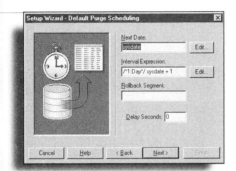

9. In the next dialog box, you can to customize the master site's settings (see Figure 26.9). For this example, we aren't customizing the master site, so simply click Next.

FIGURE 26.9

Selecting the master site enables the Customize button. You can customize the administrative users, link scheduling, and purge scheduling.

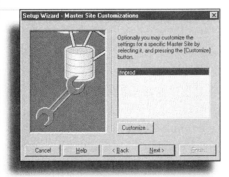

10. Click Finish in the last dialog box to accept all the values you've entered so far. The wizard creates the RepAdmin, propagator, receiver accounts, and schemas (see Figure

26.10). Clicking OK in the Setup Wizard Finish dialog box generates the master site(s). When it's completed, the wizard creates the master site, which is then visible in Replication Manager's left pane.

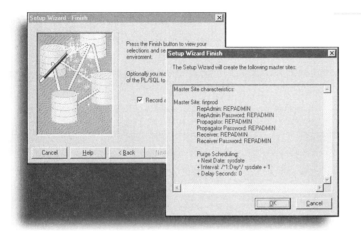

FIGURE 26.10

Select the Record a Script check box in the final wizard dialog box to have the wizard generate a script of the replication management API calls that it uses to build the system. This script can be run in SQL*Plus, SQL Worksheet, or any interactive tool.

11. After the master site is created, you can click the Configuration, Scheduling, Administration, and Database Objects folders in Replication Manager's left pane (see Figure 26.11).

FIGURE 26.11

You can view the database object by owner or by object type.

Managing Replication

The process of managing replicated sites is more complex than administering single sites. The issues are different for each configuration, whether you're dealing with multimaster, snapshot, or hybrid. Let's take a quick look at several tasks that database and replication administrators must perform for smooth operation of a replicated configuration:

- *Master group maintenance.* You can use Oracle Replication Manager to add or drop master groups. You can also modify master group properties with Replication Manager.

- *Quiescing.* This ensures that changes get propagated to all replicated sites. Deferred transaction queues are emptied at the propagation sites. The status of the queues changes from Await Callback to Quiesced when the transactions are pushed. The package called to initiate this is DBMS_REPCAT. SUSPEND_MASTER_ACTIVITY. This can be also done in Replication Manager. In Figure 26.11 on the left is a folder called Master Groups (under the Configuration folder). From here you can suspend replication.

  To suspend replication activity for a master group, click the target master group in the database connection the connects to the group's master definition site. Next, click the Properties toolbar button. On the Operations page of the Edit Master Group property sheet, click Suspend Replication.

- *Resuming replication activity.* After maintenance is completed on the master site, you can use Replication Manager to resume your sites' replication activity. The package that initiates this is called DBMS_REPCAT.RESUME_MASTER_ACTIVITY. You can execute this package in SQL*Plus or in Replication Manager. The procedure is identical to the preceding procedure for suspending replication activity for a master group, except that rather than click Suspend Replication, you click Resume Replication.

- *Conflict resolution.* Conflict resolution is used to ensure that two main objectives are achieved: data convergence and

Defining quiescing

Although the term *quiescing* isn't recognized in the dictionary, it's related to the word "quiescent," which means quiet, still, inactive. In Oracle, quiescing refers to the process of suspending replication activity between sites. This is normally done before performing administration tasks on master sites.

avoidance of cascading errors. Data convergence ensures that all sites have and share the same data. For example, conflicts can occur if two or more sites in a multimaster environment asynchronously update the same data.

You can use Replication Manager to view errors. As shown earlier in Figure 26.11, the left pane of the page has a folder called Administration. Under the Administration folder are Deferred Transactions by Dest, Local Errors, and Local Jobs. Alternatively, the view DEFERROR can be queried to see the error transactions.

A replication configuration must be designed with a specific conflict-resolution methodology in place. Oracle8 advanced replication provides system-defined routines for detecting and solving uniqueness and update conflicts. However, these system routines don't support delete conflicts, changes to primary key columns, referential integrity constraint violations, and presence of NULL values in the columns designated for conflict resolution.

Spatial Data Cartridge

Spatial data refers to location characteristics of objects as they relate to each other in real-world two-dimensional relationships. A map is an example of spatial data. Geographic information systems (GIS) that store spatial data would be likely users of Oracle's Spatial Data Cartridge, which provides a set of functions and procedures designed specifically for storing, retrieving, and analyzing spatial data. (For more detailed definitions of cartridges, see the later section "Oracle Web Server Cartridges.") Besides data from GIS systems, two-dimensional computer-aided design (CAD) drawings could be also stored as spatial data, because CAD drawings indicate the location of objects/parts (actually, primitives) in relation to each other.

In most CAD packages, data representation is done internally with primitive datatypes. A "primitive" is the most basic form of representation of an object. Different forms of geometry, such as arcs and circles, are created by using a combination of primitive

Deciding a conflict resolution mechanism for an advanced replication architecture

Designers can use a combination of several conflict-resolution techniques, depending on the business and configuration needs of their sites: minimum and maximum update, earliest and latest time-stamp update, additive and average update, priority group and site priority update, overwrite and discard update, append site name/sequence uniqueness, and discard uniqueness. A good strategy for a replication designer would be to look at individual columns and groups to decide the nature of updates, and then design the conflict-resolution mechanism.

datatypes. Oracle's Spatial Data Cartridge supports three basic type of primitives and geometries (all two-dimensional) generated by using a combination of these three types:

- *Point and point cluster type.* These elements are comprised of X and Y coordinates. These can correspond to axes in an engineering drawing, or to latitude and longitude. Point data consists of one coordinate in space—for example, (4,5), where 4 is the X value and 5 is the Y value.

- *Line strings.* When several points are joined together to form line segments, the representation is called a line string. Line data consists of two coordinates, which would represent the line segment joining the points. For example, (0,0) and (5,5) would be a line segment joining the points (0,0) and (5,5).

- *N-point polygons.* Polygons are shapes such as trapezoids, squares, and so forth, formed by joining line strings so that they form a "closed" geometry. Polygon data consists of coordinate pair values, one vertex joining the pair. Coordinates can be represented in a clockwise or counter-clockwise order around the polygon.

The Spatial Data Model

The Oracle Spatial Data Model essentially consists of elements, geometries, and layers arranged hierarchically. Elements make up geometries, which in turn make up layers:

- *Elements.* An element, the most basic datatype in the Spatial Data Model, acts as a building block for a geometry. Points, line strings, and polygons are elements. For example, a square piece of metal to be machined could be represented as a polygon; cutter paths could be represented as line strings. An example of a line string in a GIS system could be a road; a city block could be a polygon.

- *Geometries.* A geometric object is the representation created by the combination or a set of elements, arranged in an orderly manner. For example, a golf course on a map is a geometry; there would be holes (points), walkways (line elements), and boundaries (polygons). Each geometric datatype is represented by a unique identifier (GID), that stores information about the attributes of the primitives making up the geometric object.

- *Layers.* A layer is a dissimilar collection of geometric objects all having similar attributes. For example, in a facility planning layout, the foundation geometry object would normally be on one layer, storage-space would be on a different layer, machinery would be on a different layer, lighting plan would be on another layer, and so on. Layers are used extensively by architects, engineers, and contractors to see selective details about a location.

The Spatial Table Structure

Oracle's Spatial Data Cartridge uses four tables/views to store and index spatial data. These four tables make up a layer:

- SDOLAYER   This table contains summary information about a layer of spatial data. This table has two columns: SDO_ORDCNT and SDO_LEVEL (see Table 26.1).

- SDODIM   This table stores information related to the dimension (such as latitude and longitude) of the data. This table has five columns: SDO_DIMNUM, SDO_LB, SDO_UB, SDO_TOLERANCE, and SDO_DIMNAME (see Table 26.1).

- SDOGEOM   This table contains information about geometric entities stored in the data. The columns of the table are SDO_GID, SDO_ESEQ, SDO_ETYPE, SDO_SEQ, SDO_X1, SDO_Y1, SDO_X2, SDO_Y2, and so on through SDO_X*n* and SDO_Y*n*, where X*n* and Y*n* are X and Y values of the nth coordinate (see Table 26.1).

- SDOINDEX   This table contains summary index information about geometry in a layer. SDOINDEX has three columns: SDO_GID, SDO_CODE, and SDO_MAXCODE (see Table 26.1).

Syntax for tables that make up layer definition for spatial data

The syntax for these tables is *layername*_TABLE, where *layername* is the name of the layer and *TABLE* is either SDOLAYER, SDODIM, SDOGEOM, or SDOINDEX. A layer can be defined completely by using these four tables.

TABLE 26.1   **Columns of tables *SDOLAYER, SDODIM, SDOGEOM,* and *SDOINDEX***

Column Name:	Datatype:	Description:
SDOLAYER		
SDO_ORDCNT	Number	This column is the total count of ordinates per row present in the SDOGEOM table.
SDO_LEVEL	Number	This column maintains a count of number of times *layername* was tessellated during the index build stage.
SDODIM		
SDO_DIMNUM	Number	This column keeps track of the dimension to which a row refers. The minimum value is 1.
SDO_LB	Number	This column is the lower bound (LB) of the ordinate in the relevant dimension. For example, on a X-Y coordinate system with a maximum X of 100 and minimum of –100, the LB would be –100.
SDO_UB	Number	This column represents the upper bound of the ordinate in the relevant dimension. For example, if the dimension were latitude, this value would be 90.
SDO_TOLERANCE	Number	This represents the tolerance associated with points in the data. This value must be greater than zero. SDO_TOLERANCE will vary for different types of spatial data for different dimensions.
SDO_DIMNAME	VARCHAR	This represents the name used for this dimension; it can be X/Y or latitude/longitude.
SDOGEOM		
SDO_GID	Number	This column represents the geometric identifier (GID), a unique number that represents each geometrical object in a layer.
SDO_ESEQ	Number	This column represents the element sequence number. A geometrical object is comprised of primitive elements. This column lists each element in the geometry for that layer.

Spatial data indexing

Spatial data uses a special index, HHCODE, for indexing data. HHCODEs are also called "tiles." Users can adjust the number of tiles that cover a surface. In a way, it represents the granularity of a data search. The finer the grain, the longer it would take to search the data. The technique of determining how many tiles cover a surface is called "tessellation." Tile size can be fixed or variable.

Column Name:	Datatype:	Description:
SDOGEOM *(continued)*		
SDO_ETYPE	Number	This column represents the element type. For example, a POINT type has an ETYPE value of 1, a LINESTRING has a value of 2, and so on.
SDO_SEQ	Number	This column represents the sequence number of each row of data for the element.
SDO_X1	Number	This column represents the X value of the first X coordinate.
SDO_Y1	Number	This column represents the Y value of the first Y coordinate.
SDO_X*n* and SDO_Y*n*	Number	These columns represent the X and Y values of the *n*th coordinate, respectively.
SDOINDEX		
SDO_GID	Number	This column really acts as a foreign key to the SDOGEOM table.
SDO_CODE	RAW	Data representation is done in the form of tiles. This column contains the value of the bit interleaved ID of a tile that covers SDO_ID.
SDO_MAXCODE	RAW	This column is the SDO_CODE with an extra value one unit farther than the allowable maximum value of the index. Basically, it describes a logical tile.

Using Spatial Data

Spatial data must be treated differently as compared with conventional data, because the indexing and data-retrieval techniques are different. Spatial data can be entered into tables interactively from applications or by using SQL*Loader for mass/batch loads.

Spatial data is queried in essentially a two-step process. The first step, referred to as a "primary filter," uses algorithms to approximate search patterns to narrow down the search size. The output from the first filter is passed to the second stage (called the "secondary filter"). The secondary filter uses exact calculations of geometry to the smaller output of the primary filter to find a match.

Spatial data applications perform a spatial query when information contained in a bounding or a query window is requested. The query window calls the SDO_WINDOW package, which performs the data calculations.

A spatial join is the output of joining two tables (layers) with spatial operators. A spatial join would join two layers with the layername_SDOINDEX field. An example of a query that causes a spatial join could be a list of all road and railway intersections in town.

Oracle Web Server Cartridges

Reading current documentation for Oracle Web Server

Because Oracle Web Application Server is evolving rapidly and has seen at least three version upgrades in the last two years, I recommend that you use the online documentation provided by Oracle Corporation along with the Web Application Server for configuring the cartridges and Web Request Broker because this area is evolving quickly. This section covers the basic principles of Oracle Web Application Server 3.0 and is meant as an introduction. You can refer to the online documentation for the most current configuration techniques.

Oracle Web Application Server is a superset of a standard HTTP server, with extensions (cartridges) that integrate seamlessly with the Oracle server. Similar to Spatial Data Cartridges, the cartridges that ship with Oracle Web Server are functions and packages that act as extensions to the core database product of the Oracle database server. You can program cartridges in various programming languages, such as C++, C, Visual Basic, and Java.

The Web Application Server comes in two versions: advanced and standard. The advanced version is a superset of the standard version. Some notable features present in the advanced version but not in the standard version are as follows:

- *Transaction service.* Because HTTP (Hypertext Transfer Protocol) is stateless, it becomes difficult to enforce the concept of transactions, specially for data-entry applications. The advanced version of Oracle Web Server provides a transaction service—middleware software that maintains the equivalent of sessions, unlike the standard stateless HTTP.

- *ODBC cartridge.* This cartridge provides connectivity to ODBC-compliant databases other than Oracle. You use it if your site has other ODBC-compliant databases that need to work in a Web application; you don't need the ODBC cartridge to connect to Oracle.

- *Distributed cartridges.* You can run cartridges on remote nodes only if you have the advanced version. If you have the standard version, the cartridges all run on the same node.

The major components that are similar in the advanced and standard version are as follows:

- *HTTP daemons or listeners.* The HTTP daemon component (in UNIX) or listener component (in Windows NT) of the Web Application Server listens for requests from clients. The listener uses HTTP to communicate with clients and can accept connections on one or more IP address/port combinations.

- *Web Request Broker.* The Web Request Broker (WRB) keeps track of the execution of the entire system. It handles load-balancing tasks, tracks global resources such as available cartridges, and obtains the address (the object reference) of the required cartridge resource. The WRB also provides system services that all cartridges can use.

- *Cartridges.* Cartridges are server-side applications that handle cartridge-specific requests from clients. Some example of cartridges are the PL/SQL cartridge, LiveHTML cartridge, Java cartridge, and VRML cartridge.

Oracle Web Application Server 3.0 has been replaced by version 4.0, which is called Oracle Application Server. Oracle Application Server is designed to enable organizations to deploy and manage applications on a single server, rather than on hundreds or thousands of desktop PCs (the case in a two-tier architecture). Oracle Application Server 4.0 is designed to support all types of network clients, serving as a central point of access to any database, application, or legacy system.

All features of version 3.0 are available in 4.0, including backward compatibility with all cartridges. Version 4.0 also has several new cartridges, including new Oracle Call Interface (OCI) cartridge for native access to Oracle databases, an ODBC cartridge for access to any third-party database, and a new Rdb cartridge for access to Oracle Rdb database applications. A COBOL cartridge, made by Fujistu Corporation, enables access to

COBOL applications. The AppBuilder wizard, made by Borland, provides designers with step-by-step help for designing Web applications.

Using Oracle Web Application Server Cartridges

This section explains major features of two commonly used cartridges: PL/SQL and the Java cartridge. To understand the functioning of the cartridges, you need to understand the architecture of the Web Server. The Oracle Web Application Server has three major components:

Integrating Web Application Server with other major Web server listeners

You can use Web servers from Netscape or Microsoft as the listener component if you don't want to use the listener that ships with the Web Server. The *Oracle Web Application Server Installation Guide* has information on configuring other major vendor listeners to use with the Web Application Server.

- *HTTP listeners (daemons on UNIX).* The HTTP daemon (UNIX) or listener component is a process that listens for requests from clients. The listener uses HTTP to communicate with clients and can accept connections on one or more IP address/port combinations. You can specify the port on which you want the listener or daemon to listen on. Normally, port 8888 or 9999 is the default port for administration of the Web Server.

- *Web request brokers (WRB).* WRBs are software components that are implemented as CORBA-compliant object request brokers. (CORBA is a industry standard for request brokers.) WRBs can send requests to and get responses from applications running on machines on the network. One WRB keeps track of execution of the entire system. It handles load-balancing tasks, tracks global resources such as available cartridges, and provides several system services that the cartridges can use.

- *Cartridges (also called server-side applications).* Cartridges, in this sense, are server-side applications that handle cartridge-specific requests from clients. Each cartridge functions independently. An application can be designed by using several cartridges, depending on the cartridge-specific requests. On one Web Application Server, you can have multiple cartridge instances for each cartridge type. The number of cartridge instances you choose to create and deploy would depend on your application and business needs.

Web Application Server comes bundled with several cartridges, of which the following are just some:

- *Java Cartridge.* This is needed to run Java applications on the server-side.

- *PL/SQL Cartridge.* This cartridge handles requests that need to run PL/SQL procedures, functions, and packages on the Oracle server.

- *LiveHTML Cartridge.* This cartridge parses HTML documents that contain server-side include (SSI) extensions.

- *Oracle Worlds Cartridge.* This cartridge enables designers to build dynamic three-dimensional worlds and environments by using VRML.

- *Perl Cartridge.* This runs Perl scripts.

- *ODBC Cartridge.* This enables connectivity to ODBC-compliant relational databases.

Handling Requests

When the Web Application Server receives a request from a client, the listener component processes the request first and determines how it should handle the request. If the request is for a static file (a file that exists on a file system), the listener fetches the file from the operating system and sends it to the client. If the request is to execute a CGI (Common Gateway Interface) file/script, the listener executes the file and sends the results back to the client.

If the request is for a cartridge, the listener performs the following:

- Routes the request through the Web Request Broker.

- Looks up the virtual path to determine the cartridge type that this request is for. (A virtual path is the syntax of the URL that's part of the request.)

- Calls the authentication service to authorize the client.

- Sends the request to an instance of the appropriate cartridge. The cartridge instance processes the request and returns the results to the client. The URL string has all the relevant information that tells the listener what type of cartridge and instance to which to connect.

The PL/SQL Cartridge

The PL/SQL Cartridge provides the environment for developing Web applications as PL/SQL procedures stored in an Oracle database server. (PL/SQL is Oracle Corporation's procedural language extension to SQL.) When you configure the PL/SQL Cartridge, you install packages that help generate HTML pages. These packages define procedures, functions, and datatypes you can use in your stored procedures. In each HTTP request for the PL/SQL Cartridge, the uniform resource locator (URL) specifies the PL/SQL agent (which contains connection information) and the name of the stored procedure to run. The URL can also contain values for any parameters required by the stored procedure.

Before you can use the PL/SQL Cartridge, you need to load the packages listed in this section into the database schemas from which you want to run the procedures. The packages define datatypes, functions, and procedures used by the cartridge, and you can use some of them in your Web application. The functions and procedures help you generate dynamic HTML pages that contain data retrieved from the database.

Oracle Web Application Servers comes with a set of prewritten PL/SQL packages called the PL/SQL toolkit. To install the PL/SQL Web Toolkit, use the PL/SQL agent administration forms that are created with the Web server installation. The installation procedure grants the CONNECT and RESOURCE roles to the database user and executes the $ORAWEB_HOME/ admin/owains.sql script, which installs the packages in the PL/SQL Web Toolkit. When the owains.sql script is run manually; you should launch it from Server Manager or SQL worksheet (part of Enterprise Manager). If you want to run it from SQL*Plus, see the header of the script for instructions.

The PL/SQL agent and the DAD

Like the PL/SQL agent, a DAD is a named set of configuration values used for database access. It specifies information such as the database name or the SQL*Net/Net8 service name, the ORACLE_HOME directory, and NLS configuration information such as language, sort type, and date language. You can also specify username and password information in a DAD; if they aren't specified, the user will be prompted to enter a username and password when the URL is invoked. The PL/SQL agent specifies information such as which DAD to use, how much error information to return if an error occurs, a list of authorized ports that it can use, and transaction parameters. Each PL/SQL agent is associated with a DAD.

The packages are installed in the user's schema. This ensures that the user can't use the subprograms in the packages to access data in another user's schema.

Figure 26.12 shows the components of an URL. The Web Application Server comes with the Web Application Server Manager, which is a set of HTML forms you use to configure the PL/SQL Cartridge, the PL/SQL agent, and the Data Access Descriptor (DAD). On these forms you enter information such as virtual paths for the PL/SQL Cartridge, the SQL*Net/Net8 service name for the DAD, and the error-reporting level for the PL/SQL agent. Figure 26.13 shows the configuration of a PL/SQL cartridge in the Oracle Web Application Architecture. Chapter 19, "Improving Throughput with SQL, PL/SQL, and Precompilers," and Appendix A, "Essential PL/SQL: Understanding Stored Procedures, Triggers, and Packages," provide more information on PL/SQL.

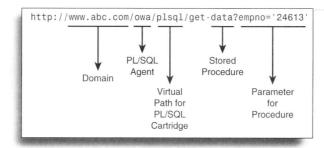

FIGURE 26.12

The basic components of an URL for the PL/SQL cartridge, showing the use of PL/SQL (functions, procedures, and packages) in the HTTP protocol. The parameters passed to the PL/SQL procedure act as a query string, which can be called from HTML forms and other Web applications.

Sequence of events observed when a PL/SQL Cartridge request is made

1. The listener component of the Web Application Server receives the request from a client and determines who should handle it. In this case, it forwards the request to the Web Request Broker (WRB) because the request is for a cartridge.

2. The WRB forwards the request to an available PL/SQL Cartridge.

FIGURE 26.13

The Web listener is a common component of all cartridges (in this case, PL/SQL and Java cartridges). After the listener interprets a request, the request is routed to the Java cartridge or the PL/SQL cartridge.

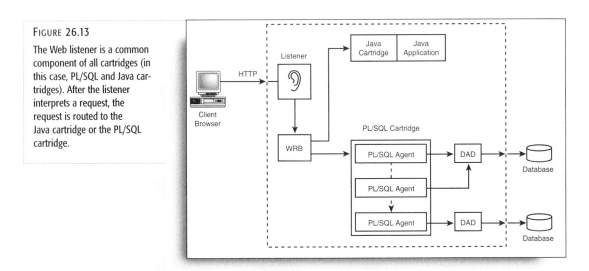

3. The PL/SQL Cartridge retrieves the name of the PL/SQL agent from the URL (request). It uses the agent's configuration values to determine to which database server to connect and how to set up the PL/SQL client configuration.

4. The cartridge connects to the database with the PL/SQL agent's configured values, prepares the call parameters, and invokes the procedure in the database.

5. The procedure generates the HTML page, which can include dynamic data accessed from tables in the database as well as static data. ("Static data" here refers to HTML pages, images, or both, which exist on a file system that's mapped to by the URL. "Dynamic data" refers to content created on-the-fly from a database query.)

6. The output from the PL/SQL procedure is returned to the PL/SQL Cartridge and the client (browser) via a response buffer.

The Java Cartridge

Java is a object-oriented programming language developed by Sun Microsystems. Java has rapidly evolved into a variety of network computing and Web architectures. What makes Java so exciting is the promise of platform independence. In keeping with the popularity of Java, Oracle Corporation has developed a Java cartridge. An HTTP request routed to the Java Cartridge is processed by running a Java application that returns the HTTP response.

The Java Cartridge doesn't support Java applets (programs written in Java that can be downloaded over the network and run in a Web browser), but supports only Java applications. Java applications are loaded from a trusted file system (which is mapped to by the Web Server).

When the listener component of the Web Application Server receives requests for the Java Cartridge from browsers, the Java Cartridge interprets information in the URL to identify the Java application that should handle the request. The Java application then programmatically responds to the client, performs interim tasks, accesses a database, or performs other computing tasks. Ultimately, the Java application sends a response back through the Java Virtual Machine (JVM) and the Web Application Server to the client. Figure 26.13 shows the Java cartridge in the architecture of the Oracle Web Application Server.

Sequence of events observed when a Java Cartridge request is made

1. The Web Application Server receives the request identified by a URL—for example,

   `http://servername.domainname/java/myfirstclass.`

2. The listener knows by the URL string that the request needs to be routed to a cartridge, and routes the request to the WRB.

3. The WRB of the Web Application Server dispatches the request. The WRB examines the URL and determines which cartridge should handle the request. If the URL is under a virtual path that belongs to the Java Cartridge, the WRB dispatches the request to the Java Cartridge.

4. The WRB finds a Java Cartridge, if available, or starts one if none is available.

5. The Java Cartridge receives the request, parses the URL, and finds the name of the application (actually, a Java class)

to call. Normally, the last part of an URL string is the Java class. In the URL mentioned in step 1, `myfirstclass` is the application (class).

6. The Java Cartridge loads the class and invokes it at its entry point, generates a response (including HTTP header and body), and returns the response. The Java Cartridge receives the response and returns it to the WRB, which forwards it to the browser client that made the request.

Oracle Advanced Queuing

Availability of Oracle AQ with Oracle Enterprise Edition

Oracle AQ isn't available with Oracle8 version of the product; it's available with the Enterprise Edition of the server. To take advantage of the full functionality of Oracle AQ option, you'll also need the Enterprise Edition version of Oracle8 with the Objects Option.

Oracle Advanced Queuing (Oracle AQ) is an Oracle8 feature that integrates a messaging queuing system with the Oracle8 Server (Enterprise Edition). This allows you to store messages into queues that can be retrieved and processed when needed. The real advantage of advanced queuing is that it's an integrated and reliable queuing system that works without any extra middleware software. Applications access the queues through a PL/SQL interface.

Oracle AQ Components and Terminology

Oracle AQ has certain terms and definitions typical to a messaging system. Let's take a quick look at some of the terms:

Using the DBMS_AQADM package

Oracle AQ provides a package called **DBMS_AQADM** that's used for creating, stopping, altering, starting, and dropping queues.

- *Messages.* A message is the smallest measurable unit of information used by Oracle AQ for messaging. Messages are inserted into and retrieved from queues.

- *Queues.* A queue acts as a container for messages. All messages in a queue must have the same datatype.

- *Queue tables.* Queue data is stored in queue tables, which are database tables that contain one or more queues. A queue table has approximately 25 columns.

- *Agents.* An agent is basically a queue user. There are two categories of agents: enqueuing and dequeuing. Users who place messages on the queue are called enqueuing agents or "producers." Users to whom a message is directed are called "consumers." Consumers act as dequeuing agents and remove messages from the queue.

- *Queue monitor.* The queue monitor is a background process that monitors queues. Parameters monitored include message expiration, retry, and delay time. The presence of this optional process depends on the values set for the AQ_TM_PROCESS initialization parameter. The AQ_TM_PROCESS initialization parameter has to be initialized and set to a value exceeding 1 for the queuing statistics to be collected. Valid values for the AQ_TM_PROCESS parameter are as follows:

    - If AQ_TM_PROCESS=0 or is unspecified, no queue monitor processes are created.

    - If AQ_TM_PROCESS=1, one queue monitor process (QMN0) is created as a background process to monitor the messages.

    - If AQ_TM_PROCESS is set 2 through 10, that many number of QMN*n* processes are created.

Major Features of Oracle AQ

Oracle AQ has the following major features:

- *SQL access.* Messaging data is stored in tables and is accessible through standard SQL functions. All principles of data access and query optimization apply to messaging data.

- *Structured payload.* You can use Oracle8 object features to structure and manage the payload. Traditional datatypes as well as user-defined objects are used for message storage and retrieval.

- *Integrated database-level operational support.* All traditional database-level activities such as import/export, use of indexes for performance enhancement, deferred rollback, backup and recovery, use of Enterprise Manager, and other tools is facilitated. In other words, messaging data is treated just as conventional or traditional data is.

- *Retention and message history.* Messages can be retained even after being read. You can specify the duration for storage.

Suggested reading for more information on AQ

For more information about Advanced Queuing, read the chapter on Advanced Queuing included in the *Oracle8 Server Application Administrator's Guide* in the Oracle documentation set. In particular, a section in this chapter titled "Advanced Queuing by Example" deserves special mention, because it has several scenarios and situations worth reading.

This history can be used for data-warehousing, auditing, and for other tracking purposes.

- *Integrated transactions.* Systems design is simplified if messaging can be "tied" to transactions versus "external" messaging systems that depend on middleware such as Transaction Processing (TP) monitors. Systems configuration is simplified because there are fewer pieces of software to configure and manage.

- *Tracking and event journals.* Relationships of messages to one another can be established because the data is stored and manipulated as relational data. Applications use these relationships to create event journals that can be used for tracking and workflow scenarios.

- *Windows of execution.* A particular message can be designated to be delivered or dispatched in a defined window of time. You can also specify a delay time after which a message should be processed. The initialization parameter AQ_TM_PROCESS is used to enable time monitoring on queue messages.

- *Multiple consumers per message.* A message can be dispatched to multiple consumers.

- *Navigation.* Navigational control is enabled between messages. You can navigate between messages in a definite order or based on an order determined by snapshots.

- *Message ordering.* The order in which messages are consumed can be set in three ways: by using a sort order based on properties by which they're sorted, by using a priority that can be assigned to each message, and by using a sequence deviation that allows you to position a message in relation to other messages.

- *Dequeue modes.* Dequeuing is the process of removing a message from a queue. If a message is browsed, it remains in the queue; if it's read, it's considered as dequeued.

- *Exception queues.* If a message isn't used with a time limit or given constraints, the message can be moved to a user-specified exception queue.

- *Message grouping.* You can group messages belonging to one queue to form a set that can be consumed by only one user at a time.

- *Retries with delays.* If a message isn't consumed for some reason, an attempt is made to retry to submit the message up to the specified limit.

- *Queuing statistics.* Oracle AQ maintains queuing statistics in a dynamic table GV$AQ. These statistics contain information about the current state of the queuing system as well as time-interval statistics.

Understanding Oracle8 Options

Overview of the Parallel Server option

Work with object types, nested tables, and methods

Create partitioned tables and indexes

Send and receive messages with the Advance Queue option

Store and query structured documents with the Context cartridge

Use one-step, two-step, and in-memory queries

The Parallel Server Option

Oracle's Parallel Server option allows multiple instances running on different *nodes* to access the same database (see Figure 27.1).

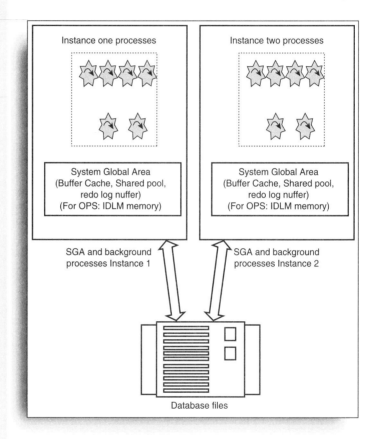

FIGURE 27.1

Oracle Parallel Server allows multiple instances to access the same database.

Use the INIT.ORA file for different instances

By keeping different INIT.ORA files for each Oracle instance in an OPS environment, you can optimize each instance's performance depending on its desired workload.

Only one instance has access to the database in single-instance mode (also known as exclusive mode). Multiple instances accessing the same database provide the following advantages:

- *Improved availability*. By general reliability theory, the probability of simultaneous failure of multiple systems should be less than the probability of failure of each individual system. Thus, multiple instances running on different systems make the database more available than a single instance. Of course, this is advantageous only when the system doesn't have any other single point of failure.

- *Improved throughput.* CPU and memory resources available from multiple machines allow increased processing power, which can be used to increase the throughput.

- *Better speed.* With the increased processing resources, the jobs can be broken into multiple smaller units, which in turn can be processed concurrently, reducing the total elapse time for the job execution.

Hardware Requirements

Oracle uses global locks to preserve data integrity and consistency while allowing concurrent read/write access to the same data files. To enable simultaneous access to the data files and to implement global locks, Oracle Parallel Server requires the following functionality at the hardware level:

- Disk accessible from all nodes
- High-speed network component for messaging

Disks Accessible from All Nodes

Oracle Parallel Server is available on several platforms where multinode systems are available from hardware vendors. Because the database in an Oracle Parallel Server environment is accessed by all instances running on all nodes, all data files, control files, and online redo log files need to be accessible to all nodes.

Various vendors have implemented this feature differently. These approaches can be divided into two categories:

- *Shared-disk systems.* In this type of architecture, a set of disks is shared among all the nodes via a common high-speed bus. VMS, UNIX, and Windows NT clusters are examples of systems using this technique. As shown in Figure 27.2, each node in a shared-disk configuration has its own CPU and memory; they do share a set of disk drives, usually a disk array. The disks are connected to each node via high-speed interconnect.

Instances share files in an OPS environment

Instances in an Oracle Parallel Server environment share all the data files and control files. However, only one instance can write to a set of online redo logs assigned to it at startup. In addition, each instance has its own initialization parameter file.

FIGURE 27.2

Disks in a shared-disk system
are connected to nodes via a
high-speed interconnect.

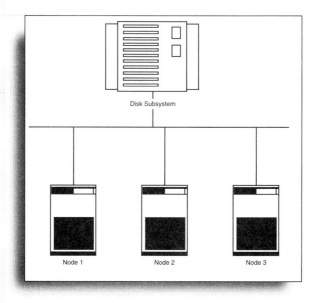

- *Shared-nothing systems.* In this type of architecture, each node has its own CPU, memory, and disks (see Figure 27.3). The disks are available to other nodes via a high-speed interconnect between nodes. Dual-ported disk drives are physically connected to two of the nodes, providing a secondary redundant disk access path in case one node fails. MPP platforms such as IBM SP-2 and Pyramid MASH are the most common examples in this category.

High-Speed Interconnect

To coordinate concurrent access to the data files and to synchronize the data in the memory of all nodes, OPS uses the Integrated Distributed Lock Manager (IDLM). IDLM requires the high-speed interconnect between nodes for messaging traffic generated for communication among nodes for synchronization.

Software Requirements

Oracle Parallel Server also requires the following special software components:

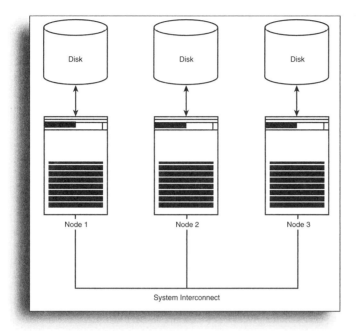

ΓIGURE 27.3
Shared-nothing systems don't have a common resource.

- *Oracle Parallel Server option.* OPS is an option priced separately from Oracle. To use Oracle Parallel Server, you must install and link it with the Oracle code. (Refer to the *Oracle8 Installation and Configuration Guide* for details on how to install and link Oracle Parallel Server.)

- *Distributed Lock Manager.* Oracle coordinates concurrent access to the data from various nodes through global locks. Global locks are implemented via special software known as the Distributed Lock Manager. Beginning with Oracle8, it's embedded into the Oracle server code itself. Hence, it's known as the Integrated Distributed Lock Manager (IDLM). To ensure data integrity, IDLM guarantees that only one master copy of the data is in the buffer cache and only one node can modify the data's master copy.

- *Cluster Manager.* This software coordinates the availability of all nodes in an Oracle Parallel Server environment. It continuously monitors the availability of all nodes by sending "heartbeat" signals. It also reconfigures the environment whenever a new member joins the cluster or when one of the existing members disappears. The Cluster Manager also performs communication between all nodes in the cluster.

Parallel Server Uses

OPS offers increased system availability

Increased system availability in an OPS environment stems mainly from the fact that if one instance of the database is down, chances are that other instances accessing the same database will make it available for users.

As mentioned earlier, the use of Oracle Parallel Server option increases system availability (because of the increased redundancy) and provides more system resources to interact with the database.

The increased system resources can be used to increase the throughput. You can do the following by using the additional CPU and memory available on the additional nodes:

- Execute more SQL statements concurrently, thus allowing more jobs or more users on the system.
- Run parts of the same SQL operation in parallel, thus increasing the speed of executing the SQL statements.

Additional system resources (to access the same database) comes with an additional cost of synchronization among the concurrent activities. Some increased resources are used to meet the overhead of the synchronization. Thus, the net amount of additional system resources available for application processing is as follows:

```
additional system resources available for processing =
resources added - resources to synchronize concurrent access
```

Therefore, OPS is advantageous as long as the cost of synchronization remains low. If the cost of synchronization becomes comparable to the resources added, the use of OPS isn't justified.

The resources consumed for synchronization depends on Oracle's internal architecture. A significant part of this cost, however, depends on the nature of the workload and the application architecture. OPS has been found suitable in the following situations:

- Compute-intensive, read-only application that rarely updates data (typical in a decision-support system or data-warehousing environment)

- Online Transaction Processing (OLTP) system with data partitioning—the OLTP application that updates disjointed data from different nodes

- OLTP with random access to a very large database

- Departmental applications—applications modifying different tables in the same database and running on separate nodes

Using Object Types with the Object Option

Oracle8 is an object-relational database because it allows user-defined object types. Oracle8 lets you define an object's attribute and the methods associated with it. For example, consider a part to be an object; its attribute can then be defined as part number, description, stock location, current inventory, and so on. Finding the location of a part, increasing the inventory on arrival of the part from the supplier, decreasing the inventory when the part is consumed, and so on are the methods you can associate with a part.

If you're involved with designing applications with a relational database, you might wonder why an object type should be used. Consider a large company, where each division and location has its own installed computer systems and information systems division. Division A needs to define a part number field for its application and decides that it should be a 12-digit number. Also consider that Division B independently defines the part number field to be VARCHAR2(12). Obviously, there's a lack of communication between the two groups. This type of inconsistency can cause problems while transferring the data between the applications. This problem won't arise if the corporate DBA defines a part_type object and all the divisions use the already-defined part_type objects in their applications. Thus, defining a part type

Security and privileges of objects

Object types are owned by the user who creates them and follow the Oracle's standard security and privilege mechanism. A user must be granted the **EXECUTE** privilege on the object types by the owner before he or she can use an object type defined by another user.

promotes standards and uniformity. The standard method to manipulate the part_type object can also be defined centrally and reused by the individual divisions. The use of object types has the following advantages:

- They let you centralize and promote application standards.

- They let you define methods and then reuse the methods, making application development consistent and efficient.

- They let you see the things as used in the business environment.

Creating and Using Object Types

An object type has a specification and a body. The specifications consist of the object's attributes and the declaration of intended methods to be used with the objects. The body consists of PL/SQL code for the methods associated with the object.

Consider the case of a research organization that needs to define an author object type. You could define an author object type as follows:

```
create or replace type author_type as object (
Last_name      varchar2(20),
First_Name     varchar2(20),
author_title   varchar(20));
```

When it's defined, you can see the attributes of an object datatype by using SQL*Plus's DESC command:

```
SQL> desc author_type
 Name                             Null?    Type
 -------------------------------- -------- ----
  LAST_NAME                                VARCHAR2(20)
  FIRST_NAME                               VARCHAR2(20)
  AUTHOR_TITLE                             VARCHAR2(20)
```

The preceding CREATE command creates an author_type datatype, which can further be referenced anywhere you would refer a standard datatype such as a number, CHAR, or VARCHAR2. For example, the following CREATE datatype command creates a paper_type datatype and uses the preceding author_type datatype definition:

```
create or replace type paper_type as object (
  paper#  number(10),
  name        varchar2(30),
  author      author_type,
  subject varchar2(20),
  price number(5));
```

① The predefined author_type datatype

② The AUTHOR_TYPE datatype as part of the new object type definition

```
SQL> desc paper_type
 Name                                Null?       Type
 ------------------------------      --------    ----
 PAPER#                                          NUMBER(10)
 NAME                                            VARCHAR2(30)
 AUTHOR                                          AUTHOR_TYPE
 SUBJECT                                         VARCHAR2(20)
 PRICE                                           NUMBER(5)
```

②

Note the AUTHOR_TYPE datatype listed under the describe output's type column. When defined, the datatype can be used in an application. The following example creates a table by using the paper_type datatype:

```
create table paper_sales (
sales_order# integer,
customer_#   integer,
paper        paper_type,
qty          number(10));
```

①

Similarly, you can use paper_type in a PL/SQL program:

```
create or replace procedure paper_sales (
customer#  IN number(10),
paper      IN paper_type)
begin ...
```

①

You need to write a statement similar to the following in order to insert a row into the table paper_sales:

```
insert into paper_sales values (123456789,999999,
paper_type(1111,'Research Paper',
author_type('Last','First','Professor'),'Oracle8',100),10);
```

To reference an element in a datatype, you have to prefix it with the datatype name. For example, to select the paper# paper name from the paper_sales table, you would write a query similar to the following:

Altering and dropping object types

When it's defined, you can drop a user object type by using the **DROP TYPE** command. You can't change an object type's existing attributes, but you can add new member subprogram specifications.

① The defined datatype

① The defined datatype

```
SQL> select sales_order#,x.paper.paper#,x.paper.name
     from paper_sales x ;


SALES_ORDER# PAPER.PAPER# PAPER.NAME
------------ ------------ -------------------------------
123456789                 1111 Research Paper
```

The following query selects the author's last and first name and title:

```
select sales_order#,x.paper.paper#,x.paper.name,
       x.paper.author.last_name,
       x.paper.author.first_name,
       x.paper.author.author_title
from paper_sales x;
SALES_ORDER# PAPER.PAPER# PAPER.NAME   PAPER.AUTHOR.LAST_NA
------------ ------------ ------------ --------------------

PAPER.AUTHOR.FIRST_N PAPER.AUTHOR.AUTHOR_
-------------------- --------------------
   123456789         1111 Research Paper            Last
First                Professor
```

Defining and Managing Object Tables and Nested Tables

An object table is a database table that's defined with an object type only—it doesn't use any relational columns. You can nest one object table inside another via an object type. Nested tables are useful in a *master-detail relationship*. The following code creates an object type employee_type and then uses it to create an object table employee_list:

```
create or replace type employee_type as object(
       EMPNO NUMBER(4) ,
       ENAME VARCHAR2(10),
       JOB VARCHAR2(9),
       HIREDATE DATE,
       SAL NUMBER(7,2),
       COMM NUMBER(7,2));


create or replace type employee_list
  as table of employee_type ;
```

An object table is shown as the list of object datatype in the DESC command's output:

```
SQL> desc employee_list
  employee_list TABLE OF EMPLOYEE_TYPE ──①

  Name                           Null?   Type
  ------------------------------ ------- ----

  EMPNO                                  NUMBER(4)
  ENAME                                  VARCHAR2(10)
  JOB                                    VARCHAR2(9)
  HIREDATE                               DATE
  SAL                                    NUMBER(7,2)
  COMM                                   NUMBER(7,2)
```

① **The object table**

The following SQL command creates the nested table dept by using the already created employee_list object table:

```
create table dept (
        dept_no number(3),
        dept_name varchar(30),
        employees employee_list)
nested table employees store as employees_list_table;


SQL> desc dept
  Name                           Null?   Type
  ------------------------------ -------- ----

  DEPT_NO                                NUMBER(3)
  DEPT_NAME                              VARCHAR2(30)
  EMPLOYEES                              EMPLOYEE_LIST
```

Using nested tables

Nested tables are a convenient way to store tables with master-detail relationship. In this example, information about all the employees in a department is contained within the **department** table itself.

Use the following command to insert rows into nested table:

```
insert into dept values (
20,'Sales',
employee_list(
   employee_type
   (7369,'SMITH','CLERK','17-DEC-80',800,NULL),
   employee_type
   (7566,'JONES','MANAGER','2-APR-81',2975,NULL)));
```

To query contents of a nested table, you need to use the THE function:

```
select e_list.ename from THE
(select employees from dept where dept_no=20) e_list;
```

Understanding Methods

A method is a PL/SQL procedure or function associated with the object. Oracle8 supports the following types of methods:

- Constructor
- Member
- Map
- Order

Constructor Method

Oracle automatically creates a constructor method for an object so that you can perform DML functions on the object. By default, the object's constructor method has the same name as the object itself, and all the object's attributes are available as parameters of the constructor method. The following example shows how constructor methods are used to insert data in the paper_sales table:

① Constructor methods

①

```
insert into paper_sales values (123456789,999999,
   paper_type(1111,'Research Paper',
   author_type('Last','First','Professor'),
     'Oracle8',100),10);
```

Member Method

A member method is a stored procedure associated with an object type. Before you can define a member method, you need to associate it with the object as its attribute. You can do this in the CREATE TYPE statement or by using an ALTER TYPE statement:

```
create or replace  type paper_type as object (
  paper# number(10),
  name       varchar2(30),
  author     author_type,
  subject varchar2(20),
  price number(5),
  stock_qty number(5),
member function STOCK_VALUE return number,
PRAGMA RESTRICT_REFERENCES( stock_value , WNDS, WNPS));
```

The member function definition can also have input parameters (although none are shown here) and it needs to specify the type of single return value.

PRAGMA RESTRICT_REFERENCES is a compiler directive that specifies what type of operations the function can perform. You need to specify this directive to prevent it from doing unwanted modifications to the object. Four options are available for PRAGMA RESTRICT_REFERENCES:

WNDS	Write no database state
WNPS	Write no package state
RNDS	Read no database state
RNPS	Read no package state

As soon as it's defined, the methods associated with an object are shown when you describe the object:

```
SQL> desc paper_type
 Name                             Null?     Type
 -------------------------------- --------- ----
 PAPER#                                     NUMBER(10)
 NAME                                       VARCHAR2(30)
 AUTHOR                                     AUTHOR_TYPE
 SUBJECT                                    VARCHAR2(20)
 PRICE                                      NUMBER(5)
 STOCK_QTY                                  NUMBER(5)

 METHOD
 ------
  MEMBER FUNCTION STOCK_VALUE RETURNS NUMBER
```

After specifying the method as the object type attribute, the next step is to define the body of the PL/SQL procedure for the intended function. The following PL/SQL code calculates the STOCK_VALUE:

```
create or replace type body paper_type as
member function stock_value
return number is
begin
        return self.price * self.stock_qty;
end stock_value;
```

```
end ;
/
Type body created.
```

When defined, the methods can be called like a PL/SQL program. However, each occurrence of an object has its own state. Because methods are used to manipulate an object's particular state, the methods need to reference a particular object occurrence. Listing 27.1 demonstrates how to use methods associated with an object. Note the usage of the STOCK_VALUE member method associated with the object PAPER_TYPE in lines 10 through 14.

LISTING 27.1   **Using the *MEMBER* method**

```
01: DECLARE
02: paper_type1 paper_type := paper_type(1,'Paper_1',
➥author_type('Last','First','Professor'),'Oracle8',100,10);
03: paper_type2 paper_type := paper_type(2,'Paper_2',
➥author_type('Last','First','Professor'),'Oracle8',200,20);
04: paper_type3 paper_type := paper_type(3,'Paper_3',
➥author_type('Last','First','Professor'),'Oracle8',300,30);
05: begin
06: dbms_output.put_line('Value for paper_type1 is:'¦¦
➥to_char(paper_type1.stock_value));
07: dbms_output.put_line('Value for paper_type2 is:'¦¦
➥to_char(paper_type2.stock_value));
08: dbms_output.put_line('Value for paper_type3 is:'¦¦
➥to_char(paper_type3.stock_value));
09: end ;
10: /
11: Value for paper_type1 is:1000
12: Value for paper_type2 is:4000
13: Value for paper_type3 is:9000
14: PL/SQL procedure successfully completed.
```

The *MAP* and *ORDER* Methods

An object type's MAP method doesn't have any input parameters. It returns a single scalar value, which can be used to compare object datatypes in SQL statements having predicates for equality, between and in, order by, group by, distinct, unique, and so on. Listing 27.2 shows how to define the MAP method for the paper_type object.

LISTING 27.2   **Using the *MAP* method**

```
01: create or replace  type paper_type as object (
02:   paper# number(10),
03:   name         varchar2(30),
04:   author       author_type,
05:   subject varchar2(20),
06:   price number(5),
07:   stock_qty number(5),
08:   map member function return_paper# return number,
09:   member function STOCK_VALUE return number,
10:   PRAGMA RESTRICT_REFERENCES( stock_value , WNDS, WNPS))
11:   /
12:
13: Type created.
14:
15: SQL> desc paper_type
16: Name                           Null?    Type
17: ------------------------------ -------- ----
18: PAPER#                                  NUMBER(10)
19: NAME                                    VARCHAR2(30)
20: AUTHOR                                  AUTHOR_TYPE
21: SUBJECT                                 VARCHAR2(20)
22: PRICE                                   NUMBER(5)
23: STOCK_QTY                               NUMBER(5)
24:
25: METHOD
26: ------
27: MAP MEMBER FUNCTION RETURN_PAPER# RETURNS NUMBER
28:
29: METHOD
30: ------
31: MEMBER FUNCTION STOCK_VALUE RETURNS NUMBER
```

Note the use of the MAP keyword in front of the MEMBER FUNCTION keyword (line 8) to define the MAP method. When defined, the MAP method can be used to order objects of that type. Here, return_paper# can be used to order the paper_type object selected from the tables papers.

The MAP and ORDER methods

The **ORDER** method is similar to the MAP method, with this difference: It can take one input argument. The MAP method, on the other hand, doesn't take any input argument.

Listing 27.3 explains the usage of the MAP method to use the ORDER clause in the SQL statement.

LISTING 27.3   Using an *ORDER* clause in the *MAP* method

```
01: create or replace type body paper_type as
02: member function stock_value
03: return number is
04: begin
05:    return self.price * self.stock_qty;
06: end stock_value;
07: map member function return_paper# return number is
08: begin
09:    return self.paper#;
10: end return_paper#;
11: end ;
12:
13: create table papers of paper_type;
14: insert into papers values  (paper_type(1,'Paper_1',
➥author_type('Last','First','Professor'),'Oracle8',100,10));
15: insert into papers values  (paper_type(6,'Paper_6',
➥author_type('Last','First','Professor'),'Oracle8',600,60));
16: insert into papers values  (paper_type(8,'Paper_8',
➥author_type('Last','First','Professor'),'Oracle8',800,80));
17: insert into papers values  (paper_type(9,'Paper_9',
➥author_type('Last','First','Professor'),'Oracle8',900,90));
18: insert into papers values  (paper_type(4,'Paper_4',
➥author_type('Last','First','Professor'),'Oracle8',400,40));
19:
20: SQL> select * from papers order by 1 ;
21:
22:  PAPER# NAME
23: ---------- -----------------------------
24: AUTHOR(LAST_NAME, FIRST_NAME, AUTHOR_TITLE)
25: ------------------------------------------------------
26: SUBJECT                 PRICE  STOCK_QTY
27: --------------------- ---------- ----------
28: 1 Paper_1
29: AUTHOR_TYPE('Last', 'First', 'Professor')
30: Oracle8                  100        10
31:
32:      1 Paper_1
```

Using the SELF keyword

The use of **SELF** keyword is optional here. It references the object's current state. It's useful if you need to pass the method's output as an argument to another method or procedure.

```
33: AUTHOR_TYPE('Last', 'First', 'Professor')
34: Oracle8                        100          10
35:
36:       4 Paper_4
37: AUTHOR_TYPE('Last', 'First', 'Professor')
38: Oracle8                        400          40
39:
40:       6 Paper_6
41: AUTHOR_TYPE('Last', 'First', 'Professor')
42: Oracle8                        600          60
43:
44:       8 Paper_8
45:
46: AUTHOR_TYPE('Last', 'First', 'Professor')
47: Oracle8                        800          80
48:
49:       9 Paper_9
50: AUTHOR_TYPE('Last', 'First', 'Professor')
51: Oracle8                        900          90
52:
53:
54: 6 rows selected.
```

Creating and Managing Object Views

A view that allows you to define the object types via a relational table's underlying structure is known as an object view. Assume that you have an existing database table whose structure is as follows:

```
SQL> describe paper
  Name                             Null?     Type
  ------------------------------   -------   ----
  PAPER#                                     NUMBER(10)
  NAME                                       VARCHAR2(30)
  SUBJECT                                    VARCHAR2(20)
  PRICE                                      NUMBER(5)
  STOCK_QTY                                  NUMBER(5)
```

You can create an object named paper_type_v based on this table's column:

```
create type paper_type_v  as object ( paper# number,
  name varchar(30),subject varchar2(20),
  price number, stock_qty number);
```

Use the following command to create an object view by using the object paper_type_v:

```
create or replace view paper_ov of paper_type_v
with object oid (paper#) as
select paper#, name, subject, price, stock_qty
from paper ;
```

You can either insert data into paper table by using the object view paper_type_v, or you can update the paper table directly:

```
insert into paper_ov values
    (paper_type_v(1,'Paper One','Using Oracle',9.99,10));
```

Because you can create the abstract datatype to insert data into the table via the object view, you can associate methods to manipulate the data in the table and thus standardize the application code. You can also use the INSTEAD OF trigger to update data in an object view.

The Partition Option

Partitions are transparent to the end user

When created, the underlying partitions of a table or an index are totally transparent to the application and users. However, users can use a partition in an SQL query's FROM clause instead of the table.

Whether it's a war or a bridge construction project, we humans have successfully adopted the "divide-and-conquer" strategy to manage things that become too large in volume and size. Oracle8's partition option is meant for a similar intent—for very large database objects. In a VLDB (very large database) environment, some objects tend to become very large, and it becomes increasingly difficult to manage them as a single entity. As the object gets bigger, the administrative tasks of restoring and backing up, loading data, building indexes, and so on become almost impossible; failure at any point forces you to repeat the operation. Imagine the ease of handling twenty 5GB pieces independently instead of handling a single 100GB table. Dividing the table into multiple partitions will provide the following advantages:

- *Increased availability.* If one partition of the table becomes unavailable due to the system failure or is made unavailable for scheduled maintenance, the rest of the table is still available for use.

- *Reduced downtime.* If a system failure affects only one or some part of the table, only that part needs to be repaired. Because the volume of the repair work (like a RESTORE) is less, it will be done more quickly.

- *Ease of maintenance.* If for any reason you need to rebuild the table in the same database or some other place, it will be much easier to manage the desired operation (such as exporting, importing, data loading, index rebuilding, and so on) independently for each partition rather than for one single, big table.

- *Balanced I/O.* You can map the different partitions to different disks to balance the I/O load and improve performance significantly.

- *Improved performance.* Some queries against the partitioned object can run faster, as the search will be limited to only the concerned partition.

What Can Be Partitioned

Oracle8 allows you to partition only tables and the indexes. Other objects—clusters, nested tables, index-organized tables, snapshots, and snapshot logs—can't be partitioned. You also can't partition a table that's part of a cluster or one that contains a column of long, LOBs, or long raw datatypes or object datatypes. You can partition an index as long as it's not a cluster index or defined on a clustered table. You can partition a bitmap index only if it's a global bitmap index on a partitioned or a non-partitioned table. You can't create local bitmap indexes on individual partitions of a partitioned table.

A partitioned table can have a local or global partitioned or non-partitioned index. A non-partitioned table can contain a partitioned index. As shown in Figure 27.4, an index that refers to rows in a specific partition is known as the "local index." On the other hand, a "global index" refers to the rows from all partitions of a table. A global index can be partitioned.

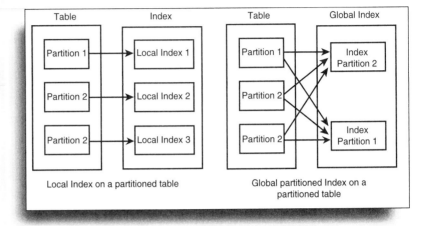

FIGURE 27.4

Partitions of a global index contain rows from any table partition.

Partitioning a Table

You can partition a table while creating it. Logical attributes such as column names, datatypes, and constraints of all the partitions of an object must be the same; physical attributes (such as storage parameters) for all an object's partitions could be different for each partition, however. The SQL command in Listing 27.4 creates a partitioned table with these characteristics.

Different partitions of an object can be placed in different tablespaces

You can specify the storage parameters of each and every partition of a table and an index in the partition's storage clause, which can include tablespace, **PCTFREE**, **PCTUSED**, initial extent, next extent, and so on.

LISTING 27.4   **Creating a partitioned table**

```
01: create table warehouse (
02:     w_id            number,
03:     w_ytd           number(12),
04:     w_tax           number(4),
05:     w_name          varchar2(10),
06:     w_street_1      varchar2(20),
07:     w_street_2      varchar2(20),
08:     w_city          varchar2(20),
09:     w_state         char(2),
10:     w_zip           char(9)
11: )
12: partition by range (w_id)
13: (
14: partition ware_P1 values less than (50)
15: tablespace TS_ware_P1
16: pctfree 95 pctused 4
17: storage (initial 2m next 1m minextents 12 pctincrease 0)
18: ,
19: partition ware_P2 values less than (100)
```

```
20: tablespace TS_ware_P2
21: pctfree 95 pctused 4
22: storage (initial 2m next 1m minextents 12 pctincrease 0)
23: ,
24: partition ware_P3 values less than (150)
25: tablespace TS_ware_P3
26: pctfree 95 pctused 4
27: storage (initial 2m next 1m minextents 12 pctincrease 0)
28: ,
29: partition ware_P4 values less than (200)
30: tablespace TS_ware_P4
31: pctfree 95 pctused 4
32: storage (initial 2m next 1m minextents 12 pctincrease 0)
33: )
34: initrans 4
35: pctfree  95 pctused 4
36: storage (initial 2m next 1m pctincrease 0);
```

The command in Listing 27.4 creates a warehouse table with four partitions. The first partition contains rows with warehouses numbered 1 to 50, the second partition contains rows for warehouses 51 through 100, and so on. This scheme of partitioning is called "range partitioned."

You can use the command in Listing 27.5 to create local indexes (line 4 of Listing 27.4) on each partition of this table.

Using ALTER to manage partitions

The **ALTER TABLE** and **ALTER INDEX** commands allow you to add, delete, move, modify, rename, split, and truncate partitions as and when needed.

LISTING 27.5   **Creating a partitioned index**

```
01: create unique index tpc.iwarehouse on tpc.warehouse(w_id)
02:    pctfree 1        initrans 4
03:    nologging
04:    local
05:    (partition iware_P1
06:    tablespace TS_widx_P1
07:    storage (initial 200K next 20K pctincrease 0),
08:    partition iware_P2
09:    tablespace TS_widx_P2
10:    storage (initial 200K next 20K pctincrease 0),
11:    partition iware_P3
12:    tablespace TS_widx_P3
13:    storage (initial 200K next 20K pctincrease 0),
14:    partition iware_P4
15:    tablespace TS_widx_P4
16:    storage (initial 200K next 20K pctincrease 0));
```

Advance Queuing

Queuing technology used in critical systems

Queuing technology is used to develop/implement high-end transaction processing solutions in banking, trading, and reservation systems, as well as other critical applications.

Oracle's advance queuing is an interprocess messaging mechanism. Messaging between processes is normally synchronous in a two- or three-tier application environment. In this type of mechanism, the client and the server follow a real-time handshake mechanism where the client sends a request to the server and then waits for acknowledgment from the server. The server responds to the client and in turn waits for its acknowledgment.

In each case, the sender of the message waits for the acknowledgment before proceeding with the next step. In certain types of processing this is a must; however, in many situations it may be acceptable for the sender to send the message and proceed without waiting for the acknowledgment. A queue mechanism can be used to exchange messages under such situations (see Figure 27.5).

FIGURE 27.5

A queue acts as intermediate message storage between sender and receiver.

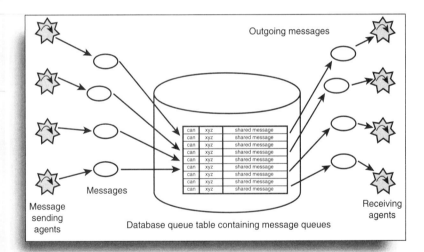

Message sending agents

Messages

Outgoing messages

Receiving agents

Database queue table containing message queues

Understanding the Components of Oracle Advance Queuing

Oracle Advance Queuing's operating mechanism can be compared to that of a mailing service; its components are very similar to that of real-life mailing services. Oracle's Advance Queuing feature consists of queues (similar to mail boxes), messages composed of the control information and the data to be sent (the envelopes containing the letter and address information), enqueue and dequeue operations (dropping the letter in the mail box and retrieving the mail designated for you), and agents (the customers using the mail services).

- *Message.* A message is the data object to be transferred from one process to another. It consists of the actual information plus the control attribute. The control attribute specifies the receiver of the message and its longevity.

  A message can be stored in only one queue but can be delivered to multiple recipients. When the last recipient retrieves the message, the message is removed from the queue.

- *Queue.* A queue is a message store. The sender puts the information in the queue, where it can be retrieved by the designated receiver. If for any reason the receiver can't retrieve the message, the message is moved to a special area called the "exception queue."

- *Queue table.* Oracle stores the message in database tables known as "queue tables." A queue table can contain multiple queues. Each queue table has an associated exception queue.

- *Agent.* Agents are the queue users who send and receive messages.

- *Time manager.* Oracle lets you define time-bound message delivery. You can specify the expiration time for a message, the retry interval in case of errors, and delayed delivery of a message by using the time manager. To enable these time-bound actions, you need to set the initialization parameter aq_tm_proccesses to 1 to create a background process that performs the necessary activity to monitor the time-bound queue activities.

- *Enqueue operation.* Putting a message in a queue to send it is known as the enqueue operation.

- *Dequeue operation.* Retrieving a message from a queue is called a dequeue operation.

- *The DBMS_AQ package.* This Oracle-supplied package lets you enqueue and dequeue messages. Oracle creates this package when you run the procedural installation script CATPROC.SQL after creating the database.

■ *The DBMS_AQADM package.* This Oracle-supplied package allows you to perform administrative tasks related to advance queuing. By using this package, you can create, alter, and drop queues and queue tables; start and stop queues; enable and disable time-management operations; add and remove recipients to queues; and browse queue contents.

Granting Necessary Roles and Privileges

Oracle creates two additional roles for advance queue operations:

■ The AQ_ADMINISTRATOR_ROLE role grants EXECUTE privileges on all procedures in the DBMS_AQ and DBMS_AQADM packages.

■ The AQ_USER_ROLE role grants EXECUTE privilege on the procedure in the DBMS_AQ package.

Before users can use or administer the advance queuing features, they need to be granted these roles. The following command appoints the user aq_admin as the queue administrator:

```
$sqlplus sys/password
SQL> grant AQ_ADMINISTRATOR_ROLE to aq_admin with admin
option ;
SQL> execute dbms_aqadm.grant_type_access('aq_admin');
```

Note that the grant_type_access procedure is used to grant necessary privileges for the administrative operations involving a multiple-consumer queue. After these commands are executed, the user aq_admin can then assign privileges so that another user can utilize the Advance Queue option. User aq_admin can also use the Advance Queue feature with this role. We will use this user for the sample commands.

Figure 27.6 shows the sequence of operations necessary for using the advance queues.

Creating the Queue Table

The DBMS_AQADM package's create_queue_table procedure is used to create a queue table (see Listing 27.6).

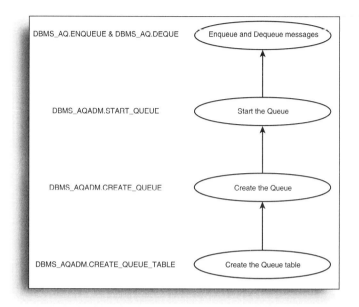

FIGURE 27.6
Perform this sequence of operations to use the advance queues.

LISTING 27.6   Creating an object to be used as a message

```
01: $sqlplus aq_admin/password
01: create or replace type event_object_t as object
02: (
03:   event_call      varchar2(2000),
04:   num_arg         number,
05:   arguments       varchar2(2000)
06: );
07: begin
08:   dbms_aqadm.create_queue_table
09:   (
10:     queue_table           => 'SAMPLE_QUEUE_TABLE',
11:     queue_payload_type    => 'EVENT_OBJECT_T',
12:     storage_clause        =>
        'storage (initial 1m next 1m pctincrease 0 )',
13:     sort_list             => 'PRIORITY,ENQ_TIME',
14:     comment               => 'sample queue table'
15:   );
16: end;
17: /
```

① Creates
event_object_t object
datatype to be used as message in advance queue

The parameters for the create_queue_table procedure are as follows:

- On line 10, queue_table is the name of the queue table.

- On line 11, queue_payload_type is the type of user message the queue will store. It can be VARCHAR2, RAW, or an object type.

- On line 12, storage_clause specifies the storage parameter for the queue table.

- On line 13, sort_list specifies the queue table columns to be used for sorting the queue data. Here, priority and enqueue time are specified as the sort keys. If this isn't specified, the queue is maintained as a first-in-first-out list.

- If multiple_consumers is left to its default value of FALSE, the queue table is defined as the single consumer queue and every message can have only one consumer. Set multiple_consumers to TRUE if multiple consumers are desired for the messages.

- On line 14, comment can be any comment that you want associated with the queue table.

- message_grouping specifies the queue's message grouping behavior.

- The auto_commit parameter can be TRUE or FALSE. TRUE causes the current transaction to commit before the operation is carried out. If auto_commit is set to FALSE, the operation is part of the current transaction and will become persistent only when the caller commits the transaction.

The command in Listing 27.6 creates sample_queue_table, which stores the user-defined datatype object event_object_t, which needs to be defined before queue creation. Users can find information about the user-owned queue from the data dictionary table USER_QUEUE_TABLES:

```
SQL> select * from user_queue_tables ;

QUEUE_TABLE                        TYPE
---------------------------------  -------
```

```
OBJECT_TYPE
- - - - - - - - - - - - - - - - - - - - - - - - - - - - - - - - - - - - - - - - - - - - - - - - - -
SORT_ORDER                 RECIPIEN MESSAGE_GROUP
- - - - - - - - - - - - - - - - - - - -  - - - - - - - -  - - - - - - - - - - - -
USER_COMMENT
- - - - - - - - - - - - - - - - - - - - - - - - - - - - - - - - - - - - - - - - - - - - - - - - -
SAMPLE_QUEUE_TABLE               OBJECT
AQ_ADMIN.EVENT_OBJECT_T
PRIORITY, ENQUEUE_TIME SINGLE    NONE
sample queue table
```

Need to see all queue tables?

The **DBA_QUEUE_TABLE**
dictionary view contains information about all the queue
tables in the database.

You can use the dbms_aqadm.drop_queue_table procedure to drop
a queue table.

Creating a Queue

When the queue table is created, users can create the desired
queue by using the dbms_aqadm package's create_queue procedure
(see Listing 27.7).

LISTING 27.7   **The *create_queue* procedure**

```
01: begin
02:     dbms_aqadm.create_queue
03:     (
04:        queue_name          => 'SAMPLE_QUEUE',
05:        queue_table         => 'SAMPLE_QUEUE_TABLE',
06:        comment             => 'sample queue'
07:     );
08: end ;
09: /
```

This procedure takes the following input parameters:

- On line 4, queue_name specifies the name of the queue to be
  created.

- On line 5, queue_table specifies the name of the queue table
  that will store the queue message in the database.

- Queue_type specifies whether the queue created will be a normal queue or an exception queue.

- Max_retries specifies the maximum number of unsuccessful attempts to dequeue the message from the queue. This count is incremented whenever the transaction that has retrieved the message issues a ROLLBACK command. The message is moved to the exception queue after the maximum allowed retries.

- Retry_delay specifies the time delay in seconds, after which the message can be retried for another dequeue operation.

- Retention_time specifies the maximum time duration in seconds for which a message is retained in the queue after the dequeue operation.

- On line 6, comment is any user-specified string to be associated with the queue.

- Auto_commit is the same as described earlier for the create_queue_table procedure in Listing 27.6.

The data dictionary view USER_QUEUES has the following columns. You can choose either all the columns or select columns from this view to receive information about the queues you defined.

Need to see all defined queues?

The **DBA_QUEUES** view contains information about all queues defined in the database.

```
SQL> desc user_queues
 Name                                    Null?    Type
 ------------------------------------ -------- ----
 NAME                                 NOT NULL VARCHAR2(30)
 QUEUE_TABLE                          NOT NULL VARCHAR2(30)
 QID                                  NOT NULL NUMBER
 QUEUE_TYPE                                    VARCHAR2(15)
 MAX_RETRIES                                   NUMBER
 RETRY_DELAY                                   NUMBER
 ENQUEUE_ENABLED                               VARCHAR2(7)
 DEQUEUE_ENABLED                               VARCHAR2(7)
 RETENTION                                     VARCHAR2(40)
 USER_COMMENT                                  VARCHAR2(50)
```

Use the dbms_aqadm.drop_queue procedure to drop a queue.

Starting the Queue

After creating the queue, the queue administrator must start the queue before it can be used to store and retrieve messages. Use the dbms_aqadm.start_queue procedure to start the queue:

```
begin

      dbms_aqadm.start_queue

      (

        queue_name     => 'SAMPLE_QUEUE'

      );

end;

/
```

The USER_QUEUES view's ENQUEUE_ENABLED and ENQUEUE_DISABLED columns show the start and stop status of user queues.

You can use the dbms_aqadm.stop_queue procedure to stop a started queue.

Enqueing and Dequeing Messages

The DBMS_AQ package has enqueue and dequeue procedures used for storing and retrieving messages through a queue. The sender process agent sends the message by using the following parameters of the enqueue procedure:

- The queue_name is the queue that will store the message. This parameter must be specified.

- The enqueue_options is an object type defined in the dbms_aq package as enqueue_options_t and is available to specify enqueue operation. This doesn't need to be specified for simple enqueue and dequeue operations.

- message_properties_t is an object type defined in the dbms_aq package as message_properties_t, and is available to specify the properties of message to be sent. You don't need to specify this parameter for simple enqueue operations. The message properties are priority, delay, expiration, correlation, attempts, recipient_list, exception_queue, enqueue_time, and state.

- payload is the actual message data to be exchanged between the sender and the receiver. It can be VARCHAR2, RAW, or a predefined object type. This is a mandatory input parameter.

- MSGID is a RAW type output returned by the enqueue operation. You can use this output to identify the message during dequeue operations.

Input parameters for dequeue
procedure

The dequeue procedure of the
DBMS_AQ package takes input
parameters similar to the one used
for enqueue procedure, except that
it uses **dequeue_options**
instead of **enqueue_options**.
Dequeue options, however, aren't a
mandatory parameter.

Listing 27.8 shows how to send and receive messages by using
advanced queuing.

LISTING 27.8   **How to use queues for sending and receiving messages**

```
01: file enqueu.sql
02: ******************************************************
03: declare
04: enqueue_options        dbms_aq.enqueue_options_t;
05: message_properties     dbms_aq.message_properties_t;
06: message_handle         RAW(16);
07: message                   aq_admin.event_object_t;
08:
09: begin
10: dbms_aq.enqueue(
11: queue_name             => 'sample_queue',
12: enqueue_options        => enqueue_options,
13: message_properties     => message_properties,
14: payload                => message,
15: msgid                  => message_handle);
16:
17: commit;
18: end;
19: /
20: ******************************************************
21: file dequeu.sql
22: ******************************************************
23: declare
24: dequeue_options        dbms_aq.dequeue_options_t;
25: message_properties     dbms_aq.message_properties_t;
26: message_handle         RAW(16);
27: message                event_object_t;
28: begin
29:
30: dbms_aq.dequeue(
31: queue_name             => 'sample_queue',
32: dequeue_options        => dequeue_options,
33: message_properties     => message_properties,
34: payload                => message,
35: msgid                  => message_handle);
```

```
36:
37: dbms_output.enable;
38: dbms_output.put_line
39:     ('Message retrieved from the queue>>>: '
40:                 || message.event_call || '    '||
41:                 message.num_arg||'    ' ||
42:                 message.arguments);
43: commit;
44: end;
45: /
46: **********************************************************
47:
48: SQL> @enqueu.sql
49:
50: PL/SQL procedure successfully completed.
51:
52: SQL> @dequeu.sql
53: Message retrieved from the queue>>>:
➥     Sample Message    1    First sample message
54:
55: PL/SQL procedure successfully completed.
56:
57: SQL>
```

Using Other *DBMS_AQADM* Functions

Many of the procedures available in this package have been discussed, and their usage should be obvious to you by now. The procedures not mentioned until now are as follows:

- STOP_ENQUEUE allows you to stop the queue, thus disabling the enqueue and dequeue operations.

- START_TIME_MANAGER used to enable the time-management process to execute its operations. Before you can enable the time-management operations, however, the time-management background process must be started by setting the INIT.ORA parameter aq_tm_process to TRUE.

- STOP_TIME_MANAGER disables time-management operations.

- `ADD_SUBSCRIBER` can be used only on queues that have been defined with multiple recipients. It adds a subscriber to the queue.

- `REMOVE_SUBSCRIBER` removes a subscriber from the queue.

- `QUEUE_SUBSCRIBER` returns the list of subscribers for the queue.

The *DBMS_AQ* Package

This package has procedures used for enqueue and dequeue operations. Please refer to the enqueue and dequeue example given earlier in this chapter for more details.

The ConText Option

ConText is a separately priced cartridge

The ConText option is released as a separate cartridge with Oracle8. This cartridge not only has powerful test/document storage retrieval capabilities, but also has powerful linguistic capabilities.

An RDBMS allows you to store and retrieve data in tabular form. This works very well for most business information that's in the form of numbers and a character string of smaller length. With the proliferation of computer technology and the popularity of personal computers, however, the soft copy of textual documents such as memos, letters, news item, bulletins, electronic mails, HTML files, résumés, reports, and so on make up a very important part of the business and need efficient and effective handling. Oracle8's ConText option allows you to store and manipulate these textual documents in the following ways:

- A table's long column is used to store the documents.

- Pointers in a database table point to the files stored at the operating system level.

Table 27.1 shows the datatypes available.

TABLE 27.1   **Storing text data in an Oracle database**

Datatype:	Characteristics:
VARCHAR2	Can store only 4,000 characters. Character strings functions can be used to manipulate the data.
LONG	Can store up to 4GB of data. Doesn't allow string functions to be used directly. Stored text can be manipulated via ConText option.
LONG RAW	Can store structured text documents. Doesn't allow string functions to be used directly. Stored text can be manipulated via the ConText option.

Figure 27.7 depicts these two methods storing text in the picture form.

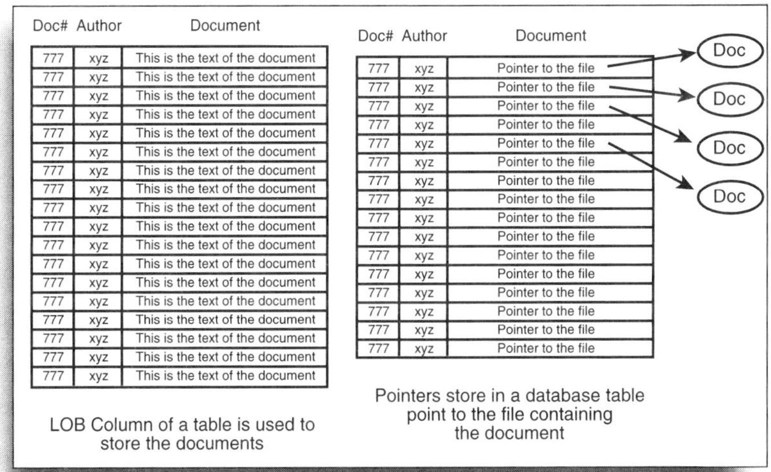

FIGURE 27.7

The Oracle8 database ConText option stores documents internally and externally.

You can view the Oracle ConText option as a set of procedures and PL/SQL programs. Once it's installed and configured, the ConText option provides application (front-end) developers with a set of functions and procedures; these things allow developers to retrieve and manipulate the text data stored in an Oracle database.

Text-enabling the database server

Before you can execute a text query, you need to text-enable the database instance by setting the initialization parameter `TEXT_ENABLE` to `TRUE` or by using the `ALTER SESSION set text_enable=true;` command.

Enable Oracle Server to process text documents

1. Install the ConText option. (Please refer to the platform-specific *Installation and Configuration Guide* from Oracle.)

2. Configure and set up the ConText option. (See the later section "Managing the Context Option.")

3. Create a table with a text column to store the documents.

4. Load the documents in the table. (See the later section "Loading the Data.")

5. Create a policy on the text column containing the text data. (See "Creating a Policy" later in this chapter.)

6. Create a text index on the column in which text is stored. (See the later section "Creating the Text Index.")

Setting Up the Sample Table for the Query Examples

The query examples use the table white_papers. The code in Listing 27.9 was used to set up the sample session.

LISTING 27.9   **Preparing a table for ConText queries**

1 Creates the table

```
01: $Sqlplus ctxdemo/ctxdemo
02: create table white_papers (paper# number primary key,
03:                            name varchar2(30),
04:                            author varchar2(30),
05:                            papers long);
```

①

2 Loads document file in sample table with `ctxload` context loader (document files located in directory from where context loader is being invoked)

```
06: $ ctxload -user ctxdemo/ctxdemo -name white_papers
➡                  -file white_paper.ld -separate
07: -log $HOME/ctxdemo/ctxload.log
```

②

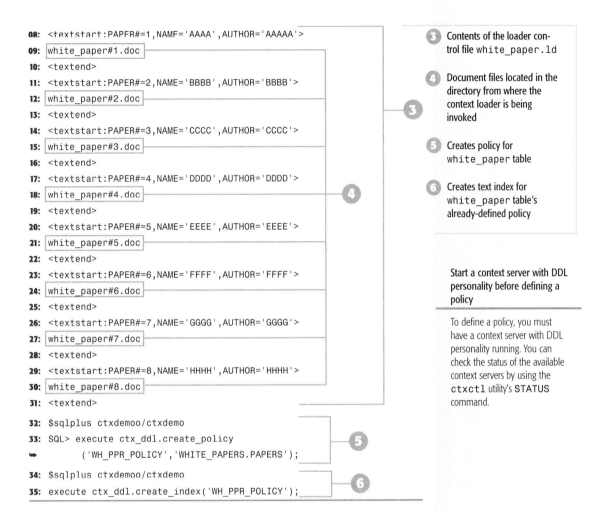

```
08:  <textstart:PAPER#=1,NAME='AAAA',AUTHOR='AAAAA'>
09:  white_paper#1.doc
10:  <textend>
11:  <textstart:PAPER#=2,NAME='BBBB',AUTHOR='BBBB'>
12:  white_paper#2.doc
13:  <textend>
14:  <textstart:PAPER#=3,NAME='CCCC',AUTHOR='CCCC'>
15:  white_paper#3.doc
16:  <textend>
17:  <textstart:PAPER#=4,NAME='DDDD',AUTHOR='DDDD'>
18:  white_paper#4.doc
19:  <textend>
20:  <textstart:PAPER#=5,NAME='EEEE',AUTHOR='EEEE'>
21:  white_paper#5.doc
22:  <textend>
23:  <textstart:PAPER#=6,NAME='FFFF',AUTHOR='FFFF'>
24:  white_paper#6.doc
25:  <textend>
26:  <textstart:PAPER#=7,NAME='GGGG',AUTHOR='GGGG'>
27:  white_paper#7.doc
28:  <textend>
29:  <textstart:PAPER#=8,NAME='HHHH',AUTHOR='HHHH'>
30:  white_paper#8.doc
31:  <textend>
32:  $sqlplus ctxdemoo/ctxdemo
33:  SQL> execute ctx_ddl.create_policy
  ➥       ('WH_PPR_POLICY','WHITE_PAPERS.PAPERS');
34:  $sqlplus ctxdemoo/ctxdemo
35:  execute ctx_ddl.create_index('WH_PPR_POLICY');
```

③ Contents of the loader control file `white_paper.ld`

④ Document files located in the directory from where the context loader is being invoked

⑤ Creates policy for `white_paper` table

⑥ Creates text index for `white_paper` table's already-defined policy

Start a context server with DDL personality before defining a policy

To define a policy, you must have a context server with DDL personality running. You can check the status of the available context servers by using the `ctxctl` utility's **STATUS** command.

One-Step Query Examples

After the operations in Listing 27.9 are complete, you can perform the text queries on the designated column of a given table. Now use the table `white_paper` to learn the use of ConText queries.

The following query looks for white papers that contain the word `Manager`:

```
select paper#,name,author from white_papers
  where contains (white_papers.papers,'Manager') > 0 ;
```

This query uses a simple method known as the one-step query. Because one-step queries are simpler to write, they're preferred for interactive use. They are slower, however, and the intermediate results aren't available for use. Oracle also offers two-step and in-memory query methods for advanced queries with improved performance; these query types are discussed later in this chapter.

The CONTAINS function lets you use several operators to combine multiple search words and conditions. Table 27.2 lists the important operators available.

TABLE 27.2   *CONTAINS* function operators

Operator:	Function:
AND or &	Selects the rows that contain both search conditions specified with AND
OR or ¦	Selects the rows that contain either search condition specified
Minus or -	Selects a record if the score of the first record minus the score of the second record exceeds the threshold
ACCUM or ,	Selects a record if the sum of search scores exceed the threshold
;	Near; returns the score based on proximity of the specified words
$	Stem; selects the rows that have stem expansions of the specified word
!	Soundex; returns a record that contains words sounding similar to the specified word
?	Fuzzy; performs a fuzzy match (expands the word to include words spelled similarly)
>	Threshold; selects all records having scores exceeding the threshold
*	Weight; assigns different weights to the scores of the searches
:	Max; selects specified number of highest scoring records
%	Wildcard; performs a multiple-character wildcard search
- ,	Performs a single-character wildcard search
( )	Grouping; specifies the order in which search criteria is evaluated
{ } ,	Escape; allows you to include a reserved word in a query by including it within braces

Operator:	Function:
SYN	Searches for all words defined as synonyms of the specified word
RT	Searches for all words defined as related to the specified word
BT	Searches for words defined as broader terms for the specified word

By using the CONTAINS function in a one-step query, you can perform the following text type queries:

- Exactly match one or multiple words and phrases. You can use logical operators AND, OR, NOT, or EQUIVALENCE to combine the multiple-word search. The following query returns the name and author of white papers containing the words cus-tomer and packets:

```
select paper#,name,author from white_papers
  where contains
  (white_papers.papers,'customer and packets') > 0;
```

The following query returns the author of white papers that contain the phrase dog and cat:

```
select name,author from white_papers where
  contains (white_papers.papers,'{dog and cat}') > 0;
```

The following query returns the author of white papers that contain the word zip but not the word dog:

```
select name,author from white_papers where
  contains (white_papers.papers,'zip not dog') > 0;
```

- Use the score-changing operators ACCUMALATE, MINUS, NEAR, and WEIGHT. These operators behave similarly to the logical operators AND and NOT; however, they adjust the returned score before returning the results, so that the score can be compared with a threshold value before the query results are returned.

The following query returns the name and author of white papers containing the words dog and zip. However, a white paper containing these words near each other returns a higher score, compared with another document that contains these words far apart.

Scores returned by the CONTAINS function

The **CONTAINS** function of Oracle's ConText option returns an integer that you can use to compare the results of multiple hits from the same **CONTAINS** function or from multiple **CONTAINS** functions.

```
SQL > select name,author,score(0)
  from white_papers where contains
  (white_papers.papers,'dog near zip') > 0
SQL> /
```

NAME	AUTHOR	SCORE0
IIII	IIII	97
JJJJ	JJJJ	93
KKKK	KKKK	73

- Use the result set operators THRESHOLD, MAX, and FIRST/NEXT. These operators help you eliminate low score documents. For example, the following query returns only the documents whose score is greater than 75:

```
SQL> select name,author,score(0)
  from white_papers where contains
  (white_papers.papers,'dog near zip') > 75
SQL> /
```

NAME	AUTHOR	SCORE0
IIII	IIII	97
JJJJ	JJJJ	93

```
select Name, Author
from WHITE_PAPERS
where CONTAINS (WHITE_PAPERS,'backup > 40') > 0;
```

Similarly, the following query will return the highest scoring document:

```
SQL> select name,author,score(0)
  from white_papers where contains
  (white_papers.papers,'dog near zip:1') > 0;
```

The following will return the 10 highest scoring documents:

```
SQL> select name,author,score(0)
  from white_papers where contains
  (white_papers.papers,'dog near zip:10') > 0;
```

- Use the expansion operators STEM, FUZZY, and SOUNDEX. The STEM operator lets you select all words that stem from the word given by the user. For example, the following query selects all documents containing `cache`, `cached`, or `caching`:

```
select name,author,score(0)
   from white_papers where contains
   (white_papers.papers,'$cache') > 0;
```

■ Use wildcard characters `%` and `-` in a query. The following query uses the multicharacter wildcard `%` and returns all rows containing words beginning with `cac`:

```
SQL >select name,author,score(0)
   from white_papers where contains
   (white_papers.papers,'cac%') > 0;
```

Understanding the *CONTAINS* Function

By looking at the examples given in the previous sections, the `CONTAINS` function's simple syntax should be clear to you by now. The `CONTAINS` function's complete syntax is as follows:

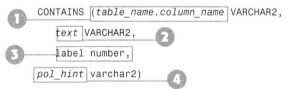

```
CONTAINS (table_name.column_name VARCHAR2,
         text VARCHAR2,
         label number,
         pol_hint varchar2)
```

① Specifies table name and column name to be queried

② Specifies text to be searched and conditions

③ Labels score generated by CONTAINS; has a default value of 0 in queries with single CONTAINS function and requires a specified label in a query with multiple CONTAINS functions

④ Specifies policy to be used for columns having multiple policies defined

Two-Step Query Example

The Oracle ConText option processes queries in two steps:

■ It searches the text index defined on the table to determine the documents that contain the search words. It assigns them a score and stores them in a temporary table. Thus, in the first phase it gathers the primary key of all documents containing the search words with associated scores.

■ In the second phase it joins the primary key values of the documents stored in the temporary results table to the main table.

Text tables require primary keys

Any table that will be used for text searches by the Oracle ConText option must have a primary key defined before a policy and a text index can be created on it.

If you try to create a text policy for a table that doesn't have a primary key, errors similar to the following are displayed:

```
SQL> execute ctx_ddl.create_policy
    ('PAPER2_policy','white_paper2.papers');
    begin ctx_ddl.create_policy
    ('PAPER2_policy','white_paper2.papers'); end;


*

ERROR at line 1:
ORA-20000: ConText error:
DRG-10503: textkey must be specified --
➥          table has no primary key
ORA-06512: at "CTXSYS.DRUE", line 180
ORA-06512: at "CTXSYS.CTX_DDL", line 1329
ORA-06512: at line 1
```

In a one-step query, the intermediate table isn't preserved by Oracle and you can't reuse its results. In a two-step query, the user creates the intermediate query before the query can be run. Use the following command to create the intermediate table:

```
create table query_temp(
  textkey varchar2(64),
  score   number,
  conid   number
  );
```

After creating the intermediate query table, you can proceed to execute the query:

```
execute
ctx_query.contains('WH_PPR_POLICY','dog','QUERY_TEMP');
select a.score, a.conid, b.paper#, b.author, b.name
  from query_temp a, white_papers b
  where  a.textkey = b.paper#;
```

In-Memory Query Example

The preceding example shows how an intermediate table is required to execute a two-step query. In-memory queries use a cursor in memory rather than in the database table to store the intermediate result (see Listing 27.10).

LISTING 27.10 An in-memory query

```
01:  variable qterm varchar2(2000);
02:  exec :qterm := 'dog';
03:
04:  set serveroutput on
05:  declare
06:     score  char(5);
07:     pk     char(5);
08:     curid  number;
09:     name   char(256);
10:     author char(30);
11:  begin
12:     dbms_output.enable(10000);
13:
14:     curid := ctx_query.open_con(policy_name  =>
                                'WH_PPR_POLICY',
15:                  text_query   =>  :qterm,
16:                  score_sorted =>  false,
17:                  other_cols   =>  'author, name');
18:     dbms_output.put_line('SCR  ID   AUTHOR          NAME');
19:     while (ctx_query.fetch_hit
              (curid, pk, score, author, name)>0) loop
20:        dbms_output.put_line(score||pk||substr(author,1,16)
                              ||substr(name,1,50));
21:     end loop;
22:     ctx_query.close_con(curid);
23:
24:  end;
```

1. Defines the query search condition

2. Defines the cursor

3. Enables the output

4. Opens the cursor for intermediate results

5. Prints the column titles

6. Fetches the results in the cursor

7. Prints the results to output

8. Closes the cursor

Managing the ConText Option

Setting up and managing the ConText option can be divided into the following tasks:

- Setting up and managing the context users
- Starting, stopping, and managing the context servers
- Managing the context queues
- Setting up the initialization parameter

Setting Up and Managing Context Users

When the ConText option is installed, it automatically creates CTXSYS and CTXDEMO users. The installation process also creates CTXADMIN, CTXAPP, and CTXUSR roles. Table 27.2 lists the functions and privileges of these users and roles.

TABLE 27.3   **Predefined context users, roles, and their functions and privileges**

Name:	Functions and Privileges:
CTXSYS	Owns the ConText data dictionary; is given the CTXADMIN and DBA roles; can start and stop the context server processes
CTXDEMO	Owns the sample ConText database objects; is given CTXAPP role
CTXADMIN	The most privileged context role; can perform all ConText administration tasks
CTXAPP	Can manage the ConText data dictionary, set up linguistics services, and perform text queries
CTXUSR	Should be given to a normal ConText user who needs to perform ConText queries

You can create additional ConText option users and assign them the appropriate roles. See Chapter 9, "Creating and Managing User Accounts," for more information.

Starting, Stopping, and Managing Context Servers

Context servers are the background processes dedicated to performing context-related operations. These processes must be started before you can perform any text operations. A context server can load data in the database, create text index, and perform text queries. You can assign specific tasks to be performed by each context server by specifying the personality mask while starting the context server. The ctxctl context control utility lets you manage the context servers interactively.

The following help session shows how start and stop context servers query their status by using the ctxctl utility:

```
*** ConText Option Servers Control ***

Servers on que_sun1.
```

```
Type help for a list of commands.


command> help


The following commands are available:


   help [command]                    - commands information
   status                            - show running servers
   start n [ling ¦ query ¦ ddl ¦ dml ¦
                      load]...  - start n servers
   stop [pid]... ¦ all               - stop server processes
   quit                              - terminate ctxctl
   exit                              - terminate ctxctl


command> start 1 query ddl dml
Enter ConText Option administrator password for
V804><password>
Waiting for servers to start up..........


command> status
+-------+-------+-------+-------+------+-------+
¦ PID   ¦ LING. ¦ QUERY ¦ DDL   ¦ DML  ¦ LOAD  ¦
+-------+-------+-------+-------+------+-------+
¦ 12981 ¦       ¦  X    ¦  X    ¦  X   ¦       ¦
+=======+=======+=======+=======+======+=======+
¦ Total ¦   0   ¦  1    ¦  1    ¦  1   ¦   0   ¦
+-------+-------+-------+-------+------+-------+
command> stop 12981
```

You can also use `ctxsrv` to start and stop the context servers from the command line:

```
ctxsrv -user ctxsys/password -personality QDML
```

Defining Personality for Context Servers

You can divide the functions performed by context servers into five categories:

- *DDL servers.* These servers are used to execute DDL commands associated with creating the underlying database objects for creating the text indexes. These servers are started with the personality mask D:

```
ctxsrv -user ctxsys/password -personality D
```

Personality and personality masks

A context server process can perform any of the functions defined here. The type of functions performed by the server gives the server its personality. A personality mask is used to define the server's personality while starting the server. To change the personality of an existing context server, use the PL/SQL procedure `execute ctx_adm.change_mask ('DRSRV_9999', 'QDML');`, which allows an existing server, `DRSRV_9999`, to perform query, DDL, DML, and linguistics functions.

- *DML servers.* When users update the text in a document, the corresponding indexes also need to be updated with these changes. DML servers perform these index updates on the user's behalf. These servers are started with the personality mask M:

  ```
  ctxsrv -user ctxsys/password -personality M
  ```

- *Query servers.* These are used to process the text-search part of the queries. These servers are started by using the personality mask Q:

  ```
  ctxsrv -user ctxsys/password -personality Q
  ```

- *Linguistics servers.* These context servers are required to process linguistics requests. Linguistic requests include theme processing and document gists. These servers are started by using the personality mask L:

  ```
  ctxsrv -user ctxsys/password -personality L
  ```

- *Loader servers.* These servers wake up at regular intervals and look in the specified directories for the files to be loaded in the database. These servers are started by using the personality mask R.

The CTX_ALL_SERVERS view gives the status information of all started context servers. The CTX_SERVERS view provides the status information for the active context servers.

Managing Context Queues

Context servers are responsible for executing the text commands received from all context-user client processes. Oracle has implemented a queuing mechanism to allow the processing of requests received from multiple clients by few servers.

Client processes put their processing requests in a queue known as the Text Request Queue. This queue is internally subdivided into multiple queues, with one queue for each function. Context servers regularly scan each request queue according to their personality and execute the desired operations. The context server informs the client process when the processing is finished. The Text Request Queue is used for query, DML, DDL, and linguistics operations only. The load operation isn't queued; instead,

Linguistics queries

The Oracle ConText option supports linguistics queries on text tables. These queries let you search documents with a search criteria containing gists and themes. A detailed discussion on setting up tables for these queries and creating these queries is beyond the scope of this book, and it's recommended that you refer to suitable Oracle documentation for this.

Viewing context queue information

You can use the CTX_ALL_DML_QUEUE, CTX_ALL_DML_SUM, and CTX_ALL_QUEUE data dictionary views to see the status of various context queues. CTX_USER_DML_QUEUE, CTX_USER_DML_SUM, and CTX_USER_QUEUE data dictionary views can be used to see user-level activity. Oracle also offers the CTX_SVC and CTX_ADM packages, which you can use to view queue information and administer queues.

the server with the loader personality detects and processes the newly placed files as described in the preceding section.

Using the Context Loader to Load Data

The context loader is an easy-to-load utility that allows you to load formatted and text data into an Oracle table's LONG or LONG RAW columns. Listing 27.11 shows a simple usage of the context loader—loading the data in the database.

LISTING 27.11   **Using the context loader to load data**

```
01: ctxload -user ctxdemo/ctxdemo -name white_papers
➡              -file white_paper.ld -separate
02: -log $HOME/vlunawat/ctxload.log ─────────①     ①  Specifies the name of the
03:                                                    loader log file
04: $ more white_paper.ld
05: <textstart:PAPER#=1,NAME='AAAA',AUTHOR='AAAAA'>
06: doc1.rtf
07: <textend>
08: <textstart:PAPER#=2,NAME='BBBB',AUTHOR='BBBB'>
09: doc2.rtf
10: <textend>
11: <textstart:PAPER#=3,NAME='CCCC',AUTHOR='CCCC'>
12: doc3.doc
13: <textend>
14: <textstart:PAPER#=8,NAME='HHHH',AUTHOR='HHHH'>
15: doc8.doc
16: <textend>
17: <textstart:PAPER#=8,NAME='HHHH',AUTHOR='HHHH'>
18: doc8.doc
19: <textend>
```

On line 1, -user specifies the username and the password, -name specifies the name of the database table in which data is loaded, and -file specifies the name of the loader control file. The contents of the loader control file used in the chapter's example are shown here.

Also on line 1: -separate specifies that the contents of the load file contain a pointer to a file holding the document and that each document is to be loaded in one row of the table.

Storing Documents in OS Files

To store the documents in OS files rather than in database tables, follow along with these prompts:

```
SQL> create table docs (doc# number primary key,
     author varchar2(20), paper long);


Table created.

SQL> execute ctx_ddl.set_attribute
     ('PATH','/home/oracle/ctxdemo');


PL/SQL procedure successfully completed.

SQL> execute ctx_ddl.create_preference
     ('COMMON_DIR','comment','OSFILE');


PL/SQL procedure successfully completed.

SQL> insert into docs values
     (1,'ABC','/home/oracle/ctxdemo/doc2.doc');


1 row created.

SQL> insert into docs values
     (2,'BCD','/home/oracle/ctxdemo/doc1.rtf');


1 row created.

SQL> commit ;

Commit complete.

SQL> exec ctx_ddl.create_policy('DOC_POLICY','DOCS.PAPER');

PL/SQL procedure successfully completed.

SQL> execute ctx_ddl.create_index('DOC_POLICY');

PL/SQL procedure successfully completed.
```

Glossary

Advanced Queuing   A messaging feature built into the database that allows message data to be accessed and updated in a manner similar to traditional relational data.

Advanced Replication   A database replication technique in which the entire contents of the database or part of the database can be replicated between several sites, all of which can update data, if desired.

application transparency   A property of a networked system wherein applications access objects in remote databases as though they were on the local database.

attribute   A term from database modeling; attributes describe modeled entities and hold specific pieces of information about the entity. They become columns in relational tables.

AUD$ The name of the table Oracle uses to store audit records. It's owned by the user SYS.

audit records   The records created as a result of auditing.

auditing   The process of recording activity as it occurs. The auditing system in Oracle allows you to record different types of database activity and access to database objects.

b*tree   An index structure that uses levels of branch blocks, each level containing pointers to the next lower level, with a set of leaf blocks at the lowest level. Oracle's b*tree indexes always have the same number of levels between the top of the index and a leaf block, regardless of the value of the index entry.

basic replication   A form of database replication in which a read-only snapshot of the database is replicated between sites.

bitmap index   An index that uses a string of bits that corresponds to rows in a table to indicate whether the indexed value is stored in the row.

bootstrap segment   A block of code used to start the database; it's stored in the SYSTEM tablespace.

branch block   An index block that contains ordered pointers to other blocks.

buffer cache   The section of the system global area in which memory buffers contain images of database blocks.

cache segment   *See* bootstrap segment.

cardinality   The number of distinct values a column contains.

Cartesian product   A mathematical term that, when applied to relational databases, refers to the result obtained by joining all the rows of one table with all the rows of another table in every possible combination.

check constraint   A constraint based on a user-defined condition that has to evaluate to true for a record to be valid.

checkpoint   A synchronization point between data files and redo log files. Every changed block is written back to disk from memory, and the redo log records a checkpoint sequence number to indicate that all changes up to this point are now on disk.

cluster   A database structure that attempts to store rows with a common value on the same blocks with each other. Rows from one or more tables can belong to a cluster and will be grouped based on value rather than table membership.

cluster key   The column or columns used to group rows in a cluster. The term is sometimes used for a particular value around which rows are clustered.

column   The basic storage unit of a table; holds one type of data and occurs once per record (row) in the table.

column constraint   A *constraint* definition that's included as part of a column definition's syntax.

complex query   A *complex statement* in which the parent statement is a query.

complex statement   An INSERT, UPDATE, DELETE, or SELECT statement containing a *subquery*.

component query   A query that's part of a *compound query*.

composite index   An index defined on more than one column of a table.

composite limit   A measure of computer resource use that combines CPU time, memory allocation, Oracle block access, and session connect time.

composite primary key constraint   A *primary key constraint* defined on multiple columns.

composite unique constraint   A *unique key constraint* defined on multiple columns.

compound query   A query containing set operators (UNION, UNION ALL, INTERSECT, or MINUS) to combine two or more component queries.

concatenated index   *See* composite index.

concentrating   *See* multiplexing (2).

constraint   A restriction on a column or columns that defines allowable values, thus preventing unwanted values from being stored.

convert file   A file used to complete the physical migration of an Oracle7 database to Oracle8.

Data Definition Language (DDL)   SQL commands that define the different structures in a database, such as CREATE TABLE and CREATE OR ALTER VIEW.

data dictionary A set of tables that contains descriptive information about the database's components, such as the data files, tablespaces, tables, and users. This information is automatically maintained by Oracle and is available for querying a series of views documented in the *Oracle8 Server Reference* manual.

data file A file containing Oracle segments and comprising all or part of a *tablespace*.

Data Manipulation Language (DML) SQL commands that allow for the manipulation of data in the database, such as SELECT, INSERT, DELETE, and UPDATE.

data segment A database segment containing rows from a table or from a clustered set of tables.

data warehouse A database used for storing historical data, which is used for data analysis.

database A collection of information that, in Oracle's case, is organized in relational tables or objects and stored in data files.

database block The smallest unit of storage moved between a data file and the database buffer cache in the *system global area*. Each block contains only one type of information, and the block header identifies the type of block.

database link A database object that identifies a pathway through Net8 to another database and an actual or im-plied userid to connect to that database.

database management system A set of computer programs that provides a formal user interface to a database while managing the internal database structures on behalf of the users.

datatype In an Oracle table, associates a specific set of properties with a column, such as the types of characters allowed and the default length.

default tablespace The *tablespace* in which a user's segments will be built, unless overridden by the CREATE command.

default value A value included in a column for which no value has been supplied with the INSERT statement.

deferred constraint A *constraint* that's not checked until its encapsulating transaction completes.

deferred writes The process of writing changed blocks back to disk when a sufficient number of changes have been made, instead of writing as a result of a transaction commit or other user-driven event.

dimension table A table, typically in a *data warehouse*, that contains further information about an attribute in a *fact table*.

driven table The table that has its rows accessed based on the result set derived from querying the *driving table*'s rows in a table join.

driving table In a *join* statement, the table that has its rows retrieved first.

dynamic performance table

dynamic performance table   A term used inaccurately as a synonym for *dynamic performance view*.

dynamic performance view   Oracle provides these views to let users see real-time information derived from the memory structures used by an instance, the contents of the control file, and header information from other database files. Although these aren't built on relational tables like a normal view, they can be queried by using standard SQL SELECT statements.

equijoin   A table join that involves selecting rows from the tables based on the equality of values in columns from each table.

Export   An Oracle utility that unloads part or all of a database's objects (including definitions of users, views, and so forth) into a formatted dump file that can be read by the *Import* utility. Generally used to restructure free space or to move a database between releases or between different platforms.

extent   A set of contiguous blocks that belong to a single *segment*.

external authentication   The process of using the operating system to authenticate users to Oracle. External authentication eliminates the need for users to log in to both the operating system and Oracle.

execute   The step in processing an SQL statement in which the data is modified.

fact table   A table, typically in a *data warehouse*, that contains the primary data.

fast full scan   A data-retrieval method that scans all the entries in an index rather than reads the blocks from the underlying table. It can be used only if all the required columns are part of the index.

fetch   The step in processing an SQL statement in which rows are returned to the application.

foreign key constraint   A *constraint* that validates a record by ensuring that the value(s) in the constraining column(s) matches values already existing in some other column(s), either in the same or in a different table.

fragmentation   An undesirable collection of disjoint free *extents* that are too small to be useful.

free list   A linked list of blocks in a table, cluster, or index that will be examined when space is required for new or relocated data.

function   A piece of code that returns a value and may accept arguments. In Oracle8, functions can be used in SQL statements, PL/SQL commands, and TYPE definitions. A number of SQL functions are provided by Oracle; additional functions, known as user functions, can be written in PL/SQL.

hash cluster   A cluster in which rows with the same hash key values are stored together.

hash join   A method of joining two tables that relies on a hashing algorithm to group related rows in a memory work area.

heap-organized table A table with rows stored in no particular order. This is a standard Oracle table; the term "heap" is used to differentiate it from an *index-organized table*.

histogram A histogram is added to an Oracle table to store information about the distribution of values throughout the table, generally used when the different values aren't uniformly distributed.

Import An Oracle utility that restores part or all of a database's objects (including definitions of users, views, and so forth) from a formatted dump file created by the *Export* utility. Generally used to restructure free space or to move a database between releases or between different platforms.

index A structure that maintains an ordered set of entries, providing fast access to specific values.

index cluster A cluster in which the rows from the participating tables are accessed via an index.

index-organized table A table whose rows are stored in an index structure, sorted by the table's primary key.

index segment A database segment that contains an index.

indicator array An array of indicator variables. Indicator variables are used to handle NULL values when programming in compiled languages because there's no native support for NULL values.

instance (1) A collection of background processes and the memory acquired for the system global area (SGA) to which they're attached. (2) An alternative name for a row in a relational table.

instance recovery The process of applying the contents of the online redo log to the data files in order to reconstruct any changes made subsequent to the most recent *checkpoint*. This procedure is performed automatically by Oracle whenever a database is restarted. If the database were closed normally, the recovery process would have nothing to do because the most recent checkpoint will be the last entry in the redo. The recovery process has two steps: During the first, a roll forward applies all changes from the redo to the blocks, and the database remains closed until this step completes. During the second step, any uncommitted changes are rolled back out, using the rollback segment entries built as part of the roll forward step. This occurs after the database is reopened and can be done by Oracle background processes or by a user process that encounters a block needing to be rolled back.

intelligent agent A process that runs on the machine that has the database you're trying to monitor. The processes can run autonomously, perform administrative tasks reactively, and provide information to OEM.

interim violation A violation of a database constraint that occurs during the processing of a statement or a transaction that may or may not be resolved by the time the statement or transaction completes.

itl   *See* transaction entry slot.

join   The process or the result of merging data from two or more tables, or multiple views of the same table.

leaf block   A block in an index that contains ordered entries and pointers to their respective rows.

LOB index segment   A database segment that contains index information for a large object (LOB).

LOB segment   A database segment that contains a large object (LOB).

local database   In a distributed database environment, a term used to distinguish between the database to which users are connected through a direct connection and any other remote database to which connections are concurrently made on behalf of users.

location transparency   In a networked system, the system's capability to make remote database objects appear local and independent of their physical location.

log buffer   *See* redo log buffer.

log buffer flush   The action of copying the unwritten contents of the *redo log buffer* to a redo log, performed by the LGWR process.

log group   A set of one or more identical *redo log files* written to concurrently by Oracle that can be used interchangeably for archiving and recovery.

method   An operation, defined in a function or procedure, that is applied to a user-defined datatype.

migrate   The process of upgrading an Oracle database from one major release to another.

Migration utility   A tool provided by Oracle to assist in upgrading an Oracle database from Oracle7 to Oracle8.

multiplexing   (1) An Oracle term used to refer to multiple copies of redo logs maintained synchronously by LGWR. (2) The process by which Net8 combines multiple client connection requests over a single transport connection through the Connection Manager.

National Language Support   A feature of the Oracle database that allows users and applications to interact with the database in their native languages.

network transparency   A network system's capability to behave and function similarly across different network protocols.

node   An independent system within a group of connected systems that share some common resources.

non-equijoin   A table join based on matching rows on a criterion other than equality.

NOT NULL constraint   A constraint that requires every record to contain a value in the constrained column.

object privilege   A privilege that allows specific SQL commands to be executed against a named object.

Open Database Connectivity (ODBC)
A standard developed by Microsoft Corporation to provide connectivity to Windows-based tools to different ODBC-compliant databases.

optimizer   The part of a relational database management kernel that's responsible for determining how the records required to execute a statement will be located and retrieved (the execution plan).

Oracle block   *See* database block.

outer join   A table join in which rows from one table are included in the result set, even if they don't contain values that match those in the other table.

package   A PL/SQL structure that's stored in an Oracle database. It can contain one or more procedure, function, global variable, or cursor in any combination.

parallel server process   An Oracle background process used with other such processes to complete an execution step of a statement in parallel, with each parallel server process being responsible for concurrently manipulating only a defined subset of the data.

parent statement   The outer portion, or main portion, of a *complex statement*.

parse   The step in processing an SQL statement in which the syntax, object validation, and user authorization are confirmed, and during which the execution is built or retrieved from memory.

partition   (1) A subset of a data or index segment, based on a value or range of values in a key field or composite set of key fields. (2) A physical section of a disk storage system.

ping   The transfer of a block of data from one instance to another in an Oracle Parallel Server database.

pipe   An operating system feature that redirects a stream of data—typically the output from a command—into another command that can process or massage it before directing to its own output interface.

primary key   A column or set of columns that comprises a *primary key constraint*.

primary key constraint   A constraint that guarantees that every record is distinguishable from every other record in a table by requiring that a uniquely defined value be inserted in each row, either in a single column or in a composite set of columns.

privilege   A right to execute a particular statement or type of statement, or to access a particular object in the database.

privilege domain   The set of system and object privileges associated with a database user.

procedure   A PL/SQL program with an assigned name that's stored in the database in compiled form.

profile   A named set of resource and password limits.

pseudocolumn   Pseudocolumns can be treated like table columns in an SQL statement, although they don't exist as part of the table definition. Oracle supports the following pseudocolumns: CURRVAL, NEXTVAL, LEVEL, ROWID, and ROWNUM.

quota   The amount of space allocated to a user in a tablespace.

RAID   A disk system that provides various options for striping, mirroring, and managing error correcting codes (often called parity checks) for balanced disk access and fault tolerance. RAID is an acronym for redundant array of independent (or inexpensive) disks.

raw partition   A disk partition used in its native, raw state without having a file system imposed over it.

recovery catalog   A database schema used by Oracle Recovery Manager to maintain information about the structure and status of the databases it backs up.

recursive SQL   One or more SQL statements executed by the system to complete the processing of a user's SQL statement.

redo log buffer   An area of the system global area where redo entries are buffered before being written to a *redo log file*.

redo log file   An Oracle database file that contains information from which transactions and their rollback information can be created. The records contain information about each change to any block and are stored in the order in which these changes were made. This allows a recovery operation to replay the changes in the exact order they occurred in the database originally.

redundancy   A number used by Recovery Manager to determine whether a sufficient number of backups are available for a data file. It's a keyword used when generating Recovery Manager reports about the status of available backups.

referential integrity constraint   *See* foreign key constraint.

relational database   A database that stores its information in two-dimensional tables (relations) that can be joined by using common data elements in one or more columns (attributes).

relink   The step in the process of building an executable program that involves the inclusion of one or more external libraries of common routines.

remote database   A database to which a connection is made, using a database link, while connected to a local database.

replication   The process by which copies of data are consistently maintained in the different databases of a distributed system.

reverse-key index   An index in which indexed values are sorted by reversing the order of the bits.

role   A named collection of privileges that can be granted and revoked like a single privilege.

rollback segment   A database segment that contains images of data recorded before changes being made to it. These "before" images are used to replace the changes should a transaction be rolled back, or should a query need to see data consistent with all other rows in the query.

row   A set of related fields in a table, one field per column, containing values or NULLS.

row piece   A row, or portion of a row, that's stored in a database block. A row that's too large to fit into a single block will be split into multiple row pieces.

rowid   A value that points to the specific physical location of a row in a table by identifying its file number, block number, and relative row number in the block. For tables in tablespaces with more than 1,200 files, the file number is a relative number, and the rowid also includes an object ID number. ROWID is a pseudocolumn that can be referenced in SQL statements. Rowids are also stored in b*tree indexes.

schema   A collection of objects associated with a particular user. In Oracle, the schema name always matches its username, so the two terms—schema and user—can generally be interchanged without confusion.

segment   An Oracle database object that requires its own storage to hold rows or entries, as opposed to an object that's stored simply as a *data dictionary* entry.

self-join   The process or the result of joining a table to itself.

self-referencing constraint   A foreign key constraint that references a column, or columns, in the same table as the constrained column(s).

sequence generator   An Oracle object that provides numbers guaranteed to be unique. The numbers can be sequential but don't need to be.

snapshot   A copy of a master table (or subset) replicated to other child sites. Snapshots can be updated at specified intervals if required.

sort run   A subset of a database sort that's copied from memory to disk due to lack of space in memory to hold the complete set of data being sorted at one time.

space utilization parameter   A parameter defined on a segment that identifies how the available space in each block will be used.

spatial data   Data that refers to and describes relative locations of objects in multidimensional space.

SQL ("sequel")   Structured English Query Language, a universal language introduced originally by IBM to allow access to data in a database.

storage parameter   A value associated with a database segment that determines a characteristic of extent allocation to that object.

striping   The process or the result of placing related data on multiple physical storage devices.

subquery   A query embedded inside another (parent) SQL statement, returning rows used by the parent.

system global area   A section of memory used to store the structures required by an Oracle instance, including the database buffer cache, the redo log buffer, and the shared pool. The system global area is frequently referred to as the SGA.

system privilege A database privilege that allows some type of general database access or use.

table A relational object consisting of one or more fields, where each field is the intersection of a column and a row (record) and has a value based on this specific, logical position. Although columns are identified by column names, which are defined in a specific order, rows have no inherent identifier or order. Unless at least one field value is different between a pair of rows, these rows are indistinguishable from one another.

table constraint A constraint definition that's not syntactically included as part of a column definition.

tablespace A named set of one or more data files that provides storage for database segments.

temporary segment A database segment that temporarily stores records that are being processed in memory but overflow the available space.

transaction A set of one or more commands issued against the database between bracketing COMMIT or ROLLBACK commands. Consequently, all or none of the database changes made by a single transaction will become permanent.

transaction entry slot Part of a block that holds information about a transaction using that block, including pointer information to the transaction's rollback information.

transaction slot *See* transaction entry slot.

trigger A PL/SQL program associated with a table's DML activity. A trigger executes when the user performs the DML activity with which it's associated.

tuple *See* row.

unique constraint A constraint that enforces all non-NULL values in a column to be different from each other.

view A logical table, storing no data itself, that allows access to one or more base tables on which the view is based, using the same SQL commands as if it were a table. Previously, views were considered pre-stored queries, but in current Oracle releases they can be used for data manipulation by DML statements.

VRML (Virtual Reality Modeling Language) A programming language used for modeling and retrieval of virtual reality environments.

Index